Spectrum Guide to
KENYA

Camerapix Publishers International
NAIROBI

Spectrum Guide to Kenya

First published 1989 by
Camerapix Publishers International
PO Box 45048
Nairobi, Kenya

First revised edition 1993
Second revised edition 1997

© 1989 Camerapix,

ISBN 1 874041 88 1

This book was designed and produced by
Camerapix Publishers International
PO Box 45048
Nairobi, Kenya

Fax: (254-2) 217244
Tel: (254-2) 334398

The **Spectrum Guide** series provides a comprehensive and detailed description of each country covered, together with all the essential data that tourists, business visitors, or potential investors are likely to require.

Spectrum Guides in print:
African Wildlife Safaris
Eritrea
Ethiopia
India
Jordan
Maldives
Mauritius
Namibia
Pakistan
Seychelles
South Africa
Sri Lanka
Tanzania
Uganda
United Arab Emirates
Zambia
Zimbabwe

Publisher and Chief Executive:
Mohamed Amin
Editorial Director: Brian Tetley
Picture Editor: Duncan Willetts
Editors: Marti Colley and Jack Crowther
Production Editor: Gail Porter and
Rukhsana Haq
Editorial Consultants: Chege Mbitiru, Bob
Smith and Jan Hemsing
Typesetting and Graphics:
Calvin McKenzie, Lilly Macharia
and Rachel Musyimi
Photographic Research: Abdul Rehman
Editorial Assistants: Maryann Muiruri
Design: Craig Dodd

Colour Separations: Universal Graphics
Pte Ltd, Singapore
Printed and bound: Tien Wah Press, Singapore

4

Editorial Board

Spectrum Guide to Kenya is one of a series of high-quality, lavishly and colourfully illustrated international *Spectrum Guides* to exotic and exciting countries, cultures, flora, and fauna.

The idea behind the series came from **Mohamed Amin**, **Duncan Willetts** and **Brian Tetley**, a three-man travel book team whose *Journey through* series on various countries have been published in many languages.

Too often they were unable to find the answers to questions — not always about guide book 'places' — that would help them to complete their work. They felt that there was need for a guide that not only lavished space on detail, descriptions, and photographs of tourist 'destinations' but tried to answer all the questions a traveller or resident might ask.

They soon discovered that such a concept involved a massive amount of research to uncover information about the other areas of a country — and its institutions and systems.

All the photographs in this guide were taken by Kenyan-born Amin and his English-born colleague and friend, Willetts, who is equally renowned for his superb photography.

Research and writing were assigned by Tetley, an English-born Kenyan with 46 years editorial experience in Europe and Africa. His knowledgeable team — each an authority on some aspect of Kenya — contributed information and helped verify facts.

For all three, Kenya is their home, so *Spectrum Guide to Kenya* holds a special place in their affections. The latest guide to the economy and investment is abstracted from the Ernst Frank company's guide to investment in Kenya which was prepared by **Geoffrey Gichangi Karuu**, one of the partners.

Text editing was the responsibility of **Marti Colley**, an English journalist, and **Jack Crowther**, an Australian editor based in Kenya, was responsible for maintaining *Spectrum Guide* in-house style and copy editing. Both relative newcomers to Kenya, but much-experienced independent travellers, their enthusiasm and eye for detail added much to this publication.

Kenyan **Nazma Rawji** was responsible for the complex co-ordination and design was by **Craig Dodd**, one of Europe's leading graphic designers, based in London.

Production Editor **Rukhsana Haq**, an experienced publishing executive and editorial assistant **Maryann Muiruri**, both Kenyans, undertook the task of preparing and revising the many draft manuscripts while Nairobi born **Abdul Rehman** spent long hours on photographic research.

Together, the diverse cultural backgrounds of the *Spectrum Guide to Kenya* team have created a guide book that seeks to answer virtually any question that any traveller or resident might ask — together with quirky stories about the early settlers, and suggested alternatives to the established tourist circuits.

With detailed route descriptions, maps, gazetteer, and address listings, *Spectrum Guide to Kenya* contains all the practical advice needed to plan and make your holiday a truly original and memorable experience.

5

TABLE OF CONTENTS

Half-title: Spanish moss festoons hagenia tree in mountain forest. Title Page: Elephant beneath Mount Kilimanjaro in Amboseli. Overleaf: Ox-bow lake in Pokomo country on the lower reaches of the Tana River. Pages 10-11: Flamingo spectacle at Lake Bogoria in the Rift Valley. Pages 12-13: Aerial view of the Kenyan capital, Nairobi.

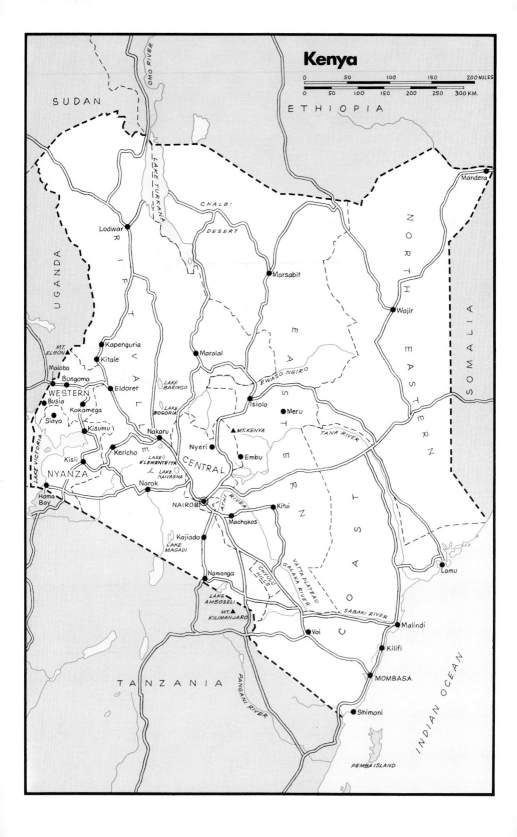

The Kenya Experience

A Welcome

The suddenness of daybreak in Kenya brings a quickening of the pulse. Now lambent colour floods the plains as the light flushes the shadows of night from the thickets, along the hidden rills, and chases them across the tawny grasslands as the sun climbs, agile, over the Equator.

The pink sky begins to dissolve into a flawless blue and the faint breath of the day's first thermal stirs the still, chill air.

To experience first light in Kenya is to be overwhelmed with a feeling of the world new-born. Across savannah plains, forest-cloaked mountains, and lakes and rivers flashing silver in the sun, the land reflects an incredible freshness.

Yet, many millions of years ago, long before our earliest ancestors evolved in the Great Rift Valley, Kenya was a flat and sterile country. It was dramatically refashioned by tumultuous forces deep inside the earth. Intense pressures, from between 160 and 250 kilometres (100-150 miles) below the surface, forced ancient foundation strata upwards.

Nascent streams of molten rock burst forth through flaws in the earth's crust as incandescent fingers of magma and fire. As the extensive lava flowed through these fissures, it slowly cooled to form the dome-shaped volcanic plateaux of central Ethiopia, Kenya, and western Uganda.

Over the aeons, with each new explosion, great cones of rock were thrust skywards. Layer upon layer, each intermittent explosion built up Mount Kenya until it stood between 7,000 and 8,300 metres (23,000- 27,000 feet) above the Equator.

As the wrack and warp slowly abated, one last spasm gave birth to the Rift Valley which runs the length of much of East Africa. When the ashes and the dust settled, the rain and sun gave flesh to Kenya's bare lava bones, leaving a sensuous skin of rich, loamy soil where lush forests of podocarpus, cedar, hagenia, and bamboo thrived. A mantle of peat, bog, and strange plants grew over the mountain skeletons, and a veneer of grass spread across the plains. The new earth was rich and fertile.

It was to become an Eden, where massive elephants, sabre-toothed tigers, giant pigs, rhinoceros and crocodiles roamed.

It was also to be the home of mankind's ancestors, for as far as we know it was in ancient Kenya that one of the earliest humans learned to stand upright and take their first faltering footsteps. Yet even as the early hominids began leaving the shores of Lake Turkana to explore the new-born fertile plains, the dying forces that gave birth to Mount Kenya were still at work. As recently as 40,000 years ago they sprang forth once more to create the Nyambene Hills on the mountain's north-eastern flank.

Thirty thousand years later, immigrants began moving down from the north to colonise this new land. The first outsiders venturing into Kenya, ancestors of today's indigenous populations, were nomads, warriors, craftsmen and farmers. For over 10,000 years, they moved south along the mighty Nile, culminating in the arrival of the Maasai and the Kikuyu during the last 1,000 years. Later came the Persians, Arabs, Europeans and Asians with their new-found faiths.

More than 40 different ethnic groups make up the mosaic of modern Kenya. Today, they're united under the national green, black, and red flag — green representing the land, black for the people, and red for the blood shed in the fight for freedom — and their unity is expressed in the national motto *Harambee*, meaning 'Let's all pull together'. Together, they make a land of harmonious contrasts.

As much as the animals and landscapes, it is these people who, each year, draw more and more visitors to this great, natural paradise. This land, where mankind took its first steps, has always invited discovery — now as much as ever before. Today, Kenya's greeting is warmer and more generous than at any time in its history.

So, *Karibu* — welcome.

Previous pages: Aerial view of Nairobi with the railway station in foreground right.

Travel Brief and Social Advisory

Some dos and don'ts to make your visit more enjoyable.

Adventure in Comfort

Almost no other resort destination in the world offers so much adventure in such safety — and comfort — as Kenya.

Visitors can spend days and nights in the wilderness at close quarters with the greatest and most ferocious natural predators on earth — apart from mankind — but with all the luxuries of civilization on hand and nothing to fear.

Luxuries include self-contained suites with private bathrooms, air-conditioning, well-stocked cocktail bars, crackling log fires, and five-course gourmet dinners.

Wherever you go in Kenya, no matter how remote or rugged, you'll find full board accommodation of at least three- and often four- or five-star comfort.

With all this, and given the climate and natural spectacle, a Kenya holiday is certain to be the adventure of a lifetime. Nonetheless, particularly in the towns and cities, unforeseen problems may arise. This section focuses on both the benefits and the potential pitfalls.

Getting Around

By Road

Road maps of Kenya vary in accuracy. The main problem is the speed at which new roads are built and deteriorate so that gradings are misleading. Unfortunately, the best maps, produced by the Survey of Kenya, are often out of print.

Similarly, there are good street maps of the major towns and cities but since these areas are also developing — and degrading — at a tremendous rate, the information is often out of date.

The A-Z guides of Nairobi and Mombasa by Kenway Publications are revised regularly, however, and though somewhat confusing in layout, are informative and clear enough to enable anyone to find their way around. Driving in Kenya is for the fatalistic and suicidal. Too many drivers have a blatant disregard for speed limits or traffic laws. Besides a good map, essential equipment for visitors who wish to drive is a large supply of sedatives.

Trucks, lorries, buses and the ubiquitous *matatus* — private freelance commuter vehicles ranging from hot-rod Peugeot 504s through minibuses down to dilapidated pickups — and darkness are the real enemies. Wherever you're going it's best to aim to arrive before sundown.

Additional hazards include potholes the size of frontline shell craters, *kamikaze* cyclists, pedestrians, cattle, goats, sheep, speed bumps that weren't there the week before, unmarked sharp bends, unannounced roadworks, and slow moving — sometimes stationary — traffic without lights.

Signposts do exist but have often been mangled in an accident or uprooted for use as building or fencing material.

Although the Mombasa to Uganda road is the main artery for much of eastern and central Africa — southern Sudan, Uganda, Rwanda, Burundi, and eastern Zaire — it should be used as little as possible, especially at night.

The top speed in unrestricted areas on main roads for private vehicles is limited to 100 kilometres (60 miles) an hour. In urban areas this varies between 50 and 80 kilometres (30-50 miles) an hour. These limits are rarely observed or enforced, except through an occasional speed trap.

This guide gives approximate distances in kilometres and miles, verified by the Automobile Association of Kenya.

Remember that for off-the-road driving, particularly in game sanctuaries and the north, especially during the rains, often only 4WD is suitable — and, even then, not infallible. Most tour groups travel in the privacy of well-maintained minibuses with drivers who, for the most part, are cautious and experienced.

For independent travellers, major towns are linked by reasonably comfortable, frequent, and — by Western standards — extremely cheap scheduled coach services.

Kenya National Parks and National Reserves

SUDAN

ETHIOPIA

UGANDA

SOMALIA

Central Island N.P.

Sibiloi National Park

LAKE TURKANA

LODWAR

South Island N.P.

LOYANGALANI

Marsabit National Reserve

MARSABIT

Nasolot N.R.

South Turkana N.R.

Losai National Reserve

Mt. Elgon N.P.

Saiwa Swamp N.P.

KITALE

Kamnarok N.R.

MARALAL

Samburu N.R.

Shaba National Reserve

ELDORET

Kerio Valley N.R.

Buffalo Springs N.R.

Bisanadi N.R.

Rahole National Reserve

Kakomega N.R.

Lake Bogoria N.R.

NANYUKI

MERU

Meru N.P.

KISUMU

Nderi N.P.

NAKURU

NYAHURURU

Mt. Kenya N.P.

North Kitui N.R.

Kora N.R.

GARISSA

KERICHO

Lake Nakuru N.P.

GIGIL

NYERI

KISII

NAIVASHA

Aberdares N.P.

Mwea N.R.

Ruma N.P.

Hell's Gate N.R.

NAROK

Longonot N.P.

THIKA

Ol Doinyo Sapuk N.P.

Arawale N.R.

Boni National Reserve

NAIROBI

Nairobi N.P.

South Kitui National Reserve

Dodori N.R.

Maasai Mara National Reserve

SULTAN HAMUD

Tana River Primate N.R.

Kiunga Marine Reserve

NAMANGA

Chyulu Hill N.P.

Ngai Ndethya N.R.

GARSEN

Tsavo East National Park

Amboseli National Park

TSAVO

MALINDI

Malindi Marine National Park
Malindi Marine National Reserve
Watamu Marine National Park
Watamu Marine National Reserve

Tsavo West N.P.

VOI

TANZANIA

MOMBASA

Shimba Hills N.R.

Mombasa Marine National Park
Mombasa Marine National Reserve

Mpunguti Marine National Reserve
Kisite Marine National Park

INDIAN OCEAN

PEMBA ISLAND

0   50   100   150   200 MILES
0   50   100   150   200   250   300 KM.

The cheapest, most uncomfortable, but certainly the most colourful and most intimate means of travel is by country bus or *matatu*.

Shoulder to shoulder, rib-to-rib, 'there's always room for one more', these vehicles are a certain way of getting close to your Kenyan neighbours, if not to understanding them altogether. Unfortunately, some local *wakora* (villains) have discovered a new trick. The guy offering you a bun, sandwich, cup of tea, or soda may well have laced it with a knockout drug.

It's not unknown for passengers to wake up long after they reach their destination to find they have been robbed of everything. So the golden rule on *matatu*, bus, or train is 'never take sweets — or anything else — from a stranger'.

By Air

Kenya has the busiest domestic flight network in Africa, with more than 200 scheduled flights a week to countrywide destinations. The national carrier, Kenya Airways, with its fleet of modern jet aircraft and Fokkers, serves major destinations. Private schedule and charter services fly to more remote areas.

From Nairobi there are several flights daily to Mombasa and from Mombasa to Nairobi. An average of at least two flights a day operate between Nairobi and the Maasai Mara, one to Lamu, seven a week to Kisumu and Malindi. Regular scheduled flights serve Amboseli, Kiwaiyu, Nanyuki, Nyeri, and Samburu.

In addition there is a daily flight from Mombasa to Lamu and eight from Mombasa to Malindi. Scheduled services to Wajir and Mandera began early in 1996.

By Train

Those who wish to travel by train in Kenya should be in no hurry. The 'Lunatic Express' is still as slow as it was almost 100 years ago when the Mombasa to Lake Victoria line was built. The metre-gauge track and severe gradients — such as the Rift Valley escarpment — limit speed.

The overnight train from Nairobi to Mombasa is perfect for romantics who wish to travel like the pioneers for whom the railway was the only link between most towns and settlements. There are two trains each night in both directions, the 'express'

leaving some 90 minutes after the 'slow' train. It takes just under 13 hours to cover the 500 kilometres (310 miles). Two highlights of the journey are when the train passes herds of wildlife on the plains at sunset, and then when dinner — with a choice of wines available — is served by white-coated waiters in the dining car.

Accommodation is two to a compartment in first class. Second class is for four occupants and is clean, comfortable and functional. Bed linen, pillows and blankets are now included in the fare. Third class offers only wooden benches and is extremely uncomfortable.

Fares are cheap by Western standards but places should be reserved in advance because the train is generally full. Special discounts are available for group bookings.

Similar facilities are available on the daily Nairobi-Nakuru-Kisumu service, the twice-weekly service from Nairobi to Malaba on the Uganda border, and the weekly service to Kampala.

On Foot

Vast open spaces, rolling hills and rugged mountain moorlands offer ideal walking country to those with time to spare.

Off the main tarmac highways, minor murram roads and cotton-soil byways pass through what are known as the 'reserves' which make up the true heart of Kenya. Much of this land is found in the central, western and north-western regions of the country and ranges between 1,200 and 2,700 metres (4,000-9,000 feet) in height. It's more strenuous than lowland walking in Europe or America, but rewarding. However, avoid cotton-soil roads during the rainy season when they become a glutinous morass.

Small hamlets and villages are sprinkled across these glorious farmlands which are tended by strong, thrifty, hardworking people with a sense of humour and always a warm welcome for passing strangers.

While much of Kenya has yet to be discovered by walkers, the main focus for trekkers and climbers is Mount Kenya, although there are other attractive ranges, such as Mount Elgon, the Cheranganis, the Aberdares, the Mau summit, the Chyulu Hills and others (see "Kenya's Mountains," Part Three).

The People

The spirit of Kenya is exemplified by its tradition of hospitality. Few people in the world are as welcoming. The peaceful stranger who visits an unknown village is greeted with an openness that many Westerners find overwhelming. And it often happens, paradoxically, that the poorer the home, the poorer the person, the richer the welcome.

In the metropolitan and municipal areas more than three decades of urbanization and rural migration to fast-growing townships has eroded this spirit.

But, nonetheless, ninety-nine per cent of Kenyans demonstrate an open-handedness and willingness to help that is hard to find elsewhere.

In a land where much of the rural population has no access to electricity, life is tuned to the sun. Activity is at its height during the early hours and in the brief cool of the late afternoon.

It's as well to remember that less than a century ago only a handful of outsiders had visited the Kenya hinterland. The cash economy was unknown and there was no modern technology — just communities of proud, independent, hardworking farmfolk who traded on barter.

In a few short decades, Kenya has travelled far and fast. The immediate descendants of a society denied access to centuries of urban living, knowledge and evolving technology, have adapted at every level to what is known as civilization.

Whatever you think of Western civilization, the structures and values of Kenyan society that have enabled the people to adapt with such dynamic success must be respected.

Long before the Western Bible or Islamic Qur'an came to Kenya, people believed in God under a variety of names. Inherent in all Kenyan cultures is a pure and simple vision of a creator who sanctifies life, predisposing no idols, totems or rituals.

This unsullied reverence for a supreme being is reflected perhaps in the manner in which Kenyans took to Christianity and Islam, both orthodox and unorthodox. In the 1990s Kenya had more registered church organizations than any other country in the world. Well over 1,700 different non-secular societies were potent proof of Kenya's commitment to freedom of expression, association, choice and worship. As you travel around the country, you'll meet many Kenyans, most of whom speak good English. They have a tradition of oral communication, and delight in explaining the history, customs, and geography of their homes. Through their eyes, their intricate social customs are woven into a rich cultural tapestry.

To enjoy your visit to the full, first familiarize yourself with some of the country's customs and taboos. Good manners aside, a knowledge and awareness of these will give you a greater insight into Kenyan culture.

The standard greeting, and always welcome to whomever it is addressed, is *jambo* — a kind of 'hello' and 'how are you?' — that should elicit the standard response, *mzuri*, meaning 'all is well'.

If, however, the reply is *mbaya,* meaning 'not so good', a commiserative *pole* — 'sorry' — will express your sympathy.

In Kenya physical contact is important. Everybody shakes hands upon meeting — even friends who last saw each other two hours ago. The proffered hand is only refused when an offence has been committed. The handshake is not just an introduction — it is a gesture of trust and peace.

Most important, 'face' — respect — is everything. Kenyans are extremely proud of their country and it ill-behoves any passing stranger to offer gratuitous or condescending criticism or advice about national or local affairs.

However, once you know a few Kenyans you may well become involved in animated but friendly discussions on the values of differing cultures; i.e., African culture as opposed to European culture. It's considered gravely insulting to shout at anybody, even with words of praise, so whatever you have to say deliver it *sotto voce*.

Anything evocative of a colonial stance will provoke even the most gentle of these gentle folk so don't call the waiter, or anybody else over the age of 16, 'boy'. The normal address when calling for service in a restaurant or bar, is a less offensive colonial hangover — 'steward' — a reminder that until the 1950s the main means of passage to Kenya was by sea. Better still, use the standard *rafiki* — 'friend' — or *bwana*, meaning 'mister'.

For anybody clearly over 40 years of age, *mzee* (old man) is a euphemistic form of address that expresses respect not only for the person but for his wisdom and experience. For women, the word *mama* carries the same connotation.

The term *mwananchi* refers to a person — the plural, *wananchi,* covers the entire community — a word which denotes patriotism and respect. The other collective for people, *watu,* has a sneering undertone.

Never use the collective 'blacks' any more than you would 'honkies' to describe whites. The normal references are Africans, *wananchi*, Asians, *wahindi,* and Europeans, *wazungu.*

Always respect lawful authority. There's talk of corruption but most visitors find the established services, especially the police, exemplary — always polite, helpful, and considerate. Tourists who unwittingly commit minor infringements of traffic laws, for instance, are usually waved on with the words, 'Enjoy your visit to our country'.

In Africa, the head of the community traditionally enjoys a great deal more status and commands more obedience than in Western cultures and this is transposed to the executive. The President is always treated with deference and you should not attempt to take his photograph unless you have permission from one of his entourage.

Since the opportunity to ask is unlikely to arise, keep your camera packed away. In the most remote regions, where superstition still persists, it's thought you are attempting to steal their soul. In more sophisticated areas it's just regarded as downright rude not to ask first. Along with social customs, always respect the law. The hiring of prostitutes, other sexual offences, and drug taking are frequent infringements.

In its application to tourists, law enforcement in Kenya is always understanding and reasonably mild, depending, of course, on which law has been transgressed and the degree of involvement. The judicial system is based on the British model so bond or bail can be granted at the police or magistrate's discretion and all cases must be brought before a court. Kenya's judiciary has won high regard for its impartiality.

Safety

Since Kenyan society is less affluent than Western society, never make an ostentatious show of wealth.

Nairobi is as safe as most capital cities; and Mombasa is a dock town. Apply common sense: muggings do take place after dark (usually unaccompanied singles or couples) and bag and watch-snatching occur even by day.

Safeguard money, passports, travellers' cheques, and airline tickets. Do not leave personal documents in your hotel room or luggage. Most hotels and lodges have safe-keeping facilities. Ask at the desk for this facility and always insist on a receipt.

Never take out cameras or other valuables in public unless absolutely necessary. Do not tempt fate by carrying around your handbag loose and open or carrying large amounts of cash.

If you are driving, do not leave anything of value in a locked car. In towns, there is usually someone who will volunteer to 'guard' it for you for a few shillings.

Be careful of the 'hustlers' in Nairobi. You may hear a hard luck story designed to get you to donate money to a 'worthy' cause.

Beggars are common. Many, but not all, are deserving cases. Although regularly moved out of Nairobi city centre and from the larger towns for relocation elsewhere, they frequently filter back.

Clothes

As Kenya rises from sea level to more than 5,200 metres (17,000 feet), and much of the country is between 1,500 and 2,100 metres (5,000-7,000 feet), visitors experience contrasting climates and extremes of temperature.

Even at 3,000 metres (10,000 feet) on the Equator, the sun can be blistering — and the nights freezing. For most of the year the standard safari outfit — tailored shirt or top jacket and trousers — is ideal for bush travel. Carry a hat to avoid eyestrain and sunstroke. At other times, shorts, casuals

Opposite: Tourists drift over Tsavo's savannah plains near Kilimanjaro.

and anything you require for sports and swimming should suffice, but bring woollens for those evenings at high altitudes.

In the cities and towns, Western business convention prevails — tailored suit, shirt, and tie. Otherwise, smart casual wear is acceptable. June to August can be overcast up-country — cool in the daytime and chilly at night — so include some warm cardigans and sweaters. Smart, medium-weight clothes will suffice for the evening.

Women will most probably find cotton dresses cooler and more comfortable than trousers, particularly for daytime wear. 'Baggy' trousers rather than skin-tight jeans are obviously better ventilated. For footwear, comfort should take precedence over style since many pavements are uneven in the cities and towns, and non-existent in the bush. Specialized sports clothes, including swimwear, should be packed. Most items are available in Nairobi and Mombasa, but in a limited range and often more expensive than back home.

Drip-dry clothing is ideal, although most hotels and lodges offer same-day laundry services. Even so, in many places the dust may make two or three changes a day necessary for the more fastidious.

Safari clothes and boots for both men and women, reasonably-priced, are available in Nairobi and Mombasa. Tailor-made safari suits can be run up in a matter of hours and men, particularly, find them a valuable addition to their holiday wardrobe. They look smart, feel cool, and cost only a fraction of a regular suit, with the added bonus of being washable.

For women, the local *kitenge* dresses and loose blouses are a most attractive and popular wardrobe addition. These are available in an infinite variety of designs and at little cost. *Khangas* and *kikois* (simple wrap-around sarongs) are also useful.

At the coast, shorts are acceptable — but bear in mind the Muslim ethic in dress. This, especially, forbids nude bathing on the beach.

What to Take

Most essentials are available anywhere in Kenya. However, if you are on specific, prescribed drugs for prolonged periods, our advice is to carry adequate dosages to cover your safari as pharmaceutical products tend to be much more costly in Kenya.

It's also worth carrying a spare pair of eye glasses and, failing that, at least a prescription that would enable you to get another pair. However, like drugs, these too are expensive in Kenya. Contact lens solutions are available in Nairobi and Mombasa but now and then supplies run out, so bring your own.

Laundry

Major hotels offer a same-day or twenty-four-hour laundry and dry-cleaning service. Elsewhere, Kenya — unlike Asia, for example — is distinguished by its lack of laundry facilities. Economy travellers staying in lodging houses or camping will have no alternative but to do their own laundry.

Health

Doctors recommend all visitors have inoculations against tetanus, polio, cholera, typhoid, and paratyphoid. A gamma globulin injection provides some protection against hepatitis and it is well worth taking this precaution.

Malaria is endemic and all visitors should take an anti-malarial prophylactic beginning two weeks before their arrival and for six weeks after departure.

Kenya has excellent medical facilities, better than most African countries. There are first-rate private hospitals in Nairobi, Kisumu, and Mombasa, and there are a surprising number of specialist physicians and surgeons, many of international reputation. There are also excellent dentists and opticians. However, medical treatment can be extremely expensive.

All visitors, therefore, should have medical insurance. It can be obtained in Kenya but usually at a higher premium than you would pay in Europe and North America for the same cover.

Temporary membership is available with the East African Medical Research Foundation — AMREF — which operates the world-famous Flying Doctor service in Kenya and Tanzania. For a token payment, AMREF guarantees to fly patients to the nearest well-equipped hospital should they fall ill or suffer injury while on safari. There is no shortage of chemists or drug stores in Kenya, all of them staffed with qualified pharmacists. Most drugs are available, although sometimes they may have unfamiliar brand names.

If your specific prescription is not available, the pharmacist will often prescribe a suitable alternative. Most chemists close on Saturday afternoons, Sundays, and public holidays. When closed, the name and location of the duty chemist is usually posted on the shop door, or may be obtained at the nearest hospital. The list of roster chemists who open at weekends in Nairobi and Mombasa is also listed in the newspapers.

Photography
Colour and black and white film, 60-minute, and one-day processing are readily available in all major centres. Camera equipment (tripods, lenses, flash, etc.) can be hired from camera shops in Nairobi and Mombasa.

It is forbidden to photograph any of the State Houses, military installations and other security areas.

When to go
The tourist season extends all the year-round with 'lows' during the two rainy seasons — which are often the best time to visit.

The 'long rains' normally fall between mid-March and the end of May, and the 'short rains' from the end of October to early December. Nairobi and the Central Highlands are cold, grey and overcast on most days between June and August.

Although some areas may be closed because of road conditions, the advantages of a low-season visit are often crystal-clear mornings and early afternoons, special hotel and lodge rates, and fewer visitors to scare off the wildlife.

The high seasons, when advance booking is mandatory, are from December to the end of March and from mid-September to the end of October, with a 'shoulder' season at the coast and in the game reserves from the end of June to mid-September.

On Safari
Many view a Kenya safari as some kind of happy endurance test which is highlighted by glimpses of stunning scenery, colourful people and herds of wild animals.

You'll enjoy Kenya all the more if you scrutinize your itinerary with care and insist on enough time in each place to enjoy it to the full.

Be selective. If it means cutting down the number of parks and reserves, it also cuts down the number of jolting kilometres you travel each day.

Remember, too, that although some animals have become used to people, they are still wild animals. Do not feed monkeys or other primates — or make excessive noise to attract their attention.

Do not leave the designated trails for that closer shot — and do not get out of your vehicle except at designated areas. Close all windows and zips when you leave your room or tent.

Many visitors believe success is related to the number of animals they check off in the shortest possible time. But this is a sad way to enjoy the unprecedented opportunities for wildlife viewing.

Instead, read up on wildlife to help you identify the smaller creatures and the birds. Then, if something catches your eye, spend time observing it and learning its habits and characteristics first-hand.

Remember that the maximum speed limit is 50 kilometres (30 miles) an hour in the game reserves — and often less. Tell your guide that, despite the watch you wear, you are in no hurry.

The more slowly you drive, the more you see; a lioness crouched in the grass, tail swishing and eyes alert, may be looking for her supper.

Stop and wait. Before the hour is up you may well witness the unparalleled spectacle of a lioness bringing down a gazelle in full flight. Always keep your camera loaded and ready for action. You never know when it's going to start.

Do not stand or sit on top of vehicles for a better view and do not forget to adhere to the park and game reserve visiting hours, 0630-1830.

The best time to see wildlife is early morning or late afternoon.

Money on Safari
A good supply of travellers' cheques is

Overleaf: Reticulated giraffe and zebra beneath Mount Kenya.

essential for anyone travelling in Kenya, but they can remain mere pieces of paper once you get to remote places far from the banks. This applies especially to almost the entire northern part of the country, where even in the larger townships the bank may only be an agency operating once or twice a week.

On the Beaten Track

The best way to travel is to take along enough cash to cover expenses en route, plus an extra sum for emergencies, say to buy that spare tyre or inner tube when you unexpectedly lose your tread.

Ideally, the rest should be in Kenya shillings travellers' cheques. These are available for a small charge and are cashed at face value, with no deductions, in any bank and most hotels.

Carrying Kenya shillings travellers' cheques eliminates any problem about fluctuating foreign exchange rates. If you do take travellers' cheques in 'hard' foreign currencies, shop around for the most favourable rate. Generally, banks give a much better rate than hotels, which often charge hefty commissions.

It is also worth noting that they charge for each cheque leaf — one charge for a single £100 cheque, but ten for ten £10 cheques.

Don't assume that large hotels with 24-hour cashier facilities will be prepared to cash your travellers' cheques unless you're staying there. If you don't have a room number they may decline to change your money on the grounds that they do not provide this facility for non-residents.

Smaller hotels tend to be more helpful, but often don't have enough cash on hand.

In Nairobi and Mombasa foreign exchange bureaux are open until 1630 daily and also Saturdays and some Sundays and public holidays.

Credit cards are invaluable for settling bills. There are several local credit cards dealing in Kenya money, but American Express, Barclaycard, Mastercard and Visa are widely accepted.

Off the Beaten Track

Most of northern Kenya, 'game country' and other places with sparse population lack normal bank facilities. The chances are that you will have problems changing large denomination bank notes, unless it is market-day in a sizeable village or trading centre. One solution is to buy something useful from a remote petrol station then use the change as needed.

You should never rely on changing travellers' cheques except at an overnight stop. Even then, if the travellers' cheques are in foreign currency, the hotel or lodge staff may not know the current exchange rate and be reluctant to take your word for it.

Ideally you should carry plenty of small denomination notes and always keep loose change for the 'helpers' who appear out of nowhere if your vehicle has a flat tyre, or gets stuck in the mud.

At such times their muscle-power can be a blessing, since the alternative could mean being stranded for hours, or even days, especially if the track is soggy 'black cotton soil', which takes ages to dry after a storm.

For lesser 'favours', the odd cigarette is always appreciated. Keep a couple of packs in the glove compartment of your car.

Sweets are always useful for persuading children to be photographed and give-away instant pictures are much appreciated.

Where to Stay

Kenya is Africa's number one tourist destination south of the Sahara, with an incredibly sophisticated tourist infrastructure and the best range of accommodation on the continent. Other options include self-service lodges in national parks and reserves, campsites, and youth hostels (see Listings).

Standards at self-service lodges vary. For most, you should carry your own bedding, food, crockery, cutlery and cooking utensils.

Camping

With more than 200 official campsites in well-chosen wilderness areas throughout the country, Kenya is ideal for those who enjoy the rugged, outdoor life.

Many people claim camping is the only way to enjoy Kenya — an inexpensive and delightful do-it-yourself holiday offering a way of life you will never forget. Wherever you camp, make sure you choose a spot to pitch your tent well before sundown. If possible, choose level ground with short grass and plenty of shade. But watch which tree you stay under. Thorn trees provide good, safe shade because they discourage snakes and climbing creatures such as leopards but the thick canopy of thorns beneath them tends to make sleeping uncomfortable.

Other trees can exude unpleasant sap and birds nesting and monkeys romping often mean droppings around the camp — and a nasty mess on the tents themselves.

Avoid dried-up river beds: sudden storms create flash floods that can sweep you away, vehicle and all. Where the climate is generally hot — in low country — pitch your tent with the largest windows facing the prevailing wind. Temperatures become unbearable without adequate ventilation.

Do not camp across or too near to game trails. Animals can be curious as well as dangerous. Ensure adequate control of camp fires. If stones are available, place them around the fireplace — and clear away all dry grass and leaves.

What you need

Tents, of course — with sewn-in groundsheets and mosquito-net windows; camp beds, sleeping bags; folding chairs and table; pots and pans (*sufurias*, Kenya-made pans, are ideal for camp fires); airtight containers for bread and biscuits, salt and sugar; at least one axe and *panga* (machete) for clearing camping sites and chopping firewood; metal bowl for washing; kettle for tea and coffee; ideally, small camping gas lamps; spade (preferably the folding type); lots of water; plates, mugs, knives, forks and spoons; food

Binoculars will add to your enjoyment. You can hire tents and camping equipment in Nairobi.

National Anthem

O God of all creation
Bless this our land and nation.
Justice be our shield and defender
May we dwell in unity
Peace and liberty
Plenty be found within our borders.

Let one and all arise
With hearts both strong and true.
Service be our earnest endeavour,
And our Homeland of Kenya.
Heritage of Splendour,
Firm may we stand to defend.

Let all with one accord
In common bond united,
Build this our nation together
And the glory of Kenya
The fruit of our labour
Fill every heart with thanksgiving.

Failure to stand for the national anthem in a public place — cinemas, theatres — could result in your being asked to leave.

Opposite: The high falls at Nyahururu 'discovered' by Joseph Thomson late last century.

PART ONE : HISTORY, GEOGRAPHY, AND PEOPLE

Above: Fossil remains of elephant that lived on the shores of Lake Turkana 1.5 million years ago.
Opposite: Maasai girl with colourful beaded jewellery.

Land of Adventure

Many millions of years ago Kenya's shape and form was dramatically remodelled — changed beyond recognition. Its ancient plateau, flat and monotonous, draining gently east to the Indian Ocean, was wrenched apart, and forced upwards in a series of massive earth movements and volcanic eruptions.

But just what caused all this violent movement is not exactly known.

The movements continued over millions of years, however, causing the earth to rise up in a dome and molten magma from deep beneath the surface to form huge volcanoes. Some, like Mount Kenya, have since been worn down to stumps by wind and rain erosion. As it continued to swell, the land split from north to south, forming a great depression in the west. This giant basin finally filled with water to become Lake Victoria.

Joined with other fissures, the main crack formed the Great Rift Valley, stretching from Jordan to Mozambique.

Thus in ancient times was Kenya transformed. Streams from the high ground on both sides of the fault began to flow into this great trough, forming a series of lakes which waxed and waned with the different levels of rainfall.

But these new highlands also created rain shadows on their leeward sides. As a result the forests in the lower and hotter sections of the valley floor began to disappear, their place taken by a new natural phenomenon — the most recent of all major environmental changes on planet earth — savannah grasslands.

Much later, some ape species on the fringes of these vanishing forests moved into the new rolling grasslands, adapting and learning to exploit their resources.

And, as the land changed, the family of apes made their home on the shores of the Rift Valley lakes and along the streams that poured down from the mountains.

In time, one of these ape species evolved into an early form of hominid — our ancestral apeman — and began to wreak far greater change on the environment than any other animal. The record of evolution

in the Kenyan Rift Valley stretches back 25 million years. Within that span virtually all stages of life's evolution are found in its fossil records.

Homo erectus was the first of the humans to walk upright. But since those first faltering footsteps along the shores of Lake Turkana, perhaps a million years ago, the fascinating narrative is void of detail. Its blank pages echo only with an oral history enriched time and again in the telling.

When the Rift formed, Arabia was divided from Africa, leaving a legacy of migrant wildlife that mingled with endemic species. Like the people who were to follow, many animals also crossed the land bridge between East and West Africa when the great rainforests of western Africa extended to the shores of the Indian Ocean.

Between five and 10,000 years ago Kenya's original inhabitants included the ancestors of today's remnant groups of hunter-gatherers — the Boni, Wata, and Waliangulu wanderers of the forest and bush.

The pan-African transmigration started about 4,000 years ago — and has since brought successive waves to this land that has always lured migrants. Through most of the second millennium BC, crop-growing Cushites from southern Ethiopia and their livestock were the major immigrants.

They were followed 1,000 years later by eastern Cushites. After them, between 500 BC and AD 500, came a floodtide of Cushitic, Nilotic, and Bantu groups — from all parts of the continent. These ancestors of today's Kenyans found the land and climate good and stayed to settle.

Smaller numbers continued to arrive until this century. They included the Arab and Persian traders who colonized the coast and, later, the Asians and Europeans.

Through this movement of people, which constantly shaped and reshaped cultures and communities, the land continued to remodel itself too. Although the immense and intense activity which created the Rift Valley slackened, it never ceased.

As recently as 40,000 years ago violent earth movements and volcanic forces gave birth to the Nyambene Hills north-east of Mount Kenya. Between 400 and 500 years ago, similar volcanic frenzies sent great cones of lava spewing upwards to form the

Chyulu Hills north of Kilimanjaro. Out of all this violence came beauty. The landscapes, flora, and fauna are as diverse — and as magnificent — as the people.

One-third of Kenya is arid or semi-arid desert: barren, brown, burnt-out land which is hauntingly lovely.

One-third is highland, mountain, forest, lake, and farmland, much of it fertile and bountiful. The remaining third is savannah grassland — home of the last remaining great wildlife spectacle in the world, where creatures such as the crocodile and rhinoceros, which evolved more than 100 million years ago, still survive.

The country's wildlife boasts more than 80 major mammal species including the Big Five — lion, leopard, elephant, buffalo, and rhino. And there are countless smaller animals, the richest birdlife on the African continent — and the third richest in the world — and a treasury of reptiles and insects so numerous and varied they have not yet all been counted and identified.

A British protectorate for more than 70 years, a Crown colony for just 43 years, Kenya's political stability and economic growth have become a benchmark for the African continent, and much of the developing world, since the country attained independence on 12 December 1963.

Concerned to improve the quality of life for all citizens, the pragmatic government has encouraged industrial development and initiated major social welfare schemes.

With its freedom and peace intact, Kenya has seen tourism grow from fewer than 100,000 visitors in 1963 to close upon an annual million. Now a major catalyst for growth and development, tourism offers holiday-makers the unforgettable magic of Kenya's panoramic vistas and untamed wildlife.

History

The Dust and the Ashes

Written in the rock of Kenya, amid the ashes of the fires which gave birth to the world, is the story of creation. And though the wind has stirred the dust and sent it eddying away, the geological notebooks remain an indelible confirmation of Kenya's claim as the 'Cradle of Mankind'. Yet though Kenya boasts the world's oldest-known palaeontological record — and perhaps, therefore, the longest continuous testament to the history of life on earth — much of it remains undeciphered. The story that is known has been uncovered with camel's hair brush, dental pic and scrupulous research, then painstakingly pieced together, fragment by fragment.

The transcription of this unique archaeological narrative has been carried out over the last 70 years by a dynasty of peerless fossil hunters. In 1926 an autocratic, eccentric Kenyan-born European, Louis Seymour Bazett Leakey, began to dig deep into the surface of East Africa. Five years later he married Mary Douglas Nicol and in the decades that followed, this fiery, iconoclastic man-and-wife team led several archaeological expeditions in Tanzania and Kenya. Together their research extended our understanding of mankind's beginnings by millions of years.

In the space of more than 30 years these unashamed Apostles of Adam uncovered an amazing collection of stone artefacts and hominid, ape, and animal fossils ranging across twenty-five million years of evolution.

The most important work done by the Leakeys was at Olduvai Gorge in Tanzania in the 1950s and 1960s. From banded sediments in this deep fissure in the Serengeti plain, they traced man's biological and cultural development back from about 50,000 years to 1.8 million years ago.

On 17 July 1959, Mary Leakey found 400 fragments of the skull of *Zinjanthropus Boisei*, 'Zinj'. The 'Nutcracker Man' was an important early 'apeman'.

Painstakingly reassembled — the reconstructed fossil is now in Tanzania's National Museum in Dar es Salaam — the skull was perhaps the beginning of a new Chapter of Revelations in the story of human evolution, one that has successfully established the East African Rift Valley — the Kenyan section, in particular — as a true Cradle of Mankind.

Some years later, in the early 1960s, the Leakeys discovered the skull and bones of a 10,000-to-12,000-year-old fossil which they named *Homo habilis*, 'Handy Man'. Physiologically he was a contemporary of

Zinjanthropus, but with a larger brain, and a gripping thumb.

Despite bitter opposition from other palaeontologists, the Leakeys considered their 'handy man' a true ancestor of modern man. Their theory was seemingly confirmed when, in 1967, their son Richard investigated the bleak, arid shore at Koobi Fora on Lake Turkana in Kenya's far north and picked up a Stone Age tool similar to those that he had found as a youngster in Olduvai Gorge.

After his father's death in 1972, Richard Leakey made even more significant discoveries — and the shores all around Lake Turkana, where he organized one of the greatest multi-disciplinary fossil hunts in the history of archaeology, have revealed more profound clues to mankind's origins than any other place in the world.

Fossil-bearing strata have preserved four million years of human and animal remains and tens of thousands of them have been studied at Kenya's National Museum. These studies have thrust back knowledge of life's beginnings on earth many millions of years before that deduced from previous evidence (see 'The Great Rift Valley: The Land that was Eden', Part Two).

Other finds by American researchers in sections of the Rift in Ethiopia confirm that the beginnings of modern man go back at least 2.6 million years — and that 'two, or even three, manlike creatures co-existed with the original *Homo* for more than a million years'.

All these spectacular finds shifted the search for the crucible where mankind was first cast from Europe and Asia to the East African Rift Valley.

Soon after our ancestral *Homo erectus* stood upright and took their first faltering footsteps, this new-found mobility inspired them to move much further afield in the search for food and water. They became wanderers and spread out across much of what is today Kenya and Tanzania. Fossil sites in the southern Rift show that *Homo erectus* and their descendants swiftly expanded their range. But although little evidence of the intermediate millennia has been uncovered, it is known that much more recently, between the last five and 10,000 years, Kenya was inhabited by the ancestors of today's remnant groups of

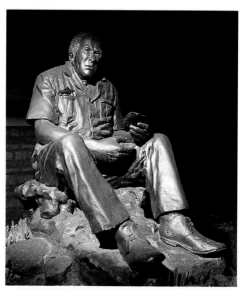

Below: Statue of Dr Louis Leakey, head of a peerless dynasty of fossil hunters.

Above: Priceless clue to mankind's beginnings. This skull of an early hominid, KNM-ER 1470 is in Kenya's National Museum.

hunter-gatherers — the Boni, Wata, and Waliangulu peoples.

These traditional wanderers of the forest and bush have a link with the 'click-speaking' Khosian peoples of southern Africa, such as the Bushmen of the Kalahari.

The Immigrants

Later began the ancestral influx of today's ethnic groups in a long series of migrations that lasted well into the 19th century. The first wave came from Ethiopia when a group of tall, lean nomadic peoples speaking the Cushitic languages moved into Kenya in a series of gradual movements spaced over the second millennium BC.

These early southern Cushites adopted the peculiar dental clicks of the Khosian as a modulation of their own tongues. They also introduced new languages and kept domesticated cattle, goats and sheep. They tilled the soil and planted crops like sorghum. Archaeological excavations have uncovered their stone bowls, earthenware pots, grindstones, pestles, as well as knives, gourds, spears, hoes and basketwork.

They also left a more enduring legacy in the irrigation systems that still exist — and many of the deep wells and large dams found in remote, arid northern Kenya were probably built by them. But when the climate changed and the lakes dried up these early settlers moved on again — southwest to the hills above Lake Victoria.

About 3,000 years ago they were followed by an eastern Cushitic pastoralist group, the Yaaku, which occupied much of central Kenya for several centuries. Even now, a small remnant group lives on, north-west of Mount Kenya at the edge of the Laikipia escarpment. Where the Yaaku settled, the hunter-gatherers who lived there adopted their language. Yaaku-speakers were also assimilated by other agricultural communities and spread across the land.

In the next millennium, between 500 BC and AD 500, the ancestors of the present-day Kenyan communities began to arrive from all over the continent. Nourished by the rich grazing and fine farmlands, well-watered by the streams and rivers, this tide of Cushitic, Nilotic, and Bantu groups stayed on. The expansion of the smaller, darker, iron-making Bantu farmers which began 2,000 years ago in south-eastern Nigeria, was explosive. Today the Bantu, who only arrived at their present locations in the 19th century, occupy a great deal of central, southern, and eastern Africa — and continue to move into new lands.

Yet, even at the conclusion of these epochs of trans-African migration and internal tribe-state expansion, the Kenyan hinterland remained as mysterious to the rest of the world as the far side of the moon.

The Taru Desert on the first inland steppe served as a forbidding natural barrier that few were brave or foolhardy enough to tackle. The Rift Valley far beyond was another vast and natural impediment. Through successive millennia, geographers and academics and others could only vaguely conjecture what lay inland.

But the Kenya coast was already known. The first unequivocal description is in the log of the Greek Diogenes, who returned to Egypt from a voyage of exploration around AD 110. His log lists the cloth, tools, glass, brass, copper, iron, olives, adzes, weapons, ivory, and rhinoceros horn loaded and unloaded at Mombasa, ruled by King Muza. Not much later the geographer Ptolemy, another Greek living in Egypt, incorporated the same details in his 'Map of the World', *circa* AD 150.

Island of War

Almost another millennium would pass before the arrival of Islam — and the dawn of the coast's golden age, around the ninth century, which gave rise to a glorious cultural and architectural heritage.

By the 14th century, a distinctive community — the Swahili — had emerged. The name Swahili derives from the Arabic plural of Sahel, meaning coast. The Islamic religion was the Arab legacy; the Kiswahili language the Bantu. The Arabian and Persian settlers developed coastal and caravan trade, established commercial centres, and made great contributions to the new literature, arts, and crafts. Their crude rag-and-coral homes gradually gave way to the architectural glories of fine houses, mosques, and monuments. Tall residences with elegantly-carved balconies overlooked each other, providing continuous shade in the narrow streets below. From the outset

Mombasa was rich in gold and ivory. Near the end of the 15th century these marked it out as a prize for the Portuguese fleets whose greatest navigator, Vasco da Gama, was ordered in 1497 by King John to round the Cape and find the sea route to India. When the Portuguese fleet entered Mombasa harbour a year later, it was repulsed by the Arabs, who cut their anchor ropes.

Da Gama sailed on to a royal welcome in Malindi from the local sultan. But Mombasa suffered for its reprisal. Two years later Cabral sailed behind da Gama and sacked the town. Five years later, in 1505, another Portuguese mariner, Almeida, came to plunder, followed 23 years later by the pillaging sailors of Nuna da Cunha.

Finally the Portuguese occupied Mombasa and, between 1593 and 1598 built the brooding bastion of Fort Jesus, overlooking the entrance to the old harbour. Its ramparts and battlements, weathered over 400 years, remain silent witness to the town's turbulent history. The stormy centuries that followed earned Mombasa its name as the 'Island of War'— Mvita.

Arab resistance was strong. They attacked from sea and land but, even backed by the forces of the Turkish corsair, Ali Bey, they were unable to shake off the tenacious Portuguese.

The first of Kenya's European colonizers remained for a century, defying siege and disease, surviving almost entirely off produce from convoys sailing from Goa, where they had established another enclave. The Portuguese downfall was the siege of Fort Jesus which began in mid-March 1696. Some 50 Portuguese, together with 2,500 locals, were barricaded inside on short rations smuggled in at night for months. The fort was relieved — in September 1697 — by 150 Portuguese and 300 Indian troops. But they did not break the siege, which continued for another 15 months until — with the help of a passing Welsh captain and crew — the Arabs finally scaled the fortress walls.

Plague, disease and famine had taken a terrible toll. Inside the fort, only 13 people survived — 11 men and two women. The merciless Arabs ran them through immediately. Finally, in 1720, the last Portuguese garrison left the Kenya coast for good. Within years it was almost as if they had

Below: Portuguese navigator Vasco da Gama.

Above: Rusting anchor outside Mombasa's Fort Jesus.

Above: Shot and cannon at Mombasa's 16th-century Fort Jesus.

never been, save for the maize, cassava, cashews, tomatoes and tobacco that they had introduced from the Americas.

Arab Renaissance

Once again the coastal towns were subject to the Arabs. But throughout the 18th century, the rival Omani dynasties reflected in their African territories the mutually destructive intrigues at home. Trade dwindled and the coast no longer prospered.

Then, in 1805, Bey Saidi Sultan Sayyid Said stabbed the incumbent ruler and seized power in Oman. Seventeen years later, secure upon his throne, he sent an army to quell the islands of Pate, Pemba, and Mombasa, which were under the rule of the Mazruis.

When the British ship HMS *Leven* visited Mombasa, the embattled Mazruis begged its commander, Captain Owen, for British protection. And on 7 February 1824, the officer proclaimed Mombasa a British 'protectorate'. In return, the Mazruis agreed to abolish slavery. Well pleased with his Christian crusade, Owen appointed his first officer, Lieutenant John Reitz, as proconsul, together with an interpreter, four sailors, and four marines. Sending messages to London and India asking for ratification of the 'treaty', he then set sail to continue his voyage.

This casual negotiation marked the beginning of British influence in East Africa. In the history of empire, there can be few instances to match such cursory presumption of imperial power but, ultimately, it led to Kenya's colonization.

Two months later, with Reitz dead from malaria, his deputy, Lieutenant John Emery, assumed the role of 'Governor' — a function that lasted for the next two years — until Whitehall, which had sat on Owen's agreement, repudiated it.

So did Britain relinquish its first brief foothold in Kenya, not to return to lay its imprint, first on Mombasa and then remorselessly inland, until more than half-a-century later.

Those 50 years were a time of unparalleled prosperity for the Sultan. From Cape Guardafui to Cape Delgado, the African coast was his acknowledged dominion and, as the slave trails ran up through the

hinterland as far as Lake Victoria, his dreams of an African empire began to flower.

But, even as they did so, Sayyid Said, who had moved the Omani government to Zanzibar, came under increasing pressure from Britain to halt the trade and, in 1845, he was forced into a treaty which severely restricted it. In 1844, the year before the treaty, the German missionary Johann Ludwig Krapf had established a British Church Missionary Society mission at Rabai just a few kilometres from Mombasa on the mainland. In 1846 he was joined by Johannes Rebmann. Both men wanted to end the slave trade and convert Africa to Christianity — and to achieve their aims they travelled far inland, where few Europeans had ever ventured.

The Explorers
From the second half of the 18th century the question of East Africa aroused an unusual degree of passion, conscience, and diatribe within the British political parties and the ruling classes.

Legions of leaders, from Prime Minister Pitt's first term of office in 1783, sought by every means to evade British involvement in this unknown territory.

In the end, the overwhelming force of Victorian puritanism and scientific curiosity — a mixture of empirical pride, the desire to explore, and Christian conscience — were enough to inspire the British to venture forth into the 'Dark Continent'. In the middle of the 19th century, the anti-slavery campaign was at its height. Missionary and explorer became one in their endeavour to end the trade in human souls and, at the same time, chart the interior and discover the source of the Nile, long believed to be part of a great watershed in the East African interior.

Greater impetus was given to British curiosity by the discovery of a permanent layer of snow on top of 5,986-metre (19,340-foot) Mount Kilimanjaro.

Johannes Rebmann saw the mountain on 11 May 1848, two years after his arrival at Mombasa, during an upcountry evangelical mission to the Chagga people. Among the learned academics of London

Opposite: Liberty Bell, Freretown, Mombasa.

his report provoked outrage. Such statements, wrote one Desborough Cooley, an important member of the Royal Geographical Society, '. . . could not fail to awaken mistrust. . . Those eternal snows . . . have so little shape . . . they take quite a spectral character'.

Cooley's wrath must have been compounded 19 months later when Rebmann's colleague, Johann Ludwig Krapf, set out from his Rabai mission (see 'Nairobi-Mombasa: A Highway to Adventure', Part Two) on a visit to Ukamba, north-east of Kilimanjaro. From a hill close to Kitui, he saw the twin peaks of Mount Kenya, also snowclad, straddled across the Equator 160 kilometres (100 miles) away. It was 3 December 1849.

Five years later Krapf produced a rough map of the interior showing the approximate locations of Kilimanjaro and 'Kenia'. It also showed a single inland sea — possibly Lake Victoria. It was largely to find out if this sea was the source of the Nile, that Richard Burton and John Hanning Speke set out from Zanzibar in 1856.

British concern, and curiosity, over East Africa reached its peak in the 1880s when the Royal Geographical Society despatched Joseph Thomson to explore the region. In spite of Stanley's advice to 'take a thousand men or die' in the warrior kingdoms of the Maasai, Thomson, then 26, set forth in March 1883 with just 143 porters and commissaries, of which only a dozen could fire a rifle. His odyssey was as remarkable for its humour as its adventure. He charted virtually all of what is today Kenya, with the exception of its great northern deserts. Keeping a steady distance between himself and the following Maasai, the Scotsman marched on from the base of Kilimanjaro to Lake Naivasha, in the shadows of the extinct volcano Longonot. Then he continued up the eastern wall of the Rift Valley to the 3,999-metre (13,120-foot) heights of the Nyandarua (Aberdares) mountain massif.

It was there, as he crested the moorlands early one morning, that Mount Kenya (*Kirinyaga*, sacred peak and abode of the Kikuyu God, *Ngai*) shed its veils of mist and revealed the startling glory of its eternal necklace of ice: glistening glaciers astride the Equator beneath the twin peaks of Batian and Nelion, which, at 5,199 metres (17,058 feet), is second in Africa only to Kilimanjaro (see 'Heartland Kenya: Magic Mountains, Moorlands Wild', Part Two).

From there he ventured northward along the floor of the Rift to Lake Baringo and then up the precipitous Elgeyo Escarpment, the western wall of the Rift. He crossed the moorlands of Mount Elgon — 4,322 metres (14,180 feet) high — and returned through the western plains of Kenya on the shores of Lake Victoria to the coast. By any standards, it was a monumental feat of endurance and enterprise.

Thomson, a genuinely modest man, was a hero back in England. His heady adventures in the wilds of Africa fired the Victorian imagination. Soon afterwards, other missions set off into the uncharted areas on either side of his route.

In 1885 James Hannington, an Anglican bishop, on his way to start a diocese in Uganda, found a lake that Thomson had missed just before Baringo. But as he went on towards the Nile, Hannington was murdered. The lake, which was named in his honour, is now known as Bogoria.

The following year, another monumental safari traversed the Kikuyu heartland and went on far north to discover a massive inland sea — Lake Turkana — which the local Samburu called, in the Maa language, *Embasso Narok* ('the Black Lake').

The leader of this 700-strong expedition was Count Samuel Teleki von Szek a rich Austro-Hungarian. With him he took Lieutenant Ludwig von Höhnel, a meticulous biographer, who painstakingly recorded every step of the epic journey. They named the lake 'Rudolf' for Austria's crown prince, who was later to shoot himself and his mistress at Mayerling.

In the 1890s, Arthur Donaldson Smith and William Astor Chanler, two Americans, surveyed the Tana River and northeastern bush, outlining the land to become known as Kenya.

Throughout all this, in an atmosphere of intensifying international rivalry, the Germans also sought to impose their influence in East Africa, particularly in what became Tanganyika, where the mercenary Carl Peters persuaded many unsuspecting and illiterate chiefs to 'sign' Treaties of Friendship — treaties which they neither understood nor could ever dispute.

Now the British

Europe's political squabble for this land of stunning beauty astride the Equator had barely begun. Thomson's written account, *Through Masai Land*, was the final thrust needed to propel Britain's imperial instincts into an East African adventure.

To Western eyes, unstructured and unhegemonic, Kenya promised only bountiful harvests and was there for the taking. Thomson's journey had been across a loosely-defined land. As now, Kenya was then a kaleidoscope of people and cultures, but local boundaries were delineated in accordance with the traditional balance of power.

The Maasai had ascendancy over grazing grounds around Kilimanjaro, Naivasha and the Mara. The Kikuyu were content to cultivate the fertile, higher grounds of the escarpments and mountains.

To the Luo, Akamba, Giriama, Turkana, Abagusii, Samburu, Abaluhya, Boran, Taita, Kipsigis, Maasai, Kikuyu, Meru and Nandi peoples the tribal territories were as well defined as the fiefdoms of Scotland and the shires of England.

Though Kenya's dynamics were tribal, its strengths were those of warriors whose history of battle honours dated back 1,000 years or more. Their characteristics of courage were noted by the incoming Europeans. There was about this yet-to-be defined nation and its people a character that set it apart from the rest of Africa.

In 1886, soon after Thomson's return, Britain and Germany agreed to the extent of the Zanzibar dominion. On the strength of Peters' treaties, what is today mainland Tanzania became the German colony of Tanganyika, and Kenya and Uganda were assigned to the British.

A fellow Scot of Thomson's, Sir William Mackinnon, was already established in East African trade and the anti-slavery campaign through his British India Steam Navigation Company's fleet, which plied regularly between Zanzibar and British ports.

Even before Thomson's epic adventure, Mackinnon had been invited by the Sultan of Zanzibar to lay down proposals for a chartered trading company that would operate throughout East Africa. Nothing came of it until 1887 when, with the back-

Above: Joseph Thomson on his walk *Through Masai Land*.

ing of the Foreign Office, he founded the British East Africa Association. Within a year it had a capital of £240,000, a Royal Charter, and an appropriate name for such an enterprise: the Imperial British East Africa Company (IBEA).

IBEA built its headquarters — a crude shantytown of iron — at Mombasa. It coined its own money, printed its own postage stamps, and published its own treaty documents. These impressive forms carried the seal of Crown authority, if not the weight. With these IBEA set about establishing its presence in the interior. Its young officers carried the flag which encapsulated the anti-slavery convictions of IBEA's founder. It bore the message: 'Light and Liberty'.

Between 1888 and 1890 they hoisted the flag over several IBEA upcountry outposts. A small contingent of British officials and soldiers carved a 500-kilometre-long (300-mile) dirt road to Machakos and beyond — to a flat, dank, fever-ridden swamp called Nyrobi by the Maasai, meaning 'place of the cold waters'. These men lived under siege for most of the time. Walk today a

Above: Kenya's earliest Anglican church — St Paul's, built at Rabai in 1887 and still in use. At right is the house that Johannes Rebmann built.

SIR WILLIAM MACKINNON, BART.

SIR FREDERICK LUGARD, K.C.M.G.,
C.B., D.S.O.

few hundred metres from Fort Smith, now aged and mellow, and in a field you'll come across the marble headstones, untended and neglected, of three British officers: one the victim of the Kikuyu, another of a lioness, the third of dysentery.

At the end of 1889 IBEA had recruited ex-Indian Army officer Frederick Dealtry —later Lord — Lugard, and assigned him the perilous task of surveying a new route to the company station at Machakos, run by John Ainsworth, who was to play a major role in the early growth of Nairobi.

Returning to Mombasa five months later, Lugard was immediately ordered to march again, this time through Kikuyuland to Uganda. He was to make alliances but he preferred to negotiate with the tribes in simpler terms than those rendered on the regal-looking treaty forms that he carried.

He struck treaties with the Kikuyu and other people through their own unshakeable bond, that of blood brother. Lugard felt it more honourable and less demanding of African credibility. One treaty he concluded was at Fort Smith with the Kikuyu chief Kinyanjui, who planted a fig tree in the compound of the fort as a symbol of the new-found friendship between his people and the British.

The Lunatic Express

The key to penetrating the interior, of course, was a railway to the great lake, Victoria — 1,000 kilometres (620 miles) away across some of the most hostile terrain in the world.

Mackinnon originally conceived this idea as a weapon against slavery and sowed the seed with 11 kilometres (seven miles) of comic track on Mombasa Island which was grandiosely called the 'Central African Railway'. It was later pulled up and re-laid as a municipal tramway powered by labourers who pushed and pulled the little rickshaw-style tramcars.

But the seed of Makinnon's vision grew in others, and blossomed in a magnificent obsession which found flower in two strange bedfellows — Lugard and Sir Gerald Portal, Britain's acting consul in Zanzibar. Lugard's experiences had turned him into an evangelist for British annexation of Uganda as a protectorate. The 35-year-old Portal, who embarked with his

Above: Fort Smith, now a private residence, near Kabete, Nairobi.

brother on what for both of them was to be a fatal fact-finding mission to Uganda, was aghast at the behaviour of IBEA officers such as Lugard. 'The combination of administration and trading is fatal,' he reported to the British Foreign Office.

Certainly it was more than IBEA could sustain. Each post required over 2,000 man-loads of between 27 and 31 kilos (60-70lbs) of supplies a year. Portal saw the impossible logistics of this. In his final recommendation, shortly before his death from fever contracted at Mumias on his return journey, he wrote: 'To effect any real improvement in property or commerce, efficiently to reap the benefit of material progress that may be made, there is but one course open. . . . The only means of effectively doing this is by a railway.'

Portal died and Lugard lived to achieve great honours, but despite their differences both had the same ambition — to establish a permanent British presence in East Africa. The idea of the railway aroused fervid opposition and ridicule on all sides. The loudest voice against was that of the radical Henry Labouchere, who warned the British Parliament that whenever Britain 'annexes some wretched, miserable jungle in the centre of Africa, we will be called upon to build a railroad to it'. The government of Lord Salisbury, however, prevailed. The estimated cost, £3.6 million (it eventually exceeded £5 million), was phenomenal for those days. Britain's sense of imperial righteousness had never been greater. But 1,000 kilometres (620 miles) of track — crossing a burnt-out desert, an infinite stretch of thorn and scrub savannah, climbing the walls of the Great Rift Valley, and down the almost sheer face for 600 metres (2,000 feet), ending with 160 kilometres (100 miles) across a spongelike morass of swamp and cotton soil plain — required an engineering miracle.

And along every mile lay in wait ferocious predators, both human and animal, little water, and endemic diseases for which no Empire had yet found the cures. Why build it at all, notwithstanding the situation in Uganda? Why, indeed?

Nobody knew, not even Sir Charles Eliot, one of the first British administrators to serve in Nairobi, who wrote in 1904: 'It

Above: Britain's Zanzibar-based Consul-General, Sir Arthur Hardinge, with the Maasai leader Lenana.

is a curious confession, but I do not know why the Uganda Railway was built, and I think many people in East Africa share my ignorance.'

Henry Labouchere anticipated him by nine years. After an acrimonious exchange during the parliamentary debate on the railway estimates, when George Curzon, Under Secretary of State for Foreign Affairs, pronounced that without a railway to the coast a British protectorate in Uganda would be absurd, Labouchere replied in satirical verse in the London magazine *Truth*:

What it will cost no words can express;
What is its object no brain can suppose;
Where it will start from no one can guess;
Where it is going to nobody knows;
What is the use of it none can conjecture;
What it will carry there's none can define;
And in spite of George Curzon's superior
lecture,
It clearly is naught but a lunatic line.

Shanty Town

Lunatic or not, a little under three years after the first rail was laid in place in Mom-

basa in August 1896, it had reached the railhead at Mile 327, where lion, cheetah, zebra, antelope, dik-dik, duiker, wart hog, and ostrich roamed in abundance.

Two or three lean-to shacks, stables for oxen and mule, an army telegraph office run by Sergeant George Ellis of the Royal Engineers, and a few tents were the only signs of human occupation. At the end of May 1899, these crude shelters were swollen by a town of tents — a camp for thousands of workers brought in like flotsam on the irreversible tide of the railway which had now assumed a will of its own and swept all before it with a purpose and direction nothing could deflect. So it was by accident, in a miscarriage of circumstances and out of recrimination and chaos, that Nairobi was born. Fifty-six kilometres (35 miles) behind, flanked by hills, and surrounded by trees, IBEA's former upcountry administrator and now Crown servant, John Ainsworth, delighted in his Machakos headquarters.

He had assumed, wrongly, that George Whitehouse, the railway's chief engineer, would centralize his operations in this

Above: R O Preston's ramp railway overcame the eastern wall of the Rift Valley in 1900.

pleasant verdure, but had watched in consternation as the railroad paused, then by-passed the ring of his beloved Iveti Hills to carve a straight scar through the Kapiti Plains to the eastern ramp of the Rift.

In three years and 530 kilometres (330 miles) the track had eased itself one-and-a-half kilometres (one mile) above sea level in a steady, equable ascent. Railhead would be at Nairobi for one reason only. There was no more flatland.

In the next 56 kilometres (35 miles) the railway would have to climb half its height again — 670 metres (2,200 feet) to the lip of the escarpment, a gradient averaging one-in-84. Machakos and Kikuyu, pleasantly situated 300 metres (1,000 feet) higher than Nairobi, with rich, red soil and great forests, had both been suggested as tentative railheads. Whitehouse had ignored the suggestions. Yet his decision to rebuild his resources and centralize the railroad's ad-

ministration in Nairobi was made only in January 1899 — when he could prevaricate no longer. It was an engineer's decision, without thought or consideration for the natural consequences he should have foreseen. Whitehouse's blinkered eyes saw only track and the long divide between Nairobi and Lake Victoria. His brilliance as an engineer was unquestionable, but his vision of the future was myopic.

Blind to all but the immense requirements of manpower and material needed to achieve one of the most remarkable feats of engineering in the history of railway construction, Whitehouse unerringly chose the most unsuitable location within a radius of 160 kilometres (100 miles) as the site from which to direct his operations — the area around the papyrus swamp into which the Nairobi, Mathari, Masongawai, and Ngong streams drained. And men and impedimenta settled remorselessly on the glutinous black soil like a swarm of flies on a carcass. As the sun drew the mists from the swamp, so the railhead drew the traders, prostitutes, gentlemen of fortune, and the swelling hordes of inevitable camp followers. Ainsworth watched the birth of this instant slum, appalled.

Whitehouse, he and others reasoned, should have chosen Machakos and failing Machakos, the administration should have beeen moved up the hill to Kikuyu. Nairobi had neither drainage nor water supplies.

Within the next ten months more than 700 men died at the Nairobi railhead, and a graveyard became the first permanent fixture of the unborn city. The little cemetery on Nairobi's Uhuru Highway near the Railway Golf Course is a grim reminder.

Thirty months after reaching Nairobi, on 20 December 1901, Florence Preston, wife of Ronald Preston, the engineer who had led the construction work all the way, hammered home the last key of the track overlooking Lake Victoria. It was nothing short of a magnificent success and remains one of the great railways of the world.

It climbs from sea level through desert, grass plain, mountain, and forest to cross the Equator at 2,785 metres (9,136 feet) before descending to the humid 1,520 metres (3,773 feet) of Lake Victoria's shores.

This unforgettable journey across almost 1,000 kilometres (620 miles) covers much of the geographic and climatic range of Africa. Whitewhouse was honoured. He was made a Knight Commander of the Order of the Bath. The 'Lunatic Line' would, wrote best-selling author, Charles Miller, 'open a wilderness to trade and cultivation. From that thin metal line a colony would grow and there would be settlers, towns and cities in the sun. . . . He had seen a vision. . . His had been the burden, his the responsibility.' Eliot noted: 'It is not an uncommon thing for a line to open up a country, but this line has literally created a country.'

Certainly the railway was the catalyst that created a sense of nationalism, though never in the sense Eliot intended. Almost as soon as work on it started, Kenya's African communities served notice they would not surrender their liberty or land freely.

Paradise Found

The first decade-and-a-half of British rule in Kenya, from 1895 to 1910, was marked by a series of uprisings, particularly in the fertile western highlands, which the British suppressed by massacre and betrayal.

Although the majority seemed to accept the takeover passively, certain groups, among them the Kamba, were not so supine. Their resistance resulted in the despatch of at least four heavy-duty punitive military expeditions before the Kamba, weakened by rinderpest and smallpox, succumbed to 'Pax Britannica'.

To counter the Kikuyu's highland forest activities the British established garrisons — at Fort Smith and near the Maasai *manyatta* on the Nairobi River at Ngong. The Nandi tribe, too, was equally defiant. In 1895, from their verdant hills above Lake Victoria, the Nandi started the guerrilla resistance which lasted more than ten years.

Eventually their leader, seer, and soothsayer, *laibon* Koitalel, was lured to peace talks under a flag of truce and then shot dead during a punitive military expedition led by Captain Richard Meinertzhagen.

Subjugated, but never acquiescent, on pain of death the Nandi were forced into compliance and by 1905 the Nandi Hills were quiet. Through most of the first decade of this century, British punitive expeditions were also busy in the north, especially around Turkana where the Turkana warriors were never wholly subjugated. Similar resistance was faced in Luhya territory, around Broderick Falls in north-western Kenya, and in the Kisii highlands of the Abagusii.

Until the dawn of the century the renowned Maasai were among the most intractable of those who opposed the colonists. In 1895, when a passing caravan on the slave trail through the Kedong Valley made too many advances to the warriors' girlfriends, the Maasai warriors cut down at least 500 of the 1,100-strong party.

This brought a response from a European — Andrew 'Trader' Dick — who happened to be nearby and decided to exact retribution on behalf of the Crown: something for which he had no authority or mandate. Attacking the Maasai and making off with a large number of their cattle, he fled up the escarpment around Uplands. When the Maasai finally caught up with him, Dick was added to the 452 Kikuyu

Above:1989 steam train excursion through the Rift Valley.

and 98 Swahili they had killed earlier. A court of inquiry found that the Maasai had been unjustly provoked and they were acquitted — but their cattle were seized.

Land was the lure that drew nearly every settler. In their minds Kenya, if not actually El Dorado, was the closest thing yet. The railway's objective was simple. It needed produce to carry to earn revenues — and farmers would provide that produce. But in such a vast country there was no way of knowing who owned land.

The administration surveyed vast tracts of the fertile 'White Highlands' which seemed to be unoccupied and sold them in parcels for settlement. Traditional tribal disputes over grazing and agricultural land paled against these massive territorial seizures. Hugh Cholmondeley, the aristocratic third Baron Delamere, who mortgaged his Vale Royal estates in Cheshire to establish large-scale mixed farming in the Rift Val-

ley, was one of the major players in this first decade. Another settler, 'Pop' Binks, was also determined to have his share of this tropical paradise and scouted around Nairobi for his own Arcadia. Eventually Binks found 65 hectares (160 acres) in the Kikuyu Forest. His experience casts some light on the difficulties of the early settlers.

The asking price from the Crown was two rupees an acre, together with 180 rupees for a Crown survey, the price payable in 32 annual instalments. It worked out at about US$10 a year. At the end of 32 years the settler was given the freehold title. But Binks soon discovered that the 'Promised Land' was not all it appeared to be.

One condition was that he put at least six hectares (16 acres) a year under cultivation. Thus, at the end of ten years, the landholder would have the entire 65 hectares under cultivation. But, as Binks put it, it would be doubtful if he 'could even sell a

Above: The highest railway station in the Commonwealth: 2,656 metres above sea level in the Timboroa highlands.

cabbage'. In his first year he paid five rupees in Nairobi for 26 kilos (60 lbs) of potato seed, but he was offered only one-and-a-half rupees for the entire crop. Binks, however, lacked Delamere's vision and determination. The Cheshire nobleman envisaged Kenya as the granary of Africa — and his faith never faltered.

Within a year of Pop's failure, potatoes were being shipped by rail and sea to South Africa, at the cost of £3 a ton. The bi-weekly rail service between Mombasa and Nairobi was already beginning to show a profit as new people and goods arrived with every ship that docked at Mombasa.

Life for many in the new British Protectorate, despite the price of imported goods and hazards of farming, had its good side.

'My pay in India,' Meinertzhagen noted on 25 July 1902, 'was exactly £108 a year and now I find myself with £400 a year under cheaper conditions for, outside luxuries such as cartridges, alcohol, etc., living is absurdly cheap. Eggs three a penny, sheep 3 rupees, a chicken half-a-rupee, and we grow our own vegetables. My daily ex-

Opposite: Jacaranda blooms on Nairobi's Kenyatta Avenue.

penditure on food is only about the equivalent of 2s a day.' The army captain who arrived in Nairobi in 1902 without a penny left in 1906 with £3,000.

Land Grab
Land sales were the great betrayal of African interests. The blame, however, was not altogether on the Crown's side, for Lenana, the Maasai chief, had welcomed the Europeans warmly and was to agree to the disposal of the tribe's highland ranges.

The key to successful large-scale farming was adequate labour, but Africans were reluctant to work for somebody else. By introducing hut taxes and other laws, however, the administration forced them into low-paid wage employment, creating a cash economy in a land of barter.

The resentment went deep. But firm in his belief in the supremacy of white dominion, Eliot was untroubled by the prospect of the Africans giving way to the European.

'There can be no doubt that the Masai and many other tribes must go under. It is a prospect which I view with equanimity and clear conscience.' In an entry in his diary on 13 July 1902, Meinertzhagen noted that Eliot was a 'scholar, philosopher and a very able man with great vision'.

But he disagreed with Eliot's vision of the day when the whole of Kenya would be a thriving European colony, the whole of the Rift Valley cultivated, and the entire country under white settlement.

'I suggested,' recalls Meinertzhagen, 'that the country belonged to Africans and that their interests must prevail over the interests of strangers. He would not have it. . . . I said that some day the African would be educated and armed.

'Eliot thought that day was so far distant as not to matter . . . but I am convinced that in the end the Africans will win.'

Meinertzhagen had much the same argument with Delamere. 'I take the view, with which Delamere has no patience, that in a hundred years time there may be 50,000 white settlers with flourishing farms and 5,000,000 discontented and envious natives; can the white man hold out against such numbers without terrible slaughter?'

In the euphoria of the new colony, however, Meinertzhagen was a voice out of tune. No realistic vision could be allowed to mar the joyous illusion of white supremacy that existed in those early days.

Meinertzhagen was not alone in his conviction. From the outset Whitehall maintained that the interests of the African were paramount in Kenya. Eliot resigned. But almost immediately on taking office, his successor, the bucolic Sir Donald Stewart, presided over the Maasai 'sellout' initialled by himself and Lenana. In this and a subsequent 1911 treaty, the Maasai surrendered all their grazing grounds in the highlands in exchange for the fragile, arid pastures of south-western and southern Kenya. Other areas, the most fertile in a country where about 80 per cent of the land is marginal, were also earmarked exclusively for European settlement. Inevitably there was bitterness — a bitterness that came to be expressed in the African struggle for *Uhuru*, the Kiswahili word for freedom.

White Settlers
Delamere, the extraordinary, titian-haired, leprechaun of an English lord, tried — and more often than not failed — in many farming ventures that did much to sow the seeds for Kenya's farm industry.

With many experiments he lost a fortune. He imported high-grade Australian sheep, but the land on which they grazed was mineral deficient. He ploughed in English clover, restocked with sheep, and watched the clover fail. The indigenous African bees were unable to pollinate it. He imported English bees — and this worked.

But with no dormant winter period to keep the crop down, and no frost to kill off the pests, the clover grew into a luxuriant, shin-high jungle. The sheep died of foot rot. Then he tried cattle, mixing good beef stock from his Cheshire estate with the long-horned, hump-backed Boran cattle of the northern tribes.

The progeny were resistant to most local viruses — but not to a new East Coast fever which came up from German East Africa and wiped them out again.

The Maasai, who had cynically watched the misfortunes of this eccentric Englishman, for some reason — perhaps admiration for the peer's tenacity, or for the new cattle breeds that he had introduced — now came to his rescue. They offered to manage Delamere's stock and, with the help of imported veterinary science, built up the cattle on those sections of the ranch where they knew the grazing could support the herds. The Maasai had won a staunch supporter for their land battles with the British administration.

As his ranching ventures gathered momentum, after months of isolation on the farm Delamere earned a reputation as a 'damned scallywag' for his party rampages through Nairobi with other fun-seeking settlers.

Their arrival in Nairobi was usually the start of a cavalry charge down Government Road (now Moi Avenue), often shooting out the glass street lamps. Other 'enjoyable' entertainment included disrupting chic garden parties and heavy drinking sprees in one of the clubs, usually Muthaiga, which Delamere often capped by riding his horse into the Norfolk Hotel to blast off his six-gun at the bottles behind the bar. Throughout his life, this controversial character remained a vigorous protagonist of a white Kenya. But although he and the young Winston Churchill took a liking to each other when they enjoyed a day's pig-sticking on Delamere's Elmenteita ranch during the latter's 1907 visit, Churchill was against an autonomous white colony.

Subsequently Churchill wrote: 'Just and honourable discipline, careful education, sympathetic comprehension are all that are needed to bring a very large proportion of the tribes of East Africa to a far higher social level than that at which they now stand. And it is, after all, their Africa.'

Yet, despite Whitehall's insistence that Kenya was a protectorate and therefore a 'foreign country' where the British code of law did not apply, in August 1907 a seven-man Legislative Council (Legco) was established with Lord Delamere as one of the settler members. The fact that four million Africans were without representation or that 600 or so settlers and the administration were the sole voice was not taken into consideration.

By 1912, however, the protectorate had begun to pay its way and the European population stood at 3,000.

When the First World War ended in 1918, the most significant political consequence was the British Government's decision to offer war veterans land in the high-lands settlement scheme. Farms were either given away to winners of a lottery or sold at nominal cost on long-term credit. The objective was to increase the European settler population and, therefore, revenue.

The scheme was bitterly resented by the African community, not least by those who had fought alongside these same soldiers in the Great War in which many Africans died. Naturally they, too, looked for gains on account of their war efforts.

But nothing was forthcoming, neither for them nor for any other sections of the African and Asian communities. Thus the scheme was seen as an overt move to advance the objective of a permanent White Man's Kenya.

By 1922 — two years after Kenya ceased to be a protectorate and became a colony— the European population had risen to more than 10,000 and in the White Highlands the settlers had laid claim to the best 27,000 square kilometres (10,500 square miles) of the country. Nevertheless, a 1923 government White Paper stated that the old principle of Africa for the Africans was to be revived and enforced:

'Primarily, Kenya is an African country. H M Government think it necessary definitely to record their considered opinion that the interests of the African native must be paramount, and that if and when those interests and the interests of the immigrant races should conflict, then the former should prevail.'

From then on, a succession of governors — with or without personal conviction — were obliged to uphold the policy. By the 1920s, many Africans, principally the Kikuyu, had found work in the rapidly growing capital of Nairobi — crossing the social and geographical divide from African bush to sophisticated, cosmopolitan town. But their traditional lifelines remained firm. The *shamba* (farm) retained its quasi-religious significance in the lives of the new urban dwellers who left their senior wives behind to ensure its maintenance.

Struggle for Freedom

Some of these young Kikuyu formed urban community groups. Their fundamental concern was land, and these early associations in Nairobi orchestrated and articulated the demand for the return of the 'alienated' Highlands. Around this time, a former mission boy, Johnstone Kamau, took a job as a water meter inspector with the Nairobi Municipal Council. As his involvement in the political organization of the Kikuyu increased, he changed his name to Jomo Kenyatta.

If the urban Kikuyu constituted the main political body in Kenya, then the Asians were the natural clients of a burgeoning civil service bureaucracy. As Churchill had forecast, they worked long hours in closed, mutually-supportive communities to establish a near-monopoly in trade, light industry, and semi-professional services. Some already had enough capital to fund local development projects in partnership with the government. Others provided credit to the settlers between harvests. Most settlers saw this purely as an economic bridge between two socially distinct communities. They reacted offensively, labelling the Asians 'the Jews of East Africa'. Others responded with resignation, bemused by the changed relationship between the Indian and the British Raj.

Essentially, Nairobi society was composed of two upper levels: officers of the Crown and officers of the British Army commanding African infantry battalions.

Although some considered the white settlers socially agreeable, many found their aristocratic eccentricity and colonial attitudes too pretentious. One officer, the Earl of Lytton, preferred the solitude of a command at Baragoi, in the desert of Samburu country, and the occasional company of the respected Baron von Otter, who led a long British campaign against the Turkana tribe, earning their respect.

Regardless of material substance, new immigrants automatically entered the upper social bracket. All were entrepreneurs of some sort — commercial speculators, professionals, skilled artisans, or remittance men and were allied to the administration since only a few 'made the settler grade'.

In Nairobi, the Muthaiga Country Club served as the settlers' hangout as well as an elegant venue for hunt balls, the occasional wild party and other revelry which, in the permissive scenario played out in the Wanjohi — 'Happy' — Valley of the highlands, was said to include wife-swapping. An acclaimed heroine of this period was

Isak Dinesen, the Baroness Blixen of *Out of Africa* fame, whose titled hunter husband, Bror, took off with another woman, leaving her to go bankrupt on their Nairobi coffee farm under the Ngong Hills. Among others, she entertained Edward, Prince of Wales, and her own tragic love story with Denys Finch Hatton was made into *Out of Africa*, an Oscar-winning film.

But looming over the early settlers eccentric — and debauched — gaiety were the Kikuyu woodsmen waiting to chop down their Elysian paradise.

In the next few years, as the settlers continued to press their claims for autonomy, Africans intensified their demands for the restoration of their liberty and the release of their lands. They were supported by many of Kenya's Asian community who, like the Africans, were denied representation in government, and placed in a social 'ghetto' between the two communities.

Several factors militated against the settlers achieving autonomy. One was the founding of the East African Association, the first pan-Kenyan nationalist movement, led by Harry Thuku, which was supported by a number of influential and militant Asians. His subsequent arrest resulted in the massacre of 23 Kenyan Africans outside Nairobi's Central police station in March 1922 (Thuku was detained and remained incarcerated for seven years).

The incident welded Kenya's African communities firmly together in their demands for freedom, which were given added impetus in the 1923 Devonshire White Paper: 'primarily Kenya is an African territory . . . [and] the interests of the African natives must be paramount'.

Another boost came from Sir Ormsby Gore who, in 1922, asserted that the 'ultimate object that I have in regard to Kenya Colony . . . [is] that it should be regarded primarily as an African country . . . that we should be there for Africans first as we are in Nigeria, and . . . it should not become an Indian colony or a white English colony'.

Gore's view was anathema to Governor Sir Robert — 'Gentlemen, you may remember that I am South-African born' — Coryndon. So, too, was Thuku's organization which, being open to all ethnic groups, represented a complete nullification of his administration's policy of divide-and-rule.

Coryndon gave an order to change its name to the Kikuyu Association. Thus, the association's complaints unheeded by the settler-dominated Legco, Kenyatta left for England in 1929 to present the association's case in Britain.

He returned in September 1930. The following year Harry Thuku was released and the Carter Land Commission was convened to adjudicate on land interests in Kenya.

Once again Kenyatta sailed to Britain to present the African case — the start of many long and lonely years of self-imposed exile. Although he gave evidence to the commission in 1932, its findings — published in 1934 — exacerbated the ever-widening rift between African and European.

The commission delineated the permanent barriers between European-owned farms in the highlands and what it described as African Land Units, henceforth labelled 'reserves'. Five years later, on the eve of the Second World War, Legco passed legislation confirming the barriers drawn in the Carter report.

As a result, the number of political organizations demanding greater African participation proliferated. But one immediate consequence of the war was that all African political associations were banned in 1940 and 23 of their leaders detained under new wartime defence regulations.

The despairing voice of the vast majority remained largely unheard, even though in 1944 Eliud Mathu, an early product of Balliol College, Oxford, became the first African to be nominated a member of Legco.

The voice of African protest was swollen by the clamour of thousands of veterans returning from the war theatres of Asia and Europe where, during the five-year-long conflict, they had been exposed to many fresh influences. As discontent grew, the tide of freedom turned into a ground swell that swept across Africa.

Two of its most articulate proponents were Kwame Nkrumah of what would become the first independent African state, Ghana, and Jomo Kenyatta. Together they participated in the Fifth Pan-African Congress in Manchester in 1945. The following year, in September 1946, Kenyatta returned home from a self-imposed exile of 15 years.

Meanwhile, well aware of his need for a base from which to speak in Legco, Mathu had formed the Kenya African Study Union. It attracted moderates such as Harry Thuku, who became its first president, and more passionate advocates of freedom, such as James Gichuru who, within a few months, replaced him.

The union's title was soon shortened to the more pragmatic Kenya African Union (KAU). In 1947, Gichuru resigned to let Kenyatta, widely acknowledged as the one man who could unite the various African political and ethnic factions and give common voice to the aspirations of all, become president. The colonial administration's response was to increase African participation in Legco to four — a token recognition of discontent far from enough to satisfy the forces of protest about to be unleashed.

Under Kenyatta, KAU grew swiftly. Political agitation spread throughout the country, and resulted in a hardening of the colonial government's attitude.

When police suppressed strikes at Mombasa port and the Uplands bacon factory on the Limuru escarpment by firing on demonstrators, the stage was set for the long drawn-out battle for freedom.

Now the Kikuyu formed secret societies. New members were sworn in through ancient and traditional oathing ceremonies. Others, including two fanatical religious groups, and politically-conscious members of the Luo, Maasai, Luhya, Kamba and Kipsigis followed suit.

The Kikuyu-dominated Mau Mau came into existence in 1948 as a natural consequence of the colonial authorities refusal to recognize African demands for the return of their land and proper representation in Legco. It was proscribed in 1950. Its aims were considered violent.

Not all saw violence as the solution. Many Kikuyu, including Kenyatta, still sought a middle road to political, economic, and social equality. Among them was Mbiyu Koinange, the son of a senior Kikuyu chief. Early in 1952 he and others formed the Kenya Citizens' Association.

They wanted peaceful change brought about by persuasion and conciliation rather than confrontation and violence. But although the majority of victims in the Mau Mau struggle were Africans loyal to their Christian Church or the authorities, Governor Sir Evelyn Baring had already demon-

Above: Britain's future King George VI on a 1920s Kenyan safari with the future Queen Elizabeth (later still, the Queen Mother).

strated that his administration was unwilling to compromise the interests of Kenya's vociferous white minority in any way.

The Final Battle

At midnight on 20 October 1952, one day after Sir Evelyn declared a State of Emergency and imposed martial law, Jomo Kenyatta and five colleagues — Paul Ngei, Kungu Karumba, Achieng Oneko, Bildad Kaggia and Fred Kubai — were arrested. Sir Evelyn's successor, Sir Patrick Renision, was to describe Kenyatta as a 'leader into darkness and death' — a slander that Kenyatta was to forgive but never forget.

The Mau Mau took to the forests to begin the war in earnest. Many innocent victims were caught in the middle, including at least 97 'loyalists' to the colonial administration who were brutally slaughtered.

While in custody awaiting trial on charges of organizing the Mau Mau — a charge he always denied — Kenyatta and his arrested colleagues heard about the 'Lari Massacre'.

Later, after what to many was a dubious trial at remote Kapenguria, in the Cherangani Hills, Kenyatta and his colleagues

were found guilty on the basis of what transpired to be perjured evidence. They were sentenced to seven years' hard labour in the scorched wastes of remote Lokitaung on the far north-western shores of Lake Turkana, known then as Lake Rudolf. There, far removed from the mainstream of Kenyan society, the administration perhaps hoped that the heat and dust of the semi-desert around Lokitaung would finish off Kenyatta, who was already in his fifties; or that, at least, his personality would cease to exercise its powerful influence on events.

In 1954 the inmates were joined by one of Mau Mau's military leaders, General 'China' Waruhui Itote, who was captured by colonial security forces in the highlands.

Now repression began in earnest. During 'Operation Anvil' carried out in Nairobi, almost 30,000 suspected Mau Mau sympathizers were rounded up and held in concentration camps.

In the months that followed, thousands of innocent men, women and children throughout the country were also incarcerated, many losing their homes and land. Two years later, in 1956, another Mau Mau leader, Dedan Kimathi, was trapped and wounded in an ambush. Brought to court, he was found guilty and later hanged — the first martyr to the cause of freedom.

Yet, even as the struggle escalated, the colonialists began to concede political ground. By 1959, twenty-five Africans were sitting in Legco together with fifteen Asians and five Arab members. But the minority Europeans still claimed forty-six seats. Not all settlers were opposed to an independent Kenya. A minority of influential Europeans — Michael Blundell, Wilfrid Havelock and Derek Erskine among them — supported the long campaign to free Kenyatta and the independence movement.

Many members of the minority Asian community, long committed to the cause of an independent Kenya, reiterated their belief in the future of Kenya under a one-man, one-vote majority rule.

But even as Kenyatta and his colleagues completed their seven-year term, Kenyatta was immediately detained and held first at Lodwar and then moved to Maralal where he remained, virtually *incommunicado*, for another two years, although at this time, Rawson Macharia, who had been a key witness at the Kapenguria trial, was jailed for twenty-one months for perjury.

The following year, though still detained at Maralal, Kenyatta was elected President *in absentia* of the newly-formed Kenya African National Union (KANU), which was the natural successor to KAU. Some months later another group was formed, called the Kenya Africa Democratic Union (KADU).

Both were anticipating the inevitable elections to come. In August 1960, the same month that KADU came into being, the eight-year-old State of Emergency finally came to an end.

The force of the African will had become irrepressible. Leaders of both KANU and KADU — except Kenyatta who remained in Maralal — were invited to the constitutional talks to discuss Kenya's future as a free nation at Lancaster House, London.

But if Kenyatta was unable to bring his incisive mind and forceful personality to bear on the talks, his influence was clearly felt. He commanded as much interest as the talks. Interviewed at his Maralal residence and asked when he would like independence he replied, 'Today'. And with the sub-

sequent announcement — after the Lancaster House talks — that Africans would vote in the general elections of February 1961, the path to full independence was open.

KANU won eighteen of the thirty-three seats with an overwhelming majority of sixty-seven per cent, against KADU's sixteen per cent. Among the first African members of the pre-independence Kenya Parliament were Daniel arap Toroitich Moi, who succeeded Kenyatta as President; Tom Mboya (later assassinated); Ronald Ngala, who died in a 1972 road accident; and Oginga Odinga, a colourful and controversial figure in the country's political history. Nonetheless, unless Kenyatta was released, KANU, and the mainly Asian Kenya Freedom Party, together with independent European and Asian members, refused to participate in government.

The bitterness between the two African parties was fuelled by the administration's invitation to KADU to form a minority government. Under increasing pressure, however, the authorities finally relented.

On 15 August 1961, Kenyatta was released, free to pursue the struggle that he had begun so long ago. On 6 November he led a KANU delegation to London to discuss Kenya's future. Soon after his return, in January 1962, Kariuki Njiri, the Member for Fort Hall (now Murang'a) resigned his Legco seat in favour of Kenyatta, who was returned unopposed.

Britain's Colonial Secretary returned Kenyatta's visit and during his stay announced the date for the second round of constitutional talks at Lancaster House.

Clear divisions now emerged between the two parties over the form of constitution they favoured. KADU sought a federal form of government, KANU opted for a strong central government.

But on his return Kenyatta agreed to form a coalition government with KADU until independence, which in May 1963 was augured by the first general elections ever held in Kenya on the universal franchise of one-man, one-vote. The result: a landslide triumph for KANU as Kenyatta swept in, unopposed, as MP for Gatundu.

Thus the first independent government with a full mandate for *Madaraka* (internal self-rule) was formed on 1 June 1963. Kenyatta was Prime Minister. In his inaugural address he revived an old African invocation that has become Kenya's clarion call, an official motto now incorporated on the country's coat of arms. He invited all, minority Europeans and Asians as well as Africans, to work in the spirit of *Harambee* —'pulling together' — in nation-building.

A firm friend of both Kenyatta and the Kenyan people, Malcolm MacDonald, Kenya's last Governor, became the first and only Governor-General.

A world leader of immense stature, few statesmen of this century, or any other, could claim to be as charismatic, visionary and pragmatic as Kenyatta. One of MacDonald's *Seven Titans,* he possessed what MacDonald described as the 'great gift of magnanimity'. Though he had suffered a long and lonely self-imposed exile in Britain, and years of incarceration, Kenyatta rose above all malice. His subsequent book, *Suffering Without Bitterness,* is testimony to the gift that MacDonald divined. It is doubtful, however, whether Kenyatta foresaw during his incarceration how soon Kenya would be free.

In later years, he even confided to one friend that in his lifetime he had never expected to see even India free. But now that freedom had finally arrived in Kenya he set about applying all his energy and vast intellect to cement it into a solid and unshakeable foundation.

Two months after taking office he invited the European farmers and entrepreneurs of the White Highlands to a Nakuru meeting to convince them of his faith in an undivided, non-racial Kenya. So evident was his sincerity and integrity that when he asked them to stay on to help build a Kenya in which all were equally free he won many over. The following month, at the final round of talks at Lancaster House, independence was set for 12 December under a constitution that abolished discrimination in all fields of life.

Three months later, at the stroke of midnight as 12 December 1963 began, the Union Jack was hauled down for the last time — and the new green, black, red and white flag of Kenya raised in its place: green for the land, black for the people, and red for the blood shed in the fight for freedom. With independence, bitterness was laid aside in the joy of nationhood. The *mugumo*

(fig tree), which Lugard and Kinyanjui had planted near the turn of the century at Fort Smith as a symbol of peace between the two peoples, still flourished, towering 40 metres (130 feet) above the compound.

The First Republic

Prime Minister Jomo Kenyatta inaugurated Kenya's birth as a member of the family of free nations — and the United Nations, Commonwealth, and the Organization of African Unity — with an address to the State opening of Kenya's first Parliament on 13 December 1963.

As a new member of the Commonwealth, Kenya's first year was a period of intense restructuring and rebuilding. Supported by the British, the government organized large land purchases on a willing-seller, willing-buyer basis intended to settle many landless Africans on former European-owned farms. Funded by the British Government, the scheme continued for some years at a cost of millions of pounds.

Social welfare and a better quality of life for all, particularly low-income and subsistence groups, were the main aims of a pragmatic policy that encouraged foreign investment and sought to diversify from economic dependence on agriculture.

One of the main concerns was to maintain the economic market that had existed before independence, the East African Common Services, as it was known, between Tanganyika — soon to become Tanzania — which had achieved independence two years earlier, and Uganda, which had become independent on 9 October 1962.

Now the market, which brought together 30 million people, became the East African Community. The main institutions were the East African Posts and Telecommunications Corporation, East African Railways and Harbours Corporation, and East African Airways. It was a bold and vigorous partnership yet, sadly, ideological differences and economic imbalances combined to work against it.

Fourteen years after Kenya's independence it collapsed. Although Kenya was firmly non-aligned, its Western-style government and economy were in glaring contrast to the socialist policies of its sister states, Uganda and Tanzania. Only the pragmatism of the three EAC leaders —

Obote, Nyerere and Kenyatta — held the federation together. In November 1964, in the spirit of nationhood and pragmatic patriotism that had marked Kenya's first year, Ronald Ngala and his KADU colleagues crossed the floor of parliament from the opposition benches to join KANU. Effectively, Kenya became a one-party state. Kenya's first year of independence was marked by many significant developments.

The Kenya Air Force and Navy were formed, Parliament Buildings were extended (the Speaker of the Senate, Muinga Chokwe, laid an air-tight cylinder containing the national flag, postage stamps, daily papers, and the names of all members of the first Parliament, in the concrete foundations), the last British troops departed, and it was announced that Kenya would become a republic.

On 10 December 1964, seventy-one years after Kenya became a protectorate and forty-four years after it was made a colony, reviewing the guard of honour formed by the last platoons of the British army, the Prime Minister thanked the troops for their help in times of flood and famine.

The bonds that now united Britain and Kenya were admiration and affection — not colonial subjugation. The following day Kenyatta gave Malcolm MacDonald a glowing valedictory on his departure for home leave at the end of his tenure as Governor-General. He achieved the unique distinction of serving in Kenya as Governor, Governor-General and, from 1965, as Britain's first High Commissioner to the former colony he had ruled in the Queen's name.

Finally, on 12 December 1964, Kenya became a republic. Prime Minister Jomo Kenyatta was sworn in as the country's first President at a ceremony in the Agricultural Society of Kenya's Mitchell Park showground, renamed Jamhuri (Republic) Park to mark this momentous step in national history. Oginga Odinga became the country's first Vice-President.

Harambee

Throughout, Kenyatta continually rallied the people to join together. He pledged to accelerate land consolidation and speed up the issue of title deeds. Initiating such major development projects as the inauguration of the Seven Forks hydroelectric scheme at Kindaruma, in a major policy statement — 'Sessional Paper No 10' — he also spelt out Kenya's blueprint for African socialism. It was based on political democracy, mutual social responsibility and dependency, and equitable distribution of income and property.

With the purchase of three Super VC-10s for East African Airways — a firm sign of Kenya's and its sister states' own confidence in their future — foreign investment began to flow into the country. Among the investors in 1965 were Philips, makers of light bulbs and electric appliances, and the Life Insurance Company of India. Although severe famine struck Kenya's drought-prone Akambaland, the last edifices of colonial prejudice were removed.

Free medical care for all children and adult out-patients became available at the former King George V Hospital, now Kenyatta National Hospital; racial discrimination was eliminated at Nairobi City primary schools, and free education for some high school students was introduced.

In March 1965, when Vice-President Odinga was under close scrutiny for alleged links with Eastern Bloc countries and China, he complained of a campaign by his parliamentary colleagues to oust him.

At a subsequent conference in Limuru, intended to reorganize and streamline KANU, Odinga was replaced as the Party's Deputy Vice-President.

Some days later, along with 27 members of the National Assembly, Odinga resigned to form the breakaway opposition party, Kenya People's Union (KPU), which was registered on 23 May 1966. A subsequent parliamentary Bill, passed the same month, stripped the dissidents of their parliamentary seats, except for twelve members who withdrew their support for Odinga.

But Kenyatta, wanting to avoid the divisions that had marred the progress and stability of other newly-independent African states, told KPU to seek a mandate at the polls. In what was described as a 'little general election', KPU won only nine seats.

Meanwhile, Kenyatta appointed Joseph Murumbi Vice-President and reshuffled the cabinet. At the same time, parliament endorsed the Preservation of National Security Act, which allowed preventative detention. Two other significant developments in

Above: Mural at Kenyatta International Conference Centre depicting the midnight arrest of Jomo Kenyatta on 20 October 1952.

Opposite: The cell at Kapenguria where Jomo Kenyatta was held during his trial.

1966 were the parliamentary merger of the lower house and the Senate into one chamber; and the opening of the Central Bank, which launched Kenya's first currency coins and notes — pegged to sterling at par value, 20 shillings to the £1.

Consolidation

Murumbi's tenure was brief. In failing health, he tendered his resignation and on 5 January 1967, Daniel Toroitich arap Moi became the country's third Vice-President.

The years that followed were ones of consolidation for the new nation. In many ways, physical independence took much longer to achieve than political independence. Four years after the Kenya flag was raised many non-Kenyans were still living and working in Kenya. Thus, from 2 November 1967, all expatriates working in Kenya had to obtain an official entry permit. This, together with the announcement — early in 1968 — of new regulations for Asian holders of British passports in Britain, triggered a massive exodus of Asians from Kenya. Other significant developments were the opening of the new Mombasa-Nairobi highway in August and the appointment of Kitili Mwendwa as the first African Chief Justice.

The following month, Kenyans were given a new vision and sense of national destiny with the country's athletics triumph in the Mexico Olympics, winning three gold, three silver, and two bronze medals to bring home a haul of eight — the highest athletic tally of any of the 118 nations competing, except the USA.

On 14 June, the first voice of Kenya's political consciousness, Harry Thuku died, aged 75. Nonetheless, the founder of the Kikuyu Central Association must have been a happy man at the progress he saw during Kenya's first seven years of freedom.

In 1969 the prospect of the first post-independence general election became the main focus, but before they were held the country was stunned by the 5 July assassination of the Minister for Economic Planning, Tom Mboya. Charismatic and popular, he was one of the vanguard who had campaigned for Kenya's independence. In the political aftermath, there was confrontation between the government and the

KPU. The opposition party was subsequently banned and its leader, Odinga, and all KPU MPs, were detained. Using the December general election to bring new faces into the cabinet, Kenyatta gave a new sense of purpose and direction to the country.

Second Decade

For Kenya, the second decade of independence represented not only a period of unprecedented growth and development, but also a challenge to the management skills of its economists and administrators.

With the 1970 opening of a satellite ground station in the Rift Valley, extensions to Nairobi International Airport, the 1972 opening of the new Central Bank building and the completion of the 33-storey Kenyatta International Conference Centre, Kenya had solid physical testimonials to its progress. In 1973, this progress was recognized when Nairobi became the first Third-World capital to host a United Nations headquarters — the United Nations Environment Programme (UNEP).

That same year Kenya celebrated a decade of independence under Jomo Kenyatta. Achievements noted included a doubling of national income, free education up to the first four grades, school attendance increased by 150 per cent, a threefold increase in tea production and a 50 per cent increase in coffee, the number one foreign exchange earner. But against this, the oil crisis resulted in a 20 per cent inflation rate.

Kenya-style democracy, based on choice of personalities not ideologies, continued to flourish. In the 1974 elections, more than half the sitting members lost their seats.

The following year was marked by the disappearance and the subsequent murder in March of J M Kariuki, a former asssistant minister with a strong following among the student community. A subsequent inquiry by a Select Parliamentary Committee left many questions unanswered but, as pressures from outside continued, particularly on the western borders with Idi Amin's Uganda, Kenya's solidarity and unity deepened. The most significant outcome of Amin's dictatorship was the collapse of the East African Community in February 1977.

Within days Kenya established Kenya Post and Telecommunications Corporation, launched its own airline, and transformed

Above: The late Jomo Kenyatta, with his successor, Daniel arap Moi, then Vice-President.

its share of the railways and harbours into a national corporation.

In 1977, because of Kenyatta's rapidly-failing health the KANU party elections were cancelled in spite of the fact that none had been held for 11 years. The 'Mzee' had earned the trust and love of all Kenyans — and throughout the world inspired respect and confidence for his statesmanship and humanity. His death on 22 August 1978 heralded a period of intense mourning.

Most Kenyans felt as if they had lost a father. But as princes, presidents, statesmen and world leaders arrived in Nairobi for his funeral on 31 August 1978, the legacy of freedom and stability that he had created remained his enduring memorial.

The Second Republic

The transition of leadership was smooth and constitutional. Within hours, Vice-President Daniel Toroitich arap Moi was sworn in as President. He marked his inauguration by exhorting all Kenyans to follow in Mzee Kenyatta's footsteps. The *Nyayo* era had begun.

In the subsequent general election in November 1978 he was returned unopposed as President of both country and party. Finance Minister Mwai Kibaki was named Vice-President. Moi made no major changes in the cabinet, but ordered a major shake-up of the security services and Immigration Department. He also cracked down on corruption, smuggling and nepotism, and pledged that political detention would be used only as 'a last resort'.

He also dissolved all tribal organizations in the interests of national unity. In his third year as President, he became Chairman of the Organization of African Unity (OAU) during its 1981 Nairobi summit, an

Above: Ministers and Parliamentarians greet President Daniel arap Moi.

office he held for an unprecedented two terms. In August 1982 a coup attempt by junior Air Force personnel was swiftly crushed. Later, two self-confessed ringleaders were court-martialled and, with ten others, sentenced to death for treason. The entire Kenya Air Force was immediately replaced by a new unit, the '82 Air Force. But most of those involved were pardoned.

A year later when Charles Njonjo, the Minister for Constitutional Affairs was suspended from the Cabinet, he resigned from Parliament. A general election was held a year ahead of schedule in September 1983. In the words of President Moi, it was 'to give the country time to clean up its house'.

A judicial inquiry into the allegations against Njonjo concluded on 12 December 1984, that Njonjo had been involved in corruption, the illegal import of firearms into Kenya, and an attempt to topple the Seychelles' Government. Although subsequently given a presidential pardon, the 64-year-old former minister did not return to politics. In 1987, Kenya staged the spectacular Fourth All Africa Games at Nairobi's 80,000-seat Moi International Stadium, one of the most modern sports complexes

in Africa, built and designed by Chinese specialists with the aid of a Chinese loan.

In 1988 a new voting system to decide nominations for KANU candidates was introduced. Electors queued up behind the candidate of their choice during the primaries. Those with more than 70 per cent support were elected unopposed. Where two or more candidates had less support they contested the election by secret ballot. It was unpopular and was later dropped.

The first decade of Moi's leadership was marked with achievements in education and social welfare. He introduced free education and free milk for all primary students, *Nyayo* wards in hospitals throughout the country, the settlement of long-standing land disputes and the issue of long-delayed land title deeds to smallholders and peasant farmers. Except for farming, the mainstay of the economy, Kenya had few real economic resources at independence. Change was swift and stunning.

Inspired by the credo of nation-building, major industrial and agricultural development continues. Tourism was an obvious avenue to develop. Indeed, from fewer than 100,000 visitors in 1963, 25 years later

Above: Elite troops of the Kenya Army.

Kenya's visitors numbered three-quarters-of-a-million a year — and tourism had become the country's major foreign exchange earner and industry. Coffee had moved into second place along with tea, another remarkable success story. A smallholder tea growing scheme launched at independence had seen Kenya become the world's third-largest producer and second-largest exporter. Kenya also produces what experts regard as the finest coffee in the world and is the world's third-largest producer of pineapples.

Undoubtedly, however, Kenya's biggest success was in education and social welfare. The number of primary schools doubled to accommodate more than five million pupils, with a sixfold increase in teachers to 150,000. Secondary schools have increased more than twelvefold to 2,500, with half-a-million students. There are now five universities with 40,000 undergraduates — and more institutes of further education have been opened.

The increase in health facilities was equally dramatic. By 1989, Kenya had 30,000 specialists — surgeons, doctors, trained nurses, and health workers — compared with only 4,000 in 1963. There were almost 2,000 hospitals, clinics and health centres and 30,000 hospital beds.

And Kenya remains one of the star sports nations of the developing world.

Stability

Despite its enormous population growth, on the whole Kenya has made great economic and social advances. When the country celebrated its 30th anniversary of independence on 12 December 1993, it could look back on thirty years of growth.

The fact that six successive parliaments had been decided in the ballot box at six general elections was testimony to the strength of Kenyan democracy, although this was somewhat diluted by the legislation of a one-party state in 1982.

Since then, however, pressure from within and from the West forced the Moi regime to rescind the constitutional one-party status, when a bundle of newly-formed political parties were registered, ready to contest the 1992 general elections. But the Opposition remained divided and Moi and KANU won a fresh five-year mandate.

The Land: Ice and Fire, Wood and Water

Like its people, Kenya's landscapes are characterized by their diversity. Covering 582,750 square kilometres (225,000 square miles), the country is a world in miniature.

Almost every known type of landform, from snow mountain and glacier to true desert, exists within its boundaries.

Similarly, all stages of landscape evolution — from Africa's oldest eroded plains to its most recent volcanic and tectonic rifts and mountains — are clearly evident.

Kenya's different facets are reflected in the aureole of pink-shrouded mist that swirls among Mount Kenya's loftiest, ice-clad spires, and on the crystal clear waters of Naivasha. And in the bubbling vivacity of the 700-kilometre-long (435-mile) Tana River as it leaps, new-born, down the shoulders of the Aberdares and Mount Kenya and on its long run to the Indian Ocean, where Kenya's magic whispers in the rustle of the palms along its Indian Ocean coast.

Kenya has 20 mountain peaks above 2,000 metres (6,500 feet) and five great massifs rising more than 3,000 metres (10,000 feet). Its western borders fall in the waters of Africa's largest lake, Victoria, and its eight major rivers, all more than 200 kilometres (125 miles) long, feature many impressive waterfalls. Gura Falls, high in the Aberdare Mountains, drops almost 300 metres (1,000 feet).

Rising from sea level to 5,199 metres (17,058 feet) at the summit of Mount Kenya, this land of contrasts is dominated by several plateaux, leading up like a series of steps and creating an impression of extensive upland plains rather than a mountainous terrain. It has given Kenya a unique landscape, with a beauty equalled or surpassed by few nations. So diverse is Kenya, in fact, that there are five distinct physiographic regions.

First, the low plateau of western Kenya, warm and fertile, enjoys year-round rain. Second, the central highlands, bisected by

the Great Rift Valley, almost all above 1,500 metres (5,000 feet), although touched in some parts by rain shadow, form Kenya's most productive and scenic region, a land of fertile farms, ancient forests, rivers, lakes and mountains.

The vast semi-arid plains and deserts of the north, where little grows and few live, make up the third area. The foreland plateau, the immediate hinterland of the coast, which seems almost a continuation of the arid north, is the fourth region.

The fifth is the semi-arid plain that runs parallel to the 480-kilometre-long (300-mile) palm-fringed coastline. Guarded by magnificent coral reefs, this has become one of the world's great holiday playgrounds.

All this beauty and grandeur were created by the tectonic disturbances spaced over many millions of years that forced Africa to arch its back, causing warps and fractures and explosive volcanoes. During the long dormant periods in between, wind and rain reshaped the lands and silt laid fresh flesh on the dry bones.

There were six vital periods of dormancy. The first one resulted in many of today's greatest land masses, usually more than 2,000 metres (6,500 feet) high — such as the Cheranganis, including the Trans-Nzoia and the Elgeyo-Suk plateaux — and the Kisii Highlands.

The second period created the landscape found between 1,800 and 2,000 metres (5,900-6,500 feet), including the Kilungu and Mbooni Hills in Ukambani, and the low bench of the Lerogi Hills near Maralal.

The third period formed the lands between 1,500 and 1,650 metres (5,000-5,400 feet) — the plains around Kajiado and Machakos.

During the fourth dormant era, the land between 1,200 and 1,450 metres (3,937-4,757 feet) settled Siaya and Busia districts and large areas of Machakos and Kitui. The last two periods resulted in the landscape be-

Opposite: Satellite image of the Rift Valley — Lakes Turkana (top) and Victoria (bottom left); Mounts Elgon (left centre), Kenya (right centre), and Kilimanjaro (bottom right). The blue lake (centre) is Baringo.

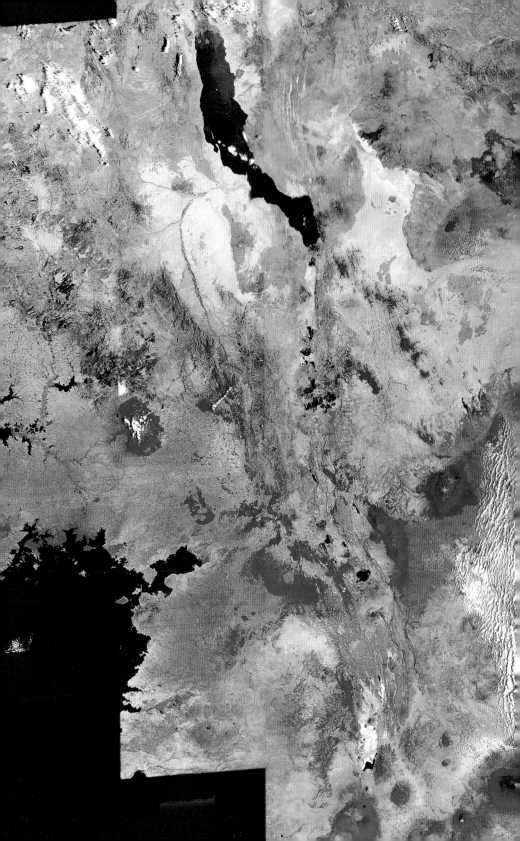

tween 900 and 1,200 metres (3,000-3,900 feet) and 300 and 750 metres (1,000-2,460 feet). These form the extremely extensive foreland plateau between the central highlands and the coast, and the coastal hinterland and littoral. Both are characterized by ubiquitous, marginal 'islands of rock' — isolated inselbergs — for in this semi-arid land many scarps retreated and there was much long-term erosion.

Undoubtedly the greatest outcome of all this geological rock and roll was the formation of the Rift Valley and its subsidiaries — the most dramatic landscape in Kenya, with sheer walls of rock up to 3,000 metres (10,000 feet) high. Although the forces that shaped the Rift are still not fully understood, clearly this — and other smaller but similar valleys — were the final result of extensive uplift as the arched land fell.

In Kenya, the greatest movements took place intermittently between five and 12 million years ago (during the mid-Miocene and late-Pliocene period) following a series of major earth movements at the close of the 45-million-year-long age of the dinosaurs (the Jurassic Period).

Subsequently, in the last million years, other minor grid faults have taken place in the floor of the central Rift Valley.

Earlier, beginning some 17 million years ago (in mid-Miocene times), stunning eruptions spread lava over the Kapiti, Simbara, Samburu, and Kericho areas.

Although Kenya appears quiescent today, the forces that shaped the country are still at work. This is evident in the immense thermal activity beneath the Rift floor, and the eruption of the Teleki volcano (and others) at the southern end of Lake Turkana as recently as 1899.

Indeed, in recent times, geologically speaking — say the last 400 to 600 years — this widespread activity manifested itself in eruptions in Menengai and Longonot and also created the Chyulu Hills.

The most dramatic eruptions in the Rift, however, took place long ago — many millions of years before the fractures that formed the present prominent scarps.

Drainage
All Kenya's main rivers were formed by the uplifting that created the great massif of the central highlands.

Spiralling down from these highlands is one of Africa's greatest-known radial river systems. Ignoring the deep depression between the two highland blocks — normally a natural route for any major river — the drainage system instead took on its now familiar pattern, seen in the parallel streams that drain both the Aberdare and the Mau dip slopes, together with the low belt between the Galana and Tana Rivers. Minor radial streams also wash the main volcanic cones as well as the interior highlands.

But, except for the Nzoia, Yala, Mara, Galana and Tana, most rivers and tributaries are seasonal. Perennial water shortage remains one of Kenya's most pressing problems. And none of Kenya's rivers are navigable except in the lower reaches of the Tana and where the Athi-Galana becomes the Sabaki.

Ecological potential
Kenya's ecological value is affected by a wide range of conditions and a rapidly-growing population. Defined by climate, soil and vegetation, Kenya has six broad ecological zones.

The close relationship between climate and altitude is also reflected in the vegetation. Where certain plant species and vegetation types occur it is possible to define climatic boundaries more accurately than by records from the relatively few 'met' stations.

Central Kenya is dominated by the three great volcanic ranges of Mount Kenya, the Aberdares, and the Mau, together with the massive trough of the Great Rift Valley which divides Kenya neatly in two.

A once dome-shaped volcanic pile, Mount Kenya, Africa's second-highest point, is the world's most perfect model of an equatorial mountain.

Both the Aberdares and the Mau ranges are essentially the product of fissure volcanic eruptions. But their inner halves have been incorporated into the down-thrown sides of the Rift Valley. Between 60 and 100 kilometres (40-60 miles) wide, the Rift Valley floor is studded with a number of small, shallow salt lakes, of which Lake

Opposite: Deep gorge in the dramatic Kerio Valley.

Magadi — a source of trona from which soda ash is extracted — has the greatest economic value.

Many prominent volcanic cones, including Longonot, Susua and Menengai, also rise above the Rift floor. The main plateaux are either lava plains or denuded surfaces created by the long and continuous erosion characteristic of this area. By comparison, the lava plains are still fairly intact and young. The best-known examples of these are the Kaputei (Kapiti) Plains, the Athi Plains, and the Yatta Plateau.

But the Laikipia Plateau is either a lava flow along a former pre-existing river valley, or an eroded remnant of lava outpouring reduced by scarp retreat. It remains a geological riddle. The eroded plateaux are confined to non-volcanic areas east of Athi River and south of Kajiado.

The hill region of Ukambani is old and dissected land with a number of plateaux plains levelled by erosion. The Mbooni, Kilungu, Ol Doinyo Sapuk and Mua Hills, together with the hills around Kajiado, are remnants of Africa's oldest erosion surface — generally regarded as late Jurassic.

Another intermediate plateau around Kajiado, Masii, Wamunyu, and between Kangondi and Kitui town, is a remnant of sub-Miocene landscapes.

The youngest surface, dominating the area east of Kitui town, is a low plateau littered with many inselbergs and rock outcrops of which Endau, Makongo, and Ithumba are examples. But the Taita Hills, and others south of Kilaguni in Tsavo West, resisted the erosion which levelled the plains.

In the volcanic south, between Sultan Hamud and Mtito Andei, the recently-formed Chyulu Hills, together with many small cones, should not be mistaken for inselbergs.

You can also see one or two similar cones on the southern edge of the Yatta Plateau, where the drainage system holds the headwaters of Kenya's two major rivers — the Tana and the Athi. The peculiar course of the Athi River in its upper section may have been caused by backtilting before the Aberdares burst out of the plains. The valley cut by the misfit Ol Keju Ado may be one of the oldest in the area — it once joined the Namanga River flowing south and eastwards before the birth of Kilimanjaro. But although there are many streams it does not mean that the area is any better-watered than the rest of Kenya.

Many streams are seasonal. Indeed, water shortage is a major problem, not only in the eastern half of the area, but also in the Rift Valley. The influence of these geophysical features on land routes is obvious.

The greatest obstacle was the precipitous drop of the Rift Valley escarpment. Both the railway line and the road had to negotiate the escarpment. The Magadi railway took advantage of the smooth watershed between Konza and Kajiado before dodging sinuously into the Rift.

The natural gap between Mount Kenya and the Aberdares also served as an important gateway to the north. But a similarly well-suited gap, between the Aberdare and Kikuyu dip slopes, created difficulties. The closely-spaced parallel streams meant there was no direct link between villages only 16 kilometres (ten miles) apart.

Yet, even if it was unhealthy, Nairobi's flat, open ground, before the final climb to the Rift wall, gave great scope for development. The Embakasi Plains proved ideal for airport development. Three airports within a radius of seven kilometres (four miles) of the city centre are something few cities claim.

Nairobi's national park, which marks its southern edge, also gives the 'City in the Sun' unrivalled charm and attraction.

Coast

Although much of the lush Kenya coast evolved in the last 30 million years, only a few kilometres inland the land becomes a barren and desolate *nyika* (scrub plain) sloping gently to the east.

Of the coastal region's three main land forms, the lowest is the coastal belt and plains that lie less than 150 metres (500 feet) above sea level. Above this, between 150 and 300 metres (500-1,000 feet), is the *nyika* proper, including the scorched Taru Desert, which almost defeated the early Eu-

Opposite: Tour group on a game drive in one of Kenya's wildlife sanctuaries.
Overleaf: Passenger train on the "Lunatic Line" descends into the Rift Valley.

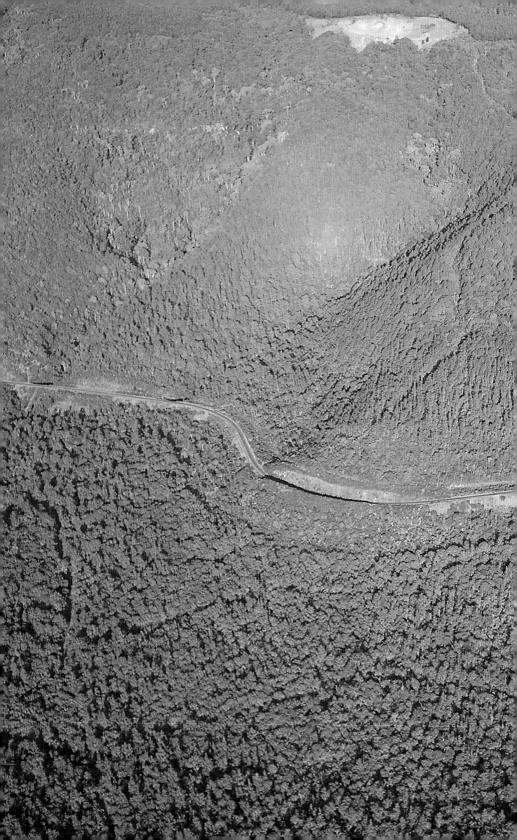

ropean explorers and railway gangs — broken only by the Shimba, Jibana, and Kulalu hills, which defied erosion because of the different composition of their stones and rocks. The third unit, part of the low foreland plateau, covers all the higher ground up to 900 metres (3,000 feet) above sea level, where the slight eastward slope is typical of Eastern Africa's general tilt.

Extensive yearly floods on the lower Tana plain, which leave the rich highland silt behind, have also created many small ox-bow lakes. But the lower reaches of the Athi-Galana-Sabaki still appear geologically young — partly because of the dramatic changes that formed the 300-kilometre-long (185-mile) Yatta Plateau.

On the slender coastal littoral many short parallel streams reach the ocean as creeks — testimony to the changes in sea level during the last million years. Where the parallel streams were closely spaced, and the hinterland was made of soft shales, following the rise in sea level which drowned the river valleys, different forms of erosion created such islands as Mombasa.

In other parts, the fluctuating sea level created different features, such as raised platforms at three distinct levels, which are clearly visible, especially around Mombasa Island. Elsewhere, raised beaches, degraded clifflines, stacks, et al, are also found.

The most outstanding feature, however, is the well-developed barrier reef which extends all the way from Shimoni in the south to Malindi in the north, without significant break — except at the mouths of rivers.

The Kenya coast has many features that make it an ideal holiday resort — beautiful, palm-fringed, white sand beaches and warm, safe lagoons and coral gardens.

Vegetation

Many forms of vegetation thrive in Kenya. But prolonged grazing, burning, shifting cultivation, or selective cutting has caused dramatic change. Forests, for instance, have been reduced to bushland or grassland by felling and burning — and overgrazing has turned grasslands to thicket or barren land. Kenya also claims a rare if dubious distinction in having two sub-types of barren land — the ecological extremes of glacier and desert.

Annual rainfall

There are strong differences in Kenya's mean annual rainfall, ranging from less than 254 millimetres (10 inches) in the north-east to more than 2,030 millimetres (80 inches) on the high mountains.

A relatively wet belt extends along the Indian Ocean coast. Another wet area covers western Kenya just east of Lake Victoria. All the mountain ranges have high rainfall with dry tongues in the valleys and basins. There are no absolutely dry seasons and rain may fall at any time in all areas. But generally rainfall follows strong seasonal patterns, most pronounced in the dry lowlands of the north and east and less apparent in the humid highlands of the central and Rift Valley areas.

Although these seasonal variations differ throughout the country, they can be classified under three main types.

Coastal area

The year starts dry and remains so until March, when rainfall gradually increases. A fairly rapid increase occurs through April and builds up to its maximum in May. After this it decreases steadily, although significant amounts are still recorded in October and November. During December it begins to fade away altogether, with minimal rainfall in January and February.

East, North-East, South-East, and Central

The two distinct rainy seasons — March-May and October-December — are separated by a dry season — June-September — which is most distinct in the lower areas of eastern Kenya.

April is generally the rainiest month but there have been years when exceptionally heavy rain gave record totals in October and November. The second minimal period — January-February — is again most pronounced in the low eastern regions.

Western Rift, Western, LakeVictoria

There is no real 'dry season'. But rainfall is highest between March and September and lowest during January and February.

The People: A Multi-Coloured Canvas of Cultures

Kenya is a cultural microcosm of Africa. People from many parts of the continent have been migrating to Kenya for centuries, each bringing some distinctive feature of their own culture and language to create a colourful mosaic of humankind.

This melting-pot of peoples, a vibrant community of 28 million citizens, will reach more than 40 million by the turn of the century. Spread all across this vast land astride the Equator, many have had to adapt their cultures and customs to the terrain in which they live — sometimes green and fertile, often harsh and arid.

Ironically, it is the smallest group, the Cushitic-speaking Kenyans, who occupy the largest area. These nomads of the north, who roam almost half the country, make up only three per cent of the population.

For two-thirds of all Kenyans, the common tongue is that of the Bantu languages. The remainder speak Nilotic languages. But these three language structures bind together a country of more than 40 different ethnic groups.

All those who migrated there during the last 4,000 years assimilated something of those who were already there, including the earliest ancestors of modern man.

Over the centuries, before the arrival of Europeans, three great waves of migrants slowly moved into the area now defined as Kenya — the largely but not exclusively agricultural Bantu, the pastoral Cushitic-speakers, and the pastoral-agricultural Nilotes.

The small groups of hunter-gatherers who lived in this then sparsely populated region were swamped as the conflicting tides of people met. Out of the eddies and whirlpools of their intermingling, today's cultures developed.

Colonial rule drew rigid and distinct divisions between different ethnic groups who most early European administrators too readily identified as time-honoured tribes.

'Tribe', as defined by Professor P H Gulliver, means 'any group . . . distinguished by its members . . . on the basis of cultural-regional criteria'. Linguistic and anthropological studies continue to reveal that such European presumptions were far from true. Populations are taken from the 1989 census.

Bajun, Swahili, and Shirazi (Bantu)
These people of the coast share a common language (Kiswahili), religion (Islam), and culture. The Bajun people (population 55,000), who live on the Lamu archipelago and coastal strip to the north, believe they originally came from further north.

Centuries of migration, conquest, transmigration, and miscegenation resulted in the Bantu-speaking Swahili absorbing immigrants of Arabic and Persian descent.

The Shirazi (numbering, together with the Swahili, 14,000), who claim to come from Persia, once made up the aristocratic families and dynasties of the Ozi kingdoms of Shaka, Mwana, Ungwana, Malindi and Mombasa.

Many of these fishing and farmfolk are skilled craftsmen, their shipbuilding and woodwork being especially famous. Their ocean-going dhows, with their distinctive triangular sails, still ply between Arabia, the Arabian Gulf, even Pakistan and India, and Lamu, Malindi and Mombasa.

Boni, Wata, Yaaka and Dahalo (Cushitic)
These small groups of hunter-gatherers live in the coastal hinterland (Boni, Wata, and Dahalo) and on the Mukogodo massif, far inland north of Mount Kenya (Yaaka). Numbering some 5,000, they once traded ivory and honey but have now become farmers and cattle herders. But they still gather wild fruits and honey and kill an occasional antelope for food.

Boran (Cushitic)
Numbering more than 80,000, of Ethiopian Oromo origin, the nomadic Boran live in an enclave in the arid north-east of Kenya around Moyale, Marsabit, along the Ewaso Nyiro River, and in Isiolo District. They raise cattle, camels, sheep and goats.

Right: Kipsigis girl at initiation.

Middle: Luhya woman with farm produce.

Below: Boni girl carries home a pitcher of water.

Above: Gusii soapstone carver in Kisii highlands.

Right: Maasai warriors with ostrich head-dresses.

Above: El-Molo family at Loiyangalani, Lake Turkana.

Buji (Cushitic)
Settled farmfolk from Southern Ethiopia, the 6,000 Buji people are one of several Oromo-speaking communities displaced by the expansionist schemes of Emperor Menelik II in the last century when they fled across the border into northern Kenya. They grow maize, *teff* (a cereal), beans, pumpkins, coffee, cotton, tobacco and bananas and claim never to have worn skins. They weave fine garments, *bado* and *kuta*, from the cotton they grow.

A law-abiding community, the Buji became farmworkers and road builders in the Moyale and Marsabit districts. Many have since moved into urban Kenya.

Dassenich (Cushitic)
Only a few thousand Dassenich live in Kenya permanently, around Ileret, in Marsabit District, at the far north of Lake Turkana. The majority live in Ethiopia where, after the rains, they farm for five or six months. Then, during the dry season they make ritual sacrifices, feast, and celebrate their annual ceremonies. In Kenya they fish instead, travelling down the east-

ern shore of Lake Turkana as far as Alia Bay and beyond in their dugout canoes, sun-drying their catch.

Their headdresses of coloured ochre and ostrich feathers testify to long hours of grooming. To avoid damage to their elaborate hairstyles, Dassenich men always carry a neck stool on which to sleep. In raids against neighbouring tribes, killings were often cruel and deliberate. The Turkana, Gabbra and Rendille bore the brunt of these attacks and retaliation resulted in periods of outright confrontation leaving villages and grazing grounds deserted.

El-Molo (Cushitic)
The 3,600-strong el-Molo, once numbering fewer than 500 people, have abandoned their two small island homes in Lake Turkana and now live at Loiyangalani, on the south-eastern shore, eking out a subsistence living by fishing from doum palm rafts.

Fresh or dried fish form their staple food, augmented by crocodile, turtle and hippopotamus meat. They also eat game and birds. But life is changing rapidly.

73

Above: Colourful traditional Akamba dance group.

They have turned to cattle herding and some now work in tourism. Commercial fishing supplements their traditional subsistence.

Larger, more permanent settlements have replaced their traditional homes of sticks covered with flimsy thatch and skins.

Embu (Bantu)

The Embu (population 256,623) who occupy the south-eastern slopes of Mount Kenya, are an assimilation of successive waves of immigrants from Meru to the north-east, Kikuyu to the west, and Mbeere to the south. Although hunting and gathering now contribute little to their economy, the Embu remain notable beekeepers.

With well distributed and abundant rainfall, the rich, fertile soil of their farmlands encourages many crops, such as coffee, tea and pyrethrum. The Embu also keep cattle, sheep and goats.

Gabbra (Cushitic)

The 36,000 camel-herding Gabbra people of Marsabit District also keep cattle, goats and sheep, but in vastly different terrain. An Oromo group forced south-west from Ethiopia in the last century, the Gabbra are now under continuous pressure from the Somali for grazing and water along their eastern boundary.

Schools at Marsabit, Maikona, North Horr, Sololo and elsewhere have created a more settled life for many but the great majority of these handsome, thrifty people still roam the vast semi-arid deserts west and north of Marsabit with their herds, and their way of life remains singularly unchanged.

Gusii (Bantu)

The Abagusii, Kenya's sixth-largest group (population 1.3 million), who live in the fertile Kisii highlands and parts of South Nyanza, claim kinship with the Kuria, Suba and Luhya.

Under pressure from successive waves of Luo immigration, they migrated eastwards about 200 years ago to settle in the Kisii highlands, subsisting on bananas, millet, eleusine and maize. Now these hills are one of Kenya's prime tea, coffee, and pyrethrum-producing areas. Passion fruit,

Above: A Bok group of the Sabaot community on the slopes of Mount Elgon.

another exotic cash crop, grows prolifically. More and more grade cattle are kept on the well-planned smallholdings that surround their thatched homesteads. Traditionally, they have close trade ties with the Luo.

Fine sculptors, too, the Abagusii fashion the soft, pinkish-white soapstone, quarried locally in the Itumbe hills, into small animal statues, candlesticks, vases and other *bric-à-brac* which are sold throughout Kenya in curio and handicraft shops.

For centuries their traditional healers practised a primitive form of trepanning, successfully performing delicate hole-in-the-head brain surgery without anaesthetics, using crude surgical instruments.

The Abagusii are also notable athletes. Several have won honours in the Commonwealth and Olympic Games.

Ilchamus (Njemps) (Nilotic)
Closely related to the Samburu and Maasai, the Ilchamus of Lake Baringo number only 16,000. But, unlike their cattle-herding relatives, the Maa-speaking Ilchamus are settled farmers and fisherfolk, grazing their stock along the receding lake shoreline dur-

ing the long dry seasons. Now that the lake resort attracts increasing numbers of visitors, however, the Ilchamus traditional way of life is changing rapidly.

But dancing is still a form of personal expression and celebration. Elevation to a new age-grade, circumcision, the birth of a baby, the onset of the rains, or simply a spontaneous need, are good enough reason to dance.

Iteso (Nilotic)
The Iteso (population 178,500) of Busia and Bungoma in Western Province, belong to the *Ateker* — 'people of one language' — family of tribes. They drifted eastwards from Uganda into Kenya between 1750 and 1850. Settling on the plains south of Mount Elgon, they came into conflict with the Luhya, especially the Bukusu, and laid waste vast stretches of country.

The aim of these raids was to rustle cattle. But, although pastoralists, they were also cultivators and, as they began to barter produce for small stock, which in turn were exchanged for the cattle they coveted, the Iteso found stability. Now they grow

Above: Gabbra camel herd in northern Kenya's 'Plains of Darkness'.

maize, cotton, sugarcane and tobacco commercially and the pace of development throughout western Kenya has made them even more zealous farmers. Iteso artisans are renowned potters and use their pots to store water, grain and other foods — and to brew millet and honey beer.

Kamba (Bantu)
Occupying the Machakos, Makueni and Kitui districts of Eastern Province, the 2.5 million Akamba are Kenya's fourth-largest ethnic group.

Originally hunters, the Kamba settled at Mbooni about four centuries ago, adopting a more sedentary life as farmers. As with most Bantu, political power lay with the elders who functioned as a 'parliament'.

From Mbooni they eventually colonized the whole area and began trading — at first with the neighbouring Kikuyu, Embu, Tharaka and Mijikenda, and later the coast.

But late last century, rinderpest decimated their herds. And with the building of the Uganda Railway and the ban on expansion into the empty land around Ulu and Yatta, Kamba prosperity declined.

Drought and famine still plague the Kamba people, especially around Kitui in the arid north-east. Poor farming and severe deforestation from charcoal production hinder development. Skilled metalworkers, potters and basketmakers, their inlaid woodwork and carvings have become a major handicraft industry, with significant local and export sales.

Keiyo (Elgeyo) (Nilotic)
A Kalenjin group — thought to have moved to their present homeland from around Mount Elgon some time in the late 16th and early 17th centuries — the Keiyo live on the almost inaccessible ledges of the precipitous Elgeyo Escarpment 700 metres (2,300 feet) or more above the sheer gorge of the river Kerio.

The Keiyo used to graze their stock on the rich grasslands of the eastern Uasin Gishu plateau, but raids by Karamojong and others in the last century forced them to seek refuge on the cliffside. Although many are farmers, cattle remain their first love. Traditionally the Keiyo were courageous and adept hunters of elephant, buffalo and rhinoceros, which provided them with meat.

Kikuyu (Bantu)

The largest of all Kenya's ethnic groups, the 4.5 million Kikuyu moved from Meru and Tharaka to their present homeland in the highlands between Kiambu, Nyeri, Murang'a, and Kirinyaga on the south and south western slopes of Mount Kenya some 400 years ago.

Land, the dominant factor in the social, political, religious and economic life of these farmers, soon brought them into conflict with the European settlers who seized large tracts of their territory.

Yet, perhaps more successfully than any other tribe, the Kikuyu adapted to the challenge of Western culture, displaying an early political awareness. This resulted in the formation of a political association in 1920 which drew up a petition of grievances to present to the Chief Native Commissioner (see 'History: The Dust and the Ashes', Part One).

Now these progressive farmers use modern methods and maintain fine livestock, benefitting from the growing markets of Nairobi and the thriving export trade in coffee, tea, pyrethrum, horticultural crops, vegetables and flowers.

They have bought most of the former White Highlands farmlands and are active in business and commerce throughout Kenya. Close to a million Kikuyu (a good percentage of the city population) make their home in Nairobi and they form a significant majority in some other towns.

Kipsigis (Nilotic)

The Kipsigis, the largest group of Kalenjin people, number 2.9 million in the Rift Valley of western Kenya and speak different dialects of the same language. Kericho is the administrative centre of the Kipsigis. Other Kalenjin groups with common affinities and customs are the Nandi, Tugen, Marakwet, Keiyo, Pokot, Terik and Sabaot.

The Kipsigis — once known as Lumbwa — have a passionate love for cattle. Raids across their borders to rustle cattle from the Abagusii, Luo and Maasai were a constant source of friction. Increasing numbers of grade cattle graze their well-kept smallholdings. The Kipsigis also grow a number of cash crops, especially tea, pyrethrum, potatoes, maize, cabbage, tomatoes, onions, peas and beans, as well as traditional crops, such as bananas and sweet potatoes.

The Kalenjin, especially the Nandi and Kipsigis, are renowned athletes. Many of Kenya's track stars are Kipsigis.

Kuria (Bantu)

The Kuria (population 112,000), astride the Kenya-Tanzania border on the cool, high ground south of Kisii and east of Lake Victoria, are separated from the lake by the Suba and the Luo communities. Even now few roads lead into their highlands with deep-cut valleys and fast-flowing streams.

Loamy soils combined with abundant and well-dispersed rainfall make for productive farming.

Cash crops include pyrethrum, coffee and, more recently, tobacco. Although they keep sheep and goats, dual-purpose cattle are the principal livestock.

The majority live across the border in Tanzania, but those in Kenya have responded to the stimulus of education. There are many primary and secondary schools throughout their region.

In the last three decades a quiet revolution has also taken place in the development of their economy. The small townships of Ntimaru, Nyabasi, Taraganya and Kihancha have become thriving markets and social venues — and are now busy trade centres for many craft industries.

Luo (Nilotic)

The largest of Kenya's non-Bantu ethnic groups, the 2.7-million-strong Luo of Siaya, Kisumu, Homa Bay and Migori districts around the Nyanza Gulf of Lake Victoria, were the most vigorous of the Nilotes who moved south from Sudan, arriving in Nyanza at least 500 years ago.

The acquisition of cattle and the constant search for pastures and fish sources dominated the minds of the first immigrants. But any expansion eastwards was blocked by the barrier of the Mau and the Rift Valley, and the warlike Maasai.

Their herds decimated by rinderpest, the Luo became increasingly dependent on farming and fishing for subsistence. But these itinerant people of the lakes and rivers are still on the move. The Luo say they

Above: Traditional Chuka dancers from Meru district.

are like the water which flows until it finds its own level. Indeed, tens of thousands have spread across the country into major towns, such as Nairobi and Mombasa, north to the shores of Lake Turkana and south to Lake Jipe.

Articulate and civic-minded, the Luo were prominent in the struggle for independence. Many leading trade unionists and politicians, in particular the late Tom Mboya (assassinated in 1969) and former Vice-President, the late Jaramogi Oginga Odinga, fanned the flame of *Uhuru* (independence) (see 'History: The Dust and the Ashes', Part One).

Luhya (Bantu)
Seventeen groups make up the 3.1 million Luhya community of Kenya's Western Province. With more than 750 people to the square kilometre, the population density between Kisumu and Kakamega, their administrative centre, is one of the highest in rural Africa and their birthrate one of the highest in the world. The earliest Luhya probably settled in the area around the fourteenth century and arrivals continued

into the 17th century. The Samia ironworkers were the most skilled of Luhya smelters, forging knives, hoes and other implements which they used as a currency over a wide area. Pottery and basketmaking are still common crafts. Groundnuts, *simsim* (sesame), maize, and later cotton, were early cash crops. Third largest of Kenya's ethnic groupings, the Luhya — like their Luo neighbours — have two major recreational passions: music and soccer.

Maasai (Nilotic)
The pastoral and nomadic Maasai (population 377,000), who live in Narok and Kajiado districts, are a fusion of Nilotic and Cushitic peoples who lived north-west of Lake Turkana 1,000 years ago.

Later the Maasai started moving south, climbing the Laikipia and Cherangani escarpments out of the Rift Valley to spread out in the ensuing centuries across the fertile grasslands of the central and southern Rift and surrounding uplands. By the last century, the Maasai had earned a reputation as powerful and ferocious warriors who raided hundreds of kilometres

Right: Pokomo fisherman with basket trap.

Middle: Pokot warrior.

Below: Swahili woman in traditional veiled dress, *bui bui.*

Above: Giriama limbo dancer.

Right: Turkana youngster collecting water from a desert *wadi.*

Overleaf: Colourfully-dressed Maasai women.

into neighbouring territory to rustle cattle. Their life, conditioned by the constant quest for water and grazing, remained unchanged for centuries.

In the more arid areas, livestock is moved seasonally, often several hundred kilometres, to undergrazed areas or to new grass stimulated by local rain.

Fresh and curdled milk, carried and stored in long, decorated gourds, is the basic Maasai diet. Blood tapped from the jugular vein of a steer or cow is mixed with cattle urine to ferment it, making a potent stimulant.

Cattle are rarely slaughtered and then only for ceremonial purposes. Game meat, with the exception of eland and buffalo, is forbidden.

In Kajiado, group ranching schemes have encouraged permanent settlement. In Narok, the fertile wheatlands on the slopes of the Mau, initially developed by entrepreneurs, are now being exploited by the Maasai themselves. Inevitably, change, long-resisted, is now reluctantly accepted.

Marakwet (Nilotic)
The Marakwet of the Kerio Valley and Cherangani Hills are another Kalenjin group. Their administrative centre is Iten. Traditionally the Kerio Valley — rife with mosquitoes and tsetse fly — was, and to some extent still is, a natural north-south route for raiding parties and as a defence against disease and enemy the Marakwet built their houses on an escarpment that, in the west, rises to 3,370 metres (11,057 feet).

Such awesome terrain limits livestock, although cattle are increasing. Crops on the escarpment ledges and in the valley are irrigated by 400-year-old furrows running from the Arror, Embebut and Embomen rivers. These furrows are still maintained by the community. Eleusine and sorghum grown on tilled land are traditional staples, together with bananas, cassava and maize. Beekeeping is also important.

Mbeere (Bantu)
The Mbeere (population 101,000) occupy 1,600 square kilometres (618 square miles) of dry savannah, thorny acacia and commiphora, bound by the Thika and Tana rivers south-east of Embu District. They share cultural and historical ties with the Embu

and their administrative centre is Embu. Skilled blacksmiths, the Mbeere obtain their iron ore from alluvial sands in the Kithunthiiri area. In their workshops, equipped with skin bellows, crude hammers, chisels, and pliers, they fashioned spears, arrowheads, axes and knives, as well as fine chains, bells and earrings.

A musical people fond of songs, the Mbeere are skilled drummers and dancers.

Meru (Bantu)
Eight groups make up the Meru community (population 1.1 million) who live on the north-eastern slopes of Mount Kenya.

Only the arrival of Europeans at the turn of the century ended the intertribal conflicts between these ethnically and culturally diverse people. The concept of the Meru as a single tribe is recent.

The region's fertile soil and abundant rainfall have made it the richest farmland in Kenya. Tea, coffee, pyrethrum, maize, and potatoes all grow in the highlands. Lower down, cotton and tobacco flourish.

Another profitable cash crop, *miraa* (khat), a mild stimulant much in demand in Somalia and Yemen, is grown in the Nyambene Hills. It is big business. Fast vehicles and light aircraft rush the bundles of fresh twigs and leaves to markets in Nairobi, Mombasa, northern Kenya and across the border into Somalia.

Mijikenda (Bantu)
Nine Bantu groups of the coastal hinterland make up the Mijikenda group ('Nine homes'), often referred to as the Nyika. They are the Giriama, Digo, Duruma, Chonyi, Jibana, Ribe, Kambe, Rabai and Kauma communities, totalling a million people in all.

Tradition has it that an Oromo invasion from the north forced them out of the hinterland into fortified hilltop villages in the south-east, some time between the late 16th and early 17th centuries. Straddling the routes into the interior, the Mijikenda were able to dominate trade with their neighbours. But these links also influenced the movement of the Mijikenda from their traditional hilltop villages into the mainstream of coastal life.

Tourism has increased the tempo of coastal development. In the drier areas of the hinterland cooperative ranches have been established to meet the demands for fresh produce from the hotels and Mombasa's growing population.

Nandi (Nilotic)

Second largest of the Kalenjin communities, the Nandi first settled in the beautiful Nandi Hills between the 16th and 17th centuries when they moved in successive waves from Mount Elgon and an earlier, still obscure, dispersal point much further north. Agricultural skills and cattle were acquired from the neighbouring Luo and Luhya and, with economic prosperity, expansion to the north and east of the Nandi Escarpment became necessary.

But their success was cut short with the arrival of the 'Lunatic Line'. This earned the Nandi a reputation almost as formidable as that of the Zulu, when they defied the British for more than a decade.

From around 1895 until 1905, Nandi *esprit de corps* and military tactics were so tenacious that they seriously held up the building of the Uganda Railway (see 'History: The Dust and the Ashes', Part One).

They had a particular penchant for the copper telegraph wire which ran alongside the track and made excellent bracelets, armlets and necklaces. Even after an armistice was arranged following the killing of their Chief, Koitalel, the Nandi were unable to resist plundering the telegraph wires. For years after, communications in this part of Kenya were erratic.

The Nandi Hills are ideal for such cash crops as tea — many large and picturesque plantations roll from one hilltop to another — pyrethrum, tobacco and coffee.

Okiek (Wandorobo) (Nilotic)

The Okiek, a small, diversified but culturally homogenous group of hunter-gatherers, are scattered throughout the highland forests. Although only 30 Okiek communities have been identified in Kenya, the last population figure was 24,000.

The Okiek use different ecosystems in their high mountain retreats throughout the year, subsisting by hunting, gathering wild fruits and edible plants, and collecting honey. Occasionally parties go down to the plains with packs of dogs to hunt. Until recently, these expert trackers hunted virtually every animal of the high forest for food. Bark and log hives hung throughout the forest heights produce honey of different flavours as the bees collect pollen from many species of flowers and shrubs.

Orma (Cushitic)

The descendants of the once all-conquering Oromo who swept through north-eastern Kenya and beyond the Tana River several centuries ago, subsequently came under pressure from the Somali. The Orma are also known as the Galla. They number 45,500. They herd cattle along both banks of the Tana River — from Garissa downstream to Garsen, where the delta drains into the Indian Ocean.

Renowned for their tall, slender physique and handsome, Cushitic features, the Orma pastoralists are also famous for their herds of white, long-horned Zebu-type cattle — among the finest in Africa. Other than a little sorghum, few crops are grown.

Pokomo (Bantu)

The thirteen subtribes which make up the Pokomo of the Tana River Valley, numbering 59,000 people, are composite, like the Mijikenda, in origin, deriving from Bantu immigrants driven south by the Oromo.

Other than the immediate banks of the Tana, the Pokomo have no land. Farming is their main pursuit and maize and rice have long been their major crops. They often harvest three crops a year from their silt-rich irrigated fields.

They also grow tobacco for cash and hunt and fish to supplement their subsistence diet. Crocodile and hippopotamus meat were once a regular part of their diet, along with fish, honey, and the fruit of the wild palm.

Expert swimmers and canoeists, the Pokomo use dugout canoes for fishing, lashing two canoes together with a platform of poles for longer journeys.

Pokot (Suk) (Nilotic)

The militant pastoralists of the plains, and the less belligerent 'corn people' of the hills, make up the Pokot.

Kalenjin by language, affinity, and traditions, they have adopted many of their neighbours' customs — the Turkana to the north and the Karamoja of Uganda to the

Above: Somali camelherd milks one of his beasts.

west. One bond with the Turkana is their willingness to eat virtually every kind of meat, except carrion-feeding hyena and jackal. Milk, blood drawn from cattle and honey supplement their restricted diet. The warriors also share the distinctive Turkana and Karamojong headdresses of painted clay which are protected by a wooden headrest when sleeping.

The pastoral Pokot herd their cattle and flocks across the waterless scrub north of Lake Baringo — from the Tiati Hills across the Kerio River to the Turkwel River and Karasuk Hills that mark Kenya's border with Uganda.

Their aggressive search for water and grazing often brings them into conflict with the Turkana and the Karamojong. Even today, the constant raids by Turkana rustlers inevitably result in retaliation. Millet, eleusine and tobacco used to be the traditional crops of the Pokot hill farmers, who also kept a few cattle and smaller stock. Such crafts as pottery, metalwork and fashioning snuff-boxes from small calabashes or horns are confined to the hill people.

Rendille (Cushitic)
The 27,000 camel-owning Rendille who roam the rocky wastes of the Kaisut Desert in Marsabit District, are north-eastern neighbours of the Samburu, with ties of kinship and economic cooperation that go back many generations, despite linguistic and cultural differences.

The Rendille live in large, semi-permanent settlements, using camels as pack animals. Watered every 10 to 14 days, the camels give enough milk even in the dry season when other milk producers have stopped lactating.

Using a small knife or blunt arrow to open a vein in the camel's throat Rendille mix camel's milk with blood. After sufficient blood has been drawn off, the wound is closed with a mixture of hair and camel dung. Following their centuries-old tradition, the Rendille herd their stock across the harsh semi-desert and scrub of the Korante Plains and Kaisut Desert, southeast of Lake Turkana.

Sabaot (Nilotic)
The Kalenjin-speaking Bok, Bongomek,

84

Kony, and Sebei are known collectively as the Sabaot. The Bok, Bongomek, and Sebei lived on the Uasin Gishu plateau before they were forced to move west on to the slopes of Mount Elgon — their women and children stolen by the neighbouring Pokot, Karamojong and Nandi. The name of Bungoma town derives from Bongomek.

Inevitably, farming replaced pastoralism, although they still own considerable numbers of cattle, sheep and goats. Not until modern times and the introduction of the ox-plough and maize did the Sabaot return to the fertile flatlands. In addition to traditional crops of eleusine, millet, sorghum, and bananas, they grow a wide range of others, including European vegetables, maize, cassava and cash crops such as sugarcane, pyrethrum and coffee.

The Sabaot have benefited from modern farm techniques and livestock development and from the improvement of communications in western Kenya. An inherited trait, shared with all Kalenjin groups, is their outstanding athletic talent.

Sakuye (Cushitic)

Today, most of the Sakuye (population 11,000), predominantly a camel owning Oromo-speaking people from the desert areas north of Buna, live along the Ewaso Nyiro River in Isiolo District. According to their folklore, their ancestors — who owned thousands of camels — were part of an original Oromo expansion from southern Ethiopia who settled at a place called Saku (Marsabit) from which they took their name. Then they moved into Isiolo District where they came into conflict with the Samburu and, more recently, the Somali.

Now, more than ever before, the Sakuye are curtailing their nomadic life. This was first forced on them in the mid-1960s by demands for closer administration during the campaign against the *shifta* (Somali bandits). With educational and health facilities available Sakuye life changed dramatically in the 1980s and 1990s.

Samburu (Nilotic)

A nomadic Maa-speaking people, the 107,000-strong Samburu group, who live in Maralal and northern Kenya between Lake Turkana and the Ewaso Nyiro River, are said to have migrated south, like the Maasai, to their present location from the north of Lake Turkana several centuries ago. These cattle-owning pastoralists, who live mainly off their herds. Milk is the principal food, supplemented with blood tapped from the veins of living cattle or from sheep and goats slaughtered for meat. Certain roots and barks are added to Samburu soups for nutritional value.

Semi-desert land restricts farming in the lowlands, but on the Lorogi Plateau and in the Karisia Hills, they grow maize, sorghum and vegetables, and large tracts are now being leased to produce wheat seed. Unlike the warlike Maasai, whose language

Top: Rendille matriarch grooming youngster.

Above: Pensive Samburu maiden.

85

Above: Traditional Taita musicians.

and cultural heritage they share, the Samburu are tolerant of other groups and place a high value on social respect.

Segeju (Bantu)
The last descendants of a once numerous pastoral people, fewer than 400 Segeju remain in Kenya. Originally, they lived around the Mount Kenya area and four centuries ago these warrior pastoralists, similar to the Maasai, owned large herds of cattle and lived on a diet of blood and milk. In 1592 the Segeju conquered Mombasa for their Malindi allies. Later, in the 17th century, the Segeju in turn were forced out of the Malindi area by Oromo pressure from the north and settled around Shimoni and Vanga at the extreme south of the Kenya coast.

During the last century the Segeju people drifted even further south. Today the majority live near Tanga, in Tanzania.

Somali (Cushitic)
Occupying some 45,098 square kilometres (17,408 square miles) — a quarter of Kenya — of the arid North-Eastern Province, the nomadic Somali camel-herders number more than half-a-million. About 140 years ago they crossed the Juba River, moving south-west, and arrived in Wajir in 1906.

Subsequently, they settled the entire north-east of Kenya, driving out or absorbing any minority hunter-gatherer groups and Bantu farmers in their path. Pastoral nomads who own large camel herds, cattle, sheep and goats, the Somali are entirely dependent on the precarious grazing and water in their semi-desert region. Highly articulate and politically aware, the Somali are united equally by family loyalty and formal political contracts.

Suba (Bantu)
Suba (population 108,000) are an agglomeration of subtribes closely allied to the Kuria, remnant groups of which occupy the Lake Victoria islands of Rusinga and Mfangano, and are now essentially Luo.

Like the Bantu-speaking people of the Lake Victoria region, the Suba say they migrated from Western Uganda, moving eastwards, then south around the shore. Apart from a small group of farmers, the Suba were hunters and fisherfolk. They hunted hippo for meat and fat, and the killing was a time for celebration, for special songs and rites. Hunters no more, the Suba concentrate on fishing, which provides a cash income that is often the envy of their farming neighbours. Canoes play a prime role in their economy. The Suba are skilled boat-builders and their craft is in great demand by the neighbouring Luo.

Taita/Taveta (Bantu)

The 218,000 people of the fertile Taita Hills and Taveta district include the Kasigau, Sagala and Dabida. Divided into seven clans, they have long farmed the land: always with many spiritual preliminaries.

Cultivation requires authority from tribal elders, sacrifices, and supplications made to the collections of skulls kept in sacred caves, which contain the ancestral spirits. Before Christianity, the Taita believed in communion with the dead as a means of arbitration and future direction.

Traditional Taita crops include millet, beans, cowpeas, cassava, sweet potatoes, sugarcane and maize — much of it grown under irrigation.

There are many banana, sugarcane, and mango plantations in Taveta, and the produce finds a ready market in Mombasa and along the coast. Other commercial crops include vegetables and coffee. Taita Hills was one of the first areas in Kenya where coffee was grown. Traditionally, hunting and trapping game was linked to trade with coastal peoples.

Meat and skins were bartered for simple manufactured goods which in turn were exchanged for livestock. Taita crafts include leatherwork, metalwork, basket-weaving, and woodwork.

Tharaka (Bantu)

The 92,000-strong Tharaka, the southernmost people of Meru District, occupy the low, hot plains east of Mount Kenya, where there are few resources. Frequent droughts often threaten famine. Malaria and sleeping sickness are endemic.

The Tharaka, once famed for witchcraft, are colourful drummers, and bee-keepers. Both drums and hives are made from hollowed logs. Some individuals may own 100 or more hives. They trade in honey and

grain and keep goats, sheep, cattle and chickens. Along the Tana and Kizita rivers they supplement their diet with fish. Grain and threshed millet is stored in large wicker granaries sealed by a slab of stone.

They grow cotton and tobacco as cash crops. Shopping baskets plaited from the leaves of the doum palm are a source of money to many women and children.

Tugen (Nilotic)

Third-largest of the Kalenjin-speaking groups, the semi-pastoral Tugen occupy a narrow rectangle of the Rift Valley floor, bound in the west by the Kerio River and in the east by the parallel ranges of the 2,500-metre-high (8,200-feet) Tugen and Kamasia hills. The administrative centre is fast developing Kabarnet. Other centres are Eldama Ravine and Kabartonjo. Like the other Kalenjin groups in the Kerio Valley, the Tugen claim to come from the Mount Elgon region. President Daniel Toroitich arap Moi, born in 1924 in the village of Kurieng'wo in Sacho Location of Baringo District and educated at Kabartonjo and Kapsabet, is a Tugen.

Turkana (Nilotic)

The 284,000-strong Turkana community inhabit the north-west of Kenya between Lake Turkana in the east and the escarpment marking the Uganda border in the west. The administrative centre is Lodwar.

Milk and blood are the main food. Men herd and water the cattle, sing and dance to them in the evening and rub their horns with fat. Camels are also important and small girls or boys herd sheep and goats which are killed for guests or minor rituals. Donkeys are used solely as pack animals.

They make dried milk by boiling large quantities of fresh milk and drying it on skins. They also make cakes from wild berries which are crushed and mixed with blood. Fishing in Lake Turkana plays little part in Turkana economics, but is practised during the dry season or famine.

Improved communications have eroded the Turkana's traditional insularity. Settlement schemes along the Turkwel and Kerio rivers and fishing cooperatives on the western shore of Lake Turkana have helped bring the community into the mainstream of Kenyan life.

PART TWO: PLACES AND TRAVEL

Above: Highland forest glade.
Opposite: One of the major hydroelectric schemes on the Tana River.

Nairobi: City in the Sun

If Nairobi were nothing more than a city that has grown in 95 years from zero population and two-and-a-half square kilometres (one square mile) to more than two million people and 700 square kilometres (270 square miles) it would be remarkable.

But it is also a brawling, dynamic maelstrom of cultures and enterprises that reflects its melting-pot heritage.

If the city sometimes seems a little contradictory and eccentric, don't be too surprised. Less than a century ago it didn't exist. Indeed, Nairobi only arose as a secondary coincidence of one man's unwavering ambition and steely determination to build a railway line across Kenya.

George Whitehouse, general manager of the Uganda Railway, was no visionary in matters metropolitan. His single-minded intent was to complete one of the most audacious feats of civil engineering ever attempted in the Victorian era — the 1,000-kilometre-long (620 mile) 'Lunatic Line' from Mombasa to Lake Victoria (see 'History: The Dust and the Ashes', Part One).

Whitehouse chose *Nyrobi* (Maasai for 'place of the cool waters') as his main up-country railhead. Then just a bleak and disease-infested swamp, it was, in engineering terms, the last piece of totally flat ground before the hard climb up the eastern shoulders of the Great Rift Valley escarpment.

The thought that one day 'Nyrobi' might be a major capital never crossed Whitehouse's mind, otherwise he might have chosen a more suitable location. The black cotton soil of the swamplands expands to become a sludge-like mass when wet, and contracts when dry. It's probably the worst imaginable foundation on which to build a city. But like so much in Kenya in the first half of this century, Nairobi evolved spontaneously.

The first resident, apart from the itinerant Maasai who brought their herds to water, was Sergeant George Ellis, from the more sedate village of Newington Butts, Surrey, England, in 1896. He built stables and an office. Then huts began to grow up around the railhead which settled, halfway between Mombasa and Lake Victoria, with

a belch of steam on 30 May 1899. Ten months after the rail-head was established, Sir Arthur Hardinge, the British Consul-General based in Zanzibar, gave it township status on 16 April 1900, when he published the first 15 clauses of the Nairobi Municipal Regulations.

The first town clerk was appointed in 1904, by which time Nairobi was a municipality covering 104 square kilometres (40 square miles). It was invested as a city on 30 March 1950, when the Duke of Gloucester presented a Royal charter on behalf of King George VI of England.

At independence on 12 December 1963, the population was about half-a-million people and it covered an area of 350 square kilometres (135 square miles). Thirty years later Nairobi's boundaries embraced 700 square kilometres (270 square miles) and its population, officially around two million, had in reality swollen to more than three million.

Now a United Nations headquarters city, Nairobi is the economic, if not political, capital of much of east and central Africa as well as Kenya. It continues to grow as it was conceived — at an astonishing speed and with great energy if, at times, seemingly without control. In some areas, Nairobi still looks and feels like an afterthought.

Despite its origins as a shantytown, to which, in 1996, many of its suburban areas seemed to be reverting, Nairobi remains truly memorable — both in the contrasts and experiences it affords, and in its setting.

Situated 500 kilometres (300 miles) from the coast and 1,670 metres (5,500 feet) above sea level, the metropolitan area stretches from the Embakasi plains in the east up the once-wooded slopes of the wall of the Great Rift Valley in the west, from the Ngong Hills in the south to the foothills of the Aberdares in the north.

When to go

Nairobi is pleasant all the year round but best in September when the jacaranda, bougainvillea and flame trees bloom, and

Opposite: Aerial view of the heart of bustling Nairobi.

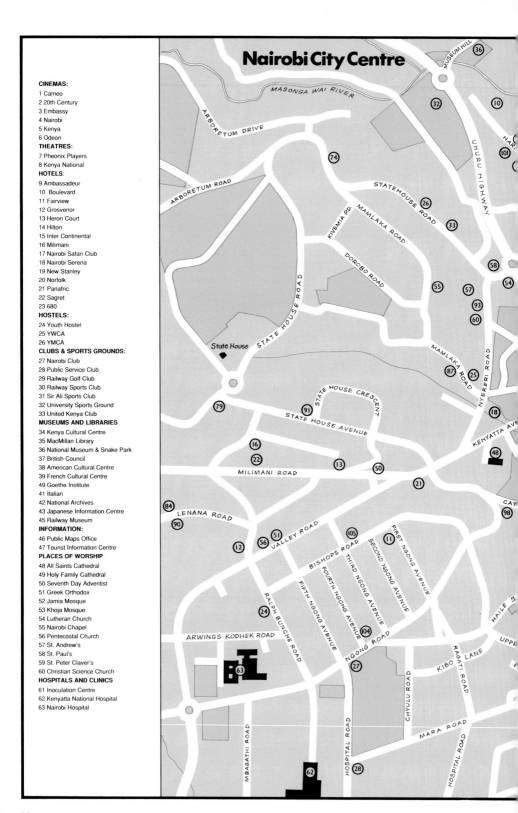

Nairobi City Centre

CINEMAS:
1 Cameo
2 20th Century
3 Embassy
4 Nairobi
5 Kenya
6 Odeon

THEATRES:
7 Pheonix Players
8 Kenya National

HOTELS:
9 Ambassadeur
10 Boulevard
11 Fairview
12 Grosvenor
13 Heron Court
14 Hilton
15 Inter Continental
16 Milimani
17 Nairobi Safari Club
18 Nairobi Serena
19 New Stanley
20 Norfolk
21 Panafric
22 Sagret
23 680

HOSTELS:
24 Youth Hostel
25 YWCA
26 YMCA

CLUBS & SPORTS GROUNDS:
27 Nairobi Club
28 Public Service Club
29 Railway Golf Club
30 Railway Sports Club
31 Sir Ali Sports Club
32 University Sports Ground
33 United Kenya Club

MUSEUMS AND LIBRARIES
34 Kenya Cultural Centre
35 MacMillan Library
36 National Museum & Snake Park
37 British Council
38 American Cultural Centre
39 French Cultural Centre
49 Goethe Institute
41 Italian
42 National Archives
43 Japanese Information Centre
45 Railway Museum

INFORMATION:
46 Public Maps Office
47 Tourist Information Centre

PLACES OF WORSHIP
48 All Saints Cathedral
49 Holy Family Cathedral
50 Seventh Day Adventist
51 Greek Orthodox
52 Jamia Mosque
53 Khoja Mosque
54 Lutheran Church
55 Nairobi Chapel
56 Pentecostal Church
57 St. Andrew's
58 St. Paul's
59 St. Peter Claver's
60 Christian Science Church

HOSPITALS AND CLINICS
61 Inoculation Centre
62 Kenyatta National Hospital
63 Nairobi Hospital

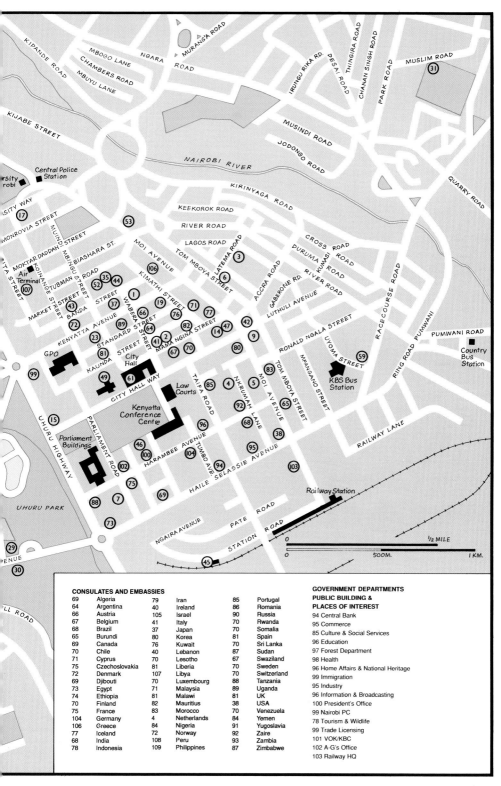

CONSULTATES AND EMBASSIES

69	Algeria	79	Iran	85	Portugal
64	Argentina	40	Ireland	86	Romania
66	Austria	105	Israel	90	Russia
67	Belgium	41	Italy	70	Rwanda
68	Brazil	37	Japan	70	Somalia
65	Burundi	80	Korea	81	Spain
69	Canada	76	Kuwait	70	Sri Lanka
70	Chile	40	Lebanon	87	Sudan
71	Cyprus	70	Lesotho	67	Swaziland
75	Czechoslovakia	81	Liberia	70	Sweden
72	Denmark	107	Libya	70	Switzerland
69	Djibouti	70	Luxembourg	88	Tanzania
73	Egypt	71	Malaysia	89	Uganda
74	Ethiopia	81	Malawi	81	UK
70	Finland	82	Mauritius	38	USA
75	France	83	Morocco	70	Venezuela
104	Germany	4	Netherlands	84	Yemen
106	Greece	84	Nigeria	91	Yugoslavia
77	Iceland	72	Norway	92	Zaire
68	India	108	Peru	93	Zambia
78	Indonesia	109	Philippines	87	Zimbabwe

GOVERNMENT DEPARTMENTS
PUBLIC BUILDING &
PLACES OF INTEREST
94 Central Bank
95 Commerce
85 Culture & Social Services
96 Education
97 Forest Department
98 Health
96 Home Affairs & National Heritage
99 Immigration
95 Industry
96 Information & Broadcasting
100 President's Office
99 Nairobi PC
78 Tourism & Wildlife
99 Trade Licensing
101 VOK/KBC
102 A-G's Office
103 Railway HQ

93

worst between June and August when it's often overcast, miserable and cold.

Getting there
There are international flights daily from many centres in Europe and regular scheduled services from America and from Asia. Gone are the days when passenger liners regularly plied their way to Mombasa and the passengers travelled upcountry on the Nairobi 'Express'. It's still possible to find passage on a cargo ship and when the trade winds are favourable it may also be possible to take a dhow from the Gulf or Mogadishu. From the west you can travel by road or railway from Kampala to Nairobi, but it's a long way.

Roads from North and West Africa are uncertain, but several overland companies out of London continue to cater for those with the spirit of adventure.

Where to stay
Just a small cross section: Fairview Hotel (4-star), Bishop's Road; Nairobi Hilton International (5-star), Mama Ngina Street; Ambassadeur (4-star), Moi Avenue; Boulevard Hotel (3-star), Harry Thuku Road; Heron Court Hotel (3-star), Milimani Road; Nairobi Inter-Continental (5-star), City Hall Way-Uhuru Highway; Grand Regency Hotel (5-star), Uhuru Highway; Hurlingham Hotel (English rustic and fine home cooking), Argwings-Kodhek Road; Jacaranda Hotel (4-star), off Waiyaki Way, Westlands; Mayfair Court Hotel (4-star), Parklands; PanAfric Hotel (4-star), Kenyatta Avenue; Meridien Court Hotel (4-star), Murang'a Road; Safari Park Hotel (5-star), Thika Road; Nairobi Safari Club (5-star), Koinange Street-University Way; Nairobi Serena Hotel (5-star), Nyerere Road-Kenyatta Avenue; New Stanley (5-star), Kimathi Street; Norfolk Hotel (5-star), Harry Thuku Road.

There are many others. See Listings for 'Hotels'.

Sightseeing
Refurbished in 1991 with many improved passenger facilities and a lavishly equipped Duty Free shopping mall, **Jomo Kenyatta International Airport**, one of the busiest and most modern in Africa, lies to the east of Nairobi in the lee of the Lukenia Hills

and Ol Doinyo Sapuk National Park. The glide path brings giant jetliners in over the Ngong Hills and Nairobi National Park in the south-west. Named after Kenya's founding father, the airport was opened five months after his death by his successor, Kenya's second President, Daniel Toroitich arap Moi.

Scheduled bus services costing a few shillings, fairly expensive taxis (you can haggle, it's a way of life), and the Kenya Airways bus will take you the sixteen kilometres (10 miles) into the city.

On your left, you pass the **Nairobi National Park**, and in the distance, Karen Blixen's favourite African panorama, the misty, blue-grey knuckle profile of the **Ngong Hills**, made famous worldwide by the film, *Out of Africa*.

The broad, dual carriageway leading into town also slices through the nether end of the city's **Industrial Area** which houses Nairobi's inland port with its giant container terminal, the General Motors assembly plant and the Firestone tyre factory.

Hard to imagine that less than two kilometres (just over a mile) away from these mundane manufacturing units a pride of lion is roaming the still pristine national park, perhaps about to pounce on a young wildebeest (gnu). An exotic first thought for travellers from less exceptional climes.

If you fly overnight on the 'red-eye' from Europe, the chances are that you will arrive in Nairobi at the start of the morning rush hour. If you intend to hire your own vehicle this will serve as an appropriate introduction to Kenya's erratic and sometimes dangerously individualistic driving styles.

The road from the airport leads to the intersection with the main Mombasa-Nairobi highway and **Langata Road** landmarked by the **Nyayo Sports Stadium**, one of the venues for the 1987 All Africa Games.

Past the stadium, you negotiate a roundabout, beyond which Nairobi's first **cemetery** lies to the left behind a stone wall. With its graves of the fallen from the 1914-18 war nearest to the road and the Jewish section in the middle, it provides an interesting perspective on colonial history. **Charles Ryall**'s grave is there, who in the year 1900 sat at night in a railway carriage

Above: Golden light illuminates Uhuru Fountain in Nairobi's Uhuru Park.

at Kima to shoot a man-eater, but the lion got him first.

The coach from which it dragged him is a macabre exhibit at the **Railway Museum** across the highway. The cemetery abuts on to the nine-hole **Railway Golf Club** course (*circa* 1922) whose ninth tee stands a two-wood drive from **Parliament Buildings**. Giant blue gums line the fairways. How many cities can boast such a sylvan recreation facility so close to their heart?

The Mombasa road now becomes **Uhuru Highway**, a celebration of Kenya's freedom. Taken from the Kiswahili, its name was changed from Queen Elizabeth Highway at independence. In the 30 or so years since then virtually every city street and district nomenclature which reflected the colonial heritage has been 'Africanized'. Good for national pride but difficult for those intent on tracking down Nairobi's historic landmarks.

Haile Selassie Avenue, for instance, which intersects with Uhuru Highway at the next roundabout after the railway bridge, was originally Ellis Avenue, named after the capital's founding citizen. To-

gether with **Moi Avenue** (previously Station Road and then Government Road), these were Nairobi's first two public thoroughfares.

The Hill
If you turn left off Uhuru Highway along **Ngong Road** and up the hill, you pass the stone-built **Railway Club** where the first game of cricket was played in Nairobi in 1899. The club's tin-and-timber predecessor also served as Kenya's first parliament. When the Legislative Council (Legco) held its initial meeting on 17 August 1907, one question the seven-member, all-European council debated was capital punishment, which was carried out by firing squad. Too often, the bullets spent themselves before they left the barrel of the old Henry-Martini rifles — salvaged from the bottom of Mombasa Harbour — and simply fell to the ground.

The consensus was that this was hardly fair on the condemned, so a bill was enacted to replace the firing squad with the gallows. It subsequently transpired that there was no official hangman but, when

Above: Jomo Kenyatta International Airport, Nairobi.

the vacancy was advertised, a former Royal Navy petty officer filled the post.

He was previously a steam-roller driver who came to Kenya along with his vehicle to improve the roads after the governor of the day muddied his shoes in Station Road (now Moi Avenue) during the rainy season. Hanging remains the official form of death penalty.

Higher up the hill, just past the **National Library** to the right, is the creeper-woven stonework of the 1913 **Nairobi Club** on the left. It replaced the original building, established in 1901, which was burnt down some time before.

It was Nairobi's first social institution and remains very much the preserve of the capital's elite. Since cash payments have always been disdained, bar chits are settled at the end of each month and members default at the peril of being blackballed. Once an exemplary bastion of male chauvinism, feminism has struck telling blows at the club's infrastructures but, to the relief of many older members, its ruling hierarchy still manages to perpetuate one men-only bar. The sprawling grounds provide a wide

range of leisure pursuits — swimming pool, bowling greens, cricket and hockey pitches, and tennis courts.

Next left, beyond the club, is the **Police Traffic Headquarters** followed by **Kenyatta National Hospital**, a free referral centre for Kenya citizens and an impressive demonstration of government commitment to social welfare. However, the neglected interior reveals the financial constraints which limit the staff's ability to care for both the institution and its patients.

Nairobi Hospital, opposite (physically and in every other sense), is a landmark of the private medical sector, employing dedicated staff and top grade specialists. Its contemporary equipment includes sophisticated intensive-care units.

Tucked away between the Nairobi Club and the Police Traffic HQ is the highly social **Kenya Regiment Association**. A survivor of the old King's African Rifles that fought valiantly in East Africa during the two world wars, the regiment's history is recorded in *The Charging Buffalo*, by Guy Campbell. Beyond the next roundabout, take the first left and you arrive at the

Royal Nairobi Golf Club, which was carved out of indigenous forest in 1904. In the past, its members were occasionally mauled by lion or gored by rhinoceros. It received its Royal accolade during the brief rule of Britain's King Edward VIII in 1936.

The forest has long gone and the course is now hemmed in on all sides by serried rows of suburban maisonettes and houses.

This entire hill area, dry and forested, was claimed by Whitehouse when the railway arrived in Nairobi. Hearing of this, the first British administrator in Kenya, Manchester-born John Ainsworth, rode up from Machakos, where he had established his headquarters and had expected Whitehouse to make the railhead (see 'History: The Dust and the Ashes', Part One). Much to Whitehouse's annoyance, Ainsworth removed the stakes which had been hammered in on Whitehouse's instructions.

In the argument which ensued, Whitehouse claimed the hill was railway land, Ainsworth that it was sovereign land: neither remembering it was African land. Announcing his intention to protect Crown interests, Ainsworth at once set up his administrative headquarters in Nairobi.

The City Centre

Nairobi's focal point is the attractively laid-out three-square-kilometre (just over a square mile) city centre, bounded in the south-east by Haile Selassie Avenue, in the south-west by Uhuru Highway, in the south-east and north-west by Moi Avenue, and in the north by **University Way**.

The skyline is dominated by the 33-storey, 105-metre-tall (344-foot) profile of the **Kenyatta International Conference Centre**, which draws its architectural inspiration from both rural Africa and ancient Rome.

At one side of the hexagonal tower is a well-appointed amphitheatre shaped like a *rondavel* (African hut), and the main plenary hall, a modern version of the Roman Senate, seats 4,000 delegates. The interior is laid out with red-tiled promenades flanked by non-functioning indoor fountains and pools.

Approaching from the direction of the airport, you turn right off Uhuru Highway into Haile Selassie Avenue, the left-hand corner dominated by the impressive marble façade built by the Central Bank Co-operative Society. The first left is **Parliament Way**, where the small precinct that occupies the corner block houses the **Professional Centre**, offices for such professional bodies as Kenya's architectural and accountants associations.

The basement is home to East Africa's best-known repertory company, the **Phoenix Players**, which emerged out of the volatile dismemberment of the Donovan Maule Theatre, Kenya's founding repertory company. This stood on the corner opposite the Professional Centre but was demolished in 1988. Continuing down Haile Selassie Avenue you pass the **Central Bank of Kenya,** on the left, and then arrive at the roundabout connecting it with Moi Avenue.

Turn right and you enter the **Nairobi Railway Station**, where the city all began, flanked on the right by the neo-classical, colonial lines of the 1929 **Kenya Railways Headquarters**. In the **Railway Museum**, located at the upcountry end of the station, are the glistening relics of old 'Lunatic Express' trains, including ancient steam engines, and the coach from which Charles Ryall was dragged to his death.

In the housed section of the Museum other *bric-à-brac*, including the old cow-catcher on which former US President Theodore Roosevelt rode in 1909 during his grand hunting safari in Kenya, commemorate the five-year drama of the railway's construction. In the middle of the sprawling marshalling yards, the **Railway Workshops**, founded by Whitehouse, still remain one of Kenya's biggest industrial undertakings, employing skilled, highly-trained personnel.

Moi Avenue, a curious mixture of some of the capital's earliest buildings, still roofed with corrugated iron, juxtaposed among its modern office blocks and hotels, marks a unique division of the city — the boundary between up-market and down-market downtown Nairobi.

The north side of this divide endows the capital with its vibrant, colourful African character.

River Road: Take a Walk on the 'Wild' Side

Moi Avenue divides the smart, metropolitan, office blocks and colonial landmarks from what many consider the real Nairobi.

This begins with **Tom Mboya Street** (previously Victoria Street), renamed in memory of the slain Kenya nationalist. There, the first bazaar and shanty in Nairobi sprang up, soon to spread down to the Nairobi River.

This is where the capital's African ambience comes to vivid life. Open-fronted shops display colourful wares, and cupboard-size radio shops blare out the latest Swahili music hits night and day.

From Moi Avenue take the turn by the **Khoja Mosque** and you come to the roundabout dominated, on the right as you enter the traffic stream, by **Nation House**. Until 1992 this was home to the country's largest-selling newspaper but was abandoned for the custom-built Nation Centre in Kimathi Street — in the city centre.

If you keep left at the roundabout you descend to the **Globe roundabout**, Nairobi's biggest, dominated at the left on the corner of **Kijabe Street,** which runs up to **Harry Thuku Way**, by the Globe Cinema (the old **Paramount Cinema**) now a victim of the video revolution, and used for offices and warehousing.

The Globe roundabout is cut by the Nairobi River, a seasonal stream born in the Ngong Hills which becomes a raging torrent during the rainy season. The roundabout, in fact, marks the head of the old swamp which gave the city its name.

Circle the roundabout and you return to Tom Mboya Street, passing on your left **Kirinyaga Road**, formerly Grogan Road after Colonel Ewart Grogan, of Cape to Cairo fame who made his fortune in colonial Kenya.

This is a street of frenetic enterprise marked by squalid lodgings and grease-stained workshops that specialize in motor vehicle parts and repairs. Its only landmark is the **colonial clock** at the far end just before it enters **Racecourse Road**.

Back at the Nation House roundabout you leave **River Road**, Nairobi's most tireless commercial centre, to your left. This mixture of upcountry *matatu* and bus operators, shops, and small-scale industrial enterprises is liberally scattered with lodging houses and cheap restaurants, both African and Asian, serving ethnic stews of *sukuma wiki* (kale or spinach) and beef and *matumbo* (tripe). River Road operates round the clock, a vibrant, colourful high street where you can haggle with the shopkeepers and snap up bargains at half the price charged on the smart side of Moi Avenue.

Above: Tourist enthuses over impressive African woodcarvings.

Above: Traditional handwoven baskets, *kiondos*, are popular buys for tourists.

Both there and on the slightly more up-market Tom Mboya Street, which is lined with shops and office blocks until you reach its intersection near the city bus station with the tail-end of Haile Selassie Avenue, you get a taste of Nairobi's inherent African character.

Turn left near the massive milling and warehouse facilities of the **Kenya Coffee Growers Co-operative Union**, into the one-way system which leads past **St Peter Claver's Church** into **Uyoma Street** with the 1963 **Siri Guru Singh Sabha Temple**, like an incongruous Earls Court of Nairobi.

Continue into **Racecourse Road**, which until the end of World War II was the road to the old racecourse at **Kariokor** (the Kiswahili phonetic for 'Carrier Corps').

There you'll find a colourful market popular for its *nyama choma* (roast meat), usually beef or goat, served with large helpings of delicious and nutritious *irio*, a Kikuyu vegetable mash of beans, peas, and potatoes (see 'Tastes of Kenya', Part Three).

Beyond the market roundabout a faceless array of middle-income maisonettes occupies the level ground that served as the city's racecourse for more than half a century — from the first meeting in 1901, when pack horses were enlisted to enliven the event and make up a decent field. It became a twice yearly gymkhana meeting, but on several occasions the start was delayed by wild game on the track — rhinoceros, lion and others.

The course at Kariokor served until the **Jockey Club of Kenya** acquired the **Ngong Racecourse** to the west of the city, said by many to be the most beautiful race track in the Commonwealth. There are now about 40 Sunday meetings a year, and the bloodstock has been refined by imported thoroughbreds.

Complete a full circle of Kariokor and return to the roundabout that marks the intersection of Racecourse Road with **Pumwani Ring Road**. Turn left into Ring Road and at the far end, leaving the mosque and police station on the left, turn left into **Landhies Road** for **Kamakunji**.

This is the country bus terminal known affectionately as **'Machakos Airport'**. In one corner, hundreds of artisans convert scrap metal into *sufurias* (pots) and old tyres into sandals. These are especially favoured by the Maasai, who name them after the distance the shoes cover before wearing out, so favourites are known as 'Loitokitok', far away on the slopes of Kilimanjaro, or perhaps as 'Kajiado', the administrative capital of a Maasai district.

'Machakos Airport' is a riot of garish colours and noise. The vivid hues of cheap plastic and cloth items flood the pavements and stalls with brilliant splashes: blaring radios, record-players and loud-hailers compete with the raucous cries of sidewalk vendors and *manambas* (touts), luring passengers onto country buses and the ubiquitous freelance *matatus*, Kenya's version of West African 'mammy wagons', which supplement the public transport system. You can find almost anything you need there and at the back of Kamakunji, which leads into the squatter township of **Shauri Moyo** and the **Hindu crematorium** and the headquarters of the Central Organization of Trade Unions (**COTU**). Hundreds of craftsmen work in this area at a large **Kamba woodcarvers' co-operative**, turning out statues and figurines of Kenya's wildlife and people which are sold by curio vendors all over the country.

Fascinating to watch, these nimble-fingered artists transform chunks and chips of mahogany and other wood into elephants, giraffes, and Maasai warriors in the space of minutes.

Past Kamakunji, at the roundabout marked on the right by the old **City Stadium** — until the 1980s the city's major sports arena — Landhies Road becomes **Jogoo Road**, the northern boundary of the industrial area, notable for its dull and endless low cost housing estates. Return to Ring Road and cross over, via the Racecourse Road roundabout, into Pangani.

The suburb was founded very early in the city's history by pioneer Asian traders and entrepreneurs and, for many, is still their inner suburban home. **Pangani** also embraces **Ngara**, with its many Asian shops selling textiles and confections.

Mainstream Nairobi

The central point of Moi Avenue is dominated by the circular **Hilton Hotel** which faces the massive ramparts of **Kenya Commercial Bank**. This could have been designed by a frustrated cotton mill architect,

Above: Jamia Mosque, Nairobi.

although some people consider it remarkably similar to the flagship of the American Sixth Fleet.

As the pivot around which all Nairobi seems to flow, the Hilton also faces the **National Archives**, repository of much treasured but faded paper relating to Kenya's recorded history. Judging by the amount of vetting a potential researcher undergoes, it may also store some state secrets. The archives are housed in the refurbished old Bank of India building (*circa* 1906), one of the city's oldest stone buildings.

New traffic lights were installed on this section of Moi Avenue in 1988 but did nothing to halt the roar and confusion of city traffic. At least now, however, you can drive straight along Moi Avenue to the

next set of traffic lights and the intersection, left, with the city's grand mall, **Kenyatta Avenue**, which was formerly Sixth Avenue, and then Delamere Avenue.

On the right is the rather scruffy **Imenti Building**, another large island of offices, shops, and restaurants, around which the tide of Nairobi's traffic swirls day and night. In 1904, the previous building on this spot formed young Nairobi's first municipal offices and, later, the first law courts.

The hole in the ground opposite Imenti building, at the corner of Moi and Kenyatta Avenues, used to be occupied by the capital's first stone building, **Nairobi House**, which was gazetted as a monument in the 1970s. Unfortunately, it occupied prime real estate space and was levelled — illegally — by the wrecker's ball. Nothing can restore it but it also seems that nothing is to occupy the hole either. The space has remained vacant since 1983 and appears to testify to the planning authority's umbrage over the building's wanton destruction.

Beyond the intersection, many of the old stone buildings which once lined either side of the road were, alas for history, being replaced in the 1990s by new ones less interesting architecturally. But the **Imperial British East Africa** (IBEA) company's 1919 building still remained.

Just a few paces farther along, again on the right, is the Ismaili **Khoja Mosque**, the place of worship for Ismaili followers of the Aga Khan, a small but devotedly patriotic section of the Kenyan community who make a large contribution, both socially and economically, to national development.

Queen Victoria

Opposite is **Jeevanjee Gardens**, the city's first recreational area, donated to the city (after the bazaars that stood there were consumed in a tinder-brush fire) by the public benefactor and philanthropist A M 'Haj' Jeevanjee, who made his fortune as a railway contractor.

In March 1906, the Duke of Connaught unveiled a bust of his mother, Queen Victoria, which now watches over lunch-time crowds who come to listen to impromptu sermons by itinerant preachers with loud-hailers. Dr Livingstone, one presumes, would be delighted to learn that evangelism is a major Kenya social recreation.

Jeevanjee Gardens is close to **Biashara Street**, the city's first bazaar, and to **City Market**, Nairobi's fruit and vegetable market. Behind City Market are local curio dealers who specialize in wicker furniture and woven baskets.

On the right of Moi Avenue, just beyond Jeevanjee Gardens, where the road turns left to become **University Way**, some of the tin huts still stand in which Nairobi's first administrator, John Ainsworth, shaped the outline of the city. Until 1980s they were the offices of the **Survey of Kenya**.

Turn into University Way and take the first turning right to come to the celebrated **Norfolk Hotel**. Not much remains of the old property, which opened on Christmas Day, 1904. Time and a terrorist bomb on New Year's Eve 1980 finished off most of the earlier west wing. But lovingly rebuilt, the Norfolk still wears its familiar red-brick and black-and-white mock-Tudor frontage.

The three large oil paintings in the Ibis Grill Room bar, originally commissioned for the **New Stanley Hotel**, depict London scenes evocative of the 1930s.

Inside the gardens an old plough and ox-wagon remind guests of the pioneering spirit in which the timbers of the Norfolk are steeped. Few hotels in the world can boast its history, or its roll call of aristocratic and rich and famous guests, many of whom are recorded in colourful detail in Jan Hemsing's excellent *Then and Now, Nairobi's Norfolk Hotel*.

Opposite is the **University of Nairobi**, **Cultural Centre** and **the National Theatre**, which was built with a British Council grant of £50,000, the support of the great Shakespearean actor Sir Donald Wolfit, and opened by Sir Ralph Richardson in 1952. One of its building stones is from Shakespeare's birthplace in Stratford-upon-Avon and the rosemary tree outside came from Shakespeare's garden. It occupies the spot where Nairobi's **Police Headquarters** once stood, where, on 16 March 1922, Kenya's first public demonstration against colonial rule took place.

The reason for the demonstration was the arrest of Harry Thuku. Still in his twenties, he was a £4-a-month telephone operator at the Treasury who lived in Pangani and was friendly with the leaders of the Indian Association which represented Indian interests in Legco. With their assistance he formed the East African Association.

On 14 March 1922, as Thuku addressed a fair-deal-for-real-Kenyans meeting in Pangani, he was arrested by Chief Inspector Satwant Bachan Singh, head of the Nairobi CID, who drove him away on the pillion of his motor cycle for interrogation by the Superintendent of Police. Two days later the mobs outside the Police HQ demanding his release were swollen by thousands of strikers and sympathizers. Attempts to disperse the protesters failed and, when Captain G S Cary was knocked to the ground, Bachan Singh gave the order to open fire. At the end of the day 21 people, including several women and one 15-

Above: Haunches of beef and venison broil at the Carnivore Restaurant.

old youth, lay dead (See 'History: The Dust and the Ashes', Part One). Thuku was Kenya's first political hero and, after independence, the road in which the Norfolk Hotel stands was renamed **Harry Thuku Road**.

The National Theatre is part of a cultural precinct occupied on one side by **Broadcasting House**, operated by the **Kenya Broadcasting Corporation**, and on the other by the **Kenya Cultural Centre**.

When you return to University Way turn right and continue past the elegant **Nairobi Safari Club**, on the left, to the roundabout on Uhuru Highway which marks the far end of the defined city centre.

Now turn left in the direction of the airport. To the left of the highway are Nairobi's newer structures, high-rise office buildings, while **Central Park** is to the right, with the children's traffic playground and the compact hexagonal-shaped **Nyayo Monument**, built late in 1988 to mark President Moi's first decade as Kenya's leader. Central Park is a favourite meeting place for Kenyans.

To the left is the **Grand Regency Hotel**, an elegant atrium-style hotel, subject of much litigation, the first new 5-star hotel in

Nairobi in 25 years and notable for a 12-storey representation of a Maasai earring on the atrium wall.

Street of History

Walk beyond the Moi monument and you come to the lush gardens of another 5-star hotel, the **Nairobi Serena**, which many envious developers consider fortunate to have been allocated land on such a prime green belt site. At least the architect had the foresight to hide the building in landscaped gardens so it doesn't look in the least intrusive. The next roundabout brings you to the intersection of **Kenyatta Avenue** and Uhuru Highway. Turn left and you're on the city's main thoroughfare. First, on the eastern corner, is the old Nairobi **Provincial Commission** office (*circa* 1913), a protected building that sits in the shadow of its 20-storey successor, **Nyayo House**, accommodating all manner of government departments, including the **Immigration Department** and, since 1990, the Kenya Television Network (KTN). On the next corner, 1992 saw the commencement of the reconstruction of a new **General Post Office** on the same site as the old GPO de-

Above: Kenya's colourful textiles.

molished in 1989, work that was still incomplete in 1996. Until 1955, the road that divides the GPO from Nyayo House was the upcountry leg of the 'Lunatic Line'—all the way to Lake Victoria or Uganda's far north – which crossed Kenyatta Avenue by courtesy of a barred, level crossing.

Opposite the GPO is **Kipande House**, another of the city's historic buildings where, both before and after independence, citizens and residents were fingerprinted and issued with identity cards. Lovingly restored, Kipande House is now a busy branch of the Kenya Commercial Bank. On the opposite side of Kenyatta Avenue, at the intersection with Koinange Street, stands the memorial to the pioneering spirit of motoring enthusiast **L D Galton Fenzi**, founder of the Automobile Association of Kenya, the first man to drive from Nairobi to Mombasa over what was then trackless bush, thorn, *wadi*, ravine, and mountain. He also pioneered the Nairobi-to-Cape Town run.

The faraway places and vast mileages inscribed on his memorial read more like an aviation navigation chart than a monument to a pioneer of the motor-age in Af-rica. Two intersections further along Kenyatta Avenue are the **memorials** to Kenya's dead of two world wars: the valiant Africans of the Carrier Corps and King's African Rifles who sacrificed their lives for a monarch and an empire that had colonized them. One monument is a plain, sombre cenotaph: the other, sculpted by Myrander in 1924, depicts three *askaris* (African soldiers). Turn left into **Wabera Street** for the **McMillan Memorial Library**, donated to the city by Lady McMillan in memory of Sir William Northrup McMillan, her husband. An anglicized American, he was knighted for his services in East Africa to Britain during World War I. Next to it, beautiful at night when it's illuminated, stands the city's main Muslim place of worship, the **Jamia Mosque**.

The next block along the left of Kenyatta Avenue contains two more historic buildings. The **Cameo Cinema**, which began its life before World War I as the **Theatre Royal**, was for many years the city's entertainment centre. Many ex-servicemen who spent time in East Africa during two world wars will remember the shows that were laid on for them at this venue. **Grindlays**

Above: Akamba arrowmaker displays his wares in a market.
Opposite: Kipande House, Nairobi: history in a living environment.

Building, once **Torr's Hotel**, on the corner of the intersection with Kimathi Street, is an elegant red brick building, *circa* the 1920s, and now converted into offices.

Diagonally opposite is the **New Stanley Hotel**, whose street-fronting **Thorn Tree Cafe** is arguably the capital's favourite meeting spot. First opened on its present site in 1913 and many times improved and extended since, the New Stanley, just like the Norfolk, has a guest register that reads like a celebrity Who's Who. The Thorn Tree Cafe is dominated by an acacia tree planted two years before independence, in 1961. A message board on its trunk is used by passing tourists and backpackers looking for companionship and by those seeking lost friends. The Hilton dominates the intersection of Kimathi Street and **Mama Ngina Street**.

Turn right and ahead of you, across Wabera Street, is **City Hall**, built in 1937. On the balcony at the front in March 1950, overlooking the colonial Law Courts, built in the 1920s the Duke of Gloucester, presented Nairobi aldermen with the Royal Charter and letters patent proclaiming it a city. On the same balcony, two years later, Prince Philip and Princess Elizabeth acknowledged the salute of Nairobi's citizens just a few days before the death of King George VI in February 1952, when Princess Elizabeth was staying with her husband at Treetops in the Aberdare National Park. The road below the balcony was for many years the start and finish of Kenya's world famous **Safari Rally** which began in 1953 as the Coronation Safari. In 1973 it moved to the ceremonial mall in the gardens of the Kenyatta International Conference Centre, whose forecourt is dominated by a magnificent stone **statue** of Jomo Kenyatta, founding father of the Kenyan nation.

Directly facing the starting ramp are Kenya's **Parliament Buildings**, built in the 1950s, the focal point of the city's master plan, which was drawn up in 1948. In its grounds is another prominent statue of Jomo Kenyatta, whose remains are buried in a **mausoleum** in **Parliament Gardens**. Lined by an avenue of flags, the mausoleum is watched day and night by ceremo-

Above: Artist works on Kenyan pottery.

nial guards. Every five years Kenya elects 202 MPs who sit, together with twelve others nominated by the president, to decide the nation's legislation and debate its progress.

A tour of these historic buildings can be arranged through the office of the Sergeant-at-Arms. It begins when you step through the splendid entrance of carved timber doors along a floor laid with Italian marble. Ten shields, one from each of Kenya's ten major tribes, line the entrance. On the left is the country's **Seal of Independence** and on the right the **Commonwealth Parliamentary Association Room** with some fascinating antique wall hangings. The old chamber that served from 1952 to 1954 now contains two despatch boxes, a gift from New Zealand to mark Kenya's independence. The striking wood panel on the landing was presented by Kabete School. Made at the end of the 1950s, each of its 32 pieces represents one of Kenya's indigenous hardwoods.

The **Long Gallery** houses a magnificent collection of 49 wool and canvas tapestries, made by members of the East African Women's League. The **tapestries** tell the picturesque, colonial history of Kenya and were presented to Parliament in 1968.

At the left, the gallery ends in the fine, blue mosaics that form the facade of the **New National Assembly Chamber** and were donated by the country's Ismaili community.

On the corner opposite Parliament Gardens is the Nairobi **Inter-Continental Hotel**, built in 1969. Facing it is the Catholic **Holy Family Cathedral**. Turn left across Uhuru Highway for **Uhuru Park** — with its tiered grass arena, behind the elegant **Uhuru Fountains** built to commemorate 20 years of independence — and **VIP pavilion** where Kenya used to celebrate its significant anniversaries and where Pope John Paul conducted mass for more than half-a-million people in 1980 and 1995.

Above the park is **The Hill**, prime real estate that houses many fine office buildings representing various government ministries. Right of the park is the Anglican **All Saints Cathedral**. Its foundation stone was laid in 1917 but work was not completed until its consecration in 1952. Inside, the

Top: Kenya schoolchildren spell out anniversary message in the Moi International Sports complex.
Above: Schoolchildren mark the 25th anniversary of Independence.

stained glass windows, nave, transept, Gothic arches and pews are reminiscent of ancient England recreated here in sentimental glory.

The **plaques** on the walls commemorate colonial pioneers and heroes such as Northrup McMillan and Baden-Powell. Some of the stones in the walls came from Lindisfarne, and from Canterbury and St Paul's cathedrals. In 1946 Britain's King George VI and Queen Elizabeth, now the Queen Mother, presented two copies of the Bible. And two of the **cypress trees** outside grew from seeds taken from the Garden of the Tomb and Gethsemane in Israel.

A plaque on the bridge that links the cathedral grounds to Kenyatta Avenue is to the memory of Railways Police Inspector Charles Ryall, killed by a man-eating lion at Kima in June, 1900.

Just beyond the cathedral is the **Pan-Afric Hotel**, built in anticipation of the tourist boom that came with independence. Turn right into treelined **Nyerere Avenue** past the Serena and the **YWCA** and you come to a cluster of churches — the Presbyterian **St Andrew's**, the **Lutheran Church**, and **St Paul's Catholic Chapel**.

Opposite, between Uhuru Highway and Nairobi University, is the Jewish **Synagogue**, formerly Vermont Hall, located next to the University campus which was upgraded after independence from the Royal Technical College.

Cross over from Nyerere Avenue into **State House Road**. On the right is the **United Kenya Club**. Continue past the University halls of residence and **Moi Girls High School** to the **Nairobi Arboretum Forest Reserve**, on the right. Little more than 32 hectares (80 acres) in extent, it contains some 270 species of indigenous and exotic trees — all labelled (see 'Flora: Forests of Flame, Streets of Mauve', Part Three). It is not advisable to go there alone.

Further on are the extensive grounds of **State House**, the official residence of the president, where photography is strictly prohibited. To get to the city centre's other **forest reserve**, return to the Globe roundabout and continue up the dual carriageway past the Ngara roundabout to the junction of **Limuru Road** with **Forest Road**, on the

right. To the left is **St Francis Xavier's Church**, built in 1933. The land on either side of Forest Road is devoted to a multitude of sports clubs — **Nairobi Gymkhana, the Premier Club**, and **the Simba Union**, formerly Sikh Union until a government ordinance banned racial or tribally aligned organizations.

Between Forest Road and Limuru Road is **City Park**, a forest reserve which was excised by Ainsworth in 1904 for use as Nairobi's first recreational area. Its gardens are magnificent, with trees and shrubs and a city parks department **plant nursery**. Follow the path down into the **sunken gardens** where there's a **playground** for children and ponds containing frogs and fish.

Also on the left is the notable **Boscawen Memorial Collection** of orchids, donated by his sister in memory of Lt Col M T Boscawen, DSO, MC.

Adjacent to the park area, within its 120 hectares (300 acres), is one of Kenya's many war **cemeteries** with the graves of 97 men, most from World War II but some from 1950 and World War I. Vervet monkeys gambol among the trees and picnickers, and the early twentieth-century **bandstand** and **maze**, remain an affectionate legacy of the colonial past.

Much of the forest remains pristine. Leopard were seen in City Park as recently as 1980 and some may still live there.

If you continue along Limuru Road, instead of turning right into Forest Road, you arrive at the city's Nob Hill estate of **Muthaiga** known to all and sundry as Millionaire's Row. Carved out of an indigenous forest, it is the most exclusive suburb in Nairobi, favoured for diplomatic residences. The **Karura Forest Reserve** backs on to its manicured lawns and landscaped gardens.

On the other side of the forest, at **Gigiri** on the Limuru Road, are the headquarters of two world organizations — the **United Nations Environment Programme** (UNEP) and **Habitat**, the United Nations Centre for Human Settlement. If you turn into Forest Road it links up with **Murang'a Road** at the Pangani roundabout, with Nairobi's second cemetery on the left. Follow the Murang'a Road to the Muthaiga round-

Opposite: Home of Kenyan democracy — Parliament Buildings in Nairobi.

Above: Young nation at play. More than half of Kenya's 26 million people are school age or under.

about. First left leads to what may well be considered the ultimate bastion of Kenya's colonial past, **Muthaiga Country Club**. In the closing stages of the twentieth century the rules of membership — although much relaxed since independence — are as anachronistic today as feudal England would have been in the Britain of the 1950s. In this conservative institution, the chef wears cotton gloves to carve the meat of the day, brought in on a trolley, and business talk over luncheon is prohibited. Featured in *Out of Africa*, Muthaiga's timbers — and members — are soaked in nostalgia.

An afternoon there may delight those who believe in an empire on which the sun never set, but it's definitely a bewildering time warp for those involved in the daily struggle for existence.

Framing the roundabout itself are the fairways of the **Muthaiga Golf Club**, home of the **Kenya Open Golf Tournament**, which features some of the great names of golf, such as Seve Ballesteros, on its roll of honour.

Murang'a Road now becomes **Thika Road**. To the right is the **Utalii Hotel and Training College** — which provides gradu-

ates for Kenya's hotel and tourist industry. The **National Youth Service** headquarters and **Survey of Kenya** are on the left and finally, to the right, the **Fox Drive-In Cinema**.

Thika Road intersects there with **Outer Ring Road**, with the **General Service Unit** (GSU) headquarters at the left of the roundabout and the first of **Kenya Breweries'** many brewing installations on the right.

Drive on past the **Safari Park Hotel and Country Club**, formerly the Spread Eagle, to the left, elegant in landscaped gardens with thorn, eucalyptus and acacia trees.

On the right, the **Moi International Sports Centre** at Kasarani is Kenya's central motif as one of Africa's, and indeed the world's, great sporting nations. Built with Chinese expertise and finance, the centre is set around a modern sports stadium, a 60,000-seat arena that was the main venue of the 1987 All Africa Games.

Nairobi National Park

The best introduction to Kenya safaris is a visit to the **Nairobi National Park**. To get there, you follow **Uhuru Highway** to the roundabout where it intersects with **Lusaka Road** on the left, and turn right up **Langata Road** Keeping **Nyayo Stadium** on the right, carry on past **Wilson Airport** — one of Africa's busiest — named after Florrie Wilson, who founded Kenya's pioneer domestic airline, Wilson Airways, in 1929. At the entrance is the **Dambusters** — a popular 'pub'. At the far end are the **Aero Club of East Africa** and the headquarters of the **Mountain Club of Kenya**. In between lie a host of enterprises, mainly concerned with aviation. Wilson Airport offers charter services throughout Kenya and Eastern Africa.

On the right, after the airport, is the **Nairobi Sailing Club**, on the eastern bank of the **Nairobi Dam** which was hastily built after World War II to boost municipal water supplies, but is no longer used.

The Sailing Club's dinghies used to cruise on the dark waters of the dam, which is outlined, opposite, by the tin roofs, timber and mud shacks of **Kibera** shantytown. The land on which these stand was presented to the city's Nubian population in 1922 as a mark of appreciation for their service and loyalty in the 1914-18 war. Now Kibera is home for hundreds of thousands of urban poor.

Nonetheless, although they may seem out of place, both the Aero Club and the Sailing Club retain a particular ambience — the aviator and yachtsman's ideal leisure resorts. Both boast good home-cooking and well-stocked bars — the Sailing Club share theirs with the **Kenya Sub Aqua Club**.

Left of Langata Road, opposite the Sailing Club entrance, the road leads to the **Carnivore**, formerly the Golf Range, now a Brazilian-inspired restaurant-cum-nightclub. There you can eat every imaginable meat, from crocodile and zebra to eland and impala steaks, and countless others, at an all inclusive price. The Carnivore is also the capital's most popular disco, headquarters of the **East African Motor Sports Club** and **Nairobi's Motocross course**. Next left from the Carnivore is **Uhuru Gardens**, where Kenya was delivered of colonial

bondage at the stroke of midnight on 12 December 1963. The gardens were neglected for 20 years until 1983, when they were transformed into a national heritage centre.

The central motif, a slender, soaring granite and marble column on three curved legs, is almost 24 metres (80 feet) high. The monument's symbol is clasped hands adorned with a dove of peace: its outliers are Kenya's freedom fighters raising the national flag, and a sentinel in front of crossed spears and a shield.

All around are lush gardens, laid out as a map of Kenya with Mount Kenya at the centre and lakes Turkana and Victoria at the peripheries. To mark 25 years of freedom, another **monument** and **musical fountains** were unveiled in 1988.

Further up the hill, past the **army barracks** at the left, and the serried, middle-income housing estates of **Langata** on the right, are the gates of the Nairobi National Park on the left and the new 1996 headquarters of the **Kenya Wildlife Service**.

Inside the administration area is a **Wildlife Conservation Education Centre** with public film shows on set days of the week and a **library** and **museum**.

The **Nairobi Animal Orphanage**, on the right as you approach the gates into the park, has suffered from the malady of planning schizophrenia. When it was founded in 1963 it was declared that it would never be a zoo although it has all the appearances of one, including two tigers — gifts from overseas.

In 1990, after months of refurbishment, it was reopened as a sanctuary for the lame and the laggard, the sick and the orphaned, who are cared for until well and strong enough to be repatriated to the wild. It was refurbished again in the mid-1990s.

However, the most threatened species — orphaned elephants and rhinos — are cared for by Daphne Sheldrick, in a compound in the west corner of the park. Daphne is the linchpin of the **David Sheldrick Conservation Foundation**, in memory of her husband who tended Tsavo National Park for many years.

The Nairobi National Park was the first Kenya national park, gazetted in 1945 and opened in 1946. Covering only 117 square kilometres (46 square miles), it incorporates a surprising number of different environments and habitats. Set at an altitude of between 1,533 and 1,760 metres (5,000-5,775 feet), only eight kilometres (five miles) south of Nairobi, the park forms a long, sloping plain of black cotton soil crossed by several deep river valleys. The **Athi River** forms part of the southern boundary.

Vegetation is mainly dry, transitional savannah with gallery forests in the valleys. This close proximity of forest cover, pasture, and permanent water makes it the focus of an animal migration area, particularly in drought years. There are more than 80 recorded mammal species, and some 500 species of birdlife.

Hippo and crocodile live in the various ponds, waterholes, and the Athi River. The park was created out of what was once a Somali reserve, Nairobi Common, a World War I training ground, and a World War II firing range. But it's difficult to believe if you're lucky enough to experience one of those days when the lion pride has made a kill, the cubs are playful, the wildebeest are gathered *en masse*, the buffalo herds have moved in through their shrinking wildlife corridor, the giraffe are cropping the thorn, and the rhino are feeding against the silhouette of the Nairobi skyline.

Fenced in on only three sides, it is still not an artificial safari park, although squatters and homesteaders are swiftly shrinking the preserved 'corridor' through the **Kitengela Conservation Area** along which most of the park species migrate.

With new factories rising directly on its northern perimeter, Athi River and its cement factory and abattoir at its eastern end, new housing estates to the west, and the noose tightening around its southern entrance, the park may now be in its last vestiges as a natural ecosystem but still a rare legacy for any city, even one in wildlife Kenya, and worth protecting fiercely.

In the east, in a murky part of the Athi-Sabaki-Galana river, lies the **hippo pool**. Signs warn you not to feed the monkeys, but take care — they will steal not only your picnic but anything else left loose in the car or held lightly in the hand.

There's no lodge in the park itself but the **Maasai Lodge**, which sits on one side of the gorge that marks its western boundary, is a pleasant place to spend a night.

Ngong Hills: The Giant's Knuckles

From Nairobi take the **Langata Road** past Wilson Airport and the National Park gates to the junction of **Magadi Road** and **Forest Edge Road**. Turn right into Forest Edge Road and first right again for the **Bomas of Kenya**, a parastatal entertainment centre.

The enclosed arena, held up with massive timber supports, is a giant auditorium where young, professional dance groups from many ethnic communities perform choreographed traditional dance routines. Visitors can also tour model ethnic villages and houses and buy traditional craftware. The restaurant in the auditorium serves ethnic food and has a well-stocked bar.

Forest Edge Road continues into a track that cuts through the thick, dark, indigenous **Ngong Forest**. Although the forest harbours an unknown number of leopards it was, nevertheless, popular with Hash House Harrier runners, and horse riders, in particular Ginger Bell's pink-coated hunt. The lure was aniseed sacks dragged along the trails by fast-running hunt servants. The track exits on **Ngong Road** near the **Jockey Club of Kenya racecourse**.

Follow Magadi Road, leaving the national park fence on the left, and plush private estates on the right, including the **Banda Preparatory School**, and continue past the **Kenya Posts and Telecommunications Training College** on the right. Turn left for Maasai Lodge, or straight on into fast-growing **Ongata Rongai**, an amazing complex of little suburban houses, basic shopping centres, and many bars and *nyama choma* eating places — all seemingly unplanned — and carry on to Kiserian, where the road to Magadi becomes the responsibility of the Soda Company. Turn right at **Kiserian** for **Ngong Hills**, keeping them to your left as you drive to **Ngong Town**. Farms, smallholdings, and smart houses in landscaped gardens are set in the dimpled valleys on the eastern slopes of these lovely hills. Amid the maize stalks stands the simple **obelisk monument** that was built to the memory of Denys Finch Hatton by his brother. Drive through Ngong Town, an unkempt and undistin-

Above: Start of one of the classic races run at Nairobi's Ngong Racecourse, Nairobi.

guished shopping centre, past **Ngong Road** on the right, and turn left up the scenic dirt trail past the **police station** to the **communications antennae** where the track ends.

Leave your car and walk uphill to look at the glorious views in any direction, particularly of Nairobi. The Kajiado County Council has installed a toll gate — in your interest. It's to keep potential muggers off the hills. But in 1996 there were more reported instances of attacks, so take care.

It takes two hours to walk up and down these ridges. From the top you gaze down the western slopes with almost sheer drops to the stark, volcanic tumult of the Great Rift Valley. From one end to the other — the highest point, **Lamwia**, is 2,460 metres (8,070 feet) — the views are one of the delights of living in Nairobi.

Maasai legend claims the hills, shaped like the knuckles of a clenched fist, were formed when a giant tripped over Kilimanjaro, more than 250 kilometres (155 miles) south-east, and clawed at the earth as he fell. Look eastward to see the suburb of **Karen** laid out beneath you. It was there that Karen Blixen settled in 1914 with hus-

band, Baron Bror Blixen, to establish a coffee farm, which she abandoned — penniless in the 1930s. Her experiences, and her love affair with Denys Finch Hatton, inspired the book *Out of Africa*, which she wrote under the pen name Isak Dinesen. In the book she expresses her love for these hills 'that had not its like in all the world'.

To reach Karen return to Ngong Town and turn left along Ngong Road, past a Kenya Broadcasting Corporation **transmitter** and a popular **night club** to the Karen shopping centre. Turn right into **Langata Road**, past a forest of radio masts on the left that denote the presence of the **BBC Monitoring Unit**, then turn first right into **Karen Road**.

A kilometre or so along there, the lush, tree-lined fairways of the **Karen Golf and Country Club** are on the left. Just before the left turn into **Bogani Road** stands Karen Blixen's old farmhouse, right, restored to the style in which she maintained it and now a **museum** in her honour. The coffee estate that she developed on 144 hectares (360 acres) was a wedding present-cum-investment from her Danish family.

113

Bror Blixen, her husband and cousin, wrote *African Hunter* and figured in the Hemingway classic, *The Short, Happy Life of Francis Macomber*. Also in the grounds is **Karen College** which was founded as a Danish gift following Karen Blixen's death in 1962.

At the junction with Bogani Road turn right into **Mbagathi Ridge** and drive along the back of the Blixen Museum. This takes you around what was her coffee *shamba*. Turn right into **Forest Lane**, left into Karen Road, then cross Langata Road and continue to the junction with Ngong Road.

Turn right and almost immediately on your right is Karen's Anglican **St Francis Church**, built in 1952, which lacks only a traditional English village church spire.

Follow the chicane as the road dips and winds through the Ngong Forest and then straightens out alongside **Lenana School**, left, formerly the Duke of York school, followed by the **Ngong Racecourse**, right.

Regarded by many as the most beautiful racetrack in the Commonwealth, the Jockey Club of Kenya runs an average of 40 Sunday race meetings a year with bloodstock imported from Europe.

Opposite the grandstand on the far side of the track is the **Commonwealth War cemetery**, beautiful in its sylvan glades, where Queen Elizabeth II of Britain celebrated Remembrance Day in 1983 among the many graves of African and British soldiers who fell in the two world wars. To visit the graves, take the next right after the racecourse. To return to the city centre take the next right turn through the forest, past the Agricultural Society of Kenya's **Jamhuri Park Showground** on the left, which annually hosts the Nairobi show, Kenya's farm and industrial trade fair. On the right is the **Rowallan Boy Scouts Camp**.

Olorgesailie and Magadi

By far the most dramatic day excursion from the capital is a visit to the Aechulian tool site of **Olorgesailie** and the soda **Lake Magadi**, little more than 100 kilometres (60 miles) from Nairobi on a well-maintained tarmac road. But the land is 1,070 metres (3,500 feet) lower, and simmers in the merciless heat of the sump of the **the Great Rift Valley**. Be sure you have a full petrol tank, or better still, take a 4WD vehicle and also carry jerricans of both water and pet-

rol. You can also drive across the Magadi salt pans to camp or picnic around its many boiling springs or just to enjoy the incredible bird life and panoramas of this magnificent, but improbable, scenic backdrop so close to cosmopolitan Nairobi (see 'The Great Rift Valley: The Land that was Eden').

The Escarpment: At the Edge of the Abyss

The **Uplands Escarpment**, near **Limuru**, cresting between 2,440 and 2,740 metres (8,000-9,000 feet) provides one of the most spectacular vantage points of the Great Rift Valley. It posed terrible problems for Ronald Preston, the chief engineer of the Uganda Railway, which reached this spot late in 1899.

Until the 1950s the track from Nairobi ran out of the city across what is now Kenyatta Avenue, through Chiromo and up past the Italian mission of the **Consolata Fathers** and the **Lady Consolata Catholic Church**. It continued through **Westlands** along an alignment now occupied by Uhuru Highway and **Waiyaki Way**. The Italian ambience was extended in the Agip Motel, now renamed **Jacaranda**.

At the Westlands roundabout Uhuru Highway ends and becomes **Waiyaki Way**, formerly Sclater's Road after the commanding officer of the Royal Engineers squad who carved this trail when they surveyed the railway route.

From the Westlands roundabout, the newly constructed dual carriageway continues for three kilometres (almost two miles) past the **All Africa Conference of Churches** conference centre to the junction with **James Gichuru Road**. Its completion marks another link in the **Trans-African Highway** that goes through Uganda to Zaire and is eventually planned to reach Lagos in Nigeria.

If you turn left into James Gichuru Road, formerly St Austin's Road, you'll come across a little piece of the city's pioneering days. The **St Austin's Mission** to the left (now with St Mary's School and the Loreto Convent) was founded by the Irish **Holy Ghost Fathers** in the 1890s when they turned much of this land into Kenya's first coffee plantation. This was after the crop failed to take root at Kibwezi, much further down the line between Mtito Andei and Sultan Hamud (See 'Nairobi-Mombasa: A Highway to Adventure').

The original coffee plantation is now largely up-market, residential **Muthangari**, still known as **Lavington**. But the devout continue to worship at St Austin's, as did Karen Blixen who wrote of it in *Out of Africa*. You can drive on through Muthangari to **Dagoretti Corner**, a colourful, if somewhat disorganized ethnic market and shopping centre. Turn north at the roundabout along the **Naivasha Road** — through **Kawangware** shantytown to **Uthiru** and **Upper Kabete**, or return to Waiyaki Way, which continues through the shantytown of **Kangemi**, largely hidden from sight, to link up with the Naivasha Road at **Kabete**.

Located on the left off the Naivasha Road just before it rejoins Waiyaki Way is the headquarters of **the International Livestock Research Institute — ILRI** (formerly ILRAD). There, cattle graze lush fields but are also used as 'test beds' — bitten by tsetse flies — in the battle to discover shields against the fatal *trypanosomiasis* (sleeping sickness).

Other veterinary and agriculturally orientated educational campuses are also here with, on the right of Waiyaki Way, the **University of Nairobi** and **Wellcome Foundation's** extensive veterinary laboratories and research institutions. Here, too, the rustic charms of the **Vet Lab Golf Club** can be enjoyed by all — membership is open to everyone.

Near this establishment, a few metres off the main road, is **Ndumbeini** — a small strip of ravaged tarmac laid on the original Sclater's Road and a stone block shopping centre with bars, butcheries and shops.

The road leads on to **Fort Smith**. This once well-stockaded, timber fort, now a private residence, was built in impenetrable forest in 1890 by Major Eric Smith as the IBEA's Company's only post in Kikuyu District. (see 'History: Now the British', Part One). In a maize field across the road from the fort are the 1898 graves of three British captains—Harrison (mauled by a lion), A J Haslam (killed by Kikuyu) and R H Nelson (who died of dysentery). Also in

Kabete is the site of the **Church Missionary Society's** first upcountry station, established in 1901. It was there that Canon Harry Leakey arrived from Reading in 1902 to build a permanent Anglican church, spread the gospel, and found the remarkable dynasty that has done more to disseminate the biblical theory of Genesis than any other family in the world — first through his son Louis, and daughter-in-law Mary, and then through his grandson Richard.

Return to Ndumbeini and turn left into **Kapenguria Road**, past the **University Farm** on the right, and the **Artificial Insemination Stud** to the left, and continue to the cross-roads with **Lower Kabete Road**. Five hundred metres (a third of a mile) along on the right the former Kenya Institute of Administration is now part of the Nairobi University campus. The training centre for Kenya's administrative personnel such as district commissioners and officers has moved some distance away. To the left lie steep hills of rich, red soil and verdant crops of maize, banana trees, vegetables and fruit. Take this road and after a few kilometres you come to **Wangige**, where the Monday Market is a riot of farm-fresh produce and haggling vendors and buyers.

Unsullied by tourists, the market is a characteristic and authentic demonstration of the lively Kikuyu entrepreneurial spirit.

Turn left at Wangige on to more smooth tarmac to rejoin the **Naivasha Road** at **Kikuyu**. The original tarmac was built by Italian prisoners-of-war in the 1940s. In 1993, it became a dual carriageway.

The Church of the Torch

If you cross the main road into **Kikuyu Road** it follows the course of the new rail alignment for some distance, leaving **Kikuyu** town, with its homely, timbered, Anglo-Saxon-style **Kikuyu Country Club**, now a school, on the right.

Under the rail bridge there are stunning views of Kikuyu farmlands, Nairobi, **Ol Doinyo Sapuk** and the Ngong Hills. After Kikuyu town, on the right, is **Alliance High School**, famous *alma mater* of Kenya's post-independence decision makers and cabinet ministers. The **Alliance Girls High School**, close by on the right, was modelled on the same lofty, idealistic but pragmatic approach to education.

Also on the right is **Thogoto**, notable for its Presbyterian **Church of the Torch** which was established by Scottish missionaries in 1898 — two years ahead of the Anglicans — and is the beacon of the Presbyterian Church of East Africa.

Jomo Kenyatta was baptized there and it still stands, well-preserved. **Monuments** in the grounds of the succeeding 1928 church give you some sense of the loneliness and hazards experienced by these first evangelists of the Christian cause almost a century ago. Since the 1990s, Thogoto has become even more widely known for the work done there at the P C E A (Kikuyu) Eye Centre.

The Kikuyu are the largest ethnic group in Kenya, numbering close to five million in 1992. The founding members of the kirk were quick to notice that there was much of the Scot about Kikuyu ways and character, finding them thrifty, industrious and clever with their hands. They lived in round thatched huts which they shared with their livestock — as the Scots did four centuries ago — and brewed a fine, colourless whisky, celebrated major occasions with the haggis (the boiled innards of goat or sheep stuffed in gut skin) and danced a passable Highland reel of their own (see 'The People', Part One).

So given the mission's early start at Thogoto, it's not surprising that the kirk — founded in Scotland by John Knox — is the strongest of Kikuyuland's secular faiths.

Rhubarb and Rabbits

At Kikuyu, from Wangige, turn right on to the Trans Africa Highway which climbs steeply, leaving the **Sigona Golf Club** — with its much-envied fairway panoramas of the Ngong Hills, Athi Plains, occasionally Kilimanjaro, Nairobi, and the Embakasi Plains — on the left, to the former Zambezi Motel, now the **Presbyterian Pastoral Institute**, also on the left, with rich farm lands on either side.

Higher up, again on the left, is **Rironi**, a typical rural shopping centre, with the **Kenya Broadcasting Corporation**'s television transmitter to the right. Half-a-kilometre (a third of a mile) later the road broadens out into a modern freeway which leaves **Limuru** town on the right and swoops up and down through green meadowlands to **Uplands**, also to the right. It then follows a hard curve right and climbs steeply to emerge suddenly above the Great Rift Valley, hundreds of metres below. This fine highway was started in 1973 by the Israeli Solel Boneh company but not finished until the 1980s. Almost immediately there's a **viewing spot** where you can pull in — if you feel up to beating off the vocal assault of vendors selling everything from giant rhubarb stems, to live rabbits, to sheepskin rugs and, when in season, pears and plums.

Almost the entire roadside, from Rironi through to Naivasha, is lined with these mainly young entrepreneurs. On the down leg to Naivasha it's mostly Kikuyu mothers and daughters with *debes* (tins) of wholesome potatoes, carrots, onions, and other vegetables and the sales pitch is more restrained (see 'Tastes of Kenya', Part Three).

Most likely you'll be so overwhelmed by the views — a magnificent panorama over **Lake Naivasha** and almost into the bowels of **Longonot** — that you'll buy something anyway. The view is as spectacular as that from Ngong Hills en route to Magadi.

It's the same grandstand scenery and immensity of scale, but without the harshness of the southern valley landscape. Instead of serried scarps, above Naivasha the Rift drops down in a single sweep, leaving towering walls on either side, with distant blue-grey mountains forming the western wall almost 100 kilometres (60 miles) away. With the white radial dishes of the Kenya Posts and Telecommunications **Longonot Satellite Station** appearing minute in the foreground, **Mount Susua** stands out in the middle of the valley and, more immediately ahead, clouds brim around the knife-edge rim of the tallest of the Rift Valley's volcanoes, 2,776-metre (9,108-foot) **Mount Longonot** (see 'Great Rift Valley: The Land That was Eden').

The alternative route, down into the Rift itself, is to turn left at Rironi on to the old Naivasha Road which, until 1994, the juggernauts had to use by law. This means braving atrocious pot-holes and bumps to arrive at the escarpment's edge. The road, with its precipitous edge, follows a series of terrifying hairpin bends along the course of the first railway alignment created at the turn of the century.

Halfway down, on the left, there was a forestry **picnic site**, complete with tumble-down grandstand and trellised benches set on the edge of the cliff overlooking the Rift Valley. There, when the wind soughs through the trees, the lyrics of silence should inspire even the most jaded muse.

Further down, on the right, a dirt road leads to the African Inland Church mission town of **Kijabe**, Kenya's own version of Salt Lake City in Utah, USA, founded by missionaries of an evangelistic American sect under strict rules of abstinence but, like the Mormons, not celibacy. Their first converts were polygamous. Missionaries have always been careful to catch their converts before reforming them.

Kijabe's sleepy monastic community is ruled by a council of elders who still invoke the same ordinances that applied in the first decade. There's a model community hospital — funded by mission money and overseas donations — but no shop sells tobacco or liquor. Former US President Theodore Roosevelt, in the course of his great African Safari of 1909, laid the church's foundation stone after an exhilarating train ride from Nairobi on the cowcatcher of the locomotive.

Though no more than 60 kilometres (37 miles) from the capital, in time and place Kijabe could be another world. When drought struck Kenya in 1984, its citizens were forced to remain indoors — or walk outside at their peril. Rampaging forest buffaloes moved down into the town in

Above: Shade trees dot a tea plantation in the Tigoni uplands near Nairobi.

search of grazing and water. The **hospital** was kept busy with casualties who had been gored. Take the right turn under the **railway bridge** for the steep climb up the richly-forested wall of the Rift to return to the new Naivasha Road. Turn left for Naivasha (see 'The Great Rift Valley: The Land that was Eden') or right for **Limuru town**, which is 15 kilometres (10 miles) or so in the direction of Nairobi, with a left turn into Limuru itself.

Set 2,160 metres (7,300 feet) above sea level, Limuru's champagne air is turbocharged by the constant thermals that thunder up the wall of the Rift and, even during the day, carry a touch of ice in their breath.

In the past, many pointed to 'Limoru', as an ideal site for a capital. If this had been so, its western suburbs would have run straight off the edge of the escarpment down into the Rift — certainly a dramatic setting for any capital city. As it is, Limuru is a bustling little farm capital and houses the head quarters of the Bata shoe company's Kenya manufacturing operations. The old **Tigoni Road** leaves the town past **Loreto High School** on the left, and the

lush fairways of the **Limuru Country Club** to the right. The golf course also hides Kenya's prettiest **cricket ground**, complete with a shingle-roofed pavilion, and an antique racecourse where once a year — with boaters, strawberries, cream and champagne — the Jockey Club used to stage a festive charity race meeting that was not just all thoroughbreds.

Continue along Tigoni Road through **Tigoni,** an imitation Surrey stockbroker village, with its fine houses cut off from public view by tall, thickset, but well-manicured hedges. These were uprooted and transplanted in a kind of ersatz Hollywood image of an English landscape — albeit with tea bushes and giant eucalyptus.

Continue past the Brooke Bond company's **Mabroukie Tea Estate,** founded in 1903 when the first clippings of *Thea sinensis* were introduced from India. They prospered well. Tea grows everywhere in the fertile, well-watered highlands and Kenya is now the world's third-largest producer and second-largest tea exporter — all premium grade. As you descend from the tea belt, past the up-market mock-Tudor

Above: Kenya's prime arabica coffee ripens in the equatorial sun.

farmhouse style **Kentmere Club,** with one of Kenya's *haute cuisine* restaurants (a quality reflected in its prices), past Brooke Bond's **Kentmere Estate,** you soon begin to enter the coffee-rich plantations of **Kiambu** district. This crop, which flourishes best at a lower altitude than tea, is Kenya's largest single foreign exchange earner after tourism. The country's *arabica* is considered the *crème de la crème* of world coffees and fetches top prices, even when the market is in glut with Latin American *arabicas.*

After lively **Banana Hill,** a rural metropolis, turn left by the speed bumps for **Chief Koinange High School,** at Kiambaa, where one of the ridges, known as millionaire's ridge, is at the right height with the right amount of sun and rain to produce the most perfect coffee ever grown. Continue through a succession of small townships, all reminiscent of the Wild West (minus stage coaches and hitching posts) into **Kiambu,** the administrative capital of the district which is surrounded by coffee plantations. Turn left at the main junction for **Cianda, Githunguri** and **Gatundu** — all beautifully rural — or right for Nairobi.

Mountain of the Buffalo

Leave Nairobi along the **Thika Road** as far as the **Kasarani roundabout,** then take the **Kasarani Road** with the **Moi International Sports Centre** on the right. This leads eventually to the **Kangundo Road.** Turn left onto this tarmac and ahead you will see the coffee hills of **Kangundo** and, to the left, the brooding hump of the Maasai **Ol Doinyo Sapuk,** the Kamba **Mountain of the Buffalo, Kilimambogo.**

The road cuts through once semi-arid ranchland, now carved up into co-operative smallholdings, and 58 kilometres (36 miles) from Nairobi finally reaches **Tala** in the heart of Kambaland, where the market is one of the most colourful in the country. **Kangundo,** seven kilometres (four miles) on from Tala, if nothing else, is a bustling, entrepreneurial trading town with lively bars. Beyond Kangundo the road is all second grade to **Machakos town.**

Instead turn left in Tala at the **BP station** and **Kwa Joe's Tourist Lodge** for **Kabaa** and **Yatta,** which brings you out at

119

Above: Fourteen Falls, near Thika, send the Athi River cascading down to the Indian Ocean.

the back of Del Monte's massive **pineapple plantation**, the largest in the world. Kenya is the world's third-largest producer of pineapples, nearly all grown on this single estate. Back on what is sometimes defined as a grade one road — though weather and abuse have taken their toll — turn left for **Fourteen Falls** and the entrance to **Ol Doinyo Sapuk National Park** (one of only a few admission-free national parks in Kenya), covering just 18 square kilometres (seven square miles). The falls are less than a kilometre (two thirds of a mile) from the clearing where you park.

Don't leave your car unattended: unfortunately, there have been nasty instances of mugging and robbery, so it is best to go with a party or large group. From the car park follow the path through the forest to the foot of the falls, pausing at a clearing

halfway down for a splendid view of the 27-metre-deep (90-foot) cataracts, a magnificent feature of the Athi-Sabaki-Galana river. Back in your car, drive across three bridges, turn right at a shantytown, and through the Del Monte **plantation** for two kilometres (just over a mile), to the park gate.

Although there's no admission charge, entrance is by vehicle only. The mountain is still home to large populations of unpredictable and bad-tempered Cape buffalo, one of Africa's Big Five animals, hence its Kamba name, *Kilima mbogo*. But it was for its wealth of bird life that the humpbacked 2,146-metre-high (7,040-foot) mountain was declared a national park in 1969. Lying 50 kilometres (30 miles) north-east of Nairobi, the park's main feature is an inselberg rising from the surrounding plains. Its soli-

Above: Cattle meadow in the Limuru Uplands above Nairobi.

tude is now slightly disfigured by the image of technology represented by the microwave **relay mast** on its summit.

Except for a small bare patch around the crest, the mountain is entirely covered with montane forest. Wildlife includes colobus monkey, leopard, black rhino, bushbuck, buffalo, duiker, impala and numerous bird species. There are two campsites.

On a clear day, from its summit, lakes and ponds shimmer below like tiny jewels in a carpet of green, while the twin spires of Mount Kenya rise in the distance.

From the entrance picnic site to the summit is nine kilometres (five-and-a-half miles) through thick, indigenous forest. Roughly halfway up the trail a bend gives way to a rugged bluff with panoramic views of the surrounding countryside — a vista beloved of Sir William Northrup McMillan and his wife.

An American, McMillan was one of the most outstanding — both mentally and physically — of Kenya's many colourful pioneer foreign settlers. He owned much of Chiromo Forest, prime land in central Nairobi, and farmed the land beneath Kilima-mbogo, where he settled in 1905 and which he named after a mysterious encounter with West African witchcraft. The family's hospitality to friends on their 8,094-hectare (20,000-acre) **Juja Farm**, now a large co-operative, was legendary.

McMillan is buried in the place he loved best, together with his wife and their faithful servant of more than 75 years, Louise Decker, who died on 1 December 1938. The three simple **graves** are hewn out of mountain rock, each set with a simple inscribed marble plaque. From the national park it's only a few kilometres into Thika town.

Nairobi-Thika

Most people drive direct from Nairobi to Thika along the new dual carriageway which roughly follows the alignment of the railway that Sir Percy Girouard, an Anglo-French governor, initiated in the second decade of this century.

Before coming to Kenya, Sir Percy, a railway engineer, had been in charge of the construction of a major line from Kano to Lagos in Nigeria. But still appalled by the cost of the 'Lunatic Line', Whitehall were

121

aghast at his suggestion that they should pay for another line. Out jogging in Nairobi one morning Sir Percy was struck by the idea that he might win their approval for a low-cost tramway instead.

His ruse worked. Built to the same gauge as the Mombasa-Kisumu line, for years afterwards the line was shown on all maps as the Thika Tramway.

But while the road journey takes only 30 minutes, it's more than 90 by rail. Queen Elizabeth II of Britain, on a sentimental return to the spot where she became Queen in 1952, rode this track on the Royal Train in 1983 — passing through **Kahawa,** the Kiswahili word for coffee, the military garrison built by the British. Completed just before independence, it was handed over to the Kenya Government by the departing colonialists and is now the **Kenyatta University** campus.

From there, the train wound through **Ruiru,** which is the headquarters for Kenya's **Coffee Research Centre.** The **Ruiru River,** flowing off the **Aberdares,** brought Nairobi its first street lighting when it was harnessed as a source of power in 1913.

Then the train travelled on to **Mangu,** where one of Kenya's oldest schools was established long ago by an order of Catholic White Father missionaries, and Thika.

The railway established its prominence as a major town. Although within sight and earshot of some of the most fertile land in the country — rich volcanic soils where coffee and fruit burgeon with prolific ease — Thika, often described as the 'Birmingham' of Kenya, now boasts tanneries, vehicle assembly plants, fruit processing factories, textile mills, grain mills, chemical factories, and packaging industries. It's odd to think that just 100 years ago this area was as wild and thick with game as the Maasai Mara today.

Unprepossessing Thika also has a **country club** to the west of the town, with rolling fairways and verdant greens for golf. In 1983, Queen Elizabeth II ate lunch there before driving on to Nyeri. The club is not far from the **Blue Posts Hotel,** built in the first decade of the century, close to the **Chania waterfalls** where Churchill camped during his African journey in 1907. He had hoped to shoot a lion but, though he heard many, was frustrated.

Machakos: Hills and Orchards

Machakos is 65 kilometres (40 miles) from Nairobi. Follow **Uhuru Highway** out on to the **Mombasa Road,** past Jomo Kenyatta Airport turnoff, and through Athi River. After 46 kilometres (28 miles), just before the **toll station,** there's a left turn and then, 16 kilometres (ten miles) on, **Machakos.** You can also make a circular excursion in either direction via Tala and Kangundo (see 'Mountain of the Buffalo').

Ringed by the green and pleasant **Ukambani Hills,** it was at **Machakos** that Britain's first up-country administrator in Kenya, Manchester-born John Ainsworth, made his headquarters in 1889. The mud-brick fort that Ainsworth built in Machakos no longer exists. In fact, his request to build it was turned down, but when the answer arrived he had already completed the work.

Machakos is the capital of Ukambani. The Akamba people have inhabited this region for at least the last five centuries. The town is named after the Akamba chief and seer Masaku, who predicted the coming of the railway — 'the iron snake'— and the pestilent plagues which followed. Smallpox and rinderpest decimated both human and animal populations throughout a large portion of the region. Masaku died in the first decade of this century.

In the hills above the town Kenya Orchards' Mua Hills **jam factory** is the legacy of missionary Reverend Stuart Watt, who, at the turn of the century, walked all the way from Mombasa with his wife. When he went lame she had to carry him for part of the journey. Apart from fruit for making jam, the Reverend also introduced wattle and eucalyptus trees.

The Church Missionary Society arrived in 1895 to add wheat and, ten years later, the South African Boers pioneered an ostrich farm. It was there that Mackinnon's Imperial British East Africa Company established the first inland African Training Centre, taken over by the Protectorate government in 1914.

The **clock tower** put up to mark the visit of Britain's Princess Margaret in October

Above: Colourful market at Tala, near Kangundo, in Ukumbani.

1956 during colonial times is the only monument of note. It still stands in the town centre at the main roundabout — though it always shows three o'clock in the afternoon whatever time you visit. Nonetheless, the clock tower and the old **pre-independence buildings** and tree-lined streets give Machakos a distinct rustic charm.

Centre of the town's social ambit is the long-established **Machakos Sports Club,** though cricket no longer continues. The discovery of a box of cricket balls in the 1980s caused undue worry to non-cricketing members of the club committee who thought they had stumbled upon a cache of revolutionary hand grenades left over from World War II.

The open-air markets of Machakos and throughout Ukambani present a colourful picture of locally grown vegetables and sun-ripened fruit, bright textiles for a variety of uses and sisal products which are a thriving local industry. The markets — selling a brilliant assortment of sisal baskets and other hand-made craft — are noticeably woman-dominated. From Machakos

the road winds down the hills on to the dry, arid, Akamba plain and continues through forlorn scrub and desperately poor smallholdings for 130 kilometres (80 miles) to **Kitui**. For an intriguing — and educational — glimpse of where most of the wood carvings which reach Nairobi and Mombasa curio shops originate, pay a visit to the wood carvers' village of **Wamunyu** — halfway between Machakos and Kitui. Set around a great grass rectangle, the verandahs of each hut are piled deep in wood shavings from years of work. A real welcome awaits visitors, especially those who enjoy a little good-natured bargaining.

Heartland Kenya: Magic Mountains, Moorlands Wild

The rugged central highlands of Kenya are crowned with 5,189-metre-high (17,058-foot) snow-capped **Mount Kenya,** the glistening, frosted coronet astride the Equator which gives the country its name. The rich volcanic soil at the base and on the mountain slopes has made this one of the most profitable agricultural areas in Kenya.

Years ago, the majority of European settlers established farms in these 'White Highlands' on fertile land that for centuries had been cultivated by local communities. Suddenly Kikuyu, Meru and Embu farmers found themselves 'squatters' on their own land. Their smouldering dissatisfaction culminated in the freedom war which, for the most part, was carried out from the forests and moorlands of Mount Kenya and the **Aberdares** to the plains beneath.

In a loose circumference, central Kenya embraces **Kiambu** in the south, Murang'a and Nyeri in the centre, the Aberdares and **Nyandarua** in the west, **Nanyuki** in the north, and **Meru** and **Embu** in the east.

As you travel through the highlands, the tremendous panoramas and rapid changes of light and colour are both surprising and rewarding. Rainbows curve over the green sunlit land as black thunder-clouds dance around the peaks of the mountains.

Dominating the landscape, Mount Kenya's twin spires thrust upwards through shrouds of mist and storm — which suddenly lift, exposing its dramatically beautiful profile. With a base diameter of more than 200 kilometres (125 miles), it is one of the largest free-standing volcanic mountains in the world.

To the east and south, the mountain slopes slip steeply away to the **Tana River** basin and the broad arid plains that end in the Ukambani hills. In the north they drop even more precipitously to the desert floor.

Westward they drop more gently to the rolling uplands of **Laikipia,** which are even drier than the east and, for the most part, treeless. The central highlands remain magically unspoilt — a pastoral idyll of

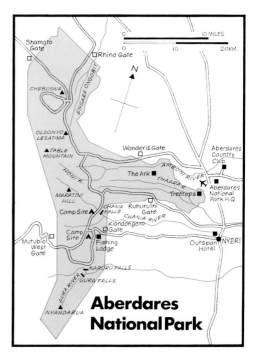

Aberdares National Park

Opposite: 275-metre-drop (900-foot) Gura Falls,Aberdare National Park.

Overleaf: Giant groundsel in rare 20-year bloom above 11,000 feet on the Aberdares.

125

Above: Fly fishing in the Aberdares — a delight of trout streams.

small market towns and well-tended small-holdings. Hotels, lodges and campsites provide accommodation to suit all tastes.

Where to stay
Mountain Lodge (4-star) (Mount Kenya Forest Reserve), book through African Tours and Hotels, Utalii House, Nairobi; Elephant and Castle (budget); Karatina Tourist Lodge (2-star); New Karatina Lamu Lodge (budget). In Nyeri, Greenhills Hotel (3-star), Outspan (4-star), White Rhino (3-star). In Mweiga, Aberdare Country Club (5-star). In Nyahururu, Thomson's Falls Lodge (homely 3-star). In Naro Moru, Naro Moru River Lodge (4-star). In Nanyuki, Mount Kenya Safari Club (5-star), Sports-man's Arms (budget and rustic). In Meru, Pig and Whistle (budget). In Embu, Izaak Walton Inn (3-star). There are many others. See Listings for 'Hotels'.

In national parks and reserves
In the Aberdare National Park, Treetops Hotel, book through Block Hotels, Rehema House, Nairobi; The Ark, book through Lonrho Hotels, Bruce House, Nairobi. In

Meru National Park, Meru Mulika Lodge (4-star), book through Msafiri Inns, Utalii House, Nairobi; and Leopard Rock Safari Lodge (self-service), book through AA Travel, Union Towers, Nairobi.

In game sanctuaries
El Karama Ranch, book through AA Travel, Nairobi; Sweetwaters Tented Camp (5-star, *circa* Adnan Kashoggi), book through Lonrho Hotels, Bruce House, Nairobi.

Sightseeing
The main road from Nairobi runs through **Thika** and continues for a few kilometres, to **Kabati** where the old road, left, used mostly by buses and *matatus,* runs on to **Saba Saba** and Murang'a.

A new road that starts there continues straight on to **Sagana**, past the **Makuyu Country Club**, a legacy from the settlers who, far from the amenities of town life, had to make their own recreations. The club, one of three golf clubs in this region, set amid olive-green coffee plantations, stands on the border between traditional Kikuyu and Kambalands. From there, a rough road, right, leads east to the **Kandara Valley** in the northern lee of **Kilimambogo**. Ruggedly beautiful, the close-cropped crests of the once-forested hills indicate why this potentially productive area is now marginal land. The dirt road is made of deep, fine-grained sand — a finger of the northern deserts only an hour's journey from the Kenyan capital.

Straight on from Makuyu, 87 kilometres (54 miles) from Nairobi and 45 kilometres (28 miles) from Thika, **Murang'a** was established in 1900 as Fort Hall, a British administrative outpost, which consisted of 'two grass huts within a stone wall and a ditch'. Today it is growing swiftly as a farm entrepôt. It sits on the brow of a cliff above the **Tana River**. A new road cuts along the lower part of the cliff, through countryside fat with farms, to Nyeri.

Perched on a hillside above the bustling town, the **Memorial Cathedral Church** of St James was consecrated by the Archbishop of Canterbury on 18 May 1955 as a memorial to the thousands of Kikuyu who died during the fight for independence.

The church has a fascinating mural by artist Elimu Njau. It depicts the Nativity, the Last Supper, and the Crucifixion — with a black Christ in a typical Murang'a landscape. The Nativity scene shows a Kikuyu manger with African shepherds and womenfolk bearing gifts. The Last Supper is set in a *banda* with giraffe and acacia trees beside it — and Kikuyu villages straggle up Golgotha's slopes.

The Kikuyu consider Murang'a their homeland, principally because between Murang'a and Nyeri, on a minor switchback road at **Mugeka**, lies Mukuruene wa Nya-Gathanga — the 'tree of the building site' — which, according to Kikuyu legend, is the Garden of Eden.

In this grove of wild fig trees the Kikuyu god, *Ngai*, commanded Gikuyu and Mumbi, the father and mother of all **Kikuyu**, to make their home. There **Mumbi** raised nine daughters who later became the founding matriarchs of the nine Kikuyu clans. The fig trees and Mount Kenya (known as *Kirinyaga*, the home of *Ngai*) are both still considered sacred by the Kikuyu. To get to Mukuruene wa Nya-Gathanga, you drive 18 kilometres (11 miles) to Mugeka. The fig grove is just beyond the vil-

lage and, although there is no longer a museum, the original fig tree, which was split by lightning, has been replaced. It could, indeed, be Eden, for there on the slopes of the Aberdares, the land is bountiful. The massif falls steeply to many enchanting valleys cultivated by smallholders.

Lured by the crisp air, open moorlands, and gushing trout streams, the Europeans were quick to settle the mountains. The scene is as pastoral today — rolling hills interspersed with green meadows and flocks of sheep and cattle herds.

On the other side of Murang'a, the old road and railway lead to **Sagana**, with its colourful **market, leather tannery, fish farm** and **railway warehouses** for coffee and grain. Turn left onto the main Nairobi-Nyeri road which clings to the north-west foothills of Mount Kenya as it climbs up the steep *Pole Pole* ('slowly slowly') hill — to **Karatina** in Nyeri district. Fertile farms, lush with groves of banana palms, vegetables, fruit, tea, coffee and flowers, all stepping down the hillsides in neat terraces, are irrigated year-round by the swift waters of the Sagana River and its tributaries.

Unkempt Karatina, 128 kilometres (80 miles) from Nairobi and 41 kilometres (25 miles) from Murang'a, was the major stronghold of the Mau Mau movement during the freedom battle, and remains the threshold to what is arguably Kenya's most magnificent country. There, the rounded foothills of the Aberdares and Mount Kenya merge in a cluster of domed crowns, many now turned into tidy farms.

During the dry season, Karatina is a swirl of dust; during the rains, it becomes a mud bath. But its **market** is one of the most colourful in Kenya — a brilliant mixture of cloths, grains, utensils, vivacious traders, and argumentative buyers. To the east, in the forest reserve of the Mount Kenya foothills, signposted by an ancient tree by the roadside, with a cleft in its bole, which was used as a Mau Mau mailbox, lies **Mountain Lodge**. Urgent messages with notice of British troop movements were left in the cleft to be picked up by other guerrilla forest units. Not far from Mountain Lodge, which stands in a forest glade, is **Sagana State Lodge** (photography prohibited) which was given to Princess Elizabeth by the colonial government when she visited

Kenya with Prince Philip in 1952. It was on the lawns of this lodge, after a night spent watching game at Treetops, that she learnt of the death of her father, King George VI. West of the lodge lies Kiganjo, the closest that the railway came to Nyeri, although for decades it was called Nyeri Station.

Today, **Kiganjo** is the base for **Kenya's Police Training College**, where many of

Above: Fading blooms of a giant senecio on Kenya's high moorlands.

the country's award-winning athletes first spring to prominence. From Karatina, the road rolls on like a roller-coaster another twenty-seven kilometres (17 miles), alongside fast-flowing streams, into **Nyeri**.

Where it enters the town, 155 kilometres (96 miles) from Nairobi, an avenue of jacaranda trees sends blossoms cascading like confetti in late September and October to carpet the road a rich purple.

Close to the Nyeri Consolata Mission, the Duke of Aosta and 650 other World War II Italian prisoners-of-war are buried in the Church Ossario Duca d'Aosta.

Home to the **administrative headquarters** of Kenya's Central Province, which occupy the former cricket ground where once a mass of brilliant flame trees grew, Nyeri has expanded into a sprawling, dynamic commercial capital.

Nestling in the middle of a broad vale, embraced by the green hills of Mount Kenya and the Aberdares, Nyeri's many **markets**, **shopping centres** and *jua kali* (self-employed) mechanics and woodworkers clearly define its entrepreneurial spirit. It was the frontline town during the war for independence and the main street, **Kimathi Way**, commemorates the famous Kikuyu freedom fighter, Dedan Kimathi. A **stone cenotaph** in 'Memory of the Members of the Kikuyu Tribe who Died in the Fight for Freedom 1951-1957' also stands.

At the far end of Kimathi Way there is a **monument** from the colonial days — a now useless **clock** and a dry **fountain** 'erected by the People of Kenya in memory of His Majesty George V'. To the right stands **St Cuthbert's Presbyterian Church**, built in 1926, but since fallen into decay.

White Rhino

The **Outspan Hotel** and **the White Rhino** were originally two settler hotels, now owned by indigenous businessmen and still flourishing after more than sixty years.

The Outspan, headquarters for **Treetops**, was built by Eric and Bettie Sherbrooke Walker, who bought the land on which it stands when it was a patch of bare scrub above the **Chania River** facing Mount Kenya. To the west stood the Aberdares, and to the north the land plunged into the fern-shrouded gorge where the Chania River boiled over the

Above: Baden-Powell's last home, Paxtu, in the grounds of Nyeri's Outspan Hotel.

rocks. The Sherbrooke Walkers could hardly believe their good fortune. 'The more we looked at it, the more strongly we felt it was the only place for our hotel.' They bought 28 hectares (70 acres) of land from the colonial government and set about building.

The **clubhouse** of Nyeri Golf Club, made of cedar bark shingles, and the **golf course** — facing Mount Kenya's glistening glaciers — already existed. All around the countryside was being transformed into coffee plantations, farmlands, and sawmills. A neighbouring sawmiller, Grace Barry, won the Sherbrooke Walker's competition to find a name for their hotel receiving a bottle of champagne for suggesting 'The Outspan' — where, 'at the end of the day's journey, the traveller outspans the weary oxen'.

The White Rhino, built by a trio of aristocrats — Berkeley Cole, Lord Cranworth, and Sandy Herd — was sometimes known as 'the hotel which charges on sight'. Sherbrooke Walker, had been private secretary to the founder of the World Scout Movement and hero of Mafeking, Lord Baden-Powell, who first visited Kenya in 1906. Later he fell in love with 'the wonderful views over the plains to the bold snow peaks of Mount Kenya. . . . The nearer to Nyeri, the nearer to bliss', he noted. In October 1938, he retired to **Paxtu,** the cottage which the Sherbrooke Walkers built within the hotel grounds for him and his wife, Chief Girl Guide, Lady Olave.

When Baden-Powell died on 8 January 1941, he was buried, amid British civilian and military graves, in the graveyard of **St Peter's** Anglican church, facing the mountain. Inscribed on his tomb is the Boy Scout's 'Gone Home' sign — a circle and a dot. The ashes of Lady Baden-Powell are interred beside him and their graves are a shrine for Scouts and Guides worldwide.

Radiating out from Nyeri, the **Great North Road** continues north through **Naro Moru** and **Nanyuki.** The road west past the entrance to the Outspan Hotel enters the **Aberdare National Park** by the **Kiandongoro Gate.** Another branches west from the town to the park's **Ruhuruini Gate.** To the left of the road to **Nyahururu,** before **Mweiga,** is the headquarters of Kenya's only gliding club. **The Ark** and **Treetops** are signposted.

The Aberdares: The Queen's Cave and Happy Valley

The road west out of Nyeri leads up into the **Aberdare National Park**. Established as a 766-square-kilometre (311-square-mile) sanctuary in 1948, this isolated volcanic massif forms part of the eastern wall of the Rift Valley. The mountain range is ringed by one of Kenya's largest forest reserves, covering more than 1,000 square kilometres (386 square miles).

The Kikuyu call this compact mountain range **Nyandarua** ('drying hide') after the shape of its silhouette. Joseph Thomson came upon the range on his wandering *Through Masai Land* in 1883, and renamed them after Lord Aberdare, president of the Royal Geographical Society.

Steeper, starker, and with denser rainforest, the Aberdares are neither as densely settled nor as extensively farmed as Mount Kenya, except in the south.

Though scaling their heights demands little mountaineering skill, it requires monumental stamina to reach the crown: the rarefied air sucks the breath from the lungs with every stride.

But the views over the Rift Valley are spectacular. The clouds curl around the 3,999-metre-high (13,120-feet) bluff of **Lesatima**, the highest point. From there, the ground falls quickly away to the broad moorland plateau which stretches south 46 kilometres (28 miles) to the second-highest and slightly more precipitous point of **Kinangop** at 3,906 metres (12,815 feet). A **stone cairn** commemorates the first ascent by a European early in the century. The two peaks and the moorlands offer trekkers some magnificent walks.

In the west, above the Wanjohi — 'Happy' — Valley, are the peaks of Kipipiri around 3,349 metres (11,000 feet) and, at 3,590 metres (11,780 feet), **'The Elephant'**. All are relatively easy to climb, given good weather (see 'Kenya's Mountains'), but remember that you can only walk in the park with the approval of the Park Warden.

Vegetation varies with altitude. The lush, well-tended vegetable, tea and coffee smallholdings give way to the bamboo-belt between the 2,100 and 2,400 metre (7,000-

8,000 feet) contours. The forest belt begins around 3,000 metres (10,000 feet).

These are some of Kenya's most ancient trees, cedar and hagenia, whose gnarled and rheumy limbs are reminiscent of Tolkien fantasies, with treetops often shrouded in clammy fingers of mist and entwined with Old Man's Beard (Spanish moss) whose wispy festoons dangle from every branch and leaf.

Higher up, the forest gives way to alpine oddities, including giant heather, tussock grass sometimes a metre or two deep, St John's wort, lobelia and groundsel, which grows to astonishing heights under the ultra-violet glare on the Equator.

Heavy rain falls through most of the year, feeding the many clear streams and waterfalls etched in deep ravines on the mountain's eastern and western flanks.

The roaring waters of **Queen's Cave Waterfall** — so called because Queen Elizabeth of Britain lunched there and the remains of the wooden pavilion testify to her visit — cascade into a small ravine resembling a fairy glade. You reach it by climbing down a cliff.

Another spectacular fall, Kenya's deepest, is the **Gura**. It plummets more than 300 metres (1,000 feet) into an impenetrable ravine opposite the **Karura Falls,** which drop almost 275 metres (900 feet) to merge downstream with the **Chania River.** These waters, rippling like a pliant ribbon in the strong winds that gust along the gorge, were filmed for the scenic aerial essay in *Out of Africa.*

All these natural wonders occur well above the Aberdare forest belt where the wildlife is fascinating (see 'National Parks', In Brief). Birdlife is abundant and varied, with more than 200 recorded species. **Trout** can be caught in the moorland streams.

During the 1950s the high moorlands above the 3,000-metre (10,000 feet) contour were the hideout of Mau Mau freedom fighters. When the British tried to flush them out with bombing runs, many a cave and impenetrable forest served as a shelter.

Moorlands wildlife includes some rare melanistic leopard, serval and genets. The high altitude and closeness to the Equator have turned their coats black. There are some mythical beasts, too, including a spotted lion which has never been seen. To

Above: Queen Elizabeth II of Britain on her return to Treetops.

the frustration of visitors — but to the benefit of the beasts and plants — the park is often inaccessible during the rains. Even in the dry season, the high altitude and rough trails make 4WD vehicles mandatory.

One gate from Naivasha lies above 3,000 metres (10,000 feet) — up a rough, rocky road that amazingly turns into tarmac near the top. It was laid for the 1959 visit of Britain's Queen Mother. Other gates lead from Nyeri, Mweiga and Pesi on the eastern face (see 'Kenya's Mountains', Part Three).

Near one gate from Nyeri, at around 3,000 metres (10,000 feet), there's a **fishing camp** with a log cabin. Both brown and rainbow trout flourish in the icy streams. Some weigh in at seven kilos (15 lbs).

The park is a delight of rolling downs, open vistas, little dells, icy tarns, bubbling streams, and waterfalls and with Mount Kenya, 80 kilometres (50 miles) away across the Laikipia plateau, it forms Kenya's major watershed. To the west, the steep Rift wall deters game, but it was there, in the lush, forested **Wanjohi Valley** below Kipipiri that — between the two World Wars — a handful of Establishment

breakaways indulged in quite a different type of sport. With their drink, drugs, low moral behaviour and high-spirited licentiousness, they succeeded in giving Kenya an undeserved bad name. In their spare time they held champagne parties which ended with keys thrown on the table and spouses departing with somebody else's husband or wife. These and similar antics earned them the name of 'The Happy Valley Set'. The murder of their acknowledged leader, Lord 'Joss' Erroll, in 1941, provided the country with an — as yet — unsolved murder mystery. The film of the novel *White Mischief* was made in Kenya.

Today, their manors and chateaux have collapsed or, fallen into shambling disrepair, are used as cowsheds and chicken houses. Kikuyu smallholders and peasant farmers tend the valley lands but little remains, except for entertaining legends told by a few remaining white settlers.

The House inspired by Peter Pan
The road from Nyeri to Nyahururu switchbacks out of the town over a series of steep hills cut through coffee plantations and

133

then arrives at a T-junction. Straight on is **Kiganjo** and the main **Nanyuki** road. Left is the **Nyahururu** (Thomson's Falls) road.

Just a few kilometres along this, left, is the turn along a track through more coffee plantations to the **Treetops** gate of the Aberdare National Park.

Perhaps the most famous hotel in its time it was Eric Sherbrooke Walker's brainchild after his wife Bettie's whimsical hankerings for a Wendy-style tree house (inspired by J M Barrie's play *Peter Pan*). The first visitors to the two-room tree house, perched in the fork of a fig tree, spent one night there in November 1932.

Twenty years later, when Princess Elizabeth was escorted through the game-filled forest to climb the ladder into the tree and to climb down a queen, she followed a distinguished list of royalty and celebrities — Tsar Ferdinand of Bulgaria, the Duke and Duchess of Gloucester, Mr and Mrs Neville Chamberlain, and Earl Mountbatten. By then the treehouse had expanded to four rooms, but in 1954 it was burned down by the Mau Mau.

Its replacement was finished in 1957 — on a site opposite the original fig tree — with 'seven wash basins and water closets'. Since then, it has grown considerably and now accommodates over 90 guests. It was refurbished again in 1996. But Treetops remains unique. It was given a royal accolade in November 1983 by the Queen's sentimental homecoming to the spot where she became Queen. Kenya's most famous lodge is usually booked months in advance.

Twelve kilometres (seven miles) from Nyeri, **Mweiga** town serves as a trade centre for a large area spread over the **Laikipia** plains between the Aberdares and Naro Moru. Its principal distinction is as the headquarters of the Aberdare and Mount Kenya National Parks.

Close by is the **Aberdare Country Club,** an elegant baronial style country home set in sprawling and superbly-landscaped gardens, on the side of Mweiga Hill. It's also the departure base for the third of central Kenya's three forest lodges, **The Ark.**

The Aberdare Country Club is worth a visit in its own right. The grounds are immaculate and colourful, with excellent golfing and horse-riding. Some 18 kilometres (11 miles) from the club and 370 metres

(1,200 feet) higher, you enter the **Ark Gate** in the Aberdare National Park to arrive soon after at The Ark, built at the end of the 1960s in the shape of an ark, in an open glade with a natural waterhole.

A drawbridge opens on to a wooden catwalk which leads to a fine 20th-century replica of what Noah used to escape the flood, with comforts he could never have dreamed of — comfortable beds, hot showers, good food, and piping hot cups of tea.

Once the guests are 'aboard' for the night they are truly a captive audience because the drawbridge is drawn up until next morning. As darkness falls, visitors take their place in front of the large, panoramic windows and wait to see which forest inhabitants will appear first. Every dawn the hunter records the number and species of animals in the Ark's log book.

Elephant, rhino, and bongo — a rare nocturnal antelope with bold black stripes on chestnut flanks — are the star players in the nightly pageant of wildlife (see 'Great and Small, Wild and Wonderful', Part Three).

Beyond Mweiga the road rides high over the flanks of the Aberdares with fantastic views over the Laikipia plateau far below and Mount Kenya rising on the other side. Some 40 kilometres (30 miles) beyond Nyeri, there's a right turn to **Ngobit.** The main road continues past the link fence that guards the western perimeter of the vast **Solio Ranch,** for many years a successful private sanctuary for Kenya's imperilled rhino population.

Ol Pejeta, another nearby private reserve on the Laikipia, covers 6,500 hectares (16,000 acres) of scrub savannah and thorn. In 1984, film star Brooke Shields spent an idyllic day there among the ranch's elephant and lion. Her memorable moment came when a pride feasted on cattle meat in the back of the pickup she was driving.

For many years Ol Pejeta was the Kenya playground of the armaments billionaire Adnan Kashoggi, but in the wake of the Iran arms deal it was seized by the Kenya subsidiary of the giant Lonrho group in settlement of debts Kashoggi owed the conglomerate. He had already transferred the Mount Kenya Safari Club to them. Lonrho have turned Ol Pejeta into a luxurious holiday resort. Guests were accommodated at

Above: Thomson's Falls, Nyahururu.

Kashoggi's Italian-style ranch house with its gold-tapped bathrooms, but now in the ranch's luxury tented camp, **Sweet Waters.**

Beyond Solio, the road continues on through **Ndaragwa,** past a right turn along a dirt trail to **Nanyuki** and **Rumuruti,** and a dirt trail leading to the **Pesi gate** which is in the northern extension of the Aberdare National Park, then on to Nyahururu, 100 kilometres (60 miles) from Nyeri.

Pesi lies just beneath Lesatima's eastern face. In the 1960s it was pure forest, but it has since been carved out as smallholdings and medium-size farms which are fertile and productive. The rolling fields of lush green grass and herds of dairy cattle which suddenly appear after the steep drive through the forest and bamboo are reminiscent of European meadowland.

Thomson's Falls

Nyahururu, one of Kenya's youngest and highest towns, sits at 2,360 metres (7,743 feet). Its name in Maa means 'where waters run deep' but it is still better known outside Kenya as Thomson's Falls — named by Joseph Thomson in 1883 in honour of

his father. In the 1920s, it was nothing much more than a log cabin for a settler angling club. But with the arrival of the railway in 1929, Thomson's Falls proper was born. The town nestles against the sweep of the great **Marmanet Forest**, from whose base the Laikipia plains stretch all the way to the black pyramid of Mount Kenya. Sleepy and undisturbed, Thomson's Falls reflects the pace of the agricultural region it serves.

It earned brief fame as the high-altitude training camp where Kenya's Olympic medallists prepared for Mexico in 1968. But it's the 72-metre (237-foot) falls which Thomson came across on his trek north that give the town its ambience.

In spate, the waters of the **Ewaso Narok River,** born on the slopes of Lesatima, gather themselves in the hippo-infested marsh and bogland that lie atop the falls and then thunder over the narrow lip in a cascade that amounts to around a million litres (220,000 gallons) a minute. In too-frequently dry Kenya, Nyahururu's planners finally succumbed to temptation, and at one side of the falls there is now an obtrusive waterworks, which supplies the town's growing population. Nonetheless, it is a popular stopover and picnic spot for those en route between the Samburu and the Maasai Mara game reserves.

For a leg-stretching diversion, if you are sure-footed and vertigo is not your problem, stone steps — tricky when wet — lead down the ravine to the bottom of the falls. A longer foot-excursion, richly-treed, follows a river walk along the opposite side of the valley. You reach this by the bridge to the left of the lodge entrance gates.

To Rumuruti
From Nyahururu, a fine new road leads 34 kilometres (21 miles) northward down the steep gradient of the Marmanet Forest to the ranching town of Rumuruti, a major gateway to the northern deserts.

Headquarters of the district administration for a large area of Laikipia, the tarmac sweeps into the dusty one-street town and out again along a gravel dirt road that eventually lands up on the shores of Lake Turkana (see 'The Great Rift Valley: The Land that was Eden').

The road has brought Rumuruti into mainstream Kenya, but the Samburu and Maasai idling around the bars and *dukas* on the one street, and the relaxed indolence of everybody else, gives you a sense of the isolation it once enjoyed as a cattle town where European settlers, raising their beef herds in the arid savannah around, met and quaffed ales in the town's old club.

The **District Commissioner's office**, with the Kenya flag flying, at the far end of the street, is just past the **post office**, where the tarmac ends and the gravel begins.

To Gilgil
Heading west out of Nyahururu, the road to **Ol Kalou** and **Gilgil** takes you through **Ol Joro Orok**, under the shadow of the northern wall of the Aberdares and Lesatima, where the hippo-infested water-bird sanctuary of **Lake Ilpolosat** dreams on, unvisited by any tourist — a hauntingly-lovely sheet of water. It's some kilometres to the left of the main road on a bumpy farm track, midway between Ol Joro Orok and Ol Kalou. Ol Kalou, 52 kilometres (32 miles) from Nyahururu, is a rapidly-growing farm and trade centre. Some kilometres

beyond Ol Kalou on the 30-kilometre (19-mile) stretch to Gilgil there's a left turn along a dirt road into the high valley between the main Aberdare massive and Kipipiri. This is Wanjohi Valley — the 'Happy Valley' of *White Mischief* infamy.

To Subukia
Another dramatic highway from Nyahururu down the eastern wall of the Rift makes a scenic route to **Nakuru** via **Subukia**. It plunges down a series of faults in the scarp to a series of breathtaking hairpin bends which wind into an African Shangrila, Subukia. Already the cool highland air has begun to change to the sweltering heat of the Rift Valley: sugar, coffee and bananas burgeon in this hothouse environment, which remains as remote as the world of the Middle Ages.

Even the little Anglican church which was built in 1951 reflects the feeling of time and setting removed. With its Norman architecture, it could have stood in its colourful gardens — overlooking the great divide of the Rift and the faraway lakes scintillating in the noonday sun — for a thousand years.

Before their eviction from Laikipia to the 'Southern Maasai Reserve' in 1911, to make way for settler farmers, Subukia's pastures were the Maasai people's retreat from the drylands. They call it *Ol Momoi Sidai* — the beautiful place — and this too the Europeans found it. By the 1920s they had already put the land under wheat, maize, barley, flax, dairy farming and — later — coffee.

There is a **police post** at **Subukia** and a number of small 'hotels'. Across a rugged but scenically impressive landscape, a short cut to **Lake Bogoria** starts a few kilometres outside the town on the road in from Nyahururu. Take the signposted **Nakuru-Bogoria** fork past **St Peter's Church**. This is a bumpy route, better suited to the intrepid traveller.

A quicker route — in better condition — is to head south to Nakuru and take the main Nakuru to Baringo tarmac, from which Lake Bogoria access roads are signposted on the right, one at the south end of the lake and another at the north. You are now in hot, dry country where a colourful road sign indicates where you actually cross that magical line, the Equator.

Mount Kenya: On God's Mountain

With its many ridges and valleys, radiating like the spokes of a wheel, the bulk of Mount Kenya straddles the Equator. Although its highest point lies 17 kilometres (10 miles) to the south, the Equator cuts across the northern shoulders at a height of 3,350 metres (11,000 feet). The mountain, 193 kilometres (120 miles) north-east of Nairobi and 480 kilometres (300 miles) west of the Kenya coast, is regarded as the perfect model of an Equatorial mountain.

Soon after his colleague Johannes Rebmann had caught that first tantalizing glimpse of the snows of Kilimanjaro, missionary Johann Krapf saw the glaciers of Mount Kenya, on 3 December 1849, from Kitui, 160 kilometres (100 miles) away.

Nineteenth-century European geographers dismissed the idea of snow on the Equator as ridiculous. But 40 years after Krapf's first sighting, Thomson's delight at his discovery was lyrical.

'Through a rugged and picturesque depression in the range [Aberdares] rose a gleaming snow-white peak with sparkling facets which scintillated with the superb beauty of a colossal diamond. It was in fact the very image of a great crystal or sugar loaf.' The twin peaks of **Batian** and **Nelion** crown one of the world's highest national parks, with 704 square kilometres (286 square miles) of forest, moorland, rock and ice.

The mountain slopes above 3,100 metres (10,170 feet), and two salients, **Naro Moru** and the **Sirimon**, down to approximately 2,600 metres (8,530 feet), were declared **Mount Kenya National Park** in 1949. The lower area, between 1,600 and 3,100 metres (5,250 and 1,020 feet), constitutes the **Mount Kenya Forest Reserve.** The park became part of a 715-square-kilometre (276-square-mile) UNESCO Biosphere Reserve in April 1978, along with 2,009 square kilometres (776 square miles) of forest reserve. The upper base of the mountain is close to 100 kilometres (60 miles) across.

Batian, 5,199 metres (17,058 feet) and Nelion, 5,188 metres (17,017 feet) are the remains of a gigantic eroded plug that once thrust another 3,000 metres (10,000 feet) or more into the sky. Its Kikuyu name, *Kirinyaga*, is derived from *Kere Nyaga* ('White Mountain').

The first Europeans to venture to any heights on the mountain were Count Samuel Teleki von Szek and Ludwig von Höhnel, who followed much of Thomson's epic route in their 1887 travels. They explored the moorlands, 900 metres (3,000 feet) beneath the peaks, and then went on to discover Lake Turkana, which they named Rudolf (see 'History: The Dust and the Ashes', Part One). Twelve years later, the great Victorian alpinist, Sir Halford Mackinder, made it to the summit with two Courmayeur guides, Joseph Brocherel and Cesar Ollier, but in those days Kenya was so remote from Europe that the significance of the achievement was underrated.

In 1929, Eric Shipton, who later became one of Britain's greatest Himalayan specialists, made the second recorded ascent. The same year, **Carr's Road** from the **Chogoria Gate** became the highest motor track in Africa when Ernest Carr drove a Model T-Ford up the trail to a height of more than 4,260 metres (14,000 feet).

Perhaps the most unusual assault, however, was made by three Italian prisoners-of-war interned at Nanyuki during the 1940s. They broke out of camp to climb the mountain equipped with a label from a tin of canned meat — showing the mountain's twin peaks as their only map — and succeeded in planting the Italian flag on Point Lenana at 4,985 metres (16,350 feet) before cold and hunger overcame them. Their exploit over, they returned to camp to resume their confinement. The epic inspired the book *No Picnic on Mount Kenya*, filmed in the 1990s as *The Ascent*.

With two major peaks above 5,180 metres (17,000 feet), Mount Kenya has many jewel-like lakes, including the **Curling Pond** beneath the **Lewis Glacier** and **Lake Michaelson.** One was the location for what may well have been the highest underwater exploration ever undertaken, when a group of aqualung *aficionados* lugged their oxygen cylinders up to its shores and plunged in.

Mount Kenya plays a crucial role in the life of the country. It is Kenya's single most important permanent watershed and its

Above: Metal cross, a gift of Pope Pius XI to Nyeri's Consolata Mission, was set in place on Point Lenana, Mount Kenya, on 31 January 1933.

largest forest reserve. The fertile loams of its lower slopes, particularly in the north-east, sustain the growth of the nation's richest farmlands. Much of the vegetation is unique. Thirteen species are endemic to the mountain. Vegetation varies with altitude and rainfall and includes rich alpine and sub-alpine flora with montane and bamboo forests, moorlands and tundra.

The **forest reserve** covers more than 2,000 square kilometres (770 square miles) and contains Kenya's greatest trees (see 'Flora: Forests of Flame, Streets of Mauve', Part Three). In the east and to the south, where the rains are frequent and heavy, the forests are thick and rich, particularly in the number of species of indigenous trees.

Their great trunks, thrusting high into the canopy, are carved by age and parasites into exotic, fluted shapes and knitted together with lianas and vines. Camphor (*Ocotea usambarensis*), one of Kenya's most valuable indigenous trees, which flourishes there, rises up to 46 metres (150 feet) high.

In the drier parts below 2,500 metres (8,200 feet), with an average annual rainfall of between 875 and 1,400 millimetres (35-55 inches), juniper and podocarpus are the giants of the forest. African olives (*Olea*

hochstetteri), smooth and straight-limbed, rise 18 metres (60 feet) high and wear a crown of olive-green leaves, ferns, mosses and 'Old Man's Beard' (Spanish moss).

Higher up, where annual rainfall is more than 2,000 millimetres (78 inches), bamboo dominates the belt between 2,600 and 2,800 metres (8,500-9,200 feet), buffered between 2,500 and 2,600 metres (8,200-8,500 feet) and 2,800-3,000 metres (9,200-9,900 feet) by stands of podocarpus.

Towards the west and north, the bamboo is smaller and less dominant. Between 2,000 and 3,500 metres (6,562-11,480 feet), where annual rainfall is up to 2,400 millimetres (95 inches), long-living hagenia is the dominant tree.

Beyond 3,000 metres (9,900 feet), where the cold is more extreme, hypericum with its more open canopy and more developed understorey, replaces podocarpus. Grassy glades are common, especially on ridges. In the glades beneath the middle canopy the profusion of shrubs, including some members of the coffee family, *Rubicae*, is thick and tangled. They rise as high as nine to 12 metres (30-40 feet) and the air is filled with the sweet, fragrant breath of their flowers. The trees are host to flowering climbers such as a rare begonia *(Begonia meyeri-johannis)* with its striking, asymmetric leaves and delicate white flowers that glow a soft pink. Underfoot, the forest floor is deep with rotting leaves, ferns and occasional plants, including the balsam 'touch-me-not' *(Impatiens fisheri).* In bloom, this plant bears remarkable scarlet flowers with spurred edges.

Among the ferns on the valley floor and by the banks of streams, where the forest is wettest, you may chance across the tall, prickly-stemmed tree fern *(Cyathea manniana)* and a smaller fern *(Asplenium hypomelas)* found in leaf scars and also around the base of the forest giants, which is closely associated with *Cyathea.*

The western forests are comparatively dry and less prolific and the north is virtually devoid of forest.

Red Hot Pokers

The high moorlands start at around 3,350 metres (11,000 feet) with a heath zone of *Erica arborea,* a weirdly-shaped bush, often as large as a tree and covered with moss and lichen. Higher up it gives way to tussock grass and a profusion of everlasting helichrysums, gladioli, delphiniums and 'red-hot pokers' — a riot of unusual flora.

Some of the world's most spectacular mountain plants flourish in the high valleys. 'Water-holding cabbages' or 'ostrich plume plants' are actually a giant mutation of the tiny alpine groundsel, there growing up to six metres (20 feet). When the leaves die they remain attached and help to keep out the cold, much like an overcoat.

Lobelias grow even higher than the groundsel — up to eight metres (27 feet). Its hairy, grey leaves, dotted with tiny blue flowers, make it look like a grotesque furry giant. The wrapping seals out the frost.

Another plant, in the shape of a huge rosette filled with water, grows closer to the ground. At night this water freezes over and the ice acts as insulation so protecting the central bud.

These plants mark the extreme range of wildlife. The only permanent residents at this altitude are rock hyrax which feed off lobelia leaves (see 'Wildlife: Great and Small, Wild and Wonderful', Part Three).

At higher altitudes, endemic mole-rat are common and there have been rare sightings of a mysterious 'golden cat'. Eland and zebra have been seen occasionally at the base of the peaks, around 4,300 metres (14,000 feet).

Moorland mammals, found lower down, include rock hyrax, Mount Kenya mouse shrew and common duiker. Buffalo and elephant sometimes roam there, and lion are permanent residents. In the mountain's thick and ancient forests black-and-white colobus monkeys leap from one branch to another in the canopy trees. Few sights are more graceful.

Wildlife in the lower forest and bamboo zone includes giant forest hog, tree hyrax, white-tailed mongoose, black rhino, suni and leopard.

Forest birds include an endemic race of green ibis, Ayre's hawk eagle, threatened Abyssinian long-eared owl, scaly francolin, Ruppell's robin-chat and many beautiful sunbirds. Moorland birds include scarlet-tufted malachite sunbirds, montane francolin, Mackinder's eagle owl and a rare, endangered swift.

Vegetation and wildlife aside, it's for the climbs on its ice-cliffs and rock faces that Mount Kenya is renowned. Much exploration was done after World War I, but it was not until 1929 that P Wyn Harris and Eric Shipton ascended Nelion, the second-highest peak, 5,188 metres (17,017 feet), for the first time, and made the second ascent of Batian.

Anyone moderately fit can attempt the third-highest peak, **Point Lenana**, 4,985 metres (16,350 feet), although its reputation as a relatively easy walk is misleading.

In all, there are now 34 difficult, technical routes to the summits which, though much lower, many experienced climbers claim to be as testing as major Himalayan climbs, offering a challenge of couloirs, ice-cliffs, secondary peaks, cornices and sheer rock walls. Kenya's location on the Equator has given it a unique seasonal characteristic. Between June and October the sun is on its north face, while the south experiences its 'winter' and is covered in snow and ice. At such a time the mountain's ice climbs are magnificent.

Between December and March, when the sun is on the south face, the rock climbs are more popular, while snow and ice prevail during the north face's 'winter'. For this reason it is best to climb in the two dry seasons — January to early March and July to early October.

The east face is generally clear of ice and snow for most of the year due to the morning sun, but the west face does not enjoy this advantage. Differing from the lower altitudes it rains on top of the mountain throughout the year.

Anywhere above 3,350 metres (11,000 feet) you notice the effects of the altitude. Take time during every stage of the ascent to allow your body to acclimatize to the altitude, temperature and thin air.

More than half the world's recorded cases of pulmonary oedema — about 50 a year — occur on Mount Kenya. Without exception, the cause is climbing too high, too quickly, without pausing for acclimatization. All those who climb Mount Kenya should be aware of the dangers.

Getting there

Leave Nyeri and pass through Kiganjo to arrive on the main Nairobi-Nanyuki road. Turn left for **Naro Moru** and Nanyuki. Naro Moru, the most popular base from which to prepare for climbing Mount Kenya, lies in the mountain's western rain shadow some 25 kilometres (15 miles) south of Nanyuki.

The tiny town is built around the railway station which frequently wins the Kenya Railways award for the nation's best-kept station. No doubt one factor in this must be the efforts of the staff, who have plenty of time to tend to the station — there are only two trains a week.

Apart from a **sub-post office** and a few scantily-stocked small *dukas* (shops), Naro Moru has few facilities. The shops are unlikely to be able to supply the food needed for the climb so buy provisions beforehand in Nairobi, Nyeri or Nanyuki.

The Routes

There are six main routes up Mount Kenya. On the western side, these include the **Naro Moru** track, the **Burguret** trail, just north of Naro Moru and, beyond Nanyuki, the **Sirimon** and **Timau** tracks. Arguably the most beautiful, enjoyable and dramatic of all the approaches to the peaks is from **Chogoria**, on the eastern side of the mountain, following **Carr's Road**. Perhaps the

toughest and most demanding, cutting as it does through the thickest and oldest of Mount Kenya's forests, is the **Kamweti** trail from the south.

Of the six, the Sirimon trail is the driest and Chogoria the wettest, demonstrating the predominant pattern of the rainfall, since the north-western slopes lie in an almost permanent rain shadow.

Above: *Kniphofia thomsoni* — Afro-alpine versions of Europe's 'red hot pokers'.

The Naro Moru route

From the village, it's 17 kilometres (10 miles) to a comfortable and economic **Youth Hostel**. From there it is a four-hour walk to the **airstrip** and the **park gate**.

Park fees are calculated according to the number of guides and porters who accompany you or your party and how many days you intend to stay in the park.

The main gate is reached along a track from Naro Moru that crosses over the railway and then the main road. Climbing gradually at first, through grasslands and smallholdings, the trail cuts through a forest reserve, climbing more steeply to the gate at around 2,430 metres (8,000 feet). It is on a ridge. Deep valleys on either side plunge down to the humid bamboo belt.

Beyond the forest, above 3,000 metres (9,900 feet), the road ends at the **Meteorological Station,** leaping-off point for moorland walks and climbing expeditions.

From the gate, the road twists and climbs up into the bamboo zone through a thick and ancient indigenous forest. The forests there are as old as in the south of the mountain but of more temperate stock, with robust cedars. Beware of buffalo and elephant — they are potentially lethal.

The final three kilometres (less than two miles) to the Met station winds up a series of steep hairpin bends, usually surmountable only in 4WD. The track then crosses **Percival's Bridge**, which was built many years ago by British army engineers to honour an officer who died attempting to climb the twin peaks.

The apt memorial commands a view over the Laikipia plains to the north-west and the panorama tells you how far and how high you have climbed. Close by is the southern ridge of the **Teleki Valley** along which the European aristocrat made his way up the mountain.

Accommodation at the **Met Station** is in comfortable log cabins (pre-booking is strongly recommended, particularly at the more popular times of the year) or in fixed tents. A sensible idea is to spend the night there to get accustomed to the altitude of 3,050 metres (10,000 feet) before making the next stage of the climb the following day. If you leave at first light you should get to Mackinder's in the early afternoon — before the weather deteriorates. From the

Met Station the trail passes through a barrier and climbs steeply up through the last of the 300-year-old forest trees. By the roadside a rare and beautiful flower blossoms in delicate pink, like a filament of fire. It is known as bottle flush. The gnarled limbs of the hagenia testify to their ancient existence, sentinels long before mankind ventured along these trails, carved over the aeons by buffalo, elephant, rhino and forest hog.

The made-up road ends at the **radio station** and soon afterwards deteriorates into a narrow foot trail through dwarf hagenia to emerge on the moorland where the forest ends as neatly as if divided by a knife. Almost immediately the hagenia is replaced by *Erica arborea* — a giant mutation of small alpine heather shrubs — endemic only to Mount Kenya.

Ahead, appallingly steep and forbidding, rises the Vertical Bog — 300 metres (1,000 feet) of treachery, a massive, sullen rampart that hides the peaks.

At the start of the rainy season water cascades down this 55° incline like whitewater rapids. Later, as its level rises, it becomes a waist-deep torrent, rushing down the steep-pitched slope. For the inexperienced, what in the dry season may take anything from 90 minutes to three hours to traverse, now becomes a day-long battle.

There the *Erica arborea* grows between lobelias and groundsels and other strange and unworldly plant forms. Enormous tussock grass, clovers, irises, larkspurs and helichrysums grow in unique form on the flanks of the high valleys.

Perhaps the most remarkable of all the world's alpine flora, many bloom only once every two decades when they adorn the entire moorlands with a glorious burst of colour, luring beautiful malachite sunbirds and others into their branches.

Near the crest of the Vertical Bog the incline slackens — still steep but not so severe. Just a few more hundred metres to a small rock bluff — and there is the south wall of Teleki Valley, the crest of a long radial ridge, with the peaks and their grand west-facing amphitheatre visible in all their glory — no more than five kilometres (three miles) away. There the path divides into two separate trails. The higher path is for the more intrepid. Though it has beauti-

ful views, it is usually wet and difficult going. The lower path, the most travelled of the two, leads down across the Naro Moru stream and carries on to Mackinder's Camp at 4,268 metres (14,000 feet) where you can spend the night. But by the time you cross the fast-flowing **Naro Moru stream** to the other side of the valley and hike the final kilometre to **Mackinder's Camp** (also known as **Teleki Lodge**) the mists have already begun to swirl and boil around the many peaks. Batian and Nelion tower majestically over the valley and a third pinnacle, **Point John,** looms even closer.

Everywhere you'll see a ubiquitous species of fat, bloated rock hyrax *(Procavia johnstoni mackinderi),* endemic only to this mountain. They thrive on scraps from **Teleki Lodge,** run by the Naro Moru River Lodge. This recent addition to the **radio station, ranger's post,** and **Mountain Club** buildings in the valley is a simple concrete-slab and tin-roof barrack room.

It is the most common departure point for the severe walk, up the steep-pitched scree alongside the **Lewis Glacier,** to **Point Lenana.** Leaving Mackinder's Camp at 0300 the hike to Point Lenana, at 4,985 metres (16,350 feet) takes about four-hours — in time to catch the sunrise. On a clear day Mount Kilimanjaro is visible to the south and, to the north, Kenya's vast northern frontier.

Many hikers recommend continuing for three hours past Mackinder's Camp to Austrian Hut at 4,790 metres (15,716 feet), where you can spend the night. From there it is only a one-hour trek up to Point Lenana. This allows time to sleep a bit longer and save energy for a trek around the peak, although most head straight back down. Instead, if you are not experiencing altitude sickness, take time to explore the tarns and glacial valleys on the northern face.

One word of warning. More often than not, nights in the huts are shared with large numbers of hyrax and other rodents, so remember to protect your food supplies.

The Chogoria Route

The Chogoria trail is by far the most scenic of all routes. It's also much longer than the Naro Moru route and it takes about three days to hike to the top. From **Mutindwa,** beyond **Chogoria village,** it's 24-kilometres (15-mile) up a rough road to the **park gate** at 2,990 metres (9,810 feet). A 4WD vehicle is necessary, even during the dry season.

Up to this point you do not need a guide. Park receipts should be saved as they will be checked on the way out.

Inside the park, close by the entrance, is **Meru Mount Kenya Lodge,** which offers comfortable, reasonably priced, self-service bandas with roaring log fires and hot showers. Run by the Meru County Council, it is the best value in accommodation anywhere on the mountain.

Some 60 minutes' walk from the gate, the Mountain Club of Kenya's **Urumandi Hut** offers an alternative to the lodge.

The joy of all this for those sufficiently acclimatized is that both the lodge and the hut are on Carr's Road, which continues up even higher from the Urumandi Hut — a 45-minute walk if you've no wheels — to a parking lot.

This road was pioneered by Ernest Carr in the 1920s. Along with two missionaries, the reverends Dr J W Arthur, and A R Barlow sent to establish a mission at Chogoria on the eastern slopes of Mount Kenya, he was among the most dedicated of the many attempting to succeed Sir Halford Mackinder and stand on the summit of Mount Kenya.

Arthur and Carr established the first two climbers' huts on the mountain — Urumandi at 3,050 metres (10,000 feet) and **Top Hut** at 4,790 metres (15,715 feet), on the Lewis Glacier besides a frozen pool known as the Curling Pond — in January 1922.

During the course of this expedition they came across the source of the **Ruguti River,** a tributary of the Tana, which is born in a steaming, boiling hot spring at 3,600 metres (11,800 feet). Arthur thought that 'here there might be formed later a health camp'. From Urumandi the landscape is spectacular. The trail to **Minto's Hut,** a stiff six-hour walk, follows the crest of a long ascending ridge to the rim of the precipice that plunges sheer to the floor of the **Gorges valley,** 300 metres (1,000 feet)

Previous pages: One of the many gemlike tarns that nestle at the throat of Mount Kenya.

below. The first man to conquer Mount Kenya, Sir Halford Mackinder, named the valley after Captain (later Brigadier-General) Gorges, who came to their rescue from Naivasha when their base camp was raided by Kikuyu.

On the other side of these sheer cliffs **Hall Tarn**, another, smaller, sheet of water was named by Mackinder after Major Francis Hall, the British officer at Fort Hall (now Murang'a) at the turn of the century.

It's a giddying but exhilarating experience to follow the trail along the edge of this stunning escarpment overlooking the valley that was scoured out by Mount Kenya's ancient glaciers. Ahead, the twin peaks beckon you forward.

Most people spend the night at Minto's Hut, perched above the head of the Gorges valley by three glittering tarns which overlook the sparkling jade waters of **Lake Michaelson,** surrounded by remarkable specimens of giant groundsel and lobelia, which spawns the Nithi River. Mackinder named the lake after one of his closest friends.

From there to Point Lenana takes between three and four hours of laborious climbing. There are two routes to choose from: one leads up a ridge west to **Simba Tarn,** and then south around the peaks, passing **Square Tarn**, climbing steeply up to the **Austrian Hut**, by the **Curling Pond**.

The tarn was 'discovered' by Arthur in 1919, when the Scotsman gave his friend, Jack Melhuish, his first and only lesson in the ancient Scottish sport of curling, thus earning the tarn its curious name.

In 1922, when they went to build the **Top Hut,** the climbers carried some skates with them and one fine morning skated for some time — at an altitude of around 4,880 metres (16,000 feet) — gliding and waltzing among the clouds that drifted over the glacier, much to the delight of the African members of the party who were amused by the behaviour of the *wazungu* (white men).

The second route from Minto's leads up a slope of loose, savage scree in the south, over a saddle, to **Two Tarns** at the head of the Hobley Valley. Another hour of hard walking from this point takes you to the base of a ridge descending from Point Lenana, at the side of which are the **Austrian** and **Top** huts. Many prefer to spend the night there and then make the climb to Lenana next morning to watch the sunrise.

The Austrian hut was built in 1973, as a gesture of appreciation from Austria for the efforts of European and Kenyan climbers in their sucessful attempt to save the life of Gerd Judmaier, a young Austrian who fell from Batian in September 1970. Unable to move because of a broken leg, he was trapped on a narrow ledge, set in a sheer cliff, for eight nights — surely one of the most dramatic rescues in climbing history.

The Burguret Route

This follows the course of the **Burguret River** from **Bantu Lodge**, some eight kilometres (five miles) north of Naro Moru on the Nanyuki road, through thick bamboo forest to the moorland. It's possible to take a 4WD vehicle up to around 3,000 metres (10,000 feet), passing some caves that the Mau Mau used as a battle headquarters.

The main blessing of this route is that it is drier than the Naro Moru trail — and avoids anything like the Vertical Bog.

The lodge management has built two huts on the mountainside — one near a natural salt lick at 3,000 metres (10,000 feet), which is known as **Bantu Secret Valley Camp.** The other, at 4,000 metres (11,500 feet), is known as the **Highland Castle.**

The Burguret route ends at **Two Tarn Hut** in the valley.

The Sirimon Route

Driest of all the major routes, after the first nine kilometres (five-and-a-half miles) through the forest reserve to the park gate at 2,640 metres (8,650 feet), the Sirimon route is virtually all pure moorland.

The trail starts 14 kilometres (eight-and-a-half miles) north of Nanyuki, by the **Sirimon River bridge** on the Nanyuki-Meru road. In such open country the wildlife is more visible and there are fantastic panoramas over the northern deserts.

This approach also provides perhaps the most stunning and least seen perspectives of Batian and Nelion — all the grandeur of their northern faces, and their smaller, but no less dramatic minions, 4,714-metre-high (15,466-feet) **Terere** and 4,704-metre-high (15,433-feet) **Sendeyo,** named after 19th-century Maasai leaders.

Nanyuki-Meru: Across the Equator

Although somnolent Nanyuki is only 23 kilometres (14 miles) from Naro Moru you could say it lies half a world away in one sense. For, just before you enter the town, the road crosses the **Equator** from south to north. The Equator is marked by two signs less than a kilometre apart. One is official, the other has been set up by a rival group of souvenir curio sellers eager to steal a march on their rivals on the real Equator.

Nanyuki's metamorphosis from a handful of Maasai *manyattas* and 'a great deal of game and nothing else', began with the arrival of the railhead at the end of the 1920s. Before then it was just a shopping centre for the largely white farming population on the Laikipia plains and the slopes of the mountain, who arrived as settlers.

Nanyuki lies on the banks of the 'Red River', the Maasai's **Ngare Nanyuki**. Today it is as a major Kenya Airforce base — as well as a training centre for the British Army under an Anglo-Kenyan treaty. Set at 1,950 metres (6,400 feet), the climate is temperate and the air bracing. The wide, tree-lined main street and monuments, such as a small **clock tower,** do much to promote Nanyuki's frontier town ambience.

The **Nanyuki Spinners and Weavers workshop**, just out of town on the **Nyahururu road**, opposite the **district hospital**, is well worth a visit. Run by a women's co-operative, it produces splendid rugs and other traditional hand-woven items.

Probably the most famous of the main street shops is **Settlers' Stores**. Almost an institution, this shop has been on the map since 1938, and many a white hunter and movie star have passed through it.

They were probably guests at what has been described as the world's most exclusive resort — a millionaire's retreat, a few kilometres east of town, on the shoulders of the mountain.

The **Mount Kenya Safari Club,** the creation of Texas oil baron Ray Ryan, a Swiss financier and the film star William Holden, is set in 37 hectares (91 acres) of lawns, bowling greens, flowerbeds and ornamental ponds, with an immaculately-kept golf course. It also boasts the only heated swimming pool on the Equator, horse riding, tennis, and wildlife safaris to the northern deserts. Sixty-seven bird species inhabit the gardens, many of them imported exotics, such as peacocks.

The service is impeccable, the food ambrosial, and the atmosphere rich — opulent contrast to the harshness of the surrounding wilderness. But you need only step outside the gates to return to reality.

On three sides the club is surrounded by 492 hectares (1,216 acres) of African bush transformed into the **Mount Kenya Game Ranch**, founded and funded by William Holden and his old friends, Don and Iris Hunt, who still run it.

Among the species kept in the sanctuary are a thriving herd of bongo, as well as the rare albino zebra, eland, oryx and gazelle. Attached to the ranch and open to club visitors is an Animal Orphanage, home to a variety of orphaned species, including cheetah, lion, chimpanzee and camel.

Also on the ranch, set in its own six-hectare (15-acre) reserve is the **William Holden Wildlife Education Centre**, established as a memorial to the film star by the William Holden Foundation with the aim of promoting knowledge and understanding of Kenya's unique wildlife legacy.

Film star Stefanie Powers was the major fundraiser, and other donations came from such people as American President Ronald Reagan.

Another conservation project in the area is the private **Ngare Sergoi Rhino Sanctuary** run by author Anna Mertz on **Lewa Downs Ranch** north of Nanyuki. It is possible to stay there in one of several exclusive, rustic cottages.

Walking or horse-back safaris through this private property are an unparalleled experience. Cuisine is entirely from home-grown produce.

Desert Panorama

From Nanyuki, on the 90-kilometre (55-mile) drive to **Meru,** you first cross the **Sirimon Bridge** (turn right for the Sirimon trail up the mountain), and then drive on to **Timau**, where staff at a trout farm restaurant pull the fish of your choice out of the tank and cook it before your eyes. Not long after this, high on the shoulders of Mount

Above: Exotic swans grace one of Mount Kenya Safari Club's ponds.

Kenya, the horizon drops down to the wastes of the northern semi-deserts far below that seem to roll on into infinity. To reach Meru, however, the road veers south-east over the shoulders of the mountain — with another dramatic change of scenery.

This time the vista is one of fertile, verdant farms, profuse with lush, green banana palms. North-east across the plains stands the rugged silhouette of the volcanic **Nyambene Hills.**

On the mountain slopes high above the town are forests and lakes sacred to the Meru, close kin of the Embu and Kikuyu (see 'The People', Part One). Beneath it, fertile lands blossom with farm produce.

Meru, an unusual town, was founded on timber. Its first enterprises were the timber yards that exploited the indigenous Meru oak — now, like Kenya's wildlife, an endangered species.

Since then, coffee and tea have become important cash crops. Others are pyrethrum, cotton, tobacco, bananas — and *miraa*, the leaf of a small tree which contains a mild amphetamine. It acts as a stimulant and also kills the appetite. The thin, freshly-plucked stems are chewed

monotonously by addicts through the day and often the night. It is a habit which — as yet — has not been prohibited by law.

Miraa grows wild in the Nyambene Hills to the north-east of Meru but so great is the demand that it is now cultivated.

Meru's **National Museum** has an interesting exhibition of Meru prehistory, tribal life, and beekeeping, a traditional agricultural activity of the indigenous people.

Outside the museum, housed in Meru's oldest stone building — the former district commissioner's office — is an exhibition of traditional Meru homesteads and plots filled with typical crops and herbs of the region, including an unusual plant, *mimosa pudica*, which shuts tight when touched. The authentic homestead comes to throbbing life when traditional Meru dances and plays are enacted.

The colourful **market** is another lively place, where stallholders offer a wide range of wares, including traditional domestic utensils, baskets, *miraa* and farm produce.

Meru National Park
Meru, of course, is the base from which to visit the **Meru National Park.** The new

147

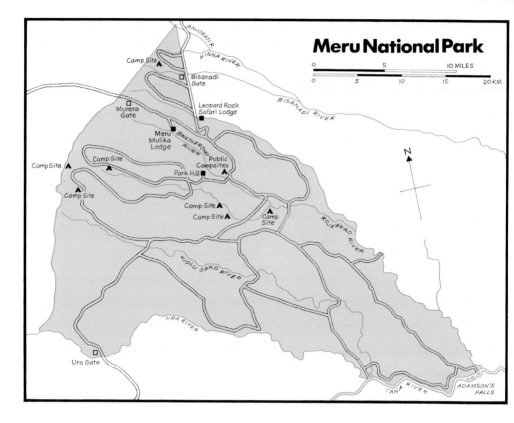

road swoops down Mount Kenya's north-eastern slopes to **Maua**, in the Nyambene Hills, and along a murram track another 30 kilometres (18 miles) to the **Murera Gate**.

Set beneath the slopes of Mount Kenya and covering a total of 870 square kilometres (143 square miles) of contrasting landscapes, wildlife rehabilitation was Meru's main *raison d'étre*. Founded as a reserve in 1959 by Meru District Council, it became a national park in the late 1960s.

The park, one of Kenya's loveliest, is where George and Joy Adamson brought Boy, son of Elsa, to rehabilitate him to the wild and hunting. There, too, Joy trained Pippah the cheetah back to her wild ways.

The park lies east-north-east of Mount Kenya at an altitude of between 366 and 914 metres (1,200-3,000 feet).

The wooded western grasslands form a hilly upland of volcanic rocks drained by 15 permanent streams. The east is an open grassland plain of red lateritic soils drained by three rivers, with considerable sections drying out seasonally. So great is the contrast between these two areas that rainfall in the west of the park is almost double that in the east (see 'National Parks' In Brief, Part Five, for wildlife and vegetation).

One area of the park has been designated a wilderness; no tourists are allowed to enter nor are there any trails to follow. Pippah's grave is marked by a simple cairn in the riverine forest near the **Rojewero confluence,** where the mighty **Tana** boils and bubbles over **Adamson's Falls**, the last of the major rapids and cataracts it encounters before broadening out on its stately journey to the Indian Ocean.

Adamson's Camp

The Tana River, some kilometres downstream, divides the Meru National Park from the **Kora Game Reserve**, once home to George Adamson who, at the age of 83, was murdered on 20 August 1989.

Kora lies at an altitude of between 250 and 440 metres (820-1,445 feet), 125 kilometres (78 miles) east of Mount Kenya and covers 1,787 square kilometres (690 square miles) of acacia bushlands from whose alluvial plains rise granite inselbergs and low hills. Bordered to the south-east by the

Mwitamisyi River, it was established in 1973 (see 'National Parks', In Brief, Part Five for wildlife and vegetation). The rivers support many amphibians, lizards, snakes, tortoises and crocodiles.

A joint Royal Geographical Society and National Museums of Kenya expedition spent 1983 and 1984 studying the flora, fauna and soils of what turned out to be a remarkable ecosystem. Out of this came *Islands in the Bush,* written by expedition leader Malcolm Coe.

When the expedition was about to end, the safari firm of Ker & Downey in Nairobi — founded by Syd Downey and Donald Ker, two famous white hunters turned conservationists — appealed for funds to help protect Kora.

The organizers also placed a brass **memorial plaque** in one of the inselbergs near a waterhole to commemorate the founding partners and their friend, Kenyan hotelier Jack Block.

Adjacent to Meru's north-east boundary is **Bisanadi National Reserve**, 606 square kilometres (233 square miles) of dry, open plain dissected by seasonally dry luggas, set at an altitude of between 320 and 660 metres (1,050-3,165 feet). This mainly thorny bushland and thicket merges into wooded grasslands with dense riverine forests of doum and raffia palm along the watercourses.

During the rains, Bisanadi serves as a vital dispersal area for wildlife from the Meru National Park, primarily elephant and buffalo. There are no visitor facilities. The reserve's eastern boundary is joined to the Kora National Reserve, while Kora's boundary in the south is formed by the **North Kitui National Reserve** and in the north-east by the **Rahole National Reserve.**

Rahole, a lowland sanctuary, covers 1,270 square kilometres (490 square miles) of as yet unsurveyed dry thorn bushland frequented by elephant, Grevy's zebra and beisa oryx.

The North Kitui National Reserve covers 745 square kilometres (290 square miles) of dense bushland, with low hills and seasonal watercourses, along the south bank of the Tana River, which demarcates 20 kilometres (twelve miles) of the northern boundary. The super-surfaced tarmac from **Meru** to **Embu** — on which speeding is a temptation — sweeps along the eastern slopes of Mount Kenya. Midway between the mountain to the west and the Tana River to the east, it crosses the Mariara, Iraru, Mutonga, Tungu, Naka, Rugutu and Thuchi rivers. Completed in 1983 by British engineers, it links Meru to mainstream Kenya.

Above Embu, flashing through the thick forest in their haste to greet the Tana, are some of Kenya's finest fly-fishing rivers. Not for nothing is Embu's timbered, cottage-style hostelry known as the **Isaak Walton Inn,** named after the grand 17th-century patron of English anglers who wrote *The Compleat Angler.* He would have delighted in the fat river bounty and forest landscapes above Embu.

There's not much in the town, however, to excite the visitor, although an avenue of jacaranda beautifies the road between the **Institute of Agriculture** and the Inn, and the **District Hospital** and the Catholic **Church of St Mary Assumption.** The main road drops between Embu's **State House** and the **Police** and **Eastern Province Headquarters,** in front of which is a flat-topped pyramid, the town's **Uhuru Monument** complete with *bas-relief.*

Some distance beyond Embu a smooth road leads south-west towards Nairobi, cutting through the 68-square-kilometre (26-square-mile) **Mwea National Reserve**, a flush of brilliant-green rice paddies, irrigated by the waters of the Tana, where wildfowling is allowed by permit, before joining the Nyeri-Nairobi road just after Sagana.

Only 100 kilometres (60 miles) north-east of Nairobi, at an altitude of around 1,000 metres (3,300 feet), Mwea's southern border is formed by the **Kamburu Reservoir** on the Tana River. In the 1980s, work was completed on the seventh project along its upper reaches. A previous scheme — on the Sagana road — created a lake 40 kilometres (25 miles) long, which is used for fish farming and as a waterfowl reserve, and may be developed as a marina.

The first hydroelectric plant, at **Kindaruma,** destroyed forever the spectacle of Seven Forks — named after the seven rivers which merged into the Tana — that plunged 137 metres (450 feet) in a roaring torrent of untapped power.

149

Western Kenya: The Source of the Nile

Western Kenya is the most populous and productive region of Kenya, but the least visited. Yet were it not for the allure of 'easy option, pre-arranged package safaris' to the coral coast and the game-rich savannahs in the north and south, undoubtedly it would be a prime tourist destination.

Its remarkable and contrasting landscapes range from silver, palm-studded flatlands bordering the eastern side of Africa's largest lake, sandy lake shores, lush hills and valleys, productive farming lands and the only tropical rainforest in East Africa, with its endemic animal and bird life.

Few inland seas measure up to Lake Victoria's proportions. Its 68,800-square-kilometre (26,563-square-mile) surface — of which Kenya claims only 3,785 square kilometres (1,461 square miles) — makes it the world's second-largest freshwater lake, and the third largest of all, exceeded in size only by the Caspian Sea and Lake Superior.

It creates a unique climate. As the sun sucks out the water, the clouds that form meet the cold air streaming from the mountain ramparts that surround the lake, resulting in heavy and consistent rainfall — particularly on the **Mau** massif, which lies on its eastern shores and is the centre of Kenya's tea-growing industry.

The densely populated region is dominated by the Luo all around the **Nyanza Gulf**, the Bantu-speaking Luhya north of **Kisumu** and the Gusii in the **Kisii Highlands**, south-east of **Homa Bay**.

Getting there

As the fish eagle flies, it's just 95 kilometres (60 miles) from the Mau, the region's eastern border massif that rises up to 3,098 metres (10,165 feet), to **Kisumu** on the shores of a deep gulf of Lake Victoria. This may be brief in distance, but in terms of contrasts, it's a long journey through many different worlds.

Where to stay

In Kericho, Tea Hotel (4-star). In Kisii, Kisii Hotel (2-star). In Homa Bay, Homa Bay Hotel (3-star). In Kisumu, Hotel Cassanova (budget); Imperial Hotel (2-star); Lake View Hotel (budget); New Kisumu Hotel (3-star); Sunset Hotel (4-star). On Mfangano Island, Mfangano Island Camp (5-star). In Kapsabet, Kapsabet Hotel (rustic charm, comfortable). In Kakamega, Golf Hotel (4-star). In Bungoma, Bungoma Tourist Hotel (4-star). See Listings for other hotels.

Sightseeing

The highway from **Nakuru** rolls up the hills towards the **Uasin Gishu Plateau** with a left turn to **Molo** and **Londiani**. From there it continues 110 kilometres (68 miles) through a rolling swathe of tea bushes and over the crest of the delightful **Mau Summit**, to **Kericho**, tea capital of Kenya which is the world's third-largest tea producer.

At first the road climbs about 910 metres (3,000 feet) in just 60 kilometres (40 miles) through fertile hills, where the land is ideal for farming and sheep rearing.

The first place you pass is the handsome pasture-land around **Njoro**, the rambling farm town where Delamere established his first Kenya estate, some 18 kilometres (11 miles) from Nakuru. The region is noted for its excellent cheeses. A left fork at Njoro leads across the **Nderit River** and up the south-eastern face of the Mau Escarpment.

The road follows a route often blazed by drivers in the Safari Rally, above the **Lake Nakuru National Park** and Naivasha, on to the summit's highest point, 3,098-metre-high (10,164 feet) **Melily**, to the capital of **Mau Narok** in the south-west. In the 1950s Mau Narok was the focus of a European settlement scheme which has since been taken over by indigenous Kenyans. Smallholdings have sprung up everywhere.

The dirt road then winds on through thick forest to **Enangipiri**. Many narrow forest trails and byways lead off the road along this massif, including one precipitous path to the ridge of brooding **Opuru**, which rises 2,854 metres (9,365 feet), and looks down on Lake Naivasha. Settlement and development are taking their toll on the primal forests on these heights. Where podocarpus and cedar once spread their roots, now wheat and barley stretch as far as the eye can see. Above the wheat fields, more forest has been cleared for potatoes. Damp, chill mists and rich soil nourish their growth.

For thousands of years these forests have been home to the Okiek, a small group of hunter-gatherers, known to the Maasai as the *il Torrobo*, Anglicized into Dorobo (see 'The People', Part One). The Okiek claim ancestral ownership of much of the Mau forest.

At the escarpment's edge, the forest stops and the walls plunge down — as does the bone-shaking murram trail — past **Mathera** with its very English-style church.

Southward, the Mau slopes down to **Narok,** gateway to the Maasai Mara and district headquarters of western Maasailand (see 'Southern Kenya: Theatres of the Wild').

West from Njoro, the main road follows the folds and contours of the gentle hills, through dales and downs, to **Elburgon**, 38 kilometres (24 miles) from Nakuru. Another 13 kilometres (eight miles) from Elburgon is **Molo,** where the evergreen grass feeds the finest sheep in the country. Molo lamb is the quintessence of Kenya's European home-cooking.

A timbered **roundhouse theatre** marks the brief tenancy of the European settlers, who also shaped the highest **golf course** in the Commonwealth — 2,440-2,590 metres (8,000-8,500 feet) — at the Highlands Hotel.

Nothing exemplifies the British capacity for nostalgia better than this half-timbered rustic hostelry complete with skittle alley. It could have been transposed straight from a 15th-century Elizabethan English village.

A few kilometres beyond Molo, the road crests 2,650 metres (8,700 feet) at its highest point. All along the great ridge, the landscape and climate is temperate and gentle — idyllic counterpoint to the harsh heat and wildlife of the savannahs and deserts.

From the summit, this great massif slopes gently down 1,830 metres (6,000 feet) to the lush, humid shores of Lake Victoria. The road bypasses **Londiani**, just 12 kilometres (7.5 miles) beyond Molo, where straggling streets of timber and stone houses, rolling fields and wooded copses, make up this sleepy rural retreat of less

than 4,000 inhabitants. Far from the hectic bustle and noise of Nairobi, the air there is as cool and exhilarating as a glass of champagne. When the railway was built at the turn of the century it required 27 viaducts to ascend the east face of the Mau. So pure is the air of the Mau highlands that the first lick of paint on these viaducts weathered until 1967 before they needed another coat.

In 1899, Sir Harry Johnston, a Special Commissioner for Uganda, visited the Mau's tranquil meadows and forests. So entranced was he that, with the same kind of nostalgia so evident at Molo, he declared Londiani would be the future capital of British East Africa — which then included Uganda. Later, however, it was discovered that the site was liable to flooding, and so another site, Njoro, was chosen. That, too, never came into existence as a capital.

The Mau range forms part of a great mountain amphitheatre that steps down, in tiers, to the lush plains of Kenya's western sugarbowl and the shores of Lake Victoria.

The old trail from Londiani, the nearest station to Kericho, cuts through what were the thick forest lands of the Okiek hunter-gatherers. During the first two decades of this century, the ancient forests were felled and the hardy tea bush took firm root.

The Londiani trail more or less follows the railway's descent to the Nyando Plains, cutting through **Fort Ternan** where a European farmer experimented with biogas during the late 1930s. So successful was this that, during World War II, he converted his car to methane gas. Fort Ternan was founded by a European pioneer in 1897. It is a rich fossil site first excavated in 1961, when animal fossils 14 million years old were revealed.

Beyond lies **Muhoroni,** sugar capital of western Kenya, where Lord Kitchener retired to farm in 1910, where Kenya's 1988 Olympic team manager, Joshua Okuthe, also now has a farm. Beyond that, well past **Kericho,** the road rejoins the main Nakuru-Kericho-Kisumu road. Above the western Mau, Kericho, 40 kilometres (25 miles) from Londiani, is almost always marked by bright, sunny mornings, but nearly every day in the late afternoon lightning flashes and thunder rumbles.

Such equal amounts of rain and sunshine combine with the rich loams of these

Above: Sheep on Kenya's highland meadowlands.

hills to make Kericho, Kisii and the Nandi Hills the most perfect tea growing region in the world. Kericho's high plateau and gentle hills are covered with a mantle of brilliant green. Plantations established as long ago as the 1920s still yield prolific, high-quality harvests. Kenya tea has earned a reputation as the *crème de la crème* of all teas, and fetches premium prices at the regular tea auctions.

Immaculately maintained, the curves, rhomboids, cubes, and triangles of these plantations, intercut with roads, create an astonishing panorama of manicured nature.

Unlike coffee, which left wild is a tree which grows to giant heights and soon becomes jungle, tea is a bush. But the strong roots serve the same purpose as the forests, binding the soil together and the thick green foliage encourages precipitation, so helping the environment to remain stable.

Westward Ho!
Kericho's first tea bush was planted in 1906 by the then acting district commissioner. The years 1916 and 1919 saw one estate and two nurseries established and large-

scale planting began around 1924. By 1932 over 12,000 acres were under cultivation.

As befits the country's tea capital, Kericho, one of the tidiest towns in Kenya, is laid out around a compact square in neat patterns that reflect the ordered geometry of the tea plantations.

Two of the town's landmarks were built in 1952: the **Tea Hotel** and the **Holy Trinity Church,** complete with clinging ivy on the tower, which looks like an import from the English shires.

The Tea Hotel is happy to organize three-hour tours of the surrounding nurseries, plantations, and the **Tea Research Institute** for interested guests. There's a first-class company-run **hospital, airstrip,** one of Kenya's loveliest golf courses at the **Kericho Club,** and a **Kericho-Sotik Fishing Association.** The forest streams in the Mau offer some of Kenya's finest, and least exploited, fly-fishing and, in the comfortable **Tea Hotel,** a river map highlights the best beats.

Kericho also has a **village green** and a **war memorial,** inscribed in the vernacular for 'We Will Remember Them', which commemorates the Kipsigis who fell in the two world wars in service of a king and empire that held them in bondage.

Aside from tea, you can also visit a Trappist monk community at the **Lumbwa Monastery** near **Kipkelion,** some 40 kilometres (25 miles) from Kericho. South-west of Kericho the road drops down the escarpment as it rises and falls over the hills, to curve south, around great bends that sweep through fertile farmland lush with sugar-cane, maize, and banana groves for 98 kilometres (60 miles) to **Kisii.** The landscape is a living, pastoral canvas, worthy of the great masters. After you pass through **Kapsuser, Chemosit** and **Litein,** the road forks just beyond **Kapkatet.** The fork is south-east along a rough and rugged trail that heads around the southern slopes of the Mau to the bustling farm town of **Bomet.** Finally it crosses over the barrier of the **Soit Olol Escarpment** and drops down to **Ngorengore** and **Ewaso Ngiro**, whence you can either travel on to Narok or turn on to the Maasai Mara trail.

Back on the Kisii road, a few kilometres beyond this fork, is **Sotik**, 53 kilometres (33 miles) from Kericho. The area around this small, sleepy town, which has a **hospital** and a **petrol station**, at 1,830 metres (6,000 feet) must be among the most beautiful and least visited in Kenya.

Soapstone cultures

Forty-five kilometres (28 miles) beyond Sotik, the road veers west into **Kisii,** centre of the Abagusii people, Kenya's most fecund community, as fertile as the lands they till for bananas, vegetables and fruit. Along with the Luhya, their Bantu kin who occupy the lower slopes of the Nandi Hills, the Abagusii community has one of the highest birthrates in the world. It's well above the national average of four per cent. Indeed, from a figure of one million in the 1979 population census, their numbers in this century's last decade have escalated dramatically.

A sadder statistic is the price that the Abagusii pay for living where they do. No region in Africa is so prone to lightning strikes as these seemingly innocent hills. In the 1980s more than 20 schoolchildren were killed after a lightning flash struck the tin roof of their classroom.

At the turn of the century, European administrators and settlers, with their alien ideas of law and order, enraged the Abagusii community (see 'History: The Dust and the Ashes', Part One). Defying British imperial might, they massed an army of spearsmen to defend their interests — only to hurl themselves at the rotating barrels of a Gatling gun and be scythed down in their hundreds. In 1908, after a British official was speared, more massacres took place. As the Abagusii fled, they were mown down, and their villages and fields razed. Fresh from his African journey, Churchill was appalled. He cabled from Whitehall questioning the need to kill defenceless people on such 'an enormous scale'.

Although the British behaviour left Abagusii society in shreds, no traces of bitterness remain. The Abagusii surely rank among the friendliest of people in a country where every community gives stranger and guest equal friendship and hospitality. The Abagusii have long been the most artistic of Kenyan ethnic groups. One of sculptor Elkana Ongesa's masterpieces, carved from the malleable pink and white soap-stone quarried out of these hills, adorns the UNESCO headquarters in Paris.

Sightseeing

Kisii is 98 kilometres (60 miles) from Kericho and straggles down a steep hillside. It is a bustling, entrepreneurial town where trader and farmer vie with one another in their nonstop enterprise. It boasts many **hotels,** a **hospital, sports stadium** and **light industrial estate,** and continues to develop at an astonishing pace.

A few kilometres south of Kisii, the soapstone quarries around the village of **Tabaka** provide almost the entire world with this fine, elegant, delicately-hued sculpting material. White is the softest, rich roseate the hardest. Wherever you go around Tabaka, families are busy crafting chess pieces, eggs, bowls, ashtrays, wine glasses, candlesticks and more.

Just five kilometres (three miles) out of town, along a road north-west from the main road, stands **Manga Ridge**, a sheer

Overleaf: Fishing canoes on a Lake Victoria shore.

escarpment which falls almost 305 metres (1,000 feet) and offers breathtaking views of Lake Victoria. To the south of Kisii you will find some of Kenya's most rewarding but least-visited landscapes and cultures.

For the adventurous, the winding road south-east leads some 50 kilometres (30 miles) to **Kilgoris**, at the base of 2,060 metre (6,760-foot) **Olasaayiet**. From this point, intrepid travellers may try the often impassable dirt road over the **Soit Olol Escarpment** to **Lolgorien** and then on to the Maasai Mara.

Most people, however, remain on the main road to fast-developing **Migori**. From Migori (all bustle and touts) a good road leads through the **border post** at **Isebania**, the least fussy crossing point between Kenya and Tanzania, to **Mwanza**.

In the high hills around these parts live the Kuria community, made up of 17 clans (see 'The People', Part One). Their lands, like so many, were divided during colonial times by the unconcerned bureaucrats in Europe who sliced up Africa like a loaf of bread. Their closest kin, the Suba fisherfolk, live beneath the Kuria Hills on the shores and islands of Lake Victoria.

Many dusty trails around there lead to remote, unspoilt beaches and fishing villages on the south-eastern shores of Lake Victoria. **Kehancha**, one of the 'undiscovered' pearls of **Lake Victoria**, is reached either from Homa Bay in the north or along the road from Migori to **Suna**, forking right at **Masara** to **Karungu**, a total of about 50 kilometres (30 miles). Situated on the wide sweep of **Karungu Bay**, this fishing village has real atmosphere and a fine beach, although like everywhere else around Lake Victoria, it is humid and malarial.

Rising from **Mungeri Bay**, the 2,270 metre (7,450-foot) **Gwassi Hills**, the highest point in this region, form the western boundary of little-known **Ruma (Lambwe Valley) National Park**.

Ruma National Park

Bound in the north by the volcanic plugs of the **Ruri Hills**, and to the north-west by the **Gembe Hills**, the eastern border of this 120-square-kilometre (46-square-mile) park is the **Kanyamwa Escarpment**. At an altitude of between 1,200 and 1,600 metres (3,940-5250 feet) Lambwe, which boasts

Kenya's only roan antelope, is infested with tsetse fly, making it unfit for human occupation. But though the tsetse are fatal to humans and their herds, wild game flourishes where they live.

The park is about 32 kilometres (20 miles) south of cluttered and untidy **Homa Bay** town along a rough dirt trail strewn with rocks. Despite its unkempt appearance, Homa Bay is the administrative centre of a large area of Nyanza Province.

There is an **airstrip** and one lone **jetty**, but the roads are little more than rough tracks. Kenya Railways' marine division operates regular scheduled steamer services on the lake, but the days when it was possible to take a seven-day luxury cruise around Lake Victoria — 1,134 metres (3,720

Above: Masterpiece in soapstone — by Elkana Ongesa.

feet) above sea level — have long gone. However, the majesty of the lakeside — a fascinating mixture of towering bluffs, great peninsulas and islands — remains to be savoured from the deck of the smaller passenger vessels cruising these busy waterways. Fares are low and timetables are posted at the port jetties.

Take the steamer out of Homa Bay and you'll enter the **Mbita Passage** at the neck of the **Nyanza Gulf** — the long inlet that leads to Kisumu, passing between the mainland and **Rusinga Island**, birthplace of Tom Mboya, who was brutally assassinated in Nairobi on 5 July 1969.

One of Kenya's founding fathers, Mboya was also one of the most outstanding and promising politicians of Africa's first generation of independence statesmen.

He lies buried there, on a rocky windswept shore, in a fine **mausoleum**, containing memorabilia and artefacts devoted to his life's work. There's also a **health clinic** dedicated to the politician's memory. His epitaph, like the man and his career, is an inspiration:

Go and fight like this man
Who fought for mankind's sake
Who died because he fought
Whose battles are still unwon

The cause to which he dedicated his life may have had its very earliest beginnings on Rusinga Island. It was there that Mary Leakey uncovered the crumbling skull of *Proconsul Africanus,* a primitive anthropoid ape that lived on Rusinga three million years ago. Even more outstanding, the earliest fossil remains found on this eroded island date back 17 million years (see 'History: The Dust and the Ashes', Part One).

Rusinga Island has recently become an up-market resort for **sport fishing** enthusiasts keen to pit their skills against giant Nile perch and tiger fish. Serviced boats and accommodation, developed by the Lonrho Group, are sufficiently sophisticated to attract anglers from all over the world. Day flights from the Maasai Mara for a day's fishing are popular. **Mfangano Island** — a centre of pre-history with its ancient rock paintings — was not slow to follow its neighbour's lead to compete with a fleet of boats and luxury accommodation

at **Mfangano Island Camp**. The islanders practise their own form of prehistoric fishing — casting kerosene lamps out from the shore at night and hauling them slowly inshore, luring squirming shoals of *dagga* (a freshwater shrimp and a much-loved delicacy for western Kenyans) to their nets.

North-east of Homa Bay rises the gaunt 1,750-metre (5,745 foot) crown of **Homa Mountain**, beneath which lime is quarried for Kenya's building industry and other manufacturing processes. The mountain is the centrepiece of a great rounded peninsula. Thunderstorms play around its peak and send jagged lightning down to sport upon Victoria's wind-lashed waters.

The lee of Homa Mountain forms the southern shore of **Kendu Bay**, a charming port village where offshore tugs tow barges along the coastline. When their funnels send straight pillars of black smoke into the still air it often heralds a sudden squall.

Just two kilometres from the town is an unusual crater lake, **Simbi**, whose emerald waters are a sea of algae. Of local legend, its source is something of a mystery. Of interest nearby is a breeding ground for the sacred ibis, the distinctive black and white birds once sacred to the Egyptians, but which are now extinct in Egypt.

From Kendu Bay it's a short and pleasant cruise across the wide span of the Nyanza Gulf to **Kisumu.** The ferry passes numerous Luo fishing fleets whose sturdy gaily-decorated canoes and sailing vessels, hand-crafted out of mahogany by the boat builders of the Suba tribe, are a picturesque part of Lake Victoria life.

Most visitors, however, take the tarmac road from Homa Bay to Kendu Bay and then cut east along the Kisumu road to **Oyugis** — famous for its pelicanry. Thousands of the birds nest there in the August-March breeding season.

From Oyugis, the road leads through the fertile sugar belt to Sondu, where a **Catholic mission** produces miniature terracotta sculptures, to **Ahero,** famous for its **heronry** which also lures ibis, cormorants, egrets and storks, and finally arrives at Kisumu, capital of western Kenya and centre of the populous Luo community. Close to three million strong, the Luo range from Homa Bay in the south to **Sio Port** on the Uganda border in the north.

Port Florence

Kisumu stands at the mouth of the **Nyando Valley,** close to where the **Nyando River** empties into Lake Victoria's **Winam** 'head of lake' and, like Nairobi, owes its position to the Uganda Railway.

This is where, on 20 December 1901, Preston triumphantly invited his wife to hammer down the last rail of his five-and-a-half-year engineering odyssey to the great lake.

The railhead was named, briefly, Port Florence — after Florence Whitehouse, wife of the General Manager and Chief Engineer, who had visited the port earlier.

The **rail terminus** is on the jetty where cargoes are loaded for Uganda and Tanzania. As East Africa's major lake port it flourishes with **customs** and **immigration** posts alongside the warehouses.

With a population of close to a million, Kenya's third-largest town is testimony to the dynamic vigour of this still young nation.

Sightseeing

Around Kisumu town, the colourful **market** by the **bus station** is full of fruit and vegetables as well as household items and, of course, fish in every shape and form, dried and fresh. If you are looking for Africana, it is there that locally crafted artefacts, such as animal figurines in stoneware, beaded stools and basketwork, may be found. The **Wananchi Craft Shop** on **Jomo Kenyatta Highway**, a women's cooperative, also sells a wide array of handmade crafts.

The twin minarets of the **Jamia Mosque** — built in 1919 but extended in 1984 — rise above **Otieno Oyoo Street**. There are also some **Hindu temples**, many **Christian churches**, and a **monument** to Archdeacon Owen at the corner of **Kakamega Road** and the road from Kericho.

Many new, white buildings dominate the skyline, but the neat administrative buildings — the town is both a provincial and a district headquarters — are well-marked. There are **cinemas, banks, post offices,** and a 1938 **clocktower** dedicated to the memory of one Kassim Lakha. The **British Council Library** is on **Oginga Odinga Road**. The **Kisumu Museum**, open daily, has fascinating exhibits of mammals, birds,

primates, amphibians, reptiles, fish and crustaceans. The **ethnographic exhibits** are also interesting, especially one devoted to traditional musical instruments. Music and dancing play a precious part in the traditional cultures of almost all the peoples who live around the lake.

Half-a-kilometre (one-third of a mile) beyond the **Yacht Club**, on the lake shore to the south, past the **Sunset Hotel**, is **Hippo Point,** an ideal place to enjoy one of the lake's spectacular sunsets and watch the hippo splashing just offshore. The **restaurant** serves cold beers and snacks and many a pleasant hour can be spent sipping drinks on the terrace.

The small fishing village of **Dunga** on a headland less than half an hour's stroll from **Hippo Point**, gives an insight with its boats, traps, nets and family homes of how fisherfolk eke out a livelihood in this and similar villages all around the lake.

Offshore, some 30 kilometres (20 miles) from Kisumu, on the north side of Winam, is one of Kenya's more recent national parks, the four-square-kilometre (one-and-half-square-mile) **Ndere Island,** which became a sanctuary in 1986.

Way out West

Thirty years after the railhead arrived at Kisumu, an extension began to wind out of town again — to cross the **Equator** at **Maseno** — and cover another 65 kilometres (40 miles) to the busy market town of **Butere**. West of this, the road forks left at **Yala**, a small market town with a railway station. The area is dominated by the malarial flat-lands and swamps of **Siaya District**, covered only with small villages linked by a few minor roads.

It is largely unvisited by tourists but from **Usenge** on the southern flanks of the large **Yala Swamp**, just a few kilometres from the district capital of **Siaya**, you can climb a nearby hill revered in Luo history as the place where the first of their ancestors arrived to settle after their long trek southwards (see 'The People', Part One).

When the Luo first arrived 500 years ago, they clashed with the existing tenants, a Bantu group whom they eventually forced into exile. You'll understand why they chose to stay when you gaze upon the island-studded lake and the lagoon below.

Above: Kenya Railways' passenger-cargo ferry on Lake Victoria.

On the northern flanks of the Yala swamp is **Sio Port**, once called Port Victoria. It was perhaps a fancy of the early rail planners that the line would one day reach there, but it never did. Sio Port is just a small desultory village that serves principally as a ferry point from which to carry lakelanders into Uganda by boat or dugout canoe.

Most visitors, however, will take the road north out of Kisumu, up the **Nyando Escarpment** for the 73-kilometre (45-mile) journey to **Kakamega**, capital of Kenya's Luhya community. After **Chavakali**, which is roughly halfway between the two towns, there's a right turn that climbs up to **Kapsabet,** set at a cool and refreshing 2,100 metres (6,400 feet) through **Kaimosi** and **Koiprak** .

Eighteen kilometres (11 miles) away is **Nandi Hills,** a beautiful farm town with a **hospital** and a **service station.**

Traditional pastoralists, the local Nandi people are skilful cattle farmers. Nandi herds produce more milk than any other district in the country. Tea and milk are in abundance there and, just a few kilometres away, on the Chemelil-Mumias plains be-

low, grows sugarcane, yielding more than 300,000 tons a year. No wonder this western sugarbowl is known as the land of milk and honey.

The contrasts between the two landscapes, separated only by the height of the escarpments, are as sharp and well-defined as the distinctive flavour of Nandi tea.

All is so quiet and peaceful in this rural wonderland it's hard to believe the Nandi were once fearsome and dedicated warriors (see 'The People', Part One). No raiders swarmed down to attack the railway builders as they carved their way to Butere in 1932, but little more than three decades earlier these warriors tormented Preston and his railhead gangs, pillaging the iron tracks for forging weapons, and telegraph wires for crafting copper bracelets.

Nandi distance runners have earned international renown in Olympic arenas as the world's finest. In one brief spell, Henry Rono accumulated an unprecedented four world records in different events.

Like the Tibetan Abominable Snowman, *Yeti*, which roams the Himalaya, the Nandi Bear, *Chemoset*, is said to roam the high for-

159

Above: Luo with conical fish basket trap on shores of Lake Victoria.

ests. Fact or fantasy, it's a story that every so often still makes headlines in the Kenya press. One of Kenya's most beautiful trees, the Nandi flame tree, takes its name from this region (see 'Flora: Forests of Flame, Streets of Mauve', Part Three).

If you return to the main road from Kisumu and continue up the north-western base of the Nandi Escarpment, you arrive at Kakamega, where the trail Sergeant Ellis carved with Captain Sclater across Kenya's backbone, from **Fort Smith** in Kikuyuland, finally reached in 1896.

Unique Forest

As you enter town the mission and Christian presence is very visible. The road passes schools and seminaries before arriving first at the colourful **market** followed by the high-walled prison. The undistinguished **clocktower** in the town centre was raised in 1935 to commemorate the silver jubilee of King George V's reign.

The town's early fame was as the seat of a 'Gold Rush' in the 1930s, when more than a thousand prospectors staked their claims on what proved to be very sparse veins of the precious ore. You still find an occa-

sional hardy local prospecting Kakamega's hillside streams, panning for alluvial treasure and in Nairobi's streets you may meet a smooth-talking confidence trickster who promises that somewhere out there in the west your fortune can be made.

But **Kakamega Forest** is the town's real treasure, a remnant of unbroken equatorial jungle that arched west to east across the continent as recently as four centuries ago and can be found nowhere else in Kenya — or East Africa, for that matter.

To reach this last of Kenya's once magnificent rainforests, take the Kisumu road south of Kakamega for about ten kilometres (six miles) and turn left at the sign opposite the service station. Carry on for seven kilometres (four miles) until you reach the fairly large village of **Shinyalu** and from there follow the route which branches to the right. After another five kilometres (three miles) turn left at the **signpost**.

There are four double bedrooms in the **Forest Rest House,** within the forest reserve, to which you should take your own food. Small and remote, it has a pleasantly quiet and friendly ambience. For a small fee, an informed resident guide will, if required, conduct you on a forest tour, surprising you with his knowledge of the birds, beasts and reptiles which make the forest their home.

Finally gazetted as a national reserve in 1985, after years of bitter debate, the **Kakamega Forest** covers some 45-square-kilometres (18-square-miles) containing Kenya's rarest arboreal, floral, faunal and avifaunal treasures. Set at an altitude of between 1,520 and 1,680 metres (4,990-5,512 feet), the hilly terrain is also scattered with seasonal swamps.

There are two major rivers, the **Isiukhu** in the north and the **Yala** in the south. These support the easternmost area of its rainforest, interspersed with grassy glades. More than 125 tree species, each averaging around 35 metres (115 feet) in height, have been identified.

Around 20 per cent of the amphibians, reptiles, birds and mammals found in this reserve occur nowhere else in Kenya.

They include bush-tailed porcupine, giant water shrew, hammer-headed fruit bat and numerous bird species.

Among the reptiles are some particularly venomous snakes, including the fat and sluggish Gabon viper. And among the primates, which include colobus and blue monkey, are high-living arboreal pottos — creatures that are active only at night (see 'Wildlife: Great and Small, Wild and Wonderful', Part Three).

The forest is also home to one of the most fascinating of all Kenya's animals — the scalytailed flying squirrel. It belongs to the peculiar group of Anomalurus rodents, now extinct outside Africa, and can 'fly' as far as 90 metres (300 feet).

Besides these two rarities, the forest, which is interspersed with open glades and grasslands, hosts abundant monkeys, small antelopes, and a wealth of bird life, including Kenya's only resident parrot population and the great blue turaco, a large, shiny bird about the size of a turkey with plumped-up plumage.

From Kakamega the road climbs for about 60 kilometres (37 miles) through scenic country to **Webuye Falls** to rejoin the 1920s spur of the Uganda Railway, which finally linked Kenya with Uganda. Until the 1970s, nothing much distinguished this place from the thick forests which cloaked the region except the 52-metre (170-foot) **waterfalls** — named after Broderick, an early European visitor to this region.

A few kilometres above the falls, on the escarpment, stands **Chetambe's Fort,** scene of an 1895 massacre by a British punitive expedition against the Bukusu tribe of the Luhya. The warriors, dug in behind a 100-metre (330-feet) moat-like rampart, had only shields for defence and spears for weapons against the fire of the British expedition's Maxim machine gun.

In the 1970s, in an Indo-Kenyan partnership organized by the World Bank, this place was chosen as the site of Kenya's paper milling industry. The falls provide an ideal source of water close to one of Kenya's great logging regions.

But in April 1996 the mill's 4,000-strong workforce woke up to find that much of the paper mill and offices had been burnt to the ground in a raging conflagration.

From Webuye the main road from Mombasa to Uganda continues, bumpy and pot-holed, through boulder-studded hills, open grasslands, smallholdings and sugar fields, to **Bungoma,** a prosperous but dull administrative town.

Marking the end of the road in Kenya is **Malaba**, where interminable queues of lorries block both sides of the border. Pedestrians, it appears, cross without difficulty.

Southwards from Webuye Falls you can follow the course of the track up to the high Uasin Gishu plateau to **Leseru.** The town is famous for its cheeses, and the lovely landscapes of the Uasin Gishu and **Trans Nzoia plateau** of north-western Kenya.

Following page: Traditional Luo dancer.

North-West Kenya: Enchanted Mountains, Unspoilt Vistas

With its high and lovely farmland plateaux, north-west Kenya, the country's most extensive and fertile wheat, grain and livestock region, is becoming increasingly popular with tourists. The great bulk of 4,322-metre (14,180-foot) Mount Elgon, the glorious Cherangani Hills, cresting more than 3,350 metres (11,000 feet), unique pristine forests, and game sanctuaries, make this one of Kenya's most spectacular regions. Exploring its many delights makes several rewarding days for any visitor.

Getting there
From Nakuru the Mombasa-Uganda highway takes you to the village of **Equator** and on through **Timboroa** and its great forest cloak to **Eldoret**, a distance of 156 kilometres (97 miles).

In the cool, dark sanctuary of the forest the railway to Uganda reaches the highest point of any line in the Commonwealth, 2,784 metres (9,135 feet), before crossing the Equator at 2,656 metres (8,716 feet) to descend to the high, level plateau of the **Uasin Gishu** and **Trans-Nzoia** farmlands.

But this journey by road or rail through one monotonous belt of conifer forest after another, is basically flat and boring.

For the most enjoyable route, and to really discover 'undiscovered' Kenya, you should turn **south-east** off the main road, on to the minor roads and dirt trails that lead to the south-eastern edge of the **Elgeyo Marakwet escarpment** of the Rift.

Where to stay
In Eldoret, Sirikwa Hotel (4-star). In Kitale, Kitale Club (pricey and somewhat run down colonial baroque). In Kaptagat, Kaptagat Hotel (3-star). In Soy, Soy Country Club. There are others. See Listings for 'Hotels'.

In national parks
Mount Elgon Lodge (3-star), book through Msafiri Inns, Utalii House, Nairobi. There are also three campsites.

Sightseeing
Prosperous farm communities exist in this Kalenjin highland wonderland, with names that seem to snap off the tongue — Kapkut, Kapsabet and Kaptagat. The first turning off the highway is the tarmac road east to **Eldama Ravine**, a sprawling town literally pitched on either side of the steep gorge that gives it its name.

It was one of Britain's first administrative centres at the turn of the century and the first District Commissioner was James Martin, the illiterate aide who joined Thomson on his epic march (see 'History: The Dust and the Ashes', Part One).

West of Eldama Ravine a **minor road** leads around the eastern base of 2,799-metre (9,184-foot) **Kapkut** to **Kamwosor**. There the road forks three ways — west back to the main road, north-west across the railway line (then left to Eldoret) or straight on to **Kapchebelel** and the glittering panorama of **World's End**, one of the most dramatic scarps in the world, and **Nyaru,** where the tarmac ends at the edge of the escarpment.

Great bluffs rise up on either side of the precipitous World's End cliffs. The name is apt. Martial eagles and other raptors circle on the constant thermals that blast up the face of the cliff and across the plateau.

Before you is a void that stuns the senses and clutches at the stomach: awesome and inspiring. Thousands of metres beneath the edge of this dizzying drop unfolds the infinite sweep of the Rift Valley.

Its great eastern wall rises blue-grey in the distance on the other side. Ahead, the valley stretches as far as the eye can see to Lake Bogoria and beyond; through searing heat and dusty desert to Marigat, Baringo, and ultimately to the cataclysmic volcanic cones that mark the southern shores of Lake Turkana. Below the magnificent cliff, **north-east** from Kapchebelel, a road leads to **Chebloch** on the tarmac road from **Kabarnet** to Eldoret. Another alternative is to take the left turn a few kilometres south

Above: Kenya's own Grand Canyon — the deep but narrow divide of the Kerio Valley.

of Eldama Ravine to Saos, under the eastern flanks of Kapkuti, and on to Kabarnet. There's also a turn west, some kilometres before Kabarnet, up the scarp through **Cheplembus** and **Kapkalelwa** to Chebloch.

From there, the smooth Kabarnet road twists and winds through the rapidly-growing towns of **Tambach** and **Iten** on the scarp that forms the southern flanks of the Cherangani Hills. Set at 1,981 metres (6,500 feet), Tambach is 37 kilometres (23 miles) from Kabarnet, and 44 kilometres (27 miles) from Eldoret. Only ten kilometres (six miles) further on, Iten is already pitched another 250 metres (800 feet) higher. Yet despite their development, the towns and the area all around remain unspoilt. It's hard to imagine 20th-century civilization amid these tranquil forests and small villages.

But the capital of this region, Eldoret, is one of Kenya's most modern towns. Surrounded by pines and giant blue gums, and rolling fields of grain and meadow pastures, Eldoret is rapidly expanding with textiles, woollen mills and other industries. Today it's the home of **Moi University,**

built on land donated by the Lonrho group, which runs one of the largest agricultural-based industries in the country.

For years, the **East Africa Tanning Extract Company** (EATEC) has tended many thousands of hectares of wattle trees, extracting tannin for the leather industry and using the trunks as telegraph poles. EATEC also diversified into mushroom farming and charcoal production. Nothing goes to waste on their farm estates.

The old charcoal kilns have been transformed into mushroom sheds. Cattle dung powers a biogas plant, which provides fuel and energy for the staff village of 4,000 people — including street lighting.

Eldoret has hotels of varying standards, ranging from top bracket down to the plain and simple. Lively discos exist at places such as the **New Wagon Wheel**, there is a thriving **sports club**, and a first-class **airport** for domestic and charter operations.

In 1996 a new international airport at Eldoret was close to completion.

To Kitale

From Eldoret to Kitale it is 69 kilometres

(43 miles). Leave the Mombasa-Uganda road where it veers west 22 kilometres (14 miles) from Eldoret, and continue northwest through Soy, four kilometres (two-and-a-half-miles) after the junction.

From Soy the great mass of **Mount Elgon** dominates the horizon as the road continues through **Moi's Bridge,** once known as Hoey's Bridge, and into **Kitale,** which stands at 1,890 metres (6,200 feet).

Avenues of giant blue gums line either side of the road of this charming rustic farm and market centre. **Kitale Station** is a reflection of the graceful days of the leisurely steam travel which inspired it.

Noted for its **fruit orchards,** and as headquarters of the giant **Kenya Seed Company,** Kitale's bracing air and relaxed life style, far from the tensions of metropolitan living, encourage longevity. It became a boom town briefly during Kenya's 1970s coffee bonanza. Ugandan coffee was smuggled across the border on the road that cuts high over the shoulders of **Mount Elgon,** the town's magnificent backdrop.

Kitale arose as a slaving station. It was right on the main caravan route between Uganda and Bagamoyo in Tanzania. The circle of stones in the car park of **Kitale Club** surrounded the ring to which the slaves were chained.

A century or more later, Kitale's business men and farmers meet in the club's bar and at weekends drive the long, lush fairways of the challenging **golf course.**

The **Kitale Museum** (or Museum of Western Kenya), originally the 'Stoneham Museum', was established by an English army officer on his Cherangani farm in 1927. In 1972, it was transferred to Kitale.

The museum contains several interesting exhibits — from agricultural to ethnographic and cultural displays. Adjacent to the museum an additional **hall** houses some striking murals depicting the domestic life of the surrounding tribes — including the Turkana, El Kony, the Nandi, the Pokot, the Marakwet and the Luo. **Laboratories** and a small **craft shop** are recent additions and, outside, there is a tortoise enclosure.

But the streamside **nature trail** of trees (and, therefore, birds, of course), footbridges, and some quite enchanting rustic **picnic sites** was allocated to a developer.

Mountain of the Breast

Covering 169 square kilometres (65 square miles) of montane forest and volcanic craters, the **Mount Elgon National Park** straddles the Uganda border. Founded in 1949, the park itself lies on the eastern flank of this massive volcanic cone, its boundaries some distance beneath the summit.

Ancient beyond comprehension, Elgon feels like a link with the beginning of time. It burst out of the Trans-Nzoia plains more than fifteen million years ago.

The topmost heights form the Kenya-Uganda border, which cuts across the rim and through the centre of the crater. Indeed, **Wagagai,** the highest peak at 4,321 metres (14,176 feet), is on the Uganda side of the crater rim, but the variation between one side of the crater and the other is minimal. **Sudek,** on the Kenya side, rises to 4,310 metres (14,140 feet), just eleven metres (36 feet) lower. For many, however, the favourite is 4,231-metre (13,882-foot) **Koitobos** (Table Rock), a flat-topped basalt peak near the edge of the caldera.

The caldera measures between six and eight kilometres (four to five miles) across, while the base of Mount Elgon is tenfold that at between 80 and 100 kilometres (50-60 miles).

At one point the rim is broken by the **Suam Gorge,** a deep rift forming the main outflow from the crater. Farther down, the **Suam River** joins the **Turkwel River,** which is spawned in the heights of Uganda's **Kadam** mountain and flows on down through Lodwar to the Jade Sea (see 'The Northern Rift: Cradle of Mankind').

Known to the Maasai, whose herds once grazed the Trans-Nzoia, as Ol Doinyo Igoon (Mountain of the Breast), Elgon is still home to a remnant group, the il-Kony (El-Kony), which lives high up its flanks.

The route to the top is generally easy, and the spectacular cliffs, deep valleys, idyllic tarns, hot springs, and excitement of an excursion into Uganda all make Mount Elgon more than worth the climb.

Getting there

The easiest approach to the mountain is from Kitale. Three gates lead into the park, through the bamboo forest into the giant stands of ancient podocarpus, and on to the moorlands. The most popular trail starts at the **Chorlim Gate** off the **Endebess road**. You reach the gate along the dirt road which cuts through the farmlands below. The other gates are approached from **Kimilili**, 50 kilometres (31 miles) west of Kitale, and 81 kilometres (50 miles) from **Kakamega**. With **Webuye** only 20 kilometres (12 miles) away, and **Bungoma** only 16 kilometres (10 miles) distant, these two towns make comfortable bases for climbs from Kimilili.

If you don't have a 4WD vehicle, you can take a *matatu* to **Kapsakwony,** for the Kimilili track, and **Endebess**. The national park road turns left up a well-maintained dirt road just a few kilometres beyond Endebess.

Angling enthusiasts who might wish to avoid the mountain heights should motor on towards **Bukwa** on the Uganda border. Some kilometres before this is one of Kenya's best-kept secrets — the delightful **Suam fishing camp**. Mount Elgon is surrounded by forest, and you should use the motor track to reach the moorland area, although the one from Mbale in Uganda has not been used for many years.

From Kitale it takes about five hours to drive to the Kimilili roadhead — in a low-ratio 4WD vehicle — and some initiative, not all entirely dependent on driving skills, to reach the top.

From Kitale the most used trail is along a well-maintained track through the national park. In dry weather it's possible to reach the roadhead in an ordinary but powerful saloon car. Although the trail is not as scenically rewarding as the Kimilili trail, an extremely pleasant campsite in the lower parkland is an attractive feature of this approach.

When to go
The crater is surprisingly cold and there's usually frost. Snow and hail are common. However, it's possible to climb Elgon at any time of the year, though the rainy seasons of April-May and August-September are best avoided. The best time to visit is between December and March.

Sightseeing
This is one of the loveliest and most un-

spoilt of all Kenya's national parks. If you are fit and hardy enough to labour up the elephant trails through its glorious forests, you can walk its moorland heights for days without meeting another soul, tramping heaths of tussock grass and wild flora, including lobelia and giant groundsel.

Burgeoning under the unique combination of rarefied air, unfiltered ultraviolet rays and freezing nights, these specimens flourish better there than on Mount Kenya or Kilimanjaro.

Different species of game lurk beneath the centuries-old trees that rise for thirty metres (100 feet) or so — clean, straight-stemmed, and crowned with evergreen foliage.

In the glades and dappled undergrowth beneath, the ever-alert, always nervous buck, duiker and other small game pause, frozen in the panic of discovery as great herds of buffalo forage for fodder (see 'National Parks', In Brief, for wildlife and vegetation).

The main peak, **Wagagai**, offers fantastic views of the crater, **Suam Gorge**, the Ugandan side of the mountain, and the distant landscapes below.

It is a seven-to-eight hour round trek from **Lower Elgon Tarn**. There is plenty of water — in the crater near the summit — but no huts. Set at 4,300 metres (14,110 feet), **Lower Elgon** is a subsidiary rocky peak with excellent views of the crater and Lower Elgon Tarn.

The tarn makes a splendid campsite, 12 hours walk from the **Kimilili Track** roadhead. It is probably the best walk on the mountain.

Lower down are a series of 'lava-tube' caves, some of which are more than sixty metres (200 feet) in diameter, set in the high basalt cliffs of the **Endebess Bluffs**. One of these, **Kitum Cave**, was the inspiration for Rider Haggard's great adventure drama, *She*.

It's also been the inspiration for a television documentary about Elgon's elephants which 'mine' the cave's salt by gouging it out during the night from walls deep inside the mountain, sometimes precipitating a roof fall that traps one or two of these great pachyderms.

The approach from Kitale takes the trekker to Kitum Cave.

Above: Groundsel on Kenya's high-altitude Afro-alpine moorlands.

Saiwa Swamp

Twenty kilometres (12 miles) north-east of Kitale, in the **Cherangani Hills**, the **Saiwa Swamp National Park**, whose two square-kilometres (less than one square-mile) form Kenya's smallest game sanctuary, is five kilometres (three miles) to the right off the main **Kitale-Lodwar road**, near the village of **Kipsain**. There's also a smart fishing camp, **Kapolet**, close to the park, and from Kipsain another road leads west to the Suam fishing camp.

Set at 1,870 metres (6,135 feet), in a basin of the meandering **Koitobos River,** filled with tall bulrushes and sedges, the Saiwa Swamp was established principally to protect Kenya's only population of between 80 and 100 sitatunga, a shy aquatic antelope.

Other mammals include monkey, nocturnal potto, spotted-necked otter, giant forest squirrel, leopard and myriad bird-life (see 'Wildlife: Great and Small, Wild and Wonderful', Part Three).

No accommodation or vehicle is allowed, but there is a **campsite**. Saiwa's rare visitors make their way along a jungle path, where black-and-white colobus monkeys swing through the trees, vervets scamper across the ground and you may catch a glimpse of the mandarin-like face of the Brazza monkey, to a wooden **walkway** above the swamp. In the canopy of trees, rare birds flit from perch to perch, including turacos, hornbills and kingfishers.

Viewing platforms are raised above the the swamp, where visitors can watch for their first sight of the sitatunga. Early morning and late afternoon towards sundown are the most likely times to see these rare, shaggy-coated antelopes.

Cherangani Hills: High Peaks and Secret Valleys

The daunting barrier of the dramatic **Cherangani Hills** hides within its forests some of the finest mountain landscapes in the world. It also embraces a place sacred to Kenyan nationalists — the small town of **Kapenguria**, where in the 1950s the colonial government staged the rigged show trial of Mzee Jomo Kenyatta. He was con-

167

Above: Mount Elgon's Kitum Cave inspired Rider Haggard's book, *She*.

victed on perjured and fabricated evidence and sentenced to a seven-year incarceration on the burning shores of Lake Turkana. The schoolroom where the trial was staged is a shrine to the the the nation's founding father and the prison compound and cell where he was held is a **national monument**. The Cherangani range rises to 3,517 metres (11,540 feet) at the northern end of the **Elgeyo Marakwet Escarpment** and in places falls 2,400 metres (8,000 feet) to the baking floor of the **Kerio Valley**, gateway to the deserts of Kenya's north.

Although the Cheranganis boast the fourth-highest point in Kenya — and one of the highest points in all Africa — surprisingly they are rarely visited.

Yet they offer some of the most diverse and splendid mountain landscapes found anywhere — from gently rolling foothills to large and rugged peaks, from thick forest to open moorland with a wealth of Afro-alpine flora — and perhaps the deepest and most precipitous escarpment in Africa.

After the highest-point, 3,517-metre (11,540-foot) **Nagen,** other major peaks are **Sigogowa,** 3,327 metres (10,915 feet); **Koh,**

2,745 metres (9,000 feet); **Morobus,** 2,269 metres (7,445 feet); **Kaipos,** 2,362 metres (7,750 feet); **Kaibwibich,** 2,689 metres (8,823 feet); **Kalelaigelat,** 3,380 metres (11,090 feet); **Tavach,** 3,298 metres (10,821 feet); **Chepkotet,** 3,370 metres (11,057 feet); and **Sondang,** 3,216 metres (10,543 feet).

But this is not all. There are **Chemnirot,** 3,355 metres (11,000 feet); **Chesugo,** 3,080 metres (10,110 feet); **Nongwasha,** 3,355 metres (11,000 feet); **Kapsiliat,** 2,604 metres (8,544 feet); and **Kaisungur,** 3,167 metres (10,390 feet). You can drive almost all the way to the top of some peaks, but others involve strenuous, high-altitude trekking. Indeed, the Cheranganis offer some of the best hill walking in Kenya — neither too hot nor too cold and with none of the giant tussock grasses that are found on the Aberdares, Mount Elgon and Kenya.

The northern end of the range, which is the higher, gives the best walking. In the south the hills are either cloaked in dense forest or thickly populated, and the eastern slopes, near the escarpment, which are the most densely settled, are generally not so appealing. It's worth noting that the drive to some of the roadheads, especially those that serve Nagen, Tavach, Chemnirot and Sondang, is extremely long and walking any distance above 3,000 metres (10,000 feet) without acclimatization is exhausting (see 'Climbing and Trekking Advisory'). A visit to the Cheranganis, therefore, may be more tiring than you expect.

Getting there
Kitale in the north and Eldoret in the south are the two main bases from which to explore the Cheranganis. The main northern access to the high peaks is the **Cherangani Highway,** starting near Kapenguria and running through **Labot** to **Iten.**

Matatus ply this route and — from **Cheptongei** to Chesoi (but not beyond) — make it possible to reach the area by public transport. This means long but pleasant walks to the base of the main peaks. Two rather long and indirect approaches take in some of the finest mountain roads in the country, well worth the travel for their own sake. They both pass through the **Kito Pass,** up the **Tot Escarpment** and off the **Kapenguria-Marich Pass.** The first, from **Chesongoch** to **Chesoi,** brings you from the Kerio Valley up the Tot Escarpment on a splendid, if extremely rough, mountain road with breathtaking views over the Kerio Valley to the Tugen Hills.

Suitable **campsites** can be found by leaving **Kapsowar** on the **Cheptongei road** and camping in clearings in the forest, at the bottom of the valley just outside town. The perpendicular slopes above are dotted with distinctive stone-built Marakwet homesteads. The escarpment itself is the location of an interesting 400-year-old irrigation system. At a time when such utilization of natural resources was commonplace in the northern hemisphere, it was unique as a concept in this part of Africa.

Some 40 kilometres (25 miles) of canals, trenches and aqueducts disperse waters from the rivulets of the Cheranganis to plots all along and down the escarpment, where the rewards are obvious. At **Chesoi,** it is still possible to see a metre-wide (three foot) channel irrigating magnificently productive land (see 'The People', Part One).

The second route takes a turn off the **Kapenguria-Marich Pass** road to pass along a valley of Himalayan proportions.

Steep in places, this road eventually joins the Cherangani Highway at **Mbanga,** some way north of Labot. There are many good camping spots on the southern section.

It also serves as a first-class shortcut for anyone travelling on to **Lodwar** from Kalelaigelat (see 'The North Rift: Cradle of Mankind'). For the road via the Kito Pass and the Tot Escarpment, head north from **Baringo** to **Loruk,** where the tarmac ends and the **Maralal road** branches right.

From there, go through **Nginyang** and then bear right at the first fork where a sign to the **post office** points left. The road now deteriorates and climbs up through the Kito Pass to cross the floor of the Kerio Valley to Tot. At the T-junction, turn left to **Chesongoch.** Continue straight through the village and turn right shortly after, on to a steep track that climbs continuously to Chesoi, high on the escarpment — one of Kenya's most spectacular roads.

The scenery changes dramatically where the road enters the foothills and forest of the main Cheranganis. You can bypass Chesoi Centre by continuing straight ahead to **Kapsowar,** a two-hour drive from Tot. Or you can bear right to **Cheptongei,** another two-hour drive. In the middle of the town a right turn takes you on to the Cherangani Highway.

The quickest route to the more southerly peaks, up to Nagen and Chemnirot, is via Eldoret and Iten. The road out of Eldoret, not signposted, begins with a right turn out of the **Sirikwa Hotel** car park followed by a left turn at the first intersection, past the **airport,** and onwards to link up with the tarmac road to **Iten.**

At Iten, turn left along a dirt road at the **signpost** for 13 kilometres (eight miles) to **Singore,** where the road swings left. After just over a kilometre (two-thirds of a mile) take the right turn north — for 22 kilometres (14 miles) — to **Cheptongei.** In the middle of the village, there's a left turn on to the Cherangani Highway. Note that some villages are so small that you miss them if you blink.

The northern approach, via **Kapenguria,** suitable for the northern peaks, is reached from Kitale along the fast tarmac road to Kapenguria. Beyond Kapenguria take a right turn, signposted **Kaibwibich** and Labot, on to the Cherangani Highway. The

Above: Scenic valley floor in the high Cheranganis.

most direct approach into the central Cheranganis is via **Cherangani Town**, turning east off the Eldoret-Kitale road at **Moi's Bridge** — or along the road from Kitale to Cherangani Town where a road leads up to the crossroads at **Labot.**

The only petrol stations are at Baringo, Kitale, Eldoret, and Kapenguria, and you should allow for increased fuel consumption because of the altitude and the rough state of some tracks. The Cherangani Highway is suitable for two-wheel-drive vehicles, apart from one rough section between Kaibwibich and Kapenguria. But note that most tracks off the highway are often completely impassable in wet weather and generally require 4WD. Other roads have been much improved, and some are so rarely used they are generally grassy and not muddy.

Sightseeing

Sigogowa (or Mtelo Mountain or Sekerr) is an excellent viewpoint. This huge mountain, which stands alone to the north, is not representative of the Cheranganis. It is best approached from the thornbush scrub of the Turkana plains and up the barren and rugged lower slopes of the mountain to a lush green 'lost world' valley inhabited by the Pokot people (see 'The People', Part One).

From Kitale follow what is possibly Kenya's most spectacular tarmac road to **Akeriamet**, at the foot of the Marich pass.

Beyond Akeriamet, several tracks lead off left to meet up at a concrete road that climbs a steep ridge to the **radio relay station.** From the first turnoff you need 4WD. Continue on a rough dirt track past the relay station to the roadhead at **Mbara.** From Kitale this drive takes between three and four hours.

Situated on a northern spur of the Cheranganis, slightly separate from the main body, **Koh** culminates in **Koh Boss**, a spectacular rock mass which has superb views. It's reached from a point near the **Weiwei River**, along the Sigor-Tot Road, where you take the track south to **Tamkal.** About three kilometres (two miles) before Tamkal, a path leads up to Koh. **Morobus**, a small but striking peak close to the Lodwar road between Kapenguria and the

170

Marich Pass, is immediately obvious once you begin the long, long descent from Kapenguria. Its craggy west face and steep south ridge are stunningly prominent. From Kitale follow the Lodwar road for about one hour until you reach a convenient stopping point to the north of the hill.

Although it's not particularly impressive as mountains go, **Kaibwibich** does give a spectacular panorama of its distant neighbours **Elgon** and Uganda's **Kadam** — and also the high Cheranganis. The nearby **rest house**, a little too remote from the main peak to be a good base, nonetheless, stands in beautiful surroundings. You need permission from the DC's office in Kapenguria to use it. The keys are held at the **chief's office** in Kaibwibich village.

Take the Cherangani Highway southeast from Kapenguria to the village. Turn right up the track signposted 'Rest House' and turn left after 400 metres (less than quarter-of-a-mile) to the top of the hill. During the dry season it is usually possible to drive right up to the **trig point** in a saloon car, but most will find it more convenient to walk the last 70 metres (230 feet) to save opening the gate.

Right in the heart of the Cheranganis, **Kalelaigelat** provides considerable sport for drivers, if not walkers, and one approach passes through delightful scenery. It has a different ambience from most — probably due to its bleak moorlands and surprisingly scanty forest. Sunrise from the summit, with views over the Trans-Nzoia, is spectacular.

It makes a convenient and easy peak to climb for those en route to **Sondang** or **Tavach**, and it is worth the detour for those returning from Nagen. The immediate vicinity is too exposed for good camping, but there are plenty of spots on the track north to Sondang. The first approach is to take the Cherangani Highway to the crossroads before Labot and then the right turn bypassing Labot to **Tangul**. There are several nice campsites in this section.

Turn left at Tangul for eight kilometres (five miles) along a well maintained rural access road to Kalelaigelat. The last section is short but unbelievably steep. You should allow about four hours for the drive from Eldoret. The second approach also starts along the Cherangani Highway, from

Kapenguria. After 35 kilometres (22 miles), take a left turn on to another rural access road at **Mbanga** through beautiful open parkland with several fine camping spots. After 14 kilometres (nine miles), turn right on to a poor 4WD track — not only extremely rough but unbelievably steep.

If you continue along the rural access road from this turnoff for another three kilometres (two miles) you arrive at the junction with the first approach. Continue for another 42 kilometres (26 miles) along one of Kenya's most spectacular roads to join the Marich Pass tarmac road. Well-maintained, the road winds up and down through a valley that would not disgrace the foothills of the Himalaya. There are splendid views of Sigogowa and Sondang.

The other end of this road is 43 kilometres (27 miles) north of the turnoff to **Saiwa Swamp National Park**, which is signposted **Kapchemogon**.

Tavach, a pleasant peak situated on a spur to the west of the main Cheranganis, offers marvellous scenic panoramas. Camping spots can be found alongside the approach road. From Kalelaigelat to Sondang, the final track gives a great feeling of passing through an untravelled world. From the summit of Kalelaigelat proceed north along the Sondang track east of a deep valley. (Another of the high peaks, **Chepkotet**, lies north-east a short walk to the west).

After about ten kilometres (six miles) you come to a small village where a fairly passable track comes in from the left. You can't miss Tavach from this point. It sits on a spur about two kilometres (little more than a mile) distant, but if you want to drive you'll definitely need 4WD. Sondang marks the end of the major spur of this part of the Cheranganis, above a steep westerly scarp with another to the east — one of the most memorable of these fine hills.

From the summit of Kalelaigelat, make your way north towards Tavach until you reach the end of the extremely rough track. Although it is only about 20 kilometres (12 miles), allow two hours.

Nagen, which is the highest point in the Cheranganis, is irresistible to all who visit the area and takes you right into the heart of the range through exquisitely varied scenery. At the top you are rewarded with stunning views of the **Weiwei Valley.** If

171

you allow enough time you can also take in Chemnirot — possibly some of the other peaks. There are two popular routes: one through parkland and woodland with splendid glades for camping, the other much longer. Drive on to Tangul, as if approaching Kalelaigelat, and then follow the signposted route straight on through Tangul to Kamelogon.

In a 4WD vehicle, which should also have high clearance, it takes about two hours to the roadhead, which is about 13 kilometres (eight miles) from Tangul. A long wheelbase, however, may pose some difficulties on the tight bends higher up. It is easy to lose the track at several points and there is one particularly weak bridge and several other poor ones.

An ascent of **Kaisungur** is easier, a relatively simple walk along a high ridge overlooking the central Cheranganis and the Trans-Nzoia farmfields — Kaisungur can also be easily climbed on the approach to Nagen from **Cheptongei**. The area to the north of Kaisungur, much less inhabited than that to the south, offers a refreshing sight.

Follow the Cherangani Highway for 24 kilometres (15 miles) from Cheptongei where it skirts the eastern flank of the hill. An obvious rough track leads steeply up to a **radio station.** Nongwasha, sometimes spelt Longoswa, is a forested mountain six kilometres (four miles) north-west of Chesoi, but you'll probably need a local guide to show you the way.

To climb **Kipkunur,** which lies along the west ridge of Kapsowar with a number of impressive cliffs, you have to walk from the road, somewhere between Labot and Kapsowar, and then through thick, well-cultivated smallholdings and forest.

A short walk up one of the most southerly outliers of this range, **Chemurkoi** is rewarded by compelling panoramas in all directions.

Follow the Cherangani Highway northwest from Cheptongei past **Kipnai Market** and a **school** for twenty kilometres (13 miles) to the start of another rural access road that heads south. Follow this new road for 62 kilometres (39 miles) until, just before a bend to the right, a rough track on the left, bears away over open grassland to a hut about one kilometre (two-thirds of a mile) from the road.

Another ingress is a left turn off the Iten road 20 kilometres (13 miles) out of Eldoret to **Moiben** and **Chebororwa.** Opposite the **chief's office** there's a right turn along a steep and winding road through thick forest to the north of the hill. Neighbouring **Kapsiliat,** north of Iten, also offers splendid panoramas.

Twenty-five kilometres (16 miles) after leaving the tarmac at Iten, just before **Chiebiemet,** take the left turn on to a small track for one kilometre (two-thirds of a mile), then cross a bridge and climb for another kilometre before taking a right fork followed by a left turn on to a parallel track, with a final turn left to a parking spot beyond some estate buildings.

Opposite: Tendrils of cloud caress the high points of the lovely Tugen Hills.

172

173

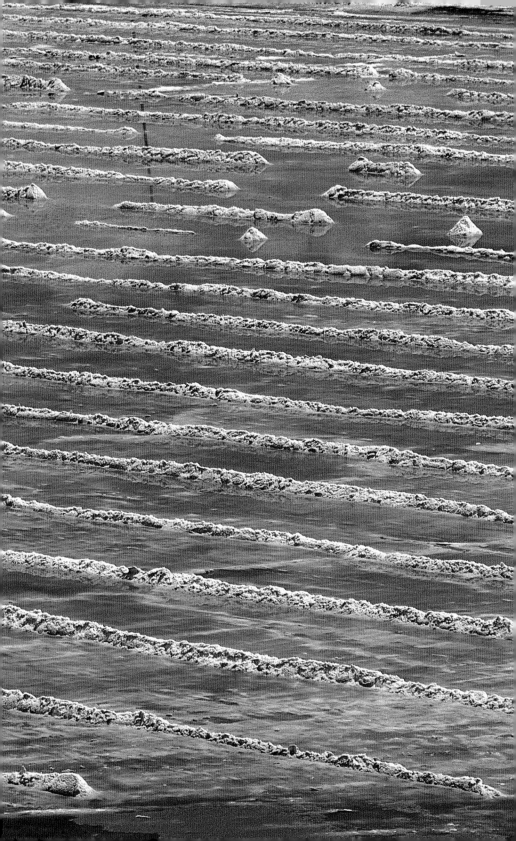

The Great Rift Valley: The Land that was Eden

The world has many great mountains, lakes, deserts and oceans. But of its valleys and gorges one alone dwarfs them all in size and dimension. Indeed, after the oceans, the Great Rift Valley is perhaps the single most dramatic feature on earth (see 'The Land', Part One).

In Kenya much of the Rift remains an expanse of raw Africa that dazzles the eye with its haunting grandeur. Nowhere is it more apparent, more dramatic, or more picturesque.

Entering the country in the north from Ethiopia through the jade waters of Lake Turkana, it slices right through the middle of Kenya like a broad knife-cut to enter Tanzania in the south at Lake Natron.

Incorporating cliffs, escarpments, sand rivers and arid plains flowing like molten lava from the north down to the low-lying, heat-ridden, soda lakes in the south, in some places this natural divide is up to 100 kilometres (60 miles) wide.

The valley floor rises from little more than 200 metres (650 feet) above sea level at Lake Turkana to reach its highest point around Lake Naivasha at 1,900 metres (6,200 feet), before descending abruptly to enter Tanzania just 580 metres (1,900 feet) above sea level.

Where the valley floor is at its highest so, too, are the valley's precipitous walls, reaching 3,964 metres (13,120 feet) in the Aberdares above Naivasha.

Where the floor is at its lowest, as at Turkana, there is virtually no distinction between the Great Rift and the stark, arid wildernesses that adjoin it. To the east, the featureless semi-desert scrub stretches across hundreds of kilometres to Somalia's Indian Ocean coastline. Yet in other places, where the floor is not much more than 610 metres (2,000 feet) above sea level, its great cliffs rise sheer above it for more than 1,520 metres (5,000 feet).

The power that transformed the face of the world is evident in the Rift's 30 active and semi-active volcanoes and countless boiling springs. They bring sodium carbonate bubbling up from deep beneath the earth, turning many Rift lakes into bitter pans of water or blistering soda flats. Today the Kenyan and Tanzanian sections of the Rift are the world's last treasury of cultures, flora, and fauna, both terrestrial and avian, that have continued unchanged for centuries.

The valley plains contain the last great assembly of African wildlife and from one end to the other, Kenya's human cultures form a cross-section of the entire African continent's cultural wealth. Little wonder, perhaps, that many think of this as Eden.

As a unique geological phenomenon, the first European to investigate the Rift was a young Scot, John Walter Gregory.

Marching up to Baringo from Mombasa in 1893, he hammered out samples from different rock layers and returned to proclaim his conclusions — that this cataclysmic rent on the face of the earth was formed 'by the rock sinking in mass, while the adjacent land remained stationary'.

It was Gregory who named it the Great Rift Valley but perhaps the name given by Austrian geologist, Eduard Suess, two years earlier best captures the imagination. He called it *graben,* derived from *grabe,* the grave. In the light of the fossil remains which have since been found on the shores of Lake Turkana no other description could be more aposite.

Suess never visited the continent but from a map of Africa he deduced that the Rift lakes were part of a connected chain created by a series of movements in the earth's surface. These movements uplifted and exposed sedimentary layers which can be dated precisely, and also preserved prehistoric fossils in a remarkably good state.

All along this majestic flaw, in the walls of its great scarps and close to the surface of its floor, lies evidence of mankind's beginnings. Much still remains to be discovered. Most of what has already been revealed was found at two of the most

Opposite: Soda pans at Lake Magadi.

significant sites in palaeontological history — **Olduvai Gorge** in the Tanzanian Rift and **Koobi Fora** on the eastern shores of Lake Turkana (see 'History: The Dust and the Ashes', Part One).

Where to stay
In Naivasha, Lake Naivasha Country Club (5-star), Safariland Lodge (4-star), Elsamere (guesthouse), Fisherman's Camp (budget). In Nakuru, Hotel Kunste; Midland Hotel (3-star); Pivot Hotel (2-star). In Baringo, Lake Baringo Club (5-star). In Kabarnet, the Kabarnet Hotel (4-star). In Lodwar, New Lodwar Lodge (budget). At Lake Turkana, Eliye Springs Lodge (basic), Lake Turkana Fishing Lodge (4-star), Oasis Lodge (basic). See Listings for 'Hotels'.

In national parks
In the Lake Nakuru National Park, Lake Nakuru Lodge; Lion Hill Camp (book through Sarova Hotels, New Stanley Hotel, Nairobi).

The Southern and Central Rift
From Nairobi take the **Langata Road** from Uhuru Highway to the **Magadi Road**, left, and on through **Ongata Rongai**. Leaving **Kiserian**, and the turnoff to **Ngong Town** on the right, drive on up the south-eastern shoulder of the Ngong Hills at some 2,134 metres (7,000 feet).

There, the ground suddenly drops between 610 and 914 metres (2,000-3,000 feet) to the stunningly stark and dramatic Maasai wilderness of arid thorn and scrub desert studded with volcanic mountains. The view inspired Karen Blixen (Isak Dinesen) to begin writing. Today, photographers leap out of cars with light meter, tripod, and lens to capture the scene.

At the scruffy hamlet of **Olepolos** turn right along the dirt road for the circular tour of Ngong Hills (see 'Ngong Hills: The Giant's Knuckles').

From there the Magadi Road takes on a serpentine aspect as it swoops down through a series of exhilarating straights and tortuous hairpins, the temperature increasing by the kilometre. One hour out on a cold winter's day in Nairobi and you're back to full-blooded equatorial warmth — a swift cure for rheumy bones and muscles. Just a little over halfway between Nairobi and Lake Magadi you pass through the straggling township of **Oltepesi.** Take the left turn to the **Olorgesailie Prehistoric Site,** well signposted, one-and-a-half kilometres (one mile) from the road. Nothing distinguishes this place as the location of what Dr Louis Leakey described as 'the most significant in the whole world of Aechulian hand axe culture'. J W Gregory stumbled over this clearing littered with bones when he crossed the Rift on his approach from the Kapiti Plains, with the **Meto Hills** — dominated by the **Black Mountain** — forming the eastern flank.

At one time this was a lake, fed by the **Keju Nyiro River.** Between 400,000 and 500,000 years ago the lake shores were inhabited by some of our earliest ancestors. The lake disappeared, however, after the river was diverted by one of the many cataclysmic movements that shaped the Rift.

When Leakey cleared the site in 1924 on the ground, all around, lay dramatic evidence of the first creature to abandon the four-legged posture and walk upright. Our earliest ancestor, *Homo erectus*, quickly became an adept pedestrian and groups soon moved south to live around **Olorgesailie**.

Other fossils found by Leakey were the broken skeletons of a race of giant baboons, long extinct. They had been slain by rough weapons of chipped stones and crude cobbles that also lay around. The weapons were fashioned from rock not found there. Man had become a hunter. Olorgesailie was declared a **national monument** in 1947 and you can see the fossils *in situ* today — a tenuous thread in the tangled and yet-to-be unravelled tapestry of mankind's story.

The knowledgeable national museum guides explain the significance of finds in the site's two square kilometres (less than a square mile). You can spend the night in one of four *bandas*, **guest houses**, or under canvas on the **camping site** — all for a nominal charge. To reach Lake Magadi you have another 45 kilometres (28 miles) to travel. The road descends all the time through the **Ol Keju Nyiro Valley**, skirting gaunt and forbidding volcanic outcrops and deep ravines, until you crest a final ridge. There, laid out beneath you, is **Lake Magadi,** shimmering with all the fires — cobalt, indigo, reds, crystalline-whites and pastel-pinks — of Dante's Inferno.

Dante's inferno

Magadi and its close neighbour, **Lake Natron**, just a few kilometres south across the Tanzanian border, are the richest of the soda lakes — the others are **Elmenteita, Nakuru,** and **Turkana** — which characterize the East African section of the Rift. Their surface heights vary in altitude from a few hundred metres to more than 1,640 metres (5,000 feet) above sea level.

Magadi is the world's second-largest single source of trona, *Sodium sesqui carbonate,* after California's Salton Sea. The lake's 100 square kilometres (40 square miles) form a drainage sump without outlet.

Set only 580 metres (1,900 feet) above sea level, the sun's rays funnel mercilessly into this arena, and intense evaporation creates ideal conditions for excavating the trona. Only after rare rains is the lake covered with water.

Mineral rights were granted to two prospectors, Deacon and Walsh, who staked a claim to Magadi in 1901. In September 1911, the company they established signed a contract with George Pauling to build a 150-kilometre-long (90-mile) railway line from Konza to Magadi. Much of the filming for *Out of Africa* was carried out along this track. The complications of World War I meant that it wasn't until 1 August 1915 that the line was handed over to the Uganda Railway — now Kenya Railways — but in 1995 the soda company began its own rail operations.

Today the lake is a prime mover of the Kenyan economy and a major foreign currency earner. Each year the company processes between 150,000 and 200,000 tonnes of soda ash for export markets in southeast Asia and the Far East.

Sightseeing

It is possible to cross the lake on specially constructed causeways — but wear sunglasses and a hat. The reflections off the soda surface are blinding.

From the air, Magadi's surface is like a covering of crumpled, melted icing mottled with patches of indigo-red where industrial excavators cut through the crust to haul up this naturally recurring source of soda ash — nowhere more than three metres (ten feet) deep — which will never dry up. Its eastern shores are dominated by the town that the Magadi Soda Company has developed during the last 80 years — complete with elegant residential suburbs, working-class flats, a smart **club** with **swimming pool, hospital, schools, mosque, churches** — and a **golf course** with 'browns', a mix of sludge and sump oil, instead of greens.

Occasionally millions of flamingos breed there, and the bleak but hauntingly lovely landscapes around have an astonishing wealth of bird life. Its western shores are beautiful, with hot springs, promontories and little valleys.

Through the Kedong Valley

The western buttress of the Rift at Magadi is formed by the formidable wall of the **Nkuruman Escarpment** topped by the **Loita Hills.** No road climbs these rugged cliffs but the dirt trails are negotiable with 4WD. The tracks cut through thick forests to the top, where, beyond the Loita Hills, the land levels out in the **Maasai Mara**. Some tour operators arrange individual safaris into these forests and up the escarpment. On your own you could get lost.

The more normal route is to return from Magadi to **Olepolos** and then take the dirt road left along the base of the Ngong Hills through the **Kedong Valley**, past **Susua**, the 2,357-metre (7,733-foot) dormant volcano to the west (see 'Kenya's Mountains', Part Three). Susua has a deep moat in its crater, surrounding an inner plateau like something from Conan Doyle's *Lost World.* Enthusiastic potholers enjoy exploring its many lava tubes.

To get to the plateau you can swing across the giddying drop into the moat over a cable that was put up by the Operation Drake adventure project in the early 1980s. In 1989, the Kenya Speleological Society — an organization of Kenyan cave explorers — held their annual dinner dance in one of Susua's caves, which is known to them as the 'Ballroom'.

Eventually, the dirt road links up with the Naivasha-Narok tarmac road. Turn right to the old Nairobi-Naivasha-Nakuru road and then left to where it cuts between the foot of the Rift Escarpment and 2,776-metre (9,108-foot) **Mount Longonot.** With its crumpled crater rim, it is the highest of

Following page: Sundown over the Rift Valley.

177

all Kenya's Rift Valley volcanoes and its sides are lined with lava funnels. If you wish to climb to the rim — not recommended if you suffer from vertigo — report at the **police station** just outside Longonot Village, where you can leave car and valuables and ask about a guide. Caution should be taken, as muggings have been known to occur — even on the rim.

From the main road a rough track leads seven kilometres (four miles) to the start of the climb. From base to summit all the way around, Longonot's flanks are creased with dozens of the ridges that inspired its Maasai name — *Oloonong'ot,* 'mountain of steep ridges' — and studded with parasitic volcanic cones.

Dark clouds often boil over its rim during the rainy season, before rolling on across the gulf and over the facing escarpment, which is almost the same height. The climb to the top and around the rim — best taken in an anti-clockwise direction — is a stiff four to five hours' walk. At 3,740 metres (9,000 feet), the air is already beginning to thin and lungs labour, but there's a small plateau on the flanks of the highest point which is ideal for a picnic. On a clear day the views are spectacular.

When Thomson climbed it during his 1883 trek he was overcome with vertigo and experienced an irresistible urge to throw himself into the abyss. The rim is very narrow and extreme caution should be taken as most of the path crosses unstable, crumbling volcanic lava. One slip could be fatal. Until recently, the crater floor and the slopes outside were notable for their steam.

Fiery Longonot is only sleeping and the nascent energy beneath its rumbling crown has now been tapped in Africa's only geothermal project. Several thousand metres beneath the surface, ground waters register an astonishing 304°C (579°F) — one of the hottest temperatures recorded. On the southern slopes, staccato jets of steam rise into the sky from the boreholes.

The railway line passes the eastern base of Longonot, but hundreds of metres above, the **scenic highway** from Limuru rides the escarpment crest at almost 2,743 metres (9,000 feet). Despite intensive settlement on its lower flanks, Longonot was declared a 52-square-kilometre (20-square-

mile) national park in the 1980s along with nearby 68-square-kilometre (26-square-mile) **Hell's Gate.** Also known as **Njorowa Gorge,** Hell's Gate is considered to have one of the most spectacular and exciting walks in Kenya, leading through a gorge lined with sheer, red cliffs (see 'National Parks', In Brief, for wildlife and vegetation). There are many birds of prey and swifts in the area — it's possible to see between 25 and 30 different species in a day.

Dominating the scene, the volcanic plug of **Fischer's Tower,** named after the German who explored this region in the 19th century, offers a stunning rock climb fraught with peril and is home to colonies of rock hyrax, or *dassies.*

If you come across fibreglass boulders and rocks among the genuine articles don't be too surprised. In the early 1980s a film crew chose Hell's Gate as one of the locations for *Sheena — Queen of the Jungle* and, in typical Hollywood fashion, decided that nature's handiwork needed some help from their props department.

From the **Naivasha YMCA** on **Moi South Road** which circles Lake Naivasha, turn left along a trail for the **park entrance.** Since it's some 26 kilometres (16 miles) there and back you'll need an early start to complete the round trip comfortably. Don't forget to carry plenty of water. There isn't another track so it's easy to follow even when, after about two kilometres (little more than a mile), the trail veers suddenly to reveal Fischer's Tower. It's thought that this volcanic stack was left standing when the water of the prehistoric lake which stretched from Naivasha to Nakuru cut through the gorge in search of an outlet.

There you may see the Lammergeiers which often nest in the high cliffs along with other raptors, of which they are the largest. Not really eagles, they are, in fact, bearded vultures (*Gypaetus barbatus*).

Another rock tower, **Ol Basta**, punctuates the end of the gorge. At this point, you have three options. One is to struggle forward another twelve kilometres (seven miles) to the end of the canyon, and from there to the Narok road, a distance of another 15 kilometres (nine miles). This is a formidable trek for which you need camping equipment, provisions, route maps and compass.

Above: 'Lost World' plateau in the crater of volcanic Mount Susua in the Rift Valley.
Opposite: Seamed and scarred profile of Longonot, a dormant Rift Valley volcano.

Lake Naivasha: Pearl In The Rift

German naturalist Gustav Fischer was the first European to see **Lake Naivasha** in 1883 — although the instant the local Maasai discovered him he sensibly turned and fled. The lake's name derives from the Maa word *Enaiposha* ('the lake') and was corrupted for ever by early Europeans who recorded the mispronunciation of their Swahili porters. The English officer who carried out the initial survey for the 'Lunatic Line', Captain Macdonald, noted in his diaries that the lake was 'full of hippo'.

It was there that John Walter Gregory paused to make his first assays of the Rift strata but, with the Maasai hostile to strangers, Gregory did not pause long. He picked up his chisels and hammers and marched on another 160 kilometres (100 miles) to Baringo.

Spread out over 110 square kilometres (43 square miles), a pearl in the bosom of

the Kenya Rift, the sweet waters of Lake Naivasha glisten silver as the sun slopes swiftly to the west. It's a popular weekend resort for Nairobi residents. Purest and highest of all the Rift lakes, Naivasha is also a bird sanctuary without peer. Over 400 species have been recorded there; more than the entire list of birds seen in the British Isles (see 'Birdlife', Part Three).

It was on these shores that Joy Adamson fostered the heroine of her wildlife classic, *Born Free*, Elsa and her cubs. Now the Adamson's home, **Elsamere,** is a living memorial — a wildlife education centre and museum to the woman brutally murdered in Shaba National Reserve in 1980. Open to the public in the afternoon, Elsamere is close to the rambling **Lake Naivasha Country Club**, which is framed by yellow fever trees in thirteen hectares (32 acres) of gardens, shrubs, flowers, and verdant lawns which sprawl down to the lake. Just after the war, this was Kenya's international air terminal when the flying boats of British Overseas Airways flew a leisurely course along the Nile and on

Above: Longonot earth satellite station in Kenya's Rift Valley.

down to South Africa. They landed at what is now the club, and passengers were ferried ashore before the 84-kilometre (52-mile) journey by road to Nairobi.

Apart from tourism and ornithology, Lake Naivasha is the fount of one of Kenya's great agro-industries. A fledgling wine industry has taken root there and carefully tended vineyards established since 1980 produce vintage Naivasha wines.

Lake waters irrigate thousands of hectares of fertile volcanic loam which burgeon with vegetables and colourful flowers. During the high season, more than a million stems a night are airlifted to winterbound Europe, taking a hint of the tropical sun to warm thousands of icebound homes with their colour and fragrance. **Naivasha town** is some distance from the lake and has little to offer tourists.

Getting there

Two kilometres (one mile) to the south of Naivasha, a right turn leads into **Moi South Road**. After a few kilometres you pass the up-market **Lake Naivasha Country Club**, right, and after another eight

kilometres (five miles), leaving scrub and farmlands to the left and vineyards to the right, there is another right turn that leads to **Safariland Lodge**. It's roughly the same distance round the lake to Carnelly's **Fisherman's Camp.**

Sightseeing

Midway between Lake Naivasha Country Club and Safariland is a **grape farm** which was once a marina. When the lake dries up, a narrow causeway links the farm to **Crescent Island**. The island takes its name from its shape. It's the visible tip of a volcanic crater rim, forming a bay in the deepest part of the lake.

The **country club** runs regular boat excursions to the island, a private game sanctuary where bat-eared foxes sport in the short grass and, undisturbed by predators, sheep graze alongside waterbuck, wildebeest and zebras. It's another rare place where you can wander among the wildlife on foot — in perfect safety. But don't go too near the wallowing hippo.

On the nearby mainland the **Naivasha polo club** welcomes visitors to watch this 'king of games', usually played on Sundays right on the shores of the lake. Just beyond Fisherman's Camp, a scenic viewpoint overlooks a small lake set in the north-western shores of the main lake. North of this, some six kilometres (four miles) past the **South Lake police post**, between the shore of the main lake and the road, lie the dark green waters of a third **crater lake**, which is something of a bovine health spa. The Maasai claim its alkaline waters offer a cure for sick cattle.

To Gilgil

From Naivasha town, the main street leads out left to the major Nairobi-Nakuru road. For 27 kilometres (17 miles) it cuts through thick groves of fever trees — acacia thorn — to bypass Gilgil on the right. This sprawling, somewhat scruffy town grew out of a small market centre. Five kilometres (three miles) out of Gilgil, along the **Nyahururu road**, under a narrow railway bridge, **Pembroke College**, right, is an élitist Kenya preparatory school.

To the left, the **Gilgil Club,** with its mellow timber buildings, is redolent with colonial ambience. Sprawling down the moorland salient from the north on the other side of the road is the club's **golf course** — rough fairways, and 'browns' instead of greens.

The **Commonwealth War Cemetery** — one of 40 cemeteries in Kenya maintained immaculately by the Commonwealth War Graves Commission — where about 200 victims of the Second World War are buried, is about two kilometres (little more than a mile) out of town along the same road. Just a little further on is a major military encampment.

Gilgil is also a training base for recruits to Kenya's famous **National Youth Service.** This remarkable institution is not centred on defence but on character training. Recruits serve two years, but after basic military training at Gilgil, they are deployed to carry out many large-scale civil projects to help maintain the impetus of national development. You can also travel north over the high moorlands to Nyahururu through **Ol Kalou,** passing the Wanjohi Valley en route, or branch off this road to **Subukia** (see 'Heartland of Kenya: Magic Mountains, Moorlands Wild').

To Nakuru

From Gilgil the main road continues on past **Lake Elmenteita.** There are a number of prehistoric sites in the cliff face and by the road, but not all of them are signposted. One of them, **Kariandus,** is next to the **diatomite mines** of the same name. The site, with a number of *in situ* Aechulian tool exhibits, about a ten minute walk from the road, is open weekday. It was cleared by Dr Louis Leakey in 1928 as he rifled through the Rift in search of mankind's origins. Next door, a mine excavates the Rift's diatomite, a startlingly-white chalky extract, composed of billions of compressed silica and the skeletons of microscopic sea organisms (diatoms) which flourished there millions of years ago. Diatomite serves as a water filter and is used in the brewing industry. It also works as a non-toxic insecticide in grain stores and was used traditionally as *karia andus* ('war-paint') by the Kikuyu. After half-a-century of excavation the mine has become a deep hole in the ground. A trail leads down its glittering white sides to the bottom where several tunnels are driven into the sides.

Just three kilometres (two miles) beyond the mine, the road cuts above **Elmenteita.** One of the smallest Rift lakes, this shallow sump dries up periodically but forms part of the Delamere family's **Soysambu** estate (see 'History: The Dust and the Ashes', Part One). Within the 80,000-acre Soysambu estate, in 1992 the fourth Lord and Lady Delamere opened their 13,000-acre Soysambu-Elmenteita Wildlife Sanctuary and twelve-tent, 24-bed luxury camp for the use of guests and friends of the Delamere family. The camp has its own air strip.

A dirt road on the left, shortly after Gilgil, skirts the lake shore to follow the old slave trail from Lake Victoria and Uganda. This trail was said to have inspired H Rider Haggard's *King Solomon's Mines.* Haggard's brother, Captain Jack, served in Lamu for years as the first British administrative officer and his letters were the author's source of inspiration (see 'Lamu: Enchanted Islands').

From Elmenteita it's another 37 kilometres (23 miles) to Kenya's fourth-largest town, Nakuru, which takes its name from the Maa word *Enakuro,* 'the place of swirling dust'.

Nakuru: The Greatest Bird Show on Earth

Photographs taken in 1900 show Nakuru as a desolate empty plain. It appears to begin abruptly at the end of the first railway platform built 'as if the bare and mysterious land beyond was forbidden territory', wrote Alastair Matheson in *Railway across the Equator*. The town that sprang up on this vast, barren plain with its bleak perspectives, soon after the arrival of the Uganda Railway, came under the patronage of Lord Delamere (see 'History: The Dust and the Ashes', Part One).

The town is perched on the western slopes of the **Menengai Crater,** the second-largest volcanic caldera in the world, overlooking the seasonal Lake Nakuru, which varies in size from five to 30 square kilometres (two-12 square miles), according to the volume of the seasonal rains.

Nakuru is also the farm capital of the country, and the administrative headquarters of Kenya's Rift Valley Province. This vibrant, noisy, dusty, entrepôt — headquarters of the giant **Kenya Grain Growers Co-operative Union** (KGGCU) and many other large national and multinational enterprises — has grown rapidly in post-independence Kenya.

It serves as a focal point for visits to the **Nakuru National Park,** and the nearby prehistoric settlement site of **Hyrax Hill** on the slopes of the Menengai Crater. It also serves as the starting point for trips into Kenya's central Rift Valley.

Sightseeing

Apart from the annual Nakuru Agricultural Society of Kenya show, Kenya's premier farm show, there's not much for visitors to see or do in the town itself. The **Rift Valley Sports Club,** however, with its **cricket ground** and splendid, colonial, solid stone, two-storey **clubhouse,** with residential rooms, is where the élite congregate.

But for tourists and bird watching buffs, the 188 square kilometres (73 square miles) of the **Lake Nakuru National Park** is something of a Mecca. During one of Kenya's cyclical wet spells, ornithologist and artist Peter Scott arrived on these fluctuating shores to marvel at a sight he described as the greatest bird spectacle in the world.

There, wading in the shallows, floating a little way offshore, with more still circling above on the Rift thermals, was a cloud of amorphous blush-pink — two million or more flamingos, one-third of the world's entire population of lesser flamingos.

But there is much more to Lake Nakuru than just flamingo. The national park, small and beautiful, is one of the easiest parks in Kenya to visit. At an altitude of between 1,753 and 2,073 metres (5,350-6,300 feet), the park is bordered to the west by one wall of the Rift Valley and to the east by a salt-dome hill. There is a crater in the north, open plains to the south and a large euphorbia forest below Lion Hill.

Wooded cliffs and shores surround swamp-fringed water, supporting a large waterbuck population and many wart hogs. Most of the parkland is covered with light acacia forest containing well-marked tracks to a variety of hides and lookouts.

The park has more than 450 recorded species of birds, including many migratory species which leave England during the northern winter. It is one of the few national parks established specifically to protect birds (see 'National Parks', In Brief).

In recent years it has also become a sanctuary for a group of Rothschild's giraffe and the endangered black rhino. You may also be lucky enough to come across the largest of African snakes, the python, which like the boa, squeezes its victims to death.

Menengai Crater and Hyrax Hill

From Nakuru town it is eight kilometres (five miles) to the rim of Menengai. A trail climbs past another of the National Museum's prehistoric sites, **Hyrax Hill,** named after the hyrax which once inhabited this area. Mankind lived there continuously for at least 3,000 years and the first *in situ* exhibit, from the Neolithic and Iron Ages, was discovered by Louis Leakey in 1926. Excavations over an 11-year period were led by Mary Leakey, with further excavations from 1965 to 1973 by other archaeolo-

Previous pages: Tourists enjoy a pioneer-style ox-wagon trek through the Rift near Naivasha.

gists. The museum displays village pottery, dating from the 16th century AD. The villagers are believed to have been semi-nomadic Kalenjin pastoralists.

One hundred metres (300 feet) below the museum, on the slope of Hyrax Hill, more Iron Age **pits** and a **trench** yielded a rare discovery — some 8,000 stone tools and six Indian coins, aged between 60 and 500 years, were found in 1974. Nearby, the contents of a **Neolithic burial mound** include parts of a human skull and bones — revealed when a huge **stone slab** was removed. Altogether 19 Neolithic and 19 Iron Age graves were discovered in this area.

Higher up the hill, an **old fort** overlooking Nakuru is believed to have been the village lookout post. From this point, 2,242-metre (7,475 foot) **Menengai** is visible to the north-west. There is a road to the crater rim from which point you look down 483 metres (1,585 feet) to the crater floor. From wall to wall the crater stretches many kilometres and beyond it sweeps the Rift with its fertile wheatlands. Lake Nakuru is several kilometres to the south.

One of the great Maasai clan battles of the 19th century — Ilpurko versus the Ilaikipiak — was fought there, and the soughing of the wind over the crater rim is said to be the sad and haunted cries of those slain in battle. Indeed, Menengai still has a sinister reputation today and local people prefer to avoid it.

Lake Bogoria: Fiery Waters, Flaming Colours

From Nakuru, the Rift Valley drops down 900 metres (almost 3,000 feet) on the 118-kilometre (73 mile) descent to the sweltering deserts and semi-deserts which mark **Lake Bogoria**, **Lake Baringo**, the **Kerio Valley**, and the **Kamasia** and **Tugen Hills**. All are easy to reach from Nakuru.

The primitive beauty of this region distinguishes it from any other part of the Rift, which is at its most spectacular there. The wall of the Laikipia escarpment, 2,440 metres (7,000 feet) above sea level, steps down in a series of terrace-like foothills. With Lake Baringo in between, the great block of the Kamasia and Tugen hills rises

32 kilometres (20 miles) away, and another 16 kilometres (10 miles) beyond that, over the grand canyon of the Kerio Valley, stands the western wall.

The **Elgeyo Escarpment** that ends in the 3,350-metre (11,000-foot) Cherangani Hills is probably the most dramatic of all the Rift escarpments. In some places it plunges straight down almost 2,440 metres (8,000 feet) to the valley floor.

Perhaps the least-visited of all Kenya's Rift lakes, Bogoria lies 50 kilometres (31 miles) from Nakuru at the foot of the **Laikipia Escarpment.** The bottle green waters, reflecting the woodlands to the east, are often illuminated by the pink and white of great numbers of flamingos. At the eastern edge the **Siracho Cliffs** rise more than 610 metres (2,000 feet).

Bogoria was originally named Lake Hannington after Bishop Hannington, who camped around the long, narrow sheet of alkaline water in the 1890s on his way to Uganda, where he was murdered. After independence it reverted to the ancient name given long ago by local communities. Gregory, the geologist, thought the lake 'the most beautiful sight in all Africa'.

Getting there

The broad, smooth Baringo road leaves Nakuru over the north-western shoulder of Menengai, past **Kabarak High School**, founded by President Moi, and on through **Kampi ya Moto.** Drive past the three shops and rail crossing to the left fork for the steep climb up the **Elgeyo Escarpment** to **Eldama Ravine** (see 'North-West Kenya: Enchanted Mountains, Unspoilt Vistas').

From Kampi ya Moto, the road veers north through **Mogotio,** with a right turn along a dirt trail for 20 kilometres (12 miles) to the **Lake Bogoria National Reserve.** An exciting alternative to the main route from Nakuru to Bogoria is to approach the lake across the **Subukia Valley** from Nyahururu in the east (see 'Heartland of Kenya').

Where to stay

If you want to camp, the **Fig Tree Campsite**, with giant fig tree groves which dominate the southern shore, provides cool shelter. There is plenty of water there: a year-round freshwater stream makes its

way directly through the campsite, inviting a dip to wash off the dust — provided you can ignore the attentions of troops of resident baboons, for whom you will be an interesting diversion.

Further west around the lake circuit are two more campsites — **Riverside** and **Acacia Tree** — and a small **picnic area** near the **Hot Springs** at the junction for the track out to the western **Maji ya Moto** gate of the reserve. A lodge stands inside the reserve near its northern entrance.

But Bogoria's natural beauty remains largely unvisited, for the most part because of its remote location and rugged terrain.

Sightseeing

Covering an area of 107 square kilometres (41 square miles), the Lake Bogoria National Reserve is between 1,000 and 1,600 metres (3,280-5,250 feet) above sea level, with thermal **steam jets** and **geysers** boiling out of the rocky ground along its western shores.

It's worth making the springs your first port of call. Resist any temptation with foot or hand to test the spectacular, though sulphurous-smelling, eruptions.

Aside from its hot springs and vast flocks of flamingo, Bogoria is particularly noted for herds of greater kudu, probably the only sanctuary in Kenya where you are virtually certain to see this unusual, powerful, and handsome antelope with its distinctive lyrate horns (see 'Wildlife', Part Three).

To Baringo

Lake Baringo lies between the two walls of the Rift Valley with the dramatic **Kamasia** block in between. Kamasia remained standing when the valley began to sink and subsequently provided Gregory with a complete geological history of the valley.

Leaving the Bogoria Reserve by the northern gate, return to the main road, which runs another 30 kilometres (17 miles) to **Marigat**. Just before you reach the town, a fine new highway on the left climbs up to **Kabarnet**, administrative headquarters of Baringo district. **Marigat** itself is a drab collection of tin huts and administrative buildings. It's another 20 kilometres (12 miles) to

the lake itself. Two decades ago this was as remote as any place in Kenya, but now it is only a three-hour drive from Nairobi.

As a result, Lake Baringo has developed into one of Kenya's major tourist resorts — particularly for ornithologists and watersports buffs. Like Lake Naivasha, Baringo's shallow, silt-stained waters make an odd contrast to the rest of the Rift lakes. These are the only two freshwater lakes along the length of the Kenyan section. Studded with islands, Baringo sustains healthy populations of tilapia fish as well as crocodile and hippo.

Sightseeing

The bird life in this area is phenomenal. Organized bird walks lead along the lowest strata of the Kamasia block on the road outside the **Lake Baringo Club**, in the club gardens, and on the lake shores. Almost 450 species of bird are resident at Baringo, either permanently or as migrants from the European winter.

Resident ornithologists can be contacted through the club, which also organizes fascinating lectures on Baringo birds, the indigenous Njemps (Ilchamus) people, and the area's wildlife. Visits to an Njemps village can be arranged.

Other activities which centre on Lake Baringo Club or the **Island Camp** include boat trips around the shores, water-skiing, and windsurfing. The crocodiles are said to be harmless and it's considered safe to swim, but early in the 1980s one attacked and ate a human and was subsequently shot.

From Baringo there are two routes north — both along dirt roads, one of sufficient quality to make the adventure worthwhile.

Some kilometres beyond the northern shore the tarmac ends and a rough trail leads down into the heart of the northern Rift. It heads in the general direction of the Suguta Valley — one of the hottest places on earth (see 'The Northern Rift: Cradle of Mankind') — to **Kapedo,** a small, remote settlement which was abandoned at the end of the 1970s. But the road east from Baringo that climbs up the folds of the Laikipia Escarpment, unfolding one magnificent panorama after another, to join the

Previous pages: Flamingos and pelicans on the shores of Lake Nakuru in the Rift.

Above: Boiling geysers on the western shores of Lake Bogoria.

Nyahururu-Rumuruti-Maralal road (see 'North-East Kenya'") — is becoming extremely popular. Returning south from Lake Baringo, you can explore the **Kamasia** and **Tugen Hills** by taking the magnificent highway, just after Marigat, that climbs the 1,370-metre (4,500-foot) western wall of the escarpment. For 57 kilometres (35 miles) this road twists and turns in a series of hairpin bends, from the last of which there is a stunning view of Baringo and the Rift.

The transition from scorched earth to the coolness of these lush green highlands is yet another of those surprises that Kenya suddenly springs forth. One of Kenya's most beautiful regions, it is at its best after the long rains from March to May. The heat is fiercest in February and early March just before the rains break.

Kabarnet, the administrative headquarters for Baringo District, is a delightful town perched like a saddle on the back of the narrow, but handsome, tree-clad ridge. It looks down on dramatic **Kerio Valley** — Kenya's own Grand Canyon — whose ridge plunges more than 1,000 metres (3,500 feet) in a few kilometres. The oppo-

site wall rises up equally dramatically and, looking down from the wooded ridge, it seems as if you could almost touch the valley floor, dappled with sunlight.

Part of Kabarnet straggles down the slopes on either side of the ridge, but most development is along the top — giving it a long, slender profile. Surrounded by prosperous and well-tended farms and small-holdings it makes a delightful away-from-it-all weekend retreat from Nairobi.

Unspoilt hills
Twenty kilometres (12 miles) to the south of the town, along the western ridge of the Kamasia Hills, a highway leads to President Moi's birthplace high above the Rift, with a panorama that takes in Baringo, Bogoria and the Kerio Valley. To the north lies the rugged saddle of the virtually impenetrable Tugen Hills. Another road to the west leads down into the Kerio Valley and up to **Tambach**.

Little explored by tourists, the **Kamasia Hills,** the **Kerio Valley**, and the Elgeyo Escarpment are among the most beautiful and unspoilt places in Kenya. In the Kerio

191

Valley a mining company has established a fluorspar industry and the company town of **Kimwarer**, which has developed rapidly as an urban centre. Neat company housing estates make an astonishing counterpoint to the tangled wilderness all around.

The **Kerio Valley Development Authority** has started to encourage fruit orchards and vegetable farms, using the waters of the **Kerio River** for irrigation.

Two nature sanctuaries, the 88-square-kilometre (34-square-mile) **Kamnarok National Reserve** and the 66-square kilometre (25-square-mile) **Kerio Valley National Reserve,** have been established along the **Kerio Gorge.**

But at the moment you can walk and drive everywhere and many charming Tugen villages — **Kabulwa, Koitilial, Chepkum, Chesetan, Chesongoch** — line the roadside.

One of the most astonishing vistas is from the Elgeyo Escarpment south of the dreamy village of **Tot**. Below the sheer cliff face a tapestry of first green and then arid scrublands extends as far as the eye can see to the **Turkana** country through **West Pokot**. The Elgeyo Escarpment road is too rocky and too steep for anything less than a 4WD car or anyone with less nerve than a very gutsy rally driver.

If you walk from Tot you can climb to the top in one day. Or you can drive 25 kilometres (16 miles) up to **Chesoi,** returning from Tot in the direction of Kabarnet and turning right halfway at **Chesongoch** for the main ascent (see 'Cherangani Hills: High Peaks, Secret Valleys').

From Tot you can continue along the Rift and join up in the desert with the Lodwar road (not recommended). Alternatively, retrace your route and climb the Kerio Hills to Kabarnet — and take the new road from there up the Elgeyo Escarpment to Eldoret.

A third option is to turn east at Tot and drive along the dirt trail through **Kolowa** to **Nginyang** on the Lake Baringo-Kapedo Road.

The Northern Rift: Cradle of Mankind

Nothing could look less like the biblical Garden of Eden than the arid badlands of northern Kenya. Yet if historical perspective has any accuracy, the eastern shores of **Lake Turkana** are one place on earth which might rightly be regarded as Eden.

The lush imagery is nowhere in evidence but the knife-edge lava wastes and petrified forests have preserved the remnants of the ancient cultures which once lived there and shaped the lifestyles of the area's contemporary groups — hardy, spartan people indifferent to materialism.

The land yields little. The soil is worn out and the only profit is survival. Simply to stay alive is indicative of both human resourcefulness and dignity (see 'The People', Part One).

When the frenzy of the tectonic forces which formed the Great Rift Valley finally abated, Africa endured one last, long, drawn-out tremor. Its spine collapsed, to form the Rift and on either side this great rupture exposed the different strata along its scarps — and the bones and teeth they contained. The grave was open. All it needed was someone to dig among the bones.

Fate might well have given that honour to Lieutenant Ludwig von Höhnel, Count Samuel Teleki's loyal geographer, biographer and friend. While Teleki's sole ambition seems to have been to slaughter East Africa's wildlife, von Höhnel diligently recorded the flora, fauna, ecology, geology, geography, and ethnic constituents which formed this part of East Africa and the Rift Valley (see 'History: The Dust and the Ashes', Part One).

At the end of March 1888, Teleki's expedition crossed the shores of Lake Turkana at **Koobi Fora**. Von Höhnel complained of walking across Koobi Fora's sandstone rocks, not thinking to look beneath them.

A week later, the tired party approached a Dassenich settlement at what is probably now **Ileret,** where two of the main fossil-bearing areas exist. Perhaps the two explorers stumbled across some fossils, for von Höhnel records: 'After an hour's walk we issued from the wood which extended in a westerly direction to the side of the lake. Then came a stretch of ground strewn with human skulls and bones.' But learned though he was, von Höhnel failed to recognize the significance of his finds. It was another 80 years, in July 1967, before Richard Leakey flew along the eastern shores of Lake Turkana. He saw below a tangle of blackened sandstone layers which looked like the slag heaps of a coal pit. Leakey asked the pilot to circle the sand pit off Koobi Fora and fly once more over this weird badland.

A camera would have recorded this ugly landscape as almost bereft of life. Leakey saw things differently, however, an inspired guess or a vision of the past as it might have been.

First, he saw graceful trees and rolling meadowlands where green grasses and vegetables grew. Mischievous monkeys gambolled in the thick foliage. Strange, elephant-like pachyderms with short trunks and thick, small tusks browsed quietly.

Nearby some hairy people, small but upright, with squat low foreheads, chattered amicably in one group. In another, workmen chipped stones to fashion new tools. Now rivers cut through the meadowlands in Leakey's inner eye, waters swift and clear. Eden was spread out before him.

He borrowed a helicopter from the American Omo Valley archaeological team, and returned to the sandstone hills near Alia Bay to check on what his inspired vision had promised. The helicopter blades had barely stopped whirling before Leakey picked up a Stone Age tool similar to those he had found in Olduvai Gorge when, as youngster, he joined his famous parents in their excavations. Within months Richard Leakey had assumed the directorship of Kenya's National Museums to begin the exploration which has made Koobi Fora the world's richest trove of hominid fossils.

Fewer than ten years later, he was summoned by his friend, Kamoya Kimeu, to a spot on the outlying edges of the Lake Turkana excavations. Leakey spent weeks piecing together thirty or more fossil fragments to reassemble a skull dating back almost three million years — evidence of *Homo habilis,* handy man, an early tool making ancestor of modern man. Other discoveries of even greater significance have since been made, including skulls of *Homo erectus,* the first species of man to walk upright. These discoveries confirmed mankind's presence on earth at least 500,000 years longer than previously believed.

Lake Turkana: The Jade Sea

Formerly known as Lake Rudolf, **Lake Turkana** covers 6,400 square kilometres (2,500 square miles) along the north-south axis of the Great Rift Valley. Turkana's blue-green waters gave the lake its other name, the **Jade Sea.**

The shores of the lake are mostly desert with occasional groups of ragged palms, stripped to ribbons by gales which blow day and night most of the year.

On the western shore two seasonal rivers, the **Turkwel** and the **Kerio,** feed the lake from deltas which spread out like the fingers of a hand. Through the swamps, which appear like lurid green oases in this land of rock and sand, the muddy flow of these rivers can be seen right out in the centre of the lake. To the south, the lake is guarded by an area of black lava boulders, terrible to walk across, which lead to the crater summit of **Mount Teleki.**

Turkana is also fed by the Omo, Ethiopia's second largest river, born 972 kilometres (600 miles) away on Mount Amara in Ethiopia's western highlands, which cuts a 32-kilometre-wide (20-mile) delta through a papyrus swamp to discharge 20 billion cubic litres of water each year into East Africa's fourth-largest lake.

The sun remorselessly sucks it out again by intense evaporation and, during the last century, the lake has shrunk dramatically. Thousands of years ago it was 150 metres (500 feet) deeper and connected to the White Nile basin by an outlet through the **Lotikipi Plain** beyond **Lokitaung** and the **Murua Rithi Hills.** Silt from the Omo has built up the lake bed in the north and some parts are now only ten metres (30 feet) deep. Around **Central Island,** however, and in the far south, the water reaches a depth of 140 metres (450 feet). Turkana is home to some of the world's most venomous reptiles — saw-scaled vipers, night- and puff-adders, and cobras. The lake also hosts a rich variety of birds; more than 350 species of resident and migratory birds live on the shores and waters of the lake, feeding on its rich, lacustrine life. Six ethnic peoples live around the lake shores and hinterland — the warrior-like **Turkana** to the west, the tiny **el-Molo** community around **Loiyangalani** on the south-east shore, the **Samburu** from Loiyangalani all the way up to Rumuruti, and the **Rendille, Gabbra,** and **Dassenich** (also known as Merille) to the east.

When to go
The Turkana region is scorchingly hot and dry throughout the year. When it rains, perhaps once every ten years, it can be humid.

Getting there
There are three springboards into the Northern Rift, which is considered by many to be one of the most exciting and adventurous places for independent travel in Africa: from Nanyuki on the shoulders of Mount Kenya to the eastern shore; from Nyahururu-Maralal to the south-eastern lake shores; and from Kitale to the western shore. However, no road connects the eastern and western shores which are barred by the virtually impenetrable barrier of volcanic rock that forms the walls of the **Suguta Valley.**

The western approach from **Kitale** is along the Kenya-Sudan highway which winds down through the **Cherangani Hills** for 355 kilometres (220 miles) to **Lodwar**. It passes the **Saiwa Swamp National Park** and through **Kapenguria,** shrine to the memory of Mzee Kenyatta. Traversing a tributary of the Turkwel River, it cuts through the **Marich Pass**, down to the south Turkana plains and skirts the **South Turkana National Reserve**, 100 kilometres (60 miles) from Kitale.

Set between 900 metres and 2,720 metres (2,950-8,920 feet) above sea level, the reserve's 1,091 square kilometres (421 square miles) of arid, thorn-bush plains are dominated by two small mountains with scattered remnant forest on their summits and higher slopes which are sanctuaries for elephant and greater kudu. The **Kerio River** forms a 25-kilometre (15-mile) boundary to the south-east and supports a gallery forest. To the west of the road, also 100 kilometres (60 miles) from Kitale, is the 92-square-kilometre (35-square-mile) **Nasolot National Reserve,** ranging from 750 to 1,500 metres (2,460-4,920 feet) above sea level.

Harsh and flat, the scorched thornbush plains, crisscrossed with seasonal watercourses, skirt the base of the **Sekerr Mountains**. There, after it leaves its gorge through the **Turkwel Dam**, one of Kenya's largest hydroelectric projects, it is joined by its tributaries, the **Suam** and the **Morun,** and enters the plains, forming the reserve's eastern boundary. Some 60 kilometres (40 miles) further on, the road passes through the small town of **Lokichar** and then on through the featureless wastes of the Turkana semi-desert to **Lodwar,** some 64 kilometres (40 miles) from Lake Turkana. Set at the foot of conical **Lodwar Mountain,** fast-growing Lodwar is the administrative centre of the 200,000-square-kilometre (77,220-square-mile) Turkana District.

It was established as a British outpost in the first decade of this century in a not too successful attempt to subdue the independent Turkana. One early colonial administrator was Captain Baron Eric von Otter, who could trek through the Turkana desert as swiftly as the nomads and was much respected. He died of skin cancer and was buried, with full British military honours, in Lodwar in 1923.

It was also there that Jomo Kenyatta was held for some time under informal house arrest before being moved to Maralal after he was released from prison at distant **Lokitaung** (see 'History: The Dust and the Ashes', Part One).

Lodwar is a major crossroad for the region. To the west, there is a road that leads to **Lorukumu** on the Rift escarpment which forms the remote border with Uganda. The main road continues north to **Lokichoggio** and the Sudanese border, and another road leads east to **Ferguson's Gulf,** a dried-up bay of the Jade Sea.

Sightseeing
Temperatures are extremely high. Constant winds whip dust around the **mission** buildings and **hospital,** and send it swirling down the streets where small shops and shanties cluster round a ramshackle beer shop. **Lodwar market** is colourful and worth a visit. The Turkana women, who

can be observed working at their various handicrafts while waiting to make an all too rare sale in this northern outpost, cheer up immensely at the sight of visitors. The town boasts only basic accommodation.

Two resorts
There are two lake resorts roughly the same distance from Lodwar. **Eliye Springs** to the east was once favoured to grow into something of a big game fishing resort and flourished in the late 1960s and early 1970s only to fade away. **Ferguson's Gulf**, northeast of Lodwar, is near the Turkana village of **Kalokol**, where the Norwegians built a massive filleting and freezing plant in the 1970s. The fish catches have fallen since Ferguson's Gulf, five kilometres (three miles) away, dried up — to leave **Lake Turkana Fishing Lodge** high and dry.

As the lodge caters mostly for weekend visitors who fly in from Nairobi, accommodation is usually available midweek. There's a campsite nearby and campers can use the lodge bar and water supply. For a modest sum you can hire fishing rods and hire a boat to go out on Turkana. Should you wish, the lodge will cook your catch for you, while you add your mark to fishing posterity on the walls of the bar.

Central Island National Park
Some 15 kilometres (nine miles) offshore lie the five square kilometres (two square miles) of **Central Island National Park**. Formed out of three large, still-steaming volcanoes, rising to 240 metres (800 feet) at their highest point, the island is a rare and fragile ecosystem. Its indigenous bushes and wild fruits form a critical link in the migration chain of bird species en route from Europe to Southern Africa.

The island's three small internal lakes have for aeons been the breeding ground for Turkana's population of Nile crocodile, the largest concentration in the world. They are survivors of an epoch long before mankind appeared on Turkana's eastern shores and live in perfect harmony with their environment. They feed on the prolific fish, which sustains a stable population of around 12,000 creatures. Some specimens reach a length of five metres (20 feet) and their form has not changed for 130 million years. During the April-May hatching season baby crocodiles chirrup in their eggs, buried deep beneath the sand to escape the predatory attention of monitor lizards and raptors. Their cries bring the parents scurrying to dig them out and carry them to the water's edge where they spend their first months.

Almost at the centre of the lake, on its north-south and east-west axis, Central Island is larger than **North Island**, which is 65 kilometres (40 miles) away, near the Omo delta. The only residents on this desolate smudge of rock are snakes, which originally drifted down from the delta on floating islands of papyrus. It is possible to explore the region north of Ferguson's Gulf. A dirt trail cuts along the featureless western shore for about 90 kilometres (55 miles) before it links up with the **Lodwar-Lokitaung-Namuruputh** dirt road.

Turn right on to this road and after 20 kilometres (12 miles) it reaches the Kenya-Ethiopian **border post** of **Todenyang**, one of the most remote police and immigration outposts in Kenya.

You can retrace your journey by turning west, where the Ferguson's Gulf trail joins the road, and visit Lokitaung, where there is a deep gorge and a great many fossil trees. Lokitaung also has vital historic significance to most Kenyans. It was there that Jomo Kenyatta and his colleagues served their seven years' hard labour.

From Lokitaung the road trails through the featureless scrub desert for 120 kilometres (75 miles) to the Kenya-Sudan highway. Turn west and it's some 160 kilometres (100 miles) to **Lokichoggio**.

Formerly an administrative centre, Lokichoggio is one of Kenya's remotest townships, with a population of around 25,000 and a floating population of aid workers, ICRC officials, and oil exploration teams.

From Maralal: Dustbowls and Oases

The second route to the Northern Rift, on the east shores of Lake Turkana, is through Nyahururu-Maralal. From the heartland of Kenya, three roads lead to Maralal (see 'North-Eastern Kenya: Sun-Scorched Plains of Darkness'), the first stage of the trip.

Above: El-Molo, fearless crocodile hunters of the Jade Sea.
Opposite: El-Molo youngster with crocodile.

Getting there

From **Maralal,** set at 1,490 metres (4,900 feet) above sea level, the rough, rocky 225-kilometre-long (140-mile) road plunges down 1,110 metres (3,650 feet) to the shores of the Jade Sea through some of the toughest terrain in the world. Skirting the base of 2,583-metre (8,475-foot) **Poror,** after some 30 kilometres (20 miles) it reaches **Moridjo** on the rim of a vast crescent-shaped escarpment, one of the most dramatic in the Rift Valley.

Plunging down more than 2,000 metres (6,560 feet), it raises the curtain on the magnificent amphitheatre of the Suguta Valley, then rolls down on to the lethal **El Barta** plains.

After 70 kilometres (45 miles), the trail degenerates into a boulder-strewn track which cuts through the ravine between the **Ndoto Mountains** in the east, where the high point touches 2,640 metres (8,650 feet) and, in the west, the 1,369-metre (4,492-foot) **Samburu Hills,** to **Baragoi.** Another 50 kilometres (30 miles) along a very rough track leads to **South Horr,** where the road enters a gorge of the **Nyiru Mountains,** with the 2,752-metre (9,029-foot) **Mowong Sowang** in the west and another 2,067-metre (6,782-foot) peak to the east.

Though it's close to the dustbowl of the **Suguta Valley,** one of the hottest places on earth, South Horr is delightfully cool. Shaded by verdant trees, nearby **Kurungu Valley** is one of the loveliest campsites in Kenya, six kilometres (four miles) beyond the town.

The camp was established by Safari Camp Services, who also offer luxury safaris. Showers and cold drinks are available at the Kurungu Valley camp and, considering its location, this amounts to luxury. Furnished *bandas* are available, but camping is more memorable.

The surrounding mountain forest hides myriad wildlife and, for a modest fee, local Samburu take you to the top of Nyiru peak and stunning views over Lake Turkana.

A *Son et Lumiére* show at the camp features traditional culture. From South Horr, the cataclysmic track descends 90 kilometres (60 miles) to **Loiyangalani** — the tiny el-Molo community's 'place of trees'.

197

Where to stay

Comfortable accommodation is available at **Oasis Lodge**, which has a swimming pool but is costly. Safari Camp Services also have a comfortable base that can fairly claim to be a lodge, and there are several campsites.

Most campers choose the **Sunset Strip** campsite south of the lodge, protected from the wind which whips down from the summit of 2,295-metre (7,530-foot) **Mount Kulal.** This haven offers showers under the palms, toilets, cooking facilities, and a small open 'bar'.

Sightseeing

Euphemistically described as the capital of the south-east region around the shores of Lake Turkana, Loiyangalani is a settlement of a few tin shacks, **police post**, **mission** and **mission school**, campsites, and two lodges. Such is its isolation that the town often runs out of beer — and is unable to restock.

There is a beach of sorts a few kilometres south of the town. Crocodile are not supposed to frequent the area, but take care.

A visit to **South Island National Park**, means a 13-kilometre (eight-mile) round trip, and you need good weather. Sudden 100-kilometre-an-hour (60-mile) storms whip off Kulal and turn the Jade Sea into a tempest. There are few places to land, but the cove in the north is perhaps the best. You'll see the narrow, crescent rim of a submerged volcano just a few kilometres north of there. Covering 39 square kilometres (15 square miles), South Island is the tip of a volcano, six-and-a-half kilometres (four miles) from the east coast and 24 kilometres (15 miles) from the south shore. All that lives there is a herd of feral goats. Volcanic ash covers the island end to end and the nightly glow of its luminous vents inspired stories of evil spirits.

South Island was also the scene of a mysterious tragedy involving an expedition led by Vivian Fuchs, later knighted for his exploratory work in Antarctica. Three days after landing, in July 1934, he returned to the mainland, sending another member of the expedition to join the col-

Right: Crater lake on Turkana's Central Island.

198

league he had left behind. Neither man was ever seen again. Few visitors set foot on Turkana's southern shore, made up of scorched black lava from centuries of volcanic eruptions, including, most recently, the **Nabuyatom Cone** and **Teleki's Volcano**. Beyond lies the forbidding **Barrier** which blocks the approach to **Suguta Valley**, where the mean yearly temperature is 54°C (130°F). Thousands of years ago Suguta was an extension of Lake Turkana. Now the only water in this vast dustbowl is **Lake Logipi's** alkaline froth.

The least known of all the Rift's soda lakes, Logipi is a haven for flamingos when there is enough water and algae. To visit the lake you need at least two 4WD vehicles and local guides. You should be absolutely fit and carry enough water and fuel.

Mount Kulal Biosphere Reserve
Another equally demanding excursion from Loiyangalani can be made to **Mount Kulal**, centrepiece of another of Kenya's four UNESCO-named Biosphere Reserves, which covers an area of 7,000 square kilometres (2,700 square miles) and embraces the South Island National Park, most of Lake Turkana, its volcanic southern shores, and the **Chalbi Desert**, an ancient lake bed.

The reserve includes many volcanic craters and lava flows, including **Teleki's** Volcano and 2,285-metre (7,498-foot) Mount Kulal with its rain and mist forests, box canyons and deep, volcanic crater. Kulal's two summits are joined by a narrow, steep ridge. The climb is straightforward if you are suitably equipped (see 'Kenya's Mountains'). Vegetation ranges from mountain forest to desert.

The Garden of Eden
Sibiloi National Park, gazetted to protect the many remarkable hominid fossil finds made by Richard Leakey's team since 1968, also embraces Central Island National Park.

Some 720 kilometres (450 miles) from Nairobi, the open, windswept plains, dominated by yellow spear grass and doum palms, are interspersed with luggas and flanked by volcanic formations, including **Mount Sibiloi** and the remains of a petrified forest. The climate is hot and windy with fierce and frequent gales. Covering 1,570 square kilometres (600 square miles)

of rock, desert and arid bush, Sibiloi has proved a unique treasury of mankind's origins. Many important prehistoric fossils were found exposed on the surface, blown clean by the ceaseless wind.

Richard Leakey recounts his discovery of the area's first *Australopithecus* fossil: 'There on the sand 20 feet ahead, in full view beside a thorny bush, lay a domed greyish-white object. Halfway to it I sat down stunned, incredulous, staring.

'For years I had dreamed of such a prize, and now I had found it — the nearly complete skull of an early hominid.'

Some of Leakey's Turkana finds have been left *in situ* at the park headquarters — including one of a prehistoric elephant. To quicken the pace of discovery, Leakey evolved a new approach involving a multidisciplinary team of scientists.

Their unique mix of skills, beliefs and nationalities, has resulted in more profound assessments about early human history than could ever have been achieved by one person (see 'History: The Dust and the Ashes', Part One).

The precise location of each discovery is marked by a concrete post bearing a reference number. The three most important finds are KNM-ER 1470, which is the skull of *Homo habilis*, and KNM-ER 3733 and 3883, the skulls of *Homo erectus.*

It is not just the fossils which have given significance to Sibiloi. The sedimentary layers have yielded important evidence of the environment three million years ago, and of the animals and plants with which early man and pre-man shared the world.

It's another backbreaking 60 kilometres (40 miles) along the eastern shore to the police and immigration outpost of **Ileret**, the 'capital' of Kenya's semi-nomadic Dassenich or Merille peoples who spill over into Ethiopia.

Getting there
Sibiloi National Park is 120 kilometres (75 miles) distant from Loiyangalani. But the only marked trail — if you can call it that — is east through the desert to the outpost of **North Horr** and then north-west to **Alia Bay**, the park headquarters. The other land route is more than 350 kilometres (220 miles) across the **Chalbi Desert** from **Marsabit**.

Southern Kenya: Theatres of the Wild

The most popular part of Kenya lies in the southern sector of the country, divided by the canyon of the Great Rift Valley.

Above the **Nkuruman Escarpment**, which forms the western wall, is the northernmost extremity of the great Serengeti ecosystem, the **Maasai Mara**, for many people incomparably the most breathtaking of all the country's game reserves, perhaps of all Africa.

To the east of the Rift, beyond the Meto Hills, which form the Rift's eastern wall, lies celebrated **Amboseli**, at the base of Africa's greatest mountain, **Kilimanjaro**. And beyond Amboseli, divided only by a narrow panhandle of wilderness plain and developing smallholdings, lies **Tsavo**, the country's largest national park, which is bisected by the Nairobi-Mombasa highway.

These arid savannah plains, covered with fragile grasslands and scrub bush, are animal sanctuaries of such magnificence that they have earned Kenya its reputation as the last great treasury of African wildlife.

Maasai Mara

At the turn of the century, Maasai territory covered more than 150,000 square kilometres (47,000 square miles) — a large portion of the southern uplands of Kenya and what is now northern Tanzania.

Four forested, mountain massifs rose out of this land — the Aberdare Range and Mount Kenya in Kenya and Kilimanjaro and Mount Meru in Tanzania — and it contained two areas outstanding for their wildlife: Amboseli and the Mara.

An extension of Tanzania's Serengeti National Park, today the Maasai Mara National Reserve, between 1,500 and 2,170 metres (5,000-7,000 feet) high, covers some 1,672 square kilometres (645 square miles) (see 'National Parks', In Brief, for vegetation). Although often described as the greatest of nature's stages, the Mara adds up to less than four per cent of the whole Serengeti ecosystem. Yet, in 1985, when the migration was at its peak, the reserve held

almost 2.5 million large herbivores together with smaller species — 1.4 million wildebeest, 550,000 gazelle, 200,000 zebra, 62,000 buffalo, 64,100 impala, 61,200 topi, 7,500 hartebeest, 7,100 giraffe, 3,000 eland and 4,000 elephant — plus uncounted antelope, rhino, wart hog, bushpig and giant forest hog. In addition there were the predators — lion, leopard, cheetah, hyena, wild dog and jackal — and many small mammals, birds, reptiles, amphibians and insects.

These creatures crowd into the Mara grasslands for three to four months during the annual migration. In its size and extent, however, the migration is a relatively new phenomenon.

When the 20th century dawned, the animals, although abundant, did not exist in anything like today's numbers. Now, when the rains bring the first green flush to the short grass plains in southern Serengeti, and the pans and pools fill with water — usually from November to January — these species crowd the area. Then, as the dry weather sets in, they pull back north and westwards into the woodlands and longer grasses, finally crowding into the golden savannah of the Mara in one of the greatest wildlife spectacles ever seen.

Getting there

From the new Nairobi-to-Nakuru road the left turn beyond Rironi takes you onto the old Rift Escarpment road. This truly atrocious road was built in the early 1940s by Italian prisoners-of-war and internees.

On the right, at the foot of the escarpment, just before it levels out on the valley floor, is the often vandalized but now restored (1989) **Chapel of St Mary of the Angels** which the road workers built as a thanksgiving. It was consecrated on Christmas Day, 1943. A few kilometres beyond the chapel there is a left turn along smooth tarmac for 148 kilometres (92 miles) to **Narok**, a major Maasai administration centre. **Kajiado**, on the south-eastern side of the Rift, is another.

A good murram-surfaced road through Maasailand links with the tarmac section of the **Kajiado-Ngong Hills road**, taking it

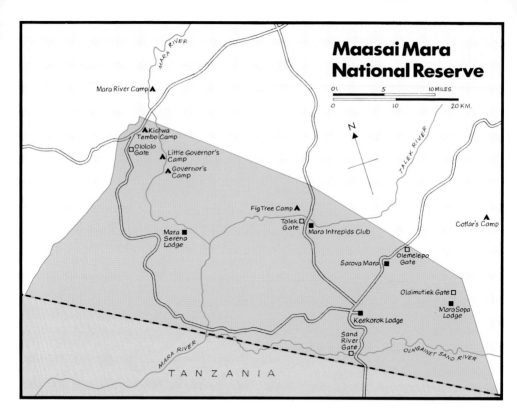

over the northern shoulders of these hills and down the escarpment past **Susua** in the **Kedong Valley** to join the existing Naivasha-Narok road. Tall silos on the horizon herald your arrival at Narok with its acacia and jacaranda trees and the Maasai who stand sentinel at every corner. The town boasts a **club** and has the one and only **petrol station** before the Mara. While waiting for your tank to be filled you'll be overwhelmed by a veritable mêlée of vendors touting curios.

You can also reach Narok from the north — from Nakuru via Njoro along steep roads twisting over the Mau Escarpment, or from the south-west hills (see 'Western Kenya: The Source of the Nile'). Both roads are rough going. And from Narok, the worst is yet to come — after the road crosses the **Engare Narok River**, 20 kilometres (12 miles) beyond Narok at **Ewaso Nyiro** the tarmac ends. But if you turn left for the eastern section of the reserve, where **Keekorok Lodge** and the **reserve headquarters** are located, there is a tarmac road straight to the reserve gate. Turn right for the western end, including

the **Mara River**, **Governor's Camps**, and **Kichwa Tembo**. The dirt tracks offer some idea of what drivers and vehicles undergo in the annual Safari Rally. You may well be easily persuaded to fly next time.

Chartered or private planes operate from Wilson Airport and there's a daily 45-minute scheduled service by vintage DC-3 which lands you without a bruise.

Where to stay

There are three kinds of accommodation: lodges, luxury tented camps, and self-service camping. Among the best lodges are Keekorok, the oldest (built at the spot where hunter Sydney Downey used to base his client's camp); the Masai Mara Sopa Lodge; Mara Serena, a 5-star Maasai *manyatta;* Kichwa Tembo — 'head of the elephant' — (a tented camp at the base of the Olol Escarpment; Governors' Camp (on one of Theodore Roosevelt's old campsites on the Mara River); Little Governors'; and Governors' Paradise Camp. Siana Springs, Mara River, Fig Tree, Mara Intrepids and Mara Sarova camps are all comfortable tented camps.

Above: Mara Serena Lodge in the Maasai Mara National Reserve.

Sightseeing

The Mara is bordered in the east by the **Loita Hills**, in the south by Tanzania, in the west by the **Soit Ololol Escarpment**, and in the north by the **Talek River**. **Leganishu**, at 2,191 metres (7,189 feet), is the highest peak in the reserve.

The **Nyangores** and the **Amala**, two large streams draining off the **Central Mau range**, merge downstream as the **Mara River**. Entering the sanctuary at its northernmost point, the river bisects the reserve from north to south, crosses the Tanzania border and turns west to Lake Victoria.

The altitude gives the region an equable climate even though it is less than two degrees south of the Equator. From the air, the visual effect of the Mara's thickets and grasslands is not unlike the spots on a leopard's or cheetah's coat. In the *Maa* language Mara means 'dappled'. The Mara plains are dominated by *Themeda triandra* (red-oat grass), a characteristic of the Serengeti, which furnishes the golden backdrop to many an East African memory.

Most trees in the reserve have no common English names. Of the many species of acacia, two stand out: yellow fever trees, *Acacia xanthoploea* (see 'Flora: Forests of Flame, Streets of Mauve', Part Three); and the stunted, shrubby, whistling thorn, *Acacia drepanalobium*, of the open plains, home to a species of ant. They drill their nests in the twigs, leaving one or two holes as entrances. When the wind blows across these holes it makes a tinny, whistling sound.

When an animal brushes against the tree, or browses on its leaves, the ants rush out to attack. So, while defending their own nests, the ants also protect the tree.

Watch a giraffe browsing on whistling thorn — it will eat only a few mouthfuls before moving on. Besides acacia, the Mara's thickets and forest patches contain many other species of tree and shrub.

Along watercourses several varieties of wild fig attract fruit-eating birds, baboons, monkeys and, at night, fruit bats. The Mara's soil is 'black cotton', which forms an almost bottomless morass during the rains. The park is well developed — some say over-developed — and well-served with rough game viewing tracks, passable to most vehicles during dry weather.

Amboseli: The Hollywood Image

Long a favourite of Hollywood film makers, the **Amboseli National Park's** 392 square kilometres (152 square miles) form the perfect auditorium for scenic views of Africa's highest mountain, 5,896-metre (19,340-foot) Kilimanjaro, the highest freestanding mountain in the world. Ringed by a halo of cumulus, its wedding cake peak floating magically in the incredible blue of the African sky, Kilimanjaro has become the clichéd symbol of Africa. But no matter how many times you've seen the movies or the magazine pictures, nothing prepares you for the breathtaking first, real vision of the monolith. Seen from the dry bed of the seasonal Amboseli lake, at around 1,200 metres (4,000 feet), Kilimanjaro rises another 4,696 metres (15,340 feet).

Relatively young by comparison with its neighbouring giants, Mounts Kenya and Elgon, Kilimanjaro burst out of the savannah a million years ago, and is covered with one-fifth of all the ice in Africa.

Besides the mountain, Amboseli is famed for its wildlife spectacle and the park is one of Kenya's earliest game sanctuaries. It was established in 1948 and in 1961 was handed over to the district council — along with an annuity — to run as a national reserve. Subsequently, 392 square kilometres (152 square miles) were excised as a national park. Vegetation ranges from equatorial rain forest, through savannah, and across true desert — at 4,570 metres (15,000 feet) — to exotic alpine flora.

Once part of the Great Southern Game Reserve, Amboseli's fragile grasslands, like those of the Mara, are under constant attack from the ravaging wheels of tourist minibuses, though it remains virtually as it was when Joseph Thomson marched across it more than a century ago.

Getting there

It's common these days to fly from the Maasai Mara, over the Rift and Magadi to Amboseli or Tsavo. Particularly for coastal visitors on a limited upcountry game excursion, a short flight of between 40 and 60 minutes saves valuable game-viewing time. Many people still travel by road, however.

Take the Mombasa highway east out of Nairobi to **Athi River**, where a smooth road forks right to head south, over the Athi Plains to **Kajiado**. There, a broad sweep of bleak grasslands, often brooding in the lowering sky of a late afternoon storm, occasionally affords glimpses of the last remnants of its once abundant wildlife — herds of zebra and wildebeest, and maybe a giraffe or two.

Twenty-eight kilometres (17 miles) from Athi River the road runs through the Maasai village of **Isenya** where the Maasai Anglican Church's **Rural Training Centre** is established in an old Mau Mau detention centre. Maasai leatherware is on sale at the local tannery. Twenty-three kilometres (14 miles) beyond Isenya, the road enters Kajiado, the administrative headquarters of southern Maasailand at the southern extremity of the **Kaputei Plains.**

Kajiado is all Maasai and cattle. Nearby a **marble quarry** provides the exterior and interior finish for many of Nairobi's new buildings. The town **cemetery** contains the graves of twenty-four casualties of the First World War, killed when General Paul von Lettow-Vorbeck's German army defeated a British force in a battle at the base of 2,629-metre (8,625-foot) **Longido**, just across the border from Namanga, in Tanzania. Another 88 kilometres (55 miles) on from Kajiado, through unromantic **Bisell**

Amboseli National Park

N

Namanga Gate

LAKE AMBOSELI

Kilimanjaro Buffalo Lodge

☐ Lemeiboti Gate

Airstrip

Observation Hut

Amboseli Lodge

Ol Tukai Lodge

Kilimanjaro Safari Lodge

☐ Kimana Gate

Amboseli Serena Lodge

Kimana Safari Lodge

KIMANA

TANZANIA

LOITOKITOK

0   5   10 MILES
0   10   20 KM.

MT. KILIMANJARO ▲

with its ruling party **KANU office**, and rolling, broken countryside of red, laterite soil and open acacia scrub, brings you to **Namanga**. As you drive, the forested slopes and rugged 2,526-metre (8,287-foot) summit of **Ol Doinyo Orok** (the 'Black' or 'Namanga mountain') rise ever higher on the horizon until, just before Namanga, the road skirts its lower slopes. Across the border looms the distant profile of another of Africa's highest mountains, 4,565-metre (14,979-foot) **Mount Meru.**

Namanga, a flourishing border town, is just a short walk through no-man's land from Tanzania, and now abustle again since the 1996 revival of East African Co-operation. It has a **petrol station** and three hotels of varying standards, including the rustic charms of **Namanga River Hotel,** which nestles beneath the mountain peak in its well-established gardens and is a useful midway stop on the journey from Nairobi to **Arusha**, 130 kilometres (80 miles) away in Tanzania. Turning left at Namanga past the petrol station it's another 70 kilometres (43 miles) to the **Meshanani Gate**.

There are two alternative routes through the park to Ol Tukai. One is to remain on the main trail, often rough and heavily corrugated depending on whether or not it has recently been graded. Keep on this route, avoiding a right fork which presents itself a few kilometres further on. The other route is over the dried-up lake bed, only passable in the very dry season.

All the time, Kilimanjaro is on the right. The airstrip built by the National Youth Service in 1973 is carpeted with tarmac.

Where to stay
Amboseli Serena Lodge; Amboseli Lodge (built of sturdy Kenya cedar and local stone); Kilimanjaro Safari Lodge (built on the site of one of Ernest Hemingway's former camps); and the sumptuous Ol Tukai Lodge which opened in April 1996.

There are other lodges outside the park and several tented camps and campsites. The self-help *bandas* at Ol Tukai, among the first in-park guest accommodation in Kenya, opened in 1950. During the filming of *Where No Vultures Fly* in Amboseli the *bandas* were occupied by the film crew. Now they have been transformed into Hollywood-style accommodation.

Sightseeing
At first glance, especially in the dry season, **Amboseli National Park** appears a dry, unattractive dustbowl — the result of two decades of tourist erosion. But Amboseli's magic and charm grow by the second. Anyone who has sat in a car, beside a herd of elephants — males, females, juveniles and the tiniest of the very young (there is a resident elephant population of some 700) will find it hard to disagree.

Set close to the Tanzanian border, beneath the north-west face of Kilimanjaro, a large area of the park is taken up by a seasonal lake. The dry soda bed of the lake gives the park its name — Amboseli derives from the Maa for 'salt dust'. During the dry season the heat creates a series of shimmering mirages over the lake basin.

Most of the park is hot and dry, covered with patches of semi-arid acacias and fragile savannah. However, there are three large **swamps** in the south-eastern area fed by **underground springs** from the melt waters of Kilimanjaro which filter through its volcanic strata to appear pure and crystal clear. These springs with their papyrus sedges are the only source of permanent water and the major watering points for the park's wildlife, including 56 species of mammal (see 'National Parks', In Brief, for wildlife and vegetation).

A lookout post on **Observation Hill,** one of the high points of the park, gives a panoramic view of this unique sanctuary and **Enkongo Narok** (Black River) and the **Engone Naibor** and **Loginye swamps** which stand out a brilliant emerald-green.

Excursions from Amboseli
Amboseli is the ideal place from which to visit both the Maasai border town of **Oloitokitok** and the 4,430-metre (7,134-foot) **Chyulu Hills**, which in the 1980s were declared a national park, virtually an extension of Tsavo. Leaving Amboseli to the south-east, the track veers along the southern edge of **Loginye Swamp**, a likely haunt of elephant, hippo, giraffe and buffalo, and past the incongruous pagoda-style **Kilimanjaro Buffalo Lodge** (this incredible essay in luxury living has its own airstrip). After some 20 kilometres (12 miles) you arrive at the **Emali-Loitokitok road,** also known as the **pipeline road.**

Turn right and then left for Tsavo West, on the road leading to the **Chyulu Gate** and the **Shaitani** lava flow, a relic of the birth of the Chyulus between four and five centuries ago. Alternatively, after turning right, ignore the left turn and carry straight on to Oloitokitok, beneath the serrated Kilimanjaro peak of 5,147-metre (16,890-foot) **Mawenzi,** some 121 kilometres (75 miles) from Sultan Hamud and virtually the same distance from Namanga.

A bustling border town, Oloitokitok is well worth a visit. Market days — Tuesday and Saturday — are particularly colourful and the panorama over the Amboseli plains to the Chyulus and Tsavo West are reward enough for the journey. A dirt link road crosses the border and runs over the eastern shoulder of Kilimanjaro to the Tanzanian town of Moshi, nestled on the south-east slopes of the mountain.

However, if instead you choose to tour the Chyulu Hills, turn **left** on the pipeline road and drive straight past **Kimana Swamp**, which is rich in wildlife. Nearby **Kimana Lodge** serves as a flower-strewn haven in the wilderness. Continue to **Makutano** and turn right along a savagely-dusty track to the northern face of the Chyulu Hills, which erupted from the savannah four or five centuries ago.

You drive up a tortuous 4WD track and along the crest of the hills, one of the toughest sections of the famed Safari Rally, and down into Tsavo.

Among the youngest of the world's mountains, the Chyulus arch their narrow back in an 80-kilometre (50-mile) east-west ridge. Much of this forms the 471-square-kilometre (182-square-mile) **Chyulu Hills National Park.** The soil is still harsh gritty lava, but after the short rains it is coated with a veneer of fragile grass. In such a mantle of green, the Chyulus are supremely beautiful, appearing like grassy moorlands.

Water percolating through the hills forms deep and fast-flowing subterranean rivers that join other underground rivers flowing from Kilimanjaro. These feed the Mzima Springs oasis in arid Tsavo West.

Deep beneath the hills lies a catacomb of eerie caves, some more than 12 kilometres (seven miles) long, maybe longer, but still unexplored.

Tsavo National Park: Last of the Great Tuskers

Tsavo is Kenya's largest national park — and one of the largest wildlife sanctuaries in the world. Among the first to be established in Kenya, in 1948, now combined with the Chyulu Hills National Park, the twin Tsavo West and East national parks cover an area of 21,754 square kilometres (8,399 square miles), more than 450 square kilometres (270 square miles) larger than Wales. In all, this adds up to more than four per cent of Kenya's total land area and is a measure of the country's concern for its natural heritage.

Almost half-a-million visitors enter Tsavo each year, providing hundreds of thousands of dollars in revenue from gate fees. Its luxury lodges also pay handsome royalties for the privilege of providing five-star comfort in the wilderness.

Located midway between Mombasa and Nairobi at an altitude that ranges from 229 to 2,000 metres (750-6,500 feet), the eastern sector of the park includes part of the 300-kilometre-long (186-mile) **Yatta Plateau,** and various volcanic hills. It is otherwise a flat plain, drained by the **Athi**, **Tiva**, **Tsavo** and **Voi rivers.**

As unique in character as in size, Tsavo is an outstanding example of how Africa constantly reshapes itself in response to animal and climatic changes. And for a discriminating minority, it is the most fascinating nature sanctuary on the African continent. More than sixty major mammal species roam its ranges, which contain more than 1,000 plant species. In the south these plants are typical of the Maasai grasslands. In the north more arid species survive best (see 'National Parks', In Brief, for wildlife and vegetation).

Birdlife is varied and exciting. Crocodile are found in pools, the Mzima Springs, and the rivers of Tsavo East which they share with schools of fish and sounders of hippo.

Once thickly-wooded, Tsavo West was transformed over the years into open grass and bushland by the great elephant herds which roamed endlessly across its red earth. In such trackless wastes, policing herds and poachers is an almost impossible

Above: Endangered rhino and elephant graze beneath the distant heights of Kilimanjaro.

task. Ironically the park's name derives from the Akamba for 'slaughter'. But with President Moi's commitment to the conservation of these wildlife giants, the 1990s saw the balance restored. Another hazard that the park wardens and rangers have to contend with is fire — either started spontaneously during the long, hot, dry summer, or by Akamba honey-hunters guided by the honey-guide bird. More than 100 of the park tracks, out of 2,000 kilometres (1,250 miles) of dirt trails, are dedicated as fire breaks. The park's network of well-graded, well-maintained murram roads is one reason why it retains its special magic.

Getting there (Tsavo West)
From Nairobi along the main Mombasa highway there are gates into Tsavo West at **Mtito Andei** and **Kyulu,** between Mtito Andei and **Voi**. From Amboseli in the south, Tsavo is 91 kilometres (56 miles) away — about a two-hour drive. Turn right on to the Oloitokitok road, then left down a corrugated road, through semi-permanent Maasai *manyattas* and homesteads, skirting the base of the Chyulu Hills. You enter the park itself, as announced by the sudden smoothness of the sandy road, well before arriving at the **Chyulu Gate.** This road is broken by the coalesced, tar-like waste of the **Shaitani lava flow** which spewed down from the Chyulus when they erupted out of the plain. The flow takes its name from the Swahili word for 'devil'. Local lore says that if you clamber to the highest point of this fascinating flow you will vanish for ever. Soon after crossing Shaitani you reach the gate.

Where to stay
Just six kilometres (four miles) from the Chyulu Gate stands Kilaguni Lodge, the first wildlife lodge built in a Kenya national park, opened by England's Duke of Gloucester in 1962. Alternatively, you can stay at Ngulia Lodge, on the edge of a high escarpment in the Ngulia Hills. Both merit the epithet 'superlative'. Kitani and Ngulia Safari Camps, two self-service camps, are a few kilometres from the main lodges.

Sightseeing
The Tsavo West National Park covers a

Above: Delicate veneer of rain flush casts a mantle of green over the Chyulu Hills.

vast region of 9,065 square kilometres (3,500 square miles) (see 'National Parks', In Brief, for wildlife and vegetation). Yet even in the small area around Kilaguni there is so much to see and explore a single night's stay is insufficient to cover it all.

Kilaguni established a concept which linked conservation to tourism. It inspired a host of other lodges that were established in wildlife sanctuaries across the country.

North of the lodge lie the **Mungai Plains,** where the grass is often as high as an elephant's eye. Combined with stunted acacia thorns, it demands a zealous and tireless game-spotter to find the animals: but this offers the same sense of excitement as the old hunting safaris.

Tsavo West headquarters, with a well-served, well-maintained campsite for do-it-yourself safari-goers, lie on these plains at **Kamboyo.**

East from the lodge, across the airstrip, the road leads up to the **Roaring Rocks** from which the scarp plunges in a sheer drop of more than 100 metres (300 feet).

The place is named after the sound of the cicadas that infest the area and the

wind which whistles over the scarp edge. It's a notable place for birdwatchers, butterfly enthusiasts and small-game hunters, with many lizards and various creepy-crawlies to study.

Another shelter nearby, which is known as **Poacher's Lookout,** was built in memory of Jack Hilton, deputy director of Kenya's national parks before independence.

The biggest attraction in Tsavo West, however, just ten kilometres (six miles) from Kilaguni, is the **Mzima Springs,** a fount of cool, clear water. One hundred kilometres (60 miles) away, the equatorial sun melts the snowcap of Kilimanjaro. The water filters down thousands of metres through the mountain's volcanic strata to join up with underground rivers flowing from the nearby Chyulu Hills. These burst out as Mzima Springs at a peak rate of almost 500 million litres (110 million gallons) a day.

Years ago a film team constructed an underwater **observation post** in the banks of the springs. Clamber down a few steps and you enter a new world: hippo move slowly across the bed of the springs rather like moon walkers. Fat tilapia swim by in great schools and a Nile crocodile glides through the water on the other side of the glass by your nose. Until the 1980s, the springs were Mombasa's sole source of water, sent gushing down a 150-kilometre (95-mile) pipeline, now supplemented by a scheme that draws supplies from the Sabaki River.

It's 30 kilometres (20 miles) along the main track from Mzima to the **Ngulia Hills**, a range of sheer cliffs which rise out of the plains 610 metres (2,000 feet) below.

A detour leads over another fascinating lava flow, **Chaimu,** and down a series of hairpin bends through Rhino Valley to **Ngulia Safari Camp,** for self-service tourists and visitors. From there the track climbs up the **Ndawe Escarpment** through thick forest to **Ngulia Safari Lodge**, built atop these cliffs in 1970.

It has created a great avian phenomenon. In October and November during the short rains, when mists are frequent, millions of migrating birds make their passage southward over this region of Kenya. Disorientated by the shadowy glow of the lodge's artificial moon, they fly down low in their thousands — enabling ornithologists to net and ring them. Many secrets of the immense distances which these birds navigate with uncanny instinct have been revealed.

The lodge is one of the few places in Kenya outside the Mara where there's a chance of seeing leopard. They haunt the cliffs and forests of these craggy hills. The waterhole draws much big and small game.

Not far from the lodge there is also a protected **rhino sanctuary.** Three of its residents were stunned with tranquillizing darts on the private Salt Lick game sanctuary to the east and relocated to form a breeding nucleus in the lee of the Ngulia Hills in the hope that in the years ahead their offspring would help to regenerate the rhino population.

The seasonal **Tsavo River** flows around the base of the hills and its valley makes a delightful route to Mzito Andei. Alternatively, follow the 57-kilometre (35-mile) trail across the park, through valleys and over hills, to the **Maktau** gate and cross the railway line to the main Voi-Taveta road.

Tsavo East: Echoes of a Forgotten Grandeur

Covering an area of 11,747 square kilometres (4,535 square kilometres), much of Tsavo East — the northern sector — is closed to the public. But the areas which are open evoke memories of Africa's former grandeur. Much of this arid landscape is a flat, uninterrupted plain of empty bush, sporadically cluttered with the bizarre-shaped 'upside down' baobab tree.

Beyond the park border, these same plains are roamed by sparse groups of hunter-gatherers and nomads of Somali stock who eke out a living in a countryside where it seems nothing could survive.

A minority of these nomads are the Wata (see 'The People', Part One), Kenya's most renowned trackers and hunters. Hundreds of years before the archermen of Plantagenet England faced the French at Agincourt, the Wata used the long bow.

There are gates into Tsavo East off the main Nairobi-Mombasa road, at **Mtito Andei, Voi,** and beyond at **Buchuma**.

Where to stay
Accommodation near Mtito Andei is available at Tsavo Safari Camp on the banks of the Galana, upstream from the Athi and downstream from the Sabaki River.

At Voi, Voi Safari Lodge offers luxurious — and Aruba Lodge self-service — accommodation. Aruba Lodge also has a shop which sells basic provisions, including firewood. It can be noisy at night, depending on which and how many animals decide to pay a visit to the nearby dam. Half-a-kilometre from Voi, there's a campsite with wooden cottages and tap water.

Sightseeing
The entrance at Mtito Andei serves primarily as the gateway to the Tsavo Safari Camp on the banks of the **Galana,** which has served for more than two decades as one of the grand African 'outback' experiences. It was originally named in honour of Glen Cottar, one of the country's legendary white hunters. The rough road travels through typical Tsavo East *nyika* for 27 kilometres (17 miles) to the river banks. If

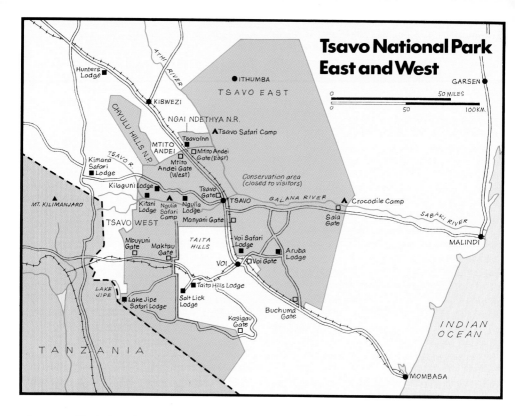

the crocodile-infested river is in spate, the crossing by rubber dinghy is both exciting and perilous — but still not as dramatic as a night spent in the camp. Buffalo might just walk through the clearing as you eat. A highlight of a stay there is a trip up the Yatta Plateau for a sundowner, where you may catch a glimpse of elephant.

Just inside the Voi gate, on the left, are the **Education Centre**, the **park headquarters** and the **house** where the late David Sheldrick, a dedicated wildlife professional, lived with his wife Daphne. His name is perpetuated in the **Sheldrick Memorial Fund**, dedicated to conservation. Daphne Sheldrick told of her husband's life in the *Tsavo Story*, and her own in *Orphans of Tsavo*.

She continues her good work at her home inside the Nairobi National Park, and for many years has been the recipient, custodian, and foster mother of the waifs and strays of Kenya's wildlife — usually orphaned infant elephants, rhinos and others whose parents were slaughtered by poachers. From the Voi gate the road to the left climbs up a hill and, just ten kilometres (six

miles) into the park, arrives at perhaps the most beautifully designed of all Kenya's wildlife lodges, **Voi Safari Lodge**.

Reflecting neither Western nor indigenous themes, it is in harmony with its setting, cut into the ledge of a craggy cliff. It offers a taste of both luxury and wildlife; as you swim in the blue-tiled pool, you can look down on elephant and buffalo at the watering hole below.

Climb up the cliff behind (strenuous for the unfit) to be rewarded by magnificent panoramas to the east and north-east. This amazing landscape seems bereft of any single, outstanding, physical feature.

From the lodge, which seems a million light years from Voi and the hurry-scurry of the lethal Nairobi-Mombasa road, drive twenty-four kilometres (15 miles) past **Irima waterhole,** to a whaleback hump of rock, **Mudanda.** Africa's answer to Australia's Ayers Rock towers over a natural dam where Tsavo East's profuse wildlife gathers in thousands during the dry seasons.

From there, retrace your path, then turn along the **Buffalo wallow**, and travel for 50 kilometres (30 miles) to the **Galana River.** Turn right and travel four kilometres (two-and-a-half miles) downstream and you come to **Lugard's Falls,** named after Britain's first proconsul in East Africa, Captain — later Lord — Lugard.

Mighty when in spate, the falls cascade through a narrow rock neck. For the brave or foolhardy only, it's said you can stand astride the top of the falls and watch the waters plunge to the pool below where crocodiles bask motionless in the sun. Do so at your own risk. In 1995 two British tourists were swept to their deaths there.

From this point, via **Sobo** to the park's **Sala Gate** (and then on to Malindi), is 110 kilometres (68 miles). Just beyond the Sala Gate, the **Galana Game Ranch** was a private wildlife reserve spread over 250,000 hectares (617,750 acres), which offered an esoteric, tailor-made safari experience for the wealthy élite. Because of the poaching problem in the area, it has been closed.

It lay under the lee of the 300-kilometre-long (186-mile) **Yatta Plateau,** one of the world's longest lava flows. The plateau overshadows the Athi-Galana River, which is spawned in the Ngong Hills close to Nairobi, for much of the river's course.

Further along the Galana, at the **Crocodile Camp**, it is said you can call the crocodiles by name and they will respond. Keep your distance, of course. If you choose not to journey from Sala through the **Jilore Forest** and **Kakuyuni** to Malindi, you can return to the Mombasa road through the waterless **Taru Desert** and by the **Aruba Dam.**

Staunching the seasonal flow of the **Voi River** off the **Taita Hills** to the south-west, the dam has created an attractive 85-hectare (210-acre) lake some 65 kilometres (40 miles) from Sala and 40 kilometres (25 miles) from Voi Safari Lodge, which provides a large reservoir for elephant and plains game.

Built by the national parks authority, the dam is a popular congregating point for wildlife. Aruba Lodge, which, with Ol Tukai in Amboseli and Kitani in Tsavo West, was among the earliest of in-park, self-help accommodation facilities, offers visitors traditional safari-style life in Africa but with much more comfort and security. There is also a camping site. **Kanderi Swamp** is easily visited from Aruba.

Excursions from Voi

Seen from a distance as a hulking mass of blue-grey rock, the rugged **Taita Hills** thrust into the white clouds sailing across the sky. Some 43 kilometres (27 miles) south of Voi they mark the road to **Taveta,** 71 kilometres (44 miles) beyond.

Although craggy and forbidding in appearance, the hills, in fact, embrace beautiful valleys, bountiful in their harvests of fruit, vegetables and flowers. The Taita-Taveta people were among the first inland Kenyans with whom the missionaries and Thomson made contact.

Getting there

From Nairobi take the right turn on the main Nairobi-Mombasa road just before the left turn into Voi Town. The road is tarmacked for 43 kilometres (27 miles), all the way to **Mwatate, Bura** and **Wundanyi**. From Bura to **Taveta** is 71 kilometres (44 miles) of often corrugated dirt road.

Where to stay

Luxury accommodation is available at Salt Lick and Taita Hills Lodges and in twelve tents surrounding the James Stewart house, all operated by the Hilton International Group. Lake Jipe Lodge is on the shores of **Lake Jipe** and **Lake Chala Lodge** stands on the crater rim of Lake Chala.

Sightseeing

Wherever you go in this volcanic landscape covered with savannah grass, scrub and thorn, the rocky spires, great bluffs, and whale-back peaks of the 2,130-metre (7,000-foot) Taita Hills dominate the view.

The road to the compact, pleasantly laid-out district capital of **Wundanyi**, on the right off the Taveta road, climbs 15 kilometres (nine miles) in a series of tortuous hairpin bends. Within 20 minutes tropical Africa seems remote and distant.

The smallholdings and neat terraces which step down the steep hillsides could be Mediterranean, except that a **Cave of Skulls**, in an out-of-town banana grove, serves as a macabre reminder of traditions whereby Taita ancestors, exhumed from their original graves, can be consulted there by their descendants, as can other skulls in less accessible caches. It was from **Vuria,** the summit of the hills, that the first

Above: Camel safari in the sprawling reaches of Tsavo East National Park.

Christian missionary in Kenya, Johannes Rebmann, saw the snows of Kilimanjaro to the distant north.

The descent is down another precipitous series of hairpin bends past gushing waterfalls to the main road and **Bura**, on the right, where the tarmac ends.

Bura was the scene of a climactic First World War battle — the British, under the command of General Jan Smuts, turned the tables on German leader, von Lettow Vorbeck. The battle is commemorated in the Teutonic Taita Hills Lodge a few kilometres beyond. With its sister Salt Lick Lodge, it's part of a privately-owned 11,000-hectare **Game Sanctuary**.

Salt Lick and Taita Hills Game Sanctuary
Situated astride the main Voi-Taita road beneath the Taita Hills, and linked by a game corridor to the Tsavo West National Park, the sanctuary is some 915 metres (3,000 feet) above sea level.

Abandoned four decades ago as a failed sisal plantation, the land has found new life as one of Africa's most exciting game parks. Predominantly flat-savannah plains,

enhanced by a man-made **dam** and **reservoir,** one border of this unfenced, wilderness reserve is marked by a green, riverine forest which follows the course of the **Bura River**.

Since it was established as a reserve, its grasslands and woodlands have drawn an abundance of zebra, buffalo, impala, gazelle, elephant, eland, waterbuck, reedbuck, giraffe, vervet monkey, lion, jackal and prolific birdlife.

Taita Hills Lodge is built like a German fortress, out of cemented sandbags. Austere and forbidding from the exterior, it is now adorned by a frenzy of climbers and flowering creepers, and is delightfully inviting inside. It served as a base for James Stewart's 1978 movie, *A Tale of Africa*. Not far from the main building is the timber hut built as part of the set and known as the **James Stewart House**, open to visitors and operated by Hilton Hotels.

Salt Lick Lodge is one of Kenya's finest and consists of rondavels built on stilts along the lines of a typical Taita homestead, connected by overhead walkways. Underneath, undisturbed by intrusive tour-

212

ists, large herds of elephant browse. Salt Lick and Taita Hills Lodges are probably the most unusual conference centres in the world, where tycoons, business magnates, and top executives meet, surrounded by lion, elephant, buffalo and countless other species. The management employs five wardens, many game rangers, all national park veterans with immense knowledge of wildlife and conservation, under the eye of a world-renowned zoologist who also runs the sanctuary's research programme. There is an established network of more than 150 kilometres (95 miles) of graded roads: off-the-road driving is banned.

Taveta

From the Taita Hills sanctuary the road to **Taveta** follows the branch railway line through the southern arm of Tsavo West. During World War I, when Tanganyika was a German colony, Taveta was a theatre of war and fell into German hands when their forces attacked the town on 15 August 1914 — just 11 days after the outbreak of war. For the next four years the region was a focal point of the conflict in East Africa.

After the German withdrawal, von Lettow Vorbeck and his men continued to harass the much stronger British forces in a drawn-out hit-and-run campaign which formed the theme of Wilbur Smith's book *Shout at the Devil,* also made into a movie.

The main railway line in Kenya was a strategic target and the Germans frequently sent out marauders from Taveta. The line was later extended across the border to **Moshi** to join up with the Tanzanian Railway system. Later still, it merged with the Uganda and Tanganyika railway systems to form the East African Railways. Taveta was linked to the main Mombasa-Nairobi railway line in 1924. In 1996 there was a thrice-weekly train from Voi and a weekly service to Moshi.

Sightseeing

The town has a well-integrated population of Taveta, Kikuyu, Akamba, Maasai and Luo and comes alive on market days — Wednesday and Saturday — when everyone rushes in for supplies. Twenty kilometres (12 miles) north of the town, an emerald at the throat of Kilimanjaro, lies four-square-kilometre (one-and-a-half-square-mile) **Lake Chala** close by the dirt road from Taveta to Oloitokitok. The Kenya-Tanzania boundary slices through the middle of this 100-metre-deep (300-foot) crater lake fed by the melting snows of Kilimanjaro. No one quite knows how its family of resident Nile crocodile came to live there.

When the white dome of Kilimanjaro is in sight, the setting is magnificent and **Lake Chala Lodge** undoubtedly claims one of the finest viewpoints in East Africa. South-east of Taveta is serene **Lake Jipe**, where **Lake Jipe Lodge** caters for lovers of solitude and peace. Bird lovers enjoy the remote lake, where many species can be spotted.

From the Voi-Taveta road, several dirt tracks lead to the lake. The best is found by turning right at the well-worn sign for **Jipe Sisal Estate** about ten kilometres (six miles) from Taveta. Tsavo Park's **Jipe Gate** is 25 kilometres (16 miles) down this dusty and bumpy track, just east of the lake's southern section. Simple *bandas* and camping facilities are available there.

The reed beds and dappled waters of Lake Jipe are set against the background of Tanzania's **North Pare Mountains** where, from small villages, slender spirals of smoke climb unwavering into the still air. Just as at Chala, the national borders slice right through the middle of the lake. To explore the waters, hire a punt from the national park office on the shore.

Floating on the lake — perhaps in Tanzanian waters, since nothing marks the division between one nation and the other — watching the sudden swoop of a cormorant as it dives for a fish beneath the surface, is euphoric.

A baroque monument near the lake shores testifies to the brevity of life and strength of man's conceit. It is a many-bedroomed mansion, designed like a medieval European fortress, known as **Grogan's Castle.** It was built by Ewart Grogan, who walked from the Cape to Cairo for the love of a woman and who settled in Kenya, like a latter-day Rhodes, to make his fortune, often without scruple. The castle is in the grounds of the sisal plantation he founded.

Nairobi-Mombasa: A Highway to Adventure

The 500-kilometre (300-mile) Nairobi-Mombasa road, the first leg of the planned Trans-African Highway — from the Indian Ocean to Lagos and the Atlantic — in 1996 resembled an antediluvian fossil. Some stretches are so bad that they are lethal.

Getting there

Many people detour via **Namanga** through **Amboseli** and the **Tsavo National Parks** (see 'Southern Kenya: Theatres of the Wild'). Alternatively, a longer route leads via Namanga, through Arusha and Moshi in Tanzania, and on to Taveta and Voi, the route pioneered by L Galton Fenzi, founder of Kenya's Automobile Association.

But for visitors interested only in seeing the coast, travel operators offer air options. Mombasa is 45 minutes from Nairobi by jet, or 90 minutes by turbo-prop. The final travel option is for those who prefer to re-live the romance of pioneer days. The Kenya Railways overnight 'Express' takes 13 hours to cover the journey in either direction. In 1901 it took as long as a week.

Yet for many the road remains the most obvious route. Frequent express coaches cover the journey in about six hours at knockdown rates in more ways than one: in 1996 the one-way ticket cost the equivalent of between US$5 and US$12, according to which bus you took. Certainly, if you've time to take in the many attractions along the way, that first journey on the road, notwithstanding the risk, can be exhilarating.

Where to stay

In Makindu, Hunter's Lodge (4-star); in Mtito Andei, Tsavo Inn (3-star); in Voi, Voi Safari Lodge (5-star). There are others. See Listings for 'Hotels'.

Sightseeing

Heading east out of Nairobi **Uhuru Highway** becomes the **Mombasa Road.** The dual carriageway leads past a drive-in cinema, night clubs, sprawling low-cost urban housing estates, until it bears off the **Jomo Kenyatta Airport** road. The next 27 kilometres (17 miles) go past junk heaps, a Minis-

try of Transport **public weighbridge** and broiler, textile and distillery plants to Athi River town. One hundred years ago the area was as interesting as any place in Kenya. When the railhead arrived there it was part of the 25,000-square-kilometre (9,650-square-mile) Great Southern Game Reserve. Less romantically, Athi River is now the base for the Kenya Meat Commission **abattoirs** — you'll know you're there by the smell — and the giant **Athi River Portland Cement works.**

With many other up and coming industrial plants, this region is beginning to look like Thika. The Athi River, which gave the town its name, rides down from the Ngong Hills through the Nairobi National Park and still supports a crocodile or two. In Tsavo East National Park it becomes the **Galana River** — and it enters the Indian Ocean at Malindi as the **Sabaki River.**

The Mombasa Road climbs out of the shallow river valley on a wide bend, past the **Small World Country Club,** and the vast game-rich ranching country of the **Athi Plains.** On the left, just past the club, is the great rock bluff of **Lukenia,** much frequented by members of the Mountain Club of Kenya (see 'Kenya's Mountains'). The road then dips down before climbing a few kilometres to the left fork to **Machakos** (see 'Machakos: Hills and Orchards').

From this point the road rises towards the undulating 'cotton soil' escarpment and reflects its foundations with great depressions where the soil has subsided. The panorama on either side is handsome — mainly large-scale ranches where domestic bovines mingle with herds of gazelle and antelope on the **Kaputei Plains.** The views to the south-west are particularly stunning —endless, sunbaked plains with the backdrop of the Ngong Hills far distant.

This fairly long, straight stretch of switchback road ends where there's a right turn to **Konza Station,** a few kilometres down the dirt trail, the junction for the railway line to **Kajiado** and **Magadi.** From there the Mombasa road veers left on to firm, smooth bedrock, through semi-arid country dotted with euphorbia and cactii, before descending through **Salama**, where scores of juggernauts park after their laborious climb up the long, steep slope of the **Ukambani Hills.** Over the years their slow progress and extreme weight has gouged deep ruts in the uphill slow lane.

When you swoop down to the base of the hills and the gentle incline of the long inland steppe which ends beyond Voi, you pass **Kima**, on the right, which was the stage for one of the grand dramas enacted during the building of the Lunatic Line.

In 1899, Charles Ryall, 25, had been engaged as an assistant superintendent of the newly-formed Railway Police, on attachment from the Punjab Police in India.

A few days before his 26th birthday he and two colleagues set up an ambush at Kima for a man-eating lion which had been attacking passengers and railway staff. Ryall left a window open in a railway carriage and offered himself as bait to tempt the creature. Unfortunately, he fell asleep and the diseased and ageing lion jumped into the coach and dragged him out.

Ryall's remains are buried in Nairobi's first cemetery, behind the Railway Golf Course, overlooking the Nyayo National Stadium (see 'Nairobi: City in the Sun').

The naming of the station as *Kima,* Kiswahili for mincemeat, may reflect a gruesome sense of humour on the part of the railway management of the day.

After Kima, the road leaves bedrock and deteriorates to slump bed as it passes the gaunt outcrop above **Sultan Hamud**. The town arose out of an 1899 railhead at Mile 250, 114 kilometres (70 miles) from Nairobi where, with some pomp and circumstance, the ruler of Zanzibar arrived to inspect the progress of this curious British enterprise.

The town already springing up around the railhead was named Sultan Hamud in his honour. The original Sultan Hamud remains, untouched by progress, much as it must have been in the first decade of this century. A newer Sultan Hamud, with **bars**, a **mosque**, **board** and **lodgings**, has sprung up to the north of the road.

Road to Amboseli

To the south-east of Sultan Hamud lie the dusty alluvial **Maasai Plains**. A spur line branched out into this wilderness to a dot

on the map called **Kibini** where rail engineers sank a borehole for water for the steam locomotives. Much later the line was upgraded for wagons to move rock quarried for the cement factory at Athi River.

A gravel road also leads south to **Loitokitok** on the slopes of Kilimanjaro, and to **Ol Tukai**, in the heart of the **Amboseli National Park** (see 'The Hollywood Image'). All this area was a natural wonderland. Greater kudu inhabited the rock outcrops and hills until the 1930s. The plains beyond were named *Simba* after the many lion that roamed there.

Emali, just a few kilometres on from Sultan Hamud, rests on the north-western edge of the Simba plains, surrounded by well-tended *shambas* (farms) and an unusually long bridge, over the railroad, just east of town. In the days when there was no tarmac road to **Namanga**, Emali was the popular turnoff point for people from up-country Kenya heading for **Amboseli.**

Immediately to the right of the bridge is the turning along the **water pipeline road** that leads to the foot of the **Chyulu Hills** and on to **Kimana Lodge**, 80 kilometres (50 miles) away. Otherwise Emali is a typical Kenyan wayside town and from there to **Hunter's Lodge** it is all Maasai country — fairly featureless and remote. The lodge at **Kiboko** (which is Kiswahili for hippo and therefore also for a hippo-hide whip) is named after J A Hunter, author of *White Hunter* (1938), *Hunter* (1952) and *Hunter's Tracks* (1957).

Born in Scotland twenty years before the turn of the century, as a professional hunter with the Game Department he killed more than a thousand rhinoceros in this area alone. After he died in 1963, his widow, Hilda, continued to run the lodge.

Hunter's Lodge is about one-third of the way from Nairobi to Mombasa and a good place to pause for refreshment in **gardens** which offer sanctuary to more than 250 species of birds. From there it's only a few kilometres to **Makindu**, with its ornate and embellished Good Samaritan Sikh temple which marks Mile 200 on the Lunatic Line.

The temple offers free food and accommodation for the weary traveller — a living example of the tenets of the Guru Nanak faith. Now the vegetation on either side of the road becomes a profusion of lush undergrowth, a reversion of grasslands to woodlands, where grotesque baobabs proliferate, as the road sweeps on to **Kibwezi**, a small dark, sombre Akamba trading centre off the main road at the **Kitui** junction.

It was there that some of the first inland missions — and Kenya's first but unsuccessful coffee and successful sisal plantations — were established in the early 1900s.

Malaria, blackwater fever, and tsetse fly were so endemic, however, that the coffee and the missions — but not the German-planted sisal — were uprooted and moved to the healthier environment of the Kikuyu uplands around Nairobi. The sisal was uprooted much later in the 1970s for an ambitious floricultural venture. But it failed. Replanted in the 1980s, it is now once again one of Kenya's premier sisal plantations.

The road north from there takes you on through the **Kibwezi Forest** to remote and arid Kitui. Off this road you could take either the first fork, right after some kilometres, to **Kanziko** and then **Mutha**, close to the **South Kitui National Reserve**, or take the sharp right turn at **Mutomo** further on which also leads to Mutha.

Covering 1,833 square kilometres (707 square miles) of arid, infertile land, the reserve embraces the seasonal **Thua River** and its floodplain, surrounded by dense bushland with low hills. Also in this vicinity but further east along the main road is the 212-square-kilometre (81-square-mile) **Ngai Ndethya National Reserve**, which protects a migration corridor between Tsavo East and West.

Forest of Vultures

From Kibwezi the road pushes on through fairly densely-cultivated countryside, with new towns developing swiftly on the north side, to **Mtito Andei** ('Forest of Vultures'). Mtito Andei is almost geometrically the halfway stage between Mombasa and Nairobi, and marks the arid boundary of the land of the Wakamba (see 'The People', Part Three). It is still little more than a sleepy halt in the desert, despite the **mosque**, the **AA post**, a **curio shop**, the **main gate** to Tsavo West, 'Greasy Joe' **restaurants**, **service stations**, the **Tsavo Inn** and the original **rail station.**

The first establishment of any note after the station was a Great War **airstrip**, just

off the road at the east end of town. From Mtito Andei the road runs for 98 kilometres (60 miles) through the heart of the Tsavo parks, alongside the railway, to Voi.

There's an element of poignancy in the signs warning: 'Elephants Have Right of Way'. Old Kenya hands remember days, even in the 1960s and 1970s, when they had to wait hours for elephants to clear off before they could leave their cars to change a tyre after a puncture. The giant baobabs, with the gouged-out trunks which the elephant used as scratching posts, still stand.

Further along the road, gaunt, forbidding mountains begin to punctuate the *nyika* (comiphora-acacia woodland). To the south the seasonal **Tsavo** ('Blood') **River** flows around the base of the impressive **Ngulia** massif. A few kilometres northeastward, just after the park's **Tsavo** (**River**) **Gate**, on the right, a road bridge crosses the main Mombasa-Nairobi railway line. The road is usually a heaving mass of baboons, so reduce speed.

On the east side there's the shell of an incongruously modern motel called **The Maneaters**. Only its name indicates that this was the location of one of the epic dramas of Victorian railroad construction. When R O Preston established the railhead there in mid-1898 he thought it would only be a matter of days before moving on. The resident wildlife thought differently.

Two lions held several thousand Indian and more than 1,300 African workers at bay in a siege which lasted for weeks. Several Africans and almost 30 Indians were killed by these maneaters in a stranger-than-fiction scenario which was later related by Colonel J H Patterson in his book, *Maneaters of Tsavo*. The military martinet, self-appointed saviour of the fear-crazed rail gangs, bungled ambush after ambush before finally dispatching the two killers. He then glorified his role by writing a melodramatic best-seller that captured the imagination of Victorian Britain. In 1996 the story was filmed in South Africa with Michael Douglas as the star. The stuffed lion skins from 1898 are exhibits at Chicago's Field Museum in America.

The bridge over the railway was a strategic German target during World War I — but the maps the Germans captured from the British were inaccurate and led them astray. The **Manyani Gate**, north, a few kilometres beyond Maneaters, leads into Tsavo East and just beyond that, on the right, is **Mbololo Hills Prison,** formerly **Manyani Detention Camp,** where the colonial authorities held what they termed 'hard-core' Mau Mau freedom fighters. Now the **Prison Industries showroom** displays well-crafted furniture, while the lush **prison farm** shows that, properly watered and tended, even Tsavo's marginal soil can bloom.

Continue towards the mass of **Voi Mountain** where in 1948 Bob Astles, who later earned notoriety as Ugandan dictator Idi Amin's henchman in the 1970s, crashed his RAF plane in thick cloud. He walked away alive, although his passenger was less fortunate and was killed instantly.

A bit further on a sign announces **Voi airstrip** — near the spot where Karen Blixen's lover, Denys Finch Hatton, crashed and died. From then on the road travels downward, past the **service station** on the left, and the **Taita Hills** and **Taveta junction** to the right, and round the outside of the rapidly developing industrial entrepôt of **Voi,** on towards Mombasa.

Voi, the capital of this region, was the first main upcountry railhead on the Uganda Railway where passengers enjoyed the first of many overnight stops. Until recently the *dak* bungalow, built to accommodate passengers, still provided dinner, bed and breakfast before the onward journey.

Mackinnon Road

From Voi the road winds another 150 kilometres (95 miles) across the treacherous Taru Desert, a scorched wilderness, entirely without water, to Mombasa. The main settlement in the Taru is **Mackinnon Road**, another memorial to the unfulfilled sense of mission of that prudent Victorian. The **Sayyid Baghali Shah Mosque** is a local landmark.

Thirty kilometres (19 miles) later comes **Samburu** with, south, a dirt road that leads to the western foot of the **Shimba Hills** (see 'The South Coast: Pearls Upon a String'). To the north the road passes through **Silanoni** and **Mbongo** along the lip of the plateau which looks down on the coast. Another 30 kilometres (19 miles) or so beyond Samburu the first palm groves, at **Mariakani**, named after the Kamba arrows used against the Maasai, announce your arrival into a world quite different from upcountry Kenya.

A busy market centre, with a **co-operative dairy processing plant**, **service station**, and always milling crowds, Mariakani marks the junction, to the left, for **Kaloleni**, 22 kilometres (14 miles) away, famous for its palm wine. Continue along the road to **Mazeras**, with its untidy, dilapidated tin-and-timber **shanty shops** and the north turn to **Rabai** and **Ribe**. In 1846 Johann Krapf, the missionary, established Kenya's first church and permanent mission at Rabai. Within the year he lost his wife and daughter to fever.

The church has long since vanished but next door to the **cottage**, where Krapf's colleague, Johannes Rebmann, lived stands **St Paul's**, built in 1887 and, hung with a litany of the previous church and mission's troubled existence, is still in use. Two years before it was built, Bishop Hannington bade farewell to his fellow missionaries at Rabai and set out for the interior and Uganda, where he met his death.

Later Krapf offered to help some Methodist missionaries from Britain build a mission at nearby Ribe. There is still a **Methodist mission** and **school** atop Ribe's hill but the jungle has grown over the hillside ruins of Krapf's mission and its **graveyard**.

At Mazeras, on the main road beyond the Rabai junction, is another Methodist venture, the **Mazeras Craft Training Centre**. It is opposite Mombasa's **Mazeras Botanical Gardens** where lily-ponds are crossed by willow-pattern bridges and coarse lawns have been planted with bamboo and palms — a cool, green place for a picnic. The gardens have official opening hours but since there is neither gate nor guardian you can enter at any time. Soon after this, the road drops down the final escarpment and enters the slums of hinterland Mombasa, marked by oil refineries, factories, rusty litter, shantytowns and milling crowds, where palms and mangoes grow incongruously against the detritus of industrial enterprise.

Overleaf: A modern locomotive follows the 'Lunatic Line', built between 1895-1901.

The Coast: The Coral Strand

Kenya's coast stretches some 480 kilometres (300 miles) from Tanzania in the south to Somalia in the north broken at intervals by ancient river mouths, now tidal creeks, and the deltas of Kenya's two biggest rivers, the **Sabaki** and the **Tana**.

Lush contrast to the deserts, plateaux and mountains up-country, it is a world removed from the primordial wildlife which roam the diminishing wildernesses inland. After hours of nonstop driving, tiredness vanishes at the sight of the *makuti* (palm-thatch) roof of your hotel and the caress of an Indian Ocean breeze. More than half of Kenya's 100 international-class hotels — five listed in the register of the world's 300 greatest hotels — are beach hotels.

As luminous, tropical night descends, fireflies perform their incandescent dance among the bougainvillea and succulents, and a pale moon strides across the lagoon. The air is sweet with frangipani which seems to bloom even in the silver glimmer of night. Early morning, while it is still dark, the calls of the *muezzins* echo from the minarets as they did centuries ago when the first Arab traders came to seek profit, and stayed to settle. They gave birth to a new culture, Swahili, and a new *lingua franca*, Kiswahili.

For much of its length — from **Vanga** in the south, 230 kilometres (150 miles) to **Malindi** in the north — the shore is protected by a fascinating coral reef. Inside its protective arms, in sheltered lagoons, grow magical marine plants and vividly-coloured fish and marine creatures. National marine parks off **Watamu**, **Malindi**, **Mombasa**, and **Shimoni**, now protect these reefs and the waters they embrace.

Holiday playground

All this has become one of the world's great holiday playgrounds. Early morning sees the first pink blush of dawn on the far horizon and sandals of cloud stepping across the sky glow briefly before fading.

The incoming tide raps the reef and floods the lagoon. Sailboards are pushed out from the shore and suddenly heel into the breeze, lithe helmsmen tacking by inclination of hip and knee. The water is always warm, ranging from 27° to 35°C (80°-95°F) and is never ruffled by storms. Kenya's climate reflects the kindness of its tropic shores. Shade temperatures rarely rise above 35°C (95°F), and although the sun shines clear almost every day — even during the rainy seasons — the heat is usually tempered by a cooling breeze. Swimming is safe on almost every beach, though at low tide wear some footwear to avoid injuries from stonefish, coral and other hazards.

Light-skinned visitors unaccustomed to the direct, vertical rays of an equatorial sun should wear a T-shirt at first when swimming or walking. Prolonged exposures have resulted in severe sunburn with the victims in hospital — no place to spend a holiday. Most come simply to enjoy sun, sea and sand, but for those inclined to snorkel and scuba dive, Kenya's reefs, coral gardens and lagoons are among the most beautiful in the world.

The reef is broken in only a few places by river mouths or creeks. Of these, the deepest, most sheltered, with a safe channel through the protecting reef, are those on either side of **Mombasa Island**. The anchorages gave the town a strategic role in the coast's turbulent history and made it Kenya's second-largest city and premier trading port.

Getting there

Mombasa is served by air, sea, rail and road. By road from Nairobi the 485-kilometre (300-mile) journey takes between five and seven hours. There are many express bus services. By air, the frequent domestic flights take either 45 or 90 minutes, depending on the aircraft. By overnight train, the journey takes 13 hours. Though passenger ships no longer ply to and from the port it might be possible to find a berth on one of the many cargo ships which sail between Europe and Kenya.

Where to stay

Castle Hotel (3-star), Oceanic (4-star), Outrigger (4-star), Hotel Splendid (2-star), Lotus Hotel (2-star), Manor Hotel (4-star), New Carlton (3-star). There are many others. See Listings for 'Hotels'.

Sightseeing

Measuring little more than 14 square kilometres (less than five square miles), Mombasa Island is grossly overcrowded. The original, narrow-streeted town, built from coral-rock in shades of buff, rose and ochre, was designed for another, more leisurely age. The island is connected to the mainland in the west by causeway, north by bridge, and south by ferry.

Arriving by air you land at **Moi International Airport,** officially opened by President Moi in August 1979. On the drive into town the road passes through **Port Reitz,** named after the 19th-century British naval lieutenant who, in 1824, established a one-man 'British Protectorate' in Mombasa. His protection was short-lived — as was he. John Reitz died of malaria aged only 23 (see 'History: The Dust and the Ashes', Part One).

Four kilometres (two-and-a-half-miles) from the airport you join the road from Nairobi, then cross the **Makupa causeway** following the railway. The road diverges from the railtrack as it arrives on the island to head another four kilometres (two-and-a-half miles) through the suburbs, straight down **Jomo Kenyatta Avenue,** to the town centre — marked by the **roundabout,** where the **Elim Pentecostal Church's** garden once boasted two **palm trees,** planted by Princess Margaret in 1956, and Queen Elizabeth, the Queen Mother, in 1959. Jomo Kenyatta Avenue is bisected by a junction to the Japanese-built **Nyali Bridge** which links the island to the northern mainland.

Drive past a police station, the **Tom Mboya Memorial Hall,** a **Baptist church** and an odd-looking **mosque,** and finally you arrive at what was, until 1989, Mombasa's traditional marketplace, **Mwembe Tayari.** There in the 1880s, the young Mr Ainsworth inspected his safari caravan of porters before setting off for his long walk upcountry to become Britain's inland representative in Machakos. Mwembe Tayari is no longer a marketplace and is now a congested bus station and snack bar area. The big street market is **Makupa,** off Mwembe Tayari in the heart of **Majengo,** the island's low-income housing district. A colourful, multi-purpose market with a lively atmosphere, it is well worth a visit. Drive along **Jomo Kenyatta Avenue,** then turn left into **Salim Mwa Ngunga Road.**

Mombasa is a good place to buy cheap fabrics — the Kenyan coast is famous for these and **Biashara Street** offers the latest in *khanga* (printed cotton wraparound) designs. It's worth comparing prices before bargaining for bulk buys. After the intersection of Biashara Street and **Kwavi Road** the emphasis is on household items.

Next to the Mwembe Tayari bus station is a sombre **war memorial,** guarded by four bronze sentinels of the King's African Rifles. It was raised, two years before the memorial in Nairobi, to honour the Kenyans who fell for an alien empire in World War I. Opposite is the **Bohra cemetery.**

Go straight ahead at the roundabout to where Kenyatta Avenue joins the main street, **Digo Road,** then turn right. To the right of Mwembe Tayari Kenyatta Avenue opposite another **mosque,** joins **Mwembe Tayari Road.** You'll pass a succession of typical Mombasa eating houses and hostelries — sign-posted by their utilitarian decor and vivacious customers — a **Khoja cemetery,** and a **Hindu temple** guarded by two, blue plaster sentinels which portray Krishna's reincarnations.

Continue along this road to Mombasa's functional **Central Railway Station,** built in 1932 when the terminus was moved from Treasury Square. From the station, it is one kilometre (two-thirds of a mile) along **Haile Selassie Road** (formerly Station Road) to Digo Road, and the main post office for Post Restante.

Follow Digo Road south past **Gusii Street,** on the right, with its magnificent **mosque** and the comfortable **Splendid Hotel,** and **Meru Road,** on the left, where there's a **Shiva temple,** past the old 'Theatre Royal', now the **Regal cinema,** to **Moi Avenue** (formerly Kilindini Road), something of a Kenyan 'costa del sol' where, curio sellers, conmen, ladies of the night, sailors, tourists and taximen patrol the long dual carriageway which leads to the docks. Moi Avenue is the best place to hire cars

Overleaf: Mombasa Island and its Kilindini port.

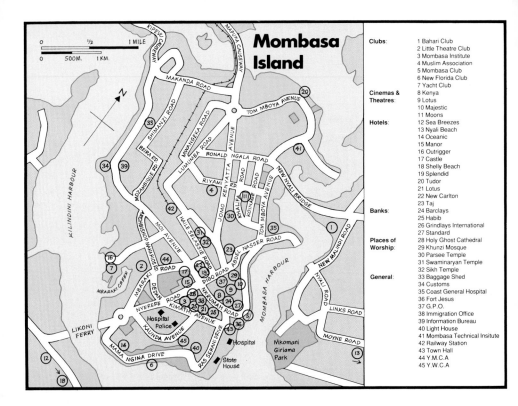

Clubs:	1 Bahari Club
	2 Little Theatre Club
	3 Mombasa Institute
	4 Muslim Association
	5 Mombasa Club
	6 New Florida Club
	7 Yacht Club
Cinemas &	8 Kenya
Theatres:	9 Lotus
	10 Majestic
	11 Moons
Hotels:	12 Sea Breezes
	13 Nyali Beach
	14 Oceanic
	15 Manor
	16 Outrigger
	17 Castle
	18 Shelly Beach
	19 Splendid
	20 Tudor
	21 Lotus
	22 New Carlton
	23 Taj
Banks:	24 Barclays
	25 Habib
	26 Grindlays International
	27 Standard
Places of	28 Holy Ghost Cathedral
Worship:	29 Khunzi Mosque
	30 Parsee Temple
	31 Swaminaryan Temple
	32 Sikh Temple
General:	33 Baggage Shed
	34 Customs
	35 Coast General Hospital
	36 Fort Jesus
	37 G.P.O.
	38 Immigration Office
	39 Information Bureau
	40 Light House
	41 Mombasa Technical Insitute
	42 Railway Station
	43 Town Hall
	44 Y.M.C.A
	45 Y.W.C.A

and change money: Barclays Bank's **bureau de change** is open Monday-Saturday 0800-1230 and 1400-1700. Most of the major car hire outlets have branches there or in neighbouring **Nkrumah Road**. After the intersection, continue past the passageway on the left to the **Fontanella bistro**, curio stands and **Castle Hotel**, famous as a pick-up point in all senses of the word. Further down are the avenue's famous 'elephant' tusks, erected in honour of Britain's Queen Elizabeth II on her 1953 coronation.

The aluminium tusks arch over Moi Avenue close to the **Information Bureau** — open Monday-Friday 0800-1200, 1400-1630; Saturday 0800-1200, with a number of leaflets and maps available. On your right before you reach the tusks is the **New Carlton Hotel**, which is nowhere near as grand as its name implies. Opposite is **Uhuru Park**, now totally hidden by the curio stalls, but with the **Uhuru Fountain** displaying an outline of Africa.

There's also the **Bella Vista** service station and restaurant, unchanged since they were built, and then a little further down, on the left, the **Sunshine Day and Night Club.** From there you pass under the **railway bridge** into the docks. East of Digo Road is Mombasa's original 'Arabian Nights' **Old Town.**

Almost inevitably, visitors first make for the grey-buffed, terracotta **fortress,** whose 15-metre-high (50-foot), two-and-a-half-metre-thick (nine-foot) battlements tower over the old town's alleys. Constructed by the Portuguese in the 16th century, **Fort Jesus** was designed by an Italian as a huge pentagon — a style common in European forts at that time — ensuring assailants were met by crossfire from all its walls.

Surrounded by a 12-metre-deep (40-foot) moat and guarded at each corner by four towers, the fort has a bloody history. Building began in 1593 and finished in 1598. The fort, which retains much of its original character, was restored between 1958 and 1960 with a £30,000 donation from the Gulbenkian Foundation.

Relics from the 17th-century wreck of the Portuguese ship *Santa Antonio de Tanna,* which sank in the harbour, were recovered in the early 1980s and are on display in the museum inside. The ship arrived from Goa

224

on 15 September 1697, and was immediately bombarded by Mombasa's Arab defenders. She dragged her anchor and drifted onto the reef and sank. Rusting 19th-century **cannon** and more modern armament from the British ship the *Pegasus*, stand outside the walls, with the guns from the German battleship *Königsberg*, which sank the *Pegasus* in Zanzibar harbour before she was destroyed as she hid up the Rufiji delta in Tanganyika.

Nearby is the **monument** which honours Muslim Major Wavell, who commanded the Arab Rifles in World War I.

The massive ramparts of this bastion slope gently down to the wide but ruined steps which lead to the old **slave harbour** where spices and slaves were shipped. Slaves were imprisoned in a cave with a freshwater well — now foul and odiferous. The port is used, less frequently each year, by the few dhows which continue the ages-old trade with the Gulf and Asia.

Leaving the fort by the **Water Gate** you enter the Old Town, keeping the **Mombasa Club**, *circa* 1885, Kenya's oldest gentlemen's club to your right, down **Mbarak Hinawy Road**, formerly Vasco da Gama Road. It was renamed in honour of the last of the Sultan of Zanzibar's governors. The narrow lanes are lined with wooden, 'Juliet' balconied houses, which are authentic Arab *mashrabia*. Between the maze of buildings are 20 or so mosques, where the faithful are summoned to prayer by the *muezzin*. Valuing their importance to Kenya's cultural heritage, measures to restore many of the Old Town's historic buildings have been put in hand.

On **Bachawy Road** stands the **Mandhry mosque**, officially the oldest, founded in 1570. In **Government Square,** is one of many galleries that sell art, Arabian carpets, carved doors and ordinary curios.

The **Jain Temple**, in **Langoni Road**, with its dome topped by a spire of gold and heavy doors carved from solid silver, is worth a visit. And the **Baluchi Mosque** in **Makadara Road** is a green, white and pink 1964 successor to the original built in 1875 by the Baluchis who migrated from the Makran coast of what is now Pakistan.

Adjacent to **Jamhuri Park** is a **Shiva temple** guarded by two plaster lions and the elephant-headed god Ganesh and a re-

markable pantheon of animal gods and devils. The temple spire is adorned by a crock of gold.

The **Dawoodi Bohra mosque,** *circa* 1902, is near Mombasa's own **Thirty-nine Steps**. These take you up to a clifftop of scrub wasteland overlooking the old harbour.

Mombasa's early buildings contrast sharply with the high-rises that sprang up in the city centre in the 1980s, particularly around **Treasury Square**. There, law courts and banks — architectural remembrances of Britain's tenure in Kenya — used to stand near the **Catholic Memorial Cathedral.** Treasury Square was once the Mombasa terminus of the Uganda Railway.

Drive to the roundabout intersecting Moi Avenue and Digo Road and turn left into **Nyerere Avenue**, past the British Council library and the **Manor Hotel**, almost a century old. It stands opposite the **Anglican Cathedral** commemorating Archbishop Hannington, who was murdered in Uganda in 1885. After the roundabout marking the intersection with **Dedan Kimathi Avenue**, formerly Ayub Khan Avenue, the road follows the line of Mackinnon's Central African Railway track.

Further along is a left turn into **Kaunda Avenue**, which leads to the entrance of the **Oceanic Hotel** with its commanding panoramic views of **Likoni Creek** and the deepwater entrance of **Kilindini Docks**.

After the left turn into Nyerere Avenue, at the roundabout, a right turn leads to **Likoni Ferry** and, east, the road becomes **Mama Ngina Drive**, Mombasa's once grand marine esplanade which leads past the **New Florida nightclub**, right, and **Fort St Joseph**, whose ancient baobab forest has now been partly uprooted for estate development. After this the drive cuts through the middle of the **Mombasa Golf Club's** nine-hole course, established in 1911, and then on along by the wall of **State House** and back into Treasury Square. Alternatively, turn right at Likoni Ferry roundabout into **Mbaraki Road**, past the baobabs that shelter the intriguing **Mbaraki Pillar**, a phallic pillar tomb of coral rag which is believed to have been the 18th-century burial place of the Sheikh of Changamwe, head of one of the 12 original tribes of Mombasa Island. Further along are some **cemeteries** containing 52 Commonwealth military

Above: Mombasa's bustling Biashara Street. Opposite: Mombasa's 'Old Town'.

graves from World War I and 146 from World War II. By the **Little Theatre Club** on the left, Mbaraki Road becomes **Mnazi Moja Road** and runs into Moi Avenue. The theatre has a regular schedule of amateur entertainment, including African and European plays, pantomimes, musicals, light and more serious drama.

First left off Mnazi Moja Road is **Archbishop Makarios Road**, which takes you to the excellent **Outrigger Hotel** and the **Mombasa Yacht Club.** Nearby stands **Kilindini Mosque**, built in the 1970s, replacing the monument established by three tribes who migrated to Kilindini in the 16th century.

The north side of the island around **Tudor Creek**, which you can explore by dhow or power boat, is mainly modern and residential. It's the anchor-point for the splendid Japanese-built **toll bridge** that connects the island to the north mainland.

Abdel Nasser Road, the continuation of **Digo Road**, leads past the **municipal** (formerly Mackinnon) **market**, right, and the Sunni mosque, **Masjid Nur**, across what the Portuguese in the 16th century christened *Cidade dos Mouros*. Probably Mombasa's first settlement, from around the 11th century, it was sacked and razed to the ground in 1505.

Behind the **Institute of Islamic Culture** on the right are the ruins of a **mosque** that may have existed at that time. The ruins are close to the 1918 **Alidina Visram High School**, formerly the Aga Khan Boys School, and the **Coast General Hospital**, which is on the left. Excavations in 1976 revealed massive ruined walls and shards of Islamic and Chinese pottery of the Ming era, dating from long before the Portuguese arrived.

Beyond is the **Lady Grigg Maternity Hospital**, built in honour of a colonial governor's wife, and a **lighthouse**. There, the old **Nyali Bridge**, a pontoon on floats, used to bridge Tudor Creek.

Nyali Beach on the north coast, over Nyali Bridge, is also close by: first right after the bridge and drive for four kilometres (two-and-a-half miles).

Mombasa's nearest beach is **Shelly** on the south coast. Take the Likoni ferry over the creek, then turn first left and continue for three kilometres (two miles).

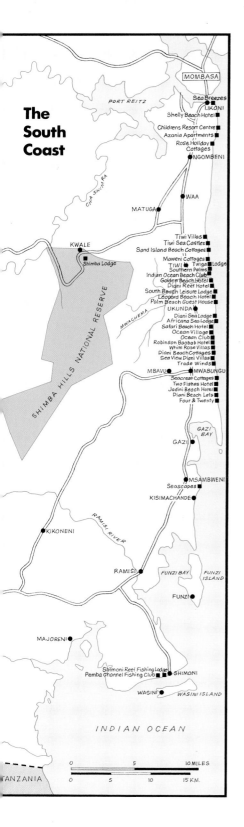

The South Coast

(map labels, north to south)

MOMBASA
PORT REITZ
LIKONI
Sea Breezes
Shelly Beach Hotel
Childrens Resort Centre
Azania Apartments
Rose Holiday Cottages
NGOMBENI
WAA
MATUGA
KWALE
Shimba Lodge
SHIMBA HILLS NATIONAL RESERVE
CHA SHIMBA
MWACHEMA
Tiwi Villas
Tiwi Sea Castles
Sand Island Beach Cottages
Maweni Cottages
TIWI — Twiga Lodge
Southern Palms
Indian Ocean Beach Club
Golden Beach Hotel
Diani Reef Hotel
South Beach Leisure Lodge
Leopard Beach Hotel
Palm Beach Guest House
UKUNDA
Diani Sea Lodge
Africana Sea Lodge
Safari Beach Hotel
Ocean Village
Ocean Club
Robinson Baobab Hotel
White Rose Villas
Diani Beach Cottages
Sea View Diani Villas
Trade Winds
MBAVU
MWABUNGU
Seacrest Cottages
Two Fishes Hotel
Jadini Beach Hotel
Diani Beach Lets
Four & Twenty
GAZI BAY
GAZI
MSAMBWENI
Seascapes
KISIMACHANDE
RAMISI RIVER
KIKONENI
RAMISI
FUNZI BAY
FUNZI ISLAND
FUNZI
MAJORENI
Shimoni Reef Fishing Lodge
Pemba Channel Fishing Club
SHIMONI
WASINI
WASINI ISLAND
INDIAN OCEAN
TANZANIA

0   5   10 MILES
0   5   10   15 KM.

The South Coast: Pearls upon a String

South of Mombasa, across Likoni Creek, lies a ribbon of lagoons and beaches strung together like pearls upon a string. From Mombasa to the Tanzanian border they are generally quieter than those to the north. But **Diani Beach** is Kenya's own Sunset Strip. At the far end of the southern coastal strip is unspoilt **Shimoni** with its relics of the slave trade and unspoilt coral gardens.

Getting there

On the drawing board in Tokyo are the plans for a new suspension bridge to cross **Kilindini Creek** to the southern mainland. But, in 1996, the way to this tropical paradise was still by old-fashioned **motor ferry**.

The usually long wait on the ferry ramp acclimatizes you to the essence of what passes for pace at the coast. *Haraka haraka haina baraka* goes the old Swahili saying, implying: 'Don't do today what you can put off until tomorrow or even longer.' The actual crossing takes four minutes, but allow at least an hour on either side. Wear a hat and suntan lotion if you have to wait in the middle of the day: it gets very hot.

Where to stay

In Likoni, Shelly Beach Hotel (4-star); In Tiwi, Tiwi Sea Castles (self-service), Tiwi Villas (self-service), Twiga Lodge (budget). There are others. See Listings for 'Hotels'.

Sightseeing

There's not much to do in **Likoni** itself, which is little more than an untidy afterthought to Mombasa town. From the ferry ramp a road runs off around the headland to the east, but there's no beach to speak of — just weed-covered coral at low tide.

But the pleasantly-comfortable **Shelly Beach Hotel,** which is the oldest of the south coast hotels and has lost none of its character, has a fine swimming pool and the ambience is all coastal. The main road southwards for 13 kilometres (eight miles) to **Waa** is single-lane tarmac. After leaving

Opposite: 15th-century pillar tomb outside Malindi's Juma 'Friday' mosque.

Above: Dinner aboard a dhow in Mombasa's Tudor Creek.

Likoni, whose southern limits are marked by the right turn for the **Kenya Naval Headquarters** at **Mtwonge**, on the south shore of Kilindini Creek, the road runs through prolific trees and undergrowth, with scattered coral rag and thatch villages and women as undulating as the road.

Just outside Waa, where the tarmac used to end, begins a smooth, broad strip of tarmac which runs all the way south to **Lunga Lunga**, the border town with Tanzania. Almost immediately to the west there is a turn which climbs twelve kilometres (seven-and-a-half miles) to **Kwale**, the administrative, tree-shaded district capital, set in the cool heights of the Shimba Hills.

The transition from languid, tropical shore to hill reserve takes no more than 20 minutes.

Kwale, where the elephant and the buffalo frequently roam, takes its name from the Swahili word for the many endemic spurfowl of the area. In 1988, customers at the one-street town's most popular bar were kept indoors long after closing hours because elephant and buffalo were grazing outside.

Shimba Hills National Reserve

Three kilometres (two miles) south of Kwale, along a corrugated but pleasant murram track, some 20 kilometres (12 miles) directly inland from the beach strip, lies the 192-square-kilometre (74-square-mile) **Shimba Hills National Reserve**, ranging in height from between 120 and 450 metres (400-1,500 feet). Basically a dissected forested plateau of conical hills, steep ridges and ravines, where many of the surviving trees are centuries-old, the hills are a major water catchment area. Fanned by strong sea breezes and frequently shrouded by morning cloud and mist, the hills are much cooler than the rest of the coast. The forested slopes and undulating grasslands are surrounded by a forest reserve covering almost 200 square kilometres (77 square miles).

It is the only place in Kenya where you can see sable antelope. Sister to upcountry Treetops the reserve's **Shimba Lodge**, is rated as the finest of Kenya's forest lodges.

Other facilities offered include two first-class campsites and a nature trail. The roads to such places as **Makadara** and

Above: Harmony with nature — glorious solitude of the Indian Ocean Beach Club seafront.

Longomwagandi forests, perhaps the only authentic African jungle at the coast, are well-graded and signposted. There lianas — parasitic climbers — are locked in deadly embrace with their ancient and gigantic hosts: all in perpetual gloom, with borassus fruit (which make the elephant tipsy) and butterflies and, of course, leopard. You can also visit the open areas and such vantage spots as **Giriama Point** and **Pengo Hill Lookout,** the highest point.

Still unspoilt, the rolling downs and thick, ancient rain forests offer occasional glimpses of the reserve's elusive wildlife, especially on early morning game drives.

Back on the main coast road, the first resort after the Kwale turnoff and, after Likoni, the oldest on the south coast, is **Tiwi.** Located six kilometres (four miles) from Waa, turn left down a coral sand road for another two kilometres (little more than a mile). Tiwi has many self-catering bungalow resorts. You can reach Tiwi Beach from another turn, one-and-a-half kilometres (one mile) beyond the first turn. Go left again, then follow the road down to the **Mwachema River estuary**.

Diani: An Original Tropical Paradise

Diani is Kenya's original tropical paradise: palm-fringed beaches, caster-sugar sands and translucent, cornflower-blue sea. The offshore reef which stretches the length of the south coast is a 20-minute swim away. Even at low tide, the water is deep enough for swimming and snorkelling.

Beneath the sea's placid surface, an inner universe of strange rock formations, swaying weeds and sculptured corals are dazzlingly lit by shoals of angel, jewel, zebra and parrot fish. Every resort hotel hires out snorkelling equipment and many offer aqualung facilities for those who wish to swim down to 30 metres (90 feet) depth.

Getting there

From Tiwi at low tide you can cross to Diani at **Kongo**, on a sweep of the estuary guarded by giant sentinel baobabs, where the magnificent and well-preserved 15th-century **Mwana Mosque** still stands. The

231

vaulted roof of its prayer-room is intact and worshippers still come to recite their prayers to Allah. But from Kongo it's a long and tiring walk to Diani Beach so most will return to the main road to continue another five kilometres (three miles) to **Ukunda**. It sprawls between the shopping centre along the hinterland main road — with a **bank**, a **post office** and **dukas** — and the Diani Beach strip, with two shopping centres, and an **airfield**. Turn left at the main road for what is now universally known as Kenya's Sunset Strip.

Where to stay
Africana Sea Lodge, Diani Reef, Diani Sea Lodge, Golden Beach, Jadini Beach, Safari Beach, Leisure Lodge, Leopard Beach, Nomad Beach Bandas, Robinson's Baobab, Trade Winds, Two Fishes and Block Hotels' Indian Ocean Beach Club — a mixture of 5- and 4-star hotels with a comfortable beachcomber-style alternative in Nomad Beach Bandas. There are many other options, including self-service chalets, cottages and camping sites. See Listings for 'Hotels'.

In Shimoni, the Pemba Channel Fishing Club (4-star) and Shimoni Reef Fishing Lodge (4-star). There are others. See Listings for 'Hotels'.

In national reserves
Shimba Lodge (5-star), Kwale. Booking through Block Hotels, Rehema House, Nairobi, or at Nyali Beach Hotel, Mombasa or Indian Ocean Beach Club, Diani Beach.

Sightseeing
The strip is divided into north and south. Turn left, off the slip road from Ukunda, to go north; right to go south. The north is a johnny-come-lately but has magnificent hotels. But south is where Diani started years ago when Dan Trench, scion of one of Kenya's settler families, built the original Jadini Beach Hotel. The first hotel along this road is **Trade Winds**, which retains all its original atmosphere. Offering bar games, it is something like a good English village pub.

Directly opposite the track to Trade Winds is a monolithic **baobab tree** with a 22-metre (72-feet) girth, so ancient that it is protected by presidential decree. It's a survivor of the once impenetrable **Jadini Forest** which used to clothe all this section of

the coast. As you head south you'll come across remnants of the forest here and there, with their diminishing primate and avian populations. But tread warily for snakes also find refuge there from encroaching *Homo sapiens*. Those eyes glittering in the dark at night are probably only bushbabies, though locals like to recount tales of leopard.

The most atmospheric spot along Sunset Strip is **Nomad's**, which also run the only beach bar along the whole coast — set in the cemented remains of a wrecked dhow.

Diani's night-life includes discotheques and live bands at all the hotels — lively and exhausting. There's also traditional Giriama dancing. But be careful on the beach at night. Mugging is common.

To Shimoni
From Ukunda the road runs south through palm plantations, swamps and abandoned sugar plantations, to **Shimoni,** the first permanent British settlement in Kenya. Ten kilometres (six miles) out of Ukunda a right turn leads up to the back door of the Shimba Hills while there is a left turn to **Kinondo**, a jungle-shrouded peninsula where, offshore, **Chale Island** is now a German-owned resort.

Another ten kilometres (six miles) brings you to the sleepy little village of **Gazu**, where the **primary school** was once the home — and headquarters — of Sheikh Mbaruk ('Baruka') bin Rashid, a rebellious Mazrui leader who tortured the opposition and suffocated them with the smoke of burning chillies.

Two-and-a-half kilometres (one-and-a-half-miles) beyond that is East Africa's largest **coconut factory**, processing millions of nuts a year, the flesh laid out to dry for three or four days to turn into copra. **Msambweni**, a once neglected fishing village, just 25 kilometres (15 miles) from Ukunda, derives its name from the Kiswahili for 'place of the antelope'. But Msambweni's 17th-century slave pen testifies to the misery that thousands suffered.

Walk along the beach, negotiating difficult coral impediments, and eventually you'll reach **Funzi Island**, where a deluxe fishing resort, completed in 1991, offers superb opportunities for deep sea fishing. If it is your intention to wade across the

Above: Ancient Kongo Mosque marks the Mwachema Estuary between Tiwi and Diani beaches.

channel which divides the island from the mainland, choose low tide. There are no difficulties about camping on Funzi, providing you are self-equipped in all respects.

Return to the main road and go on another 13 kilometres (eight miles) to the **Ramisi River**, where land on either side of the road and river was once cultivated as one of Kenya's biggest sugar plantations. The chief local occupations now have reverted to fishing, mangrove pole cutting, and domestic and market gardening.

From Ramisi the main road runs another 35 kilometres (21 miles) to the **Lunga Lunga** border post.

But to discover the definitive end of the south coast turn left to **Shimoni**, just three kilometres (two miles) beyond Ramisi where signs mark the turning to the old headquarters of Sir William Mackinnon's IBEA enterprise.

Shimoni is famous for its deep-sea, big game fishing in the reaches of **Pemba Channel,** which divides the coast from Tanzania's **Pemba Island**, 40 kilometres (25 miles) away. Shimoni is the Swahili word for 'place of the hole' — a reference to the

15-kilometre (nine-mile) cave where slaves were penned before being shipped. It is possible to enter the cave from several places, including a climb down a ladder. At first, most visitors are overwhelmed by the stench of bat guano which covers the floor several centimetres deep. The shackles which held the slaves are still in place.

But Shimoni's greatest attractions lie offshore. For this is the home of one of Kenya's great marine national parks, the 28-square-kilometre (10-square-mile) **Kisite Marine National Park** and the adjacent **Mpunguti Marine National Reserve,** 11-square-kilometres (four-square-miles).

Wasini Island

Located in the coral gardens about one kilometre (half-a-mile) south of **Wasini Island**, this trapezoid section of the Indian Ocean encompasses four small, arid coral islands and a considerable area of fringing reefs and surrounding sand.

The government has declared the entire area surrounding the island **Wasini Marine National Park** (see 'National Parks', In Brief). You can walk around 17-square-kilometre (six-and-a-half-square-mile) **Wasini**

233

— just five kilometres (three miles) long and one kilometre (half-a-mile) wide — in a couple of hours. The island boasts a small pillar tomb set with many shards of Chinese pottery, and its shores are a beachcomber's delight.

Many finds include pieces of glass and a variety of shells, both natural and manufactured. The scrap metal is detritus from World War I when Wasini was used as a firing range.

Wasini Island Restaurant at the southern tip of the island, **Ras Mondini**, has a liquor licence for diners only — lest offence be given to the Muslim islanders. The management arrange snorkelling trips to the fabulous reefs around Kisite Island in a large dhow with a seafood lunch included.

Seventeen kilometres (ten-and-a-half miles) south of Shimoni, across the bay from the peninsula, is **Vanga,** which can also be reached by a murram road off the main road just before Lunga Lunga. Untouched by Kenya's tourist industry, Vanga lies in a tangle of mangrove swamps.

A **causeway**, flooded every so often by spring tides, leads over one of the swamps to the town. If you want to explore the mangroves, you can hire one of the precarious local dugouts.

Above: Moray eel and underwater photographer in coral lagoon at Kenya coast.

Opposite top: Angel fish in one of Kenya's coral gardens.

Below: Starfish in a marine national park.

Opposite: Underwater marine garden off Kenya's south coast.

Mombasa to Malindi: Sun, Sand, Sailing and Surfing

For years, the northern springboard from Mombasa was a toll bridge floating on pontoons that rose and fell with the tide. Today an elegant new Japanese single-span bridge arches over **Tudor Creek**, dramatic evidence of the changes that independence and package tourism have wrought. This route, which incorporates tarmac, gravel, dirt road, and boat, stretches 386 kilometres (240 miles) to the Somali border.

Getting there
From Kenyatta Avenue, travelling inland, take the intersection, right, to **Nyali bridge.**

Where to stay
Just a small cross-section of hotels on the north Mombasa mainland covering Nyali, Bamburi and Shanzu beaches: Bahari Cottages (self-service); Bamburi Beach Hotel (4-star); Bamburi Chalets (self-service); Casuarina Hotel (4-star); Coral Beach Hotel (4-star); Dolphin Hotel (5-star); Mombasa Inter-Continental (5-star); Kenya Beach Hotel (4-star); Mombasa Beach Apartments (self-service); Mombasa Beach Hotel (5-star); Neptune Beach Hotel (5-star); Nyali Beach Hotel (5-star); Reef Hotel (5-star); Seawaves Beach Hotel; Serena Beach Hotel (5-star); Severin Sea Lodge (4-star); Whitesands (4-star). In Kikambala, Sun 'n Sand Beach Hotel (4-star); Whispering Palms (4-star); Kanamai Holiday Centre; Kenya Marinas. In Kilifi, Mnarani Club Hotel (5-star); Sea Horse Hotel (budget). There are others. See Listings for 'Hotels'.

Sightseeing
Leaving the bridge, turn right on to the **Kisauni headland** which accommodates more five-star hotels along its **Nyali**, **Bamburi**, and **Shanzu** strip than any other area of the country.

Almost immediately you'll come to a right turn which takes you through **Freretown**, Kenya's first colony for liberated slaves. It was established in the last century by Sir Bartle Frere, a former governor of Sind in India (now in Pakistan). Continue along to **Cement Road** for the **Tamarind,**

perhaps the coast's most up-market restaurant. The Tamarind overlooks Tudor Creek and the jetty below where you can board the Tamarind dhow to cruise and dine, under the stars.

The road goes on to **English Point** past the **Krapf Memorial,** which records the sad fate of the wife and child of the coast's first Christian missionary — and marks their graves. It also records the spot where he made his pledge to attempt the conversion of the African continent.

Nearby is the 1910 **Mombasa Swimming Club** and on the left **Moi Park,** formerly Princes Park, which was presented to the city by the (then) Prince of Wales and the Duke of Gloucester and is the site of the annual **Mombasa Show**. The park borders the residential estate of Nyali which in the first decade of the century was developed as a sisal estate. Now spacious houses, an 18-hole golf course and smart hotels adorn this stretch of coastline and its neighbouring beaches.

Just a kilometre (half-a-mile) inland from Nyali Beach Hotel **Bamburi cement factory,** once the tenth-largest in the world, stands near several hectares of quarried limestone coral that have since been rehabilitated, in one of the most exciting environmental successes ever achieved, by Swiss ecologist René Haller. He transformed the gaping scars into a forest-clad wonderland of nature trails, fish ponds, wildlife and birdlife sanctuaries which now constitutes a major tourist attraction as well as profit-making farm.

One of Kenya's latest national marine parks lies off the Nyali headland. The ten-square-kilometre (four-square-mile) **Mombasa Marine National Park** is surrounded by a 200-square-kilometre (77-square-mile) marine national reserve established in 1986.

At the far end of the Nyali-Bamburi beach strip, the **Mamba Crocodile Village** earns substantial money from the sale of crocodile skins as well as drawing thousands of visitors daily to see the reptiles and other attractions. The road runs past the **Kipepeo Aquarium**, with its splendid display of tropical marine life, a **German beer garden,** and on through **Kenyatta** and **Shanzu Beaches.** Kenyatta Beach is where the late President Kenyatta had his old coast home. There are more hotels along

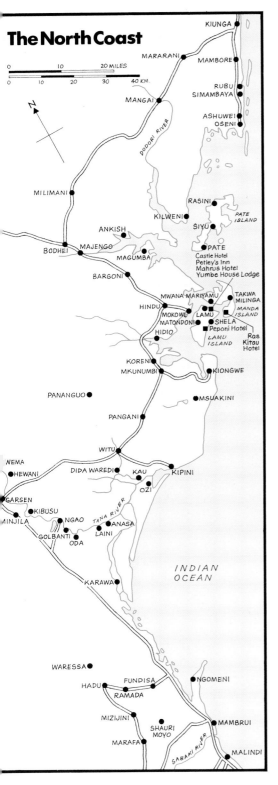

the strip at Shanzu, ending in the African Safari Club's **Palm Beach Hotel**, 12 kilometres (seven miles) off the main road.

Turn left, inland, past the maximum security Shimo la Tewa **jail** and after three kilometres (two miles) you'll come to another of the club's enterprises, the **Shimo la Tewa Sports Centre**. After another two kilometres (one-and-a-third miles) or so a 'Danger' sign announces your arrival at the south bank of **Mtwapa Creek** where, for many years, a hand-hauled rope ferry was manoeuvred by a crew singing ballads in the style of Paul Robeson. Now, however, on the main road just beyond the prison, another Japanese-built **suspension bridge** leaps across the mirror surface of the creek.

The shores on either side are lined with marinas and water sport centres. Rarely ruffled by a breeze, they are protected on either side by the cliffs, topped by elegant villas with sweet-scented gardens.

On the far bank, turn right along a sand road for one-and-a-half kilometres (one mile), to the **Kenya Marineland and Snake Park**. There you'll find turtles, sting rays, small but colourful fry, hand-fed sharks — and a writhing mass of deadly mambas as well as other venomous species in the serpentarium. In the grounds a Belgian couple transformed an old snackbar into **Le Pichet**, a true gourmet experience.

North of Mtwapwa Creek immense sisal plantations border the route, baobabs, kapoks and later — beyond Kilifi — jungle. Some 16 kilometres (10 miles) beyond the bridge is the lost city of **Jumba la Mtwana** ('House of Slaves'). To get there, turn right again off the main road. Like the better-known lost city of Gede, it was abandoned some time between the 14th and 15th centuries and was swiftly shrouded in jungle.

It lay for more than 400 years until it was discovered in the late 1960s. The jungle was hacked away in the early 1970s. The revealed city was smaller than Gede but still fascinating, with four **mosques**, a **cemetery**, and **houses**.

Five kilometres (three miles) beyond this monument a right turn continues for two kilometres (little more than a mile) to **Kikambala Beach** with the **Whispering Palms** and, further north, the **Sun 'n Sand**, one of Kenya's earliest coast resorts. Apart from the Sun 'n Sand, the original, airy,

high-pitched, *makuti*-thatched hotels favoured for their simplicity and coolness have been replaced by massive blocks of concrete annexes for rooms, service, and entertainment areas — to most people's regret. From Kikambala, the coast remains commercially unspoilt and undeveloped until Kilifi, the midway point between Mombasa and Malindi. The only exception is the sprawling **Vipingo sisal estate**, which was established more than half-a-century ago on 8,100 hectares (20,000 acres) and has its own town, factories and narrow-gauge railway.

Forty-four kilometres (27 miles) from Mombasa, a right turn leads five kilometres (three miles) to **Takaungu**, a charming Arabic village of whitewashed houses. Close by, overlooking a mangrove creek, is the forgotten grave of an Omani sultan who died there in the 19th century. Now a traditional woodcarving industry thrives there, turning out intricately-carved doors with Arabic inscriptions.

Kilifi Creek

Ten kilometres (six miles) along the main road from the turn-off the tarmac arrives at

Above: Dugout *ngalawa* (canoe) in coast lagoon.

Mnarani, at the southern headland of **Kilifi Creek**, a kind of tropical Dartmouth that stretches inland some 15 kilometres (nine miles).

On the brow of the headland to the right, along a snaking trail, is the former **Mnarani Club**, complete with an **airstrip**, swimming pool and a **jetty** for yachts and power boats. Still famous for its big-game fishing competitions, the club has now become a more formal hotel. To the left of the brow is another **serpentarium** and, close behind, some 17th-century **ruins**, including a **mosque** and several **pillar tombs.** The ruins were cleared in the early 1970s.

High cliffs line the entrance to this natural deep-water harbour and only the entrance through the reef limits the draught of vessels capable of mooring within. Gracious Mediterranean-style houses step down the cliffs overlooking the ocean-going yachts which bob at their moorings.

Kilifi Creek was bridged in 1991 by the Japanese. Though an undisputed boon to travellers, however, many see the bridge as a defacement of the creek's unspoilt tranquillity. Kilifi serves as a natural water sports arena with windsurfing, water-skiing, powerboat racing and sailing. It lures other *aficionados,* too, including bird lovers.

Millions of carmine bee-eaters make their nests in the mangrove swamps at the far end of the creek. With their long beaks, tapering bodies, and elongated tails, they swoop at dusk in great clouds. After capturing the insect, bee-eaters carefully tap the venomous sting out before swallowing the bee. The sound of their wings fills the air with a vibrant humming noise (see 'Bird-life: An Avian Spectacle without Equal', Part Three). Kilifi town spreads along the north side of the creek to the right of the main road. Private residences occupy much of the beautiful beach-front north of the town, making access by others virtually impossible.

Nature reserve

Just out of the town, to the left, lies the **Arabuko-Sokoke Forest**, an ornithological treasure house and an area rich in rare fauna. It is the last of the great indigenous coastal forests and, although under threat, offers protection to some rare trees. It was established as a forest nature reserve in 1943 and, with the addition of 16 square kilometres (six square miles) in 1977, now covers 417 square kilometres (161 square miles). One of the most important nature conservation sites in East Africa, the forest is the only surviving lowland coastal forest of any size with many important and threatened plant species.

Mammals include Ader's duiker, blue duiker, golden-rumped elephant shrew, bristle-tailed elephant shrew and coastal races of the bushbaby. There is also a remnant endangered herd of 80 elephants. Threatened birds include the Sokoke Scops owl and Clarke's weaver, both endemic to this forest, east coast akalat, Amani sunbird, and Sokoke pipit. Migratory visitors include pitta and spotted ground thrush.

Sokoke Scops owl is grey-white with a tonal 'tonk tonk' call which one forester imitates so well he can usually lure an owl close enough for nocturnal visitors to see.

Ader's, or Zanzibar duiker, all of 35 centimetres (14 inches) high, now feared extinct on Zanzibar, is also found around the Gede ruins, and in the Boni National Reserve. Another rare creature is the astonishing golden-rumped elephant shrew. Bushbabies are endemic.

The forest also has a prolific variety of rare, brilliantly-coloured butterflies, and a frog, *Leptopelis flavomaculatus,* only known from this forest and the Shimba Hills.

Sadly, some trees have been cut down by sawmillers, but most hardwood forest and many rubber trees remain untouched. These have been fenced off and the gates locked. If you inquire at the **forestry office** you may be allowed to wander in the nature sanctuary. You'll find a compass useful if not essential.

Back on the main road northwards to the lost city of Gede, the next 40 kilometres (25 miles) is through thatched villages which slumber drowsily, offering glimpses of life styles little changed over the years.

Unaffected by increasing numbers of tourists, and birthplace of Kiswahili, the *lingua franca* of Eastern Africa, some of these villages have been there for 1,000 years or more. One of the world's great living languages, initially Kiswahili was a fusion of Arabic and indigenous vernaculars. Like all great languages it continues to borrow freely from others. When the British arrived there was no word for Commissioner so it was adapted phonetically as *Kamishina*. The language grew and developed in cities like **Gede** — turn right at the **signpost** marked Watamu — whose mystery has never been solved. Gede vanished in the 16th century, swallowed by voracious trees and lianas.

The 18 hectares (45 acres) of ruins show that it was inhabited by a cultured and gracious community, but no records survive to reveal its history. Walking through the relics of these old buildings, including the **Dated Tomb**, *circa* 1399, it's not difficult to sense the brooding spirits which remain.

In the ruins and the adjacent jungle, Sokoke's golden-rumped elephant shrew has found a second home. You'll see it nowhere else but in these two places.

Gede was gazetted as a **national monument** in the 1920s. The National Museums run a small on-site **museum** with evidence that shows Gede once traded actively with Arabia and Asia, although it is now five kilometres (three miles) from the sea and two kilometres (one-and-a-third miles) from **Mida Creek.**

Watamu

From Gede village the road runs another six kilometres (four miles) to a fork left, for 10.5 kilometres (six-and-a-half-miles) to **Watamu**. Set around **Turtle Bay**, a curve of aquamarine water, Watamu's coral gardens and atolls sweep inland into the recesses of **Mida Creek.** Watamu's somnolent days have long gone. Up-country Europeans, package tourists from Germany and Italy, Samburu and Maasai *moran* dominate the waterfront. The village has a **post office**, a **mosque**, *dukas* and a **serpentarium** all overhung by palms and tropical creepers.

Covering ten square-kilometres (four square-miles), the **Watamu National Park** is surrounded by a 32-square-kilometre (12-square-mile) national marine reserve — embracing a 30-kilometre-long (19-mile) , five-kilometre-wide (three-mile) strip of coast and sea, including Mida Creek. At the northern end of the marine reserve is the six-square-kilometre (two-square-mile) **Malindi Marine National Park**, which is surrounded by another 213-square-kilometre (82-square-mile) national marine reserve some 20 kilometres (12 miles) further

north. These ocean sanctuaries became one of Kenya's four biosphere reserves in May 1979. They contain an ecosystem of rock platforms, cliffs, coral reefs, lagoons and sandy beaches with three major marine habitats. The coastline is bordered by fringing reefs on the seaward side plunging down vertically many metres.

Between limestone cliffs stretch beautiful sandy beaches. **Mida Creek** contains tidal mudflats with fringing mangrove swamp. Between March and May, waders are thick on the mudflats as they halt to rest and hunt food on their long migratory journey. Watamu's central motif, **Whale Island**, a hump-backed piece of coral opposite the entrance to the creek, is also a bird sanctuary. Between June and September it is a nesting ground for roseate and bridled tern and many shore birds, including sanderling, curlew, sandpiper, whimbrel, grey plover, greater sand plover and Mongolian plover. Non-breeding visitors include Saunder's little tern, lesser crested tern, and sooty gull.

Both national parks and reserves were established in 1968 to stop the depradation of coral and cowrie by tourists and locals. But the most significant impact on the area is the Sabaki River, which carries a heavy load of silt during the rainy seasons.

The **coral gardens** are breathtaking, and scuba-divers, for their part, delight in the discoveries deep below where brilliantly-coloured fish swarm to eat out of their hands.

At high water divers can visit an underwater cave where *tewa* (giant rock cod), weighing up to 400 kilos (880 lbs), hang suspended upside down, disoriented by the glimmering ceiling. But the swift under-currents are unpredictable.

Malindi: Swell for Surfers

Malindi was where Vasco da Gama first set foot in East Africa in 1498, having veered away from Mombasa where his anchor ropes were cut. His monument now stands on the headland where he stepped ashore.

Immediately he arrived, da Gama made friends with the Sultan whose welcome

Opposite: 17th-century Mnarani ruins at Kilifi.

241

Above: Catamaran racing off the Kenyan coast.

was memorable: 'For nine days we had fêtes, sham fights and musical performances.' Finally, the Sultan saw the Portuguese mariners off, loaded with fruit and provisions, to Calcutta. In the last century the missionary Krapf found Malindi derelict, but the Sultan of Zanzibar reinvigorated trade in 1860 and settled the town with traders.

But ever since author Ernest Hemingway arrived to game fish in the 1930s, only to spend more time tippling gin in the bar of the Blue Marlin than out on the water, Malindi has been the locale for most of Kenya's big game fishing tournaments. From all over the world deep sea sports anglers fly in to joust with the giants of the deep. Package tourists followed and now, with Kiswahili and English, German and Italian, many dialects echo in the markets.

Established in the 13th century, Malindi stands on the panoramic sweep of a wide bay — where the Indian Ocean swell over the broken reef makes surfing possible the year round. The best months are between late June and early September when the seasonal monsoon sweeps in truly magnificent rollers. Watersports are undoubtedly Malindi's prime tourist attraction.

Where to stay
Blue Marlin (4 star), Club Che Shale (4 star), Coconut Village, Driftwood Beach Club (upmarket beachcombing), Eden Roc (3 star), Lawford's (3 star), Silversands Beach Cottage (self service). There are others. See listings for 'Hotels'.

Sightseeing
Malindi Airport on the main Mombasa-Malindi road, 13 kilometres (eight miles) from the Gede turnoff, is marked by an injunction to drivers to dim their lights to avoid dazzling oncoming aircraft. The town itself lies two kilometres (little more than a mile) beyond, marked by churches on the left and **roundabout** with bypass, right, leading to the national park and the beach strip of **Silversands**.

Further on, on a headland overlooking the marine park, stands the **Vasco da Gama Pillar,** a cross fashioned from Lisbon stone, which the navigator raised next to what was the Sultan of Malindi's palace, in

January 1499. It was saved from collapse in 1873 by the crew of a British ship who protected it with a cone of concrete. More work was undertaken in the 1930s and 1940s to shore up the cliffs on which it stands. South of the monument, the road leads to **Silversands,** shaded by a swaying backdrop of casuarina, tamarind and whispering palms with many campsites, ending at the **Driftwood Club.**

The nearby **Birdland aviary** contains about 1,000 birds covering some 230 species, including carmine bee eaters, hornbills, a tame ostrich and other wildlife, such as baboons, monkeys and mongooses. Closer to the **marine park headquarters** the **serpentarium** contains species endemic to the Malindi area — including deadly black and green mambas — in coral snake pits.

The headquarters of Malindi Marine National Park is at **Casuarina Point.** In the coral heads and grass-shrouded hollows of these underwater gardens, snorkellers and scuba-divers swim alongside rainbow coloured fish, over potato, staghorn and mushroom coral. Off **Barracuda Reef,** the deeps of **Stork Passage** teem with big game fish. **Tewa Reef** and the caves by **Sail Rock** are other attractions.

In Malindi, the 'old town' of the 1930s to 1950s is an interesting Swahili quarter, with a large and busy market (where buses and *matatus* arrive), shops and hotels, stretching down to what the pre-war European retirees thought of as the village green, now the town's **Uhuru Gardens,** with its Second World War **memorial**.

To the right is the **Bohra Mosque** built in 1928, close to the Vasco da Gama monument unveiled by a Portuguese envoy in 1960. The **brass plaque** was subsequently removed by thieves. Beyond this, the **offices** of the Malindi local authority, marked by four ancient **cannons** and a **bell,** were originally built by the IBEA Company in 1890.

Lawford's Hotel, on the main road was established in 1934 by Leo Lawford, a retired district officer. There are close to a dozen mosques in the old town, including **Juma'a Mosque** which stands where slaves were auctioned off each week until 1873. Alongside it is the phallic 15th-century **Pillar Tomb** containing the mortal remains of Sheikh Abdul Hassan. Next to it stands a much abbreviated 19th-century **tomb.** Offshore, out in the Indian Ocean, are found some of the finest and largest fighting fish in the world — barracuda, wahoo, tunny (longtail, yellowfin and skipjack), bonito, kingfish, sailfish, dorado and marlin (Pacific blue, black and striped). There are also shark (tiger, mako and hammerhead), and rainbow runner.

In the peak season, between October and February, many classic international fishing contests are held. These are usually run from the **Malindi Sea Fishing Club,** along the seafront, close to the **fish market.**

Some distance beyond, on the right, what might well have been the first **church** in East Africa forms part of a 16th-century chapel near the spot where St Francis Xavier paused to bury two soldiers on his 1542 journey to Goa. When the church was refurbished in 1933, decorators stripped off the plaster to discover a painting of the crucifixion.

In the north of the town **Malindi Snake Park** also has cages of monkeys and tortoises, including a large and venerable specimen from Seychelles. The nearby **Blue Marlin** — built in 1931 as the Palm Beach Hotel — is where Hemingway once stayed and caroused over split gins instead of deep sea fishing.

Habari Night Club and **St Anthony's Catholic Church** stand cheek-by-jowl along this strip of beach, where Karen Blixen once picnicked with Denys Finch Hatton. Italian, Swahili and German restaurants are interspersed with the **Lutheran** and **St Andrew's churches** and a number of hotels, including the **Eden Roc,** the **Malindi Safari Club** and **Malindi Chalets**. At the north end of the strip there's a left fork to the **Suli Suli Sporting Club,** and a sand track straight on to the **Malindi Golf Club,** where visitors can either play tennis or nine holes of golf.

Speed bumps on the approach to the bridge across the **Sabaki River** herald the scenic, if bruising, road to Lamu and Kenya's remote north — a journey through still unspoilt forests and sleepy coastal villages.

The river was the northern border of Zanzibar's 16-kilometre-wide (10-mile) coastal strip. Runaway slaves used to settle on the far bank — only to discover the only market for their crops was Malindi.

The Road to Lamu: Mad Dogs, Eccentric English

For many people the essence of Kenya's coast is best savoured in the 222-kilometre (138-mile) stretch north of Malindi.

From Malindi, the Tana River, Tawaka, and Malindi Taxi services send their buses rumbling north on a journey which takes anything from half-a-day to possibly two days, depending on whether the **Tana** is in flood and the state of the track.

You can also sail by dhow from Mombasa's Old Port, which means at least two full days spent wallowing in the Indian Ocean swell. Or you can drive from the other side of the **Sabaki suspension bridge** through a succession of sunny Giriama villages set in baobab and fruit groves, where the traditional dress of the coast still prevails (see 'The People', Part One).

Sightseeing

Some little distance from Malindi there's an east fork to **Marafa village,** then another right turn for half-a-kilometre (a third of a mile) to a strikingly-coloured lunar landscape of eroded pinnacles and cliffs, dubbed by locals **Hell's Kitchen.**

Dating geologically from the Pliocene era these 30-metre-high (100-foot) pillars of buff, russet, pink and maroon sandstone are known as 'demoiselles'. Steep paths take you through the odd and tortured landscape where different layers of rock have been exposed by wind and rain.

Returning to the Lamu road, you travel another 13 kilometres (eight miles) to **Mambrui,** thought to have been surveyed in the 15th century by the Portuguese. The old cotton plantations worked by slaves still flourished in the 1930s. Near the decaying **cemetery** a **pillar tomb** is inset with Ming dynasty porcelain bowls. The 1962 **Riadha Mosque,** which overlooks the village from the only high point, has a lime-green dome inscribed with quotations from the Qur'an. Similar inscriptions have been carved on the **school** next to it.

At **Gongoni** the road reaches a **signpost** marking a track on the right to the Italian **space research centre.** The ancient Bajun settlement is indicated by an interesting ruin which marks the harbour. This was an anchorage superior even to those at Mombasa and Malindi. Folklore suggests Gongoni was destroyed by a 13th-century flood — a divine act of retribution against the women who persisted in bathing in milk.

Some distance from the village at the end of the peninsula is **Ngomeni** where the Arabian Nights ambience of the village — minarets, castellated mosques, and discreet maidens dressed in veils — are juxtaposed with twentieth-century technology. Out at sea, in the wide sweep of **Formosa Bay,** stands the **San Marco satellite launching pad,** and its sister platform, built by the Italians in the late 1960s. To get there, follow a track through a marshy estuary, past some man-made lagoons built to trap the tide to recover salt by evaporation.

Further north along the Lamu Road is **Fundi Issa,** some 33 kilometres (21 miles) from Malindi, where a right turn leads along four kilometres (two-and-a-half miles) of sand trail to **Robinson Island.** A descendant of one of Kenya's old European settler families, David Hurd, turned the sandbank into an idyllic castaway island, complete with *cordon bleu* seafood and watersports. At low tide you can walk from the mainland to the desert *pied-à-terre* in ankle-deep water. Hurd's success inspired another desert-island resort, only five kilometres (three miles) further on along the Lamu road. Known to the locals as the *Mto wa Mawe* (River of Rocks), **Giriama Village Island** has a restaurant and bar, four *makuti*-thatched huts, and serves lunches and dinners of crab and other crustacea.

Another 13 kilometres (eight miles) beyond Fundi Issa take an east turn to **Karawa** on the magnificent sweep of **Formosa Bay,** which is unprotected by a reef and pounded by breakers, which make for enthralling surfing.

From the turn-off, the Lamu road cuts through the delta of the Tana River where its many fingers treble and quadruple back on themselves. Then from a final ridge, with the broad green delta spread out below, the track drops gently down past the left turn to **Hola** and **Baomo Lodge** and on to **Garsen,** some 30 kilometres (19 miles) inland from the sea, and exactly 111 kilometres (69 miles) between Malindi and

Lamu. The narrow **causeway** ends on the south bank of the Tana. Garsen is the capital of the heartland of the Orma and Pokomo people. No tourist resort, it has only one street of desultory *dukas*, often dry petrol pumps, and not a single hotel.

The **ferry** is unpredictable. Travellers have been stranded there for days. In the dry season, it is easy enough to cross, but during the rains when the Tana is in spate, it often spills out on either side for ten kilometres (six miles) or more and the road is either awash or a sea of glutinous mud.

With the current too swift to risk the perilous passage, the antiquated ferry comes to a standstill. At such times, Pokomo boatmen use their *ngalawas* (dug-out canoes) to ferry waiting tourists, backpackers, and local itinerants across.

There, if you're lucky, you may find a bus waiting to take you on to **Mokowe** and the ferry to **Lamu Island.** The 48 kilometres (30 miles) of tarmac to the next major village, **Witu**, is notable only for the green thread of the jungle, flooded plantations and smallholdings, borassus palms, ibis and egret. But hidden in the delta's tangled mangrove swamps are the remnants of rubber plantations and other ventures initiated by Europeans and locals who settled there around the turn of the century.

In the 1860s the Sultan of Witu cut a canal across the swamps between the Tana and the small stream of **Ozi** to exploit the Tana waters. Two decades later, in 1892, it engulfed his plantations and the flooded Tana adopted the canal and changed course permanently.

The main channel pours into the Indian Ocean at **Kipini**, 21 kilometres (13 miles) south-east of Witu along a jungle-lined track. Witu, with its abundant mango plantations, was once proclaimed the State of Swahililand by a former Sultan of Pate, who fled the northern island in 1862 after offending the much more powerful Sultan of Zanzibar. Calling himself Simba — 'the Lion' — he produced his own currency and issued his own Swahililand stamps. The end came after the 'sultan' signed an 1888 alliance pact with the Dendhart brothers from Germany. The Berlin treaty of 1890 swept aside this puny alliance, and when nine Germans stayed on to establish a sawmill in the princedom it angered his successor, his son, who saw them as a threat. During an argument, one of the Germans shot the 'sultan's' guard and was killed in return, along with the others. The 'sultan' refused to discuss this matter with the new administration, so a British expeditionary force of almost 1,000 men razed the town and surrounding plantations.

There must be something that induces madness in the air of this region. At least three early colonial officers are reputed to have committed suicide at Kipini, where the wreck of the launch *Pelican* — in which one district commissioner flew the British flag as far upstream as Garissa — lay rusting on a mudbank for years.

Before World War I another settler, Charles Edward Whitton, set up a new plantation. When it failed he retired to his house in Lamu and never set foot outside the island — where he was much-loved and a Justice of the Peace, also known as the Lord Mayor or 'Coconut Charlie' — for 40 years.

An even more eccentric contemporary, Percy Petley, also experimented disastrously with Witu agriculture. After he went bankrupt he set up **Petley's Inn** in Lamu which acquired a reputation as an unusual hostelry. Surprised guests were often told to cook their own food and if they objected, were ordered off the premises.

Today, all that remains of this and subsequent history is a **plinth** and **flagstaff** (*circa* 1949) which is guarded by two **cannons** brought from Lamu by the British.

One is dedicated to Khalifa, the 'sultan's' son, and the other displays a **plaque** recording its manufacture in Cossipore, India, in 1852. The town mosque, **Masjid al-Nur** (the House of Light) built in the 1900s, was refurbished in 1968.

Near Witu, around one of the largest of the delta's lakes, **Kenyatta**, a settlement scheme for Kenyans expelled from Tanzania after the breakup of the East African Community in 1976 to 1977, has become a self-sufficient township of some 20,000 people. From Witu it's another 32 kilometres (20 miles) to **Mkunumbi,** where you turn east for **Kiongwe** on the **Ras Tenewe** headland that protects the Lamu archipelago.

Back on the main road it's 25 kilometres (16 miles) from Mkunumbi to **Hindi** and then east for 11 kilometres (seven miles) to

Mokowe, where a motor boat takes you on the 30-minute voyage to Lamu Island. If you're driving yourself, you have to leave your vehicle in the car park and pay an *askari* (watchman) to guard it.

From Mokowe

From Hindi it's 40 kilometres (25 miles) through Bargoni and Majengo to Bodhei, where a barely discernible trail, right, leads through Milimani, Mangai and Mararani to Dodori and Boni national reserves and Kiunga National Marine Reserve. Alternatively, you can drive on north-west another 40 kilometres (25 miles) to Ijara beyond which a left turn, on to the Bura road, passes the Tana River Primate Reserve.

The road to Bura continues another 44 kilometres (27 miles) skirting the Arawale National Reserve, sanctuary for Kenya's only herd of Hunter's hartebeest with their lyre-shaped horns. For both reserves there is an entrance charge, but for Arawale it is only a token gesture. There is no place to enter.

The Dodori National Reserve ranges from sea level to 100 metres (300 feet) high and covers 877 square kilometres (339 square miles) in the coastal zone of north-eastern Lamu District, extending towards Somalia. It's bisected by the Dodori River, which flows along an alluvial valley of short-grass flood plains where Pleistocene sand dunes run parallel to the coast. The reserve's creeks and inlets also serve as a substantial breeding ground for the rare mermaid-like dugong and green turtle. It is a buffer zone between the Kiunga Marine National Reserve and increasing human settlement.

There is one campsite, but with the incursion of ruthless armed bandits since the 1980s — and in the 1990s of desperate refugees from war-torn Somalia — it is essential to check with police and park authorities before attempting to enter the area.

Nearby Boni National Reserve, covering some 1,339 square kilometres (517 square miles) flush alongside the Somali border, separated from the sea by a narrow coastal strip, is the only coastal, lowland, groundwater forest in Kenya with dry lowland bush and grassland in drier areas. And the whole of the neighbouring 60-kilometre (37-mile) coastal reef and lagoon, from the

Somali border in the north to Oseni in the south, forms the 250-square-kilometre (37-square-mile) Kiunga Marine National Reserve, rising from sea level to thirty metres (100 feet). It contains more than 50 offshore islands, sandy beaches, mangrove swamps, coral reefs, mainland sand dunes and forest and became one of Kenya's four biosphere reserves in 1980 — an important breeding ground for a strange aquatic mammal, the dugong, that gave rise to the mermaid legends.

Poaching of green turtles and their eggs has been reduced but there is still some poaching of dugong. On the offshore islands lesser kudu, bushbuck, monkeys, porcupines, and wild pig roam; and wild birds nest in the cliffs — particularly in the breeding season between June and August.

Accessible only by air or boat, thatched Kiwaiyu Safari Village, on the mainland opposite Kiwaiyu Island, is a truly 'away-from-it-all' retreat. The administrative centre for the area is Kiunga, a remote, unspoilt village about 150 kilometres (95 miles) by road from Lamu, and about 100 kilometres (60 miles) by air. An old colonial officer's house is the sole evidence of Britain's far-reaching imperial ambitions.

Lamu: Enchanted Islands

The islands of the Lamu Archipelago are the last survivors of a 1,000-year-old civilization that developed between the ninth and 19th centuries (see 'History: The Dust and the Ashes', Part One). Lamu, some 100 kilometres (60 miles) south of the Somali border, was for centuries one of the trading ports from which ivory, rhino horn and slaves were exported. The Swahili *Lamu Chronicle* claims the town was founded by Arabs in the seventh century, but the Pumwani Mosque dates from 1370 and there is no mention of Lamu until 1402.

Like Mombasa and Malindi, Lamu was a thriving port and sultanate during the 18th and 19th centuries when it was frequently at ritualized war with its neighbours — Pate, Siyu and Faza — all island kingdoms of this northern archipelago. Every so often boats would sail across, pennants flying, richly-uniformed soldiers orchestrating their battle cries with style and dignity, to taunt their rivals. Actual conflict was rare but in 1813, the Nabhani of Pate fatally miscalculated the ebb of the tide when his fleet sailed into Shela, a Lamu beach, to fling what was probably meant to be a metaphoric gauntlet at the sultan's feet. Enraged, the sultan ordered an advance and the Pate battalions retreated swiftly to their boats — now left high and dry by the tide. The result was a grisly massacre and Lamu entered its golden age.

For 60 years Lamu controlled all trade until the British forced Zanzibar to sign an anti-slaving pact. British naval patrols blockaded slave ships and brought missionaries and crusaders, such as Stanley, to assert authority over this island kingdom.

The first resident agent, a Frenchman, arrived in the 19th century and was followed later by American traders, and German colonizers. Britons contributed much to Lamu's idiosyncratic traditions. The Freelanders, a group who intended to reach Mount Kenya and set up a 'socialist Utopia', never went any further — and appalled the islanders by their immorality.

Although rapidly-decaying, the town today is a living monument to its past. The old houses, built with walls of coral two-thirds of a metre (two feet) thick, have a series of alcoves about three metres (ten feet) wide, rather than rooms. Their width is decided by the length of the mangrove poles used for the flooring and ceiling. Many are three-storeys high, with precipitous staircases to a flat roof where much of the community's life goes on.

Lamu town looks across the channel to **Manda Island.** Although its seaboard is obscured by mangrove swamps, Lamu is still a busy port, mangrove poles being the major export. The creeks around the island and on the mainland constitute 450 square kilometres (174 square miles) of gazetted forest reserve. Lamu's appeal derives from the unique character of its people. Their culture is very old and of mixed origin.

Although staunchly Islamic, most customs derive solely from the Swahili culture, a people of mixed Bantu and Arab blood who many centuries ago were prosperous and politically powerful (see 'History: The Dust and the Ashes', Part One). Outwardly, little has changed in this strictly Islamic enclave, where the only motor car belongs to the district officer who can travel little more than two kilometres — none of it in the built-up area. The elegant centuries-old houses with their fountains in flower-filled *cortiles* (courtyards) reflect a heritage that had running water, plumbing and simple air-conditioning while Europe was still in bondage to the Dark Ages.

In the alleyways walk women clad in the *bui-bui* (the all-embracing black robe that denotes the modesty of their faith), with only their eyes revealed to public gaze. By turning its back on the world, perversely Lamu attracted its attention.

Getting there
The **Makowe Jetty** serves not only Lamu but Manda and Pate. The airstrip on Manda, however, serves air passengers who are taken by dhow to Lamu.

When to go
Lamu is pleasant at any time of the year but the tourist class hotels are closed between May and June for renovation and holidays.

Where to stay
Mahrus Hotel (budget), Peponi Hotel (one of the world's 200 great *little* hotels), Petley's Inn (4-star), Castle Hotel (4-star).

Sightseeing
Wherever you decide to go, your main form of transport, apart from walking, will be donkey — or dhow. Only 19 kilometres (12 miles) long, by eight kilometres (five miles) wide, Lamu island consists mainly of high sand dunes and waving palm trees.

In the north, the two towns, **Lamu** and **Shela**, are separated by more than two kilometres (one-and-a-half miles) of beach.

On the **quayside** there's **Petley's Inn** (founded by Percy Petley, who hunted, it is said, with a fist that felled leopards, and acquired in 1957 by a former British consular officer in Ethiopia and Djibouti), the **Castle Hotel** and the Lamu **National Museum**.

Much of the museum, which opened in 1971, was established by James de Vere Allen, who collected many outstanding examples of local arts and crafts, including carved doors which rival those of Zanzibar, made from the mahogany bean tree; ebony

thrones inlaid with bone and ivory; 'Arab' chests made from Tanzanian teak; scale-model dhows and jewellery.

There is also a reconstruction of an *mtepe* (large canoe) which Lamu invented with the British Navy's help. These 12-metre-long (40-foot) canoes had planks sewn with coir because the sultan mistrusted metal. The museum also houses *siwas* (great horns of ivory or brass) jealously-guarded symbols of kingship blown only on state occasions.

All these and much more you can see in the museum, opened in 1971. But it does not have Charles — 'Coconut Charlie' — Whitton's art collection, which he bequeathed to Mombasa's Fort Jesus Museum. The museum was once the British DC's house and its architecture is redolent of those imperial days. The first British proconsul in Lamu was Rider Haggard's brother, Captain Jack Haggard, whose letters inspired the author (see North-West Kenya: 'Enchanted Mountains, Unspoilt

Above: Dhow drifts gracefully on the mirror surface of a Lamu backwater.

Opposite: Launching a hand-crafted dhow at Lamu.

Vistas'). He caught two legendary three-metre-long (ten-foot) 230-kilo (500-lb) dugong, 'mermaids', now displayed in London's Natural History Museum.

The **brass cannon** the British used to subdue Witu's Swahililand stands in front of the museum. To the right is the **Riyadha Mosque** and to the left the **Catholic church** of Mary Mother of Jesus. Before it was built Catholics, mostly visitors, used the **Presbyterian kirk.** The church is set discreetly back from the street. All the land about the museum was reclaimed from the sea by dumping garbage. Before that, according to one of East Africa's first administrators, Sir Frederick Jackson, the shore was a 'public, very public latrine'.

To the left of the church is Petley's Inn, where extensive restorations were completed in 1992, including traditional-style bedrooms and an open-air poolside bar.

Beyond this, the waterfront — **Kenyatta Road** — is dominated by administrative offices, the **Customs** compound and the three-storey Arab-style **Castle Hotel**.

In the town itself a colourful **market** is held each morning in front of the old **Sultan's Fort**, begun by the Omani in 1808, completed some 12 years later and restored in 1857. It became a prison but when it was restored again in 1987 it became a museum.

Lamu's main street — formerly *Usita wa Mui*, now **Harambee Road** — used to be the waterfront before last century's reclamation. Alleys run off it in an uphill east-west direction which ensures that the yearly monsoons wash away the dust and odiferous droppings. These alleys are extremely labyrinthine, so make sure you have a map (the museum sells a good one) to guide you through them.

The other national monument in Lamu is the fluted 14th-century **pillar tomb** behind the **Riyadha Mosque** on the town's upper slopes. The mosque, built in 1900-1901, is perhaps the most senior of the town's 42 mosques, all of which are involved in the island's famous **Maulidi celebrations,** a major festival in the Islamic calendar.

This was established by Sheikh Habib Salih who, after he left the Hadhramaut in the 1880s settled in Lamu and became the town's patron. He made Lamu famous for its Qur'anic college and for Maulidi, the

Above: Ritual sword fight marks Lamu's yearly Maulidi festival.

Prophet's birthday celebration. For a week, religious festivities, feasting and dancing draw Muslim pilgrims from all over East Africa and the Indian Ocean. It's the best time to be in Lamu; but you need to be there at least a week early to secure a room.

Another interesting 15th-century **tomb** in Lamu contains the remains of Mwana Haddie Famau, a local woman. Located near a betel plantation, the tomb is now walled up and the porcelain-embedded pillars at each corner have long vanished.

For those keen on reliving Lamu's past, some of its 18th-century town-houses have been restored by the Lamu Society. History and Lamu's Arabian Nights ambience are the main reasons for visiting the island. As you might expect, the nightlife wouldn't shatter the coterie on the Champs Elysées.

The walk from Lamu to Shela Beach takes between 40 and 60 minutes. **Shela**'s most notable landmark was once the 1829 **Friday Mosque**. Fifty-eight steps, each one of a different height, take you to the top where there is a marvellous panorama of the Shela sand dunes, which are said to cover **Hadibu**, the island's first seventh-century Arab settlement, and the scene of

the 18th-century massacre. Shela's waterfront is now marred by a huge block-style hotel. In the scrub above the beach lie the neglected **graves** of a former IBEA officer, Mr Sandys and Lt Col Pink, who took over Petley's Hotel. The beach beyond Shela, unprotected by a reef, is one of the few places on the coast where you can surfboard. And the beaches on **Manda**, opposite Shela, are enhanced by the mysterious cannon scattered around.

The five hectares (12-and-a-half acres) of ruins of **Takwa**, an ancient city on Manda razed between the 16th and the 17th centuries, cleared by Kirkman in 1951 were documented between 1977 and 1979 by Thomas Wilson. You can only reach Manda by dhow — from either Lamu or Shela.

You wade the last few metres and then walk through the baobab groves to the **Takwa National Monument**.

Takwa's doors all face north to Mecca, as does the main street with the **mosque** at the end of it. The town still attracts occasional pilgrims from Shela, some of whom claim descent from Takwa, and come to pray for rain. On the left there's a 17th-century seven-metre (22-foot) **tomb** with corner pinnacles and, in the centre of the north wall, a ruined **mosque** with a lofty column and a restored *mihrab* (pulpit).

Apart from this, Manda and its somewhat distant neighbour, **Pate Island**, boast at least 12 major and 14 minor historical sites, including Pate's **Siyu fort**.

Pate

Pate is two hours by boat from Lamu, landing at **Mtangawanda** and **Faza** on the north shore. By air, a grass **landing strip** carved out of tropical forest is all that denotes Pate's place in the 20th century. Its impressive ruins sets it apart from the other islands.

Pate has to be explored on foot and the most popular route starts in Pate Town and leads, via **Siyu**, to Faza — making the return journey to Lamu from there. If you're worried about accommodation, carry a tent. Normally, however, you'll be besieged by generous islanders inviting you to stay. Carry water and food also since supplies are unpredictable.

From the **dock** an hour-long jungle trail leads through mango and coconut plantations and dense bush to Pate Town. The **Nabhani ruins** outside Pate Town are rich with walls, tombs, mosques and mysterious edifices.

According to the *Chronicles of Pate*, the town was founded by Arab immigrants in the early years of Islam. Archaeological evidence shows the existence of a flourishing port on the present site as early as the 10th century. In the 13th century, however, a dispossessed group of Arab rulers, the Nabhani, arrived. In the 17th century the Portuguese exerted some influence on the island but to little avail.

Throughout the late 18th century, Pate and Lamu were at war and the 1813 massacre marked Pate's fall from city status. Siyu, facing north-west in the middle of the island, is not so well-documented, but during the 17th and 18th centuries it became a Mecca for students of Islam.

Unlike the other towns, Siyu showed little or no interest in trade and so passed the avaricious eyes of the Portuguese despite its having been likened, at the end of the 17th century, to the district's pulse. Instead of trading, Siyu's inhabitants concentrated with great skill on peaceful artistic and artisan occupations — many of them religion-inspired — and for which Siyu is still renowned. Siyu lost its independence to the Sultan of Zanzibar in 1847.

Today the town's stout 19th-century **fort** and its rusting **cannon**, its mirror image reflected in the still waters of the mangrove creek, is Siyu's most striking building, giving no indication of its mysterious builder.

Pate Island's greatest historical site, far out on the south-eastern shore, is the 1,200-year-old city-state of **Shanga**.

Donkeys carry the few visitors from the grass airstrip along a jungle trail of mango and coconut plantations, across the unspoilt hinterland, pausing briefly in their passage through thatched villages, to the recently uncovered ruins of the oldest-known settlement on the coast. First settled between the eighth and ninth centuries, Shanga vanished almost overnight.

In the mid-1950s the indefatigable James Kirkman landed on the island's shores and stumbled upon its ancient ruins, overgrown in a thick jumble of creeper, baobab, bush and weed. But real excavation did not begin until 1980 when an Operation Drake team, led by archaeologist Mark Horton, dug through several layers of houses and streets to its ninth-century level.

The dry fossils and ancient ruins they found reveal the bare bones of a fascinating drama covering several centuries. High-class merchants and their women lived in splendour in this busy port-state until, centuries after it was established, the retreating sea left it high and dry.

Now only echoes of the past haunt the eight hectares (20 acres) of ruins, some with recesses where ceramics and works of art were displayed.

The mosque, with its *kiblah* pointing to Mecca, denotes the prevailing faith, but as the inhabitants slowly left, only the legacy of a graceful age remains.

The ruins are vivid contrast to the cultures inland on the mainland, which they plundered for slaves and artefacts as the source of their wealth.

Overleaf: Local regatta between inshore dhows at Lamu.

North-Eastern Kenya: Sun-scorched Plains of Darkness

The desolate, arid badlands of north-eastern Kenya are a vast, magnificent, and still largely-unexplored wilderness. Although they constitute more than one-third of Kenya, less than five per cent of Kenya's people live there. Patrolled by scouts on camelback, during the 1960s it was the scene of a bitter guerilla conflict by Somali *shifta* (bandits) who claimed the region for Somalia.

After independence, the area was closed to visitors for many years, although work continued on such projects as oil exploration and water drilling. Most of those who inhabit this region are hardy nomads, Kenya's ethnic Somalis and the Gabbra, who call it *Dida Galgalu* (Plains of Darkness) — and walking anywhere you wonder how anyone or anything could survive.

The security situation in the far north and north-east, particularly near the long and lonely stretches of the Ethiopian and Somali borders, has deteriorated considerably over recent years. And in 1996 Somalia was still continuing its own internal war.

Featureless to all but those who roam its hidden trails, it's easy to get lost in what was once romantically known as Kenya's Northern Frontier District (NFD).

Where to stay

Three kilometres (two miles) out of Maralal on the Lake Turkana road, cedar-built 66-bed Maralal Safari Lodge is spacious and comfortable, with pool and small conference facilities. Maralal campsite is just past the lodge. There is also a youth hostel.

In national parks

In the Marsabit National Park, 4-star Marsabit Lodge (about three kilometres — two miles — from the main park gates, in a superb location). Marsabit campsite is near the main gate.

In national reserves

Samburu Lodge, on the northern bank of the Ewaso Nyiro with riverside bars and a restaurant, (5-star); Samburu River Lodge, (5-star). In Buffalo Springs Reserve, Buffalo Springs Lodge (3-star). In the Shaba Reserve, Sarova Shaba opened in 1989 and arguably the last word in safari comfort, (5-star). Larsen's Camp in Samburu evokes the old days of affluent safari camps.

Champagne Ridge Campsite (Buffalo Springs) is not far from first gate. There are also three campsites in Shaba.

Getting there

There are two gateways into this semi-desert terrain — from Nanyuki on the shoulders of Mount Kenya, and from Nyahururu above the Marmanet Forest. The road from Nyahururu sweeps through the forest to dusty **Rumuruti** (see 'Heartland of Kenya', Part Two), southernmost border of Samburuland.

From there a gravel road roughly follows the course of the **Ewaso Narok River**, for the first half of the 145-kilometre (90-mile) journey to **Maralal**, past **Colcheccio**, a large ranch offering facilities to tourists.

At roughly the halfway stage, a north turn leads to a well-graded track — with great views over the Rift Valley — which leads down to Lake Baringo. Further on, at **Kisima,** just a few kilometres before Maralal, a sharp right turn to **Archer's Post** and **Isiolo**, offers magnificent views over the northern badlands.

Maralal

Maralal, the Samburu administrative centre and district capital, is an exciting town nestling west of the **Ol Doinyo Lenkiyo** mountains. It offers all the ambience of a frontier town. Even the climate is appropriate — scorching heat by day with log fires a necessity at night.

Two dusty main streets, a few *dukas*, a bank, and a hotel or two are the major facilities. Home for many years of Wilfred Thesiger — author, British Arabist, eternal nomad and seeker of unknown lands — Maralal is a good place to study the large

Above: Sundown over the Ewaso Nyiro in Samburu National Reserve.

numbers of colourfully decorated Samburu women and young warriors (*moran*) who almost always congregate there.

Remember that if you are heading north to Lake Turkana or east, through **Wamba** and the Great North Road, to Marsabit and Moyale, Maralal is your final point to stock up with all the essentials to carry you there and back — petrol, oil, foods, bottled beer and mineral water. It is also the northern-most outpost of bank and post office services, and only unrelieved desert country lies ahead.

Maralal is home to one of Kenya's most significant national monuments, **Kenyatta House**, the bungalow where Kenyatta was detained prior to his final release in 1961. There's not much else, apart from the **Samburu Rural Development Centre**, outside the town and local soothsayers and blacksmiths.

To venture into the Northern Frontier District proper, retrace your footsteps to Kisima and take the dirt road through **Wamba**, a typical Samburu town which lies at the foot of **Warges**, the southernmost and highest summit of the **Ol Doinyo Lenkiyo** mountains. Martial eagles circle on the strong thermals and hunt for prey in the sheer ravines below. Another summit in this range, 2,375-metre (7,790-foot) **Mathews Peak**, was named by the Teleki expedition in appreciation of the help they received from Sir Lloyd Mathews, commander-in-chief of the Sultan of Zanzibar's army. From there the road continues to the Great North Road, joining it north of Archer's Post, at the foot of the **Lololokwe Mesa**.

From Nanyuki

From Nanyuki, the road climbs through the crisp mountain air, past wheatfields and verdant smallholdings to **Timau**, and then on up over the shoulders of Mount Kenya before the dramatic descent to the scorching, semi-desert of the Northern Frontier District. The road plunges down more than 2,135 metres (7,000 feet) from 3,050 metres (10,000 feet) in fewer than 40 kilometres (25 miles).

Somewhat unimpressive in harsh sunlight, in darkness **Isiolo** presents a more romantic face, shining out across the indigo desert in a sparkling necklace of light. Beyond the **mosque** on the outskirts, the tin

255

roofs of the town close in on either side. For all its squat, nondescript, single-storey main street — reminiscent of the Wild West — Isiolo is gateway, if not capital, to a good one-third of Kenya. The tarmac peters out at the **checkpoint** on the town's northern boundary, where the road becomes the **Great North Highway** which leads to Addis Ababa, the Ethiopian capital, much of it in Kenya over a sea of corrugations while a dirt road leads eastward into the trackless wastes of the desert.

Sightseeing
In Isiolo you'll find many local souvenir vendors selling 'traditional' copper, brass and aluminium Samburu bangles, plastic 'elephant hair' bracelets, short 'Somali swords' in red leather scabbards, and other trinkets.

Apart from its mosques and one main street, with typical basic but comfortable board and lodging — try an early morning bucket shower in the backyard looking up at Mount Kenya's silhouette against the blush of dawn for a real sense of adventure — there's not a great deal to see in Isiolo but plenty of atmosphere. The frontier ambience — Kikuyu women selling fresh produce from their highland shambas, Somali and Boran cattlemen arguing the price with camel and cattle dealers, and the itinerant Samburu, Gabbra, Turkana, and resident Meru — make this town a real melting-pot of cultures.

Isiolo is the main departure point for the four major destinations of this vast desert area — **Marsabit, Moyale, Wajir**, and **Mandera**. The journey to Marsabit takes between five and six hours, five to six hours more from Marsabit to Moyale. In another direction it's nine hours to Wajir and four more hours to Mandera. These times assume that there are no hold-ups, both literally — bandits are still rife in the remote areas — and in the mechanical sense.

The roads could also be out of action because of rains and floods. However, plans have been in hand for years to tarmac the Great North Road from Isiolo to the Ethiopian border at Moyale. This would provide a first-class all-weather road between Nairobi and Addis Ababa. The plan was first launched in the 1960s but in 1996 the stretch between Isiolo and Moyale had still to be carpeted. For most tourists, the first destination, 45 kilometres (38 miles) out of Isiolo to the north, is **Samburu National Reserve**. This covers 165 square kilometres (64 square miles) to the north of the **Ewaso Nyiro River**, 90 kilometres (56 miles) north of Mount Kenya. Set at between 800 and 1,230 metres (2,625-4,036 feet), the reserve is a lava plain with steep-sided gullies and rounded basement hills. The Ewaso Nyiro River forms 32 kilometres (20 miles) of the southern boundary and is Samburu's central feature.

Upstream, the same river plummets over Thomson's (Nyahururu) Falls. In spate its waters quickly become a raging torrent. Early in 1986, and in 1987, it dried up during a prolonged drought, which came to an abrupt end as a flash flood sent a wall of water three metres (10 feet) deep rolling down its dry bed.

In this landscape, battlements made of scarps and fallen boulders rise up out of the thorn scrub, and where the stone and dirt road lurches down a dip and over a *wadi* (dried-up river) the rugged hills to the north-west vanish from view.

Vegetation consists of acacia woodland with bush, grass and scrubland with a narrow, riverine woodland of doum palm along the Ewaso Nyiro River.

Samburu is one of the few sanctuaries in Kenya which are home to Grevy's zebra, which, with bat-like ears and single-direction stripe, is notably different from the Burchell's (common) zebra. Rare beisa oryx and blue-shanked Somali ostrich can also be seen (see 'National Parks', In Brief).

Adjoining the reserve, more or less a contiguous extension of the same environment, is the **Buffalo Springs National Reserve**, covering some 131 square kilometres (51 square miles) of rolling, lowland plains interspersed by seasonally dry luggas and the Ewaso Nyiro River — its northern boundary. Unlike most rivers, these waters never reach the sea. They bury themselves in the **Lorian Swamp** near the desert town of **Habaswein** in the east.

Shaba National Reserve
A few kilometres to the east, across the rutted surface of the Great North Road, lies the **Shaba National Reserve**, the third re-

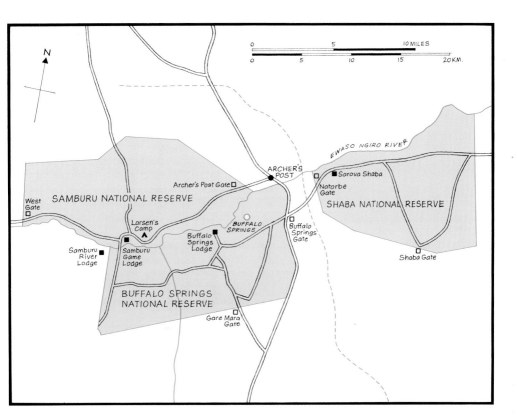

serve of the Samburu complex beloved by Joy Adamson, who continued her work on rehabilitating leopard to the wild there. She was murdered there in 1980. A **plaque** raised on her old campsite by Samburu County Council honours her memory.

Although a luxury lodge opened in 1989, Shaba remains one of Kenya's most pristine game reserves. Covering an area of 239 square kilometres (92 square miles), the reserve is set at the base of the Mount Kenya foothills, 70 kilometres (43 miles) north of the main massif, at between 700 and 1,500 metres (2,300-4,920 feet).

Beyond the foothills, the reserve covers a lava plain with ridges dominated by the **Shaba Massif**. The northern boundary includes 34 kilometres (20 miles) of the **Ewaso Nyiro River** and there are numerous springs and a large swamp. Beyond the **Sharinka Falls** in Shaba's far eastern section, **Chanler's Falls** are named after William Astor Chanler, who mapped out the region in the late 1800s.

Great North Road
The Great North Road, which divides Shaba from Buffalo Springs and Samburu, now thrusts northward through **Archer's Post**, 48 kilometres (30 miles) from Isiolo, some 320 kilometres (200 miles) from Nairobi, into a stark, dramatic wilderness.

Pitted with giant corrugations the road is difficult to drive over, even at speed. There is a military training ground south of the river. After Archer's Post — named for an early British administrator Geoffrey Archer (later Sir) who made camp there in 1911 — the road heads for the sugar-loaf of 1,853-metre (6,080 foot) **Lololokwe**.

Just before its base a dirt road veers west, through **Wamba**, into Samburu country and the lush forests of the **Lorogi Plateau** in the **Karisia Hills**, on to Maralal.

From Lololokwe the Great North Road heads through arid and ravaged land to **Seredupi** and **Lodosoit,** after which it cuts through the eastern extremities of Kenya's least known game sanctuary, the **Losai National Reserve**, located in the mountains that rise out of the **Kaisut Desert**.

Losai National Reserve
Situated 175 kilometres (110 miles) north of

Mount Kenya at an altitude of between 625 and 1,750 metres (2,050-5,740 feet), the 1,806-square-kilometre (698-square-mile) reserve is a lava plateau dissected by dry luggas with scattered volcanic plugs and cones covered with thorny bushland.

It is virtually impenetrable, even by a 4WD vehicle, although the medical mission of **Ngoronet,** with its airstrip, is in the middle. The reserve touches the fringes of both the **Ndoto** and **Ol Doinyo Lenkiyo** mountains, visible to the west. The Ndoto Forest is one of Kenya's biggest, with almost 1,000 square kilometres (390 square miles) of indigenous, virgin timber.

Set on the Great North Road, at the northern edge of the reserve, is the mission town of **Laisamis.** Before World War I an English aristocrat making a hunting trip in this region with Colonel J H Patterson, the martinet of the *Maneaters of Tsavo* melodrama, pitched camp near there. Returning from a foray into the Kaisut desert he found his wife locked in the colonel's arms, in *flagrante delicto*, and returned to the desert where he shot himself.

Another lurching 100 kilometres (60 miles) across the Kaisut Desert, a tumultuous landscape of raddled lava and rocks resembling lumps of rusted cannon ball and shot, takes you to **Logologo.** The neat little mission town, its two-storey houses strangely incongruous in the desert wilderness, has grown up around the airstrip.

There the **Milgis Lugga** passes under one of the bridges built by the youth service. Before it was built, flash floods tumbling down from the mountains delayed travellers for days.

Shortly after Logologo, the road crosses the border of the **Marsabit National Reserve** and climbs the slopes of the volcanic mountain, which rises abruptly out of the desert, to **Marsabit,** a bleached, monochrome of a town. Capital of a sprawling administrative region, Marsabit is where the Gabbra, Rendille and Borana people meet on common ground. There is a **bank, post office, service station** and **workshop,** although the petrol pumps often run dry.

The town is as hot as the surrounding desert. But two kilometres (little more than a mile) away, the dirt track halts at the gate of the 2,088-square-kilometre (806-square-mile) Marsabit National Reserve.

Marsabit National Reserve

Situated 560 kilometres (348 miles) north of Nairobi, **Marsabit National Reserve** is a forested mountain oasis with several volcanic craters, many filled with freshwater lakes. Lower down, the forest merges into acacia grasslands which, in turn, give way to thorny bushland on the lower slopes.

Once through the gate and round the first bend, you enter another world where the forest closes in and is reflected in two magic crater lakes. Born out of volcanic fire, Marsabit is often swathed in mists.

Each night as the desert air cools, clouds form and, an hour or two before dawn, clamp their clammy fingers around the western peak. The mist rarely releases its grip before early afternoon. The forests, watered by the mists, sustain elephant which are famous for their giant tusks. The reserve is also renowned for its herds of greater kudu (see 'National Parks', In Brief, for wildlife).

At least 52 species of eagle, hawk, and falcon nest in the sheer 200- to 215-metre (650-700-foot) cliffs, amid stands of juniper and podocarpus, which give the reserve's craters a green fur lining. Altogether there are 350 recorded bird species. Rare lammergeier bearded vultures nest on the sheer cliffs of **Gof Bongole** — the largest crater — which has a ten-kilometre (six-mile) rim.

Higher up Marsabit Mountain, another amphitheatre called **Lake Paradise** lies at the bottom of the bowl, below an old 150-metre-high (500-foot) caldera rimmed with forest trees laced with Spanish moss. There, American film makers Martin and Osa Johnson made their home for four years in the early 1920s, writing articles, books and shot some of the earliest wildlife films, which aroused interest in Kenya.

Other interesting places to visit include **Gof Redo** crater, just out of town. It's near enough to tackle on foot but best to do it in company. You can also visit the **Singing Wells** at **Ulanula** which are owned by the Borana. The wells plunge vertically, some four to 15 metres (15-50 feet) down.

Each morning, the well-masons work in mud and water to fashion a trough in the quick-drying sun. Four men form a human ladder, the lowest one standing chest-deep in the water below, the second perched on a rocky ledge, the third balanced expertly on two slender poles, and the fourth at the top. They swing three buckets of stitched giraffe hide up and down in harmonic rhythm, singing a hymn-like song as they work. The trough fills quickly and Borana women hurry to take home the day's water as their livestock drink eagerly. These desert people hold their animals in high esteem. Rather than risk them dying in Marsabit's chill night air, they opt to walk up to 70 kilometres (45 miles) to the warmth of the desert floor before returning in a day or two to water them again.

If you continue across the pitiless glare of the Chalbi Desert for 350 kilometres (220 miles) you will to **North Horr** and from there you can drive to **Koobi Fora** and the **'Cradle of Mankind'**. The signpost at the edge of Marsabit town gives the distance to the eastern shores of Lake Turkana as more than 350 kilometres (220 miles) across the Chalbi, a vast salt desert, which used to be the bed of an ancient lake. Even now, during extraordinary rains, which fall perhaps once every 50 years (as in the early 1960s), Chalbi becomes a shallow inland sea covering thousands of square kilometres.

From Marsabit the Great North Road continues north across the inhospitable wastes of the *Dida Galgalu* ('Plain of Darkness') and then veers east over the **Ngaso Plain** to Moyale. It takes between five and six hours of rugged travel to cover the 245 kilometres (150 miles) from Marsabit in a 4WD vehicle.

Sightseeing

Moyale consists of a small **mosque**, one main street, a few sandy side streets, row of *dukas*, ubiquitous **bar**, **camel corral**, **post office**, **police station**, **small market** and two abandoned petrol stations. It is attractive for its **Burji architecture** — which depends entirely upon local materials.

Sticks, thin branches, tree trunks, mud, dung and every other sundry usable is employed with ingenious, if unexpected, results to sophisticated eyes. From what land and nature provide, a cool living space is created in a land where outside temperatures are upwards of 32°C (90°F) all year-round. Safe, high and dry in every sense of the phrase, it is customary for the smaller domestic livestock — chickens and goats —

to spend from sundown to sunrise on the flat mud roofs. From Moyale it is possible to enter Ethiopia. Immigration officials need to see your visa — Kenyans do not need one. Customs searches are quite thorough due to smuggling. After leaving Kenya, you climb a wide stretch of tarred road into **Ethiopian Moyale,** which is more prosperous than its Kenyan counterpart.

Northern Frontier: The Harshest Desert

If you have incredible stamina and a penchant for risks, you may consider taking the desert trail from Moyale east to **Mandera** and **Wajir**. But remember that, although the route is clearly shown on all maps, you may have to carve your own trail to Mandera, set snug against the Ethiopian and Somali border. On rare occasions Kenyan police or army vehicles go this way, but otherwise there is nothing apart from camel trains on the move. By the beginning of the 1990s the Somali *shifta* (bandits) had again become active in the region, so you would be best advised to make the long journey back to Isiolo and explore the north-eastern desert from there.

Getting there

Tackling the route north-east from Isiolo you will be very much out on your own, crossing scorching desert over which the horizon merges with ruthless persistence into the heat, haze and dust which envelop everything in front. So monotonous and spotted with thorn bush is the landscape that if you stray just a few metres from the trail you become disoriented in minutes and hopelessly lost.

Sightseeing

The trail drives through this featureless plain, past the village of **Kula Mawe**, and the right fork through **Garba Tula**, and on to **Modogashe**, the meeting point for Eastern and North-Eastern provinces.

In the late 1960s American teams swept across the desert with drilling rigs to sink boreholes for local townsfolk and nomadic communities. But more often than not the water was too alkaline to use. In the

Above: Forbidding volcanic mountains guard the approach to Suguta Valley.

waddies around town you'll see Borana and Somali camel herders digging deep into the sand to tap the residue of the last rains, hidden well below the surface.

From this dusty shantytown with its two provincial **police headquarters**, it's a bumpy, sandy, sweltering 50 kilometres (30 miles), past the western extremity of the **Lorian Swamp**, where the desert finally sucks the Ewaso Nyiro dry, and across the **Sabena Desert** to **Habaswein** which looks like a Hollywood set for *Beau Geste*. From Habaswein it's another 110 kilometres (70 miles) to **Wajir**, some 50 kilometres (30 miles) from the Somali border. Thorn bushes grow out of the sand that stretches away to an ill-defined horizon.

There is no surface water for hundreds of kilometres in any direction, but around Wajir more than 100 wells are scattered across 70 square kilometres (30 square miles) of desert. These wells, only about six metres (20 feet) deep, have been in use for centuries. Indeed, legend has it that some 3,000 years ago the Queen of Sheba watered her camels there. White buildings, with little minarets rising above the flat-roofed houses, endow Wajir with all the ambience of Arabia. Set at 900 metres (2,950 feet) above sea level, Wajir is a major administrative centre for thousands of square kilometres of north-eastern Kenya, with a **district commissioner's office**, **police station**, **hospital** and **army camp**.

A plaque on the wall behind the DC's desk records the names of illustrious predecessors. An odd-looking building houses the **Royal Wajir Yacht Club**, though there is no sea or lake within 500 kilometres (310 miles). The club acquired the 'royal' prefix after entertaining a member of Britain's royalty. Wajir's sandy streets see few vehicles, but a circle of whitewashed stones at one end of the main street serves as a roundabout.

Hidden behind a low stone wall, overgrown by weeds and encroached on by the desert sands, is the **cemetery**. There's little of inspiration, save perhaps for the colourful **market** which sells domestic ware, pottery, and an ingenious locally-made air freshener. Marabou storks sit hunched around the town's garbage pit.

Mandera

From Wajir to Mandera it is another 185

kilometres (115 miles) across the trackless wastes of the **Gora Dudu Plains**. The route veers east at the fork just after **Tarba** to the dusty settlement of **El Wak** — Somali for 'the Wells of God' — which was once an outpost for a camel patrol. Just beyond the town a right turn loops across the border.

From there it's about 100 kilometres (70 miles) along what ostensibly is a main road to **Ramu** which lies on the Ethiopian border by the seasonal **Daua Parma River**. Ramu boasts a **National Christian Council of Kenya** shelter where you can spend the night if a room is available. There is also a Kenya Army garrison plus the most virulent mosquitoes you'll find anywhere.

From Ramu, the tarmac continues to **Mandera**, tucked in against the Somali-Ethiopian borders.

Sightseeing

As at Moyale, the border between Kenya and Somalia is freely open for the local people. Indeed, Somali currency is accepted in the town though, with the state of affairs in Somalia in 1996, the currency was worthless.

But, civil war or no, Mandera is a thriving black market entrepôt, although the town is little more than a collection of dilapidated administrative buildings. Essentials such as detergents, tea, coffee and *miraa* cross into Somalia in exchange for electronic goods, cameras and other luxuries from the Arabian Gulf.

The main focus is the **market**, which does brisk business in *miraa*, a leaf which, when chewed, acts as a mild amphetamine.

If you're lucky, the **Mandera Club**, members only, may allow you in to buy a beer. The only licensed premises in town, it opens in the late afternoon.

From Garissa

The other gateway to the north-east is **Garissa**, on the Tana River, only 380 kilometres (235 miles) from Nairobi through Thika or Machakos and Kitui. A fairly good road will deliver you to this dusty administrative centre so long as there is no bandit ambush en route. Garissa is located just 400 metres (1,310 feet) above sea level, and is the last place on its course from source to sea where the Tana River is bridged. Further down it has to be crossed by ferry.

Temperatures and humidity are high in Garissa, but petrol and beer should be available and a bank follows conventional banking hours. Accommodation is basic.

Sightseeing

Garissa is the base from which to explore the Tana basin as the river rolls down to the sea beyond **Garsen**. A thrice-weekly bus service to Wajir and Mandera follows the road that joins the Isiolo-Wajir road at Modogashe.

The road to Garsen leads straight along the southern bank of the Tana for 150 kilometres (90 miles) through **Tula** to **Hola**, passing both the extensive **Bura settlement scheme** and the 533 square kilometres (206 square miles) of the remote **Arawale National Reserve** to the north.

You can cross the Tana at Hola by ferry and then turn back, westwards for a few kilometres, to the reserve set on a flat plain dissected by sandy-bedded rivers and covered with thorny bushland (see 'The Road to Lamu: Mad Dogs, Eccentric English').

Hola, which falls in the Coast Province of Kenya, is the administrative headquarters of Tana River District with a **post office**, **hospital**, **police station** and **petrol station**.

It's another 87 kilometres (55 miles) downstream, all along the south bank, to **Garsen**. Roughly halfway between the two is one of Kenya's most wonderful wildlife sanctuaries, the **Tana River Primate Reserve**, which covers 169 square kilometres (65 square miles) of flood plains, sand levees, old river channels, ox-bow lakes, and ponds in a 50-kilometre (30-mile) belt along the Tana's north bank. This highly diversified range of riverine forest with patches of bush and grasslands provides cover and food for almost 300 species and is one of the last sanctuaries for the endemic red colobus and mangabey monkeys in Eastern and Central Africa. They are survivors of a time when the Ituri rainforest used to stretch across Africa in a broad swathe from east to west.

There are five other primates, including Sykes monkey and yellow baboon (see 'National Parks', In Brief, for wildlife). More than 240 bird species have been recorded as well as 22 species of fish. There is one **tented camp**.

PART THREE: SPECIAL FEATURES

Above: Lush harvest of Kenya's tropical orchards.
Opposite: Sun-up over the Kenya wilderness.

Wildlife: Great and Small, Wild and Wonderful

Kenya boasts one of the greatest wildlife populations in the world: some unique, much of it rare, and a few whose lineage goes back long before the first ancestors of mankind evolved on the shores of Lake Turkana, northern Kenya's remote inland sea. A large area on its eastern shores forms one of more than 50 nature sanctuaries established to preserve for future generations a wildlife, marine and prehistoric heritage which has few equals.

Kenya's first national park, Nairobi, opened its gates in 1946. By independence in 1963 there was a network of 12 parks and reserves. Expansion was swift. Within the next 25 years their number had increased to more than 50. They range from the combined area of the twin Tsavo parks, which cover more than 21,750 square kilometres (8,399 square miles), to the Saiwa Swamp National Park, which covers two square kilometres (less than a square mile).

Kenya has more than 80 major animal species — from the 'Big Five', the most cherished trophies among the old hunting fraternity — to tiny antelope, such as the dik-dik, slightly larger than a rabbit.

The Big Five: Elephant

The **African elephant** weighs anything from three-and-a-half to six-and-a-half tonnes. It eats between 90 and 270 kilos (200-600lbs) of fodder and drinks between 200 and 300 litres (44-66 gallons) of water a day. It depends almost entirely on its trunk for scent and communication, washing and cleaning, carrying and clearing, and for drinking and eating. The tusks, upper incisors, are simply secondary lifting, carrying, and clearing tools. An elephant's life span depends on its lower teeth. As one is worn away, the next one moves down the jaw to push it out. When the last one is worn down, at anywhere between 50 and 70 years, the elephant dies of starvation.

Gestation takes close to two years. The young weigh between 120 and 135 kilos (265-300 lbs) at birth. During labour the mother is attended by two other females — 'midwives' — which accompany her when she withdraws from the herd to give birth in discreet privacy. Although their sight is poor, elephants have an excellent sense of smell and well-developed hearing. Their brain weighs three times that of a human brain — up to five kilos (8-11lbs).

Rhinoceros

The **black rhinoceros**, the smaller of the two rhino species, weighs around 907 to 1,364 kilos (2,000-3,000lbs). The average size of its horns varies between 50 and 90 centimetres (one-and-a-half to three feet) for the front horn and just over 50 centimetres (almost two feet) for the rear horn.

With its relatively small three-toed hoofs and pointed prehensile upper lip, the black rhinoceros is a browser found anywhere from sea level up to 3,500 metres (1,150 feet), in vegetation ranging from savannah to montane forest.

The **white rhinoceros** is not white but derives its name from the Afrikaans 'weit', wide-mouthed. With their square lips, white rhinos are grazers, and more sedentary and gregarious than black rhino. They move in families and groups of between two and five. The white rhinoceros is normally a good 15 centimetres (six inches) higher at the shoulder and weighs between 2,000 and 4,000 kilos (4,400-8,900lbs), making it the second biggest land animal.

Buffalo

African buffalo need plenty of fodder to maintain strength and stamina. Voracious eaters, they browse and graze on a variety of grasses, leaves, twigs and young shoots for most of their 15 to 20 years. Gregarious, they often form herds of 500 up to 2,000. Buffalo are found everywhere in Kenya, from sea level to mountain forests above 3,000 metres (9,840 feet), always close to water. They are particularly dangerous.

Lion

The **lion**, largest of Kenya's three big cats, weighs up to 280 kilos (620 lbs). Its amber-coloured eyes, like those of the leopard, differ from those of most cats in that they

Above: Endangered white rhino in one of Kenya's wildlife sanctuaries.

are circular, not oval. Inherently lazy, the lion, nevertheless, is extremely powerful. At one leap it can clear a barrier almost four metres (13 feet) high or a chasm up to 12 metres (30 feet) wide.

Lion hunt communally by running down their prey at a top speed of around 64 kilometres-an-hour (40 miles). They pounce on the victim's back, drag it to the ground and seize it by the throat. Another method is suffocation by holding the victim's muzzle in its mouth. A lion or lioness accounts for 19 head of game a year at an average weight of about 115 kilos (250lbs).

Prides, which number up to 30 animals, mostly females and young, mark their range — up to 160 square kilometres (525 square miles) — by urination. The lion's roar, rarely heard during daytime, carries as far as eight kilometres (five miles) and signals territorial ownership.

Leopard
The **leopard** is much smaller than the lion and weighs between 30 and 80 kilos (65-

180lbs). Its sandy fur is exquisitely-patterned with dark rosettes. Leopard move mainly at night, resting up during the day in the branches of a shady tree. Superb hunters, they prefer to kill by leaping from branches and seizing the neck or throat.

Leopard kill anything from small rodents to fairly large gazelle and antelope. They eat fish and come readily to carrion. What they cannot eat immediately, they haul up a tree, out of reach of scavengers.

Cheetah
Cheetah are the most slender of the three big cats and weigh between 45 and 65 kilos (95-140lbs). With their deep chest, slender body, and long thin legs, cheetah are built for speed. The fastest animal in the world they have recorded speeds of more than 112 kilometres-an-hour (70 miles). But the burst of energy is brief and always leaves the cheetah gasping for breath. Sometimes cheetah are so short of air that their victims escape the capture hold — a slashing, claw-

Overleaf: Majestic elephant — their future in peril.

Above: Crested crane struts in front of a Cape buffalo.

raking blow to the flank — and make off. At other times, a more dominant killer or scavenger will move in and steal the kill.

Giraffe

Nature has given the **giraffe**, the world's tallest creature, several systems to help it cope with life as the 'skyscraper of the bush'. These include a prehensile upper lip and a 45-centimetre (18-inch) tongue — the longest in the world. They also have a unique system of canals and valves which maintain constant blood pressure whether the giraffe is standing tall — or bending down to drink.

Giraffe, more closely related to the deer family than any other living creature, run in a fascinating loping gallop at speeds of up to 56 kilometres (35 miles) an hour.

Measuring anything from four-and-a-half to five-and-a-half metres (15-18 feet), giraffe weigh up to 1,270 kilos (2,280lbs). Already more than one-and-a-half metres (five feet) high at birth and around 70 kilos (150lbs) in weight, the young continue to grow for the first seven to ten of their 25 years. Two races of giraffe are common in Kenya. Maasai giraffe are found mainly to

the south-west of the Athi River while Rothschild giraffe, with their distinctive white 'stockinged' forelegs, are now seen only in the Lake Nakuru National Park and at the AFEW Giraffe Sanctuary, Nairobi. The much less common reticulated giraffe, is found mostly in the country's north.

Hippopotamus

Weighing up to four tonnes, **hippo** are the third-largest land animal. But they can stay totally submerged for three or four minutes. True amphibians, they eat, mate and give birth under water and spend most of the day sleeping and resting, usually in the water, coming up frequently to blow air and recharge their lungs.

At sundown the schools (or 'sounders') leave the water, adult bulls at the back, to spend the night within the limits of their 'home-range', marked by well-defined pathways.

There, they search for fodder, eating around 60 kilos (130lbs) nightly. Usually born in the water, the young are suckled at first on land. Disobedient young are chastised, sometimes with a bite, and the youngster is made to cower in submission.

Top: Lion cub.

Above: Mating lion and lioness.

Above: Leopard lazes in a Maasai Mara tree.
Opposite: Cheetah on an Amboseli acacia thorn.

Crocodile

For all its sinister-looking teeth, the **crocodile** is unable to chew. To eat large prey, the reptile clamps on to its victim's legs and threshes around in the water, rotating several times until the limb is wrenched from the trunk. Then it raises its head and the food falls to the back of its throat. Digestion is slow. Bodies recovered from crocodiles 15 hours after the kill have been unmarked. Crocodiles kill with a blow of either the head or tail.

These cold-blooded saurians depend entirely on external temperatures and regulate their body heat according to the time of day. They leave the water early in the morning to warm up, return to the water to escape the excessive heat of high noon, and bask later in the cooler part of the day until around sundown, when they return to the water for the night. They stay submerged for up to an hour.

Other cats

The **serval** has long legs, large oval ears, a medium build, and weighs between 13 and 15 kilos (30-35 lbs). Its main food is rodents, but it also eats lizards, fish, vegetables, birds, and small antelope, depending on what is available. To catch birds it leaps high into the air as the victim takes off. Serval cats can be found throughout Kenya — from lowland savannah to high mountain moorland.

Caracal

The **caracal**'s flat head, long legs and powerful shoulders give it the proportions of a lynx. With hind legs longer than forelegs, the caracal can suddenly spring into the air, sometimes as high as three metres (10 feet) — for its size, a phenomenal distance — and pull down a bird in mid-flight. Few cats can emulate this feat.

Copy cats

Civets, long-legged, dog-like creatures, are the largest of the viverrid family, weighing from nine to 20 kilos (20-45lbs). Their long body has a varied pattern of black spots.

Civets are found in savannah and sometimes dense forest. They hide during the day in old burrows. They have a low-pitched cough and growl. Another species,

271

Above: Gregarious hippos in a Mara waterhole.
Opposite: Hippo and young thunder into the Mara River.

the less common **palm** (or two-spotted) **civet**, spends most of its life in trees or vines and mews like a cat. **Small spotted** (or **Neumann's**) **genet** are widespread through Kenya's savannah country. Mainly solitary and nocturnal, they are equally at home on the ground or in trees. So slender and flexible is the genet's body that it can follow its head through any opening. **Large spotted** (or **bush**) **genets** are longer than the more common small-spotted genet, and lack a dorsal crest. They have shorter fur and larger body spots.

Widespread throughout Kenya, they favour woodland and forest. When angry or threatened genet spit and growl like cats. Their normal call is a clear, metallic note.

Mongooses

The **dwarf mongoose**, smallest of Kenya's six or seven species, is active during the day looking for grubs, insects, larvae, spiders, rodents, reptiles, eggs and young birds. They roam in packs of up to 15 and attack live prey *en masse*, swooping down on the victims with a savage growl. Stock-ily-built, with a short snout and speckled brown or reddish-brown coat, mongoose live in dry savannah woodlands, taking refuge in old termite hills, rock crevices or hollow trees. Nomadic creatures, they seem to have little concern for safety and are seen frequently. They communicate with a range of bird-like chirrups and whistles.

The biggest of Kenya's mongooses is the **large grey mongoose**. Another species, the slender (**black-tipped**) **mongoose**, is often mistaken for a ground squirrel because it runs with its tail up straight. The **white-tailed mongoose** varies its behaviour according to its habitat. It favours almost any environment — from wooded areas, bush, open plains, to locations close to water where they eat molluscs and crabs.

The **banded mongoose** moves around in packs. Highly social animals, their groups often grow to between 30 and 50 gregarious and appealing creatures.

Hyrax

The **tree hyrax** is perhaps best known both as the elephant's closest relative and for its

scream. Delivered in the dead of night, it sounds like the Devil incarnate. In fact, it serves as a territorial call much like the lion's roar. Tree hyrax are nocturnal and well adapted for climbing trees.

The soles of their feet are made sticky by a substance secreted from a gland. Tree hyrax are found in almost any forest from sea level to around 4,000 metres (13,125 feet).

Lighter in colour, **rock hyrax** have feet that enable them to move with agility among boulders and precipices. Their soles have semi-elastic, 'rubber' pads which provide a grip on all inclines in all conditions.

Dogs and Jackals

Wild dog are social animals which live and hunt in packs of as few as ten to as many as 100. They can sustain speeds of 50 kilometres-an-hour (30 miles) for almost two kilometres (just over a mile). When one is exhausted, another takes its place.

The pack eats on the run, tearing the flesh off the prey and often ripping out its entrails until the luckless victim drops. A pack of 12 can consume a full-grown impala within ten minutes. The pack hunts only at sun-up and sundown. A pack's kill averages just under two kilos (four-and-a-half lbs) of flesh a day for each animal.

Lame and sick dogs which trail after the hunt are well cared for. When they come upon the kill they are made welcome. Colleagues regurgitate semi-digested meat for them to eat, as they do for their young.

Black-backed (or **silver-backed**) **jackal**, the most common of Kenyan jackals, are distinguished by a broad black band, similar to that of a German shepherd dog, along the back, and their white underbelly. Resourceful animals, they hunt and scavenge, in packs of up to 30, on small antelope.

The most elusive of the three, the **side-striped jackal**, gets its name from the indistinct light stripe along its flank.

Golden jackal are very adaptable and have been found even in the suburbs of Nairobi, where they scavenge on garbage dumps at night.

The **bat-eared fox**'s enormous ears provide acutely-tuned antennae for picking up the location of the insects on which it feeds, and also help in defence. Its ears twitch left or right only to be flattened close against

Top: Greater kudu.
Above: Rock hyrax.

Opposite: Lone acacia and rhino on a deserted Kenyan savannah plain.

274

Top: Reticulated giraffe.
Above: Bat-eared fox.

the side of its face when danger threatens. Bat-eared fox are active at night and spend the day drowsing outside the burrow. They mate for life and are the only one of the seven African foxes found in Kenya.

Although dog-like in appearance and behaviour — males cock their legs to urinate — **hyena** are probably more closely related to the mongoose. For many years considered scavengers, they are, in fact, ruthless hunters. Spotted hyena hunt in packs of up to 30. Their prey is varied and their appetite indiscriminate. They cut down wildebeest, zebra and gazelle at up to 64 kilometres-an-hour (40 miles).

These voracious killers follow pregnant female prey, snatching their new-born as they are delivered. Strong teeth and powerful jaws allow hyena to crack bones to suck out the marrow. Spotted hyena attack humans and frequently their own kind.

Marked by dark vertical stripes, the **aardwolf's** sandy-brown coat, makes it look a more elegant miniature of the striped hyena, to which it may be distantly related. Some experts suggest it is a form of hyena which has degenerated into a genus of its own.

Baboons and Monkeys

Unlike other primates, Kenya's two species of baboon display many canine characteristics, including barking, walking on all four limbs, and omnivorous habits.

The larger **olive baboon**, the most common, is found everywhere in Kenya except the east, where the **yellow baboon**, smaller in height, is dominant. They cover up to 18 kilometres (10 miles) a day for food — shoots, roots, seeds, bushes, flowers, insects and an occasional kill. They prey on timid mammals — hares and young gazelle — whose defence is to 'freeze' to the ground. They also snatch up fledgling birds.

Baboon normally use trees only to escape danger and to sleep. They are extremely social, living in well-organized groups, known as troops, which average between 40 and 80 animals. Each troop is permanent, ruled by a dominant male which assumes authority by force. When it becomes senile, a younger leader usurps its place in a vicious battle for power. Baboon are fierce fighters and predators regard them with respect. They are well-equipped for defence, with acute hearing and eyesight allied to extremely effective teeth. They often inflict severe, sometimes fatal, wounds on their enemy.

Colobus

Black-and-white colobus monkeys differ from most other monkeys in two respects. They have no thumb, and spend virtually their entire lives above ground. Rarely, if ever, do they come down to earth.

Few creatures equal their climbing ability or their leap — as much as 30 metres (100 feet). They differ, too, from most other monkeys in their capacity to remain silent, often for hours. Colobus live in troops of up to 25 made up of many families.

Vervet

Vervet are the guenon group of tree-dwelling, daytime monkeys confined to tropical forest. The one exception is the **black-faced vervet** (or green monkey) which live on the savannah. They use the gallery forests and thick bush for refuge and sleep, but forage widely on open ground, often over long distances of up to 400-500 metres (436-545 yards), in troops of six to 20, although groups of up to l00 have been observed.

Vervets have acute vision and excellent hearing but a poor sense of smell. They communicate with a wide range of facial expressions, lowering eyebrows, raising and jerking their heads, and threatening with bared teeth and open mouths.

Patas

The **patas monkey**, also known as red hussar, are the only primates which do not mix with other monkeys. Large, tall and long-legged, they live almost exclusively on the ground and stand erect to walk on their hind legs. The patas weigh up to ten kilos (22lbs) and are known as the 'greyhounds of the apes'. They have been clocked at 56 kilometres-an-hour (35 miles). Patas use trees and termite hills as vantage points.

Sykes

Sykes monkeys have a distinct white throat and chest patch, although they are members of the blue monkey races which are larger and stouter. They hold their thick long tails, with curved tip, higher than the body when walking. Sykes have narrow, elongated purplish-black faces, no beards, but dense, bristly tufts of hair on their foreheads, earning them also the name of 'diadem'. Moving in a distinctive, gentle, trotting gait, they are found wherever there are forests. Sykes are related to the extremely rare and beautiful **golden monkey**, distinguished by its greenish-gold back merging to orange on its flanks. Golden monkeys live in small numbers in isolated areas of western Kenya.

Bushbaby

The **lesser galago**, a nocturnal primate better known as the **bushbaby**, are small and slim with thick, woolly fur, and a conspicuous white stripe down the nose. Widespread and common throughout Kenya — they hide in coastal bush, acacia woodlands, and forests. Bushbabies are well-adapted to life in the trees. Their tail acts as a counterweight and they use their hind legs for grasping branches before leaping from one to another. On the ground, they walk upright or in a crouch. They can jump an incredible three metres (l0 feet) on their extremely powerful hind legs.

Zebra

The zebra's vivid and eye-catching stripes are unique. No two are alike. Just as a fingerprint distinguishes one human from another, so the zebra's stripes mark each creature as a distinct individual.

Of the two species, **Grevy's zebra** are considered the more attractive. Larger, heavier and taller than the common (or **Burchell's**) **zebra**, its black or dark brown stripes are more numerous and much narrower. Its ears are round and fringed.

Burchell's zebra is smaller, more like a pony, with fewer, broader, more clearly defined stripes, especially on the rump.

Zebra stallions fight ferociously for mates and dominance. The clashes are spectacular. Rival stallions rear and plunge, lashing out with hind and forelegs and slashing at each other's necks.

The Antelopes

Eland, the heavyweights of Kenya's fragile pastures, weigh close to a tonne. But they can leap more than two metres (six-and-a-half feet), virtually from a standing position. Between 170 and 180 centimetres (five-and-a-half to six feet) at the shoulder, they are the largest of Kenya's antelope.

Their large, twisted horns average around 80 centimetres (two-and-a-half feet) long — the record length being more than one metre (three feet). To collect twigs, they grasp them between their two horn pedicles (or stalks), breaking them loose with a shake of their head.

Kudu

Weighing between 280 and 320 kilos (600-700lbs), **greater kudu** can easily clear two metres (six-and-a-half feet) at a jump despite their impressive weight.

Distinguished by what are among the most magnificent horns in the antelope kingdom, their spiral horns average around 130 centimetres (over four feet) long, with the record a fraction under 180 centimetres.

Their acute hearing is accentuated by an ability to turn their large rounded ears in almost any direction. These large, slender antelopes, grey with six to eight prominent vertical white stripes on either flank, raise their tails when alarmed. **Lesser kudu,** smaller and more graceful than the greater, display more stripes — between 11 and 15.

Above: Rare mandarin-faced de Brazza monkey, in the Saiwa Swamp National Park.

Bongo

The **bongo** is the largest of Kenya's forest antelopes, with 12 to 14 vertical white stripes down the flanks of its bright chestnut coat. With age, the coat darkens. Unwilling jumpers, bongo are shy and easily disturbed. Living in pairs and groups of up to 30 to 35, old bulls leave to live out the last of their 12- to 14-year life span alone.

Sitatunga

The **sitatunga**, or **marshbuck,** is unique among antelopes and easily distinguished. Its two-toed, elongated hooves, which spread widely to dissipate its weight, enable it to move about on floating weeds.

When alarmed, they bark and sink into the water until only the tip of their nostrils shows. The only place they can be seen in Kenya is in the tiny Saiwa Swamp National Park.

Waterbuck

Waterbuck have scent glands that give off an unpleasant musky smell so powerful that it serves as a telltale indication of their presence. Their majestic horns are unmistakable. Around an average of 70 centimetres (little more than two feet) long, the record length is a fraction over one metre (three feet). With a short, glossy, brown to greyish-brown coat, the **common waterbuck** is distinct from the **Defassa waterbuck**, by the white crescent across its rump — the Defassa having pure white buttocks.

Oryx

Oryx wield their long horns with dexterity in the cut and thrust of the wild, often with such force the horns pass through the body. The horns average 70 centimetres (just over two feet), with a record length of more than a metre (three feet). Some experts suggest that the oryx's distinctive black and white facial markings serve as a warning to predators.

Beisa oryx are found north of the Tana. **Fringe-eared oryx,** marked by a distinctive tassel on their ears, and heavier and darker brown coats, are found south of the Tana.

Topi

The **topi** is prime flesh for all the predators which follow the Maasai Mara migration. Large and robust, the topi's shoulders are

Above: Wildebeest and zebra on the annual migration from Serengeti to Maasai Mara.

higher than their rump, giving them the familiar hartebeest look. Overall reddish-brown to purplish-red, they have dark patches on the face, upper forehead, legs, hips and thighs.

Jousting males, each of which has its own territory, drop to their knees and clash horns. Rutting males mark out their territory with dung heaps and by rubbing facial and foot glands on the ground. They then take guard on the nearest high ground. Topi are found in the Mara, north of the Tana River, and east of Lake Turkana. **Tiang**, a related species, lives on Lake Turkana's north-westernmost shores.

Hartebeest

Much topi behaviour also characterizes the **hartebeest.** Males keep watch from knolls or high ground after defining their territory and winning the courtship battle for a harem. But for a good part of their 12 to 15 years, hartebeest bulls are celibate. The losers form bachelor herds but old bulls are cast out to die.

The most common, **Coke's hartebeest**, is around 120 centimetres (four feet) high at the shoulder and weighs between 62 and 90 kilos (132-198lbs). **Jackson's hartebeest** are larger, and **Hunter's** smaller. Hunter's are unmistakable because of the shape of their horns and the white chevron between their eyes.

Coke's are widespread in southern Kenya; Jackson's only in the extreme northwest; and Hunter's between the Tana River and Somalia and Tsavo East National Park.

Wildebeest

The **wildebeest** is the star of the world's greatest animal spectacular — the annual migration from Serengeti to the Maasai Mara. More than a million of these strange-looking creatures are joined by zebra and topi to march from southern Serengeti to the northernmost corner of the Mara.

Thousands swarm into the swollen rivers behind their leaders in such numbers that many hundreds die. On the hoof, wildebeest move in a single-file formation which is unique among plains game. They provide a veritable banquet for predators which grow fat on the abundant pickings of the migration. Not surprisingly. Weighing between 160 and 220 kilos (350-720lbs), the wildebeest is a meal on its own.

Above: Bongo, a rare nocturnal mountain antelope.

Roan

Roan antelope the third-largest of Kenya's antelopes, are aggressive animals, with weapons to match. The male's horns, on average, are 70 centimetres (just over two feet) long. Rutting males joust with rivals by going down on their knees and making sweeping movements of the horns. The roan depends almost entirely on grass throughout its 15-year life span, living in herds of up to 20. In Kenya they are found only in Lambwe Valley on the shores of Lake Victoria and in the trans-Mara region.

In the Shimba Hills are Kenya's only remaining **sable antelope**, similar to the roan but slightly smaller. The sable is one of the most beautiful of large antelopes: the male's satin-like coat appears almost pure black, the female's dark reddish-brown.

Gazelles

Both grazers and browsers, **Grant's gazelles** endure extreme heat and go without water for long periods during their ten to 12 years of life. Moving about throughout most of an active day, rarely seeking shade, their herds vary in size from six to 30, usually with a male in charge of a harem of about a dozen or so does. Their call is an alarmed grunt or bleat. They are often found together with **Thomson's gazelles**, their smaller lookalikes, on the Maasai plains. The only way of telling them apart is that the white on the buttocks reaches above the tail in the Grant's and on the Thomson's it ends below.

Short stumpy tails rotating in perpetual motion, Thomson's gazelles are flesh for almost every predator. They have no alarm call: instead, they signal danger by rippling or flexing the muscles in their flanks. They also leap in a stiff-legged, standing-still jump known as 'stotting' or 'pronking'.

Impala

Emblem of the East African Wildlife Society, the **impala** is also food for almost every large predator, yet it continues to maintain itself in large populations.

One reason is its prodigious leap when threatened. In a series of spectacular bounds it soars over obstacles up to three metres (10 feet) above the ground or jumps ditches up to ten metres (33 feet) wide. Changing direction upon each landing, the zigzag course disconcerts any predator.

Bushbuck

The **bushbuck**'s dappled white markings are perfect natural camouflage. Blending into rock and bush, this shy, mainly nocturnal creature of forest and thicket flits elusively in and out of cover.

Bushbuck need the camouflage to avoid their principal enemy, the leopard. When cornered they defend themselves and their young with courage. Their short, bushy tails are white underneath. Raised on the run, this serves as a warning for others.

Reedbuck

The **bohor reedbuck**, an elusive antelope, shy and easily startled, is normally seen at sun-up and sundown. During the day these small, graceful antelope lie up in reed beds or tall grasses, shaping the stems around them into a shelter. When alarmed, they squat on the ground, only bolting at the last moment. They run with a peculiar gait — like animated rocking horses.

Reedbuck are hunted by all the large predators. The bohor reedbuck is widespread in southern Kenya, west of the Tana River. The slightly larger **Chanler's mountain reedbuck** is found in central and western Kenya on open, grass slopes up to 4,000 metres (13,125 feet).

Dik-dik

The **dik-dik**, a gentle, greyish fawn, darts through the thickets in shy and elusive flight around twilight. They live in pairs, or occasional family groups, and establish middens up to a metre (three feet) in diameter to mark out their territory.

Kirk's dik-diks have hindquarters taller than their front shoulders, long, thin legs and a sloping back.

In flight, they run in a series of zigzag bounds. Their alarm call is a shrill whistle, a bit like a bird call — or a zik-zik cry — hence their name.

Guenther's long-snouted dik-dik is found in northern Kenya.

Klipspringer

The **klipspringer** measures around 50 to 55 centimetres (one-and-a-half to two feet) high from hoof to shoulder, and weighs between 11 and 18 kilos (25-40 lbs). It is a phenomenal jumper. It bounces on the tips of its rubbery hooves and this tip-toe effect makes its exceptionally strong legs look even longer.

The klipspringer's olive-yellow coat, speckled with grey, is stiff and brittle, serving as a cushion to ward off the shocks of hitting rock walls when they jump. Living only in rocky hills, klipspringer mark their territory with a secretion from scent glands.

Oribi

The **oribi** is another of Kenya's beautiful small antelopes, with a long slender neck and silky coat, varying from pale fawn-grey to bright reddish-brown. Oribi live in pairs or small groups and, when alarmed, give loud shrill whistles or sneezes and leap straight up in the air in a standing-still jump before bounding off. Some experts suggest they do this to scan a larger area of bush for signs of predators.

Steinbok

Steinbok (or Steenbok) often elude their predators by darting down an old aardvark burrow in which, in more placid times, a female may also raise her young. Living alone, pairing only during the mating season, steinbok avoid hilly country. They are often found in sand dunes along the coast.

Gerenuk

In the Somali language **gerenuk** means 'giraffe-necked'. This unique antelope's neck has evolved through the ages to become longer, making it easier for the gerenuk to feed. It has also learned to stand on its rear legs so as to reach the leaves higher up on acacia thorns and other desert shrubs.

These elegant creatures are fascinating to watch in motion. Extremely swift, they bring their long necks down in line with their slender backs, making them appear to be about half their height. Gerenuks were only 'discovered' as a species in 1878.

Suni

Suni, a forest antelope, are only 30 centimetres (one foot) tall weighing eight kilos (18lbs). They are rarely seen and move mostly at sun-up and sundown.

But suni leave one telltale clue to their presence — a strong, musky scent which lingers long after leaving a location. A large gland below their eyes gives off the pungent odour.

Below: Kirk's dik-dik.

Below: Agama lizard with striped sand snake.

Above: Gerenuk, the giraffe-necked gazelle.

Above right: Klipspringer

Right: Chameleon, nature's camouflage artist

Above: Python ready to swallow a young gazelle.

Duiker

The **bush** (or **grey**) **duiker** stands around sixty centimetres (two feet) from hoof to shoulder and weigh between 11 and 13 kilos (25-29lbs).

They are widespread throughout the country, though there are many local variations in body size, horn length, colour and thickness of coat.

Mountain duiker, the only duiker found in open range, are the most widespread. They live from sea-level desert to snowline. They are often found on farms — even in small vegetable gardens.

Forest duikers are red and their characteristic hunched posture, with their heads close to the ground, enables them to move more easily through thick undergrowth, using well-marked trails and passages. When alarmed, all duiker plunge into thick cover.

Their name, given by early Afrikaner settlers in Africa, is Dutch — meaning 'diver'.

Birdlife: An Avian Spectacle without Equal

Of the world's estimated 8,600 bird species, Africa south of the Sahara boasts about 1,750, of which East Africa claims 1,294, and Kenya 1,054 species, making Kenya the greatest country in Africa for bird-watching. Indeed, the number of bird species is surpassed only in the Latin American countries of Columbia, Venezuela and Peru, where most forest birds are not easily seen.

Bird-watchers in Kenya stand a good chance of seeing at least 60 per cent of all African avifauna. More than 50 per cent of Kenya's birds have been recorded within the radius of Nairobi. To see more than 100 species in a day is quite common.

With its vast deserts, rolling grasslands, massive mountains and tropical coast, Kenya encompasses many habitats which serve as home or resting place for great numbers of endemic and migrant species.

Waterbirds

Kenya's Rift Valley lakes support an immense number of waterbirds and many other species abound in the grasslands and acacia woodlands that surround them. Apart from Baringo and Naivasha, all the Rift Valley lakes are alkaline.

More than 400 species — greater than the total bird species of the British Isles — have been recorded at freshwater Lake Naivasha alone. There you are likely to see two species of cormorant. The **greater cormorant** is black with white on the foreneck and breast; the **long-tailed cormorant**, also black, usually rests on rocks or tree trunks in the water, wings outstretched.

Cormorants dive and swim beneath the water for their prey, bringing it to the surface where it is tossed in the air, caught, and swallowed. After this, when perched, they stretch their wings to dry.

The **African darter** behaves in a similar fashion, but it's distinguished by its much longer neck, which assumes an S-shape at rest. This neck enables the bird to dart its bill forward and pierce the fish. Other large waterbirds readily visible, either standing at the water's edge or wading in the shallows waiting to catch fish, are different species of **heron, ibis** and **stork**. The most outstanding, the **Goliath heron**, is the largest of all herons. The smaller **black-headed heron**, which also feeds onshore off insects and rats, is grey, white and black.

Even smaller, the wings of the thickset, biscuit-coloured **squacco heron** turn white during the breeding season. When searching for food, this stealthy heron stands stock still, as it waits for prey. Some herons move their head from side to side to get a proper fix on the target.

Ibises are identified by their down-curved bills. The loud shriek of the **hadada ibis** is heard around sundown and sun-up — and on bright, moonlit nights. This sociable bird has olive-brown feathers with bright metallic-green reflections.

The **sacred ibis** is seen more frequently. Flocks often gather on waste ground in Nairobi, at the lakes, and in lagoons and estuaries at the coast. They are identified by their white feathers, bare black head and neck, and down-curved bill.

Ducks and Geese

The freshwater lakes also play host to many ducks, some resident, others migrant, of different sizes. Because their flight feathers all moult at once, ducks and geese cannot fly for some weeks after breeding, making them extremely vulnerable. The biggest, a tree duck known somewhat misleadingly as the **spurwing goose**, has a dark red bill, glossy metallic black upper parts, and white belly.

The much smaller **white-faced whistling duck**, also a tree duck, has a distinctive clear whistling call, white face, reddish plumage and barred flanks.

Of the geese, the **Egyptian goose**, with its predominantly brown plumage, white shoulders, and honking call, is common in Kenya. Although of similar size, the **knob-billed goose** is almost silent. Identifiable by its black and white plumage, during the breeding season the male develops a distinctive knob at the base of its bill. One of the most beautiful of the large African birds, the **crowned crane**, with its straw-coloured crest and black crown, is also one of the most distinctive.

The **hammerkop**, which has a wide range in tropical Africa, is the only member of its family in Kenya. It has a conspicuously long, backward-pointing crest, resembling a hammer; hence its name. The hammerkop's nest is an astonishing work of sticks and vegetation, lined with mud or dung, often balanced in the fork of a tree .

Between 90 centimetres and one metre in diameter (two-and-a-half and three feet), it has a side entrance which leads to an enclosed chamber. Hammerkop add to the old nest year after year until eventually it collapses. Hammerkop feed off frogs and tadpoles, often from the back of a hippo.

Birds of prey
Three birds of prey are common on the Rift lake shores. The **fish eagle**, with its striking white head, chest, back and tail, chestnut belly and black wings is the most frequently seen, usually perched on the limb of some tall tree on the shoreline. They will suddenly leave this perch to swoop down to the surface and pluck their wriggling prey from the water with consummate ease. Their echoing cry is one of the familiar sounds of Kenya.

Also seen close inshore as it darts among the reeds and papyrus, the **malachite kingfisher** lives off Naivasha's abundant tree frogs and fish. Its colouring — cobalt-blue crown barred with black, bright ultramarine blue on the back, and reddish underparts — is glittering contrast to the black-and-white pied kingfisher often seen hovering over creeks and estuaries.

Immediately its prey is spotted, the **pied kingfisher** plunges into the water, eyes closed, giving it a success ratio of about one-in-ten.

Kenya's waters attract many different gulls. The **grey-headed gull**, found almost exclusively on the lakes, is identified by its grey head, generally white and pale grey colours, and red bill and legs.

The **red-knobbed coot**, another familiar resident — very plain, slate-black colour — is distinguished by the red knob on its forehead. Feeding off plants just beneath the surface, they perform a valuable service — keeping water free of weeds. Another

bird, the curious **African jacana**, appears to walk on water. Its splayed feet and long legs enable it to walk on water-lilies. Jacanas have diminished with the introduction of the beaver-like coypu which, with their voracious appetites, have all but destroyed Naivasha's water-lilies.

Alkaline lakes
Lake Nakuru is world-famous for its hordes of **lesser** and **greater flamingo**. Of the world's six-and-a-half million flamingos, the lesser are the more numerous. About four million live in the alkaline lakes of the Rift Valley — in Ethiopia, Kenya, and Tanzania. **Greater flamingo**, outnumbered almost 100-to-one, are distinguished by height. Males reach 180 centimetres (six feet), twice that of the lesser flamingo. The female is smaller.

Both species are pink with red legs, webbed feet, a long sinuous neck and a unique bill, specially adapted for their food needs. The inside of the mouth is an efficient filter. Lake Nakuru sustains both flamingos and a substantial number of **white pelican**. The white pelican, almost entirely white with black flight feathers, is often seen with the **pink-backed pelican**, distinguished by its smaller size, grey plumage, and head crest. Besides pelicans and fla-

Above: Pied kingfisher.

285

mingos, attractive smaller species live at Nakuru, among them the black and white **avocet**, recognized by its grey-blue legs and upturned bill.

Another black-and-white species, with a straight long bill, and vermilion-red legs is the **black-winged stilt**, the only other bird, apart from flamingo, whose legs are longer in proportion to its body. When breeding parents are disturbed they walk away from the nest, dragging a wing on the ground.

Two species of stork are frequently seen on Kenya's lakes and waterways. The distinctive **yellow-billed stork**, with black and delicately-hued pink-white plumage, red legs, and down-curved orange bill, catches fish and frogs with astonishing speed.

The ugly, unmistakable **marabou stork**, associated with town tips because of its scavenging habits, hunts flamingo chicks by stampeding a flock.

Of the migrant **waders** and **plovers**, by far the most common is the **ruff**. Their breeding plumage is extremely spectacular and elegant, but they are seen in Kenya in their rather dull, non-breeding colours.

The resident **blacksmith plover**, commonly found inland near water surrounded by short grass and muddy shores, has a distinctive black, white and grey plumage, and a conspicuous white crown. Normally silent, it becomes extremely noisy when breeding and flies fearlessly at any enemy, uttering the characteristic cry which gives it its name.

Coastal areas

European visitors find many migrant species difficult to identify because their summer, or breeding, plumage differs considerably. Identification is further complicated between April and May, when some waders begin to change into their northern summer plumage ready for the flight back to their breeding grounds.

Although the **greenshank** a sizable wader with a slightly up-curved bill, is common to all Kenya's wetlands, the largest numbers are found at the coast.

The **little stint**, the smallest of the wintering shorebirds, arrives from its breeding grounds in Russia early in August after making its way along the eastern

Left: Bateleur eagle — one of Kenya's raptors.

Mediterranean. Running at breakneck speed as it feeds along the water's edge, the **sanderling,** a small, dumpy bird from eastern Greenland, Siberia and Arctic America, always seems in a hurry.

Among the visiting birds, the **great white egret,** a member of the heron family, is readily distinguished from its close relatives, the **yellow-billed egret** and **little egret,** by its all-white plumage, all-black legs, and long black or yellow bill.

Another bird with all-white plumage, bare red legs and face, the **African spoonbill** takes its name from its long, spatulate bill.

With its large head and big yellow eyes which help it to see at night, the **water thicknee** is widespread along the creeks and islands of the Kenyan coast.

The bushy grassland hosts many **bee-eaters** — attractive birds with long bills and a brilliant plumage, which hunt bees, wasps, hornets and similar insects. Back on the perch, the bee-eater knocks the insect briskly against a branch until the venom is discharged.

The **white-fronted bee-eater** is readily identified by its brilliantly-coloured plumage. The **carmine bee-eater,** the most eye-catching with greenish and cobalt-blue head, neck and rump, breeds in the Lake Turkana basin in the north and travels to the coastal lowlands between November and March. They roost in their thousands in the mangroves north of Mombasa. The **little bee-eater,** in sharp contrast, is mostly green with a yellow throat.

Woodland birds

The **golden palm weaver** is another common bird found in trees, bushes and reeds along coastal rivers or streams. Almost entirely yellow, this bird has a bright orange head and black eyes. Its lookalike, the **golden weaver,** has a chestnut head and pale red eyes.

The **secretary bird,** the sole member of its family, found only in Africa from sea level to 3,000 metres (10,000 feet), is usually seen in pairs. This terrestrial bird of prey stands almost one metre (three feet) high and has a wingspan of more than two metres (seven feet). It's easily recognized by its grey and black plumage, long legs with black 'plus-fours', and a conspicuous crest

which can be raised like a halo. It spends most of its life strutting on the ground, looking for snakes, insects and rats. It pounds the snakes to death with sledge-hammer blows of its feet.

Perhaps the most frequently seen bird of prey in Kenya is the **augur buzzard,** which chooses particularly high vantage points in the branches of a tree, on top of high rocks, or even telegraph posts to scout for prey.

Not long ago the **helmeted guinea-fowl** could be seen in flocks numbering as many as 2,000. But in recent years they have been killed extensively for the pot. Generally black, thickly-freckled all over with white, the bird sports a bony crest or horn on its crown.

Another game bird, the **yellow-necked spurfowl** of open bush country, is plentiful, particularly along the edges of forest and woodland. About the size of a chicken, its most conspicuous feature is its yellow throat.

There are 16 species of pigeon in Kenya, of which the **speckled pigeon** is the largest. Extremely widespread, it is found between 500 and 3,000 metres (1,600-10,000 feet) in acacia woodlands, on cliffs, and sometimes around houses. With its brownish-back and wings, grey underparts and marked 'dominoes' round its eye, it's easy to identify.

Attractive birds

Kingfishers, hoopoes, bee-eaters, and hornbills are distant kin to the **rollers,** which run kingfishers close for beauty.

Perhaps the most eye-catching of all, the **lilac-breasted roller,** is tawny-brown on top, rich lilac on the throat and breast, with the rest various shades of bright- and greenish-blue. The birds earned their name from the aerobatics they perform when courting.

A large, unusual, down curved prominent bill with a large casque is the most noticeable feature of **hornbills.** When trees are in fruit in the thickly-wooded coastline, raucous brayings and grunts betray the presence of the **silvery-cheeked hornbill.** The plumage of the largest member of the family, the **ground hornbill,** is generally black with a red face and throat in the male and usually blue in the female.

When breeding, the female **red-billed hornbill** finds a suitable hole or hollow in a tree and walls herself in with mud, dung and saliva, regurgitated by the male. The female puts these into the entrance hole until the opening narrows to a slit and she cannot leave the nest. As she settles down to lay three to six eggs, the male feeds her through the opening. When the eggs hatch, the male works hard to feed his demanding family until the female grows new feathers and breaks out. By this time the young are still only half-grown. The chicks repair the damaged exit by re-plastering as soon as the mother has left. Now both parents feed them until the young are ready to break out of the nest.

Woodpeckers

Among the woodpeckers, the **Nubian woodpecker** has short legs and strong feet. With these, and its stiff, wedge-shaped tail, it climbs trees easily. Its extraordinarily long tongue, coated with mucous, is projected to catch ants, and sap from trees, or to 'spear' large insects. It uses its chisel-like bill to drill into wood for larvae, and to excavate nest holes.

There is a large family of **flycatchers**. The male **paradise flycatcher**, with its glossy-chestnut and indigo-black plumage and long tail, is probably the most attractive. It is more common along the coast in its white phase, when the tail, back and wings are white. It uses cobwebs to bind together and anchor its nest of twigs, grass, and lichen.

One of the most photographed birds in Kenya, the **superb starling**, is notable for its metallic greenish-blue back, black head, and narrow white band across the breast separating the metallic-blue upper parts from the bright chestnut belly. Although the **blue-eared glossy starling** is seen less often than the more common **superb starling**, it glitters with a metallic, iridescent-green sheen in bright sunshine. In other light, it seems bluish, violet, even golden. The yellow-orange eye is characteristic.

Perhaps the most spectacular of Kenya's brilliantly-coloured starlings, with their metallic gloss, is the male **violet-backed starling**, which has white underparts and an iridescent purple back and head. In some light it appears plum-coloured, even crimson. When the wild fig trees come into fruit, flocks of these starlings feast themselves for three to four days. When the fruit is gone the birds also disappear.

Desert birds

Found in dry-bush and semi-desert country, the **pale chanting goshawk** was named for its melodious call — repeated hour on hour at the start of the breeding season. The chant is also made on the wing when the pair soar together in circles.

Pale grey, with bright reddish-orange legs, a finely-barred belly and a white rump, the bird spends much of its time on the ground, unlike other hawks.

Bustards, their strong legs adapted to life on the ground, are well-suited to desert life. The **kori bustard**, the biggest member of the family in Kenya, is easily identified by its size and broad wings. Though its flight is laboured, it is powerful and rapid.

The ornamental plumes of loose feathers on the head, nape and long neck are used in remarkable breeding displays. When threatened they hide by crouching low. These birds are omnivorous.

The **spotted thicknee** — once known as the spotted stone curlew — is the dry country counterpart of the water thicknee, with the same large eyes. Habitually watchful, thicknees spend the day in shade where their cryptic appearance makes them virtu-

Above: Saddle-billed stork.

289

ally invisible. When approached they flatten themselves on the ground, head and neck outstretched.

Living in hot, arid lands and eating grain, **sandgrouse** need to drink at least once a day. The young rely on the male, which often flies 80 kilometres (50 miles) to water. It crouches down and thoroughly soaks its belly feathers before the long journey back to the nest. There it fluffs out its feathers as the chicks crouch beneath it to draw the water with their beaks. The belly feathers hold three times as much water as any other bird. The **chestnut-bellied sandgrouse**, living in arid bush and plains, is the most common species in Kenya.

If you visit the dry country of the southern Rift Valley you may well hear a remarkable and unmistakable birdsong — the call of the **red** and **yellow barbet**, whose song, in fact, is a duet, sometimes even a chorus.

Another common family, the **weavers**, all share the ability to tie knots and build completely enclosed woven nests. Placing a long piece of grass at the tip of a branch, weavers hold one end down with a claw and use their beak to weave the other end in, out and over, until it forms a suspended ring. With the bird in the middle of the ring, it fashions more and more strands, meticulously working each piece of grass, until a hollow ball is made.

Inhabiting wooded grassland below 1,400 metres (4,500 feet), the **white-headed buffalo weaver** is seen often. Its nest, an untidy structure hanging from the branch of a thorn tree, with an entrance from below, is made of thorn twigs for protection, and lined with grass or feathers.

The entrance to the hanging nest of the **Vitelline masked weaver** is also at the bottom, but it contains a partition to stop the eggs from falling out. Suspended from the end of a branch, its occupants are safe from predators.

Other weavers build even more elaborate nests, with long vertical entrance tunnels hanging at the side. Other safety measures include building nests close to the hives of stinging insects, large birds or even people.

The **white-browed sparrow weaver,** whose rather loose and untidy nests are seen on acacia trees, is extremely common

in dry country. Another member of the family, the male **red-naped widowbird**, in its striking breeding plumage, has an entirely black body with a scarlet crown and nape. The female is a nondescript tawny buff colour. After breeding, the male loses its tail feathers and scarlet colouring and looks the same as the female.

The female **Holub's golden weaver** is extremely demanding. The male may build as many as six large, rough, and loosely woven nests before she is satisfied.

Quelea and **mousebird** are agricultural pests which destroy and damage grain and fruit. The **red-billed quelea**, a member of the weaver family, often found in flocks of more than a million, is a menace to small grain crops.

The **speckled mousebird**, a member of a small family peculiar to Africa, is no bigger than a sparrow, but its long tail, made up of ten stiff, graduated feathers, gives it an overall length of 30 centimetres (one foot). They have extremely large feet with strong claws and outer toes which move forwards and backwards, enabling them to climb easily.

Grassland birds

The **ostrich**, measuring between two to three metres (six-and-a-half to 10 feet) high, is the largest living bird and cannot fly. However, its strides of four metres (13 feet) are enough to leave all but the swiftest of predators behind. Ostrich can maintain speeds of 50 kilometres (30 miles) an hour for up to 30 minutes.

On the run, however, they often vanish abruptly from view. They stop in full stride and drop suddenly into a squatting position, extending their neck all along the ground. In full stride they can bound up to a height of one-and-a-half metres (five feet). Their lethal kick can bend an iron bar at right angles. They share the distinction of being a flightless running bird with the South American rhea, the emu and cassowaries of the Antipodes.

Millions of years ago there were nine species of ostrich, but now only the African ostrich survives. It is characterized by its height, half of which is made up of its neck, and its two-toed foot, legs and thighs.

Females are shabby brown with pale edgings to their feathers. Males are much more dandy with vivid black and white plumes on the wings and tail. The adult male stands two-and-a-half metres (eight feet) and weighs more than 130 kilos (300 lbs).

Eggs average 15 to 16 centimetres (six inches) long and weigh up to one-and-a-half kilos (three lbs). One is equal to two or three dozen domestic chicken eggs and tastes the same. Chicks can run almost as soon as they hatch. After only a month — they grow at a rate of six to eight centimetres (one-and-a-half to two inches) a week — they can reach a speed of 55 kilometres (35 miles) an hour.

Ostrich have tough gullets and voracious appetites and have been known to swallow coins, nails, horseshoes and other metal objects. Reared from the young, they make faithful pets.

On the plains among the herds of wild or domestic animals, flocks of large, white birds are a familiar sight. **Cattle egrets** are one of the few bird species which benefit from human activity. They prey on the insects disturbed by the movements of the herds.

Vultures
Circling slowly, gliding on the rising thermals, **vultures** remain aloft all day watching herds of animals and the movements of jackals and hyenas. When a vulture sees a corpse it planes down swiftly and is soon joined by others. They eat up to six kilos (13 lbs) of food at one sitting and become so bloated they cannot take off and must wait until the meal is digested.

The largest African vulture, the **lappet-faced vulture**, with its massive bill and a pinkish bald head, is most frequently seen in the national parks.

The smaller **Ruppell's vulture**, with its dark-brown plumage and creamy-white edges that give it a spotted appearance, is much more common.

The **black-shouldered kite**, a member of the hawk family, is thickset, pale grey above and white below, with black shoulders, a short, white square tail and striking red eyes. This bird of prey hovers like a kestrel.

The **black kite**, one of the most familiar and obvious, is seen near human habitations in Kenya up to 3,000 metres (10,000 feet). It is readily recognizable by its dark brown plumage, yellow bill and markedly forked tail.

Plovers
Although most plovers are found near the sea, lakes, rivers, mudflats and swamps, the **crowned plover** is a wanderer of grass bushlands up to 3,000 metres (10,000 feet) above sea level. Notable for its black head with a white ring on the crown, this handsome bird has a white abdomen, a pale greyish-brown back, red legs and a red bill with a black tip.

Its nest, like that of all plovers, is built in a shallow, quite often unlined, indentation on the ground. The chicks' marking is perfect camouflage. When warned by the parent they crouch down as the adult bird diverts attention by spreading one of its wings wide as if injured — a form of distraction display common among plovers.

Ground-living **larks** are usually softly-coloured, but their exquisite song, serving as both courtship and territorial defence, more than compensates. They prefer open country and normally sing from a perch.

On the open grasslands in Kenya larks and **pipits** predominate, but although somewhat alike in appearance, the two are not closely related. The pipit family con-

Above: Ostrich.

sists of graceful and slender birds, with an upright stance.

Rhinoceros, giraffe, zebra, buffalo, various antelope, even wart hog, and most domestic stock are visited by **oxpeckers**, known as tick-birds. These belong to the starling family.

The **red-billed oxpecker** walks about on buffalo, its stiffened tail and sharp, curved claws enabling it to move about with ease. It feeds mainly on bloated ticks, but also flies, scar tissue, blood, living tissue, and the discharge from open wounds, making it unpopular with cattle breeders.

Garden birds

Strikingly beautiful, the **hoopoe's** unmistakable main body plumage is bright pinkish-cinnamon with wings and tail having alternate black and white bars. The erectile crest feathers are pinkish with black tips, and the black bill has a slight downward curve.

Hoopoes nest in holes in trees, rocks, banks, or even buildings. Pairs are often seen on lawns hunting for large insects, larvae, worms and lizards. Their monotonous call of 'hoop, hoop, hoop' is low and penetrating.

Looking rather like thrushes, to whom they are related, **babblers** keep up a continuous chatter as they move around on bushes or on the ground searching mainly for insects.

The **robin chat**, with its reddish-orange throat and chest, well-marked white eye-stripe, and a grey belly, is an excellent mimic of other birds and often gives a full concert repertoire. Its natural song seems to have territorial and advertising functions.

Robin chats feed mainly on the ground and, although shy, can be relatively tame in gardens. Chats are often parasitized by the **red-chested cuckoo.**

The potential host is kept under close observation by the female cuckoo when building its nest. She sneaks in to lay her egg when the nest is unattended, sometimes removing one of the robin chat eggs.

The cuckoo egg hatches first and the chick's first instinct is to eject any other object in the nest. Either the eggs or the young of the robin chat are manoeuvred to the edge and pushed out, leaving the cuckoo chick in sole possession.

The host parents seem unconcerned and feed the large, demanding interloper until it leaves the nest. Even then, the foster parents continue to feed the growing cuckoo until it is independent.

In many respects **sunbirds** are similar to humming birds but they are not related. Both groups have long curved beaks, brilliant plumage, and draw nectar from flowers which helps pollination. Sunbirds are a distinct family of small birds, with slender, pointed, down-curved bills. In most species the male has brilliantly-coloured plumage, most of it with an iridescent metallic sheen. The females are generally drab.

The **waxbill** family of small to very small seed-eaters includes the **red-billed firefinch**, perhaps the most familiar bird in Africa. The female is dull brown with a tinge of red on the tail, but the male plumage is entirely pinkish-red with a few whitish spots on the breast. The nest, with its side entrance, is an untidy ball of dry grass, lined with feathers and placed low down in bushes.

The bird is known to be parasitized by the **indigobird**, a member of the parasitic division of the vast weaver family.

Above: Secretary bird.

Flora: Forests of Flame, Streets of Mauve

Myriad and marvellous botanical glories adorn Kenya. To a great extent, from rare orchids to precious hardwood forests, the beauty of its flowers, shrubs and trees characterizes the country. After the rainy seasons flowers burst into riotous colours — even in semi-desert and desert regions.

Throughout the year, rivers in drier areas are lined with doum palms and large acacias; mountain foothills are clothed in forests; and the plains of the game parks are dotted with baobab and thorn.

Besides trees, there are many shrubs, herbs, grasses, ferns, mosses, orchids, lianas, fungi and lichen.

Kenya's indigenous forests enjoy a great diversity of trees. Where European and North American forests have no more than 25 species, Kenya's forests have no less than 50 and some a good deal more — the forest on Mount Elgon contains 62 tree species.

Other completely indigenous forests grow in vital watershed areas such as Mount Kenya, the Aberdares, Shimba Hills, Kakamega, Nandi Hills and the Mau Range.

Kenya's forests fall into several categories. The lowland forests are small patches, mainly confined to local hill ranges, such as the Taita Hills and Mount Kasigau. Set less than 330 metres (1,080 feet) above sea level, these patches consist of mixed evergreen forest with much *afzelia* and *trachylobium*, and *brachylaena* in drier areas. Higher up, between 800 and 1,600 metres (2,625-5,250 feet) above sea level, there are *ocotea* and *Newtonia buchananii*.

Upland forests are predominant in Kenya, beginning with plateau forests which lie between 1,300 and 2,000 metres (4,265-6,560 feet) in places where the annual rainfall is 875-1,000 millimetres (34-40 inches), such as Nairobi, Ngong, Nyeri and Kiambu. There, where the climate is equable and cool, mixed evergreen forests of *brachylaena* and *croton* flourish. Above 2,000 metres (6,560 feet) on Mount Kenya, Mount Elgon, the Aberdares, the Kikuyu-Laikipia Escarpment, and the Mau, Elgeyo and Cherangani mountain ranges, the mixed evergreen forests are of *ocotea, juniperus, hagenia* and bamboo.

Along the coast, particularly in the sheltered estuaries of Mida Creek and the Tana River, and on the leeward side of the Lamu archipelago, mangrove swamp forests flourish. These have great commercial value. Mangrove timber is used for building poles, charcoal, and leather tanning. **Mangrove swamps** play a critical ecological role in filtering organically-rich material carried down to the sea, and serve as a breeding ground for various forms of marine life.

In Kenya's non-indigenous forest plantations, **conifers** are cropped for paper manufacture, furniture, packaging, and particle and building board. The non-indigenous hardwood **eucalyptus** is cropped for building and woodfuel. None of these forests has as much diversity of species or fauna as the indigenous forests.

The original home of the ubiquitous **coconut** is a mystery. Some authorities consider it to be Polynesia, while others maintain the first nut came from South America, drifting on ocean currents. The coconut palm furnishes almost everything man needs for survival and shelter — food and drink through its nut, while husk fibres make ropes and mats and are used to stuff mattresses. The shell is turned into charcoal. The leaves are used to thatch houses or woven into baskets and mats. The trunk is used to build houses. The major economic product is dried nut flesh, copra. It is processed to yield coconut oil for cooking, and coconut meal, a valuable high-protein livestock food.

The indigenous **doum palm** is the only one of its family which grows branches. Its long slender stems divide regularly into two, giving the tree its distinctive appearance. It often grows to a height of more than 15 metres (50 feet). The orange-brown fruit has edible skins, but are not very tasty. Elephants often eat them and subsequently disperse the seeds far and wide in their dung. Traditionally, the fruit is used to make buttons and necklaces and the leaves for weaving baskets and mats.

Wild **date palms** are also widespread throughout Kenya, particularly in hot, dry areas alongside streams and swamps where there is a high water table. Although edible, its fruit is disappointing to taste and the commercially-cultivated variety has a bigger, fleshier and more tasty fruit.

Arab traders introduced the tree to Kenya long ago but, although it has great potential as a food, it has been little exploited. However, its leaves are used for basketwork and sleeping mats.

The exotic **golden wattle**, a member of the acacia family, was introduced from Australia. Widespread in Kenya it has light, greyish-green foliage and beautiful yellow flowers.

But exotic acacias apart, Kenya has more than 40 indigenous species, including flat-topped **red thorn acacia**, which grows in many parts of the Great Rift Valley and in other areas. Its extremely heavy and durable hardwood is used to build bridges, and as fence posts, pulley blocks and rough farm buildings.

One of the most beautiful of Kenya's acacias, found besides streams and lakes throughout the Rift, is the yellow-barked **fever tree**. Early travellers who camped in its shade linked the tree with their bouts of malaria and gave it its once common name (fever tree).

Acacia trees serve many functions. They are used to feed goats, and as fencing posts and fuel. Where they grow on river banks, they anchor the soil: where they drop their nutrient-rich leaves at the beginning of the rainy season, they add nitrogen to the ground.

Acacia hardwood timber, a lasting building material, is also used for carving. It supplies the leather industry with tannin and one species yields a high-quality industrial gum.

The **baobab**, with its 'upside-down' look, central to many African legends and superstitions, is revered. The rotund, glossy trunk sprouts a crown of thick branches which look more like roots since they are bare of leaves for most of the dry season. Found in many parts of Kenya less than 1,300 metres (4,000 feet) above sea level, baobabs — which grow to a diameter of be-tween five and seven metres (15-20 feet), and not much more than that in height — live for many centuries. The tree is a ubiquitous gift of nature. Its hollowed-out trunk can store water or be split lengthways to make canoes. Bark fibres are twisted into ropes and baskets. Leaves and fruit-pulp are used medicinally and the seeds and leaves are edible.

The attractive **camel's foot tree** takes its name from its two-lobed foliage which bears some resemblance to a camel's hoof. A native of Asia, its branches are adorned with fragile, delicate-pink flowers, strikingly like some orchids. It is also known as the orchid tree.

Australian flame trees rise more than 33 metres (100 feet) high, and their crimson mass of blooms are visible for a considerable distance. However, they flower all too rarely.

Native to Madagascar, the magnificent **flamboyant** was first discovered in 1824. Since then it has been introduced to tropical areas all over the world. In Kenya it thrives at heights beneath 1,370 metres (4,500 feet), especially where it is warm and dry. With its canopy of scarlet flowers, the flamboyant is well-named. Its blossoms cast a glow over Mombasa's streets and gardens.

One of the most striking Kenyan trees, the **Nandi flame tree**, also known as the African tulip tree, is spectacular in bloom with large orange-red flowers fringed in gold. Native to the Lake Victoria basin and

Above: White and pale yellow-flowered frangipani — the scent of angels.

western Kenya, its buds are filled with water which spurts out if punctured, hence its other name, 'fountain tree'. Another Australian exotic, the **bottle-brush**, owes its name to the red or white flowers that drape its stem like a bottlebrush.

The pink blossoms of the **Cape chestnut** make it one of the most beautiful of Kenya's indigenous deciduous trees. It fills the mountain forest homelands with sweet-scented fragrance and vibrant colour and is also cultivated in many gardens and parks.

Introduced from tropical America, the fast-growing deciduous **cassia** readily took root in Kenya where its yellow blossoms warm the streets, parks and gardens. It grows about nine metres (30 feet) high.

An exotic from Brazil, the **kapok**, or floss-silk tree, reaches close to 30 metres (98 feet) and is often confused with its **bombax** lookalike. The seed is protected by a cotton-like material used to stuff cushions. Its smooth, green trunk is covered with spines and its flowers, which vary from vivid-red to pink, have five petals.

One of Kenya's more easily recognized native trees, even when it is not in bloom, is the **red-hot poker tree**, or Kaffirboom.

This deciduous tree with its bright red upright flowers is extremely widespread, and reaches a height of around 14 metres (45 feet). Its red and black seeds were once used to weigh gold and jewellery.

Unlike other members of Australia's eucalyptus family, the **red flowering gum** does not reach great heights but is much admired for the ornamental beauty of its pink and red flowers. Another widespread member of the Australian eucalyptus family, the **blue gum tree** which lines many streets, can be recognized by its habit of continuously shedding bark.

The delicate, bell-shaped flowers of the **jacaranda**, an exotic from Brazil, blossom between September and November, when Nairobi and many other Kenyan towns are strewn with a thick carpet of blue-violet petals.

The quick-growing, well-shaped, deciduous *Himalayan Prunus* (**bird cherry tree**) blossoms twice a year — at the beginning of each rainy season. Its delicate pink flowers can be seen in many gardens and streets. The drooping branches of the **pepper tree** from Peru look like those of the weeping willow. Its round red-ripe berries hang in loose clusters. It produces a strong resin. The **tipu** (Pride of Bolivia) has a splendid crown of light, small-leaved foliage and plentiful clusters of yellow, pea-shaped flowers.

Shrubs

More than 200 species of *Acalypha* shrubs flourish in Kenya. They have a varied foliage, ranging from deep-pink, red, brown, greenish-brown, to various shades of green. One species, **copperleaf**, is a native of the South Sea Islands.

Despite its name and pretty pink flowers, the **desert rose** (mock azalea), found in Kenya's semi-desert lands, is lethal. Its milky sap, a potent toxin, is used as arrow poison.

Yesterday, today and tomorrow takes its name from its dark purple-blue blossoms, which change to mauve, cream and white as they age. An evergreen from Brazil, it gives off one of nature's sweetest fragrances.

Candle bush, a wild indigenous shrub of grassland, scrub and forest edge, is most obvious during the flowering season. Its bright yellow flowers form clusters of upright spikes like candelabra.

Moonflower (devil's trumpet), the fast-growing, soft-wood shrub bears large, trumpet-shaped, sweet-scented white flowers. But the fragrance conceals the kiss of death: the flower is extremely poisonous.

From Guatemala, **snow on the mountain** is reminiscent of a miniature poinsettia. Its tiny cream bracts, sometimes tinted rose, completely cover the one- to three-metre-high (three- to ten-foot) compact bushes and make an arresting sight.

As characteristic of a tropical Christmas as holly is in northern latitudes, **poinsettia** (Christmas star) is used as decoration and to illustrate Christmas cards and calendars.

A native of tropical America, the extremely beautiful rosette-shaped coloured bracts range from scarlet to pink to pale yellow but with insignificant flowers. **Hibiscus** (Chinese rose), originally from China, is probably the world's best-known tropical flower. Widespread in Kenya, it produces a host of beautiful flowers of various colours, all with prominent yellow stamens and red stigmas — blooms that

Hawaiian maidens weave into traditional garlands called *leis* to greet visitors.

Christ thorn (the crown of thorns), imported from Madagascar, is perhaps the best-known member of the euphorbias. With its formidable thorns, it makes an excellent hedge that grows to about two metres (six feet) high. It can also be clipped back to edge flower beds or allowed to grow into a large, attractive bush covered in red flowers.

Found particularly along the coast and in upcountry Kenya, the nostalgic fragrance of **frangipani** (the temple tree) makes it, perhaps, the loveliest of Kenya's exotic shrubs. It takes its name from the 12th-century perfume developed from its flowers by the Italian nobleman Frangipani. The white variety is a native of the West Indies. The pink-flowered frangipani comes from Central America.

Oleanders, with their single or double delicate pink, red or white flowers, are found in Kenya's cultivated gardens and parks both upcountry and at the coast.

A much-branched evergreen shrub from Columbia, the **fire bush**, carries a great profusion of orange-yellow flowers, hence its alternative name, oranges and lemons.

Cape honeysuckle, as its name suggests, originates from South Africa. In full sun and dry conditions, it produces wonderful orange-red spikes of flowers in terminal clusters.

Thevetia (yellow oleander), from tropical America, has elongated leaves reminiscent of oleander. The attractive lemon-yellow blossoms, with their sweet, delicate fragrance, flower for most of the year. But the milky sap is dangerously poisonous.

Climbers

If any shrub is symbolic of colourful Kenya, it has to be the **bougainvillea**. Clinging to fences or any other neighbouring natural or contrived support, it will often climb to the tops of the tallest trees by its long, spiny tendrils.

The many different forms and shades of commonly-cultivated bougainvillea create a fantastic mosaic of colours, ranging from deep magenta-purple, through crimson and soft-pink, to brick-red and bronzy-gold, even white. A native of Brazil, it was first taken to Europe by an 18th-century French navigator, Louis de Bougainville, who found specimens in Rio de Janeiro.

One of the most beautiful climbers, with large tresses of deep-violet flowers, is **petrea**, known as purple wreath. It, too, is a native of Latin America.

Perhaps the best-known of the Bignoniaceae, **Golden shower**, which grows freely and blooms in profusion in full sun, is a native of Brazil. Its gorgeous clusters of orange-coloured flowers catch the eye everywhere. Drought-resistant, it flowers most of the year.

Succulents

Aloes are African members of the lily family, and Kenya has many species ranging from four to seven metres (13 to 23 feet) in height. The sap of the spiny, sharp-pointed leaves has long been used to relieve burns, insect bites, and other inflammations. Today aloes are grown commercially for making cosmetics, shampoos and suntan lotions.

The **giant cactus,** a tall, sturdy branched species from South America, has five- and seven-sided branches, covered in spines, which develop large, whitish, trumpet-shaped flowers on their edges, that only blossom at night.

The **candelabra tree**, a succulent cactus-like euphorbia, grows as high as 15 metres (50 feet). From its relatively short, thick trunk a number of spiny branches spread in candelabra fashion. It is usually seen in savannah country, sometimes on a termite mound, and is extremely common in parts of the Rift Valley, where the Lake Nakuru National Park's euphorbia forest is one of the largest in Africa.

A plant which often reaches five metres (15 feet), the **prickly pear** is also a member of the cactus family. The 'leaves', in fact, are really stems and branches: the real leaves have been transformed into spines and bristles.

Feathery bamboo, a vigorous-growing bamboo, is used to make fences and scaffolding, and for a variety of other building purposes.

Opposite: Bougainvillea — emblem of Kenya's gardens.

Tastes of Kenya: A Culinary Safari

Most of Kenya's traditional food is high in fibre, protein, iron, fructose and complex carbohydrates. They're mainly vegetable-oriented, although the array of ethnic dishes reflects the country's culinary diversity. Flavours range from rather bland dishes from upcountry, through exotic recipes from Arabia and the Asian sub-continent, to those brought in from Europe.

Most Kenyans breakfast on sweet, milky tea and bread, followed by lunch and dinner of *sukuma wiki, irio, githeri, matoke* or *ugali* served with stew, roast meat or fish. *Ugali* is Kenya's equivalent of Western bread, potatoes or pasta. Together with potatoes, it is the basic food of many and, apart from milk, the only staple available in some poorer areas.

It is a 'bread' made from ground maize flour served steaming hot. Kenyans eat *ugali* by rolling it into a small ball and using this to scoop up the gravy of the accompanying side dish of meat or fish stew or vegetables. It is also delicious with *maziwa lala* (a cross between yoghurt and sour cream). Black or brown finger millet or cassava are sometimes used to make different versions of *ugali*.

Spinach

Sukuma wiki (kale) was introduced to Kenya by Europeans as cattle fodder. It was gradually adopted into ethnic diets throughout the country and is now eaten everywhere. Less bitter than spinach, chopped fine and stir-fried with onions and tomatoes, it is particularly delicious.

There are two other common kinds of spinach: one introduced by immigrant Italians and the other, *mchicha*, native to Kenya. It has a chartreuse coloured leaf. Cooks often add a pinch of bicarbonate of soda to turn the leaves darker green.

Githeri, mataha, njahi and *irio* are Kikuyu dishes which are served in ethnic restaurants and cafés nationwide. *Githeri* is a simple red beans and maize mixture to which potatoes, carrots, spinach, tomatoes, onions and, occasionally, diced meat are added. *Mataha* is *githeri* with potatoes and pumpkin leaves instead of spinach. *Njahi,* made with black beans, is generally served only at celebrations, and is a beautiful pale, purplish-pink, often garnished with raw banana slices.

Irio, the most popular dish, is made with green peas soaked overnight, then cooked for two hours or more until tender. Fresh maize kernels and potatoes, sometimes sweet potatoes, are added and it is cooked again until the maize is soft. Then the mixture is sprinkled with salt and mashed together. *Irio* is served with meat stew in gravy or tomato-based sauce. It is eaten the same way as *ugali*, though it is also delicious served cold the next day, cut into slices and dabbed with spicy mustard. *Irio* can be any colour, from pale green to pale lavender, and has the double advantage of being filling, cheap — and nutritious.

Meat, fish and poultry are generally served as accompanying side dishes. How they're prepared depends on the people and the region. Maasai nomads enjoy boiled goat soup flavoured with roots, with the meat eaten separately afterwards.

Other people slaughter and roast or boil beef for celebrations, reserving certain portions for specific age and gender groups, with *wazee* (elders) receiving the choicest cuts. The Kikuyu are traditionally supposed to prefer stewed, boiled or roast mutton and beef to poultry or fish, which are widely eaten elsewhere.

They make a passable haggis and sausages of blood and intestines called *mutura*. It's close to the black pudding enjoyed in Europe. They also enjoy sheep or goat brains and ox and sheep's tongue.

Chicken is a favourite among the Abaluhya and other highland people, who serve it curried or cooked in oil, tomatoes and onions.

Fish

Fish is most popular in coastal areas, and among the Luo. At the coast, sea-perch, parrot-fish, red snapper, kingfish, giant crayfish, jumbo prawns, crabs, oysters and sailfish are readily available. In the Lake

Victoria region, Nile perch, tilapia and trout are the main catches. Nile perch is a favourite throughout Kenya, mainly because its firm texture and mild taste make it a versatile ingredient.

It can be roasted or baked in its skin over charcoal and served with vegetables. At the coast, the Swahili simmer it in lime juice and coconut milk with ginger, garlic, tomatoes and onion. Asians eat it with small hot rings of green pepper. Europeans consider it delicious when it is steamed and served with a few herbs and butter or with fresh slivers of green onion and ginger.

Thinly-cut, smoked sailfish, battered sea perch, trout, parrotfish, and tilapia are also popular. Tilapia is often gutted, deboned, laid out like paper, and left to dry in the sun. Dried Nile perch and *omena*, a tiny iridescent fish, are also sold for fish stew made with onions, spices, and other vegetables. Although they smell rather pungent, once soaked and cooked, these dried fish are quite palatable.

Dried foods apart, absolute freshness and simplicity of ingredients are the key to Kenyan cuisine. Although the same ingredients are used, recipes vary from region to region.

The Borana of Marsabit cook with curry; Somali people add *jira* (cumin), cardamom, cinnamon, cloves and ginger; the coastal Swahili add coconut; the Luo around Lake Victoria prefer *dhania* (coriander) to eastern spices, and the Kikuyu do not traditionally use any herbs at all.

Most traditional dishes are mild, salt-free, and have a subtle blend of flavours. As ethnic groups move and resettle, however, and European and Asian influences continue to spread, so African tastes are rapidly changing. Spices, peppers, wine, coconut and other condiments are increasingly used and add a new range of flavours to the traditional Kenyan menu. But traditions persist — even in urban areas.

Most Kenyans come from rural backgrounds and many people still have a smallholding or well-tended vegetable garden. Even in Nairobi, *sukuma wiki*, *mchicha*, tomatoes, dhania, sweet potatoes and some types of pumpkin are found in virtually every garden — often at the expense of flower beds and lawns. Maize, the most popular crop of all, grows on every spare piece of land, not only in farms, but along the roadside, in the median strips of dual carriageways, and even in flower-pots.

Kenyans nibble fresh, charcoal-roasted maize much as Westerners eat French fries or chips. Vendors can be seen roasting the maize ears on black stoves and, at the coast, they also fry hot cassava chips and boil strong coffee served in small cups without handles. These are Kenya's traditional 'fast foods', sold in dusty lanes, along main thoroughfares, and in markets everywhere.

Fresh foods

Market days are colourful and noisy — a time to gossip, socialize, sell and buy foods not grown at home. Most large towns have a central market, either indoors or in the open. But these markets differ greatly in character between towns and regions.

At Oloitokitok, a small, busy trading town beneath Mount Kilimanjaro on the Tanzania border, the market appears an almost perfect square of colour on the dusty landscape. Informal, *khanga*-clad highland women are joined by Maasai women from the plains below, who are festooned like Christmas trees, with beads wreathed around their necks, and hanging off their ears like tinsel. On the ground, on brown burlap sacks, stacks of tomatoes, carrots, potatoes, *sukuma wiki*, small hot green peppers, ginger root, and plump, purple eggplants are laid out for inspection.

All this is vivid contrast to the Lodwar market on the flat, white-hard desert sand of Turkana in the north-west of Kenya. The dark, graceful Turkana women dress entirely in brown goat skins, relieved only by mounds of opaque beads, whose effect is as muted as Loitokitok dress is vibrant.

But the Lodwar market, the most exotic in Kenya, is well-organized and spotless. The central section, reserved for cattle sales, is the exclusive domain of men.

Neither is Kisumu market easily forgotten. Lake Victoria spreads out beyond the town in the sparking sunshine, making Kisumu like a miniature San Francisco. In summer it is hot and humid, but in the Kenyan winter the weather is mild and the large market is packed with an abundance of food. Green or purple-black avocados,

Above: Some traditional Kenya dishes — *githeri*, *irio*, and others.

the size of small footballs, are ranged alongside pineapples so sweet and non-fibrous they taste like candy. Red onions are sold in 15-kilo (30-lb) sacks and garlic by the bunch. All manner of pumpkins and peppers are on display, together with many varieties of rice, corn meal, flour, brown and finger millet, red beans, chick peas and dried maize kernels.

Different again is the Mombasa market, where sights and smells are flavoured by Indian and Arab spices, giving it the feel of a bazaar.

Largest of all is Nairobi's City Market, where fresh dill, watercress, dhania, parsley, fennel and basil are usually available.

Most produce is brought daily to market from nearby farms, especially fresh fruit. With some 30 varieties, bananas are always available.

In the central highlands, potatoes, cabbages, carrots, onions, oranges, pawpaw and mangoes are particularly abundant.

Live chickens, rabbits, honey, plums and pears can be bought on the escarpment road, only a few kilometres north-west of Nairobi.

Many different varieties of potatoes, cassava, yams and peppers are widely grown. Other vegetables include radishes, Brussels sprouts, mushrooms, asparagus, cauliflowers, zucchini and cucumbers.

Sporting Kenya: Third World Superstars

For most people, the mention of Kenyan sport conjures up images of top athletes powering their way to success at the Olympics, or all the drama and spectacle of the Safari Rally. But it would be a mistake to think that these are what Kenyan sport is all about. Kenya is a veritable playground in the sun. For resident and visitor, player and spectator, an unlimited choice of sports is offered.

Although sport was once the preserve of the Europeans and Asians, they have since become an African success story. Today's sports stars produce world-class performances and considering the financial constraints that face developing nations, Kenya's triumphs since independence are remarkable.

Participatory sports
Kenya's reputation as a sports haven is best illustrated by the host of participation sports available to resident and visitor alike. From appraising a rally of veteran and vintage cars, enjoying a sedate game of bowls or croquet to games that are more strenuous, such as tennis, squash, rugby, cricket or watersports, Kenya has something for everyone — including white water canoeing and rafting.

Golf
There are many scenic courses to choose from, where green fees are inexpensive and caddies are always available. The Muthaiga Golf Club plays host each year to the Kenya Open Golf Championship. Though the prize money may not be as much as elsewhere, the Open is an important stepping stone to the European PGA Circuit.

Stars such as Seve Ballesteros, Nick Faldo, Ian Woosnam, Sandy Lyle and Tony Jacklin have all played in the Open. The opening in 1991 of an 18-hole international standard course at the Windsor Golf and Country Club 12 kilometres (seven miles) north of Nairobi made a valuable addition to the golfing circuit. Kenya is probably the only country in the world with the following rule: 'If a ball comes to rest . . . close to a hippopotamus or crocodile, another ball may be dropped at a safe distance, but no nearer the hole, without penalty.'

Tennis, squash and table tennis
Africans and Asians have long excelled at these sports with considerable enthusiasm and some success. Kenya won the East and Central African Squash Championship in 1984 and Paul Wekesa is the first Kenyan to play the men's professional tennis circuit.

Although Kenyan tennis is not highly ranked internationally Kenyans compete in the Davis Cup and host the Kenyan Open.

Visitors wishing to play tennis, squash and table tennis will find facilities and traditional Kenyan hospitality at any Kenyan sports club or international hotel.

Bowls and croquet
A select number of sports clubs cater for lawn bowls and croquet with world-class facilities and standards. Kenya regularly competes in major international tournaments, such as the Commonwealth Games. You should carry your own kit.

Darts
Those who prefer to smoke and drink while playing their 'sport' will find Kenya is a nation of darts lovers. Keenly contested competitions are held all over the country. Linked as they are to bars, cigarette and drink manufacturers are pouring large amounts of money into developing both the popularity and the standard of the game. Table-top games such as billiards, pool, and snooker are almost exclusively found in sports clubs and hotels, though there is a pool table in Nairobi's Cameo cinema bar.

Gym and health clubs
Body-builders and weight-watchers need not worry that all their hard work will turn to flab on their Kenyan safari. Saunas and masseurs are also available for those who need them. Costs are fairly high but compare well with Western prices. Some international hotels provide these facilities.

Above: Bowls competition at the Nairobi Club.

Swimming

Those looking for exercise and relief from the heat will find swimming pools at all international hotels. Guests are admitted free of charge. There are also Olympic-size swimming pools at Nairobi's Nyayo Stadium and Moi International Stadium.

Action and adventure

Many people come to Kenya for gliding, hang-gliding, ballooning, scuba diving, sailing, sailboarding, surfboarding, water-skiing, climbing, trekking and fishing.

Hang-glider enthusiasts will find dozens of places to jump off into space — although conventional glider pilots have to go to Mweiga, near the Aberdare Mountains.

Almost continuous thermals there make it possible for gliders to stay aloft for hours and travel considerable distances, above some of the most spectacular scenery on earth.

And you can always go to Wilson Airport to do a spot of parachuting. Or paraglide at the coast — hanging from a parachute while it is being pulled along by a speedboat. Serious fly-fishermen find some of the gamest fish in the world in the lakes and rivers of Kenya. Fly-fishermen should also note that Kenya manufactures flies and lures for a growing international market at a fraction of the cost elsewhere. Kenya's lakes provide more successful hunting grounds. Large-mouth bass, fighting tiger fish, sweet-tasting tilapia, and huge Nile perch await the angler in lakes Victoria and Turkana.

Fishermen will need to bring their own equipment and pay a nominal fee for a fishing licence. In all, fishermen are well catered for, with access roads and simple huts provided for their convenience.

Kenya also offers some of the world's best deep-water, offshore fishing with marlin, sailfish, shark, swordfish, tuna and wahoo luring all those who see themselves in the Hemingway mould. The main bases for this sport are Shimoni, Mombasa, Kilifi, Watamu and Malindi. There, anything from small outboard dinghies to fully-crewed luxury yachts with every conceivable convenience and the most up-to-date equipment can be hired. The season lasts between November and March when the gentler north-east monsoon blows and the Somali current runs along the coast, bringing with it nutrients from the Arabian Sea which, in turn, attract the fish.

Kenya's palm-fringed coastline is much more than a place to lie in the sun and paddle in the almost tepid waters of the Indian Ocean. Just offshore lie Kenya's coral gardens — a magnet for snorkellers and scuba divers.

Those wishing to explore the shark-free reefs will find many outfits — all professionally run and offering top quality equipment for hire — catering to every level of experience. Scuba divers will be required to produce a certificate of competence, though there are plenty of scuba schools for the beginner.

Most hotels and independent operators provide sailing and windsurfing equipment and training, if required.

Standards have rapidly improved to the point where Kenyans have started winning international regattas, some of which are now held in Kenya.

More conventional sailors find opportunities to tack, reach and run with the wind on lakes Naivasha and Victoria.

Water skiiers are able to indulge their passion at the coast, and lakes Naivasha and Baringo.

The Safari Rally
The Safari Rally has become synonymous with Kenya. For 3,000 kilometres (1,850 miles) the world's best rally drivers hurtle through the Kenyan outback, battling with thick mud, blinding dust, unpredictable wildlife, and the clock for the winner's laurel.

The first Safari Rally (then known as Coronation Rally) was held in 1953. On that occasion, 57 local European drivers wound their way through East Africa. Despite the organizers' attempts to keep the rally a strictly amateur event, it stirred the imagination of the world.

Once it gained international status in 1957, the rally (then known as the East African Safari Rally) was soon contested by drivers and major works teams from overseas. Today the Safari Rally is an important event with successful drivers and works teams being awarded valuable points in the World Rally Championship. Foreign drivers with their formidable reputations and multinational backing were the winners in 1988, 1989, 1990, 1991, 1992, 1995 and 1996.

A full programme of local events that are used to determine 'Motorsportsman of the Year' is held throughout the year. They include road safety, training, economy-run, fun and national rallies, and even go-cart races.

Athletics
Few countries have done so well in any one sport as Kenya in athletics. By the late-1980s Kenya's dominance of middle and long-distance running had been established beyond all doubt. Yet Kenyan athletes did not compete in their first international meet until 1952 — and did not win a gold medal until 1962 in the Perth Commonwealth Games. International attention first came with the superlative performances of Kipchoge ('Kip') Keino and Naftali Temu. In 1965 Keino claimed his first gold medal when he won the 1,500 metres at the First All Africa Games in Brazzaville. The following year he won two gold medals in the Jamaica Commonwealth Games for the one mile and three mile events.

At the same games, Temu won gold for the six-mile, following that with a 5,000 metres win in the 1967 World Games at Helsinki. In the 1968 Mexico Olympics Temu got the ball rolling by winning the 10,000 metres. Amos Biwott won Kenya's second gold in the 3,000 metres steeplechase. Keino put the icing on the cake when he won the 1,500 metres. The Kenyans returned home to a heroes' welcome with three gold, four silver and one bronze medal.

At the 1970 Edinburgh Commonwealth Games, Keino again won gold in the 1,500 metres. Robert Ouko (800 metres), Charles Asati (400 metres), and the men's 4 x 400 metres relay team also proved Mexico was no fluke and, in all, Kenya won four gold, one silver, and four bronze.

Keino made gold again in the 3,000 metres steeplechase at the 1972 Munich Olympics, but lost his 1,500 metres crown. The men's 4 x 400 relay team snatched Kenya's second gold. It was Keino's last Olympics and Kenya's last until 1984, having chosen to boycott the Olympics at Montreal and Moscow. With five gold, one silver, and six

Top: Front-runner in the gruelling 3,000-kilometre-long Safari Rally.

Above: Kenyan athletes — the cream of the world's middle and long-distance runners.

Above: Soccer is Kenya's most popular sport.

bronze medals Kenya literally ran away with the 1974 Commonwealth Games in Christchurch. Mike Boit and Benjamin Jipcho emerged as new but short-lived stars. In 1978, Henry Rono, burst on the scene — setting world records in the 3,000 metres, 5,000 metres, 10,000 metres, and 3,000 metres steeplechase.

Kenya brought back five gold, four silver and two bronze medals from the 1978 Edmonton Commonwealth Games and one gold (Korir), one silver and three bronzes at the 1982 Commonwealth Games. A blank World Championship followed in 1983 and only a two-medal haul (Korir again) at the 1984 Olympics at Los Angeles.

Not until 1987 was Kenyan pride fully restored when their athletes won the 800 metres, 10,000 metres, and marathon at the

World Championships in Rome. The following year they won the 5,000 metres, 3,000 metres steeplechase, 1,500 metres, and 800 metres at the Seoul Olympics.

The remarkable John Ngugi also won the World Cross Country Championships and Ibrahim Hussein won the Boston Marathon for the third time in 1992.

Kenya took four golds in the 1991 World Championships in Tokyo, mainly on long distances, and 11 more in the Fifth All Africa Games in Cairo, again mainly on long distances. The 1992 Olympics in Barcelona brought Kenya two gold, four silver, and two bronze medals.

Boxing
Boxing is the second sport to have brought international fame to Kenya. Kenyan box-

305

ers have consistently performed well at international levels in both the Commonwealth Games — their best performance was in Brisbane in 1982, when they won five gold, one silver, and one bronze medal — and the King's Cup, where they were runners-up in 1982. Following the 1987 All Africa Games, Kenya were the undisputed African champions with eight gold and two bronze medals. The next year, Robert Wangila won Kenya's first Olympic gold medal in Seoul. Wangila later turned professional but died after a knockout.

Football

To the hundreds of thousands of football fans in Kenya who cram the stadiums each weekend, nothing is more exciting than watching their favourite team in action. Yet for all its popularity, Kenya footballers have still to perform well at the highest level.

In the annual event in which seven or eight teams from the region compete for the East and Central African Championships, Harambee Stars — the Kenyan national team — eight times the winners since 1967, were defeated in 1991 by Zambia 2–0 but qualified among the ten best teams to go to Tunisia for the finals (held every two years) of the Africa Cup of Nations in 1994.

At club level, Gor Mahia (winners of the Nelson Mandela Cup in the Africa Cup Winners Tournament in 1987) and AFC Leopards, remain Kenya's top two clubs.

Hockey

From the 1950s until the early 1970s, hockey grew from strength to strength as Kenya performed well in the international arena. After the 1956 Olympics Kenya was ranked tenth in the world: following the 1964 Olympics this had improved to sixth. But the high point of Kenyan hockey came in 1971 when the Kenyan team came fourth in the first World Cup and won the East Africa Hockey Championships for the sixth consecutive year.

Since then, Kenyan hockey has slipped into the doldrums. Kenya's gold medal in the 1987 All Africa Games, went some way to restoring lost pride.

Cricket

Like hockey, for a long time cricket was largely a Kenyan Asian affair. But in the 1990s and 1980s Africans began to make their mark felt. In 1986 the captain of the national team on tour of the UK was an African.

Unlike hockey, Kenyan cricket made little impact in the international arena until 1996 when it beat West Indies in an early round of the World Cricket Cup.

Although Kenya was represented in the 1975 World Cup it was as members of a composite East African side. Kenyan born-and-bred cricketers, however, have gone on to play at the highest levels — Derek Pringle for England, Qasim Omar for Pakistan, and Dilip Patel for New Zealand.

In 1994, as an associate member of the International Cricket Conference, in 1995-96, Kenya hosted the ICC mini-World Cup Tournament, finishing second in the 20-nation tournament to emerge as one of the three nations to earn a place in the 1996 World Cricket Cup staged in India, Pakistan and Sri Lanka which was when they beat the West Indies in a result that sent shock waves around the cricketing world.

Other spectator sports

For those who enjoy the 'sport of kings', Nairobi's Ngong Road Racecourse offers an eight-race card almost every Sunday afternoon and on most public holidays, except during August-September. The racing is well patronized and professionally-run, with stipendary stewards, a qualified handicapper, bookmakers, and tote facilities.

With the excellent amenities and catering, an afternoon at one of the world's prettiest courses is surprisingly inexpensive and extremely enjoyable.

airkenya aviation

- **Nairobi**   - **Nanyuki**   - **Samburu**   - **Amboseli**   - **Masai Mara**
- **Lamu**   - **Malindi**   - **Kiwayu**   - **Ukunda**   - **Mombasa**

Airkenya Aviation is the largest private airline in East Africa, with 190 staff including 28 multi-national pilots. From its base at Wilson Airport, Nairobi it provides a network of scheduled services within Kenya and operates charter flights throughout the region.

The fleet of 18 aircraft ranges in size from a 40-seat Fokker F27 to a five-seat, twin-engine light aircraft. The latest additions to the fleet are two fully air-conditioned 34-seat Shorts 360-300 turbo-prop aircraft and a Kingair which is ideally suited for VIP charters.

The company operates daily scheduled services to all the main tourist destinations and in addition has introduced "The Coastline Connector" which offers a twice daily scheduled service linking Mombasa, Malindi, Lamu and Kiwayu with regular departures from Ukunda on the South Coast.

Reservations may be made directly with the company or through a Kenya-based travel agent or tour operator.

For further details contact: John Buckley, Airkenya Aviation Ltd.,
PO Box 30357, Wilson Airport, Nairobi.
Tel: (254-2) 501601/501421/501501   Fax: (254-2) 500845

the friendly airline

Your stay in Kenya is made twice as memorable at a Serena Hotel or Lodge.

Nairobi Serena Hotel

Mara Serena Safari Lodge

Samburu Serena Safari Lodge

Amboseli Serena Safari Lodge

Mombasa Serena Beach Hotel

At Serena Lodges and Hotels we uphold the highest standards of service, efficiency and comfort.

The Nairobi Serena Hotel, overlooking Nairobi Central Park, is a member of the 'Leading Hotels of the World'. Dine at the Cafe Maghreb by the poolside, or at the Mandhari Restaurant with its international à la carte cuisine. The energetic Maisha health and fitness club is also available.

The Mara Serena Safari Lodge, set high on a ridge, offers panoramic views of the surrounding Maasa Mara Game Reserve, with its multitude of wildlife.

The Samburu Serena Safari Lodge situated on the banks of the Uaso-Nyiro river in the Samburu Game Park, is the ideal place to view Kenya's exotic birdlife and rare animals. These include Grevy's Zebra the reticulated Giraffe, the long necked Gerenuk and the blue shanked Somali Ostrich.

When in Amboseli, stay at the Amboseli Serena Safari Lodge. Overlooking Mount Kilimanjaro, the lodge is a perfect getaway. A sun terrace with views of the lush plains makes it the ideal place to view the plains game.

The Mombasa Serena Beach Hotel, a member of the 'Leading Hotels of the World', is situated on the white sandy beaches on Mombasa's North Coast. The hotel combines traditional coastal architecture with modern facilities.

Come to Serena and we will ensure your stay with us is made as comfortable as possible.

SERENA HOTELS
SAFARI LODGES • HOTELS • RESORTS

Travellers come to Travellers Beach Hotel for . . .

The beach ...
White sandy beaches with sun and fun all year round. An elegant new beach resort hotel on Mombasa's north coast.
Superbly Travellers.

The restaurants ...
Exquisite, exceptional with superb variety. There is 'La Pergola' pizzeria and pasta bar, the exotic 'Sher-e-Punjab' Indian restaurant and two convenient snack bars.

Also the "Suli-Suli" fish grill and "Vunja-Joto" ice cream parlour, "Bahari" grill, Kisima Bar".
Uniquely Travellers.

The accommodation ...
Contemporary, spacious and air-conditioned rooms complete with satellite colour television.
Luxuriously Travellers.

The entertainment ...
Dynamic, high energy, powerful. There is the modern underground "Show Boat" night club. Exciting traditional cabarets with performing acrobats and live bands.

The holiday ...
Exciting, vibrant and full of energy. Windsurfing, scuba diving, deep sea fishing and lots more.
Out and about the Travellers way.

Out of Africa — a

Unlock the secrets of

The only way to discover Kenya in all its infinite beauty —
from snow-capped mountains to Indian Ocean beaches,
from endless game-filled plains to sparkling lakes.

5-star luxury in the wild

Treetops • Outspan • Samburu Lodge • Larsens Camp • Nyali Beach Hotel • Keekerok Lodge • Shimba Lodge •
Lake Baringo Club • Lake Naivasha Country Club • Jacaranda Hotel • Indian Ocean Beach Club • Ol Tukai Lodge

out of this World
nya with Block Hotels

We not only accommodate you but your wishes too.

block
hotels
all the best places

STAYING IN NAIROBI?
Try The Country Hotel In Town,
Set Within 5 Acres of Luxuriant Tranquil Gardens.
Just 2Kms from The City Centre.

- The Fairview Hotel -

Arrivals relax in the spacious Reception

A comfortable Lounge to receive guests

Fairview
THE COUNTRY HOTEL IN TOWN

Bishops Road, Nairobi Hill, P.O. Box 40842, Nairobi, Kenya, East Africa.
Tel: (254-2) 723211, 711321   Fax: (254-2) 721320

Kenya's Mountains and Hills

All of Kenya's mountains have been mapped and photographed and all but some peaks in the distant north have been climbed. The narratives found in archives and diaries of the ascents of some of the major peaks are interesting. Most smaller mountains, however, were climbed only for some scientific or administrative pursuit — and the record is scattered in obscure works.

Although not particularly high, some of the hills along the Nairobi-Mombasa road are spectacular. These and the Taita Hills were visited by many early travellers, including three Germans, Baron von der Decken, Johann Krapf and Johannes Rebmann, and two Britons, Charles New and Joseph Thomson. Indeed, Rebmann travelled by the Sagala Hills as early as 1847.

New, who climbed the 1,640m (5,383ft) south-western shoulder of Kasigau in July 1863, remembered, 'Never did I perform a harder three hours' task. . . .'

Surrounded by perpendicular cliffs, Kasigau reminded him of St Paul's Cathedral. New also visited the Taita Hills, climbed a spur of Vuria, and finally reached the 1,146m (3,760ft) crest of Marimba south of the Voi-Taveta road. Twenty years later Joseph Thomson took three hours to reach the summit of Ndara and journeyed to a valley running deep into Bura mountain, where 'the stupidity of our guide who took us the wrong road' landed him at the bottom of a steep precipice — '1,000ft from the top'.

The North

The area offers a variety of mountains ranging from dramatic steep isolated peaks such as Baio to the extensive podocarpus-clad forest of the Mathews Range. The hills, which all create their own climate, rise out of semi-desert.

Guides: Because of the thick vegetation and forest, a guide is essential on most peaks.

Logistics: These mountains are fairly remote and care must be taken. Many prefer to travel in convoy as security against a breakdown. Water is rare and, whether travelling by car or on foot, you should not only carry adequate supplies but also fill up at all the sources listed.

Camping: Generally camping is possible anywhere in the area, but care should be taken to achieve some privacy. Along the route of the various Turkana 'buses', there are a number of campsites, with water, showers and toilets. They are usually full of Turkana bus passengers and you are likely to be pestered by trinket-sellers and professional photograph-posers.

Public Transport: In most areas there is no transport, let alone public transport. But it may be possible to reach Wamba from Isiolo by hitchhiking or *matatu*.

Security: Security is generally quite good, except for Losiolo. Although *shifta* (bandits) have been reported in the gap between the Mathews and the Ndoto ranges and on the El Barta Plains around Baragoi they do not seem to have troubled vehicles.

FOROLE 2,007m (6,584ft)

Forole lies on the Ethiopian border to the north of the **Huri Hills**. A long craggy ridge, steep on both the Kenyan and Ethiopian sides, it is covered and surrounded by thicker bush. Although **Forole** is a dramatic mountain, many other peaks give nicer walks.

But undoubtedly Forole's attraction is standing with one foot in Ethiopia and reflecting on the inevitable excitements of the journey to the top. A series of small springs on the Kenyan side have paths running to them, penetrating the thicker lower bush. It is essential to use the paths and best to hire a guide from the **village**.

JABISA 1,544m (5,065ft)

Views like those from the top of Jabisa don't come any grander. You can see **Lake Stephanie (Chew Bahir)**, **North Island**, the **Lapurr Range**, **Forole, Mount Kulal** and the **Mega Escarpment** in Ethiopia. The area is particularly hot and, for the traverse of the main peaks, you should carry at least five litres of water. The nearest sources are at Sabarei and El Sardu.

PORR 668m (2,191ft)

This mountain forms a perfect pyramid on the north side of El Molo Bay on Lake Turkana. Rising 300m (1,000ft) above the lake, it is more of an enjoyable trek for hill-walkers than for serious mountaineering. The track passes through a number of dry luggas bordered by thorn trees and other bushes. They provide a break from the winds off Mount Kulal which rise suddenly as the sun sets.

KULAL 2,285m (7,498ft)

Covered by thick and ancient green forests, Kulal, like **Marsabit**, is an incredible and almost unbelievable contrast to the lava wastes around Lake Turkana. The exciting approach and spectacular views of the lake and deep mountain gorges make it one of Kenya's most rewarding mountains. The highest point lies on a narrow ridge near the **Arabel** end. **Ladarabach** to the south is easier to reach. The ridge between Ladarabach and the **summit** has been crossed only two or three times. It's very challenging — long traverses on loose soil above steep drops and extremely severe climbing grades. The eastern side of the ridge forms the head of the **El Kajarta Gorge**, the most spectacular on the mountain. With difficulty you can reach it from the road to the east. The spectacular drive up

Ladarabach is rough. Just short of the **roadhead** at **Gatab Mission**, you can hire guides and obtain water. A **campsite** at the edge of the roadhead offers a magnificent panorama over Lake Turkana. From there a day's easy walking through lush forest and attractive meadowlands takes you to another fine viewpoint overlooking the lake — and yet another overlooking El Kajarta Gorge to Arabel. The drive up Arabel, which has less spectacular views of the lake, is also very rough.

NYIRU 2,752m (9,030ft)

Rising out of thorn scrub, this impressive, large and bulky mountain with stunning views of the northern deserts, shares with Marsabit and Kulal the blessing of thick, cool forests and pleasant meadowlands which shroud its summit. During the dry season the Samburu take their cattle up **Nyiru** and some live there permanently, creating a bewildering array of cattle trails.

Water is always available near the **summit** and there are plenty of campsites if you want to spend a night or two at the top. Again, you'll need to find shelter from the strong early night wind. The most common approach, via **Tum**, gives the shortest ascent with easy access to the most spectacular of the peaks and a pleasantly cool early morning ascent in the mountain's shadow. This also allows you a detour down the mountain into **Suguta Valley**, where temperatures rarely drop below 38°C (100°F).

Turn left 12km (7.5mls) before Tum and follow the track past the Pakati **mission post** down into the valley. Bear right at an obvious fork for the trail to **Lake Logipi**. Be prepared. It is rarely visited and the boulder-strewn track is steep and incredibly rough — you'll drive most of it in low-ratio first gear, so allow a full day for the 60km (40mls) to Lake Logipi and back.

SUPUKO 2,067m (6,780ft)

This highest point on the spectacular eastern ridge of the **South Horr Valley** is generally neglected in favour of its bigger neighbour on the other side. But a circuit of the two main peaks, **Porale**, 1,990m (6,530ft), and **Supuko**, 2,067m (6,780ft), offers some fascinating, if difficult, ridge walks with fine views of **Nyiru,** the **South Horr Valley,** and the northern deserts.

The best place to start from is **Kurungu Camp** using guides. Two obvious rock faces that lead up to the summits can be seen above Kurungu Camp: one in the north, **Porak**; the other in the south, **Mumusia**. Hidden by a subsidiary north-west peak, Supuko is 2km (almost 1.5mls) to the north of Porak and not too obvious from the road.

Ndoto Range

ALIMISION 2,637m (8,650ft)

Located in the centre of the range, an extremely narrow ridge which forms the highest part of Alimision offers splendid scenic landscapes. The climb is mainly along cattle trails and not much obscures the views. The last leg is an enjoyable airy scramble but not for those who suffer vertigo. A **spring** near the summit is sometimes dry. Much bigger than it looks, **Alimision** towers 1,676m (5,500ft) above the roadhead at **Arsim**. It is possible to approach it via **Lesirikan**, but it means an extremely tiring walk.

POI

Climbers rate **Poi** in the northern **Ndoto Range** the most challenging climb in the country after Mount Kenya — and technically almost as demanding. The easiest route is a Grade V climb. Poi is surrounded on three sides by almost sheer cliffs between 300 and 610m (1,000-2,000ft) high — a rock climbing paradise that amounts to 5km (3mls) of cliffs. The fourth side is a ridge which creates a barrier between **Arsim** and **Ngurunit**.

BAIO 1,751m (5,746ft)

Baio rises almost sheer out of the desert for 1,219m (4,000ft) some 30km (20mls) from the main **Ndoto Range**. Its southern face is a dramatic 600m (2,000ft) overhanging precipice, invisible until you reach the **summit**. The reasonably short climb means you can stay on the summit for some time to enjoy the stupendous scenery — Baio itself, **Holilugum Nder**, the **Ndoto Range**, **Poi**, the **Mathews Range**, **Marsabit** and the **Kaisut Desert**.

If lucky you may see some of the greater kudu which live on the mountain. Another attraction is the pleasure of camping at Ngurunit and bathing in the **rock pools**. It is worth hiring a guide and also an *askari* to guard your vehicle. These can be arranged through the local chief.

There are two routes: The first, which is extremely steep and direct, avoids most of the thorn bush but involves some airy scrambling, which is avoided by the second route, although this is much longer and through dense bush.

From **Ngurunit** drive for 40km (25mls) along the **Laisamis road** to where a track on the right leads to a **UNESCO research station**.

You can't miss it because of the large herds of camels all around it. Continue past the station for another 4km (2.5mls) to the foot of the mountain.

Mathews Range

OL DOINYO LENKIYO 2,286m (7,505ft)

This remote and rarely visited mountain is at the northern end of the **Mathews Range**. From **Isiolo** you drive 119km (74mls) along the **Great North Road** towards **Marsabit** to a left turn and on to a track for **Lodosoit**. Five km (3mls) along this, take the left fork and drive another 15km (10mls) to a vermiculite **mine**. From the mine it's another 20km (12mls) to a col between **Il Bision** and the main range.

MATHEWS PEAK 2,375m (7,792ft)

Covered in lush and beautiful podocarpus forest, this is the highest mountain in the main part of the remote **Mathews Range** with delightful walks through the cool of the forest. You can stay at the Wildlife Department's **campsites** lower down the valley. Water is available everywhere and the **Ngeng River** has some marvellous large **rock pools** ideal for swimming. You can hire a ranger from the **game post** as a guide.

From Isiolo follow the Marsabit road to the **Wamba turnoff** on the left, 20km (12mls) beyond **Archer's Post**. Follow this road for 40km (25mls) to the next turnoff signposted Wamba, right, and immediately left onto the **Barsaloi road**. Drive along this road for 18km (11mls) to a right fork that leads on 15km (10mls) to **Ngalai**. Just before Ngalai bear right along a rough track for 10km (6mls) to **Kishishi Game Post** where you sign in.

MATHEWS SOUTH PEAK 2,285m (7,497ft)
Much easier to climb than **Mathews**, which takes the form of a U-shaped ridge, the south peak is notable for the excellent viewpoint on **Londoma** in the south-west. **Ukut**, the forested high point, is in the south-east corner. The Kishishi Game Post lies at the head of the U-shaped ridge, the outside of which is made up of many steep and rocky faces. You'll need a guide as the inside of the ridge is shrouded with thick forest and it is easy to lose your way. There is also a great deal of confusion over names and you may be taken to the wrong place.

WARGES 2,688m (8,820ft)
This extremely large and attractive mountain with its magnificent panoramas lies to the southeast of the Mathews Range. The **campsite** in the **Wamba Valley** is a delightful place to stay. The lower parts of the mountain are covered with thick and sometimes impenetrable bush. Its crest sports another of the many lush and ancient podocarpus forests of these northern mountains.

How much you enjoy the first part of the climb through the bush depends on how easily you find a decent game trail to follow. They become rarer as the game diminishes and after the rains, when the wildlife spreads out, they often don't exist. So what should take between four and five hours can sometimes involve up to two days. You'll need a guide and you should rely on his judgement. From **Wamba**, bear right at the end of the main street to take the extreme right fork to the **Forestry house** where you can hire a guide.

LOLOLOKWE 1,853m (6,080ft)
Surrounded on three sides by sheer 300m (1,000-ft) cliffs, this spectacular mountain is a distinctive landmark for travellers on the **Great North Road**. Its main attraction is the walk round the top of its bluff. To the north, the smaller hill with a microwave **relay station** also offers splendid views. From **Isiolo** drive north on the **Marsabit** road past the Wamba turnoff and past the main wall of **Lololokwe** until you can see a valley to the north of the main mountain. Turn off there and drive up the valley to the **roadhead**. You should take an *askari* to guard your vehicle. The journey from Isiolo is about one hour.

LOSIOLO 2,470m (8,104ft)
On a clear day from the **summit** of Losiolo you can take in one of the most spectacular panoramas Kenya offers — the **Ndoto Range**, the **Cherangani Hills** (including **Sekerr**), **Mount Nyiru**, **Lake Baringo**, and **Tiati** in the **Tugen Hills**. The **roadhead**, one of two in Kenya known as **World's End**, is an extremely popular **viewpoint**. From Maralal drive north for 18km (11mls) along the **Baragoi road** to the **Poror turnoff** on the left, and follow this track through Poror **village** for 3km (just over 2mls) to a **T-junction**. Take the left turn for just over 7km (4mls) to reach World's End.

The Tugen Hills

The Tugen Hills offer many delightful and relatively short walks, all with magnificent and varied views. They make an extremely pleasant excursion from Nairobi.

Kabarnet, the administrative capital of the region, has a good, reasonably-priced hotel. A few km east of Kabarnet the road to **Tenges** is one of the most scenic in Kenya, with incredible views of the Rift. A third tarmac road heads north from Kabarnet to **Kabartonjo** and a fourth to Iten across the floor of the Kerio Valley.

TIATI 2,351m (7,713ft)
Tiati, a large northern outlier of the **Tugen**, is separated from them by the **Kito Pass**. It's a long hot climb through rugged scenery to an extremely good viewpoint.

A small forest below the summit makes a pleasant **campsite**, but you need to carry your own water. The nearest water is at the **Barpello mission**. A guide is essential. You drive through the Kito Pass from the Cheranganis. After a long flat straight section near the top of the pass the road turns right and drops steeply.

From this point the Barpello mission, where you hire guides and askaris, is about one km (0.7mls) off the main road some 7km (4mls) from the summit of the pass. From the mission turnoff continue along the main road another 2km (just over a mile) towards **Tot** to a right turn signposted 'Freedom from Hunger' and follow this for 11km (7mls) to the campsite at the roadhead.

SAIMO 2,501m (8,207ft)
Rising out of heavily cultivated farmland, the summit of this forested eminence consists of three peaks, the highest being the middle one. The forest is host to brilliant butterflies and many orchids. There are splendid views over

Baringo. The approach road also gives good views of the **Cheranganis**, the northern part of the **Kerio Valley**, **Tiati** and **Saimo** itself. There are many tracks through the farms and forest. Saimo is an enjoyable morning's outing from Kabarnet. From **Kabarnet** drive 19km (12mls) north to **Kabartonjo** and then continue along a rough dirt road — that gets rougher — to **Bartalimo**. It takes an hour.

MAROP 2,306m (7,567ft)

This mountain, with panoramic views of the Rift Valley and the Tugen Hills, is a short excursion from Kabarnet. Drive from **Kabarnet** along the **Marigat road** to the point where it passes the southern end of an obvious ridge leading south from **Marop**. There is a track, signposted to **Kasare** and **Kapkomoi Primary Schools**, along the west side of the ridge. Leave the car by the main road, or drive along the track for some way. It becomes increasingly rough. From the main road, follow the track for about 3km (just over 2mls) to a fork which you should ignore and continue north for one km (0.7mls). This brings you north-west of the summit to a point where an old motor track, to the right, zigzags up the hill to a col below the summit. From there it's a short scramble to the summit.

KIBIMJOR 2,347m (7,699ft)

With its impressive knife-edge ridge leading to the summit climbers are rewarded with mind-boggling views, from both the top and the approach roads. The first approach is suitable for saloon cars.

The second, though slower and rougher, is much more scenic, circuiting **Eldama Ravine**. From Kabarnet drive to **Tenges** and continue south for 3km (almost 2mls) to the road, opposite an old forest station, leading west to a quarry.

KAPKUT 2,800m (9,185ft)

With its spectacular viewpoint overlooking the southern end of the **Kerio Valley**, **Kapkut** is reached by a long drive through rolling farmland followed by a short walk.

Densely-populated and intensely cultivated, camping is only possible at the roadhead. Follow the **Nyaru** road from Eldama Ravine for about 20km (12mls) to **Kipsaos**.

Just before the village, take the right turn to a good dirt road that runs east along the rim of the Kerio Valley with splendid views. Continue to the **roadhead**. A gentle 15-minute walk, past a school and through forest, brings you to the grassy **summit**. From the roadhead you can also walk to Kaisamu, opposite Kapkut.

The Mau

The **Mau Escarpment** forms the western wall of the Great Rift Valley with a north-western extension as far as **Tinderet** which overlooks **Lake**

Victoria. Although within easy reach of **Nairobi**, the hills are rarely explored and have suffered severe deforestation and dense settlement. But the craters on the volcanic outliers of **Buru** and **Londiani** make extremely pleasant excursions.

TINDERET 2,640m (8,663ft)

This impressive mountain, overlooking the eastern shores of Lake Victoria, is clearly visible from the **Nakuru-Kericho road**, with splendid scenic approach roads. Thick bamboo and forest on the **summit** severely limit the views. Follow the **Londiani-Fort Ternan road** towards Londiani to a left turn to **Tinderet Tea Estate** and follow this road for 8km (5mls). There you come to a road heading north across the range and returning in a large semicircle to a **roadhead** near a ridge running north of the peak. It's between 30 and 35km (19-22mls) from **Kipkelion**. You'll need to locate an old footpath to the **summit**.

LONDIANI 3,011m (9,878ft)

You can reach the summit by road and the twin craters of this large forested volcano are fascinating. Follow the **Eldoret** road from Nakuru to a right turn signposted **Molo Forest Station** just before Molo. Follow this road past the forest station for 5km (3mls) to a **crossroads** at the start of a **village**.

Take the right turn and drive for 10km (6mls) to the forest where the road continues for another 2km (just over a mile) to the crater rim. There's a rough track for 3km (almost 2mls) down into the crater, to a lovely campsite in a clearing by a stream. There are also some campsites on the inner crater rim and in the inner crater. For the summit, which is densely forested with bamboo, follow the main Eldoret road from Nakuru for 50km (30mls) where it veers left and another road continues straight on. Take this road for 12km (7mls) to a right turn on to a murram road. Follow this for 12km (7mls) to a fork and keep left. Continue for another 12km (7mls) to a right turn which leads 6km (almost 4mls) to the **police station** and the **post office** on the summit.

MELILI 3,098m (10,165ft)

The road passes close to the highest point of the **Mau**, but the approach roads are extremely rough. From **Njoro** take the **Narok** road past **Egerton College** for 44km (27mls) and through **Mau Narok** to a left turn. Follow this past some **sawmills** for another 21km (13mls) then sharp left for the last 9km (6mls) to the **summit**.

BURU 2,854m (9,365ft)

Isolated from the **Mau** range, this fascinating volcanic peak with many craters stands between **Naivasha** and **Elmenteita** in the Rift Valley. Although the mountain is settled on its lower and middle slopes, you will spend most of the walk in forest with tantalizing glimpses of **Mount Longonot** and **lakes Elmenteita** and **Nakuru**.

From Naivasha follow the new **Nakuru road**. Turn left, on to the **Moi South Lake Road**, and continue for almost 9km (6mls) to a **three-way junction** where the road branches left.

Take the road on the right bearing towards **Eburru** for 14km (almost 9mls) until you come to a fork. Take the track on the left for 2km (just over a mile) to another left fork which leads to **Eburru** village. After passing **Eburru Harambee Secondary School**, bear sharp right on to the road that climbs the hill behind the village.

Follow this for 3km (almost 2mls) to the crest of a slope past a triangular fork where roads lead right and left, and a private track goes half right. Continue straight on into the floor of a large crater and a large levelled apron where the road starts to bear left. From the **parking spot**, the summit is very evident and from the corner of the apron a wide footpath climbs parallel to its right hand side. Follow this to the rim of the large crater, passing a much smaller crater on the right.

After about two hours, the track bears right across level ground and descends steeply to a level section with an ill-defined path to the left. Follow this, keeping a large steep-sided crater on your right, to the bamboo-covered summit.

The Aberdares

The third-highest mountain range in Kenya after Mount Kenya and Mount Elgon, there is much to enjoy — and to frustrate you— in the Aberdares. There is a well-maintained network of roads running on the broad moorland plateau in the central part of the range between **Naivasha** and **Nyeri** which allow you to visit most waterfalls. There is one approach to **Lesatima** and the northern moorlands, and some rarely-used approaches to **Kinangop**. It's advisable whatever the time of year or weather to use 4WD.

Where to stay
There is a small **fishing lodge** offering bunkhouse accommodation where you can also camp. For weekends in January, February and March, book at Mountain National Park HQ, Mweiga. At other times, it is hardly ever used.

KIPIPIRI 3,349m (10,987ft)
Standing to the west of the range and divided from it by the deep cleft of the Wanjohi Valley, Kipipiri is an outlier with a flat topped dome offering views to the west over the Rift. It is much less covered by cloud than the main range. It is quite possible to climb it in a long day from Nairobi. The foot of the mountain is densely-populated and heavily-cultivated, making camping less than ideal, but by no means impossible. The schoolmaster at **Geta** allows parties to camp on his **playing field**. It is possible to climb Kipipiri from any direction, but the approach from the north is easiest. Carry water. From **Gilgil** follow the **Nyahururu road** for 25km (15.5mls) to

the first stretch of the wheat-fields and a right turn, signposted **Wanjohi**.

Drive south through Wanjohi towards Geta, taking the first major dirt road right. From this climb a track up an evident spur running north. The journey takes about three hours from Nairobi. Follow the ridge, which is covered in bamboo in places, to many of the false summits. The climb takes between two and three hours.

LESATIMA 3,999m (13,120ft)
The highest point of the Aberdares is nothing more than a strenuous high-altitude walk but with splendid views over **Laikipia** and **Mount Kenya**. There are two approaches. Both require a 4WD vehicle and the walks are entirely on the high moorland ground. Carry all your water.

From Naivasha
From Nairobi, just before the Naivasha turnoff on the **Nairobi-Nakuru road**, there is a right turn signposted **North Kinangop**. Follow this until the tarmac ends with a left turn on a rough track to the Aberdare National Park. Follow this to the **Mutubio Gate**. The final leg before the gate, astonishingly, is tarmac. From the gate it's 3km (almost 2mls) to a crossroads.

The right-hand track heads to the 300m-deep (1,000ft) **Karuru Falls** and the **fishing lodge.** Continue straight across for another 3km (almost 2mls) to a second crossroads where a disused track joins from the left and the right track leads to the fishing lodge and the **Kiandongoro Gate.** Continue straight across for another 9km (almost 6mls) then bear left at a fork. The right fork goes to the **Ruhuruini Park Gate**. Another 10km (6mls) on, you come to the **Wandares track**, left, marked by a fire tower on a hill beyond.

From Nyeri
From Nyeri follow the **Nyahururu** road for 13km (8mls) through **Mweiga** to a left turn clearly signposted **Wandares Park Gate**, and the start of the **Wandares track.**

Follow the Wandares track to a small timber cabin and continue along the extremely rough trail to the roadhead. Camping there exposes you to strong winds, camping lower exposes you to strong lions. Stay in the cabin. Either approach takes about four hours from Nairobi. Follow the track from the roadhead north-west, following the southern contours, beneath the ridge, along the game trails until you reach the last col below Lesatima.

From there you can climb straight up to the lower north peak or bear south-west to the true **summit**. Most of the walk is on gentle gradients but you'll certainly feel the altitude on the final climb. It takes about three hours.

From Nyahururu
From Nyahururu follow the **Nyeri road** for 6km (almost 4mls) to a signposted right turn through **Kaheho** to the **Shamata gate**. There is a more direct but much rougher approach to this gate via

Ol Kalou. After the gate ignore the signs to the campsite and continue for 6km (almost 4mls) to the junction with the disused **Virgin's Lane** and continue another 3km (almost 2mls) to a fork. Bear right (left here, and left again, brings you to **Chebuswa Hut**; left but then right takes you down **Elephant Entry Road** to the **Ngobit Gate**). Continue to the roadhead. The last 2km (just over a mile) is usually extremely muddy and soggy. Follow the track from the roadhead and then bear south on the game trails to a ridge that overlooks the **Dragon's Teeth**.

Walk down into the basin keeping the Teeth to the west and you eventually reach some ridges which you can follow up to Lesatima. The walk takes between three and four hours.

TABLE MOUNTAIN 3,971m (12,438ft)
South-west of **Lesatima**, right on the edge of the main escarpment, **Table Mountain** is the end of a ridge which is mostly higher than the peak. Two approaches are possible.

The first, rarely used, climbs the escarpment above **Wanjohi** through various bands of vegetation. The second approach is along the rarely travelled ridges south of Lesatima. From the summit of Lesatima continue south along the main ridge of the Aberdares. After an initial steep descent, you'll reach a small pool.

Fill up there for the night's camp then climb the next peak on the ridge, and the rather lower one that follows, to descend to a col which has reasonable camping and can be reached in a day from Nairobi. From Lesatima it takes between one and two hours. From there continue to the next high point and turn sharp right to the rock castle (mentioned in route one), down into a valley and straight up the side of the ridge leading to Table Mountain. Alternatively, continue straight on before bearing right to follow a subsidiary ridge leading into the basin at the head of the valley. From there you climb straight up the side of the ridge and follow it to the summit. It takes between two and three hours from the campsite. The round trip from Nairobi is feasible over a weekend.

THE ELEPHANT 3,590m (11,780ft)
This distinctive peak, which owes its name to its shape when seen from South Kinangop, offers fine views of the **Kinangop** and over the Kinangop Plateau. It is normally tackled en route for the Kinangop. From **South Kinangop** village drive east along the winding **Thika road** to the **Kiburu forest station** where you may be obliged to pay fees, or hire a guide in lieu.

Turn left there and drive north for 22km (14mls) to a T-junction where you take a right turn on to the **Fort Hall** (Murang'a) **track**. From there continue straight past all junctions for another 2km (just over a mile), leaving your vehicle just before a steepish downhill slope.

Continue on foot along the Fort Hall Track past a small landslide and the crest of the ridge. Descend for a short section in a south-easterly direction into a clearing on your left. The climb to the Elephant starts at the top of the clearing.

Follow the path along the main ridge to a small clearing on a grassy knoll with views of the steep ridge ahead.

Avoid the game trails to the east and continue straight up the ridge through some bamboo after which the going becomes much easier. There is a **derelict hut** about three hours walk from the **roadhead** with some possible camping spots nearby — or you can sleep in the hut.

From there you continue in a northerly direction for about another hour to the Elephant, which has four summits, all of equal height. To climb all four takes about an hour.

THE KINANGOP 3,906m (12,816ft)
Perhaps the grandest and most impressive peak in the Aberdare massif, **Kinangop** stands tall among an array of large ridges, in contrast to the rolling moorland of the northern Aberdares.

The true **summit** is reached by an airy scramble up a volcanic outcrop. From the **Elephant**, climb down the col between the two westernmost summits heading west and down the gullies to reach relatively flat ground at the foot of a ridge leading to the Kinangop, a subsidiary of the main ridge. Follow this along the crest to avoid tussocks. It does not involve a great deal of switchbacking. Where the ridge merges into the mountain, strike straight up the side, and then follow the crest to the summit, the third of the volcanic outcrops.

Mountains and Hills of Maasailand

This large group of very different mountains is spread widely over southern Kenya.

SUSUA 2,357m (7,732ft)
Susua is much neglected in favour of its neighbouring volcano, **Longonot** (see 'The Land that was Eden', Part Two). This is probably because the mountain appears unimpressive from a distance, due to the relatively gentle angle of its outer slopes — although it makes for a much more pleasant walk. It is also possible to drive up into the floor of the outer of its two craters where you encounter an extraordinary sense of isolation.

The **inner crater** is concealed until you reach its very lip, with a large central plug, shaping the crater like a ring. Susua also has some fascinating **lava caves**. The outer crater is occupied by Maasai, who may ask for water. Take all water with you. Cars should not be left unattended in secluded spots, though they are probably safe when left in prominent positions by the summit roadhead. You may be able to climb Susua from the main **Narok road**, which can be reached by public transport, but it's a long hot walk to the base. Camp either by the caves for seclusion and shade, or by the roadhead for better views. Leave **Ngong town** on the right turn at the T-junction and then bear right at an offset round-about. Follow this road down into the Rift. At a small group of *dukas* turn right, signposted **'Rifle Range'**. Follow the road, ignoring both a frequently used left turn to the rifle range and a second minor left turn, to head north past the rock faces of **Ndeiya**, and a large drop in the Rift Valley floor. Follow the road down this and head towards the east side. At the base of the eastern flanks, the main track forks right, but take the left branch which leads to a small group of *dukas*. From there a rough track, with deep water runnels at the side, heads straight up for 7km (4mls). Turn left for the cave area or right to follow the track for a meandering 8km (5mls) to reach the edge of the inner crater. From the roadhead follow game tracks anti-clockwise around the rim, staying close to the rim. It takes between one and two hours to the summit and the circuit takes between 6 and 8 hours. It can be unpleasant because of the sharp lava fields.

NGONG 2,461m (8,074ft)

On a clear day, from this pleasant, undulating ridge perched on the edge of the Rift Valley, you can see some of the best views in the country — with vistas over **Ol Doinyo Sabuk**, **Mount Kenya**, **Aberdares**, **Longonot**, **Suswa**, **Shambole**, **Nkuruman Escarpment**, **Lengai**, **Mount Meru**, **Kilimanjaro**, and many others, all visible from **Lamwia** (**Ol Lemoya**), the highest point.

Unfortunately, in 1996 muggings had become not only commonplace but terrifying. A Kenya sports cyclist disappeared while training on the hills. It is essential to visit the Ngong Hills only in large and escorted parties — taking care to report to the local police station beforehand.

ESAKUT

A delightful mountain in the Rift Valley behind the Ngong Hills. Although only two hours from Nairobi, it is hardly ever climbed. It gives a pleasant ridge walk and good views. Wear boots as the ground is very stony. Watch out for ticks — the hill is notorious for them. Take water.

At Ngong town turn right at the T-junction and then bear right at an offset roundabout. Follow this road, the Ngong circular road, for 8km (5mls) from Ngong. At this point the road to Ndeiya and Susua branches off right. Continue for another 8km (5mls) and then turn right on to a rocky track and carry on for a few hundred metres to the fork left.

Follow the road for about 4km (2mls) until it suddenly heads north. Just after the sudden right hand bend is a left turn. Take this rough track, which heads initially west and then south, over a ridge of Esayeti into the basin between the two mountains. Park anywhere.

OLOOLKISAILI 1,760m (5,774ft)

This prominent hill lies to the south of the Magadi road, and offers good ridge walking, but it's a long hot climb. The hill is a roughly north-south ridge that curves round the remains of a crater to the east. Of the two summits, at both ends of the ridge, the northern one is highest by about one metre (3ft). There are three approaches. The first two give access to the north and south summits respectively, the third to the centre of the main ridge from where either summit can be tackled. In all cases, just follow the best-looking line, but be prepared for some steep ground. Take plenty of water. Boots are recommended. It is possible to stay at the *bandas* at the **Olorgesailie Prehistoric Site** (convenient for the first ascent) or camp at the foot of the climb to get a suitably early start.

SUBUGO 2,683m (8,802ft)

This is the highest point of the rolling, grassy **Loita Hills**, a pleasant range to the west of the **Nkuruman escarpment**. The easy-going underfoot and the wide open spaces make an enjoyable walk. The area is sparsely inhabited by Maasai, some of whom have settled. For rock climbers, **Lost Aloe Crag** is worthwhile. Drive west from **Narok**, turn left on to the **Keekorok road**, and after a few metres fork left again on to the **Narosura road**.

Follow this through Narosura to climb the Loita escarpment, the top of which is about 80km (50mls) from Narok.

From there a rough 4WD track used to lead up to Subugo, although the first part is very steep. Alternatively about 3km (almost 2mls) from where the road finally levels off completely is a deep valley on the right. It is possible to drive some way into there to find a suitable campsite. The campsite is at 2,133m (7,000ft) and extremely cold at night. Lost Aloe Crag lies on the north-east side of the valley, about 1.5km (almost a mile) from the road.

CHYULU 4,430m (7,134ft)

The highest point of a lovely range of hills running parallel to the Nairobi-Mombasa road offers scope for hill walking and good views of Kilimanjaro. The hills are mostly grass covered with extensive stands of forest. Conditions vary with the rains and the grass is either very high or very short. Fires occur frequently and destroy much vegetation. There is no water. *Miraa* grows in places and you'll probably see people gathering it for sale. There is a lot of game, but the elephant and buffalo are extremely shy. 4WD recommended.

NZAUI 1,830m (6,003ft)

This dramatic-looking peak is obvious to those driving to Nairobi from Mombasa. **Nzaui** is now best known for the rock climb, **'The Nose'**. The summit is covered in forest but there is a good viewpoint nearby. There is a small network of roads on the mountain, and a **forest station** with a pleasant **rest house**, recently repaired by the Mountain Club of Kenya. There is a water supply at the rest house which also has excellent camping nearby. Nzaui makes a pleasant, if long, day trip, or a good lazy weekend. Drive down the Mombasa road to Emali and turn left along a murram road for several kilometres, through **Matiliku market**, continuing north with the rock face to your right. A little before **Nziu village** a track turns right on the crest of the hill. A battered **signpost** facing the other way is marked 'Nzaui Forest, Kyense Highway, 8mls'. Follow the track, crossing a wide sandy **river bed** and soon after turn right. The track is very stony in places and can be impassable after heavy rains. It is usually passable by 4WD or high clearance cars. After traversing horizontally for a km or two (about a mile) it gradually climbs to the summit. Near the top the track divides: the left branch leads to the Rest House, and the right to the **summit**.

Taita Hills

The Taita Hills are surprisingly green, lush, rugged, and give good views. Except for their highest peaks they are densely inhabited by friendly people. There are no security problems.

VURIA 2,209m (7,248ft)
The highest point in the Taitas, this excellent viewpoint looks out over **Kasigau**, **Mawenzi**, **Kibo**, **Ngulia** and the **Chyulus**. The plains of **Tsavo** seem to be vertically below. From **Voi** take the **Taveta road** past **Bura**. About one km after the Bura turnoff go right to follow a murram road up a dramatic but pretty valley.

Yala is the rock peak to the right of the valley head: **Vuria**, the highest point, is to the left. Over 15km (9mls) from the main road, some *dukas* mark the col at the head of the valley. Turn left to drive right round the northern flank of Vuria. After just over 3km (2mls) a track goes off left. It is generally good, but steep and leads 3km (almost 2mls) to the **radio station** on the **summit**. It is pleasant to camp by the track on the last but one bend below the top, though it can be extremely cold. The best views are directly away from the summit at the last bend.

KASIGAU 1,641m (5,383ft)
Standing completely alone on the plains south of **Voi**, this impressive mountain is steep on all sides and features a number of large precipices.

Guides can be hired from the chief's office or possibly the forest post. The best place to camp is a few kms along the **Mwatate-Rukanga** road in clearings in the bush.

The drive round **Kasigau** is recommended. The walk starts in **Rukanga village**. Drive down the **Mombasa road** 30km (20mls) south of the **Voi** to **Maungu** turnoff and turn right. Alternatively, from the Taitas, turn south off the **Voi-Taveta** road onto an unlikely track 500m east of the Wundanyi turnoff. After 5km (3mls) turn left then right between some buildings, and look for signs to '**Kasigau Road**' to avoid getting lost in the sisal. From the main road, walk along the branch going to the town centre, then bear right to follow a water pipe into a forested gully to the right of a large castle-like buttress. Water is available at the head of the pipe. Climb steeply through the forest to the main ridge. At this point you may find you have circled round behind the ridge without realizing it, so turn right, not left as you might expect. Follow the ridge through the forest, until a final steep ascent brings you to the summit. It is worth reaching the tops of some buttresses for the views.

Climbing and Trekking Advisory

Any reasonably fit person can trek, but the fitter you are, the more you will enjoy it. Do as much walking and exercise as possible to prepare yourself for Kenya's highland trails. The best time for climbing or trekking is in the dry seasons — January to March, and July to October. You can organize your trip through one of Kenya's specialized tour operators (see Listings).

Trekking demands strong, comfortable boots with good soles. Higher up, good boots are essential, and in snow or ice these should be large enough to allow for one or two layers of heavy woollen or cotton — never nylon — socks. Carry several pairs. Wearing light shoes or sneakers after the day's walk help to relax your feet.

Loose-fitting trousers, hiking shorts or, for women, wrap-around skirts are ideal. It is better to wear two light layers of clothing than one thick one. If you get too hot, you can peel off a layer. At very high altitudes wear thermal underwear. Your pack should be as small as possible, light and easy to open. The following gear is recommended: Two pairs of woollen or corduroy trousers or skirts; two warm sweaters; three drip-dry shirts or T-shirts; ski or thermal underwear; at least half-a-dozen pairs of woollen socks; one pair of walking shoes; one extra pair of sandals; light casual shoes or sneakers; woollen hat; gloves or mittens; a strong, warm sleeping bag with hood; a thin sheet of foam rubber for a mattress; padded anorak or parka; a plastic raincoat; sunglasses and sun lotion; toilet gear; towels; medical kit; water bottle; and a light day pack. It is better to carry too many clothes. Drip-dry fabrics are best.

Your medical kit should include pain killers (for headaches); mild sleeping pills (for insomnia); streptomycin (for diarrhoea); septram (for bacillary dysentery); tinidozole (for amoebic dysentery); throat lozenges and cough drops; eye ointment or drops; one broad spectrum antibiotic; alcohol (for massaging feet to prevent blisters); blister pads; bandages and elastic plasters; antiseptic and cotton; sun block; and a transparent lip salve.

In addition, most of which can be bought in Kenya, you should carry food, torch, candles, lighter, pocket-knife, scissors, spare laces, string, safety pins, toilet paper, and plastic bags to protect food, wrap up wet or dirty clothes, and take away your litter. Your tent and photographic equipment may be cheaper at home. Also carry high-energy food — chocolate, dried fruit, nuts — and whisky, brandy or vodka for a soothing nightcap.

Cooking and eating utensils are normally provided by the trekking agency and are carried by porters. Lock your bag against theft or accidental loss. Water is contaminated below 2,900m (9,500ft) so don't drink from streams. Chlorine is not effective against amoebic cysts. All water should be well boiled or treated. Walk at your own pace. Drink as much liquid as possible to combat high altitude and dehydration. Never wait for blisters. Pamper your feet with an alcohol massage.

Mountain Sickness

Both trekkers and climbers are at risk of mountain sickness. Sudden ascents above 3,600m (12,000ft) and more, without acclimatization, can lead to an accumulation of water, on the lungs or the brain. If this occurs it is *essential* to descend immediately to seek medical attention. Untreated, it can be fatal. Pulmonary oedema is characterized by breathlessness and a persistent cough, even when resting, accompanied by congestion of the chest. If these symptoms appear, descend at once. Cerebral oedema is less common. Its symptoms are extreme tiredness, vomiting, severe headaches, staggering when walking, abnormal speech and behaviour, drowsiness and even coma. Victims must descend at once. There have been more cases of mountain sickness on Mount Kenya than on any other mountain, mainly because of the quick ascent to extreme heights. Youth, strength and fitness make no difference. Above 3,000m (9,840ft) the air is thinner. Plan frequent rest days between 3,700 and 4,300m (12,000-14,000ft), sleeping at the same altitude for at least two nights. Climb higher during the day but always descend to the same level to sleep. Never pitch camp more than 450m (1,500ft) higher in any one day

At 4,300m (14,108ft) the body requires three to four litres (five-seven pints) of liquid a day. At low altitude try to drink at least a litre (two pints) a day. If you suffer early mountain sickness, go no higher. If more serious symptoms appear, descend immediately to a lower elevation. Mild symptoms should clear in between one and two days. Some victims are incapable of making correct decisions and you may have to force them to go down against their will. The Mount Kenya National Park runs a Mountain Rescue Team.

Kenya's Mountains, Rivers, Lakes and Falls

Mount Kenya:
Batian 5,199m, Nelion 5,188m, Lenana 4,985m.

Mount Elgon:
Wagagai 4,322m, Sudek 4,310m, Koitobos 4,231m.

Aberdare Range:
Lesatima 3,999m, Kinangop 3,906m, Kipipiri 3,349m. Table Mountain 3,971m

Cherangani Hills:
Chemnirot 3,505m, Kalelaigelat 3,380m, Chepkotet 3,370m, Kaisungur 3,167m

Sekerr Range:
Mtelo 3,325m.

Mau Range:
Melili 3,098m.
Londiani 3,011m.

Ndoto Mountains:
Bokhol 2,534m.
Alimisian 2,637m.

Nyambene Range:
Itiani 2,513m.

Ngong Hills:
Lamwia (Ol Lemoya) 2,461m.

Taita Hills:
Vuria **2,209m.**

Individual peaks
Nyiru 2,752m.
Longonot 2,776m.
Supuko 2,067m.
Ol Doinyo Orok 2,553m.
Chyulu Hills 4,430m.
Ol Doinyo Sapuk 2,146 m.

Kenya's major rivers
Tana 708km; Athi-Galana-Sabaki 547 km; Mara 290km; Nzoia 258km; Turkwel-Suam 354km; Arror-Kerio 350km; Ewaso Nyiro (North) 330-km; Voi 210km; Yala 180km; Ewaso Nyiro (South) 140km; Melawa 110km; Miriu 110km; Sondhu 110km; Kuja 90km.

Kenya's major lakes
Victoria 67,493 sq km; Turkana 6,405 sq km; Baringo 129 sq km; Naivasha 114-991 sq km; Magadi 104 sq km; Amboseli 0-114 sq km; Jipe 40 sq km; Bogoria 34 sq km; Nakuru 5-30 sq km; Elmenteita 18 sq km.

Kenya's major waterfalls
Gura 273m; Seven Forks (Kindaruma) 135m; Nyahururu (Thomson's) 73m; Swift-Rutherford 67m; Webuye (Broderick) 52m; Yala 40m; Selby 35m; Chania 25m; Thika 25m.

PART FOUR: BUSINESS KENYA

The Economy

Kenya's 1994 gross domestic product (GDP) was Ksh 322,340 million. The government encourages investment and introduced significant economic reforms in an attempt to accelerate economic growth and increase external trade. The reforms include privatization of state corporations, removal of most regulatory constraints, liberalization of foreign-exchange controls and the creation of various economic incentives. The economy is based primarily on agriculture.

Real GDP has declined over the past five years. The slowing of the country's economic growth was largely the result of a prolonged drought that reduced agricultural output, high inflation resulting from excess growth in money supply and depreciation of the Kenya shilling. However, the economy is recovering; a GDP growth rate of three per cent was recorded in 1994.

This recent expansion can be attributed to improved weather and the implementation of appropriate macroeconomic reforms, including tighter monetary policy, liberalization of foreign-exchange controls and trade regimes, and deregulation of several sectors of the economy.

The high inflation and interest rates reported in 1993 and 1994 declined in 1995 following measures taken by the government to contain the money supply.

There are no reliable statistics for unemployment, mainly because of difficulties in assessing the scale of the informal (*jua kali*) sector. However, unemployment and under-employment are both high. Approximately one million people are unemployed out of a labour force of close to ten million. It is estimated that of the nine million employed, around 1.2 million are engaged in the informal sector, and six million in agricultural activities.

The official currency in Kenya is the Kenya shilling which floats freely, although the Central Bank of Kenya (CBK) exercises control over the shilling's exchange rate by dealing in foreign currency.

Kenya has a free enterprise economy. State intervention is limited to semi-autonomous agencies that generally support services and infrastructure, and serve as marketing, administrative and advisory boards. The economy is based primarily on agriculture, which contributes almost 30 per cent of GDP.

Tourism and light industries are becoming increasingly significant. Kenya's principal crops are coffee and tea, which are also the country's major exports, together with cereals, sugar and horticultural crops, such as cut flowers, pineapples, French beans, and other fruits and vegetables. Small quantities of pyrethrum, a locally grown natural insecticide, are also exported. Several light industries and canning factories have been started, located mainly in Nairobi, Mombasa and Thika.

Motor vehicle assembly plants and an oil refinery supply local and export markets. Fuel deliveries are made by pipeline from the Mombasa refinery to Nairobi and Kisumu. Oil is Kenya's principal import. Several international oil companies have expressed interest in drilling for oil in Northern Kenya.

Tourism is Kenya's largest source of foreign exchange, with gross receipts in 1994 of an estimated US$450 million. The country's infrastructure, particularly energy, roads and water supply — which directly affect tourism — needs some improvement. Problems of poor personal security must also be addressed. However, despite these shortcomings, gross tourism earnings were expected to reach US$470 million in 1996.

Many commercial banks, building societies and financial institutions, including branches of several US, Asian and European banks, operate in Kenya.

The government has in the past participated in commercial enterprises. But in a 1992 policy paper on the reform and privatization of public enterprises, it identified 207 non-strategic commercial organizations for privatization.

The majority of these companies operate in the following sectors: cement, sugar, hotels, banking, textiles, supermarkets, wine and spirits imports, insurance and property. After privatisation, this will leave only 33 'strategic' enterprises, including those involved in energy, railways and telecommunications, under state control. The government intends to complete the entire privatization programme by the end of 1997.

Government and Business

Governmental policy encourages growth of the business sector by reducing controls over some industries, cutting direct tax rates and providing financial incentives, particularly to export-oriented businesses. Industries still regulated by the government include banking and finance, insurance, health and utilities.

All businesses must comply with various laws relating to antitrust, labour relations, environmental protection, consumer protection and civil rights. Antitrust laws prohibit monopolies and other unfair business practices. Labour laws regulate minimum wages, conditions of employment (such as dismissal, working hours and safety), discrimination and collective bargaining.

The Kenya Bureau of Standards is responsible for consumer protection with respect to product quality. Local governments regulate town plans by establishing zones for different purposes.

Environmental Law

There is currently no comprehensive law on environment and development in Kenya. The Kenya National Environment Action Plan — NEAP — was published by the Ministry of Environment and Natural Resources in June 1994. The plan sets out the government's policy objectives and strategies and discusses sectoral issues, including pollution control and waste management.

The NEAP recognises that, as a consequence of outdated provisions and weak deterrents, existing legislation is often difficult to enforce and therefore advocates the creation of a single institution with the legal authority to co-ordinate the management of environmental resources.

The government also recognizes the need to harmonize, update and strengthen existing laws for the sustainable management of natural resources. Hence a two-stage process has been initiated, with the technical financial assistance of the United Nations Environment Programme, to review the laws.

The first stage will entail the development of new 'umbrella' legislation; the second stage will include the review of current sectoral legislation to ensure that it conforms to the umbrella legislation. Because such legislation transcends territorial boundaries — measures taken in one country will affect its neighbours — the government is collaborating with the governments of Uganda and Tanzania to develop regional environmental protection legislation.

Financial Sector

Kenya has a well-developed financial system comprising the CBK, commercial banks, non-bank financial institutions, development finance institutions, building societies, savings and credit societies, and insurance companies.

The CBK is responsible for licensing and supervising commercial banks and other financial institutions. It also issues currency and is the government's bank and main lender.

Investors (both foreign and domestic) may obtain funds from Kenya's commercial banks, non-bank financial institutions, insurance companies, building societies and savings and credit societies.

Development finance institutions, owned mainly by the government and international lending organizations, provide funds for industrial and agricultural development. A number of

financial institutions became insolvent in 1986 and 1993. The CBK is now exercising strict controls over these institutions.

Among the strengthened controls are the following:
• Maximum deposit-taking capacity: Paid-up capital and unimpaired reserves should not be less than 7.5 per cent of deposit liability.
• Maximum advance limit: Lending to any one person should not exceed 100 per cent of share capital and unimpaired reserves.
• Minimum liquidity level: Liquidity reserves should be 20 per cent of deposit obligations.
• Establishment of deposit protection fund.
• Conversion to banks of non-bank financial institutions: Non-bank financial institutions (NBFI) are encouraged to convert into banks. Stricter controls apply to the NBFI; for example, the minimum liquidity level is 24 per cent, compared with 20 per cent for banks.

Most of the large commercial banks are branches or subsidiaries of foreign banks from Europe, the United States and Asia. Foreign banks must be approved by the Ministry of Finance before commencing operations.

Financial institutions are controlled by the Ministry of Finance through acts of parliament.

Securities Exchange

Kenya's only stock exchange, the Nairobi Stock Exchange (NSE), is the third-largest stock market in sub-Saharan Africa (after South Africa and Zimbabwe). Established in 1954, it is also one of the oldest in Africa. The exchange is a limited liability company licensed by Kenya's Capital Markets Authority (CMA); the operations of the CMA are regulated by the Capital Markets Authority Act.

The restructuring of the NSE in 1992 involved the establishment of a permanent secretariat, the creation of a trading floor and the change to a more modern, 'open outcry' trading system. The market has responded with significant increases in turnover and capitalization; turnover rose from 5.8 million shares (worth Ksh 164 million) in 1992 to 42.8 million shares (worth Ksh 2,710 million) in 1994.

Essential Industries

Agriculture is Kenya's major economic sector, accounting (with forestry and fishing) for 30 per cent of GDP and 19 per cent of wage employment in the formal sector. Its share of informal-sector jobs is higher, although no data are available. More than half of agricultural output is for subsistence, while two cash crops, tea and coffee, together with horticulture, provided 52 per cent of merchandise export revenue in 1993.

Manufacturing is the second-largest sector,

contributing 14 per cent of GDP. Agro-processing is this sector's major industry. Other significant industries include vehicle assembly, rubber and plastic products, and petroleum refining.

The largest industries in the service sector are the following: trade (imports and exports), restaurants and hotels, which together account for around 15 per cent of GDP; finance, insurance, real estate and business services which, combined, constituted nine per cent; and government services, which account for 16 per cent.

Natural Resources

Kenya's main source of energy is oil, which accounts for 80 per cent of total commercial energy. Electricity, coal, fuelwood and solar and wind energy account for the balance. Kenya has no known oil reserves and relies on imported oil.

At the end of 1994 the government announced the deregulation of the oil industry, giving oil companies the right to set their own pump prices and import their own finished products. The country's sole oil refinery, located in Mombasa, will be protected for two years by a suspended duty of 50 cents a litre on finished products (other than jet and illuminating kerosene and automotive diesel).

Electricity is the second most widely used source of energy by commercial and industrial establishments and households. It is generated from hydro, thermal and geothermal plants.

Kenya produces 95 per cent of its electricity requirement and imports the balance from Uganda.

The country is in the process of implementing some power stations and is expected to be self-sufficient in power when the projects are complete (most likely before the end of the century). Most rural areas do not have electricity; however, the government is in the process of implementing a rural electrification programme.

Kenya has limited mineral resources. The mining and quarrying sector accounts for just 0.3 per cent of GDP, and the main mineral resources are soda ash, fluorspar, salt and limestone. Soda ash and fluorspar are exported, as is cement (which the country reports under industrial, not mineral, output). Other natural resources include water, fisheries and wildlife, which attract many tourists.

Foreign Trade

Kenya's leading exports are agricultural products, both primary and processed, including coffee, tea, horticultural products and pyrethrum extract. Non-agricultural exports include petroleum products, soda ash and cement.

The United Kingdom is the leading market for Kenyan goods and the second-largest supplier of imports. The UAE is the largest; it provides most of Kenya's crude oil requirements.

The United Kingdom's prominence is the result of the presence of several large UK-based multinationals in Kenya. The European Union (EU) as a whole purchased 36 per cent of total exports in 1993 and was the origin of 35 per cent of imports. Regional trade has increased in importance, particularly Kenyan exports to members of the Preferential Trade Area (PTA), which encompasses 21 Central and East African countries. Other important trading partners are Japan and Germany.

Trade Associations

In November 1994 the 21 member nations of the PTA and the 10 member nations of the Southern Africa Development Community (SADC) ratified a treaty for the Common Market for Eastern and Southern Africa (COMESA), bringing the 31 countries together into one trading bloc. The countries aim to have a full-fledged common market in operation by 2000 and common currency agreements in place by 2020.

Kenya, along with Uganda and Tanzania, has signed a protocol for the East African Co-operation Council. The association, when fully operational, is intended to ease the free movement of people and goods among the three countries. Discussions are under way on the harmonization of tariffs. Kenya's membership in international trade associations includes the following:

• The Lome Convention: Under this association, exports from Kenya, as well as from 68 other African, Caribbean and Pacific states, entering the EU are entitled to duty reductions or exemptions and freedom from all quota restrictions. Trade preferences include duty-free entry of all industrial products and a wide range of agricultural goods.

• Generalized System of Preferences (GSP): Under the GSP, a wide range of Kenya's manufactured products is entitled to preferential duty treatment in the United States, Japan, Canada, Switzerland, Norway, Sweden, Finland, Australia, Austria, New Zealand and most East European countries.

In addition, no quantitative restrictions are applicable to Kenyan exports of the goods eligible for GSP treatment.

Investment

Exchange controls were progressively abolished between 1994-96 as part of the continued liberalization of the Kenyan economy.

Current regulations allow for the free flow of capital and repatriation of funds subject to payment of applicable taxes. There are no restrictions on residents' holding of foreign currency. However, individuals entering or leaving the country with foreign currency in excess of the equivalent of US$5,000 are required to declare it at the point of entry or departure. Commercial banks must also report foreign-currency transactions in excess of the equivalent of US$5,000 to the Central Bank of Kenya (CBK), which entails completion of a simple statistical form.

Residents of Kenya may freely invest up to a maximum of US$500,000 outside the country; commercial banks may process such applications without reference to the CBK. Investments involving funds in excess of this amount require CBK approval, which is usually granted without undue delay for all bona fide transactions.

Although payments for technical, management, royalty and patent fees are freely remittable, the relevant agreements and renewals are subject to approval by the Ministry of Finance's Capital Issue Committee.

The Finance Bill for 1995-1996 proposed the repeal of the Exchange Control Act which would result in the full liberalization of the nation's economy, and allow the free movement of capital. It is likely, however, that the government will retain some reserve powers.

Foreign Investment

Business sectors that have generally been reserved for Kenyans (through the trade licensing system) include minor service areas, distribution channels, basic transport and, until recently, telecommunications and power generation. The government has announced that it would welcome foreign participation in the latter two sectors.

Foreigners or foreign-owned companies acquiring real estate except for agricultural land or sea-front plots face no restrictions. No foreigner may acquire agricultural land without presidential approval, which is granted only in exceptional cases.

There is also strict control in the mining and oil sectors. Approval for foreign investment depends on the type and scale of operation, geographical location, environmental impact, employment potential and potential benefits for the state and the district. Negotiations are usually lengthy.

Foreign ownership in listed Kenyan companies is generally restricted to 40 per cent in the aggregate and five per cent for each individual investor. Foreign investors are required to obtain approval from the Ministry of Finance and trade licences appropriate to the nature of the business.

Incentives

The investment allowance is designed to encourage industrial growth and attract foreign investment. The allowance takes the form of a deduc-

tion from taxable income. It is granted for capital expenditure on hotels and manufacturing.

From 1 January 1995, the rate of the allowance was 60 per cent. For enterprises manufacturing under bond the rate is 100 per cent. From 1 January 1996, an enterprise may claim a 100 per cent investment allowance for both new and old machinery in any factory that the customs authorities have licensed for manufacturing under bond for export. This allowance is not withdrawn even if the assets are sold within five years of the year of deduction.

A 40 per cent allowance is granted for purchases by residents of new ships larger than 495 tons. However, if such a ship is sold within five years after the end of the year of the deduction, the allowance is withdrawn and the amount deducted is treated as taxable income.

Exemption from Customs Duties and VAT

Certain imports may be exempt from customs duties and value-added tax (VAT). Such imports include capital goods and plant and machinery acquired for projects with a net foreign-exchange savings or earnings, and capital goods for investment in small-scale industries. The Ministry of Finance must approve the exemption.

Materials imported for use in manufacturing for export are eligible for duty remission under a duty exemption scheme, which is administered by the Export Promotion Programmes Office (EPPO) of the Ministry of Finance.

To attract large-scale foreign investment, the government allows importers of approved capital goods to set off import duty paid on such goods against the income tax liability of the project. To qualify, a project must involve expenditure on productive physical assets in excess of US$5 million within a two-year period and must generate net economic benefits to Kenya.

Companies may negotiate tax exemptions and reductions on contracts with government or quasi-government institutions. These concessions vary according to the benefits to the Kenyan economy expected to result from the contract and the extent to which contract financing is provided from foreign aid.

To encourage manufacturing for export, in 1989 the government instituted an in-bond programme open to operations producing entirely for export. Enterprises operating under the programme are exempt from all customs duties and VAT on plant, machinery and equipment, raw materials, components and any other imported inputs. Such enterprises are eligible for a 100 per cent investment allowance and are exempt from all export taxes and levies. Currently, enterprises manufacturing under bond are licensed to operate in Eldoret, Kisumu, Mombasa, Nairobi, Nakuru, Nyeri and Thika, or within the immediate environs of these localities.

The Export Processing Zones Act of 1990 introduced the Export Processing Zones (EPZ) scheme. Six EPZs have been established, and another three are at an advanced stage of development. The Export Processing Zone Authority, which regulates the operations of the EPZs, has approved over 40 enterprises to operate in the zones.

Enterprises operating in the EPZs enjoy the following benefits:
• A 10-year tax holiday and a reduced 25 per cent tax rate for the following 10 years.
• Exemption from withholding taxes on payments to non-residents during the first 10 years;
• Exemption from import duties on machinery, raw materials and intermediate inputs;
• Exemption from import and export quotas;
• Exemption from VAT;
• Exemption from exchange controls; and
• Unrestricted employment of foreigners in managerial, technical and training positions.

The government created the Investment Promotion Centre (IPC) to serve as the primary contact point for investors. The IPC provides information to potential investors on various matters, including the following:
• General investment climate;
• Details of investment rules and procedures;
• Major investment opportunities; and
• Obtaining financing.

The IPC assists in arranging site visits and suggests ways to succeed in the Kenyan business environment. The IPC also provides support services to investors and recommends necessary policy and legal reforms.

Kenya as a Regional Centre

Kenya is a suitable location for a regional office for operations in Eastern and Central Africa. It has the most developed infrastructure in the area, including efficient transportation and communication systems as well as readily available accommodation for expatriates. The country has a large number of banks and financial institutions, and funds may be easily obtained without restriction.

Commercial banks and financial institutions provide the major sources of finance for foreign investors. In 1996 there were 37 commercial banks, 44 non-bank financial institutions, 43 insurance companies, 6 development finance institutions and 5 building societies. The non-bank financial institutions are being pressured by the government to convert into commercial banks by merging either with their parent banks or with one another, or by applying to become banks themselves.

Interest rates have in the past been controlled by the government but commercial banks are now free to set their own interest and exchange rates, depending on supply and demand.

All of the usual short-term funding facilities — including overdrafts, short-term loans, inter-company borrowing, discounting of trade bills, commercial paper, and factoring — are available from Kenya's commercial banks and non-bank financial institutions. The most common instruments are overdrafts and short-term loans. Medium- and long-term local-currency financing remains largely the preserve of the development finance institutions and is still scarce. Foreign-currency financing for the medium and long term is available through bilateral or multilateral lenders, often the development finance institutions. Insurance companies also lend for construction and land acquisition. Savings and credit societies provide both short- and medium-term funds to members.

Funds may also be obtained from the capital market (the Nairobi Stock Exchange) with the approval of the Capital Markets Authority.

There are no government controls over lending to foreign investors. Lending institutions exercise their normal credit policy in assessing the viability of potential loan proposals; these institutions usually require collateral for the loan and financial projections for the project.

There are currently no credit guarantees in operation. However, the Ministry of Finance is in the process of establishing an export credit guarantee scheme.

Importing and Exporting

Import licensing was virtually abolished in 1993, but the Imports, Exports and Essential Supplies (Imports) (Amendment) Order 1993 still prohibits the import of certain goods completely and requires that others be subject to prior approval or comply with technical, sanitary, health and environmental conditions.

Those that are prohibited include bones, horn, teeth and ivory of animals on the endangered species list, coral and seashells, and nuclear and other toxic waste. Goods subject to prior approval include weapons, ammunition and fireworks, and those that must comply with various standards include live animals, fish, plants and certain chemicals. The liberalization is intended to make local manufacturers more competitive and to increase the diversity of available goods.

The Ministry of Finance may control imports and exports by imposing variable tariffs in accordance with the World Trade Organization regulations.

There are no restrictions on exports; however, the Imports, Exports and Essential Supplies (Exports) (Amendment) (No 2) Order 1994 requires exporters of certain goods to obtain a licence. Such goods include the following: military equipment and munitions; special engines; vessels, aviation and transport equipment and vehicles, and parts thereof; antiques and other works of art; live animals other than livestock and pets; seashells and coral; and ivory, rhinoceros horn and other products of endangered species. Commercial banks are required to submit to the CBK statistical information with respect to all exports and export proceeds channelled through them.

Tariffs are classified according to the Harmonised Commodity Description and Coding System. Under the June 1995 budget, the number of rates was reduced from seven to six; the rates now range from 40 per cent to 0 per cent.

Goods imported from other Preferential Trade Area (PTA) countries carry duties equal to 40 per cent of the regular tariff rate. The PTA countries plan to eliminate all tariffs on intra-PTA trade by 2000, as well as establish a common external tariff with a maximum rate of 30 per cent. Duties are usually levied on the cost, insurance and freight (CIF) invoice price of goods. Documents required for imports include a certificate of origin, commercial invoice, shipping documents and pre-shipment inspection certificate. Clearing agents assist with documentation and filing procedures for both imports and exports.

Anti-dumping Regulations

Goods considered to have been dumped in Kenya and goods subsidized by a government or other authority outside Kenya are subject to a number of variable anti-dumping duties. The duties were introduced in 1994 — on maize, sugar, iron, steel, tyres, tubes, paper, newsprint and paper bags — to protect farmers and local manufacturers from subsidized imports. Goods are regarded as having been dumped if the export price from the country in which the goods originated is less than the fair market price of the goods in that country. No quotas are imposed on any products.

Intellectual Property

Patent, trademark and industrial design laws follow the British pattern. Kenya is a member of the following: The Paris Convention for the Protection of Industrial Property, 1883-1967; the Convention Establishing the World Intellectual Property Organization, 1967; the Patent Co-operation Treaty, 1970; The Africa Regional Industrial Property Organization Protocol, 1984; and the Berne Convention (signed 1993).

The Industrial Property Act (IPA) of 1989 provides for registration of patents, utility designs and industrial designs in Kenya, but the sophisticated enforcement and administration required to implement the regulations are generally lacking.

Application for a patent is made by the owner or the owner's legal agent to the director of the Kenya Industrial Property Office (KIPO) at the Ministry of Research, Technical Training and Technology. The application must contain details about the applicant and about the inventor's claims, one or more drawings (if necessary), an abstract and, if applicable, a declaration claiming priority and a declaration of novelty.

Applications are subject to an international search and to an examination as to substance and novelty. Upon acceptance of the application, a patent is granted, issued, registered and advertised in the Kenya Gazette.

The duration of a patent is seven years, effective from the filing date. A patent may be renewed for two five-year periods.

Trademark applications may be filed with the Registrar of Trademarks by the owner or owner's legal representative. The application is examined and advertised in the Kenya Gazette; if no objection follows within 60 days from the advertisement, the trademark will be registered. Trademarks are valid for seven years from the date of the original application and renewable for 14-year periods thereafter. If a mark is not used for five years, application may be made for its removal from the register.

Copyrights

Registration of copyrights is not required but is possible by registering the work with the appropriate association, such as The Music Copyright Society of Kenya. A number of such associations are co-operating with the Registrar-General (in the attorney-general's office) to establish a tribunal to hear complaints of copyright infringement. The tribunal, which will help plaintiffs avoid the costly process of High Court resolution, is not yet in operation.

Copyrights are conveyed under the Copyright Act. Works eligible for protection include literary works, musical works, artistic works, audio-visual works, sound recordings, broadcasts and programme-carrying signals.

Copyrights are conferred to individuals who are citizens or residents of Kenya or corporate bodies incorporated under or in accordance with the laws of Kenya. Protection in certain types of copyright is extended to nationals of countries that are parties to the 'Universal Copyright Convention' and to the 'Convention for the Protection of Producers of Phonograms against Unauthorised Duplication of their Phonograms', to which Kenya is a party.

Protection is granted for a period of 50 years from the first year of publication or broadcast, and 50 years after the death of the author in case of literary, musical and artistic works other than photographs. Photographs are protected for a period of 50 years from the year the work was made lawfully accessible to the public.

Computer Technology

Computer technology is not yet well developed in Kenya. Rights are in accordance with the requirements of the supplier of the respective technology. Industrial design applications should be made to the director of KIPO. The application must be accompanied by four samples or photographic representations and drawings. Industrial design licences are valid for five years from the date of application and may be renewed for two consecutive periods of five years.

Licensing Arrangements

Many overseas manufacturers have licensed established Kenyan companies to produce their products, especially cosmetics, pharmaceuticals, soaps, detergents, food and household items. These arrangements are often temporary, with a successful operation leading to production by the licensor itself or to outright acquisition of the brand by the licensee. Licensing arrangements can also give overseas firms access to the PTA.

At present all licensing agreements involving remittance of royalties and fees must be approved by the CBK, which in turn refers them to KIPO. This office will allow royalties of up to two per cent of net invoiced sales under trademark licensing agreements in which the trademarks are registered in Kenya. In certain cases it will agree to royalties of up to three per cent of net invoiced sales where export sales of the licensed goods are shown to earn substantial foreign exchange for Kenya. KIPO will agree to similar fees for patent and design licenses, but only if the patent and designs are registered in Kenya.

Withholding tax of 20 per cent of the gross amount of royalties is deductible under the Income Tax Act from any royalties payable under a licensing agreement. Different withholding tax rates may apply to management and technical know-how fees, depending on the nature of the service supplied.

Companies

The provisions concerning public and private limited liability companies are contained in Kenya's Companies Act (revised 1978), which is modelled closely on the UK Companies Act 1948, before amendments.

A limited liability company (LLC) is an independent legal entity. A shareholder's liability for any deficiency on a winding up of a company's affairs is usually limited to the amount, if any, unpaid on his or her shares. Shares may be transferred without affecting the continuity of the business.

Limited liability companies may be public or private. A private company is prohibited from inviting the general public to subscribe to its shares. It may not have more than 50 members (excluding past and present employees), and its shares are not freely transferable, even between members. A public company, as its name suggests, may offer its shares to the general public. There is no limit on the maximum number of shareholders, but it must have a minimum of seven. Its shares are freely transferable.

The law relating to partnerships is contained in the Partnership Act 1962. A partnership is restricted to a maximum of 20 persons; if this number is exceeded, the partnership must convert into a company and be registered under the Companies Act. A partnership agreement need not be formal (filing in a public registry is not even required) but must generally be in writing.

If the partnership does not trade under the names of the partners, its trading names must be registered under the Business Names Act 1962.

A limited partnership may be formed when at least one partner is a general partner liable without limit for all the firm's debts. A limited partner may not take part in the enterprise's management. Limited partnerships are governed by the Limited Partnership Act 1962, which requires them to be registered with the Registrar of Companies.

The death, resignation or retirement of any individual partner dissolves a partnership unless, as is generally the case, the partnership agreement provides otherwise.

A partnership is not regarded as a separate taxable entity or assessed as such although it must file an income tax return (also referred to as a return of income). Once the taxable income of a partnership has been determined, it is allocated among the partners in accordance with their profit-sharing ratio. Partners are taxed on their share of taxable income together with any taxable income they have received from other sources.

Joint Ventures

Joint ventures may be conducted as partnerships or organized as limited liability companies in which all parties are shareholders. Trusts may trade as unit trusts. Members of the public may acquire interest in unit trusts, which must buy back the interest if requested by the holder.

Unit trusts are exempt from income tax except for payment of withholding tax on interest income and dividends as a resident person.

There are no restrictions on the establishment of a branch of a non-resident company except that it must be recorded with the Registrar of Companies. The following documents must be submitted to the registrar:

• Certified copy of the company's memorandum and articles of association or equivalent constitution documents (with an English translation if necessary);
• Names, addresses, nationalities and occupations of the company's directors and secretary;
• Statement of initial capital, and existing mortgages and charges, if any, incurred by the company in Kenya;
• Names and addresses of one or more Kenyan residents who are authorised to accept legal notices on the company's behalf; and
• Address of the company's registered principal office.

If satisfied that these documents and particulars comply with the provisions of the Companies Act, the registrar issues a certificate of compliance.

Branches may repatriate management and

other fees and may use local overdraft facilities in the same way as subsidiary companies. Initial losses may be written off against the parent company's taxable income. A higher rate of corporation tax (42.5 per cent) is applicable to branches of non-resident companies than to resident companies (35 per cent), but dividends to non-resident shareholders attract a withholding tax of 10 per cent, which does not apply to remittance of branch profits.

The private limited liability company, rather than a branch or partnership, is the preferred form for most foreign investors establishing subsidiaries in Kenya. Kenyan law does not require private companies to issue financial statements or to accord equal voting rights to all shareholders. Other advantages of setting up a company include limited liability and lower tax rates.

A foreign investor may prefer to open a branch in cases in which operations are expected to be minimal. A company's name is reserved and approved by the Registrar of Companies. To form a company, the founding members (also known as subscribers), who may be nominees for the actual shareholders, must sign the memorandum and articles of association.

The memorandum states the company's name and objectives, the location of its registered office (which must be in Kenya), its limited liability status and the amount of authorized share capital. The articles of association are the company's bylaws, which regulate its internal management and the rights of its members.

The signed memorandum and articles, together with other statutory forms, are submitted to the Registrar of Companies in Nairobi. If the registrar is satisfied with the documents, he or she issues a certificate of incorporation, which brings the company into existence. A private company may commence business upon receipt of the certificate of incorporation. A public company, however, may not start operations or borrow money until a certificate of entitlement to commence business has been issued by the registrar, which generally follows additional formalities.

It normally takes approximately six weeks to complete the steps required to establish a company in Kenya, although formation can be completed in a shorter period of time if necessary.

The formation cost for a small private company is approximately Ksh 50,000, including stamp duties and legal fees. Stamp duty is charged at a rate of 1 per cent on the authorized share capital. The maximum registration fee is Ksh 4,500.

The minimum number of founder members is two, with a maximum of 50, for a private company, and seven for a public company.

No minimum share capital is prescribed by law for a limited liability company. However, the minimum capital requirement for quotation of a public company on the Nairobi Stock Exchange is Ksh 2 million. All authorized share capital need not be issued, and all issued share capital need not to be paid up. The directors do, however, occasionally make calls on members for unpaid contributions. Directors are not required to be Kenyan nationals or residents. In general, a director need not be a shareholder, although in some cases the articles of association may require a director to hold a specified number of shares to qualify for appointment.

All companies are required to appoint an auditor to disclose the annual financial statements to the shareholders.

The company's first auditor may be appointed by the directors subject to confirmation by the shareholders at the first annual general meeting. Thereafter the auditor is reappointed automatically unless he or she resigns or becomes unqualified to perform his or her duties or the shareholders appoint a replacement. The auditor must be independent of the company being audited and must hold a practising certificate issued by the Registration of Accountants Board.

Every limited liability company must file an annual return with the Registrar of Companies. The return contains the names of directors, the company secretary, shareholders and details of charges against its property.

In addition, public companies must file their annual financial statements with the registrar. An annual filing fee of Ksh 50 is charged.

A company is required to file an annual self-assessment return together with its accounts with the Commissioner of Income Tax within four months after the end of its financial year. As of 1996, companies must also submit four instalment returns and pay instalment tax at the end of the fourth, sixth, ninth and twelfth months. The implementation of this requirement began in 1990.

Companies must file annual pay-as-you-earn (PAYE) income tax returns for employees. They should be reconciled with the monthly returns. The Companies Act requires companies to have their financial statements audited annually.

Mergers are defined as taking place when two or more business concerns dealing in the same or similar goods or services combine; takeovers occur when one such business acquires 50 per cent or more of the voting power of another company. In both cases, prior approval from the treasury minister must be obtained. This restriction does not apply if one business already owns 50 per cent of the other business and seeks to purchase additional shares or assets.

The Commissioner of the Restrictive Trade Practices, Monopolies and Price Controls Act (RTPA) may be required to give a recommendation on a proposed merger or takeover to the Treasury.

The RTPA establishes guidelines for the commissioner to consider when making their recommendation. A proposed merger or takeover that increases production efficiency and lowers production costs, expands exports and increases employment will generally be regarded by the commissioner as advantageous.

Labour Force

In 1993 an estimated one million people were unemployed. The majority of the population is engaged in agriculture and in the informal sector, which together employ 7.2 million. The large pool or surplus labour caused by nearly 10 per cent unemployment plus under-employment in agriculture and the informal sector provides an inexhaustible supply of unskilled workers. Intense competition for unskilled and semi-skilled jobs has resulted in docile unions and good labour relations.

Foreign workers may be employed if there is a shortage of qualified Kenyans. There are no restrictions on the methods of production.

Technical and managerial skills are no longer scarce. Higher education is producing more technicians and managers. There are many more locally trained accountants now than ever before and a surplus of lawyers. Recent legislation prohibits foreign nationals from being admitted to the bar.

Absenteeism is low at the unskilled and semi-skilled levels and negligible at the technical and managerial levels. Although retirement at age 55 is not compulsory, it is common for employees in the private sector; the National Social Security Fund makes contributors eligible for benefits at 55. Civil service employees also retire at age 55 but may be required to retire at 40 to extend opportunities for government employment to a larger portion of the population.

Salaries paid to executives are competitive, especially in the private sector. Compensation usually takes the form of cash combined with benefits such as housing, utilities, motor vehicles and medical insurance. In 1996, the average executive salary was Ksh 50,000 a month.

Wages

Minimum wages are set by the General Wages Advisory Board and the Agricultural Industry Wages Council, which include representatives of the government, employers and workers. The two bodies advise the Minister of Labour and Manpower Development, who adjusts minimum wage levels periodically, normally on 1 May, through amendments to the Regulation of Wages General Order (for the industrial sector) and the Agricultural Industry Order. In 1996, the minimum wage was Ksh 1,700 a month in Nairobi and Mombasa, Ksh 1,567 a month in other municipalities and Ksh 955 in rural areas. However, the average monthly wage was approximately Ksh 5,000.

The legal maximum working week for regular employees is 45 hours spread over six days. Workers in certain sectors, including agriculture, public service, hotels, retail trade and essential domestic work, are not subject to this limit. In practice, employees in both the public and private sectors work an average five-day, 40-hour

week. In practice, it is difficult to dismiss an employee after the standard initial probationary period (customarily three months) unless the worker deliberately damages company property, is absent without approval or good reason, displays gross inefficiency or commits gross misconduct.

Because dismissal is difficult, employers often prolong the probationary period, for example, by prescribing a further period of training.

In the rare event of an employee's dismissal, provisions for compensation, notice and appeal are included in the Employment Act 1976, revised in 1984. The regulations covering redundancy of employees are contained in the 1994 amendments to the Employment and Trade Disputes Acts. These regulations require notice to be given to the union concerned. They dictate minimum levels of compensation and provide that such termination may be the subject of a trade union dispute.

It is generally accepted that an employer must give at least one month's notice of the intention to terminate employment or one month's pay in lieu of notice. Payments due on termination include accrued holiday pay, if any, and severance pay.

Severance is paid at a rate of 15-days' pay for each completed year of service (based on the employee's pay at the time of termination) to employees with more than five years of service. Accrued pay is normally due whether an employee ceases employment after ordinary notice or upon summary dismissal for a lawful cause or for personal reasons such as poor performance or redundancy. In cases in which a union agreement exists, the conditions of termination are specified in the agreement.

Labour Legislation

Employment conditions and employee protection in Kenya are regulated by the following principal laws:

The Employment Act 1976; the Regulation of Wages and Conditions of Employment Act 1967; the Industrial Training Act 1971; the Trade Unions Act (revised 1970); the Workmen's Compensation Act (revised 1988); the Trade Disputes Act 1965; the Shop Hours Act of 1925 and the Mombasa Shop Hours Act of 1949.

The Ministry of Labour and Manpower Development recorded 68 strikes in 1993, down from 97 in 1992. There was an increase in mandays lost to strikes in 1993, to 67, 139 from 49,436 in 1992. High rates of unemployment have made dismissals the most common motive for striking; rarely do strikes last longer than a week.

Thirty-three trade unions are registered under the Trade Unions Act. They are organized by craft rather than industry and belong to a central body, the Central Organization of Trade Unions.

In 1993 approximately 330,000 workers (excluding teachers) belonged to unions. Because of the current shortage of jobs, unions have little negotiating power. Union membership is not compulsory in any industry, although in some industries an agreement may exist under which the remainder of a company's workforce must join the union if a specified percentage of the workers does. The interests of employers are represented by the Federation of Kenya Employers (FKE). Most large- and medium-size businesses are FKE members.

The Trade Disputes Act 1965 provides regulations covering the legality of strikes, industrial dispute-settlement procedures and arbitration. If necessary, the government arbitrator may intervene or the matter may be referred to the Industrial Court.

Employers must contribute an amount equal to five per cent of each employee's gross salary to the National Social Security Fund (NSSF) up to a maximum of Ksh 80 an employee a month. A matching contribution is withheld from each employee's salary and paid over to the fund. The Fund provides benefits to the following individuals:

• Members of the fund who have reached the age of 55 and who have retired from their regular employment;
• Members of the fund who have reached the age of 50 and who have not been employed during the immediately preceding three months;
• Members of the fund who emigrate from Kenya and do not have the present intention to return permanently to Kenya;
• Members of the fund who become disabled; and
• Survivors of members of the fund.

Persons not permanently resident in Kenya do not have to contribute to the NSSF if they are employed in Kenya for periods not exceeding three years at any one time and are covered by a programme in another country providing similar benefits. On leaving Kenya, foreign employees may obtain a refund of their own and their employers' contributions.

Other Payroll Taxes and Employee Benefits
Individuals who earn Ksh 1,000 a month must contribute monthly to the National Hospital Insurance Fund (NHIF). The required contribution is calculated on a graduated basis, with Ksh 30 the minimum monthly contribution and Ksh 320 the maximum contribution. Married women with employment income are exempt from this contribution if their husbands are contributors. The fund covers in-patient hospital expenses of up to Ksh 450 a day.

Overtime is payable at one-and-a-half times the normal hourly wage, except for Sundays and public holidays, when the rate is twice the normal hourly wage.

Employees are entitled to a minimum of 24 days annual paid vacation after a year of continuous employment. Some employers offer more days to those employees with seniority. In addition, employees have 11 annual legal holidays. Employees are entitled to 30 sick days a year at full pay and 30 more days at half pay. Employers must provide two months of paid maternity leave. However, this leave takes the place of paid annual vacation for the year in which it is taken.

Employers must carry workers' compensation insurance for their employees.

Most large employers set up pension or provident plans for their employees. Additional benefits normally provided to employees include medical insurance and job training. Senior employees and expatriate staff are often furnished with a car, housing, domestic services, utilities and passage to and from Kenya.

In most sectors of the economy, the employer is required to pay a training levy for each employee.

Foreign Nationals
A foreign national intending to work in Kenya must have a work permit, which is obtained by the employer on the expatriate's behalf. Before a permit is issued, the employer is required to justify the employment of a foreigner instead of a Kenyan. Work permits are issued for an initial period of two years and may be renewed, provided that the permit holder can prove that the conditions of employment are unchanged.

There are no official percentage limits on employment of foreigners, but the number of expatriate employees is closely monitored by the Department of Immigration (DI), which issues the work permits. The DI is among the most efficient of government departments, acknowledging permit applications within two weeks and handing down decisions within a month.

Self-employment (class H) permits were once the easiest to obtain on the grounds that they did not take jobs that would otherwise be given to Kenyans. However, the frequent disguising of full-time jobs as self-employment has led the DI to clamp down on class H permits, which are now issued sparingly. Applicants are now advised to apply for class A permits, which stipulate a particular employer. In many cases, class A applicants must first establish their own companies, bringing in foreign exchange to capitalize them, and then apply for the work permits. Approximately 9,120 expatriates held valid work permits in Kenya in 1996, compared with nearly twice that number 20 years ago.

Taxation

The central government of Kenya levies direct taxes, such as personal and corporate income taxes, and indirect taxes, including VAT and customs and excise duties. Local authorities raise revenue primarily through the imposition of real estate taxes, trading licences and service charges. The Income Tax Act 1973, as amended, contains the income tax law for both individuals and companies. The Ministry of Finance normally announces taxation charges and amendments in the budget speech in June each year. Such charges are usually effective from 1 January of the following year. In general, the Income Tax Department does not issue advance rulings on proposed transactions. However, foreign investors may be able to obtain through negotiation with the Ministry of Finance specific tax concessions for major projects of particular importance to the Kenyan economy.

The taxes levied by the central government are administered by the Kenya Revenue Authority (KRA). The KRA assesses and collects taxes, administers and enforces tax-related laws and performs other related duties. The KRA has three departments: the income tax department, the VAT department and the customs and excise duty department. Each department is headed by a commissioner. A company's tax year is its financial year, while an individual's tax year is the calendar year.

In 1992 Kenya adopted a self-assessment system. Under this system companies and individuals engaged in business must file self-assessment returns accompanied by financial statements within four months after the end of each tax year. Companies must file instalment tax returns and pay estimated tax at specified times during the tax year. For accounting periods beginning on or after 1 January 1996, companies must file instalment returns by the end of the fourth, sixth, ninth and twelfth months of the tax year.

These returns must be accompanied by four equal instalment tax payments, which are based on either the assessed tax for the preceding year or the estimated tax for the current year. Any balance of tax due must be paid by the date for filing the annual self-assessment return.

Individuals must file instalment returns unless they meet any of the following requirements:

• Their only income is employment income taxed at source;

• Their non-employment income does not exceed 50 per cent of their employment income; or

• Their total tax payable does not exceed Ksh 20,000

Employers must withhold tax from employees' salaries under the pay-as-you-earn (PAYE) system and remit the tax withheld monthly. Employees may credit tax withheld against tax payable. An overpayment of tax is refundable to the taxpayer or may be used to offset future tax liabilities.

If a self-assessment return in not filed or if the Commissioner of Income Tax doubts a self-assessment, the commissioner may issue a new or revised assessment.

A taxpayer may object to an assessment within 60 days of the date of issue by filing a document stating the precise ground of the objection. If the income tax department refuses to amend the assessment, the taxpayer may appeal to one of the local committees located around the country. If dissatisfied with the decision of the local committee, the taxpayer may appeal to the High Court and the Court of Appeal. Tax authorities conduct random audits of taxpayers. Tax authorities assess penalties for failure to furnish the required financial statements or for filing incorrect returns. Late payments are subject to a penalty of 15 per cent plus two per cent a month of the sum of the tax due and the 15 per cent penalty. In the absence of a specific penalty, the general penalty for offences under the Income Tax Act is a fine of up to Ksh 8,000, imprisonment for up to six months or both.

The Commissioner must issue assessments on executors or administrators of decedents' estates within three years after the income year the decedent died. All other assessments must be issued within seven years after the income year to which the assessment relates. However, no time limit is imposed on the issue of an assessment in cases of fraud or gross or wilful neglect.

Resident Corporations

Corporations, unincorporated organizations and associations (excluding partnerships) are subject to Kenyan income tax at the corporate rate. Religious, charitable, educational and pension trusts as well as some other bodies are exempt from tax. The income tax rate for resident corporations is 35 per cent. Corporations also must pay certain licence fees, real estate taxes and service charges to local authorities.

Kenya taxes income accrued in or derived from Kenya. However, if a resident company conducts business both inside and outside Kenya, its worldwide profits are deemed to be derived from Kenya. Consequently, profits derived by foreign branches of resident companies are subject to tax in Kenya. This provision does not apply to unearned income such as dividends, interest, royalties and rents received from foreign sources. Such income is exempt from Kenyan income tax.

A corporation is a resident in Kenya for tax purposes if it is incorporated under the laws of Kenya, it is managed or controlled in Kenya during the tax year, or the Ministry of Finance declares the corporation to be resident in Kenya by a notice in the Kenya Gazette.

Taxable income is accounting income arising or deemed to arise in Kenya, adjusted for nontaxable income, such as dividends and capital gains, and for non-deductible expenses such as depreciation. Income from the following sources must be computed separately:

• Rent, premiums and similar income from the leasing of real estate;

• Income from agriculture, forestry, fishing and similar activities; and

• Profits from any business not falling within the first two categories.

Companies may offset losses from one of the specified sources only against subsequent income derived from the same specified source.

Dividends, Interest, Rent and Royalties

Dividends paid by Kenyan companies are subject to a final withholding tax of 10 per cent. However, dividends are not taxable to resident recipients who directly of indirectly control 12.5 per cent or more of the distributing company's voting power.

From 1 January 1996, the withholding rate on dividends paid to residents was reduced to 7.5 per cent. A resident corporation's taxable income includes non-exempt interest from Kenyan sources. Such interest is subject to a 10 per cent withholding tax, but the gross interest payment before deduction of the withholding tax is included in taxable income. The withholding tax is creditable against the corporation's income tax liability. Taxable income includes rental income and royalties from patents and trademarks.

Capital gains derived from transactions taking place after 13 June 1985 are not subject to tax. However, the capital gains tax is only suspended and may be reactivated in the future. Gains derived from transfers of property regarded as business transactions for tax purposes are treated as ordinary business income.

Valuation of Assets

No income tax regulations exist for the valuation of inventory (stock). Obsolescence provisions may be challenged in certain circumstances.

Fixed assets may be revalued for financial statement purposes, but such revaluation does not affect the assets' tax value. Any surplus created by a financial statement revaluation is tax-free, and tax depreciation allowances continue to be based on the original acquisition cost.

Expenses are deductible only if they are incurred wholly and exclusively in the production of income. However, expenses are not deductible if they are incurred in the production of income from non-Kenyan sources or in the production of tax-exempt income from Kenyan sources, such as dividends from associated companies incorporated in Kenya. Private or capital expenditure is not deductible.

General expenses that are not directly attributable to either taxable or non-taxable income are apportioned, and only the portion attributed to taxable income is deductible. Expenses are usually apportioned on a pro rata basis, but permission may be obtained from the tax authorities for the use of a more favourable basis. Expenses are deductible on an accrual basis.

Depreciation charged in the financial statements is not deductible for tax purposes. For machinery, it is replaced by a fixed rate depreciation allowance, known as a wear-and-tear allowance, which must be calculated annually. A straight-line depreciation deduction is allowed for industrial buildings, hotels and farm works.

The term 'machinery' is not defined in the Income Tax Act, but in practice, it includes vehicles, ships, aircraft, equipment, tools, furniture, fixtures and fittings. Machinery is divided into four classes or pools, for which different rates of wear-and-tear are allowed under the declining-balance method. Individual assets are not separately depreciated.

A wear-and-tear allowance of 12.5 per cent for furniture, fixtures and fittings is granted only by concession.

The cost of newly acquired assets is added to the relevant pool, and proceeds from disposal of assets in the pools are deducted.

For the purpose of the wear-and-tear allowance, capital expenditure for automobiles other than commercial vehicles is deemed not to exceed Ksh 100,000. When a company sells a vehicle on which allowances have been limited under this rule, the amount of sales proceeds deducted from the appropriate pool is calculated with reference to the proportion that Ksh 100,000 bears to the purchase price of the vehicle.

If sales proceeds exceed the amount in the pool, the excess is taxed as a trading receipt. Resident associated companies that transfer machinery to each other may make an election to avoid this tax . The wear-and-tear allowances are deducted from the pools at the end of the tax year, and the resulting amounts represent the opening balances in the pools for the following tax year.

If a company ceases to do business, it may write off any positive balance remaining in a pool as a 'balancing deduction' against income in the final year of operations. This deduction may be carried back to the preceding six years if income earned in the final year is insufficient to take advantage of the deduction.

Companies may claim wear-and-tear allowances for the whole year in the year in which assets are purchased. In any subsequent year, companies may claim a whole year's allowance even though an asset may not have been used for some months during the year. A company may not claim an allowance for an asset in the year of disposal of the asset. If an accounting period is longer or shorter than 12 months, the allowances are adjusted proportionately.

A straight-line depreciation deduction of 2.5 per cent a year is allowed for capital expenditure on industrial buildings. The annual rate for hotels is 4 per cent. The investment allowance reduces the depreciable cost of a building. Land may not be depreciated. Companies may apply to the income tax department for an increase in the relevant depreciation rate if the expected useful life of a particular building is shorter than normal because of the building's construction or use.

Broadly, industrial buildings are buildings or structures that are used for specified purposes, including manufacturing, transportation, storage or power production.

The term includes hotels, houses built for and occupied by company employees, buildings used for the welfare of workers and any other buildings specifically designated as industrial buildings by the Ministry of Finance in the Kenya Gazette. An office, retail shop or private residence qualifies for the industrial building allowance if it forms part of a larger building that otherwise qualifies as an industrial building and if the cost of the non-industrial part is 10 per cent or less of the total cost of the building. The balancing adjustments available to sellers of machinery are not available to sellers of industrial buildings. The purchaser of a used industrial building takes the asset at its written-down tax value. The purchaser then continues to claim annual allowances at 2.5 per cent or four per cent as appropriate, based on the cost to the original owner.

Farm Works Allowance

Capital expenditure on the construction of farm works is deductible over three years beginning with the year of the expenditure. When sold, farm works are transferred at their tax written-down values.

The category of farm works includes: one-third of the expenditure on a farmhouse, labourers' quarters, any other immoveable buildings necessary for the proper operation of the farm, fences, dips, drains, water and electricity supply works other than machinery, windbreaks and other works necessary for the proper operation of the farm. Amortization of goodwill, patents, copyrights and trademarks is not deductible.

A company may deduct scientific research expenditure in the year incurred if the research is for the purpose of the company's business.

Reserves

In general, all reserves are regarded as appropriations of after-tax income and therefore are not deductible. Bad debts that have been written off and allowances for specific doubtful debts are deductible if the relevant debts are owed to the business and the amounts have been included in income in the current year or in a previous year. Any recoveries of bad or doubtful debts must be included in gross income. General provisions for bad debts are not deductible.

Repair expenses are deductible if they relate to business or rental property or to assets used for the production of income. For example, expenditure on structural alterations to maintain the current rent revenue of a rental building is an allowance deduction. However, expenditure on the construction of additions or improvements or on putting newly acquired assets into workable condition is not currently deductible. Such expenditure must be capitalized, and tax depreciation allowances may be claimed.

Operating taxes paid, such as customs and excise duties and VAT, are deductible. In general, income taxes are not deductible. Tax penalties and interest on overdue or underestimated

income tax are not deductible. Legal expenses incurred by a company in the ordinary course of business are deductible if the expenses are not capital in nature. For example, legal expenses relating to the recovery of debts, the defence of product liability claims, wage disputes and similar operating matters are fully deductible. All legal and incidental costs incurred with respect to a public issue of shares, debentures or similar securities are deductible.

Legal expenses incurred in acquiring depreciable assets may be capitalized as part of the cost of the asset. Legal expenses relating to company formation, the issue of share capital (except public issues), registration of mortgages and debentures, transfers of real estate and the defence of actions resulting from non-business activities are generally disallowed. However, legal expenses incurred in leasing real property for less than 99 years are deductible.

Finance Expenses

Expenses incurred to obtain loans for working capital are normally deductible. Fees, commissions and expenses incurred in obtaining loans for other purposes are not deductible unless incurred by banks and other institutions.

Interest

Interest expenses are deductible if the debt was incurred wholly and exclusively to produce taxable income. If proceeds from a loan are used wholly or partly to finance loans to directors, a corresponding proportion of the interest payable is not deductible. The variable amounts payable on participating debentures are treated as interest and are therefore deductible.

In principle, interest is not deductible until a company has paid any applicable withholding tax. However, by concession, this requirement is normally waived if the company can produce evidence of payment after the end of the relevant accounting period.

The deductibility of interest on loans is restricted for a foreign-controlled company with a debt-to-equity ratio exceeding 3 to 1. However, banks and financial institutions licensed under the Banking Act are not subject to this rule.

Lease Payments

Lease payments are deductible only if the commissioner is satisfied that the sole consideration for the payments is the use of or right to use an asset and that the entire payment is taxable income in the hands of the recipient.

The Income Tax Act does not contain any special rules concerning the deductibility of royalties. In practice, a company may deduct royalties paid to non-residents only if it has paid the applicable withholding tax.

Non-deductible Expenses

Preliminary organizational expenses such as legal and accounting fees and stamp duties on registration are not deductible. However, for the first year of its business operations, a company may deduct business expenses that were incurred before the commencement of its business and that are otherwise deductible. In general, a company may only deduct donations from which the company derives a direct benefit, such as a contribution to a related trade association.

Exceptions to this rule include certain grants and scholarships for technical education related to a company's business and donations made solely for industrial research or experimental work related to a company's business. Other items that are not deductible include dividends payable, expenditure or losses recoverable under insurance or through indemnity, and fines.

Foreign–Exchange Gains and Losses
Foreign-exchange gains from revenue and capital transactions are subject to tax. Similarly, all realised exchange losses are generally deductible. However, exchange-loss deductions are restricted for foreign-controlled subsidiaries.

Foreign-exchange losses relating to a loan from foreign sources are deferred if a foreign-controlled subsidiary's debt-to-equity ratio exceeds 3 to 1. Any excess losses may be carried forward.

Foreign Tax Relief
In principle, only income derived from Kenya is subject to Kenyan income tax. However, certain types of income that may normally be considered to be derived from foreign sources are deemed to be derived from Kenya. These types of income include the profits of foreign branches of resident companies and income from services performed outside Kenya by resident workers.

Kenya grants relief for foreign taxes paid in accordance with tax treaties with other countries. If foreign tax is paid to a country that does not have a tax treaty with Kenya, the tax paid is unilaterally treated as a tax-deductible expense in Kenya. Foreign withholding taxes on dividend or interest income from outside Kenya are not deductible because such income is not subject to Kenyan income tax.

A company may offset a loss derived from any of the specified sources only against subsequent income from that source.

Under these rules, a company may carry forward indefinitely its business losses and offset them against future business income until the losses are exhausted. However, a company may not offset business losses against incidental rental income because this is income from another specified source. Similarily, a company may not offset business losses against dividend and interest income, which is income from an unspecified source.

Losses may not be carried back. In the event of a corporate reorganisation, a company may not carry forward the unrelieved losses of another company to offset its profits.

Treatment of Groups

The income tax law does not allow consolidated return, which combine profits and losses of affiliated companies, or the transfer of losses by loss-making companies to profitable members of the same group of companies. If companies under common control transfer between themselves assets qualifying for wear-and-tear allowances, the tax law deems the consideration for the transfer to be the fair market value of the assets. However, if this treatment would result in a taxable balancing adjustment to the transferrer company, the two companies may jointly elect to substitute the transferrer's written-down tax value for the asset as the consideration.

Related-Party Transactions
Anti-avoidance provisions apply to all transactions between residents and related non-residents that result in the residents' earning less than the profit that would have been expected if the two parties had not been related. These provisions substitute an arm's-length profit in the residents' tax computations.

No comparable provisions apply to transactions between related residents. However, the commissioner has the general power under Section 23 of the Income Tax Act to challenge tax-avoidance arrangements.

For purposes of the anti-avoidance rules, parties are related to one another if either party participates directly or indirectly in the management, control or capital of the business of the other party, or a third party participates directly or indirectly in the management, control or capital of the business of both parties.

Corporate Distributions on Liquidation
The tax status of companies in liquidation is generally the same as that of ongoing companies. Taxable income in the liquidation period is computed and taxed according to the normal corporate tax rules. Liquidating companies may not carry back losses incurred on termination of their activities, but they may carry back balancing deductions for undepreciated capital expenditure. Liquidating distributions in cash or in kind are taxed to recipients as dividends to the extent that the distributions represent profits earned by the company before or during the company's wind-up.

Dividends, Interest and Royalties
A final withholding tax is imposed on dividends, interest and royalties paid to non-residents. The following are the applicable rates:
- Dividends: 10 per cent;
- Interest: 12.5 per cent; and
- Royalties: 20 per cent.

Non-resident Corporations
In general, Kenyan branches of foreign compa-

nies compute their taxable profits in the same manner as resident companies. However, interest, royalties, and management and professional fees paid by Kenyan branches to foreign head offices are not deductible. In addition, tax avoidance through artificial intercompany pricing practices is limited by anti-avoidance provisions.

A branch's expenses incurred outside Kenya are deductible only if the branch receives adequate consideration. This rule applies particularly to executive and general administrative expenses, which are deductible only if the commissioner considers the expenses to be just and reasonable.

Restrictions also apply to the deductibility of payments by a branch for services rendered by non-resident directors of the branch's foreign parent.

A branch's sales abroad of items that the branch manufactures, produces or grows in Kenya generate income deemed to be derived in Kenya. Such income is therefore taxable in Kenya. Branches of foreign banks operating in Kenya are required to include in their taxable income any income derived from assets the branch holds outside the country.

Branches need not withhold tax on remittances of profits to their head offices. In contrast, dividends distributed by a subsidiary to its foreign parent are subject to a 10 per cent withholding tax. However, branches pay corporate income tax at a rate of 42.5 per cent, which is higher than the 35 per cent rate applicable to locally incorporated subsidiaries.

Partnerships and Joint Ventures
Partnerships must file information returns, but they are not assessed as separate taxable entities. The taxable income of a partnership is allocated among its partners. The partners then aggregate their own shares of the partnership taxable income with any taxable income they receive from other sources.

The tax treatment of joint ventures depends on the organizational structure of the venture. Ventures organized as partnerships are taxed as partnerships, while ventures organized as limited companies are taxed under the corporate tax rules.

Trusts
In general, trusts are taxed like companies. Unit trusts pay withholding tax on interest and dividend income as resident persons. Otherwise, unit trusts are exempt from income tax.

A unit trust is any scheme or arrangement in the nature of a trust in which the public, as beneficiaries under the trust, are permitted to own an interest or an undivided share in one or more groups or blocks of specified securities and to participate proportionately in the income therefrom.

Taxation of Individuals
Resident and non-resident individuals are subject to tax on their income derived from Kenya. All employment income earned by resident individuals is deemed to be derived from Kenya, regardless of where the employment is performed or the income is paid. As a result of this rule, resident individuals are effectively subject to Kenyan income tax on their worldwide employment income. In addition, resident individuals are subject to tax on any profits they receive from a business carried on both inside and outside Kenya.

Non-resident individuals are subject to Kenyan income tax at the normal graduated rates on income from employement with a resident employer or a Kenyan permanent establishment of a non-resident employer. A non-resident is also subject to various flat-rate withholding taxes, which are final taxes.

Special rules apply to foreign nationals working for a regional office of a non-resident employer.

Definition of Resident
An individual resident in Kenya for 183 days or more during a tax year or for an average of 122 days or more in that year and the two preceding years is considered taxable. If an individual has a permanent home in Kenya, any time spent there will cause them to be a resident.

Taxation of Residents
An individual's taxable income includes the following:

- Gains or profits from business activities;
- Employment income;
- Rents and premiums from leasing real estate;
- Dividends and interest; and
- Pension and annuity payments in excess of Ksh 150,000 a year.

The first three of the above categories are 'specified sources' for purposes of the loss relief rules.

Employment Income
Employment income includes virtually all cash and non-cash remuneration, allowances and benefits derived from employment.

Taxable benefits in kind include the use of a company car and the services of domestic servants. The commissioner periodically sets the taxable values of employer-provided vehicles and utilities. Employers may deduct the cost of providing non-cash benefits.

The taxable benefit resulting from the use of company accommodation is generally deemed to be 15 per cent of total compensation including benefits in kind, other than the value of the accommodation. For agricultural employees, the percentage is 10 per cent. For 'higher-paid' employees, the housing benefit is valued at the higher of 15 per cent of total compensation and the market rental value of the premises.

A higher-paid employee is an individual

earning annual income of Ksh 600,000 or more, excluding the value of the company accommodation. The value of the taxable benefit is reduced by any rent paid by the employee to the employer. Full-time service directors are normally treated as employees for benefit purposes. For example, directors' fees are considered employment income.

A full-time service director is a director of a company who must devote substantially all of their time to the service of the company. A full-time service director may not be the beneficial owner of or be able to control, directly or indirectly, more than five per cent of the share capital or voting power of the company. If directors control more than five per cent of the voting power of the company or if they do not devote substantially all of their time to the company, their housing benefit is valued at 15 per cent of their total taxable Kenyan income from all sources.

Benefits that have an aggregate value of less than Ksh 24,000 a year and that are received with respect to employment or services rendered are exempt from tax. This exemption does not apply to employer-provided housing or any employer-paid life insurance premiums.

The following items are exempt from tax:

The value of any medical services provided by employers to employees and full-time service directors; employer contributions to pension and provident funds; the first Ksh 150,000 a year of pension income and retirement annuities; the withdrawal of benefits from a pension fund to a maximum of Ksh 360,000, and from a provident fund of a maximum of Ksh 240,000; and, for non-citizens recruited outside Kenya and their families, the cost of passages on joining, for annual leave, and on departure.

The following expenses are deductible in determining employment income:

• Membership in professional and technical associations. However, expenses for educational and training courses are not deductible.
• The cost of special clothing or necessary tools.
• Interest, up to a maximum of Ksh 56,000, on borrowings from specified financial institutions to finance the purchase of owner-occupied residential property.
• Travelling expenses incurred during the performance of duties, to the extent not reimbursed by the employer. However, the cost of commuting between home and work is not deductible.
• Contributions to pension and registered provident funds. The combined ceiling for contributions by employers and employees is Ksh 3,000 a month. From 1 January 1996, this ceiling was increased to Ksh 5,000 a month.
• Income derived from real property includes royalties, rents, premiums or similar consideration received for the use or occupation of the property.

• Expenditure on structural alterations necessary to maintain the existing rent revenue of a rental building is deductible. However, the cost of enlarging or replacing the premises is not deductible.

Dividends and Interest
Dividends paid to residents are subject to a final withholding tax of 10 per cent. From 1 January 1996, the rate is reduced to 7.5 per cent.

A 10 per cent withholding tax is imposed on non-exempt interest payments to residents, who must include the gross amount of the payment in taxable income. The withholding tax is considered a prepayment of tax.

Interest is exempt from tax if it is derived from post-office savings bank ordinary accounts, tax-reserve certificates or home-ownership savings plans. Capital gains are not subject to tax.

Alimony.
Alimony is not included in the taxable income of the recipient, and it may not be deducted by the payer.

Deductions
In general, to be deductible, expenses must be incurred wholly and exclusively to produce income and may not be reimbursable under an insurance policy, contract or indemnity.

Allowances and Exemptions
Resident individuals may apply the following annual tax credits, known as personal reliefs, to reduce the amount of their income tax payable.

Married taxpayers supporting dependent children receive no additional relief other than the standard family relief. Individuals are taxed at progressive rates.

Married Women and Dependent Children
The income of a married woman living with her husband is generally aggregated with the income of her husband. However, a married woman's professional income, self-employment income or income from employment is assessed separately if her employer is not her husband, a partnership in which her husband is a partner or a company in which her husband holds 12.5 per cent or more of the equity. Partnership income is not considered employment income and consequently is aggregated with a married woman's husband's income.

Single person's relief is allowed against a married woman's tax on professional, self-employment and employment income. A married woman is not treated as living with her husband if they permanently live apart or if she is resident in Kenya and her husband is non-resident.

Children are taxed on their own income as single individuals. However, income paid to or for the benefit of a child under a settlement created by a parent is generally regarded as the parent's income.

Loss Relief

Losses are deductible if incurred wholly and exclusively in the production of income and not recoverable under any insurance policy, contract or indemnity.

Losses attributable to any of the specified sources of income may be deducted only from subsequent income arising from the same source. Individuals may not carry back losses.

Taxation of Expatriates

Expatriates who are resident in Kenya are taxed on their worldwide employment income regardless of the place of employment or residence of their employers. Tax credits are available under double tax treaties.

Taxation of Non-residents

Non-residents are subjects to tax at the normal progressive rates on their employment income in Kenya if their employers are resident or have permanent establishments in Kenya. Non-citizens of Kenya may deduct from their taxable income one-third of the income derived from employment in Kenya if they meet the following requirements:

• The employer is a non-resident company or partnership trading for profit.
• The employee is in Kenya solely to perform duties relating to the employer's regional office, which has been approved by the commissioner.
• The employee is absent from Kenya for the performance of the duties described in the preceding item for at least 120 days in the year.
• The cost of the employment is not deductible in determining the employer's income subject to Kenyan income tax. (For example, the salary expense for a regional director who is in Kenya for only a part of the year is not deductible in Kenya.)
• Non-residents are not entitled to personal reliefs or other tax credits.
• Non-residents are subject to final withholding taxes at flat rates on dividends, interest, fees, rents, royalties and pensions received from Kenyan sources.

Withholding Taxes

Certain payments to non-resident companies and individuals without a permanent establishment in Kenya are subject to final withholding tax, which fully satisfies the recipient's tax liability with respect to the relevant income.

The withholding taxes are assessed on gross payments. Withholding tax deducted from payments to a resident or to a non-resident with a permanent establishment in Kenya is creditable against the recipient's ultimate corporate or personal income tax liability unless the withholding tax is a final tax.

Profits remitted by Kenyan branches of foreign companies to their home offices abroad are not subject to withholding tax.

Salaries and Wages

Employers must withhold income tax from all salaries, wages and taxable benefits derived from Kenya under the PAYE tax collection system.

PAYE deductions are made monthly in accordance with tables supplied by the PAYE section of the income tax department.

These tables apply the normal progressive income tax rates to salaries, including the value of housing and other taxable benefits in kind.

Failure to follow PAYE procedures is punishable by a fine of Ksh 8,000, imprisonment for up to six months or both.

Payment of Withholding Taxes

PAYE deductions must be remitted to the tax authorities by the ninth day of the month following the deduction. All other withholding taxes must be remitted within 30 days of the date of deduction. Estate and gift taxes are not levied in Kenya.

Indirect Taxes

Kenya introduced the VAT on 1 January 1990. The VAT system in Kenya is based on the same principles as the VAT systems in Europe. VAT is a broad-based consumption tax levied on the supply of taxable goods and services, including hotel and restaurant services, by a taxable enterprise in the course of business. Imports of goods and services are also subject to VAT.

Enterprises must register for VAT if they have an annual turnover of Ksh 2 million or more. However, no minimum VAT threshold applies to designated jewellers, designated pre-recorded music dealers, persons who sell more than four vehicles a year and saw-mill operators.

Supplies are divided into taxable supplies and exempt supplies. The standard rate of VAT on taxable supplies is 15 per cent. A few supplies and the export of goods and services are zero rated. A VAT rate of six per cent applies to essential items including food supplies, restaurant services, farming and food processing equipment. A VAT rate of 25 per cent applies to luxury goods, including jewellery and electronic entertainment equipment.

Suppliers are enterprises that are registered for VAT or that are required to be registered for VAT. Suppliers must account for VAT by charging VAT on all taxable supplies. In general, suppliers may claim as a credit VAT paid on inputs to the extent they use the inputs in the production of taxable supplies. VAT returns, together with the net amounts due, must be filed with the VAT department by the 27th of the month following the month in which the supplies are made.

Customs and Excise Duties

Kenya levies customs and excise duties on imported, exported and excisable goods. The Customs and Excise Act contains the rates applicable to various categories of goods.

The rates of duties are applied to the cost, insurance and freight (CIF) value of the goods. Under the Preferential Trade Area for Eastern and Southern African States (PTA) Treaty, Kenya must reduce progressively the rates of duty levied on imports of specific commodities from other PTA countries.

Customs duty rates are zero, 5 per cent, 10 per cent, 15 per cent, 25 per cent and 40 per cent. The high rate of 40 per cent is imposed to discourage the importation of non-essential goods.

Excise duties are levied on luxury goods including cosmetics and bottled water. The rate is 10 per cent for most items. Both customs and excise duties may be levied on the same goods.

Other Taxes
Kenya charges stamp duties on many legal documents and agreements. Ad valorem duties are imposed on transfers of real estate in urban areas at the rate of four per cent; on transfers of real estate in rural areas at the rate of two per cent; and on transfers of securities at the rate of one per cent.

A real estate transfer is free from stamp duty if the beneficial ownership of the property transferred does not change. This rule covers transactions such as transfers between wholly owned subsidiaries and transfers between a wholly owned subsidiary and its parents.

The stamp duty is due within one month of the execution of an instrument. The late payment penalty is 25 per cent a quarter or part thereof of the amount remaining unpaid.

Training Levy
Employers in most industries must pay a training levy semi-annually. In agriculture, construction, saw-milling and related industries, the levy is based on turnover. In other industries, the levy is based on the number of employees a company has. Employers who introduce a training programme and receive permission from the Director of Industrial Training may obtain refunds of the levy for their employees who attend approved training institutions.

National Social Security Fund
Employers must make contributions to the National Social Security Fund (NSSF), which provides retirement benefits.

Local Goverment Service Charges
All natural and legal persons resident in Kenya must pay service charges to their local authorities. The maximum monthly charges are Ksh 200 for employees and Ksh 900 for self-employed individuals and legal persons.

Financial Reporting and Auditing
The Companies Act requires companies to maintain proper books of account in English. The required books include a cash receipts and expenditure book, a sales and purchases book and a record of assets and liabilities.

The act does not specify a required accounting method, but it provides a schedule of items that must be disclosed in the accounts. In practice, the methods used by companies comply with generally accepted accounting principles (GAAP).

Financial Statements
The directors of a company are responsible for ensuring that audited financial statements are prepared and presented to the shareholders at the annual general meeting. Financial statements are prepared in accordance with Kenyan accounting standards, which are developed by the Institute of Certified Public Accountants.

Accounting Principles and Practices
The fundamental concepts of going concern and consistency apply to the preparation of accounts. Assets are stated at the lower of cost and net realisable value. Although use of the accrual basis is not mandatory, it is generally adopted in Kenya. If financial statements are prepared using assumptions that differ from the fundamental concepts, the variance must be disclosed in a note. Notes also must disclose any changes in accounting policies.

Inventory is valued at the lower of historical cost and net realisable value. Historical cost consists of the cost of purchases and production overhead necessary to bring the inventory to its present location and condition. The historical cost of current inventory is accounted for using the first-in, first-out (FIFO) method, the unit cost method or the weighted-average cost method.

The last-in, first-out (LIFO) or base stock formula may be used if the statements disclose the difference between the amount of the inventories shown in the balance sheet and either of the following: the lower of the amount as determined by one of the methods noted above and net realisable value; or the lower of current cost at the balance-sheet date and net realisable value.

Fixed Assets
The gross value of property, plant and equipment is stated at either historical cost or a revalued amount. Fixed assets are stated net of accumulated depreciation. Expenditure that increases the expected future benefit from an existing fixed asset is added to the carrying value of the asset. If permanent impairment causes an asset's recoverable value to fall below its net accounting value, the net accounting value is reduced to the recoverable amount, and the difference is charged immediately to income.

PART FIVE: FACTS AT YOUR FINGERTIPS

Visas and immigration regulations

Citizens of Eritrea, Denmark, Ethiopia, Finland, Germany, Holland, Ireland, Italy, Norway, Spain, Sweden, Turkey and Uruguay do not need visas. Neither do Commonwealth citizens, unless they are nationals of Australia, Nigeria or Sri Lanka. All other nationalities require visas issued (or approved) beforehand. Visitors not requiring a visa and holding an onward or return ticket normally obtain a 'Visitors Pass' on arrival at any Kenyan port of entry free of charge. These are usually valid for three months. No visitor can take up work or residence without the authority of the Principal Immigration Officer.

Since visa regulations are subject to change, it is advisable to double-check visa requirements with airline offices, tour operators, or Kenyan Government offices abroad well ahead of your intended visit. Visa applications normally take six weeks to process and usually allow a maximum stay of three months.

Health requirements

As a precaution, visitors arriving from places where there is cholera should bring evidence of recent inoculation. Malaria is endemic year-round throughout Kenya in all areas below 2,000m (6,500ft) and visitors should take a recommended prophylactic two weeks before their arrival and for six weeks after their departure.

International flights

Kenya is well served by flights from around the world. Over 30 international airlines provide scheduled services. The approximate flying time to Nairobi from Europe is eight hours; from North America 16 hours; from the Indian subcontinent six hours; from the Gulf four hours; from the Far East and Australasia 16 hours.

Kenya has two main points of entry by air: Jomo Kenyatta International Airport, Nairobi, and Moi International Airport, Mombasa. Both are among the most modern in Africa, with full passenger facilities — including 24-hour currency exchange facilities, post office, shops, restaurants, snack bars and bars. A porter service is available both inside and outside the customs area. For arrivals without health certificates, a vaccination service is also available. For transport into town, Kenya Airways provide regular bus services; taxis and self-drive hire-cars are available; and for those on a group tour, minibuses are provided by tour operators. There is also a Kenya Bus Service (KBS–Stagecoach) bus to Nairobi. An international airport at Eldoret is expected to be operational by 1998.

Air fares

The usual range of fares is available: first, business or club, and economy classes; excursion fares, bookable anytime for stays of between 14 and 45 days; and Advance Purchase Excursion (APEX) fares bookable two weeks in advance, allowing for stays of between 19 and 90 days. The price of the cheaper APEX fare varies according to the season, with June–September and December–January the 'high' seasons. You can make stopovers en route with all fares except APEX.

Departure tax

In 1996 the airport departure tax was US$20 a person, payable in US dollars, pounds sterling or Kenyan shillings. For internal flights there is a departure tax of Kshs100.

Arrival by sea

Kilindini Port, Mombasa, is one of the busiest docks on Africa's eastern seaboard. Regular passenger services were suspended early in the 1970s but there is a full range of customs and immigration posts for arriving passengers. Some cargo liners offer limited passenger berths and cruise liners call for short stop-overs.

Arrival by rail and lake steamer

There are two points of entry into Kenya by rail — at Malaba on the Kenyan-Ugandan border, and at Taveta on the Kenyan-Tanzanian border. Arrivals undergo full customs and immigration checks. Kisumu also serves as an entry point by inland waterway with full customs and immigration stations at Kisumu docks.

Arrival by road

Kenya is bordered by Somalia in the north-east, Ethiopia in the north, Sudan in the north-west, Uganda in the west, and Tanzania in the south. There are many land entry points. There main customs and immigration check post on the Somali border is at Mandera. The border posts between Kenya and Ethiopia are Moyale, Fort Banya (Ileret), and Todenyang; between Kenya and Sudan, Lokichoggio; and between Kenya and Uganda, Oropol, Katikekile, Bukwa, Malaba and Busia. The border posts between Kenya and Tanzania are Sirari (Migori) in the south-west, Namanga and Oloitokitok in the south, and Taveta and Lunga Lunga in the south-east.

Customs

Customs formalities are kept to a minimum. Unused personal effects, unexposed film, cameras and accessories (except cine and slide projectors) may be temporarily imported duty free. Visitors are also permitted to carry in 200 cigarettes or 50 cigars duty free, one litre of alcohol, and a quarter-litre of perfume. Refundable deposits may be required for radios, tape-recorders, musical instruments and similar equipment. Visitors wishing to bring in video cameras and recorders should consult the nearest Kenya tourist office, consulate or embassy, as a customs bond is normally required while the equipment is in the country. The import of firearms, agricultural and horticultural produce, and pets is forbidden.

Road services
There are bus services between all major towns in Kenya, run by reputable companies. They are swift and economic in well-maintained vehicles. It is advisable to book ahead. In addition, many bus companies and transport operators run express saloon car services on the same routes. Many other, less reliable, services are available.

Taxi services
There are taxi services in Nairobi, Mombasa and most large towns. They can be found at designated taxi ranks and outside the larger hotels.

The biggest taxi operator, the parastatal Kenatco, operates a large fleet of Mercedes-Benz saloon cars in Nairobi and Mombasa.

Car hire
There are many car hire companies in Kenya, offering everything from small sedans to 4WD vehicles. While some offer a flat weekly rate, most charge a daily rate, plus mileage and insurance. Vehicles can be hired on a self-drive basis or with driver.

Driving
Drivers require a valid international driving licence. Visitors may use their domestic licences for up to 90 days providing they are endorsed at the Road Transport Office, Nyayo House, Nairobi. Those with their own vehicles require a *Carnet de passage* and *Triptique* and International Certificate of Insurance. Petrol is sold in litres and driving is on the left.

Rail and ferry services
Kenya Railways operates a total network of 2,733 route kilometres (1,698 miles) of track, consisting of the main lines from Mombasa to Kisumu and from Nakuru to Malaba. Branch lines are Nairobi-Thika-Kiganjo-Nanyuki; Voi-Taveta; Konza-Kajiado-Magadi; Gilgil-Ol Kalou-Nyahururu; Rongai-Solai; Leseru-Kitale; and Kisumu-Butere. There are 137 stations. Kenya Railways also operate the inland marine services — passenger and cargo — on Lake Victoria.

Climate
Temperatures rarely fall below 24°C during the day and 10°C at night. Warm woollens are advised for late evenings. Warmer clothing should be worn in up-country areas. Kenya has two rainy seasons — between October and December and from March to early June.

Currency
The Kenyan shilling is divided into 100 cents. Notes are issued in denominations of 1,000, 500, 200, 100, 50, and 20 shillings. There are 10 shilling, five shilling and one shilling coins and 50 cents and 10 cents coins.

Banks
Banking hours vary but are normally between 0900 and 1500 weekdays and from 0900 to 1100 on first and last Saturdays of the month. Banks at international airports open 24 hours a day. There are many exchange bureaux.

Credit cards
American Express, Diners Club, Visa, Access, Barclaycard, and MasterCard are widely accepted throughout Kenya. American Express, Diners Club, Visa and MasterCard all have offices or agents in Nairobi and Mombasa.

Government
Kenya is an independent republic within the Commonwealth, a member of the United Nations Organization and the Organization of African Unity. It covers 582,644 sq km (225,000 sq mls) astride the Equator. The population is about 30 million. The capital Nairobi, which covers an area of 700 sq km (270 sq mls), has a probable population of about three million. It was incorporated as a city by Royal Charter in March 1950. Other major towns include Mombasa, Kisumu, Nakuru, Meru and Eldoret.

The government operates under an executive President who is also Commander in Chief of the Armed Forces. He is assisted by a Vice-President and a Cabinet chosen from the legislature, the National Assembly. In addition to the 200 members who are elected to Parliament every five years, there are 12 nominated MPs, a Speaker, and the Attorney-General. In 1996 executive wing of the government consisted of 32 ministries, each headed by a minister and two assistant ministers, and administered by a permanent secretary. The judiciary consists of the High Court, presided over by a chief justice, magistrate's courts, and a court of appeal. Kenya's eight provinces are each headed by a provincial commissioner and each of the 54 districts by a district commissioner, who is assisted by district officers. In addition, there are chiefs and assistant chiefs at sub-district level. The provision of various services and utilities is undertaken by county councils, municipal local authorities and, in Nairobi, the City Council.

Language
The official language is English. The national language is Kiswahili. Kiswahili or vernacular is the language of instruction in lower primary schools, English in upper primary, secondary

and university. There are more than 80 vernaculars. Many people involved with tourists speak German, French, Italian, or all three.

Religion
All major faiths are represented in Kenya. There are more than 1,700 registered religious organizations. The majority (about 70 per cent) are Christian — Anglican, Baptist, Catholic, Coptic, Orthodox, Pentecostal, Presbyterian and numerous Afro-Christian sects. The largest minority faith (about 20 per cent) is Islam. The remainder are Sikhs, Hindus, or traditional religions. Most services are conducted in English or Kiswahili.

Time
Kenya is three hours ahead of Greenwich Mean Time (GMT).

Daylight
Sun-up and sundown at around 0630 and 1845 — varying only by 30 minutes a year — maintains an almost constant 12 hours of daylight.

Business hours
Government offices observe a 5-day-week; most other businesses operate 0800 to 1700, Monday to Friday, and 0830 to 1300 on Saturday. They are closed on Sunday. Some general stores or dukas (shops) stay open well into the evening and over the weekend. In Mombasa, trade may start as early as 0700 with a long siesta break between 1230 and 1600.

Security
Walking alone at night is inadvisable. Use taxis, which are found outside most hotels. Do not leave valuables in hotel rooms and do not carry large sums of cash. If you have valuables, use a safe deposit box.

Communications
A first-rate communications system links every corner of Kenya to every country of the world. The Kenya Posts and Telecommunications Corporation provides international direct dialling and subscriber trunk dialling services to all major cities and telex, facsimile, data communication, and related services through the satellite earth station. In 1996 overseas calls cost about US$3 a minute and to the Far East about US$5 a minute. Cheap rates apply from Monday to Friday between 1800 and 0700, and at weekends from 1400 Saturday to 0700 Monday. The charge is about 60 per cent of the normal. There is also a communication tax of 18 per cent on all calls. International telegraph, telex and facsimile services are available, and telex and facsimile rental services are provided by most major hotels. Costs range from one US$1.5 a minute to the United Kingdom, and US$2 a minute to the United States.

Media
In addition to four daily and several weekly newspapers (in English or Kiswahili), Kenyans have a choice of periodicals and in 1996 three television stations. Large country areas are served by fortnightly 'rural' newspapers and, in more remote rural areas where people have difficulty in obtaining access to these media, Ministry of Information offices are organized along provincial, district and sub-district lines. Radio and television programmes are broadcast in English, Kiswahili and, in the case of radio, vernacular languages, by the parastatal Kenya Broadcasting Corporation (KBC). Documentary and film-makers require a licence.

Energy
The electricity supply is 240 volts (50 cycles AC), although in some hotels wall sockets are provided for 110-volt American appliances. US visitors should, however, still bring a small step-down voltage converter.

Medical services
Overall, medical facilities are better in Kenya than in most other African countries. There are first-rate hospitals in Nairobi and at the coast, and specialist physicians and surgeons, as well as good dental surgeons, dentists and opticians

Medical insurance
Cover can be bought in Kenya at reasonable cost from indigenous and locally represented multinational insurance firms. Another option is to buy insurance from the African Medical Research Foundation — AMREF — which runs the famous Flying Doctor Service in Kenya and East Africa. In the event of serious illness or accident on safari, the doctors fly out from their headquarters at Wilson Airport and either treat the casualties or fly them to hospital in Nairobi.

Chemists/Drugstores
There is no shortage of chemists or drugstores in Kenya, all staffed by qualified pharmacists. Most drugs are available, although sometimes under unfamiliar brand names. If a visitor's specific prescription is unavailable, the pharmacist will often prescribe a suitable alternative without the need to visit a doctor. Advice and treatment for minor ailments is always generously available. Most chemists close on Saturday afternoon, Sunday, and public holidays. When closed, the name and location of the duty chemist is usually posted on the shop door, or may be obtained at the nearest hospital. Weekend chemist opening times are published in the national newspapers.

Liquor
Licensing hours are liberal. Local spirits and wines as well as imported brands are available. Kenyan beer is a frequent winner of international brewing awards for light lagers.

Tipping
In the better restaurants and hotels a service charge is included in the tariff. If you should

want to tip someone who has been especially helpful, ten per cent is reasonable.

Otherwise, do as you see fit — remembering that while not to tip can result in poor service, too large a tip can make it difficult for the next customer.

Clubs

Clubs are a prominent feature of upper class life. Some are organized around sport; others are religious, cultural and philanthropic. Most have excellent facilities and are happy to welcome visitors, especially members of international clubs and societies represented in Kenya.

English-Kiswahili Dictionary

Hello	Hujambo
How are you?	Habari?
I am well (good, fine, etc.)	Mzuri
Thank you very much	Asante sana
Goodbye	Kwaheri
Hotel	Hoteli
Room	Chumba
Bed	Kitanda
Food	Chakula
Coffee	Kahawa
Beer	Bia or Pombe
Cold	Baridi
Warm	Moto
Hot	Moto sana
Tea	Chai
Meat	Nyama
Fish	Samaki
Bread	Mkate
Butter	Siagi
Sugar	Sukari
Salt	Chumvi
Bad	Mbaya
Today	Leo
Tomorrow	Kesho
Now	Sasa
Quickly	Upesi
Slowly	Pole-pole
Hospital	Hospitali
Police	Polisi
Mr	Bwana
Mrs	Bibi
Miss	Bi
I	Mimi
You	Wewe
He, She	Yeye
We	Sisi
They	Wao
What?	Nini?
Who?	Nani?
Where (Place)?	Mahali gani?
Where (Direction)?	Wapi?
When?	Lini?
How?	Namna gani?
Why?	Kwanini?
Which?	Ipi?
Yes	Ndio
No	La, Hapana
To eat	Kula
To drink	Kunywa
To sleep	Kulala
To bathe	Kuoga
To come	Ijayo
To go	Kwenda
To stop	Kusimama
To buy	Kununua
To sell	Kuuza
Street/road	Barabara
Airport	Uwanja wa Ndege
Shop	Duka
Laundry	Dobhi
Money	Pesa
Cent	Senti
One	Moja
Two	Mbili
Three	Tatu
Four	Nne
Five	Tano
Six	Sita
Seven	Saba
Eight	Nane
Nine	Tisa
Ten	Kumi
Eleven	Kumi na moja
Twelve	Kumi na mbili
Thirteen	Kumi na tatu
Twenty	Ishirini
Twenty-one	Ishirini na moja
Twenty-two	Ishirini na mbili
Twenty-three	Ishirini na tatu
Thirty	Thelathini
Forty	Arobaini
Fifty	Hamsini
Hundred	Mia
Thousand	Alf, Elfu

Phrases

Where is the hotel?	Hoteli iko wapi?
Good morning	Habara ya asubuhi
Good afternoon	Habari ya mchana
Good evening	Habari ya jioni
Please come in	Karibu ndani tafadhali
Please sit down	Keti tafadhali
You're welcome	Una karibishwa
Where do you come from?	Ume kutoka wapi?
I come from . . .	Nime toka . . .
What is your name?	Unaitwaje?, Jina lako ni?
My name is . . .	Naitwa, Jina langu ni . . .
Can you speak Swahili?	Unaweza kuongea Kiswahili?
Only a little	Kidogo tu
I want to learn more	Nataka kujifunza zaidi
How do you find Kenya?	Unaonaje Kenya?
I like it here	Hapa napapenda
The weather is hot isn't it?	Hewa hapa ni joto, sivyo?
Yes, a little	Ndiyo, kidogo
Where are you going?	Unakwenda wapi?
I am going to . . .	Nakwenda . . .
Turn right	Pita kulia
Turn left	Pita kushoto
Go straight	Enda moja kwa moja
Please stop here	Simame hapa tafadhali
How much?	Pesa ngapi?
Wait a minute	Ngoja kidogo
I have to get change	Ni badilishe pesa kwanza
Excuse me	Samahani
Where is the toilet?	Choo kiko wapi?
In the back	Upande wa nyuma
Where can I get a drink?	Naweza kupata kinywaji wapi?
One cup of coffee	Kikombe kimoja cha kahawa
How much does this cost?	Bei ngani?
That's quite expensive	Bei ghali sana

In Brief

Kenya National Parks

Kenya's national parks are wildlife and botanical sanctuaries set aside to conserve their special species and for educational and recreational enjoyment by Kenyans and overseas visitors.

Parks and Reserves Legislation
The original national parks administration, established in 1945, was combined with the Game Department under the Wildlife (Conservation and Management) Act of 1976. The combined departments regained independent status as a single body when they became the self-funding and semi-independent Kenya Wildlife Service parastatal in July 1989.

National parks and national reserves may be established on any type of land with the consent of the appropriate district authority or the National Assembly. Under certain conditions, within national reserves, the land may be used for other purposes than nature conservation.

Within marine national parks and reserves swimming, sailing and water-skiing are allowed, but permission is required for the passage and anchorage of boats. All fishing is prohibited, except by traditional methods, which have permission to continue.

Forest reserves and nature reserves, for the protection of forest, coastal and watershed resources, are declared under the Forest Act.

Biosphere Reserves
In the 1990s there were almost 300 dedicated biosphere reserves throughout the world — four of them in Kenya. Biosphere reserves are protected environments which contain special landforms, landscapes and systems of land use.

While national parks may not serve scientific research, biosphere reserves do. Their management is undertaken by the host government, with different ministries responsible for each different land use. Funds for specific research projects and scientific and administrative training are provided through UNESCO.

The major research project at the Mount Kulal Biosphere Reserve is International Protection of Arid Lands (IPAL). The Mount Kenya Biosphere Reserve is to have one devoted to research on African mountains.

World Heritage Sites
There are little more than 100 World Heritage Sites, which are more strictly protected under international law than biosphere reserves. They are either unique cultural sites — the Pyramids, the Acropolis, Taj Mahal — or unique natural sites, such as Australia's Great Barrier Reef, or Tanzania's Selous National Park.

Designated culutural sites in Kenya are Fort Jesus, the Gede ruins, and the Koobi Fora fossil beds. Natural sites are Mount Kenya, Hell's Gate, and the Maasai Mara National Reserve.

Parks and Reserves Administration
National parks are the responsibility of the Director of the Kenya Wildlife Service. National reserves are administered by the local authorities, but staffed by national parks staff. Kenya's total wildlife conservation area is 44,359 sq km (17,127 sq mls), or 7.6 per cent of Kenya's 582,644 sq km (225,000 sq mls).

Nature and Forest Reserves
Nature reserves and forest reserves are managed by Forest Department staff within the Ministry of Environment and Natural Resources.

Those of most interest are often given additional protection under national parks and national reserve legislation which, in turn, makes them more accessible than many other forests.

There are over 210 gazetted forest reserves in Kenya (83 under government administration and 126 under trust, or local government administration). This means that 16,916 sq km (6,531 sq mls) or 2.97 per cent of Kenya's total land area is devoted to forests.

There are also 130 non-gazetted forests (11 under government protection and 119 under trust protection), giving Kenya another 5,034 sq km (1,944 sq mls) devoted to forestry.

Biosphere Reserves

Kiunga Biosphere Reserve
Size: 250 sq km
Province: Coast
District: Lamu
Geographical location: North-eastern coastal border of mainland Kenya and Pate Islands, Indian Ocean
Altitude: Sea level-30m
Vegetation: Reefs, interspersed with 50 limestone islands — which provide vital nesting areas for migratory birds — with microscopic marine plants, marine angiosperms, and dugong grass. On the mainland there are coastal scrublands and mangroves.
Fauna: Dugong and green turtle are common. Abundant reef fish population.
Bird life: Many seabirds in large nesting colonies.
Visitor facilities: Swimming, sailing, water-skiing and diving are all permitted.

Mount Kulal Biosphere Reserve
Size: 7,000 sq km (South Island National Park 39 sq km).
Province: Eastern
District: Marsabit
Geographical location: South-east of Lake Turkana
Altitude: 378-2,416m
Vegetation: Ranges from mountain forest to

desert with rainforest, mistforest, grasslands, dry evergreen forest, woodlands, bushlands and saltbush scrublands.

Fauna: Greater kudu, oryx, gerenuk, giraffe, zebra, dik-dik, gazelle, elephant, cheetah, lion, black rhino, leopard, ostrich and crocodile.

Cultural heritage: Long but probably discontinuous history of human occupation with archaeological evidence of pastoral and fishing populations near the old Chalbi Lake.

Visitor facilities: None.

Malindi/Watamu Biosphere Reserve

Size: 261 sq km (Malindi Marine National Park 6; Watamu Marine National Park 10; Malindi Marine National Reserve 213; and Watamu Marine National Reserve 32 sq km)

Province: Coast

District: Kilifi

Geographical location: A strip of coast and sea 30km long and 5km wide, including Mida Creek; just south of Malindi and 88km north of Mombasa.

Altitude: Sea level

Vegetation: Algae, microscopic marine plants, marine angiosperms, mangroves, palms and casuarina.

Fauna: Various crabs, corals, molluscs, cowries and marine worms.

Bird life: Whale Island is a nesting ground for roseate and bridled tern and there are numerous shore birds.

Visitor facilities: Boat trips, watersports and coral viewing.

Mount Kenya Biosphere Reserve

Size: 715 sq km (Mount Kenya National Park 580 sq km)

Province: Central/Eastern

District: Nyeri/Meru

Geographical location: Mount Kenya straddles the Equator, 193km north-east of Nairobi and 480km from the Kenya coast.

Altitude: 3,000-5,199m

Vegetation: Rich alpine and sub-alpine flora with montane and bamboo forests, moorlands and tundra. Between 3,800 and 4,500m many bizarre species flourish, notably giant rosette plants of which 13 species are endemic to Mount Kenya.

Fauna: In the lower forest and bamboo zone there are giant forest hog, tree hyrax, white-tailed mongoose, elephant, black rhino, suni, duiker and leopard. Moorland mammals include the Mount Kenya mouse shrew, hyrax and duiker. At higher altitudes the endemic mole-rat is common and the golden cat rare.

Special features: Several mountain peaks with isolated glaciers. The highest peaks are Batian, 5,199m, and Nelion, 5,188m. There are about 20 glacial tarns (small lakes) and numerous glacial moraine features.

Visitor facilities: One lodge, several climbing huts, and three campsites.

National Parks

Aberdare National Park (Opened May 1950)

Size: 767 sq km

Province: Central

District: Nyeri/Murang'a

Geographical location: Central highlands, west of Mount Kenya, 180km from Nairobi.

Altitude: 1,829-3,994m

Vegetation: Rich alpine and sub-alpine flora giving way at lower altitudes to bamboo forests and montane forest.

Fauna: Mammals of the forest zone include blue monkey, colobus, leopard, elephant, wart hog, black rhino, giant forest hog, bushbuck, buffalo, red duiker and suni. The open moorlands have serval, eland, several species of duiker and bongo.

Bird life: More than 250 recorded species.

Special features: Trout in moorland streams.

Visitor facilities: Two lodges, two self-help fishing lodges, and five campsites.

Amboseli National Park (Opened April 1948)

Size: 392 sq km

Province: Rift Valley

District: Kajiado

Geographical location: Along the Tanzanian border, north-west of Mount Kilimanjaro.

Altitude: Up to 1,155m

Vegetation: Semi-arid acacias and grasses with papyrus sedges in the swamplands.

Fauna: The park's 56 mammal species include lion, cheetah, leopard, elephant, zebra, hippo, black rhino, Maasai giraffe, oryx, wildebeest, gerenuk, impala and Grant's gazelle.

Bird life: More than 425 recorded species.

Visitor facilities: Four lodges and several campsites.

Hell's Gate National Park (Opened February 1984)

Size: 68 sq km

Province: Rift Valley

District: Nakuru

Geographical location: South of Lake Naivasha.

Altitude: 1,560–2,187m

Vegetation: A wide variety of succulents.

Fauna: Eland, giraffe, zebra, impala, Grant's and Thomson's gazelle, klipspringer, hyrax and mountain reedbuck.

Bird life: Many birds of prey and swifts. More than 100 species of bird have been recorded.

Visitor facilities: None

Lake Nakuru National Park (Established 1968)

Size: 188 sq km

Province: Rift Valley

District: Nakuru

Geographical location: Central Kenya, 157km north-west of Nairobi.

Altitude: 1,753-2,073m

Vegetation: The lake is fringed by swamps. Surrounding areas support a dry transitional sa-

vannah with dry forest in more elevated areas.
Fauna: Mammals include the rare long-eared leaf-nosed bat, colobus, spring hare, clawless otter, rock hyrax, hippo, leopard, waterbuck, impala, Thomson's gazelle, striped hyena, hunting dog, bat-eared fox, wild cat and golden cat. Rothschild's giraffe and black rhino have been introduced.
Bird life: More than 400 recorded bird species. One of the few parks established specifically for the protection of birds, flamingo in particular.
Visitor facilities: Two lodges, three camps, two campsites and one self-help banda.

Malkamari National Park (Opened October 1989)
Size: 876 sq km
Province: Eastern
Geographical location: Along north-eastern border with Ethiopia. No more information available.

Meru National Park (Opened April 1968)
Size: 870 sq km
Province: Eastern
District: Meru
Geographical location: East-north-east of Mount Kenya, 348km from Nairobi.
Altitude: 366-914m
Vegetation: Mainly thorny bushland in the north, wooded grasslands in the west and open grasslands elsewhere. Dense riverine forests of doum and raffia palm grow along the watercourses, and sedges occupy riverine swamps.
Fauna: Large mammals include lion, leopard, cheetah, elephant, zebra, black rhino, reticulated giraffe, hippo, lesser kudu, oryx, gerenuk, hartebeest and Grant's gazelle.
Bird life: There are more than 300 recorded species, including Pel's Fishing Owl.
Visitor facilities: One lodge, two tented camps, two self-help lodges, and several campsites.

Mount Elgon National Park (Opened April 1968)
Size: 169 sq km
Province: Rift Valley
District: Trans-Nzoia
Geographical location: On the western border with Uganda, 470km from Nairobi.
Altitude: 2,336-4,321m
Vegetation: Ranges from wet montane and bamboo forests to Afro-alpine moorlands and tundra.
Fauna: Colobus, elephant, leopard, giant forest hog, bushbuck, eland, buffalo, duiker, black-and-white colobus, blue monkeys and golden cat.
Special features: A flat-topped basalt column known as Koitobos (Table Rock) and the 'lava-tube' caves, some over 60m in diameter, which are visited by elephants in search of salt.
Visitor facilities: Three campsites.

Mount Kenya National Park . . . see **Mount Kenya Biosphere Reserve**

Mount Longonot National Park (Opened January 1983)
Size: 52 sq km
Province: Rift Valley
District: Nakuru
Geographical location: South of Lake Naivasha, in the Rift Valley, 90km from Nairobi.
Altitude: 1,875–2,187m
Vegetation: V-shaped valleys and ridges with impenetrable forest around the crater.
Fauna: Similar to Hell's Gate but not as common.
Bird life: Many recorded species.
Visitor facilities: None.

Nairobi National Park (Opened December 1946)
Size: 117 sq km
Province: Nairobi
District: Nairobi
Geographical location: 7km south of Nairobi city centre.
Altitude: 1,533-1,760m
Vegetation: Dry transitional savannah on the plain with gallery forests in the valleys.
Fauna: The close proximity of forest cover, grass and permanent water makes the park the centre of an animal migration area, particularly in drought years. Concentrations of larger mammals with over 80 recorded species, except elephant. Hippo and crocodile can be found in various ponds, waterholes and the Athi River.
Bird life: More than 400 recorded species.
Visitor facilities: No lodges or campsites.

Ol Doinyo Sapuk National Park
Size: 20 sq km
Province: Eastern
District: Machakos
Geographical location: East-south-east of Thika, 65km north-east of Nairobi.
Altitude: 1,524-2,145m
Vegetation: Montane forest
Fauna: Colobus monkey, leopard, black rhino, bushbuck, buffalo, duiker and impala.
Visitor facilities: Two campsites.

Ndere Island National Park (Opened November 1986)
Size: 4.2 sq km
Province: Nyanza
District: Kisumu
Geographical Location: Lake Victoria
Altitude: 1,200-300m
Vegetation: Grasslands and wooded interior
Fauna: Impala, crocodile and hippopotamus.
Vistor facilities: None.

Ruma National Park (Established 1966)
Size: 120 sq km
Province: Nyanza
District: Homa Bay
Geographical location: 10km east of Lake Victoria in western Kenya, 140km from Kisumu.
Altitude: 1,200-1,600m

Vegetation: Grassland savannah, woodlands with extensive acacia thickets, rivers and hills.
Fauna: Roan antelope, Bohor reedbuck, leopard, buffalo, Jackson's hartebeest, Rothschild's giraffe, serval cat, hyena, zebra and ostrich.
Visitor facilities: Two campsites.

Saiwa Swamp National Park (Opened 1974)
Size: 3 sq km
Province: Rift Valley
District: Trans Nzoia
Geographical location: Situated below the Cherangani Hills, 20km north-east of Kitale.
Altitude: 1,860-1,880m
Vegetation: Tall bulrushes and sedges.
Fauna: Primarily established for the protection of 80 to 100 sitatunga. Other mammals include monkey, nocturnal potto, spotted-necked otter, giant forest squirrel and leopard.
Visitor facilities: One campsite.

Sibiloi National Park (Opened August 1973)
Size: 1,575 sq km (Sibiloi National Park 1,570; Central Island National Park 5 sq km; South Island 39sq km)
Province: Eastern
District: Marsabit
Geographical location: Situated on the eastern shores of Lake Turkana, 800km from Nairobi.
Vegetation: Grassy plains with yellow spear grass and doum palms. Scrubby salvadora bush is found on Central Island.
Fauna: Mammals include zebra, gazelle, oryx, hartebeest, topi, lion and cheetah. The world's largest crocodile population (12,000) breeds on Central Island and there are 60 species of fish.
Bird life: More than 350 recorded species.
Special features: Koobi Fora palaeontological site, known as the 'Cradle of Mankind'.
Visitor facilities: Three campsites at Alia Bay, the park headquarters. Visitors must carry their own supplies, including petrol.

Tsavo National Park (Opened April 1948)
Size: 21,283 sq km (Tsavo East National Park 11,747; Tsavo West National Park 9,065; and Chyulu National Park 471 sq km).
Province: Eastern/Coast
District: Kitui/Machakos/Taita-Taveta
Geographical location: South-east Kenya, inland from the coast, 240km from Nairobi.
Altitude: 229-2,438m
Vegetation: Bush grasslands and acacia woodlands, dotted with baobab and ivory palm, with saltbush, doum palm, tamarind and fig trees by riversides and the Mzima Springs.
Fauna: Larger mammals include lion, leopard, cheetah, elephant, black rhino, hippo, giraffe, lesser kudu, eland, oryx, Cape buffalo, zebra, yellow baboon, waterbuck, gemsbok, Coke's hartebeest, gerenuk and gazelle. Crocodile can be found in pools and in Mzima Springs along with hippo and various fish.
Bird life: More than 500 recorded species.
Visitor facilities: Several lodges and campsites.

Marine National Parks

Kisite Marine National Park/Mpunguti Marine National Reserve (Opened June 1978)
Size: 39 sq km (Kisite Marine National Park 28; and Mpunguti Marine National Reserve 11 sq km)
Province: Coast
District: Kwale
Geographical location: South of Wasini Island off Shimoni, on the south coast near the Tanzanian border.
Altitude: Sea level to about 5m
Vegetation: Sea grasses and marine algae.
Fauna: Corals, sea urchins, cowrie, starfish, various crabs, sergeant-major fish, parrot fish and butterfly fish, in all more than 250 recorded species.
Visitor facilities: None

Malindi/Watamu Marine National Park . . . see **Malindi/Watamu Biosphere Reserve**

Mombasa Marine National Park (Opened December 1986).
Size: 10 sq km
Province: Coast
District: Mombasa
Geographical location: Offshore from Mombasa.
Altitude: Sea level
Vegetation: Sea grasses and marine algae.
Fauna: Corals, sea urchins, cowrie, starfish, various crabs, sergeant-major fish, parrot fish and butterfly fish, in all more than 250 species.

National Reserves

Arawale National Reserve (Opened 1974)
Size: 533 sq km
Province: North-Eastern
District: Garissa
Geographical location: 5km from Tana River and 130km north of Malindi.
Altitude: 85-100m
Vegetation: Thorny bushland.
Fauna: Hunter's hartebeest. Other mammals include zebra, elephant, lesser kudu, buffalo, hippo and crocodile.
Visitor facilities: None.

Bisanadi National Reserve (Opened September 1979)
Size: 606 sq km
Province: Eastern
District: Isiolo
Geographical location: Adjacent to the north-eastern boundary of Meru National Park.
Altitude: 320-660m
Vegetation: Mainly thorny bushland and thicket merging into wooded grasslands. Dense riverine forests of doum and raffia palm occur along watercourses, with various sedges in swamps.
Fauna: During the wet the season, the reserve is

a major dispersal area for wildlife from the Meru National Park, primarily elephant and buffalo, but also some other species.
Visitor facilities: None.

Boni National Reserve
Size: 1,339 sq km
Province: North-Eastern
District: Garissa
Geographical location: North-east coast
Altitude: 0-100m
Vegetation: The only coastal lowland ground-water forest in Kenya. Lowland dry bushlands and grasslands in drier areas.
Fauna: Large concentrations of elephant in the dry season, giraffe, topi, gerenuk and Harvey's and Ader's duiker.
Visitor facilities: None.

Buffalo Springs National Reserve (Opened 1960s)
Size: 131 sq km
Province: Eastern
District: Isiolo
Geographical location: 85km north of Mount Kenya, 343km from Nairobi.
Altitude: 900-1,000m
Vegetation: Riverine forest of acacia and doum palm, acacia woodlands, bush, grass and scrublands.
Fauna: Elephant, zebra, reticulated giraffe, gerenuk, oryx, cheetah, buffalo and crocodile.
Bird life: There are 320 recorded species.
Visitor facilities: One lodge and five campsites.

Dodori National Reserve (Opened 1976)
Size: 877 sq km
Province: Coast
District: Lamu
Geographical location: North-east coast.
Altitude: 0-100m
Vegetation: Densest, most varied mangrove swamps in Kenya, lowland dry forest, marshy glades, and groundwater forest.
Fauna: Major breeding ground for the East Lamu topi. Larger mammals include lesser kudu, giraffe and lion. The reserve also has substantial breeding grounds of dugong and green turtle along the shoreline.
Bird life: Prolific bird life, especially pelican.
Visitor facilities: One campsite.

Kakamega Forest National Reserve (Opened May 1985)
Size: 240 sq km
Province: Western
District: Kakamega
Geographical location: North of Kisumu.
Altitude: 1,520-1,680m
Vegetation: The easternmost area of the Congo-West African equatorial rainforest, the fairly dense forest is interspersed with grassy glades. There are at least 125 tree species with an average height of 35m.
Fauna: Some 10-20 per cent of the amphibians, reptiles, birds and mammals found there occur nowhere else in Kenya — bush-tailed porcupine, giant water shrew, and hammer-headed fruit bat. The forest also supports numerous species of primates, including colobus and blue monkey.
Bird life: More than 350 recorded species, including rare snake-eating birds.
Visitor facilities: One guesthouse, self-help bandas and two campsites.

Kamnarok National Reserve (Opened June 1983)
Size: 88 sq km
Province: Rift Valley
District: Baringo
Geographical location: Close to lakes Baringo and Bogoria
Altitude: 1,520-1,680m
Vegetation: Diverse, 4,000ft deep valley with semi-tropical vegetation on the slopes, dry thornbush at the base.
Fauna: Bush pig, waterbuck, buffalo, elephant, Rothschild's giraffe, dik dik and wart hog.
Bird life: Pelicans, grebe and many other water birds.
Visitor facilities: None

Kerio Valley National Reserve (Opened 1983)
Size: 66 sq km
Province: Rift Valley
District: Baringo
Geographical location: In the Rift Valley, close to the Tugen Hills.
Vegetation: Semi-tropical vegetation on the slopes, dry thorn bush at the base. An area of immense importance because of its bio-diversity.
Visitor facilities: None

Kora National Reserve (Opened November 1989)
Size: 1,787 sq km
Province: Coast
District: Tana River
Geographical location: On the Tana River, 125km east of Mount Kenya, 289km from Nairobi.
Altitude: 250-440m
Vegetation: Mostly acacia bushland with riverine forests of doum palm, acacia and Tana River poplar.
Fauna: Elephant, black rhino, hippo, lion, leopard, cheetah, serval, caracal, wildcat, genet, spotted and striped hyena and several species of antelope. The rivers support a wide range of amphibians, lizards, snakes, tortoise and crocodile. Famous as the last home of George Adamson who was murdered there, at his camp, in July 1989.
Visitor facilities: None

Lake Bogoria National Reserve (Opened November 1970)
Size: 107 sq km
Province: Rift Valley
District: Baringo

Geographical location: 50km north of Nakuru.
Altitude: 1,000-1,600m
Vegetation: Mainly bushland with small patches of riverine forest. Grasslands along shoreline.
Fauna: Greater kudu.
Bird life: Flamingo
Special features: Thermal areas with steam jets and geysers.
Visitor facilities: One lodge and three campsites

Losai National Reserve (Opened January 1976)
Size: 1,806 sq km
Province: Eastern
District: Marsabit
Geographical location: Situated in the Losai Mountains south-west of the Marsabit National Reserve in northern Kenya, 175km north of Mount Kenya.
Altitude: 625-1,750m
Vegetation: Wild, semi-desert with thorny bushland.
Fauna: Elephant, black rhino, greater and lesser kudu, gerenuk and Grant's gazelle.
Visitor facilities: None.

Maasai Mara National Reserve (Opened November 1974)
Size: 1,510 sq km
Province: Rift Valley
District: Narok
Geographical location: South-west Kenya, bordering the Serengeti National Park and Tanzania.
Altitude: 1,500-2,170m
Vegetation: Open grasslands with patches of acacia woodland, thickets and riverine forests.
Fauna: During the dry season (July-October) the reserve is a major concentration area for migratory herbivores including about 250,000 zebra and 1.3 million wildebeest. There are also gazelle, elephant, topi, buffalo, lion (Kenya's largest population), black rhino, hippo, hyena, giraffe, leopard and mongoose.
Bird life: Prolific, including 53 birds of prey.
Visitor facilities: Many lodges and campsites.

Marsabit National Reserve (Opened 1967)
Size: 1,482 sq km
Province: Eastern
District: Marsabit
Geographical location: Northern Kenya, 560km north of Nairobi
Altitude: 420-1,700m
Vegetation: Higher altitude forest merges into acacia grasslands in the middle altitudes. Arid thorny bushland dominates the lower zone.
Fauna: Elephant, greater kudu, monkey, baboon, hyena, aardwolf, caracal, cheetah, lion, klipspringer, gazelle, oryx and reticulated giraffe. There are 13 recorded species of bat.
Bird life: More than 350 species, including 52 birds of prey.
Special features: Volcanic craters, several containing freshwater lakes.
Visitor facilities: One lodge and three camp-

sites.

Mwea National Reserve (Opened January 1976)
Size: 42 sq km
Province: Eastern
District: Embu
Geographical location: 100km to the north-east of Nairobi
Altitude: 1,000-1,100m
Vegetation: Mainly thorny bush with patches of woodland. Scattered baobab.
Fauna: Small numbers of elephant, buffalo, lesser kudu, crocodile and hippo.
Bird life: Many water fowl, other water birds and other species.
Visitor facilities: Two picnic sites.

Mwingi National Reserve
Size: 745 sq km
Province: Eastern
District: Kitui
Geographical location: Next to Meru National Park.
Altitude: 428-675m
Vegetation: Bushland and riverine forest.
Fauna: Crocodile and hippo along the Tana River.
Visitor facilities: None.

Nasolot National Reserve
Size: 92 sq km
Province: Rift Valley
District: West Pokot
Geographical location: 100km north of Kitale in north-western Kenya, near the Ugandan border.
Altitude: 750-1,500m
Vegetation: Mainly thorny bushland.
Fauna: Elephant, giraffe, black rhino, lesser kudu, bushbuck, duiker, dik dik, lion, leopard, spotted hyena and jackal.
Bird life: More than 150 recorded species.
Visitor facilities: Two campsites.

Ngai Ndethya National Reserve
Size: 212 sq km
Province: Eastern
District: Machakos
Geographical location: South-eastern Kenya between the Tsavo East and Tsavo West National Parks.
Altitude: 650-750m
Vegetation: Thornbush and thicket with scattered baobab.
Fauna: Migration corridor between Tsavo East and Tsavo West.
Visitor facilities: None.

Rahole National Reserve
Size: 1,270 sq km
Province: North-Eastern
District: Garissa
Geographical location: 150km east-north-east of Mount Kenya.
Altitude: 250-480m
Vegetation: Dry thorny bushland.

Fauna: Elephant, Grevy's zebra, beisa oryx, hippo and crocodile.
Bird life: More than 100 recorded species.
Visitor facilities: None.

Samburu National Reserve (Opened 1960s)
Size: 104 sq km
Province: Rift Valley
District: Samburu
Geographical location: 90km north of Mount Kenya, 343km from Nairobi.
Altitude: 800-1,230m
Vegetation: Narrow riverine woodland of doum palm. Otherwise acacia woodland with bushland, grassland and scrubland.
Fauna: Elephant, cheetah, reticulated giraffe, oryx, gerenuk, vervet monkey, zebra, buffalo and crocodile.
Visitor facilities: One lodge, two luxury tented camps and three campsites.

Shaba National Reserve (Opened 1985)
Size: 239 sq km
Province: Eastern
District: Isiolo
Geographical location: 70km north of Mount Kenya.
Altitude: 700-1,500m
Vegetation: Acacia woodlands, bushlands, and grasslands. Riverine communities dominated by acacia and doum palm.
Fauna: Gerenuk, gazelle, oryx, zebra, giraffe, cheetah, leopard, lion, hippo and crocodile.
Bird life: More than 350 recorded species. Famous as the last home of Joy Adamson who was murdered there in 1980.
Visitor facilities: One luxury lodge and three campsites.

Shimba Hills National Reserve (Opened September 1968)
Size: 320 sq km
Province: Coast
District: Kwale
Geographical location: 30km south-west of Mombasa.
Altitude: 120–450m
Vegetation: Forests and grasslands interspersed with woodlands, riverine forests, coastal bushland, and scrubland.
Fauna: Antelope, buffalo, waterbuck, reedbuck, hyena, wart hog, giraffe, elephant, leopard, baboon and bush pig.
Visitor facilities: One luxury lodge, self-help bandas, two campsites, a picnic site and a nature trail.

South Kitui National Reserve (Opened September 1979)
Size: 1,833 sq km
Province: Eastern
District: Kitui
Geographical location: Adjacent to the north boundary of the Tsavo East National Park.
Vegetation: Bush grasslands and acacia woodlands, dotted with baobab, ivory palm and saltbush.
Fauna: Larger mammals include lion, leopard, cheetah, elephant, black rhino, hippopotamus, giraffe, lesser kudu, eland, oryx, Cape buffalo, zebra, yellow baboon, waterbuck, gemsbok, Coke's hartebeest, gerenuk and gazelle.
Visitor facilities: None.

South Turkana National Reserve
Size: 1,091 sq km
Province: Rift Valley
District: Turkana
Geographical location: North-western Kenya, 100km north of Kitale.
Altitude: 900-2,270m
Vegetation: Dense thorn bush, riverine forest and scattered forest.
Fauna: Elephant and greater kudu.
Visitor facilities: None.

Tana River Primate Reserve (Opened 1976)
Size: 169 sq km
Province: Coast
District: Tana River
Geographical location: Inland from the Indian Ocean, 120km north of Malindi on the Tana River between Hola and Garsen.
Altitude: 40-70m
Vegetation: Highly diversified riverine forest with nearly 300 species. Some bush and grasslands.
Fauna: Seven primates include endemic red colobus, mangabey monkey and baboon. Also elephant, hippo, gazelle, duiker, river hog, giraffe, lion, waterbuck, bush squirrel, crocodile.
Bird life: 248 bird species have been recorded.
Visitor facilities: Limited accommodation is available at Muchelelo Research tented camp, by prior arrangement with Kenya Wildlife Service.

There is some security risk due to the reserve's closeness to the Somalia border where in 1996 there was an ongoing civil war.

Marine National Reserves

Kiunga Marine National Reserve — see **Kiunga Biosphere Reserve**

Malindi/Watamu Marine National Reserve — see **Malindi/Watamu Biosphere Reserve**

Mombasa Marine National Reserve (Opened December 1986)
Size: 200 sq km
Province: Coast
District: Mombasa
Altitude: Sea level.
Geographical location: Offshore from Mombasa.
Vegetation: Marine grasses.
Fauna: Myriad species of reef and deep-sea fish, corals and other forms of marine life.

Game Sanctuaries

Kisumu Impala Wildlife Sanctuary (Opened October 1992)
Size: Less than 1 sq km
Province: Nyanza
Altitude: 1,149m
Fauna: Holding ground and sanctuary for 'problem' animals such as leopard, hyena and baboon who settle too close to human populations in this densely populated area.

Laikipia Plateau Reserve (Opened October 1991)
Province: Rift Valley
District: Laikipia/Isiolo
Altitude: 1,200m
Vegetaion: Semi-arid scrub thornbush.
Fauna: Elephant, gerenuk, eland, Grevy's zebra, buffalo, bushbuck, bush pig, duiker, cheetah, leopard and lion.
Bird life: More than 100 recorded species.
Visitor Facilities: None.

Maralal Game Sanctuary
Province: Rift Valley
District: Maralal
Altitude: 1,400m
Vegetation: Semi-arid grasslands, thorn bush.

Fauna: Elephant, gerenuk, buffalo, zebra, antelope, leopard and lion.
Bird life: More than 150 recorded species.
Visitor Facilities: None.

Mkogodo Forest Reserve
Province: Rift Valley
District: Laikipia
Altitude: 1,800m
Vegetation: A belt of riverine forest along the Ngare Ndare River.
Fauna: Elephant, gerenuk, eland, buffalo, bush pig, bushbuck, duiker, zebra, cheetah, leopard and lion.
Bird life: More than 200 recorded species.
Vistor facilities: None.

Salt Lick Sanctuary
Size: 113 sq km
Province: Coast
District: Taita-Taveta
Geographical location: South-eastern Kenya, next to the Tsavo West National Park.
Altitude: Up to 914m
Vegetation: Savannah and woodlands.
Fauna: Zebra, buffalo, impala, gazelle, elephant, eland, waterbuck, reedbuck, giraffe, vervet monkey, lion and jackal.
Visitor facilities: Two lodges and luxury tented camp.

Nature Reserves

Arabuko Sokoke
Cheptugen-Kapchem-utwa
Kaimosi Forest
Karura
Katimok-Kabarnet
Langata
Mau South West
Mbololo
Nandi North
Uaso Narok

Addresses
Kenya Wildlife Service
Langata Road
PO Box 40241 Nairobi

Provincial Wildlife Officer
(Marine National Parks)
PO Box 82144 Mombasa

Gazetted Forests

Forest Department,
Ministry of
Environment
& Natural Resources,
PO Box 30513 Nairobi

Aberdare
Size: 1,030 sq km
Province: Central
District: Nyandarua/
Nyeri/Muranga

Arabuko-Sokoke
Size: 418 sq km
Province: Coast
District: Kilifi

Bahati
Size: 102 sq km
Province: Rift Valley
District: Nakuru

Buda
Size: 7 sq km
Province: Coast
District: Kwale

Dagoretti
Size: 8 sq km
Province: Central
District: Kiambu

East Ngambeni
Size: 107 sq km
Province: Eastern
District: Kitui

Eastern Mau
Size: 650 sq km
Province: Rift Valley

District: Nakuru

Eburru
Size: 87 sq km
Province: Rift Valley
District: Nakuru

Eldoret
Size: 1.5 sq km
Province: Rift Valley
District: Uasin Gishu

Escarpment
Size: 0.7 sq km
Province: Central
District: Kiambu

Gongoni
Size: 8 sq km
Province: Coast
District: Kwale

Gonja
Size: 8 sq km
Province: Coast
District: Kwale

Kamiti
Size: 2 sq km
Province: Central
District: Kiambu

Kapolet
Size: 16 sq km

Province: Rift Valley
District: Trans-Nzoia

Kapsabet
Size: 12 sq km
Province: Rift Valley
District: Uasin Gishu

Kaptagat
Size: 130 sq km
Province: Rift Valley
District: Uasin Gishu

Karura
Size: 10 sq km
Province: Nairobi
District: Nairobi

Kiambu
Size: 1.3 sq km
Province: Central
District: Kiambu

Kibwezi
Size: 59 sq km
Province: Eastern
District: Makueni

Kiganjo
Size: 3 sq km
Province: Central
District: Nyeri

Kijabe Hill

Size: 7 sq km
Province: Rift Valley
District: Nakuru

Kikuyu Escarpment
Size: 419 sq km
Province: Central
District: Kiambu

Kilombe Hill
Size: 16 sq km
Province: Rift Valley
District: Baringo

Kipipiri
Size: 50 sq km
Province: Central
District: Nyandarua

Kipkabus
Size: 57 sq km
Province: Rift Valley
District: Uasin Gishu

Kitale
Size: 24 sq km
Province: Rift Valley
District: Trans-Nzoia

Lerogi
Size: 910 sq km
Province: Rift Valley
District: Samburu

Leshau
Size: 2 sq km
Province: Central
District: Nyandarua

Londiani
Size: 1 sq km
Province: Rift Valley
District: Kericho

Loitokitok
Size: 8 sq km
Province: Rift Valley
District: Kajiado

Loriak
Size: 50 sq km
Province: Rift Valley
District: Laikipia

Losai
Size: 3 sq km
Province: Rift Valley
District: Laikipia

Lugori
Size: 22 sq km
Province: Rift Valley
District: Samburu

Magumo North
Size: 2 sq km
Province: Central
District: Nyandarua

Magumo South
Size: 4 sq km
Province: Central
District: Nyandarua

Mailuganji
Size: 17 sq km
Province: Coast
District: Kwale

Maji Mazuri
Size: 77 sq km
Province: Rift Valley
District: Baringo

Mangrove forests (5)
Size: 450 sq km
Province: Coast
District: Kilifi, Kwale,
Lamu, Mombasa, Tana
River

Marmanet
Size: 233 sq km
Province: Rift Valley
District: Laikipia

Marsabit
Size: 153 sq km
Province: Eastern
District: Marsabit

Mathews Range
Size: 938 sq km
Province: Rift Valley
District: Samburu

Mau Narok
Size: 8 sq km
Province: Rift Valley
District: Nakuru

Menengai
Size: 60 sq km
Province: Rift Valley
District: Nakuru

Mkogodo
Size: 302 sq km
Province: Rift Valley
District: Laikipia

Molo
Size: 9 sq km
Province: Rift Valley
District: Nakuru

Mount Elgon
Size: 733 sq km
Province: Rift Valley
District: Elgon

Mount Kenya
Size: 2,009 sq km
Province: Central/
Eastern
District: Kirinyaga,
Nyeri, Meru and Embu

Mount Londiani
Size: 297 sq km
Province: Rift Valley
District: Baringo/Nakuru

Mount Nyiru
Size: 459 sq km
Province: Rift Valley
District: Samburu

Muguga
Size: 2 sq km
Province: Central
District: Kiambu

Muringato Nursery
Size: 0.3 sq km
Province: Central
District: Nyeri

Mwachi
Size: 4 sq km
Province: Coast
District: Kwale

Nabkoi
Size: 30 sq km
Province: Rift Valley
District: Uasin Gishu

Nairobi Arboretum
Size: 0.3 sq km
Province: Nairobi
District: Nairobi

Nakuru
Size: 7 sq km
Province: Rift Valley
District: Nakuru

Namanga Hill
Size: 118 sq km
Province: Rift Valley
District: Kajiado

Ndare
Size: 56 sq km
Province: Eastern/Rift
District: Meru,
Laikipia

Ndotos Range
Size: 972 sq km
Province: Rift Valley
District: Samburu

Ngong Road
Size: 13 sq km
Province: Nairobi
District: Nairobi

Ngong Hills
Size: 31 sq km
Province: Rift Valley
District: Kajiado

North Tinderet
Size: 262 sq km
Province: Rift Valley
District: Uasin Gishu

Nyamweru
Size: 8 sq km
Province: Central
District: Kiambu

Nyeri
Size: 11 sq km
Province: Central
District: Nyeri

Ol Arabel
Size: 94 sq km
Province: Rift Valley
District: Laikipia

Ol Bolossat
Size: 33 sq km
Province: Central
District: Nyandarua

Rumuruti
Size: 64 sq km
Province: Rift Valley
District: Laikipia

Sekhendu
Size: 8 sq km
Province: Rift Valley
District: Trans-Nzoia

Shimba
Size: 192 sq km
Province: Coast
District: Kwale

South Laikipia
Size: 35 sq km
Province: Central
District: Nyeri

South-Western Mau
Size: 869 sq km
Province: Rift Valley
District: Kericho,
Nakuru

Timau
Size: 3 sq km
Province: Eastern
District: Meru

Timboroa
Size: 60 sq km
Province: Rift Valley
District: Baringo

Tinderet
Size: 279 sq km
Province: Rift Valley
District: Kericho,
Nandi

Tumeya
Size: 2 sq km
Province: Rift Valley,
Western
District: Uasin Gishu,
Kakamega

Uaso Narok
Size: 21 sq km
Province: Rift Valley
District: Laikipia

Western Mau
Size: 198 sq km
Province: Rift Valley
District: Kericho,
Nakuru

West Molo
Size: 3 sq km
Province: Rift Valley
District: Nakuru

Witu
Size: 39 sq km
Province: Coast
District: Lamu

Non-gazetted Forests

Boni
Size: 185 sq km
Province: Coast
District: Lamu

Hewani
Size: 27 sq km
Province: Coast
District: Tana River

Kazuki Hill
Size: 2 sq km
Province: Central
District: Murang'a

Kokani
Size: 62 sq km
Province: Coast
District: Tana River

Kingatua
Size: 0.6 sq km
Province: Central
District: Kiambu

Mangrove forests (4)
Size: 267 sq km
Province: Coast
District: Kilifi,
Kwale, Mombasa,
Tana River

Mwina
Size: 34 sq km
Province: Coast
District: Tana River

Wayu
Size: 420 sq km
Province: Coast
District: Tana River

Wildlife Profile

Eastern Africa's open plains, particularly in Kenya, hold a greater number and diversity of species than any other continent. There are almost 100 species of grazers (ungulates) whereas the whole of Asia can claim only 70, South and Central America only 16, Europe only 13, and North America only 11. Together with predators, scavengers, reptiles, insects, oddities and the rich bird life — third in the world in number of species — it gives Kenya rightful claim to be called the Last Eden. In fact, of the whole range of fauna, only the tigers and the major primates — chimpanzee and gorilla — are missing.

MAMMALS

(Swahili names, if any, in brackets):

Elephant, *Loxodonta africana* (Tembo/Ndovu): Widely distributed. Rain forests, secondary forests, highland forests, open woodlands, savannah, dry bush, and swamps. Tsavo, Mount Kenya, the Aberdares, Meru National Park, Amboseli, Samburu, Shimba and Maasai Mara.

Rock hyrax, *Heterohyrax brucei* (Pimbi): Widely distributed. Cliffs, rocky hills and stony mountain slopes.

Tree hyrax, *Dendrohyrax arboreous* (Perere): Widely distributed. Forests. Nocturnal. More often heard than seen.

Black rhinoceros, *Diceros bicornis* (Kifaru): Widely distributed but few remaining. Bush, savannah, light forests, highland forest and high-altitude moorlands. Tsavo, Nairobi, Amboseli, Mount Kenya, the Aberdares and Nakuru national parks and Samburu, Maasai Mara national reserves.

White rhinoceros, *Diceros simus* (Kifaru): Introduced. Maasai Mara National Reserve.

Burchell's zebra, *Equus burchelli* (Punda milia): Widely distributed in grasslands, open savannah, and grassy flats surrounded by bush. Large numbers seen at Amboseli and Maasai Mara.

Grevy's zebra, *Equus grevyi* (Punda milia): Dry grassy bush country. Seen in Samburu, Marsabit, Meru National Park and northern Kenya, east of Lake Turkana and north of the Tana River.

Buffalo, *Syncerus caffer* (Nyati/mbogo): Widely distributed. Rainforests, secondary forests, highland forests, open woodlands, savannah, bush and swamps. Large numbers in Tsavo, Meru, Amboseli and mountain national parks and Samburu and Maasai Mara national reserves.

Wildebeest, *Connochaetes taurinus* (Nyumbu): Widely distributed. Grassland, savannah and open woodlands. Southern Kenya, north to Mau Forest and Thika River. Their mass migration in Maasai Mara is one of nature's great spectacles.

Coke's hartebeest, *Alcelaphus buselaphus cokei* (Kongoni): Widely distributed. Grasslands and grassy savannah. Southern Kenya, north to Lake Naivasha, upper Tana and Galana rivers. Nairobi National Park, Amboseli and Maasai Mara.

Lelwel hartebeest, *Alcelaphus buselaphus lelwel* (Kongoni): Savannah. North-western Kenya. A hartebeest resembling the Lelwel lives in the Lambwe Valley of western Kenya, another on Laikipia, north of Mount Kenya.

Hunter's hartebeest, *Damaliscus hunteri* (Kongoni): Restricted to an area of sansevieria bush with grassy clearings extending from the Tana River to southern Somalia. Some have been transferred to Tsavo Park.

Topi, *Damaliscus korrigum jimela* (Nyamera): Grasslands and open savannah. Western Kenya, along Kenya coast from the Sabaki River to the Somalia border. Numerous in Maasai Mara.

Harvey's red duiker, *Cephalophus harveyi* (Funo): Widely distributed in forests, bush and high grass jungles. Being secretive in their habits, duikers are only encountered accidentally.

Blue duiker, *Cephalophus monticola* (Paa): Widely distributed in forests, gallery forest and bushlands.

Yellow-backed duiker, *Cephalophus sylvicultor* (Paa): Forests with plenty of undergrowth, gallery forest and dense savannah. Mau Forest.

Grey (Bush) duiker, *Sylvicapra grimmia* (Nsua): Widely distributed. Bush, forest edges, cultivations and high grass.

Suni, *Nesotragus moschatus* (Paa): Locally in highland forests, coastal forests and dense bush.

Steinbok, *Raphicerus campestris* (Dondoro): Widely distributed. Grasslands, with a certain amount of scattered bush. They are found as far north as Laikipia, and at the foot of Mount Elgon.

Klipspringer, *Oreotragus oreotragus* (Mbusi mawe): Widely distributed but only on rocky hills and mountain ranges. Hell's Gate and Tsavo.

Oribi, *Ourebia ourebi* (Taya): Widely distributed. Grasslands, open savannah woodlands, and hilly country, scrubby bush.

Kirk's dik dik, *Rhynchotragus kirkii* (Dikidiki or

Taya): Widely distributed in dry bush country. Often seen in Tsavo, Amboseli and Maasai Mara.

Guenther's dik dik, *Rhynchotragus guentheri* (Dikidiki or suguya): Northern Kenya. Samburu.

Waterbuck, *Kobus ellipsiprymnus* (Kuro): Widely distributed. Savannah, bush and gallery forests. Eastern Kenya. Tsavo, Amboseli and Nairobi national parks have both common and defassa.

Defassa waterbuck, *Kobus defassa* (Kuro): Widely distributed in western Kenya, east of Nairobi National Park to the Maasai Mara. Laikipia Plateau and Nakuru National Park.

Bohor reedbuck, *Redunca redunca* (Tohe): Widely distributed in grassy areas with patches of bush, and reedbeds, never far from water. Can be seen well in Nairobi and Nakuru National Parks.

Chanler's mountain reedbuck, *Redunca fulvorufula chanleri* (Tohe): Rocky slopes, escarpments and stony ridges. Central and western Kenya. Seen in Nairobi National Park.

Impala, *Aepyceros melampus* (swara pala): Widely distributed in Kenya north to Wamba and northern Ewaso Nyiro (Samburu). Can be seen in large numbers in Tsavo, Nairobi National Park, Amboseli and Maasai Mara.

Thomson's gazelle, *Gazella thomsoni* (Swara tomi): Grasslands and savannah. Laikipia Plateau, southern Kenya, west to Lake Victoria, east to Tsavo West.

Grant's gazelle, *Gazella granti* (Swara granti): Grasslands, open savannah and dry bushland. Widely distributed in Kenya, east almost to Indian Ocean, west to Lake Victoria. Can be seen in Tsavo, Nairobi National Park, Amboseli, Maasai Mara and Samburu. Grant's gazelle of north-west Kenya is known as **Bright's gazelle.**

Gerenuk, *Litocranius walleri* (Swara twiga): Dry bush country. Northern and eastern Kenya, Lake Magadi region. Tsavo, Meru, Samburu and Amboseli are good places to see this species.

Beisa oryx, *Oryx beisa* (Choroa): Desert scrub, dry bush, and grasslands with scattered trees. Northern Kenya, south to Laikipia Plateau and Tana River. Can be seen in Samburu, Marsabit and Meru National Park.

Fringe-eared oryx, *Oryx beisa callotis* (Choroa): Dry bush country and grasslands. From Tana River south to Kilimanjaro area and west of Lake Magadi. Can be seen in Tsavo and Amboseli.

Sable antelope, *Hippotragus niger* (Palahala, mbarapi): Rare in Kenya. Savannah with patches of bush and open meadow, especially of the miombo forest type. Coastal areas north to Bamba, inland from Kilifi. Shimba Hills National Reserve near Mombasa.

Roan antelope, *Hippotragus equinus* (Korongo): Rare now in Kenya. Savannah interspersed with grassy patches, rolling uplands with bush and open forest. Ruma (Lambwe Valley) National Park.

Eland, *Taurotragus oryx* (Pofu or mbunja): Although widely distributed, numbers have become much reduced in densely settled areas. Grasslands, savannah and mountain moorlands. Nairobi National Park, Tsavo and Maasai Mara.

Bushbuck, *Tragelaphus scriptus* (Mbawala or pongo): Widely distributed, wherever bush and undergrowth offer cover. Nairobi and mountain national parks are good places to see them.

Greater kudu, *Tragelaphus strepsiceros* (Tandala mkubwa): Rare in southern Kenya, more common on the mountains of the northern regions. Dense savannah, especially of the miombo forest type, rocky hills covered with forests, and thorn thicket belts of dense bush along rivers. Seen at Marsabit and Lake Bogoria.

Lesser kudu, *Strepsiceros imberbis* (Tandala ndogo): Northern Kenya, south through eastern part of country to Kilimanjaro region and southern Ewaso Nyiro. Tsavo, Amboseli and Meru national parks.

Bongo, *Boocercus euryceros*: Rare. Highland forests of Kenya, usually between 2,100 and 3,300m (6,890-10,830ft). Mount Kenya, the Aberdares, Mau Forest and Cherangani Hills.

Sitatunga, *Tragelaphus spekei*, (Nzohe): Swamps. Western Kenya. Can be observed in the Saiwa Swamp near Kitale.

Maasai giraffe, *Giraffa camelopardalis* (Twiga): Dry thorn country, acacia grasslands, savannah, bushlands and highland forest. Widely distributed in southern Kenya, north to the Tana River. Tsavo, Amboseli and Nairobi national parks, Maasai Mara and many other places.

Reticulated giraffe, *Giraffa camelopardalis reticulata* (Twiga): Northern Kenya. Meru National Park, Samburu and Marsabit. A sub-species is known as **Rothschild's Giraffe**, *Giraffa camelopardalis rothschildi*. Nakuru National Park.

Bush pig, *Potamochoerus porcus* (Nguruwe mwitu): Widely distributed. Forests, gallery forests and bushy savannah. Crepuscular and nocturnal. Rarely seen.

Giant forest hog, *Hylochoerus meinertzhageni*: Rain forests, gallery forests and highland forest. Mount Elgon, Cherangani Hills, Mau Forest, Mara River, the Aberdares and Mount Kenya.

Wart hog, *Phacochoerus aethiopicus* (Njiri): Widely distributed. Savannah and bushy grasslands. Common in Nairobi National Park and many other reserves.

Hippopotamus, *Hippopotamus amphibius* (Kiboko): Widely distributed. Rivers, lakes and swamps. Good places to see this species are the Mzima Springs (Tsavo West), the Hippo Pools of Nairobi National Park and the Mara River.

Carnivores

Lion, *Panthera leo* (Simba): Still widely distributed. Grasslands, savannah, open woodlands, bush and semi-deserts. Nairobi park, Maasai Mara, Tsavo West and Samburu are good places to see and study lions.

Leopard, *Panthera pardus* (Chui): Widely distributed. All types of forest, savannah, bush, grasslands, semi-deserts and rocky mountain areas. Usually secretive and rarely seen.

African wild cat, *Felis sylvestris lybica* (Paka pori): Widely distributed. Nocturnal.

Cheetah, *Acinonyx jubatus* (Duma): Fairly widely distributed in grasslands and open savannah. Can usually be seen in Nairobi National Park, Amboseli, Samburu and Maasai Mara.

Serval cat, *Felis serval* (Mondo): Widely distributed, but rarely seen. Dry bush country and savannah. Shy, solitary and mainly nocturnal.

Spotted hyena, *Crocuta crocuta* (Fisi): Widely distributed. Mainly nocturnal.

Striped hyena, *Hyaena hyaena* (Fisi): Nocturnal and rarely seen.

Aardwolf, *Proteles cristatus* (Fisi ndogo): Looks like a small striped hyena and is sometimes encountered in daytime.

Spotted-necked otter, *Lutra maculicollis* (Fisi maji): Widely distributed. Rivers, lake shores, papyrus marshes, reed beds and quiet backwaters. Especially common around Lake Victoria.

Clawless otter, *Aonyx capensis* (Fisi maji): Found in rivers, streams and swamps up to 3,000m (9,843ft).

Honey badger, *Mellivora ratel* (Nyegere): Nocturnal. Can be seen regularly near several lodges and do-it-yourself camps.

Grey or golden jackal, *Canis aureus* (Mbweha): Grasslands and savannah. Amboseli.

Black-backed jackal, *Canis mesomelas* (Mbweha): Widely distributed. Savannah and grasslands. It is most commonly seen in Nairobi National Park, Amboseli, Maasai Mara and many other places.

Side-striped jackal, *Canis adustus* (Mbweha): Very nocturnal, rarely seen.

Hunting dog, *Lycaon pictus* (Mbwa mwitu): Widely distributed, though much reduced in numbers. Bush, light forest, savannah, and grasslands. Seen in Tsavo, Maasai Mara, Samburu and Nairobi National Park.

Bat-eared fox, *Otocyon megalotis* (Mbwela masikia): Widely distributed. Grasslands and open woodlands. Often seen in Amboseli, and occasionally in Nairobi National Park.

White-tailed mongoose, *Ichneumia albicauda* (Nguchiro): Widely distributed. Nocturnal.

Black-tipped mongoose, *Herpestes sanguineus* (Nguchiro): Widely distributed. Diurnal.

Dwarf mongoose, *Helogale undulata* (Nguchiro): Widely distributed. Diurnal and gregarious. Often seen on termite hills.

Banded mongoose, *Mungos mungo* (Nguchiro): Grasslands. Diurnal and gregarious. Often seen in Maasai Mara.

Genet, *Genetta spp.* (Kanu): Widely distributed. Nocturnal. Have become tame at several lodges.

Primates

Bushbaby, or **greater galago**, *Galago crassicaudatus* (Komba): Widely distributed. Gallery highland forests and bamboo thickets. Nocturnal. Can be often heard wailing and screaming. **Senegal galago**, *Galago senegalensis*, are found in savannah and woodlands.

Potto, *Perodicticus potto* Western Kenya: Nocturnal, rarely seen. Found in Kakamega, Kaimosi and Mau Forests.

Olive Baboon, *Papio anubis* (Nyani): Savannah, gallery forests, bush, rocky mountains. Most of Kenya, particularly Nairobi National Park and the Aberdares.

Yellow baboon, *Papio cynocephalus* (Nyani): South-eastern Kenya, Amboseli and Tsavo West.

Tana mangabey, *Cercocebus galeritus*: Lower Tana, Witu and Lamu hinterland.

Red colobus, *Colobus badius*: Tana River and Sokoke-Arabuko Forest near Malindi.

Black-and-white colobus, *Colobus polykomos* (Mbega): Forests, especially highland forest of Mount Kenya, the Aberdares, Mount Elgon and Nakuru National Park.

Vervet monkey, *Cercopithecus aethiops* (Tumbiri or tumbili): Widely distributed. Savannah, woodlands, mountain forests and gallery forest.

Blue or Sykes monkey, *Cercopithecus mitis* (Kima): Favours denser and more extensive forests. Large and very variable in colour.

Red-tailed monkey, *Cercopithecus nictitans*: Evergreen and gallery forests. Western Kenya.

De Brazza monkey, *Cercopithecus neglectus*: Forests, especially along rivers and swamps. Western Kenya, particularly Mount Elgon and Kitale.

Patas monkey, *Erythrocebus patas*: Savannah, acacia scrub. North-western Kenya, Uasin Gishu and Laikipia districts.

Bird Profile

With landscapes ranging from glacial mountains and alpine moorlands, through close-canopy forest and mangrove swamp, to savannah and semi-desert, and with many freshwater and alkaline lakes, and a tremendous variety of botanical species, Kenya hosts some 1,500 bird species. Some of the more common or spectacular species — excluding the many migrants from the north — are:

Ostrich: Two subspecies: **Maasai Ostrich**, *Struthio camelus massaicus*: Widely distributed in grasslands and open savannah. North to Tana River; **Somali**, or **blue-shanked ostrich**, *Struthio camelus molybdophanes*: Dry bush country in northeastern Kenya. Samburu.

Pelicans: **Pink-backed pelican**, *Pelecanus rufescens*: White, greyish on wings, head and belly, tinged pinkish on back and rump. Inland lakes. **White pelican**, *Pelecanus onocrotalus*: Somewhat larger, white, tinged with pink during breeding season. Common on Lake Naivasha and on Lake Nakuru.

Cormorants: **White-necked cormorant**, *Phalacrocorax carbo*, and **pigmy cormorant**, *Phalacrocorax africanus*: Common on lakes Naivasha and Nakuru. **Darter**, *Anhinga rufa*: Related to cormorants. Widespread on lakes and rivers. Long, thin neck.

Herons: **Blackheaded heron**, *Ardea melancocephala*: Common and widely distributed. Lake shores, river banks and swamps; often quite far from water. **Goliath heron**, *Ardea goliath*: Largest African heron. Never far from water. Can be seen at Lake Naivasha. **Night heron**, *Nyciticorax nycticorax*: Lakes, rivers and marshes.

Egrets: **Yellow-billed egret**, *Mesophoyx intermedius*: Swamps, rivers, and lakes. Locally numerous. **Little egret**, *Egretta garzetta*: Smaller with black bill. **Cattle egret**, *Bubulcus ibis*: Widely distributed, usually in flocks, often accompanying game or domestic stock. Feeds on insects disturbed by grazing animals.

Storks: **Saddle-billed stork**, *Ephippiorhynchus senegalensis*: Swamps, marshes and reedy lake shores. Singly or in couples. Seen fairly regularly in Buffalo Springs, also Amboseli and Maasai Mara. **Yellow-billed stork**, *Ibis ibis*. Widely distributed. Flat shores and sandbanks of shallow lakes and rivers. Often in small parties. **Open-billed Stork**, *Anastomus lamelligerus*: Lakes, marshes and large lagoons. Sometimes in large flocks. Often seen on the Galana River and Aruba Dam (Tsavo East). **Marabou**, *Leptoptilos cruminiferus*: Widely distributed. Open savannah, often in big flocks. A stork with the habits of a vulture. **Hammerkop**, *Scopus umbretta*: Rivers, pools and shallow lake shores. Big spherical nest can be seen in riverine forests. **Abdim's stork**, *Sphenorynchus abdimi*. Visits East Africa from Sudan, often in large flocks.

African Spoonbill, *Platalea alba*: Shallow lakes, lagoons and dams. Seen in Rift Valley lakes.

Ibises: **Sacred ibis**, *Threskiornis aethiopicus*: Widely distributed. Lakes, rivers and marshes. Often in flocks. **Hadada**, *Hagedashia hagedash*: Well-watered and well-wooded areas. Usually singly or in pairs. Seen in Nairobi National Park and at Lake Naivasha.

Flamingos: **Lesser flamingo**, *Phoeniconaias minor*: Bill dark red, tipped black. Common at lakes Magadi, Nakuru, Bogoria and Elementeita. **Greater flamingo**, *Phoenicopterus ruber*: Bill pink and black. Recorded breeding at Lakes Magadi, Elmenteita and Nakuru. Often in close association with smaller species.

Geese: **Egyptian goose**, *Alopochen aegyptiacus*: Common and widely distributed. Lakes, ponds, dams, rivers and marshes. In pairs and family parties. Outside breeding season also in flocks. **Spurwing goose**, *Plectropterus gambensis*: Lakes and rivers, often in big flocks. **Knob-billed goose**, *Sarkidiornis melanotos*: In small flocks on lakes, pools and wooded swamps. Can be seen at Lake Naivasha.

Ducks: **African pochard**, *Aythia erythrophthalmus*: Common on lakes, often in flocks of 50 or more. **Yellow-billed duck**, *Anas undulata*: Open waters, reedy ponds and rivers. Gregarious. **Red-billed duck**, *Anas erythrorhyncha*: Common in swamps, reedy pools and inlets of lakes. **Hottentot teal**, *Anas punctata*: Shallow saline and freshwater pools with mud banks, shallow grassy coves. Can be seen at Lake Nakuru. **Cape wigeon**, *Anas capensis*: Large and small sheets of saline water and marshes. **White-faced tree-duck**: *Dendrocygna viduata*: River flats, swamps, saltwater lagoons, estuaries, pools and rivers. Often in large flocks. **Fulvous tree-duck**, *Dendrocygna bicolor*: Inland lakes and marshes.

Secretary bird, *Sagittarius serpentarius*: Often seen in grasslands, savannah and light bush. Forages on ground.

Vultures: Animal carcasses very quickly attract vultures of several species, especially **hooded vultures**, *Necrosyrtes monachus*; **white-backed vultures**, *Pseudogyps africanus*; and **Ruppell's griffon vultures**, *Gyps ruppellii*. They all give way to the large **lappet-faced vulture**, *Torgos tracheliotus*. The **Egyptian vulture**, *Neophron percnopterus*, uses stones to break ostrich eggs.

Lammergeier or **bearded vulture**, *Gypaetus barbatus*: Rather scarce, but can be seen around Elgon, Rift Valley (Hell's Gate), Mount Kenya.

Kites and buzzards: **Black-shouldered kite**, *Elaus caeruleus*: Savannah, dry grasslands and cultivated areas. Often seen Nairobi National Park. **Yellow-billed kite**, *Milvus migrans*: A subspecies of the European black kite. Common in savannah, along lakes, rivers, and also in towns. **Augur buzzard**, *Buteo rufofuscus*: Common in mountains, open savannah and cultivated areas.

Eagles: **Verreaux's eagle**, *Aquila verreauxii*: Rocky hills, mountains and gorges. Has bred in Nairobi National Park. **Tawny eagle**, *Aquila rapax*: Widely distributed. Common in open savannah, cultivated areas, bush and semi-deserts. **Martial eagle**, *Polemaetus bellicosus*: Widely distributed. Woodlands, savannah and thornbush. Can be seen in Nairobi National Park. **Long-crested hawk eagle**, *Lophaetus occipitalis*: Fairly common in riverine forests, bush, wooded and cultivated areas. Can often be seen perched on telegraph poles. **Bateleur eagle**, *Terathopius ecaudatus*: Fairly common in open savannah and thornbush country. Flight is swift and rocking. **African fish eagle**, *Cuncuma vocifer*: Common along rivers, lakes, estuaries and seashore. Loud, ringing call.

Falcons: Many different species of this group of raptors haunt different arid, semi-arid and savannah areas of Kenya. **Peregrine**, *Falco peregrinus*: A small race of the well-known cosmopolitan species. The **African hobby**, *Falco cuvieri*: A distinct species. Savannah and thornbush country. **Lanner**, *Falco biarmicus*: Seen fairly often in savannah and in dry country, usually near rocks. Shrike-sized **pigmy falcon**, *Poliohierax semitorquatus*: Thorn-bush and semi-desert areas. Especially common in the northern part of Kenya (Samburu). Smallest African raptor.

Hawks: There are several species of goshawks and sparrow-hawks. **Pale chanting goshawk**, *Melierax poliopterus*: often seen in acacia and bush country.

Goshawk, *Melierax mitrata*: often seen in acacia and bush country.

Guineafowl: **Helmeted guineafowl**, *Numida mitrata*: Widely distributed and often seen in big flocks. **Vulturine guineafowl**, *Acryllium vulturinum*: Dry bush. Northern and eastern Kenya. Especially common in Samburu.

Yellow-necked spurfowl, *Pternistis leucoscepus*: Widespread and common in dry open bush and grasslands, in the vicinity of cultivated areas. **Jackson's francolin**, *Francolinus jacksoni*: Mountain forests. Can be seen in the Aberdares and Mount Kenya National Park.

Black crake, *Limnocorax flavirostra*: Common and often seen. Marshes, swamps, river banks and lake shores. Will walk around on a hippo's back. **Red-crested coot**, *Fulica cristata*: Lakes, dams and swamps. **Purple gallinule**, *Porphyrio porphyrio*: Swamps, papyrus marshes.

Crowned crane, *Balearica regulorum*: Widely distributed. Swamps, lake shores and grasslands. In pairs, small parties or flocks.

Bustards: **Kori bustard**, *Ardeotis kori*: Open savannah, thornbush and grasslands. Nairobi National Park, Amboseli, Samburu and Maasai Mara. **Black-bellied bustard**, *Lissotis melanogaster*: Fairly common in open grasslands and cultivated areas. Maasai Mara, Tsavo National Park. **White-bellied bustard**, *Eupodotis senegalensis*.

Stone curlews: *Burhinus* spp: Of the three species of stone curlews, two are mostly found near water, one in dry scrub, bush and open woodlands.

Jacana, or **lily trotter**, *Actophilornis africanus*: Walks on floating vegetation. Common at Lake Naivasha and Amboseli.

Plovers and related species:**Crowned plover**, *Stephanibyx coronatus*: Not bound to the vicinity of water. Very common on grasslands, especially in short grassy areas. **Blacksmith plover**, *Haplopterus armatus*: Common near rivers, swamps and lakes. **Spur-winged plover**,*Haplopterus spinosus*: Along rivers and lakes. Can be seen in Rift Valley lakes and Samburu. **Wattled plover**, *Afribyx senegallus*: Swamps and damp areas with short grass. Western Kenya. Of the smaller species, **Kittlitz's plover**, *Charadrius pecuarius*, and the **three-banded plover**, *Charadrius tricollaris*, are widely distributed on sand banks and mud flats along lakes, rivers and dams. **Chestnut-banded plover**, *Charadrius pallidus venustus*: Found at Lake Magadi only. **Black-winged stilt**, *Himanto-pus himantopus*: Marshes and salt lakes. Very common at Lakes Magadi and Nakuru. **Avocet**, *Recurvirostra avocetta*: Mud flats, estuaries, lagoons and lakes Nakuru and Magadi.

Coursers: Several species on grasslands and dry bush country. **Temminck's courser**, *Cursorius temminckii*: Can often be seen on recently burnt ground. **Heuglin's courser**, *Hemerodromus cinctus*: Occurs in Tsavo National Park.

Gulls: **Grey-headed gull**, *Larus cirrocephalus*: Most common gull on East African inland waters. **Sooty gull**, *Larus hemprichii*: Occurs on the coast.

Sandgrouse: Several species. **Yellow-throated sand-grouse**, *Eremialector gutturalis*: One of the most common and widely distributed. It can be seen at Amboseli and in many other places coming to water holes in large flocks.

Pigeons and doves: Numerous in species and numbers. **Speckled pigeon**, *Columba guinea*: One of the most handsome. **Ring-necked dove**, *Streptopelia capicola*: Widely distributed. Very common in savannah bush and cultivated areas. **Namaqua dove**, *Oena capensis*: Dry bush and semi-desert areas. Very pretty.

Cuckoos: Well represented in East Africa. **Red-chested cuckoo**, *Cuculus solitarius*: Calls 'tit-tit-whoo'. Also known as 'rainbird'. **White-browed coucal**, or **waterbottle-bird**, *Centropus superciliosus*: Skulks in dense bush, especially near rivers and in reed beds. Has a bubbling call, like water being poured out of a bottle. **Emerald cuckoo**, *Chrysococcyx cupreus*, **Didric cuckoo**, *Chrysococcyx caprius*, and **Klaas' cuckoo**, *Chrysococcyx klaas*: Distinguished by the metallic colouration of their upperparts.

Parrots: **Grey parrot**, *Psittacus erithacus*: Largest African parrot. A renowned 'talker'. Found locally in western Kenya. **Red-headed parrot**, *Poicephalus gulielmi*: Mountain forests. Seen quite regularly along the Naro Moru River.

Turacos: Several species of *Green red-winged turacos, Touraco* spp: Coastal highland and mountain forests. **Grey turacos** or 'go-away' birds are partial to savannah and dry bush. **White-bellied go-away bird**, *Corythaixoides leucogaster*: Common at Samburu.

Rollers: Represented by several species. **Lilac-breasted roller**, *Coracias caudata*: Commonly seen in savannah and bush. **Broad-billed roller**, *Eurystomus glaucurus*: Forests, savannah, riverine forests and mountains, up to the bamboo zone.

Bee-eater, *Meropidae*: Represented by a number of species. **Little bee-eater**, *Melittophagus pusillus*: Widely distributed. **White-fronted bee-eater**, *Merops bullockoides*: Often seen in the Lake Naivasha region, including Hell's Gate. **Cinnamon-chested bee-eater**, *Merops oreobates*: Often seen at the Naro Moru River. **Carmine bee-eater**, *Merops nubicus*: Common in coastal areas from November to April.

Kingfishers: Some kingfishers are always found close to water. **Giant kingfisher**, *Megaceryle maxima*, and **Pied kingfisher**, *Ceryle rudis*: Large rivers and lakes. **Malachite kingfisher**, *Corythornis cristata*: Along streams, rivers and lake shores fringed with reeds, papyrus and other dense vegetation. Very pretty **grey-headed kingfisher**, *Halcyon leucocephala*: Seen far away from water. **Brown-hooded kingfisher**, *Halcyon albiventris*, and **striped kingfisher**, *Halcyhon chelicuti*: Mainly birds of savannah and woodlands.

Hornbills: The **tokos**, *Tockus erythrorhynchus*, and others: Widely distributed. Savannah and bush country. Large forest hornbills, such as **trumpeter hornbills**, *Bycanistes bucinator*, and the **silvery-cheeked hornbill**, *Bycanistes brevis*: Coastal, riverine and mountain forests. **Ground hornbill**, *Bucorvus leadbeateri*: Grasslands and savannah. Forages on the ground.

Hoopoes and **wood hoopoes**: The **African hoopoes**, *Upupa* spp: closely resemble the European species. Wood hoopoes are long-tailed, iridescent green, black, or blue in colour. **Green wood hoopoe** or **kakelaar**, *Phoeniculus purpureus*: Woodlands and riverine forests. Usually met in small, noisy flocks.

Nightjars: Some nightjars have distinctive calls, but when seen flitting at night, or sitting on a road in car lights, the many different species are not easy to distinguish from each other.

Owls: **African marsh owl**, *Asio capensis*: Quite frequently flushed out of high grass. **Verreaux's eagle owl**, *Bubo lacteus*: Often discovered sitting on an acacia tree in riverine forest or savannah country.

Mousebirds: **Speckled mousebird**, *Colius striatus*: Common and widespread along forest edges, bushy savannah, thick scrub and cultivated areas. **Blue-naped mousebird**, *Colias macrourus*: Dry bush.

Trogons: **Narina's trogon**, *Apoloderma narina*: Highland and mountain forests. One of the most beautiful of East African birds.

Barbets: Many species. **Red-and-yellow barbet**, *Trachyphonus erythrocephalus*: Often seen perched on termite hills in dry bush country. Samburu reserve and Tsavo National Park. One of the most striking, **D'Arnaud's barbet**, *Trachyponus darnaudii*: Less colourful, but worth watching for its mating behaviour. Male and female sing and posture together, bobbing, bowing and wagging their tails.

Honey guides: **Greater** or **black-throated honey guide**, *Indicator indicator*: So named because they guide humans or honey badgers to bees' nests.

Woodpeckers: Many species. One of the most

common and widely distributed is the **Nubian woodpecker**, *Campethera nubica*: All types of savannah country.

Swifts: Various species. Seen practically everywhere, from the streets of Nairobi (**Little Swift**, *Apus affinis*) to the crags of Mount Kenya (**Alpine Swift**, *Apus melba*).

Passerines: Too many species to mention. Among the more colourful are two **Glossy starlings**, the **Blue-eared** *Lamprocolius chalybaeus* and the **Splendid**, *Lamprocolius splendidus*. **Superb starling**, *spreo superbus*: Very tame around lodges and picnic sites. **Golden-breasted starling**, *Cosmopsarus regius*: Can be observed and photographed at Kilaguni Lodge.

Sunbirds: Many varieties. Small, often colourful birds which dip their beaks into flowers. Not to be mistaken for hummingbirds. **Scarlet-chested sunbird**, *Chalcomitra senegalensis*: Very striking and often seen.

Weaver birds: Make beautifully woven nests, often arranged in such large colonies they can't be missed. Yellow, or a combination of yellow and black. **Sparrow weaver**, *Plocepasser mahali*: One of the most common and widespread. Brown and white plumage. **White-headed buffalo weaver**, *Dinemellia dinemelli*: Common and very characteristic of dry bush country. Black, white and red. **Common buffalo weaver**, *Bubalornis albirostris*: Male is black.

The enormously long-tailed **wydahs** and **widow birds** are related to the weavers. **Pintailed wydah**, *Vidua macroura*: Black and white. **Long-tailed widow bird**, *Euplectes progne*: Black with some red and white on the wings. Seen between Nanyuki and Nyeri. At mating time, widow birds perform interesting courtship dances.

Finches: There are many small and colourful species, especially the **Red-cheeked Cordon bleu**, *Uraeginthus bengalus*; **Purple grenadier**, *Uraeginthus ianthinogaster*; and **Fire-finch**, *Logonosticta rubricata*.

Shrikes: No traveller in East Africa can miss the black and white **Fiscal shrike**, *Lanius colluris*, of which in some places there seem to be two to every bush. The shrike family, as a whole, is very well represented, but many species are shy and less easily seen than the fiscal and its close relations.

Oxpeckers: Game watchers will soon become aware of two oxpeckers: **Red-billed oxpecker**, *Buphagus erythrorhynchus*, and **Yellow-billed oxpecker**, *Buphagus africanus*. They climb around on rhinos, buffaloes, giraffes and other animals in search of ticks.

Reptile and Amphibian Profile

Nile Crocodile, *Crocodylus niloticus*: Widely distributed in rivers, lakes and swamps, but much reduced through uncontrolled shooting and trapping. There is often a spectacular concentration at Crocodile Point, below the Lugard Falls of the Galana River in Tsavo East. During the last few years crocodiles have been on the increase in Samburu's Ewaso Nyiro River and a few can usually be seen at Mzima Springs, the Hippo Pools of the Nairobi National Park, Lake Baringo and on the Mara and Tana rivers. One of the last great sanctuaries for crocodiles is Lake Turkana.

Lizards: **Monitor lizards**: Can attain a length of two metres (six feet) or even more. **Nile Monitor**, *Varanus niloticus*: Mainly found along rivers. Known to dig up crocodile's nests and to eat the eggs. **Spotted Monitor**, *Varanus occelatus*: Dry bush and savannah country, at a considerable distance from any water.

Small geckos have established themselves in human habitations. The adhesive pads on their toes allow them to run up and down walls and even to walk on ceilings.

Rock agama, or **rainbow lizard**, *Agama agama*: Very beautiful. Can be seen around many of the lodges and do-it-yourself camps. Males are blue, with red heads. Fascinating to watch their colours become more intense or fade away, according to their state of agitation.

Chameleons are represented by a number of species, some of which are armed with horns.

Turtles are common in streams, rivers and the sea and **Terrapins**, *Pelomedusa subrufa*, live in many of Kenya's rivers.

Tortoises — especially the **Leopard tortoise**, *Testudo pardalis* — can often be found in grasslands and savannah.

Snakes: Visitors are usually surprised by the apparent lack of snakes. However, these reptiles are shy and secretive and some are predominantly nocturnal. Only rarely does a tourist travelling by car catch a brief glimpse of one as it slithers across the road. But in the country, moving about on foot, you soon come to realize that snakes are not uncommon. Most venomous species tend to get out of the way of any human being, warned by the vibration of the ground.

Black mamba, *Dendroaspis polylepis*: Has a sinister reputation of occasionally attacking without provocation, but this usually happens when it finds itself cut off from its hiding place. Not common in Kenya.

Puff adder, *Bitis arietans*: Widespread and fairly numerous. The most dangerous of Kenya's snakes. Relying on its wonderful camouflage, it usually does not take evasive action but remains motionless. A person walking through scrub or high grass can easily put his foot close enough to make it strike with lighting speed.

Black-necked or **spitting cobra**, *Naja nigricollis*: When cornered accidentally, it ejaculates its venom, aiming, if possible, at the face of its presumed enemy.

Green tree snake or **boomslang**, *Dispholidus typus*: May be seen slithering along a branch. It carries its poison fangs so far back in its jaws that to be bitten, a human being would have to put a finger into its mouth.

Rock python, *Python sebae*: Widely distributed and not uncommon in some places but not often seen. A truly magnificient snake which quite often attains a length of up to 5m (16ft). There are records of pythons over 11m (37ft) long.

Amphibians are represented in East Africa by **caecilians**, **toads** and **frogs**. There are no newts or salamanders. Frogs are especially numerous, ranging from tiny **Tree frogs** with adhesive pads on their toes, to the huge **Bullfrog**, *Pyxicephalus adspersus*: Up to 25cms (10 inches) in length and able to dig itself into the earth, vanishing from sight within about 20 minutes. **Clawed frog**, *Xenopus laevus*: Only rarely leaves the water. Has a flattened body, small forelimbs, large hindlimbs, and carries sharp, black claws on the first, second, and third toe. Males make rattling calls which can be heard a considerable distance away. The legless, worm-shaped **caecilians** spend most of their time underground or under stones, fallen leaves, in rotten tree trunks, or termite hills, and are rarely seen.

Insects and Arachnids

Most tourists who come to Kenya to collect insects are looking for **butterflies**, **moths**, or **beetles**. These groups occur all over Kenya, with some species only in confined areas. Around 600 species of butterflies are found, with closely defined limits for the coastal, dry-country, upland species, and those which occur in western Kenya. Some of those most likely to be seen are depicted on Kenya's definitive postage stamps issued in 1983.

Along the coastal belt, from the Tanzanian border northwards to Malindi, there are several interesting species. *Euphaedra neophron*, a purplish-brown butterfly, is to be found in the forests and under the cashew-nut and coconut plantations. A browner form is also found in Taveta Forest, around Meru, and near Mount Kenya. Quite a number of coastal butterflies can be found as far inland as Meru, having made their way across the dry semi-desert plains.

Also occasionally found in this area is *Papilio ophidicephalus*, the emperor swallowtail, a magnificent, large, black and yellow butterfly whose long tail has a brilliant blue and red patch at its base. It is sometimes quite common in Kibwezi Forest near the Mombasa road.

Between the coastal belt and just short of Nairobi are the great grassy plains of Kenya, which also cover the Rift Valley. Generally speaking, there is not enough rain to allow trees to grow, and a special group of butterflies has evolved to cover this vegetation: *Colotis* are white butterflies with brilliant red or orange tips and are common. So are the blue and yellow pansies, *Precis* spp, which can be seen settled on their territories of dry earth among the grass.

Where forest has been cut, for example for housing in the Nairobi area, these butterflies are also to be found. The northern deserts of Kenya are a major extension of this area, which is poor in species even during the infrequent rains.

Small mountains and hills are much more interesting. On the Taita Hills live a blue and black swallowtail, *Papilio taita* and *Cymothoe taita*, a creamy-white and black butterfly. Both of these are also found in Mbololo Forest on the top of the hills close to Voi. Kakamega Forest in western Kenya is the same as the great rainforests of the Congo Basin and attracts similar butterflies. The best butterfly areas are also good for moths, particularly during the rains. The first night of the rains is always the most productive.

Use either a black-white or an ordinary pressure lamp and a white sheet for collecting, or the moths may be badly damaged by large beetles in some areas. During the rains any light will produce magical results. Clouds of moths, along with millions of termites, will always come.

The best areas for **beetles** are the same as for butterflies, except that during the first nights of the rains, the area around Voi is very good for **dung-beetles**, *Scarabaeidae* spp.

A spectacular manifestation of insect life are the **termite hills** all over the countryside. Up to 3m (10ft) in height, they're often crowned by a series of turrets containing air-shafts, or running straight up in one single hollow tower that resembles a miniature factory chimney.

Termites are often referred to as 'white ants' but, in fact, they are related to cockroaches. They may have been the first creatures on earth to establish a social organization. Deep in the centre of the termite castle lies the strongly cemented royal cell where the gigantic queen spends her life tended by an army of workers and well-armed soldiers, and produces eggs at a rate of about one every two seconds. During the wet weather columns of **soldier ants**, also known as 'safari ants' or *siafu*, meander in thick black bands for hundreds of metres through bush and forest. These bands are formed by a two-way stream of bush ants and guarded on both flanks by aggressive, large-pincered 'soldiers'.

If you look closely where the column fans out, you'll see a wholesale massacre of spiders, cockroaches, crickets, caterpillars, even of frogs, lizards and small snakes.

An arthropod not classified among the insects is the **giant millipede**, popularly known as the 'Tanganyika Train'. This glossy black creature with reddish-brown legs, up to 30cms (12in) in length, is perfectly harmless. However, the big **centipedes** which lurk under tree trunks and fallen leaves have a venomous bite.

There are a number of species of **scorpions** in Kenya. Most of them are small with disagreeable but harmless stings. In hot, dry, bush country, however, there are scorpions up to 20cms (8in) long, which are as dangerous as they look. Scorpions are related to **spiders**, among which are some striking and beautiful species.

The huge, yellow and black *Nephilia spiders* construct amazingly tough, golden yellow webs. They are harmless, as are practically all other East African spiders. The one known exception is an uncommon species related to the black widow, *Latrodectes*, of America. It is black with dark red markings and a globular body. Its bite is quite venomous, though not necessarily fatal.

Animal Checklist

Mammals

INSECTIVORES
Rufous Spectacled Elephant Shrew
Yellow-Rumped Elephant Shrew
Rwenzori Golden Mole
East African Hedgehog
Otter Shrew
Giant White-Toothed Shrew

BATS
Straw-Coloured Fruit Bat
Epauletted Fruit Bat
Hammer-Headed Fruit Bat
Mouse-Tailed Bat
White-Bellied Tomb Bat
Hollow-Faced Bat
False Vampire Bat
Yellow-Winged Bat
Lander's Horse-shoe Bat
Lesser Leaf-Nosed Bat
Giant Leaf-Nosed Bat
Long-Eared Leaf-Nosed Bat
African Mouse-Eared Bat
Banana Bat, or African Pipistrelle
Yellow-Bellied Bat

Angola Free-Tailed Bat
White-Bellied Free-Tailed Bat
Flat-Headed Free-Tailed Bat
Giant Free-Tailed Bat

POTTOS, GALAGOS, and MONKEYS
Potto
Greater Galago
Bush Baby
Tana Mangabey
Black-Faced Vervet Monkey
Blue, or Sykes' Monkey
de Brazza Monkey
Red-Tailed, or White-Nosed Monkey
Patas Monkey
Olive Baboon
Yellow Baboon
Black and White Colobus
Red Colobus

PANGOLINS
Lesser Ground Pangolin

CARNIVORES
Hunting Dog
Golden Jackal
Black-Backed, or Silver-Backed Jackal
Side-Striped Jackal
Bat-Eared Fox

Zorilla
Ratel, or Honey Badger
Clawless Otter
African Civet
Neumann's, or Small-Spotted Genet
Bush, or Large-Spotted Genet
African Palm Civet
Marsh Mongoose
Dwarf Mongoose
Large Grey Mongoose
Slender, or Black-Tipped Mongoose
White-Tailed Mongoose
Banded Mongoose
Aardwolf
Spotted Hyena
Striped Hyena
Cheetah
Caracal
African Wild Cat
Serval
Golden Cat
Lion
Leopard

ANT BEARS
Ant Bear (Aardvark)

HYRAXES
Tree Hyrax
Rock Hyrax

ELEPHANTS
African Elephant

ODD-TOED UNGULATES
Black Rhinoceros
Square-Lipped, or White Rhinoceros
Grevy's Zebra
Burchell's, or Common Zebra

EVEN-TOED UNGULATES
Hippopotamus
Giant Forest Hog
Wart hog
Bush Pig
Common Giraffe
Reticulated Giraffe
Coke's Hartebeest, or Kongoni
Jackson's Hartebeest
White-Bearded Gnu or Wildebeest
Hunter's Hartbeest or Hirola
Topi
Zanzibar, or Ader's Duiker
Yellow-Backed Duiker
Blue Duiker
Bush Duiker
Klipspringer
Suni
Oribi
Steinbok
Kirk's Dik Dik
Guenther's Dik Dik
Common Waterbuck
Bohor Reedbuck
Chanler's Mountain Reedbuck
Impala
Thomson's Gazelle

Grant's Gazelle
Gerenuk
Roan Antelope
Sable Antelope
Oryx
Bongo
Sitatunga
Bushbuck
Greater Kudu
Lesser Kudu
Eland
African Buffalo

HARES and RABBITS
African Hare
Spring Hare

RODENTS
Cane Rat
Porcupine
Striped Ground Squirrel
Unstriped Ground Squirrel
Bush Squirrel
Giant Forest Squirrel
Scaly-Tailed Flying Squirrel
African Dormouse
Crested Rat
Giant Rat
Kenya Mole Rat
Naked Mole Rat

362

Bird Checklist

OSTRICH
Ostrich

GREBES
Little Grebe

PELICANS
White Pelican
Pink-Backed
Pelican

CORMORANTS
White-necked
Cormorant
Long-tailed
Cormorant

DARTERS
African Darter

**HERONS and
EGRETS**
Cattle Egret
Black-Headed
Heron
Goliath Heron

HAMMERKOP
Hammerkop

STORKS
Marabou Stork
Yellow-Billed
Stork
Saddle-billed
Stork
Open-billed Stork

**IBISES/
SPOONBILLS**
Sacred Ibis
Hadada Ibis
Wood Ibis
Glossy Ibis
African Spoonbill

FLAMINGOS
Greater Flamingo
Lesser Flamingo

DUCKS and GEESE
Eygptian Goose
Fulvous Tree
Duck
Pygmy Goose
Spur-winged
Goose
Knob-billed
Goose

BIRDS OF PREY
Bateleur Eagle
Martial Eagle
Steppe Eagle
Wahlberg's Eagle
Verreaux's Eagle
Long-Crested
Eagle
Tawny Eagle
African Fish Eagle
Secretary Bird
White-Backed
Vulture
Pale Chanting
Goshawk
Augur Buzzard
Black Kite
Black-Shouldered
Kite

GAME BIRDS
Crested Francolin
Yellow-Necked
Spurfowl
Helmeted
Guinea-Fowl
Vulturine
Guinea-Fowl

CRANES
Crowned Crane

**CRAKES, RAILS,
and COOTS**
Black Crake
Red-Knobbed
Coot

BUSTARDS
Kori Bustard

JACANAS
(or Lilly trotters)
African Jacana

**PLOVERS and
ALLIES**
Blacksmith Plover
Crowned Plover
Black-Winged Stilt

GULLS and TERNS
Grey-Headed Gull
Caspian Tern
Roseate Tern
Bridled Tern

SANDGROUSE
Chestnut-Bellied
Sandgrouse
Black-Faced
Sandgrouse

DOVES and PIGEONS
Speckled Pigeon
Red-Eyed Dove
Ring-Necked
Dove
Laughing Dove
Namaqua Dove

TURACOS
Schalow's Turaco
Hartlaub's Turaco
White-Bellied Go-
Away-Bird

**CUCKOOS and
COUCALS**
Red-Chested
Cuckoo
White-Browed
Coucal

OWLS
African Marsh Owl
Spotted Eagle Owl
Verreaux's Eagle
Owl
Pearl-Spotted Owlet
Scops Owl

SWIFTS
Little Swift

MOUSEBIRDS
Speckled
Mousebird
Blue-Naped
Mousebird

KINGFISHERS
Pied Kingfisher
Malachite
Kingfisher
Grey-Headed
Kingfisher

BEE-EATERS
Little Bee-Eater
Carmine Bee-Eater
Cinnamon-
Chested
Bee-Eater
White-Fronted
Bee-Eater

ROLLERS
Lilac-Breasted
Roller
Rufous-Crowned
Roller

HOOPOES
African Hoopoe
Green Wood
Hoopoe

HORNBILLS
Red-Billed
Hornbill
Yellow-Billed
Hornbill
Silvery-cheeked
Hornbill
Casqued Hornbill
Jackson's Hornbill
von der Decken's
Hornbill

BARBETS
Red-Fronted
Barbet
Red-Fronted
Tinkerbird
Golden-Rumped
Tinkerbird
D'Arnaud's Barbet
Red and Yellow
Barbet

WOODPECKERS
Nubian
Woodpecker
Brown-Backed
Woodpecker
Grey Woodpecker
Fine-Banded
Woodpecker

LARKS
Rufous-Naped Lark
Fischer's Sparrow
Lark

**SWALLOWS and
MARTINS**
Wire-Tailed
Swallow
Red-Rumped
Swallow
Striped Swallow

**WAGTAILS and
PIPITS**
African Pied
Wagtail
Golden Pipit

Yellow-Throated
Longclaw

BULBULS
Yellow-Vented
Bulbul

SHRIKES
White-Crowned
Shrike
Black-Headed
Tchagra
Tropical Boubou
Black-Headed
Gonolek
Slate-Coloured
Boubou
Fiscal Shrike

**THRUSHES and
ALLIES**
Stonechat
Capped Wheatear
Anteater Chat
Spotted Morning
Warbler
White-Starred
Bush Robin
Robin Chat
White-Browed
Robin Chat
Olive Thrush

**BABBLERS and
CHATTERERS**
Rufous Chatterer

WARBLERS
Hunter's Cisticola
Rattling Cisticola
Tawny-Flanked
Prinia
Black-Breasted
Apalis
Grey-Backed
Camaroptera
Crombec

FLYCATCHERS
White-Eyed Slaty
Flycatcher
Silverbird
Chin-Spot Fly-
catcher
Blue Flycatcher
Paradise
Flycatcher

TITS
White-Breasted
African Penduline

SUNBIRDS	Bunting	WEAVERS and ALLIES	Widow-Bird	Tailed Starling
Amethyst Sunbird		Reichenow's	Yellow Bishop	Violet-Backed
Scarlet-Chested	FINCHES	Weaver	Black-Winged	Starling
Sunbird	Yellow-Rumped	Golden Palm	Bishop	Hildebrandt's
Variable Sunbird	Seed-Eater	Weaver	Red Bishop	Starling
Eastern Double-	Brimstone Canary	Taveta Golden	West Nile Red	Superb Starling
Collared Sunbird	Streaky Seed-Eater	Weaver	Bishop	Golden-Breasted
Mariqua Sunbird		Masked Weaver	Long-Tailed	Starling
Tacazze Sunbird	WAXBILLS and	Vitelline Masked	Widow-Bird	Wattled Starling
Red-Chested	ALLIES	Weaver	Jackson's	Redwing Starling
Sunbird	Green-Winged	Speke's Weaver	Widow-Bird	
Beautiful Sunbird	Pytilia	Black-Headed	Red-Billed Buffalo	ORIOLES
Malachite Sunbird	Yellow-Bellied	Weaver	Weaver	Black-Headed
Bronze Sunbird	Waxbill	Chestnut Weaver	White-Headed	Oriole
Golden-Winged	Common Waxbill	Spectacled	Buffalo Weaver	
Sunbird	Purple Grenadier	Weaver	White-Browed	DRONGOS
Kenya Violet-	Red-Cheeked	Red-Headed	Sparrow Weaver	Drongo
Backed Sunbird	Cordon-Bleu	Weaver	Grey-Capped	
Collared Sunbird	Red-Billed	Cardinal Quelea	Social Weaver	CROWS
	Firefinch	Red-Billed Quelea		Pied Crow
WHITE-EYES	Cut-Throat	White-Winged	STARLINGS	Indian House Crow
Kikuyu White-Eye	Bronze Mannikin	Widow-Bird	Blue-Eared	Cape Rook
	Pin-Tailed Wydah	Red-Collared	Starling	Fan-Tailed Raven
BUNTINGS	Paradise Wydah		Ruppell's Long-	White-Naped
Golden-Breasted				Raven

A Demographic Profile

Kenya is inhabited by all three of the great language families of Africa. With the exception of recent immigrant communities, Kenyans can be divided into three distinct generic groupings: Bantu, Nilotic, and Cushitic (also known as Hamitic).

Each group belongs to a different language family — the Bantu to the Niger-Kordofanian family, Nilotic to the Nilo-Saharan family and Cushitic to the Hamito-Semitic family of Afro-Asiatic origin. Within Kenya the Bantu languages are further classified geographically into Western, Central, and Eastern. The Nilotic languages are divided into Western, Eastern, and Southern — although Maa, an Eastern Nilotic language, is spoken far south of any Southern Nilotic language.

The Cushitic family is represented in Kenya by two different branches, the Eastern and Southern Cushitic. Dahalo is the sole example of the latter still spoken in Kenya.

Many languages may be mutually intelligible and decisions as to their status are made with many reservations. Two-thirds of Kenya's people speak a Bantu language as their mother tongue; 30 per cent are Nilotic speakers and only three per cent speak Cushitic languages. However, the mainly nomadic people of this group range across 40 per cent of Kenya's territory.

Most early European administrators too readily identified tribes as time-honoured units. But, as linguistic and anthropological studies are continuing to reveal, this was far from the truth. The names of the ethnic groups are those in common usage. However, the Kiswahili plural prefix 'Wa' is frequently used by Kenyans when referring to these groups, as in Wakikuyu, Wakamba, Wataita, Wamaasai, Wanandi, and so on. The Western Bantu groups incorporate their own plural prefix 'Aba', as in Abaluhya, Abagussii, Abasuba, and Abakuria.

Population by Tribe/Ethnic grouping
Burji: number unknown, Moyale district.
Dassenich: 418, Todenyang, Marsabit districts.
El Molo: 3,600, Loiyangalani.
Embu: 256,623, Embu district.
Gabbra: 36,000, Marsabit district.
Gusii: 1.3 million, Kisii & South Nyanza districts.
Ilchamus: 15,872, Lake Baringo.
Iteso: 178,455, Busia & Bungoma districts.
Kamba: 2.5 million, Machakos & Kitui districts.
Keijo: number unknown, Elgeyo Escarpment.
Kikuyu: 4.5 million, Central Kenya.
Kipsigis: 2.9 million, Kericho district.
Kuria: 112,236, south of Kisii
Luo: 2.7 million, Kisumu district.
Luhya: 3.1 million, Kakamega district.
Maasai: 377,089, Narok and Kajiado districts.
Marakwet: unknown, Elgeyo-Marakwet district.
Mbeere: 101,007, Embu district.
Meru: 1.1 million, Meru district.
Mijikenda: 1,007,371, Kilifi district.
Nandi: Number unknown, Nandi district.
Okiek: 24,363, highland forests.
Orma: 45,562, north-east, Tana River district.
Pokomo: 59,000, Tana River district.
Pokot: number unknown, West Pokot district.
Rendille: 27,000, Marsabit district.

Sabaot: number unknown Trans Nzoia district.
Sakuye: 11,000, Isiolo district.
Samburu: 107,000, Samburu & Marsabit districts.
Segeju: 364, Kwale district.
Somali: 45,098, Mandera, Wajir & Garissa districts.
Suba: 108,000, South Nyanza district.
Taita/Taveta: 218,000, Taita-Taveta district.
Tharaka: 92,528, Embu district.
Tugen: number unknown,
Turkana: 284,000, Turkana district.
Population by province
Nairobi: 700 sq kms, 2,000,000+ (2,857+ to a sq km)
Coast: 83,040 sq kms, 1,342,794 (16 to a sq km)
Central: 13,173 sq kms, 2,345,833 (178 to a sq km)
Eastern: 155,759 sq kms, 2,719,851, (17 to a sq km)
North Eastern: 126,902 sq kms, 373,787 (2 to a sq km)
Nyanza: 12,525 sq kms, 2,643,956, (211 to a sq km)
Rift Valley: 163,883 sq kms, 3,240,402, (19 to a sq km)
Western: 8,196 sq kms, 1,832,663, (223 to the sq km)

Gazetteer

(First line indicates kilometre distance to major towns)

ARCHER'S POST
Nairobi 323, Isiolo 48, Nanyuki 123, Marsabit 239, Wamba 56, Maralal 110.
Alt: 790m (2,600ft). Post Office. Police post. Pop: 807. Samburu District, Rift Valley Province. Archer's Post Dispensary (Mission). Nearest hospital: Isiolo. Petrol/diesel usually available.

ATHI RIVER
Nairobi 27, Machakos 38, Mtito Andei 209, Namanga 138, Mombasa 458.
Alt: 1,520m (5,000ft). Post Office. Police Tel: 20222. Pop: 9,760. Machakos District, Eastern Province. Athi River Health Centre (Govt) Tel: 20368. Nearest hospital: Nairobi. Petrol/diesel.

BARAGOI
Nairobi 441, Nyahururu 243, Loiyangalani 225, Maralal 97.
Alt: 1,520m (5,000ft). Police Tel: 4. Pop: 2,592. Samburu District, Rift Valley Province. Baragoi Health Centre (Govt). Nearest hospital: Maralal. No petrol/diesel.

BARINGO (see Lake Baringo)

BUNA
Nairobi 793, Wajir 156, Moyale 101.
Alt: 940m (3,100ft). Police. Pop: 500. Wajir District, North Eastern Province. Buna Dispensary (Govt). Nearest hospital: Moyale. No petrol/diesel.

BUNGOMA
Nairobi 402, Eldoret 90, Kakamega 74, Kitale 127, Kisumu 127, Webuye 35.
Alt: 1,430m (4,700ft). Post Office. Police Tel: 20847. Pop: 25,161. HQ Bungoma District, Western Province. Bungoma District Hospital (Govt) Tel: 20345. Petrol/diesel usually available.

BUSIA
Nairobi 479, Bungoma 65, Eldoret 155, Kakamega 92, Kisumu 130.
Alt: 1,190m (3,900ft). Post Office. Police Tel: 2ll0. Customs Tel: 2038. Immigration Tel: 2027. Pop: 24,857. HQ Busia District, Western Province. Busia District Hospital (Govt) Tel: 2720. Border post with Uganda. Petrol/diesel.

BUTERE
Nairobi 408, Bungoma 43, Busia 71, Kakamega 53, Kisumu 59. Alt: 1,370m (4,500ft). Post Office. Police Tel: 20004. Pop: 1,044. Kakamega District, Western Province. Butere Health Centre (Govt) Tel: 20028. Nearest hospital: Mumias Mission Hospital. Petrol.

CHIEBIEMET
Nairobi 372, Eldoret 60, Iten 25.
Alt: 2,590m (8,500ft). Police Post. Pop: 1,000. Elgeyo Marakwet District, Rift Valley Province. Chiebiemet Dispensary (Govt). Nearest hospital: Kapsowar Mission Hospital. Petrol.

CHEPKORIO
Nairobi 313, Eldoret 39, Nakuru 157, Eldama Ravine 57.
Alt: 2,500m (8,200ft). Police Tel: 2Y6. Pop: 500. Elgeyo Marakwet District, Rift Valley Province. Chepkorio Health Centre (Govt) Tel: 1Y2. Nearest hospital: Plateau Reformed Church Hospital. No petrol/diesel.

ELBURGON
Nairobi 194, Molo 13, Nakuru 38, Njoro 20.
Alt: 2,410m (7,900ft). Post Office. Police Tel: 5. Pop: 5,343. Nakuru District, Rift Valley Province. Elburgon Health Centre (Govt) Tel: 33. Nearest hospital: Molo. Petrol.

ELDORET
Nairobi 312, Nakuru 156, Kitale 69, Bungoma 90.
Alt: 2,100m (6,900ft). Post Office. Police Tel: 32223. Pop: 50,503. HQ Uasin Gishu District, Rift Valley Province. Eldoret District Hospital (Govt) Tel: 33472; Uasin Gishu Hospital (Private) Tel: 32720. Petrol/diesel.

ELIYE SPRINGS
Nairobi 799, Kitale 418, Lodwar 63.
Alt: 375m (1,230ft). Pop: 500. Turkana District, Rift Valley Province. Nearest hospital: Lodwar. Nearest petrol: Lodwar.

ELDAMA RAVINE
Nairobi 216, Eldoret 96, Nakuru 60.
Alt: 2,130m (7,000ft). Post Office. Police Tel: 52222. Pop: 2,692. Baringo District, Rift Valley Province. Eldama Ravine Health Centre (Govt) Tel: 52012; Mercy Mission Hospital Tel: 16. Petrol.

EL WAK
Nairobi 822, Wajir 185, Mandera 177.
Alt: 427m (1,410ft). Post Office. Police Tel: 2002.
Pop: 500. Mandera District, North Eastern Province. El Wak Sub Health Centre (Govt). Nearest hospital: Wajir or Mandera. Petrol sometimes available.

EMBU
Nairobi 139, Embu 137, Murang'a 52, Nyeri 96, Sagana 40.
Alt: 1,372m (4,500ft). Post Office. Police Tel: 20102. Pop: 16,155. HQ Embu District and HQ Eastern province. Embu District Hospital (Govt) Tel: 20487. Petrol/diesel.

FERGUSON'S GULF
Nairobi 800, Kitale 419, Lodwar 64.
Alt: 375m (1,230ft). Pop: 500. Turkana District, Rift Valley Province. Nearest hospital: Lodwar. Petrol.

GARISSA
Nairobi 380, Mombasa 468, Wajir 321 (via Modo Gashi), Mwingi 202, Modo Gashi 161.
Alt: 100m (320ft). Post Office. Police Tel: 2005. Pop: 14,076. HQ Garissa District and HQ North Eastern Province. Garissa Provincial Hospital (Govt) Tel: 2284. Petrol/diesel.

GARSEN
Nairobi 715 (via Mombasa), Mombasa 230, Malindi 111, Garissa 238, Lamu 111.
Alt: 30m (100ft). Police Tel: 44. Pop: 1,007. Tana River District, Coast Province. Garsen Health Centre (Govt) Tel: 35. Nearest hospital: Ngao Mission Hospital. Ferry: 0600-1800 only. Petrol.

GILGIL
Nairobi 116, Nakuru 40, Naivasha 27, Nyahururu 82.
Alt: 2,010m (6,600ft). Post Office. Police Tel: 2222. Pop: 9,103. Nakuru District, Rift Valley Province. Gilgil Health Centre (Govt) Tel: 2214. Nearest hospital: Naivasha. Petrol.

HABASWEIN
Nairobi 527, Wajir 110, Modo Gashi 50, Isiolo 242.
Alt: 275m (900ft). Police Tel: 4. Pop: 500. Wajir District, North Eastern Province.
Habaswein Dispensary (Govt) Tel: 9. Nearest hospital: Wajir. Petrol.

HOLA
Nairobi 802 (via Mombasa), 531 (via Garissa), Mombasa 317, Garissa 151, Malindi 208.
Alt: 60m (200ft). Post Office. Police Tel: 2009. Pop: 5,352. HQ Tana River District, Coast Province. Hola District Hospital Tel: 2025. Petrol.

HOMA BAY
Nairobi 423, Kericho 157, Kisii 59, Kisumu 104 (115 via Kendu Bay), Mbita 35.

Alt: 1,145m (3,750ft). Post Office. Police Tel: 22626. Pop: 7,489. HQ South Nyanza District, Nyanza Province. Homa Bay District Hospital (Govt) Tel: 22004. Petrol.

ISIOLO
Nairobi 285, Marsabit 277, Meru 57, Nanyuki 85, Modo Gashi 192. Archer's Post 38, Garba Tula 125.
Alt: 1,220m (4,000ft). Post Office. Police Tel: 2008. Pop: 11,331. HQ Isiolo District, Eastern Province. Isiolo District Hospital (Govt) Tel: 2031. Petrol.

ITEN
Nairobi 346, Eldoret 34, Tambach 10, Kabarnet 60, Kaptarakwa 27, Tot 108, Kapkerop 33.
Alt: 2,225m (7,300ft). Police Tel: 2063. Pop: 743. HQ Elgeyo-Marakwet District, Rift Valley Province. Iten District Hospital (Govt) Tel: 2014. Petrol/diesel.

KABARNET
Nairobi 282, Marigat 42, Nakuru 146, Tambach 37, Eldoret 88, Mogotio 104.
Alt: 2,060m (6,750ft). Post Office. Police Tel: 2333. Pop: 3,621. HQ Baringo District, Rift Valley Province. Kabarnet District Hospital (Govt) Tel: 2064. Petrol.

KAHAWA
Nairobi 12, Thika 30, Nanyuki 188.
Alt: 1,555m (5,100ft). Pop: 30,958. Nairobi Area. Kahawa Health Centre (City Council). Nearest hospital: Nairobi. Petrol/diesel.

KAJIADO
Nairobi 76, Namanga 88, Athi River 51.
Alt: 1,740m (3,520ft). Post Office. Police Tel: 21222. Pop: 3,520. HQ Kajiado District, Rift Valley Province. Kajiado District Hospital (Govt) Tel: 21021. Petrol/diesel.

KAKAMEGA
Nairobi 402, Bungoma 74, Kisumu 73.
Alt: 1,525m (5,000ft). Post Office. Police Tel: 20222. Pop: 32,025. HQ Kakamega District and HQ Western Province. Kakamega General Hospital (Govt) Tel: 20020. Petrol/diesel.

KALOLENI
Nairobi 473, Mombasa 52 (via Mariakani), Mariakani 20, Kilifi 35, Mazeras 22.
Alt: 210m (700ft). Pop: 1,171. Kilifi District, Coast Province. Saint Luke's Kaloleni Mission Hospital Tel: 16. Petrol/diesel.

KAPENGURIA
Nairobi 413, Eldoret 101, Kitale 32, Lodwar 323.
Alt: 2,135m (7,000ft). Post Office. Police Tel: 2622. Pop: 2,752. HQ West Pokot District, Rift Valley Province. Kapenguria District Hospital (Govt) Tel: 2621. Petrol/diesel.

KAPSABET
Nairobi 325, Eldoret 48, Kakamega 68, Kisumu

85, Nandi Hills 18.
Alt: 1,950m (6,400ft). Post Office. Police Tel: 2004. Pop: 2,945. HQ Nandi District, Rift Valley Province. Kapsabet District Hospital (Govt) Tel: 2005. Petrol/diesel.

KAPTAGAT
Nairobi 320, Eldoret 34, Nakuru 164, Eldama Ravine 61.
Alt: 2,380m (7,800ft). Post Office. Police Tel: 9. Pop: 500. Uasin Gishu District, Rift Valley Province. Kaptagat Dispensary (Govt). Nearest hospital: Plateau Reformed Church Hospital. Petrol.

KARATINA
Nairobi 128, Murang'a 41, Nanyuki 72, Nyeri 27. Alt: 1,770m (5,800ft). Post Office. Police Tel: 71222. Pop: 2,980. Nyeri District, Central Province. Karatina Health Centre (Govt) Tel: 71358. Nearest hospital: Nyeri. Petrol/diesel.

KEDOWA (Lumbwa)
Nairobi 240, Nakuru 84, Kericho 73, Kisumu 156, Kipkelion 38.
Alt: 1,920m (6,300ft). Post Office. Police Post. Pop: 4,875. Kericho District, Rift Valley Province. Lumbwa Health Centre (Govt). Nearest hospital: Londiani. Petrol.

KERICHO
Nairobi 266, Kisii 98, Kisumu 83, Nakuru 110, Molo 52.
Alt: 2,010m (6,600ft). Post Office. Police Tel: 20222. Pop: 19,192. HQ Kericho District, Rift Valley Province. Kericho District Hospital (Govt) Tel: 20116; Kericho Nursing Home (Private) Tel: 20270. Petrol/diesel.

KERUGOYA
Nairobi 132, Embu 31, Nyeri 41.
Alt: 1,555m (5,100ft). Post Office. Police Tel: 21002. Pop: 3,552. HQ Kirinyaga District, Central Province. Kerugoya District Hospital (Govt) Tel: 21058. Petrol.

KIAMBU
Nairobi 16, Ruiru 16, Limuru 27.
Alt: 1,675m (5,500ft). Post Office. Police Tel: 22221. Pop: 3,669. HQ Kiambu District, Central Province. Kiambu District Hospital (Govt) Tel: 22333. Petrol/diesel.

KIBOKO
Nairobi 160, Mombasa 325, Mtito Andei 76.
Alt: 900m (3,000ft). Pop: 500. Machakos District, Eastern Province. Nearest hospital: Makindu (Govt) Tel: 8. Petrol/diesel.

KIGANJO
Nairobi 147, Nanyuki 50, Nyeri 7.
Alt: 1,740m (5,700ft). Post Office. Police Tel: 86022. Pop: 2,234. Nyeri District, Central Province. Kiganjo Dispensary (Mission). Nearest hospital: Nyeri. Petrol.

KILIFI
Nairobi 543 (via Mombasa), Mombasa 58, Malindi 61, Kaloleni 40.
Alt: Sea level. Post Office. Police Tel: 2109. Pop: 5,866. HQ Kilifi District, Coast Province. Kilifi District Hospital (Govt) Tel: 2525. Petrol/diesel.

KIMILILI
Nairobi 409, Eldoret 97, Kakamega 81, Kitale 50, Bungoma 16, Webuye 20.
Alt: 1,675m (5,500ft). Post Office. Police Tel: 18. Pop: 2,143. Bungoma District, Western Province. Kimilili Health Centre (Govt). Nearest hospital: Misikhu Mission. Petrol.

KINANGO
Nairobi 490, Mombasa 58, Mariakani 37, Mazeras 46, Samburu 55.
Alt: 215m (700ft). Pop: 1,691. Kwale District, Coast Province. Kinango Hospital (Govt) Tel: 4. Petrol/diesel.

KISII
Nairobi 364 (via Nakuru), Kericho 98, Kisumu 121, Nakuru 208.
Alt: 1,675m (3,750ft). Post Office. Police Tel: 20222. Pop: 29,661. HQ Kisii District, Nyanza Province. Kisii District Hospital (Govt) Tel: 20473; Kisii Nursing Home Tel: 20034. Petrol/diesel.

KISUMU
Nairobi 349, Kakamega 53, Kericho 83, Kisii 121, Homa Bay 142.
Alt: 1,145m (3,750ft). Police Tel: 44444. Pop: 1,000,000. HQ Kisumu District and HQ Nyanza Province. Nyanza Provincial General Hospital (Govt) Tel: 40152: Victoria Hospital (Govt) Tel: 2563. Petrol and diesel. Main port of entry on Lake Victoria.

KITALE
Nairobi 381, Eldoret 69, Kapenguria 32, Nakuru 225.
Alt: 1,890m (6,200ft). Post Office. Police Tel: 20895. Pop: 28,320. HQ Trans-Nzoia District, Rift Valley Province. Kitale District Hospital (Govt) Tel: 20951; Mount Elgon Hospital Tel: 20025. Petrol/diesel.

KITUI
Nairobi 195, Garissa 269, Mtito Andei 184, Thika 153. Alt: 1,160m (3,800ft). Post Office. Police Tel: 22804. Pop: 4,402. HQ Kitui District, Eastern Province. Kitui District Hospital Tel: 22206. Petrol/diesel.

KWALE
Nairobi 516, Mombasa 31, Mariakani 64, Kinango 30, Ukunda 20.
Alt: 370m (2,200ft). Post Office. Police Tel: 4014. Pop: 2,200. HQ Kwale District, Coast Province. Kwale Hospital (Govt) Tel: 4024. Petrol/diesel.

LAKE BARINGO
Nairobi 274, Nakuru 118, Marigat 15, Kabarnet

57, Eldoret 145.
Alt: 975m (3,200ft). Pop: 500. Baringo District, Rift Valley Province. Kampi ya Samaki Health Centre (Govt). Nearest hospital: Kabarnet.

LAKE TURKANA
See separate entries for Eliye Springs, Ferguson's Gulf, and Loiyangalani.

LAMU
Nairobi 826 (via Mombasa), Mombasa 341, Malindi 222, Garsen 111, Witu 66.
Alt: Sea level. Post Office. Police Tel: 3217, Customs Tel: 3039, Immigration Tel: 3032. Lamu District, Coast Province. Lamu District Hospital (Govt) Tel: 3012. Ferry operates from 0600-1900. Cars can be left on the mainland at a guarded car park. Secondary port of entry by sea.

LIMURU
Nairobi 35, Naivasha 54, Nakuru 121.
Alt: 2,225m (7,300ft). Post Office. Police Tel: 40222. Pop: 1,728. Kiambu District, Central Province. Limuru Health Centre (Govt) Tel: 41274. Nearest hospital: Tigoni. Petrol/diesel.

LODWAR
Nairobi 736, Kitale 355.
Alt: 460m (1,500ft). Post Office. Police Tel: 21071. Pop: 500. HQ Turkana District, Rift Valley Province. Turkana District Hospital (Govt) Tel: 21622. Petrol/diesel.

LOITOKITOK (see Oloitokitok)

LOIYANGALANI
Nairobi 569, Nyahururu 371, Maralal 225, North Horr 88, Marsabit 276 (via North Horr).
Alt: 380m (1,250ft). Police Post. Pop: 1,060. Marsabit District, Eastern Province. Loiyangalani Dispensary (Mission). Nearest hospital: Maralal. Petrol sometimes available from Mission.

LOKITAUNG
Nairobi 944, Kitale 563, Lodwar 208.
Alt: 730m (2,400ft). Post Office. Police Post. Pop: 500. Turkana District, Rift Valley Province. Lokitaung Hospital (Govt).

LONDIANI
Nairobi 219, Nakuru 63, Kericho 52, Kisumu 135.
Alt: 2,285m (7,500ft). Post Office. Police Tel: 64004. Pop: 2,994. Kericho District, Rift Valley Province. Londiani Hospital (Govt) Tel: 64019. No petrol.

LUNGA LUNGA
Nairobi 604, Mombasa 119, Msambweni 50.
Alt: 60m (200ft). Pop: 1,671. Police Tel: Kwale 4001, Customs Tel: 14, Immigration Tel: 120. Kwale District, Coast Province. Lunga Lunga Dispensary (Govt) Tel: 30. Nearest hospital: Msambweni. Border with Tanzania. Petrol.

MACHAKOS
Nairobi 65, Athi River 38, Mtito Andei 209.
Alt: 1,615m (5,300ft). Post Office. Police Tel: 21221. Pop: 84,320. HQ Machakos District, Eastern Province. General Hospital (Govt) Tel: 21911; Machakos Nursing Home (Private) Tel: 21168. Petrol/diesel.

MAGADI
Nairobi 107.
Alt: 610m (2,200ft). Post Office. Police Tel: 9. Pop: 2,515. Kajiado District, Rift Valley Province. Magadi Soda Company Hospital (Private) Tel: 78. Petrol/diesel.

MALINDI
Nairobi 604 (via Mombasa), Mombasa 119, Garsen 111, Lamu 222, Kilifi 64, Mambrui 16.
Alt: Sea level. Post Office. Police Tel: 20485. Customs Tel: 20165. Immigration Tel: 20149. Pop: 23,275. Kilifi District, Coast Province. Malindi District Hospital (Govt) Tel: 20490. Secondary port of entry by sea. Petrol/diesel.

MAMBRUI
Nairobi 618 (via Mombasa), Mombasa 133, Malindi 14.
Alt: Sea level. Pop: 1,256. Kilifi District, Coast Province. Mambrui Dispensary (Govt). Nearest hospital: Malindi. No petrol.

MANDERA
Nairobi 999, Wajir 362, Isiolo 714, El Wak 177, Garissa 683.
Alt: 305m (1,000ft). Post Office. Police Tel: 2003. Customs. Immigration. Pop: 946. HQ Mandera District, North Eastern Province. Mandera District Hospital (Govt) Tel: 2004. Border post with Ethiopia and Somalia. Petrol.

MARALAL
Nairobi 344, Nyahururu 146, Loiyangalani 225, Baragoi 97.
Alt: 1,495m (4,900ft). Police Tel: 2622. Pop: 10,230. HQ Samburu District, Rift Valley Province. Maralal District Hospital (Govt) Tel: 2623. Petrol sometimes available.

MARIGAT
Nairobi 253, Nakuru 97, Kabarnet 29, Lake Baringo 21, Eldoret 130, Mogotio 62.
Alt: 1,070m (3,500ft). Police Tel: 9. Pop: 865. Baringo District, Rift Valley Province. Marigat Health Centre (Govt). Nearest hospital: Kabarnet. Petrol.

MARSABIT
Nairobi 562, Isiolo 277, Moyale 245, North Horr 188, Loiyangalani 276 (via North Horr), Archer's Post 239.
Alt: 1,675m (5,500ft). Post Office. Police Tel: 2022. Pop: 8,739. HQ Marsabit District, Eastern Province. Marsabit District Hospital (Govt) Tel: 2006. Petrol sometimes available.

MASENO
Nairobi 372, Kisumu 23, Butere 36, Bungoma 79, Kisii 110, Kericho 84, Homa Bay 142, Kakamega 42. Alt: 1,435m (4,700ft). Post Office. Police Tel: 150. Pop: 1,639. Kisumu District, Nyanza Province. Maseno Mission Hospital Tel: 6. Petrol/diesel.

MAUA
Nairobi 338, Meru 48, Nanyuki 133, Isiolo 105. Alt: 1,615m (5,300ft). Post Office. Police Tel: 21022. Pop: 1,805. Meru District, Eastern Province. Maua Mission Hospital Tel: 21002. Petrol.

MERU
Nairobi 290 (via Nanyuki), Nanyuki 90, Isiolo 57, Embu 137.
Alt: 1,220m (4,000ft). Post Office. Police Tel: 20223. Pop: 72,049. HQ Meru District, Eastern Province. Meru District Hospital (Govt) Tel: 20370. Petrol/diesel.

MIGORI
Nairobi 435 (via Nakuru), 350 (via Narok), Kericho 169, Kisumu 192, Kisii 71, Homa Bay 78. Alt: 1,370m (4,500ft). Police Tel: Suna 28. Pop: 6,135. South Nyanza District, Nyanza Province. Migori Health Centre (Govt) Tel: 58. Nearest hospital: Rapogi Hospital. Petrol/diesel.

MODO GASHI
Nairobi 477, Isiolo 192, Wajir 160, Habaswein 50, Garissa 161.
Alt: 300m (1,000ft). Police Post. Pop: 500. Isiolo District, Eastern Province. Modo Gashi Dispensary (Govt). Nearest hospital: Wajir.

MOLO
Nairobi 207, Nakuru 51, Elburgon 13, Kisumu 156.
Alt: 2,470m (8,100ft). Post Office. Police Tel: 21006. Pop: 5,350. Nakuru District, Rift Valley Province. Molo Hospital Tel: 21112. Petrol.

MOMBASA
Nairobi 485, Malindi 119, Lamu 341, Mtito Andei 249, Lunga Lunga 119.
Alt: Sea level. Post Office. Central Police Station Tel: 225501. Customs Tel: 3l4044. Immigration Tel: 311745. Pop: 600,000. HQ Mombasa District and HQ Coast Province. Coast Provincial General Hospital (Govt) Tel: 314201; Aga Khan Hospital (Private) Tel: 312953; Mombasa Hospital (Private) Tel: 312190. Main port of entry by sea and air. Petrol/diesel.

MOYALE
Nairobi 807, Marsabit 245, Wajir 257.
Alt: 1,070m (3,500ft). Post Office. Police Tel: 20l4. Customs. Immigration. Pop: 7,478. Marsabit District, Eastern Province. Moyale Sub-district Hospital (Govt) Tel: 2022. Border post with Ethiopia. Petrol sometimes available.

MTITO ANDEI
Nairobi 236, Mombasa 249, Voi 98.

Alt: 730m (2,400ft). Post Office. Pop: 2,067. Machakos District, Eastern Province. Nearest Hospital Makindu. Petrol.

MURANG'A
Nairobi 87, Nanyuki 113, Nyeri 68.
Alt: 1,280m (4,200ft). Post Office. Police Tel: 22600. Pop: 15,343. HQ Murang'a District, Central Province. Murang'a District Hospital (Govt) Tel: 22780. Petrol/diesel.

MUTOMO
Nairobi 274 (via Kibwezi), Kitui 68, Mtito Andei 116.
Alt: 1,010m (3,300ft). Police Tel: 2. Pop: 500. Kitui District, Eastern Province. Mutomo Mission Hospital Tel: l6. Petrol.

MWEIGA
Nairobi 167, Nyeri 12.
Alt: 1,890m (6,200ft). Post Office. Police Tel: 55002. Pop: 500. Nyeri District, Central Province. Mweiga Dispensary (Mission). Nearest hospital: Nyeri. Petrol.

MWINGI
Nairobi 178, Thika 136, Garissa 202, Kitui 78.
Alt: 1,070m (3,500ft). Police Tel: 32. Pop: 2,303. Kitui District, Eastern Province. Mwingi Dispensary (Govt). Nearest hospital: Kitui. Petrol.

NAIROBI
Mombasa 485, Malindi 604, Nakuru 156, Eldoret 312, Kitale 381, Kisumu 349.
Alt: 1,645m (5,400ft). Head Post Office. Central Police Station Tel 222222. Pop: 3 million+. Kenyatta National Hospital (Govt) Tel: 726300; Aga Khan Hospital Tel: 742531/740010; Nairobi Hospital Tel: 722160, and MP Shah Hospital Tel: 742763. Petrol/diesel.

NAIVASHA
Nairobi 89, Nakuru 67, Gilgil 27.
Alt: 1,890m (6,200ft). Post Office. Police Tel: 20l99. Pop: 11,491. Nakuru District, Rift Valley Province. Naivasha Hospital (Govt) Tel. 20052; Naivasha Nursing Home. Petrol/diesel.

NAKURU
Nairobi 156, Eldoret 156, Kisumu 193, Kitale 225. Alt: 1,830m (6,000ft). Post Office. Police Tel: 42222. Pop: 92,851. HQ Nakuru District and HQ Rift Valley Province. Nakuru Provincial General Hospital (Govt) Tel: 42563; Nakuru War Memorial Hospital (Private) Tel: 43444. Petrol/diesel.

NAMANGA
Nairobi 164, Kajiado 88.
Alt: 1,295m (4,250ft). Post Office. Police Tel: 2. Customs Tel: 9. Immigration Tel: 19. Pop: 2,017. Namanga Hospital (Govt) Tel: 15. Border post with Tanzania. Petrol.

NANDI HILLS
Nairobi 307, Eldoret 66, Kakamega 86, Kisumu

103, Kapsabet 18.
Alt: 1,980m (6,500ft). Post Office. Police Tel: 43005. Pop: 1,419. Nandi District, Rift Valley Province. Nandi Hills Hospital (Govt) Tel: 43024. Petrol.

NANYUKI
Nairobi 200, Isiolo 85, Meru 90, Nyahururu 97.
Alt: 1,850m (6,400ft). Post Office. Police Tel: 22222. Pop: 18,986. HQ Laikipia District, Rift Valley Province. Nanyuki District Hospital (Govt) Tel: 22033; Nanyuki Cottage Hospital (Private) Tel: 22684. Petrol/diesel.

NARO MORU
Nairobi 177, Nanyuki 23, Nyeri 33.
Alt: 1,980m (6,500ft). Post Office. Police Tel: 62003. Pop: 500. Nyeri District, Central Province. Naro Moru Health Centre (Govt) Tel: 62009. Nearest hospital: Nanyuki. Petrol.

NAROK
Nairobi 148, Nakuru 188 (via Naivasha), Kisii 157.
Alt: 1,980m (6,500ft). Post Office. Police Tel: 2367. Pop: 5,690. HQ Narok District, Rift Valley Province. Narok District Hospital Tel: 2300. Petrol/diesel.

NGONG
Nairobi 26.
Alt: 1,980m (6,500ft). Police Tel: Karen 564055. Pop: 4,004. Kajiado District, Rift Valley Province. Ngong Health Centre (Govt). Nearest hospital: Nairobi. Petrol/diesel.

NORTH HORR
Nairobi 657, Loiyangalani 88, Marsabit 188.
Alt: 550m (1,800ft). Police Post. Pop: 1,325. Marsabit District, Eastern Province. North Horr Dispensary. Nearest hospital: Marsabit.

NYAHURURU (Thomson's Falls)
Nairobi 198, Gilgil 82, Nanyuki 97, Maralal 146, Nyeri 100, Nakuru 72, Rumuruti 48.
Alt: 2,350m (7,700ft). Post Office. Police Tel: 22333. Pop: 11,277. HQ Nyandarua District, Central Province. Nyahururu District Hospital (Govt) Tel: 22114. Petrol/diesel.

NYERI
Nairobi 155, Nanyuki 57, Murang'a 68, Embu 96.
Alt: 1,770m (5,800ft). Post Office. Police Tel: 2222. Pop: 35,753. HQ Nyeri District and HQ Central Province. Central Province General Hospital (Govt) Tel: 2480. Mount Kenya Hospital (Govt) Tel: 2033. Petrol/diesel.

OL KALOU
Nairobi 146, Nakuru 70, Nyahururu 52.
Alt: 2,380m (7,800ft). Post Office. Police Tel: 72003. Pop: 1,911. Nyandarua District, Central Province. Ol Kalou Hospital Tel: 72033. Petrol.

OLOITOKITOK (Loitokitok)

Nairobi 235 (via Emali), Namanga 123.
Alt: 1,680m (5,500ft). Post Office. Police Tel: 22007. Customs Tel: 6. Immigration Tel: 22003. Pop: 2,071. Kajiado District, Rift Valley Province. Loitokitok Hospital Tel: 22040. Border post with Tanzania. Petrol/diesel.

RONGAI
Nairobi 189, Nakuru 33, Eldoret 131.
Alt: 1,890m (6,200ft). Post Office. Police Tel: 32011. Pop: 583. Nakuru District, Rift Valley Province. Rongai Health Centre (Govt) Tel: 32023. Nearest hospital: Nakuru. Petrol/diesel.

RUIRU
Nairobi 23, Thika 19, Nanyuki 177.
Alt: 1,525m (5,000ft). Post Office. Police Tel: 22222. Pop: 1,718. Kiambu District, Central Province. Ruiru Health Centre (Govt) Tel: 22545. Nearest hospital: Thika/Nairobi. Petrol/diesel.

RUMURUTI
Nairobi 232, Nyahururu 34, Nanyuki 131, Maralal 112.
Alt: 2,130m (7,000ft). Post Office. Police Tel: 32803. Pop: 1,487. Laikipia District, Rift Valley Province. Rumuruti Hospital (Govt) Tel: 23806. Petrol.

SAGANA
Nairobi 99, Nanyuki 101, Thika 57, Nyeri 56, Embu 40, Murang'a 12.
Alt: 1,190m (3,900ft). Post Office. Police Tel: 46002. Pop: 2,098. Kirinyaga District, Central Province. Sagana Rural Health Centre (Govt) Tel: 46020. Nearest hospital: Murang'a. Petrol/diesel.

SIAYA
Nairobi 418, Kisumu 69, Butere 46, Bungoma 89, Busia 70, Kakamega 85.
Alt: 1,280m (4,200ft). Post Office. Police Tel: 21428. Pop: 4,022. HQ Siaya District, Nyanza Province. Siaya District Hospital (Govt) Tel: 21060. Petrol/diesel.

SOTIK
Nairobi 319 (via Nakuru), 260 (via Narok), Kericho 53, Kisii 45, Narok 112.
Alt: 1,830m (6,000ft). Post Office. Police Tel: 8. Pop: 1,334. Kericho District, Rift Valley Province. Sotik Dispensary. Petrol.

SOY
Nairobi 338, Eldoret 26, Kitale 43, Nakuru 182.
Alt: 1,950m (6,400ft). Police Tel: 9. Pop: 500. Uasin Gishu District, Rift Valley Province. Soy Health Centre (Govt) Tel: 14. Nearest hospital: Eldoret.

SULTAN HAMUD
Nairobi 114, Mombasa 371, Kiboko 46, Mtito Andei 122.
Alt: 1,250m (4,100ft). Post Office. Police Tel: 5. Pop: 1,360. Machakos District, Eastern Province. Sultan Hamud Health Centre (Govt) Tel: 7.

Nearest hospital: Makindu Tel: 8. Petrol/diesel.

TAMBACH
Nairobi 356, Eldoret 44, Kabarnet 37, Iten 10.
Alt: 1,980m (6,500ft). Police Post. Pop: 654. HQ
Elgeyo Marakwet District, Rift Valley Province.
Tambach District Hospital Radiocall: Nairobi
3772. Petrol.

TAVETA
Nairobi 448, Mombasa 265, Voi 114.
Alt: 760m (2,500ft). Post Office. Police Tel: 4.
Customs Tel: 18. Immigration Tel: 2024. Pop:
1,812. Taita-Taveta District, Coast Province.
Taveta Hospital (Govt) Tel: 2620. Border post with
Tanzania. Petrol.

THIKA
Nairobi 42, Nanyuki 158, Murang'a 45, Kitui
153, Mwingi 136, Garissa 338.
Alt: 1,495m (4,900ft). Post Office. Police Tel:
2l999. Pop: 41,328. Kiambu District, Central
Province. Thika Hospital (Govt) Tel: 21621.
Petrol/diesel.

THOMSON'S FALLS (see Nyahururu)

TIGONI
Nairobi 26, Nakuru 127, Limuru 6.
Alt: 2,135m (7,000ft). Post Office. Police Tel:
40222. Pop: 500. Kiambu District, Central Province. Tigoni Hospital (Govt). Petrol.

VOI
Nairobi 334, Mombasa 151, Mtito Andei 98.
Alt: 550m (1,800ft). Post Office. Police Tel: 2106.
Pop: 7,397. Taita District, Coast Province. Voi
Hospital (Govt) Tel: 2016. Petrol/diesel.

WAJIR
Nairobi 637, Garissa 321 (via Modo Gashi),
Moyale 257, Mandera 362, Isiolo 352, Modo
Gashi 160.
Alt: 240m (800ft). Post Office. Police Tel: 21002.
Pop: 6384. HQ Wajir District, North Eastern
Province. Wajir District Hospital (Govt) Tel:
2103l. Petrol.

WAMBA
Nairobi 389, Isiolo 104, Nanyuki 189, Meru 161.
Alt: 1,675m (5,500ft). Post Office. Police Tel: 4.
Pop: 2,256. Samburu District, Rift Valley Prov-
ince. Wamba Hospital (Mission).

WITU
Nairobi 760 (via Mombasa), Mombasa 275,
Garsen 45, Lamu 66.
Alt: Sea level. Post Office. Police Tel: 7. Pop:
2,288. Lamu District, Coast Province. Witu
Health Centre (Govt) Tel: 9. Nearest hospital:
Kipini Hospital (Govt).

WUNDANYI
Nairobi 377, Mombasa 194, Voi 43.
Alt: 1,250m (4,100ft). Post Office. Police Tel:

2002. Pop: 500. HQ Taita-Taveta District, Coast
Province. Taita District Health Centre (Govt) Tel:
2041. Nearest hospital: Wesu Tel: 5. Petrol.

Kenyan Administrative Areas

Province	District
Coast	Kilifi
	Kwale
	Lamu
	Mombasa
	Taita-Taveta
	Tana River
Eastern	Embu
	Isiolo
	Kitui
	Machakos
	Makueni
	Marsabit
	Meru
	Tharaka-Nithi
North Eastern	Garissa
	Mandera
	Wajir
Central	Kiambu
	Thika
	Kirinyaga
	Murang'a
	Nyandarua
	Nyeri
Nairobi	Nairobi
Rift Valley	Baringo
	Keiyo Marakwet
	Kajiado
	Kericho
	Bomet
	Laikipia
	Nakuru
	Nandi
	Narok
	Mara
	Samburu
	Trans-Nzoia
	Turkana
	Uasin Gishu
	West Pokot
Nyanza	Kisumu
	Nyamira
	Kisii
	Siaya
	Homa Bay
	Migori
	Kuria
Western	Bungoma
	Elgon
	Busia
	Kakamega
	Vihiga

National Museums

From prehistoric fossils to the origins of mankind to the more recent past, more than 400 historical sites illustrate Kenya's rich and diverse history. Established by Kenya's National Museum, most of these sites are the subject of ongoing scientific research — archaeological and palaeontological.

Most of these sites are restricted to the public because of their size, inaccessibility, or vulnerability to damage and pilfering. In many cases, they are of little apparent interest to the non-scientific community.

There are, however, 24 sites which are open to the public. Accessible and well documented, these sites are of immediate interest to the most casual observer.

In addition to the National Museum headquarters in Nairobi, there are also branch museums in Kisumu, Kitale, Lamu, Meru and Mombasa.

The Museum also acquires new land and initiates new projects. Local residents and visitors can now enjoy the **Ololua Forest Recreation Area** near Karen, Nairobi which provides a safe, peaceful atmosphere for family outings, nature walks, picnics, and horse riding.

There schoolchildren learn forest appreciation through lectures and guided walks. The Museum is developing a Visitor's Centre offering information and refreshments.

Historic Sites

Chetambe Fort
Province: Western
District: Bungoma
Features: Palaeontological site.

Diani
Province: Coast
District: Kwale
Features: Ancient mosque, still in use.

Fort Jesus, Mombasa
Province: Coast
District: Mombasa
Features: 16th-century Portuguese fort, overlooking the Indian Ocean. The museum illustrates the ancient culture of the coast.

Fort Ternan
Province: Rift Valley
District: Kericho
Features: Palaeontological site, described as Africa's richest known source of animal fossils dating back fourteen million years.

Gede
Province: Coast
District: Kilifi
Features: Ruined city of Islamic origin dating from the 13th century.

Hyrax Hill
Province: Rift Valley
District: Nakuru
Features: Prehistoric site, including artefacts, Iron Age settlement, hill fort and Neolithic cemetery.

Kariandus
Province: Rift Valley
District: Nakuru
Features: Prehistoric site, including artefacts and fossils.

Kenyatta House, Maralal
Province: Rift Valley
District: Samburu
Features: Kenyatta's place of detention during Kenyan struggle for Independence.

Kijabe
Province: Central
District: Kiambu
Features: Church built by Italian Prisoners-of-War.

Kiunga
Province: Coast
District: Lamu
Features: Islamic ruins, including mosques and tombs.

Koobi Fora
Province: Eastern
District: Marsabit
Features: Palaeontological site, including evidence of the existence of a relatively intelligent hominid two million years ago. There is a museum and campsite.

Malindi
Province: Coast
District: Kilifi
Features: Vasco da Gama's pillar, erected 1499.

Mambrui
Province: Coast
District: Kilifi
Features: Pillar tomb decorated with late-Ming bowls.

Mbaraki
Province: Coast
District: Kwale
Features: Portuguese pillar.

Mnarani
Province: Coast
District: Kilifi
Features: 16th-century mosque and tombs.

Mtwapa
Province: Coast

District: Mombasa
Features: Ruins of a 14th-15th century slave-trading settlement.

Muhanda Fort
Province: Western
District: Bungoma
Features: Palaeontological site.

Olorgesailie
Province: Rift Valley
District: Kajiado
Features: Prehistoric site, hand axes and other stone tools preserved *in situ*, together with fossils of extinct mammals.

Selangai
Province: Rift Valley
District: Kajiado
Features: Maasai circumcision stones and Maasai water wells.

Shanga
Province: Coast

District: Lamu
Features: Seven acres of Islamic ruins dating from the 10th century.

Sibiloi
Province: Eastern
District: Marsabit
Features: Petrified forest.

Songhor
Province: Rift Valley
District: Kericho
Features: Palaeontological site.

Takwa
Province: Coast
District: Lamu
Features: Fifty hectares (125 acres) of Islamic ruins dating from the 16th and 17th centuries.

Thim Lich
Province: Nyanza
District: South Nyanza
Features: Stone structures and ancient fortress.

Public Holidays

January 1	New Year's Day
March/April	Good Friday
	Easter Monday
May 1	Labour Day
June 1	Madaraka Day (anniversary of Self-Government)
October 10	Nyayo Day (anniversary of President Moi's inauguration)
October 20	Kenyatta Day (anniversary of Jomo Kenyatta's release from detention)
December 12	Jamhuri/Uhuru Day (anniversary of Independence and formation of Republic)
December 25	Christmas Day
December 26	Boxing Day
Variable	Idd-ul-Fitr (Muslim holiday celebrating the end of Ramadan, which is decided by the lunar calendar)

Calendar of Annual Events

January	International Bill Fishing Competition, Malindi
February	Mombasa Fishing Festival
March	Kenya Open Golf Championship
pre-Easter	Safari Rally
Mid-June	Nakuru Agriculture Show
End-August	Mombasa Agricultural Show
End-September	Nairobi Agricultural Show
November	Malindi Fishing Festival

LISTINGS

Airlines

Nairobi offices

Aeroflot
Corner Hse
PO Box 44375
Tel: 224555

Aero Zambia
International Hse
Mama Ngina St
PO Box 58834
Tel: 246519

Air France
International Hse
PO Box 30159
Tel: 219855/229265

Air Botswana
Hilton Hotel
Mama Ngina St
PO Box 60418
Tel: 331648/58

Air Burundi
Jubilee Insurance
Exchange
Mama Ngina St
PO Box 61165
Tel: 215216

Air Canada
Lonrho Hse
Standard St
PO Box 30601
Tel: 218776/7

Air India
Jeevan Bharati Hse
Harambee Ave
PO Box 43006
Tel: 334788

Air Madagascar
Hilton Hotel
City Hall Way
PO Box 41723
Tel: 225286/226494

Air Malawi
Hilton Hotel
City Hall Way
PO Box 42676
Tel: 333683/340212

Air Mauritius
Union Towers
Moi Ave
PO Box 45270
Tel: 229166/7

Air Namibia
Hilton Hotel
Mama Ngina Way
PO Box 60418
Tel: 331648/58

Air Seychelles
Lonrho Hse
PO Box 46163
Tel: 229359

Air Tanzania
Chester Hse
Koinange St
PO Box 20077
Tel: 336224/397

Air Zaire
Consolidated Hse
Koinange St
PO Box 46282
Tel: 230143/244440

Air Zimbabwe
Chester Hse
Koinange St
PO Box 14515
Tel: 339522

Alitalia
Hilton Hotel
Mama Ngina St
PO Box 72651
Tel: 224361-3/822351

Austrian Airlines
Grindlays Building
Kenyatta Ave
PO Box 30139
Tel: 214465/66

British Airways
International Hse
PO Box 45050
Tel: 334400/822555

Cameroon Airlines
Rehani Hse, HFCK
Kenyatta Ave
PO Box 45749
Tel: 337788

Egypt Air
Hilton Hotel
PO Box 44953
Tel: 226821/2

El Al
KCS Hse
Mama Ngina St
PO Box 49316
Tel: 228123/330935

Emirates
View Park Towers
Tel: 212990

Ethiopian Airlines
Bruce Hse
Muindi Mbingu St
PO Box 42901
Tel: 330837/57

Gulf Air
International Hse
Mama Ngina St
PO Box 44417
Tel: 219710

Iberia
Hilton Hotel
Mama Ngina St
PO Box 60418
331648

Iran Air, 6th floor
View Park Towers
PO Box 22378
Tel: 229464

Japan Airlines
International Hse
Mama Ngina St
PO Box 42430
Tel: 220591/333277

KLM
Fedha Towers
PO Box 49239
Tel: 822376/332673

Kenya Airways
Barclays Bank Plaza
Loita St
PO Box 41010
Tel: 229291/332750

Lufthansa
IAM Bank Hse
University Way
PO Box 30320
Tel: 335819/846

Nigeria Airways
Hilton Hotel
PO Box 57058
Tel: 336555/436

Olympic Airways
Hilton Hotel
PO Box 42536
Tel: 338026/822259

PIA
ICEA Building
Banda St
PO Box 47365
Tel: 822386/333900

Royal Swazi
Reinsurance Plaza
Taifa Rd
PO Box 58716
Tel: 210670

Sabena
International Hse
Mama Ngina St
PO Box 43706
Tel: 222185/333198

Saudia
Anniversary Towers
University Way
PO Box 58452
Tel: 334270/335612

South African Airways
Lonrho Hse
Standard St
PO Box 34203
229663/227486

Sudan Airways
Travel Hse
General Kago St
PO Box 48492
Tel: 225129

Swissair
Corner Hse
Mama Ngina St
PO Box 44549
Tel: 250288-9

Uganda Airlines
Uganda Hse
Kenyatta Ave
PO Box 59732
Tel: 221354/228668

Varig
Lonrho Hse
Standard St
PO Box 48997
Tel: 220961/337097

Zambia Airways
Kaunda St
PO Box 42479
Tel: 224722/221007

Air Charter

NAIROBI
A-D Aviation
Wilson Airport
PO Box 47906
Tel: 891180

AfricAir
Wilson Airport
PO Box 45646
Tel: 501219/210

Afro Aviation
Wilson Airport
PO Box 39422
Tel: 226944

Aim Air
Wilson Airport
PO Box 21099
Tel: 501612/610

Air Kenya
Wilson Airport
PO Box 30357
Tel: 501601/4

CMC Aviation
Wilson Airport
PO Box 44580
Tel: 501421/501222

Cassman Brown
Wilson Airport
PO Box 46247
Tel: 501421

East African Air
Charters
Wilson Airport
Tel: 501431/500506
Fax: 254-2-502358

Executive Aviation
Wilson Airport
PO Box 17152
Tel: 332382/822655

Falconair
Wilson Airport
PO Box 30603
Tel: 501523

Pioneer Airlines
Wilson Airport
PO Box 43356
Tel: 501399

Rent-A-Plane
Wilson Airport
PO Box 42730
Tel: 500506/501431

Safari Air Services
Wilson Airport
PO Box 41951
Tel: 501211/3

Skymaster
Wilson Airport
PO Box 58771
Tel: 501608

Tradewinds Air-
ways
Bruce Hse
Standard St
PO Box 42474
Tel: 223071

Mombasa
Sunbird Aviation
(Coast Air)
Moi International
Airport
PO Box 84700
Tel: 433320/332

Malindi
Air Mara
Lamu Rd
PO Box 146
Tel: 20287

Airports

Jomo Kenyatta
International Airport
PO Box 19001
Nairobi
Tel: 822111

Wilson Airport
PO Box 30163
Nairobi
Tel: 501216

374

Kisumu Airport
Nyerere Rd
PO Box 431, Kisumu
Tel: 43900

Malindi Airport
Mombasa Rd
PO Box 67, Malindi
Tel: 20851/20060

Moi International
Airport
PO Box 93939
Mombasa
Tel: 433211

Nanyuki Airport
PO Box 54, Nanyuki
Tel: 21116

Diplomatic Missions

Nairobi
Algeria
Comcraft Hse
Haile Selasie Ave
PO Box 53902
Tel: 334227/178

Argentina
Town Hse
Kaunda St
PO Box 30283
Tel: 335242

Australia
ICIPE Hse
Riverside Drive
PO Box 39341
Tel: 445034

Austria
City Hse
Wabera St
PO Box 30560
Tel: 333272/228281

Bangladesh
Ole Odume Rd
PO Box 49866
Tel: 562815

Belgium
Silopark Hse
PO Box 30461
Tel: 220501/225143

Brazil
Jeevan Bharati Bldg
Harambee Ave
PO Box 30754
Tel: 338975/337722

Bulgaria
Kabarnet Rd
PO Box 44778
Tel: 567308

Burundi
Development Hse
PO Box 44439
Tel: 338721/735

Canada
Comcraft Hse
Haile Selassie Ave
PO Box 30481
Tel: 334033/6

Chile
International Hse
PO Box 45554
Tel: 337987/934

China
Woodlands Rd
PO Box 30508
Tel: 722559

Colombia
Tchui Hse
Muthaiga Rd
PO Box 48494
Tel: 765911

Costa Rica
Wilson Airport
PO Box 30750
Tel: 569522

Cyprus
Eagle Hse
Kimathi St
PO Box 30739
Tel: 220881

Czechoslovakia
Embassy Hse
PO Box 30204
Tel: 210494

Denmark
HFCK Building
Koinange St
PO Box 40412
Tel: 331088/098

Djibouti
Comcraft Hse
Haile Selassie Ave
PO Box 59528
Tel: 339633/640

Egypt
Harambee Plaza
PO Box 30285
Tel: 225990/2

Ethiopia
State Hse Rd
PO Box 45198
Tel: 723027/035

Finland
International Hse
PO Box 30379
Tel: 336717/334777

France
Embassy Hse
PO Box 41784

Tel: 339783-4/
339973-4

Gabon
Othaya Rd, Lavington
PO Box 42551
Tel: 569429

Germany
Williamson Hse
4th Ngong Ave
PO Box 30180
Tel: 712527/30

Greece
Nation Centre
PO Box 30543
Telex: 22008
Tel: 340722/744

Holy See (Vatican)
Manyani Rd
PO Box 14326
Tel: 442977/975

Hungary
Ole Ndume Rd
Lavington
PO Box 61146
Tel: 560060/560453

Iceland
Norwich Union Hse
PO Box 45000
Tel: 338522

India
Jeevan Bharati Bdg
PO Box 30074
Tel: 224500/222566

Indonesia
Utalii Hse
PO Box 48868
Tel: 215848/215873

Iran
Corner State Hse
& Dennis Pritt Rds
PO Box 49170
Tel: 720343/796

Iraq
Lower Kabete Rd
PO Box 49213
Tel: 725510/87

Ireland
Maendeleo Hse
PO Box 30659
Tel: 226771/4

Israel
Bishops Rd
PO Box 30354
Tel: 722182

Italy
Prudential Bdg
PO Box 30107
Tel: 337356-7/016-7

Japan
ICEA Building
PO Box 60202
Tel: 332955-9

Korea (South)
Kencom Hse
PO Box 30455
Tel: 322839/333581

Kuwait
IPS Building
PO Box 42353
Tel: 338558/330901

Lebanon
Maendeleo Hse
Monrovia St
PO Box 55303
Tel: 223708

Lesotho
International Hse
PO Box 44096
Tel: 337493/224876

Liberia
Bruce Hse
PO Box 30546
Tel: 222604-5

Libya
Jamhiriya Hse
Loita St
PO Box 60149
Tel: 226183/224318

Madagascar
PO Box 30793
Tel: 226494

Malawi
Bruce Hse
PO Box 30453
Tel: 221174/220435

Malaysia
Eagle Hse
Kimathi St
PO Box 48916
Tel: 229724/5

Mauritius
Union Towers
PO Box 45270
Tel: 330215

Mexico
Kibegare Way
Loresho Ridge
PO Box 41139
Tel: 582850/579

Morocco
Diamond Trust Bldg
PO Box 61098
Tel: 222361/264

Netherlands
Uchumi Hse
PO Box 41537
Tel: 332420/227111

Nigeria
Lenana Rd
PO Box 30516
Tel: 564116/8

Norway
HFCK Building
Koinange St
PO Box 46363
Tel: 337121/22/24

Pakistan
St Michaels Rd
Westlands
PO Box 30045
Tel: 443911/912

Peru
Longonot Place,
Kijabe St
PO Box 75732
Tel: 336398

Philippines
State Hse Rd
PO Box 47941
Tel: 725897/721791

Poland
Kabarnet Rd
PO Box 30086
Tel: 566288

Portugal
Reinsurance Plaza
PO Box 34020
Tel: 338990/339853

Romania
Norfolk Towers
PO Box 48412
Tel: 227515

Russia
Lenana Rd
Hurlingham
PO Box 30049
Tel: 722462

Rwanda
International Hse
PO Box 48579
Tel: 334341/336365

Saudi Arabia
Muthaiga Rd
PO Box 58297
Tel: 7627881/4

Somalia
International Hse
PO Box 30769
Tel: 224301

Spain
Bruce Hse
PO Box 45503
Tel: 336330/335711

Sri Lanka
International Hse
PO Box 48145
Tel: 227577/78

Sudan
Minet ICDC Hse
Mamlaka Rd
PO Box 48784
Tel: 720853/54

Swaziland
Transnational Plaza
PO Box 41887
Tel: 339231/3

Sweden
International Hse
PO Box 30600
Tel: 229042/5

Switzerland
International Hse
PO Box 30752
Tel: 228735/6

Tanzania
Continental Hse
PO Box 47790
Tel: 331093/104

Thailand
Grevillea Grove
Westlands
PO Box 58349
Tel: 715801/796

Turkey
Gigiri Rd
PO Box 30785
Tel: 520404

Uganda
Uganda Hse
Kenyatta Ave
PO Box 60853
Tel: 3308801/834

United Kingdom
Bruce Hse
PO Box 30465
Tel: 335944/60

USA
Moi Ave
PO Box 30137
Tel: 334141/50

Venezuela
International Hse
PO Box 34477
Tel: 332300/340167

Yemen
Lenana Rd
PO Box 44642
Tel: 564379

Yugoslavia
State Hse Ave
PO Box 30504
Tel: 720670-2

Zaire
Electricity Hse
Harambee Ave
PO Box 48106
Tel: 229771/2

Zambia
Nyerere Rd
PO Box 48741
Tel: 224796/724799

Zimbabwe
Minet ICDC Hse
Mamlaka Rd
PO Box 30806
Tel: 721045/4971

Mombasa
Denmark
PO Box 99543
Tel: 316051

Finland
PO Box 99543
Tel: 229241/223898

France
PO Box 86103
Tel: 315446/221008

Germany
PO Box 90171
Tel: 228781

India
PO Box 90614
Tel: 311051

Italy
PO Box 84958
Tel: 311532/26955

Netherlands
PO Box 90230
Tel: 311434/5

Norway
PO Box 83058
Tel: 485494/471771

Switzerland
PO Box 30752
Tel: 228735-6

Missions Abroad

Australia
PO Box 1990
Canberra, ACT 2600
Tel: 474788

Belgium
1-5 Ave de La
Joyeuse Entrée
1040 Brussels
Tel: 230365/3100

Canada
Gillin Building
141 Laurier Ave
West Ottawa
Ontario KIP 5J3
Tel: 613563

China
No 4 Xi Liu Jie
San Li Tun, Beijing
Tel: 523381

Ethiopia
PO Box 3301
Addis Ababa
Tel: 180033/136

Egypt
20 Boulos Hanna St
Dokko
PO Box 362, Cairo
Tel: 704455-6

France
3 Rue Cimaros
75016 Paris
Tel: 5533500

Germany
Villichgasee 17
5300 Bonn-Bad
Godesberg 2
Micael Plaza
Tel: 353066/356041

India
66 Vasant Marg
Vasant Vihar
New Delhi
Tel: 672280/053

Italy
Via Del Circo
Massimo Rome 00153
Tel: 5781192/0995

Japan
24-20 Nishi-Azobu
3 Chome, Minato-Ku
Tokyo
Tel: 794006

The Netherlands
The Hague
Tel: 636175

Nigeria
52 Queen's Drive
Ikiyi,
PO Box 6464, Lagos
Tel: 682768/685531

Pakistan
8 St 88
PO Box 2097
Islamabad
Tel: 823819

Russia
Bolshyaya Ordinka
Dom 70
Moscow
Tel: 2373462/4702

Rwanda
PO Box 1215
Kigali
Tel: 2774

Saudi Arabia
Baladia St
PO Box 6347, Jeddah
Tel: 6656718/6601885

Somalia
PO Box 618
Mogadishu
Tel: 80857/58

Sudan
PO Box 8242
Khartoum
Tel: 940386

Sweden
2TR Birger
Jarilsgatan 37
71145 Stockholm
Tel: 218399/04/09

Switzerland
80 Rue de Lausanne
1202 Geneva
Tel: 327272/038

Tanzania
NIC Investment Hse
Samora Ave
PO Box 5231
Dar es Salaam
Tel: 31526

Uganda
60 Kira Rd
PO Box 5220, Kampala
Tel: 231861/233146

United Arab Emirates
PO Box 3854
Abu Dhabi
Tel: 366300

United Kingdom
45 Portland Place
London WIN 4AS
Tel: 01/362371-

United Nations
866 United Nations
Plaza
New York 10017
Tel: 4214740

USA
2249 R St NW
Washington DC
20008
Tel: 440215

Zaire
5002 Ave de 1,
Ouganda
Zone de Gombe
PO Box 9667
Kinshasha
Tel: 30117

Zambia
5207 United Nations
Ave
PO Box 50298, Lusaka
Tel: 212531/361

Zimbabwe
5 Park Lane
PO Box 4069
Harare
Tel: 790847

Tourist Offices

France
2 rue Volney
Paris 75002
Tel: 260-66-88

Germany
6000 Frankfurt
A Main 1
Hosch-strasse 53
Tel: 282551/552

Hong Kong
1309 Liu Chong Hing
Bank Building
24 Des Voeux Rd
PO Box 5280
Tel: 5-236053/4

Japan
Yurakucho Building
1-10 Yurakucho
Chome
Chiyoda-ku, Tokyo
214-3595

Sweden
Birder Jarilsgatan 37
2TP
PO Box 7692
Stockholm 11145
Tel: 218300/04/09

Switzerland
Bleicherweg 30
PO Box 770
8039 Zurich
01-202-22-43/44/46

United Kingdom
25 New Bond St
London W14 9HD
01-355-3144

USA
424 Madison Ave
New York
NY 10017
486-1300

Suite 111-12 Doheny
Plaza
9100 Wilshire
Boulevard
Beverly Hills
California 90121
274-6635

Hotels

NAIROBI

ABBEY HOTEL
Gaberone Road
Tel: 331487

ABERDARE SAFARI
University Way
Tel: 337060/215840

AFRICANA HOTEL
Dubois Rd
Tel: 220654

BAHARINI STAGE
LODGE
Duruma Rd
Tel: 211981

BAHATI FACE
PO Box 17058
Tel: 558305

BENPER HOTEL
Shiriku Rd
Tel: 722542

BLUE SAFARI CLUB
Maasai West Rd
Tel: 890444/184

BONUS SQUARE INN
9th St, Eastleigh
Tel: 760408

CASSANOVA INN
PO Box 28047
Tel: 761443

CASTLE INN
PO Box 74411
Tel: 802193

CHAMUWAJI
TRADERS HOTEL
PO Box 32047
Chamuwaji Hse
Ngariama Rd
Tel: 721903/222832

CHIPOLOTA HOTEL
Igoji Hse
Tsavo Rd
Tel: 218208/600363

CHIROMO HOTEL
Chiromo Rd
PO Box 44677
Tel: 745927

CITY VIEW HOTEL
PO Box 16029
Tel: 765051

CONTINENTAL
HOTEL
PO Box 73893
Rhapta Rd
Tel: 440420/444772

CREST HOTEL
Baringo Square
Tel: 504676/91

DEKA HOTEL
PO Box 53511
Tel: 760493

DILBAHAR HOTEL
Ngara Road
Tel: 747867/761893

DIPLOMAT HOTEL
Tom Mboya Street
Tel: 245050/6114

DOLAT HOTEL
Murigo Mansion Hse
Mfangano St
Tel: 222797/228663

DRYWOOD HOTEL
PO Box 51912
Kanyaki House
Ole Sangale Rd
Tel: 500948/4829

EL PASO HOTEL
PO Box 47415
Tel: 566578

EMBASSY HOTEL
Bazaar Mansion Hse
Tubman Rd
Tel: 224087

ESPERIA HOTEL
Parklands Rd
PO Box 14642
Tel: 742818

EVEREST HOTEL
PO Box 44822
Tel: 741450

FAIRVIEW HOTEL
Bishops Rd
PO Box 40842
Tel: 723211/711321

FIG TREE HOTEL
Ngara Rd
PO Box 31938
Tel: 743697

GRAND HOLIDAY
HOTEL
PO Box 69343
Tel: 214159
Fax: (254-2) 216876

GRAND REGENCY
Uhuru Highway
PO Box 57549
Tel: 211199/219481
Fax: 217120

GREENVIEW HOTEL
Nyerere Rd
PO Box 42246
Tel: 729923

HADHRAMUT
HOTEL
River Rd
Tel: 210017

HAKIMA HOTEL
PO Box 11500
Tel: 764445

HANNAH'S LODGE
4th Ave, Parklands
PO Box 44181
Tel: 742864/741957

HERON COURT
Milimani Rd
PO Box 41848
Tel: 720740/1/2/3

HILLCREST ANNEX
Tom Mboya St
Tel: 336842

HILLCREST HOTEL
Waiyaki Way
PO Box 14284
Tel: 444208

HILTON NAIROBI
Mama Ngina St
PO Box 30624
Tel: 219611
Fax: 254-2-339462

HOME PARK
HOTEL
Jogoo Rd
Tel: 545124

HOTEL
AMBASSADEUR
Moi Ave
PO Box 30399
Tel: 336803

HOTEL BOULEVARD
Harry Thuku Rd
PO Box 42831
Tel: 337221/227567

HOTEL COMFY
Keiya Rd
PO Box 20320
Tel: 743969/959

HOTEL COUNTY
Parliament Rd
PO Box 41924
Tel: 226190/337621

HOTEL EMSLEY
Tsavo Rd
PO Box 49860
Tel: 223437

HOTEL GRETON
Tsavo Rd
Tel: 242891/242834

HOTEL HERMES
Haile Selassie Ave
PO Box 62997
Tel: 313558

HOTEL GLORIA
Ronald Ngala St
PO Box 32087
Tel: 228916

HOTEL INTER-
CONTINENTAL
City Hall Way
PO Box 30353
Tel: 335550

HOTEL MECCA
Kenchic House
Mfangano St
Tel: 219225

HOTEL MERCURY
Tom Mboya St
PO Box 13083
Tel: 220068/338063

HOTEL SALAMA
Tom Mboya St
PO Box 28675
Tel: 225898

HOTEL TERMINAL
Moktar Daddah St
Tel: 228817/8

HURLINGHAM
Arwings Kodhek Rd
PO Box 43158
Tel: 721920/723001

IMPALA HOTEL
Parklands Rd
PO Box 14144
Tel: 742346/7

INDIANA HOTEL
PO Box 34060
Tel: 242151

INTERNATIONAL
HOTEL
Muranga Rd
Tel: 742210/746145

JEI KEI HOTEL
PO Box 49446
Tel: 218453/4/3408

JOKAGI HOTEL
Kamae Lane Off
Luthuli Ave
Tel: 331176

KARANGI HOTEL
Monrovia St
Tel: 333568

JACARANDA HOTEL
Westlands
Block Hotels
Rehema Hse
PO Box 47557
Tel: 335807/830
Telex: 22146
Fax: 340541

KENYA
INTERNATIONAL
Murang'a Rd
PO Box 22411
Tel: 742210/746145

KIRIMA SAFARI
HOTEL
New Pumwani Rd
Tel: 229136

KWALITY HOTEL
Arwings Kodhek Rd
PO Box 44275
Tel: 721285

LENANA MOUNT
HOTEL
Ralph Bunche Rd
Tel: 717048/4

MAKADARA NEW
HOTEL
Hamza Rd
Tel: 790536

MALAIKA HOTEL
Tom Mboya St
Tel: 338329

MANG' HOTEL
Haile Selassie Ave
Tel: 336055/340692

MARBLE ARCH
HOTEL
PO Box 12224
Lagos Rd
Tel: 245656
Fax: 245724

MAYFAIR COURT
Parklands Rd
PO Box 66807
Tel: 740920/740906
Fax: (254-2) 748823

MERIDIAN COURT
Murang'a Rd
PO Box 30278
Tel: 333675

MILIMANI HOTEL
Milimani Rd
PO Box 30715
Tel: 720951

NAIROBI SAFARI
CLUB
University Way
PO Box 43564
Tel: 330621

NAIROBI SERENA
Kenyatta Ave
PO Box 46302
Tel: 725111
Fax: 725184

NEW NYERI BAR
& HOTEL
PO Box 26001
Tel: 543773

NEW STANLEY
Kimathi St
PO Box 30680
Tel: 333233-6/217294-5
Fax: 254-2-229388

NGONG HILLS
PO Box 40485
Tel: 567137
Fax: 229938

NORFOLK HOTEL
Harry Thuku Rd
PO Box 40064
Tel: 335800

NYOTAL HOTEL
Latema Rd
Tel: 220664/227816

OAKWOOD HOTEL
Kimathi St
PO Box 40683
Tel: 220592

ORIENTAL PALACE
Arrow Towers
Taveta Rd
Tel: 217600

PANAFRIC HOTEL
Kenyatta Ave
PO Box 30468
Telex: 22454
Fax: 2-211472/
726356/721878

PARIS HOTEL
Mfangano St
Tel: 337483

PARKLANDS
SHADE HOTEL
Ojijo Rd
PO Box 33003
Tel: 749870/042

PARK–PLACE
PO Box 70069
Magadi Rd
Tel: 890456/95
Fax: 890270

PARKSIDE HOTEL
PO Box 53104
Monrovia St
Tel: 333329

PARK VILLA
Harambee Plaza
Uhuru Highway
Tel: 217353

PARSONIC HOTEL
Kirinyaga Rd
Tel: 225010/220208

PLAZA HOTEL
Mogadishu Rd
Tel: 534200

PLUMS HOTEL
Ojijo Rd

PO Box 40747
Tel: 745222

PORTVIEW HOTEL
2nd Ave
Tel: 642236

PRINCESS HOTEL
Tom Mboya St
Tel: 214640/212806

RAMADA HOTEL
11th Eastleigh St
Tel: 765999

SAFARI PARK
Thika Rd
PO Box 45038
Tel: 802493

SAGRET HOTEL
Milimani Rd
PO Box 18324
Tel: 333395/720933

SAMAGAT HOTEL
Pak House
Accra Rd
Tel: 230435/217668

SAYTA'S HOTEL
South B
Tel: 559200

SELDOM HOTEL
PO Box 33145
Tel: 762272

SELENGEI
PO Box 7834
Tel: 228765

SHADE HOTEL
Ngong Rd
Karen
Tel: 882298

SILVER SPRINGS
Arwings Kodhek Rd
PO Box 61362
Tel: 722451

SIMARY SAFARI
PO Box 31166
Tel: 750623

SIRONA HOTEL
Keiyo Rd
Tel: 742730/7439697

SIXEIGHTY HOTEL
Muindi Mbingu St
PO Box 43436
Tel: 332680

SOLACE HOTEL
Tom Mboya St
PO Box 48867
Tel: 331277

SOSMAR HOTEL
PO Box 23067
Tel: 250890

SPORTVIEW HOTEL
Kasarani
Tel: 803890/861648

STAY HILL HOTEL
Kirinyaga Rd
Tel: 216156

SUN COURT INN
University Way
PO Box 51454
Tel: 221418/413/458

SUPREME HOTEL
Keekorok Rd
Tel: 225241/331586

SWISS COTTAGE
PO Box 65063
Tel: 803075

TERMINAL HOTEL
Moktar Daddah St
PO Box 43229
Tel: 228817/8

TIGER HOTEL
Gnl Waruingi St
Tel: 764161

TIMBOROA HOTEL
Sheikh Karume Rd
Tel: 216896

TRAVELLERS HOTEL
Ronald Ngala St
Tel: 334826

UTALII HOTEL
Thika Rd
PO Box 31067
Tel: 802540

VISA HOTEL
PO Box 76534
Tel: 512392

WAB HOTEL
PO Box 40013
Tel: 794100/799867

WAGON HOTEL
PO Box 22581
Tel: 763869

WAMBUGU GROVE
Parklands Road
Tel: 741684

WANDA HOTEL
Off Thika Road
Tel: 803387

WARGADUD HOTEL
PO Box 69083
Tel: 764882

WINDSOR GOLF &
COUNTRY CLUB
Ridgeways
PO Box 45587
Tel: 802259/862300
Fax: 254-2-802322

YASMIN HOTEL
River Rd
Tel: 226958

YOUTH HOSTEL
Ralph Bunche Rd
Tel: 723012

YMCA Hostel
State Hse Rd
PO Box 30330
Tel: 724116

YWCA Hostel
Mamlaka Rd
PO Box 40710
Tel: 724699

The Coast

MOMBASA

ABC LODGE
Kwa Shibu Rd
Tel: 313340

AFRICAN SAFARI CLUB
PO Box 81443
Tel: 485520/485906

AL MASHREQ
PO Box 41784
Tel: 311061/6

AL-IQBAL HOTEL
Raha Leo St
Tel: 221988

AQUARIUS WATAMU
Watamu Rd
Tel: 32069

BAHARI BEACH
PO Box 81443
Tel: 471603

BRISBANE HOTEL
Mombasa/Malindi Rd
Tel: 485659/7

CASTLE HOTEL
Moi Ave
PO Box 84231
Tel: 223403

COCONUT BAR HOTEL
Box 85430
Tel: 471641

CONTINENTAL
GUEST HSE
Haile Selassie Ave
Tel: 315916

COSY GUEST HSE
Haile Selassie Ave
Tel: 313064

CROWN HOTEL
Mombasa/Nairobi Rd
Tel: 485321

FISHERMAN'S INN
Mwamba Drive
Tel: 471343/472214

FONTANA HOTEL
PO Box 86291
Tel: 485934/20

HOTEL FORTUNA
PO Box 81914
Tel: 20594

HOTEL HERMES
Msanifu Kombo St
PO Box 98419
Tel: 313599

HOTEL SAPPHIRE
PO Box 1254
Tel: 492257/494893
Fax: 495280

HOTEL SEA BREEZES
Likoni Rd
PO Box 960222
Tel: 451218

HOTEL SHIMO LA
TEWA
PO Box 81443
Tel: 485226

HOTEL SKYWAY
Moi Ave
PO Box 83933
Tel: 313536

HOTEL SPLENDID
PO Box 90482
Tel: 220967/221694

HOTEL STRAND
Moi Ave
Tel: 223294/9398

HUNTER'S HOTEL
Jomo Kenyatta Ave
PO Box 98583
Tel: 493072

KENYA BEACH
PO Box 95748
Tel: 485821/2/3

LOTUS HOTEL
Cathedral Rd
PO Box 90193
Tel: 313207/313234

MAKUTI SAFARI
HOTEL
Moi Ave
PO Box 99753
Tel: 313082

MANOR HOTEL
Nyerere Ave
PO Box 84851
Tel: 314643

MANSON HOTEL
PO Box 83565
Tel: 222356

MANSOUR
NAJISAID TANAN
Jamhuri Rd
Tel: 220657

MAUNGA HOTEL
PO Box 83386
Tel: 316339

MOMBASA HOTEL
PO Box 83652
Tel: 223015

MONIQUE HOTEL
PO Box 99702
Tel: 474231

NAROK LODGE
PO Box 93465
Tel: 432048

NEW CARLTON
Moi Ave
PO Box 86779
Tel: 223776

NEW MARKET
HOTEL
Old Biashara St
Tel: 222792

NEW MERMAID
Moi Ave
PO Box 84899
Tel: 313082

NEW OUTRIGGER
Ras Liwatoni
PO Box 82345
Tel: 220822/3

NEW PALM TREE
Nkrumah Rd
PO Box 90013
Tel: 311756/313560

NEW SPORTS VIEW
Ronald Ngala Rd
PO Box 87444
Tel: 494625

OCEANIC HOTEL
PO Box 90371
Tel: 311191-2

POLANA HOTEL
Maungano Rd
PO Box 82923
Tel: 222168

SILVER STAR
Mt Kenya Rd
Tel: 472542/3/4

TAJ HOTEL
Digo Rd
PO Box 82923
Tel: 223198/313545

THREE COINS
Ganjoni Rd
Tel: 221548

South Coast

AFRICANA SEA
LODGE
PO Box 84616 Msa
Tel: (0127) 2624
Fax: 254-127-2145

AZANIA APARTMENTS
PO Box 85965 Msa
Tel: 451548

BEACHCOMBER CLUB
PO Box 54
Msambweni
Tel: 52074/33/2426

CHALE ISLAND
PARADISE
PO Box 4
Msambweni
Tel: 3235/6
Fax: 3319/20

CHILDREN'S RESORT
CENTRE
PO Box 96048 Msa
Tel: 451417

CLUB GREEN OASIS
PO Box 80
Msambweni
Kwale District
Tel: 52206

CORAL BEACH
COTTAGES
Diani
Tel: 2413

DIANI BEACH
COTTAGES
PO Box 14, Ukunda
Tel: 3471

DIANI REEF HOTEL
PO Box 35, Ukunda
Tel: 2602

DIANI SEA LODGE
PO Box 37, Ukunda
Tel: 2115/2398

DIANI SEA RESORT
Beach Rd
Tel: 3081-3

FOUR 'N' TWENTY
PO Box 90270 Msa
Tel: 312449

FUNZI ISLAND
CLUB
Diani Beach Rd
Tel: 2044/2346

GOLDEN BEACH
PO Box 31, Ukunda
Tel: 2625

INDIAN OCEAN
BEACH CLUB
Block Hotels
Rehama Hse
PO Box 47557 Nbi
Tel: 335807/830
Telex: 22146
Fax: 254-2-340541

JADINI BEACH
PO Box 84616 Msa
Tel: 2622

KASKAZI BEACH
PO Box 135 Ukunda
Tel: 3725
Fax: 2233

LAGOON REEF HOTEL
Diani Beach
PO Box 83058 Msa
Tel: Diani 2627

LEISURE LODGE
PO Box 84383 Msa
Tel: (01261) 2011-2

LEOPARD BEACH
PO Box 34, Ukunda
Tel: (01261) 2110-1

MARENJE HOTEL
Lunga Lunga Rd
Msambweni
Tel: 52064

MAWENI COTTAGES
PO Box 96024 Msa
Tel: 51008

NEPTUNE PARADISE
Galu Beach
Tel: 3620/3061
Fax: 3019

NOMAD BANDAS
PO Box 1, Ukunda
Tel: 2155

OCEAN VILLAGE
PO Box 2188,
Ukunda
Tel: (01261) 2725

ROBINSON'S
CLUB BAOBAB
PO Box 84792 Msa
Tel: 2623

SAFARI BEACH
PO Box 84616 Msa
Tel: 2726
Telex: 21428
Fax: 254-127-2357

SAND ISLAND
BEACH COTTAGES
Tiwi
PO Box 96009 Msa
Tel: 51233

SEA CREST
COTTAGES
PO Box 44053 Nbi
Tel: 22728/9
(Nbi booking)

SEASCAPES
PO Box 45541 Msa
Tel: 334996/20486
(Nbi booking)

SEA VIEW DIANI
VILLAS
PO Box 45626 Msa
Tel: 2138/2089

SHELLEY BEACH
PO Box 96030 Msa
Tel: 451001-4

SHIMBA LODGE
Block Hotels:
Rehema Hse
Nairobi
Tel: 335807
Telex: 22146
Fax: 254-2-340541

LEISURE LODGE
Diani
PO Box 84383 Msa
Tel: 2011-2

TIWI SEA CASTLES
PO Box 96599 Msa
Tel: 803158/802336

TIWI VILLAS
PO Box 24752 Nbi
Tel: 4080 4065

TRADE WINDS
PO Box 8, Ukunda
Tel: 2016

TWIGA LODGE
PO Box 80820 Msa
Tiwi 51267/51210

TWO FISHES
PO Box 23, Ukunda
Tel: 2101-4

WARRANDALE
COTTAGES
PO Box 11, Ukunda
Tel: 2186
Nairobi: 29898

SHIMONI
PEMBA CHANNEL
FISHING CLUB
PO Box 44
Msambweni
Tel: 313749/225417

SHIMONI REEF
FISHING LODGE
PO Box 82234 Msa
Tel: 471771

North Coast

AL-WAHAT
BEACH RESORT
PO Box 85039 Msa
New Nyali
Tel: 485733/48

BAHARI BEACH
Bamburi Rd
PO Box 81443 Msa
Tel: 471603

BAMBURI BEACH
HOTEL
PO Box 83996 Msa
Tel: 485611

BAMBURI CHALETS
PO Box 84114 Msa
Tel: 485706/485594

COWRIE SHELL
APARTMENTS
Bamburi Rd
PO Box 10003 Msa
Tel: 485971

DHOWS INN
PO Box 431 Kilifi
Tel: 22028

DOLPHIN HOTEL
PO Box 81443 Msa
Tel: 485801

GIRIAMA BEACH
PO Box 86693 Msa
Tel: 486720/485726
Fax: 486191

HOTEL INTER-
CONTINENTAL
PO Box 83492 Msa
Tel: 485811

HOTEL MALAIKA
Shanzu
PO Box 81443 Msa
Tel: 485101

HOTEL SEAHORSE
PO Box 81443 Msa
Tel: 2515

KANAMI HOLIDAY
CENTRE
Kikambala
Tel: 32101/32046

KENYA BEACH
Bamburi Rd
PO BOX 95748 Msa
Tel: 485821

KENYA MARINAS
PO Box 15070
Kikambala
Tel: 485738/866

MKWAJUNI MOTEL
Mombasa/Malindi Rd
Tel: 22472

MOMBASA BEACH
PO Box 90414 Msa
Tel: 471861
Fax: 472970

MOMBASA BEACH
APARTMENTS
PO Box 89362 Msa
Tel: 473231/474848

MTWAPA BEACH
Malindi Rd
Tel: 228367/8/9

NEPTUNE BEACH
Bamburi
PO Box 83125 Msa
Tel: 485701

NYALI BEACH
Block Hotels
Rehama Hse
PO Box 47557 Nbi
Tel: 335807/830
Telex: 22146

OCEAN VIEW
BEACH HOTEL
Malindi Rd
PO BOX 81127 Msa
Tel: 485308

OCTOPUSSY
BAMBURI
Malindi Rd
PO BOX 83135 Msa
Tel: 485395
Nairobi 315430

OYSTER BAY
BEACH HOTEL
Shanzu Beach
Tel: 485061

PALM BEACH
Malindi Rd
Shanzu
PO Box 81443 Msa
Tel: 485906

PARADISE BEACH
Shanzu Rd
Tel: 468104

PICCOLO BEACH
PO Box 82671
Mombasa/Malindi Rd
Tel: 485236

PLAZA HOTEL
Bamburi Rd
PO Box 88299 Msa
Tel: 485321/325

REEF HOTEL
PO Box 82234 Msa
Tel: 471771-2

SERENA BEACH
PO Box 90352 Msa
Tel: 485721/277

SEVERIN SEA LODGE
Bamburi Rd
PO Box 82169 Msa
Tel: 485001

SHANZU BEACH
PO Box 81443 Msa
Tel: 485604

SILVER BEACH
PO Box 81443 Msa
Tel: 471471

SUN & SAND
BEACH HOTEL
PO Box 2, Kikambala
Tel: 32621/32055

TRAVELLERS
BEACH
Bamburi
Malindi Rd
Tel: 485121

WHISPERING PALMS
PO Box 5 Kikambala
Tel: 32620/32004/5

WHITESANDS
PO Box 90173
Mombasa
Tel: 485911-3
Fax: 485652/485405

Kilifi
KILIFI HOTEL
PO Box 3, Kilifi
Tel: 22263

MNARANI CLUB
PO Box 81443 Msa
Tel: 2318-9
Nairobi 336859

SEA HORSE HOTEL
PO Box 70, Kilifi
Tel: 2390/2364
Nairobi 220592

Watamu
BUSTANI YA
EDEN HOTEL
Off Turtle Bay Rd
Tel: 32262

CLUB TEMPLE
POINT
PO Box 296
Mida Creek
Tel: 32057/32275

HEMINGWAY'S
PO Box 267
Tel: 32624/32052
Fax: 32256

OCEAN SPORTS
PO Box 100
Tel: 32624/32008

TURTLE BAY
BEACH HOTEL
PO Box 457
Tel: 32080/32226

WATAMU BEACH
PO Box 300,
Tel: 32001

WATAMU PARADISE
Tel: 32062/32436

Malindi
AFRICAN DREAM
VILLAGE
Casuarina Rd
PO Box 939
Tel: 20442/3/4

AFRICAN PEARL HOTEL
Lamu/Ngowe Rd
Tel: 30988/17

ANGEL'S BAY VILLAGE
Off Lamu Rd
PO Box 857
Tel: 31268/4/6/87

BLUE MARLIN
PO Box 54
Tel: (0123) 20440

BOUGAN VILLAGE
HOTEL
Lamu Rd
Tel: 21205/20382

CASUARINA VILLAS
Tel: 20857

CLUB CHE SHALE
PO Box 492
Tel: 20063

COCONUT VILLAGE
PO Box 868
Tel: 20928

CORAL BEACH
Malindi Rd
PO Box 84231 Msa
Tel: 23403

DRIFTWOOD
BEACH CLUB
PO Box 63
Tel: 20155

EDEN ROC HOTEL
Lamu Rd
PO Box 350
Tel: 20480

GARRODA CORAL
BEACH
Mida Creek Rd
PO Box 163
Tel: 32098

KINGFISHER
LODGE
PO Box 29
Tel: 30261/21168

KIVULINI VILLAGE
BEACH HOTEL
Hospital Rd
Tel: 20898/21267

LAMBERTIS
HOTEL
Lambertis/Ngowe Rd
PO Box 543
Tel: 30508/30507

LAWFORD'S
PO Box 20
Government Rd
Tel: 30092

MALINDI SEA
FISHING CLUB
PO Box 364
Tel: 20410

NEW LAMU HOTEL
PO Box 333
Sheikh Nasser Rd
Tel: 20864

PALM GARDEN
HOTEL
Harambee Rd
Tel: 20115/31895

PALM TREE CLUB
Lamu Rd
PO Box 180
Tel: 20397

SILVERSANDS
VILLAS
Tourist Rd
PO Box 91
Tel: 20385/20842

TANA HOTEL
Jamhuri Rd
PO Box 776
Tel: 20657/20116

WHITE ELEPHANT
SEA LODGE
PO Box 948
Tel: 20223

Lamu
HOTEL POLE POLE
PO Box 242
Tel: 33204

ISLAND HOTEL
PO Box 179
Shela Village
Tel: 33568/33290

KIJANI HOUSE
PO Box 266
Tel: 33235/33374
Fax: 33237

KITENDETINI
BAHARI HOTEL
PO Box 83470 Msa
Tel: 3231

MAHRUS HOTEL
PO Box 25
Tel: 33001

PALACE HOTEL
PO Box 83
Tel: 33164/33272

PEPONI HOTEL
PO Box 24
Tel: 33029/33423

PETLEY'S INN
PO Box 4
Tel: 33107
Nairobi: 229612

RAS KITAU BEACH
Manda Island
PO Box 99
Tel: 3206

Kiwaiyu
KIWAIYU SAFARI
VILLAGE
PO Box 48287 Nbi
Tel: 331231

Up-country Hotels

Bungoma
BUNGOMA
TOURIST HOTEL
PO Box 972
Tel: 126

BUNGOMA SIMBA
PO Box 663
Tel: 20804

EGRET HOTEL
PO Box 1100
Tel: 41241

KANDUYI INN
PO Box 664
Webuye/Malaba
Tel: 20013

PARK VILLA
Webuye/Kitale Rd
Tel: 41290/41621

Busia
FARMVIEW
Hospital Rd
Tel: 2470/2300

PARADISE LODGE
Busia/Kisumu Rd
Tel: 2056/2212

Chogoria
CHUKA FARMERS
PO Box 394
Tel: 30285

Eldoret
ELDORET VALLEY
PO Box 734
Uganda Rd
Tel: 32314/33560

MAHINDI HOTEL
Uganda Rd
Tel: 31520

SIRIKWA HOTEL
PO Box 3361
Tel: 31655
Telex: 35010

SOSIAN VIEW
Arap Moi St
Tel: 33215

WAGON HOTEL
PO Box 2408
Tel: 33578/62270

Embu
IZAAK WALTON INN
PO Box 46527 Nbi
Nbi booking
Tel: 227828

TEL AVIV HOTEL
Mama Ngina St
Tel: 20951/20028

Gatundu
NEW GATUNDU HOTEL
PO Box 671
Tel: 74121

Gilgil
GILGIL MAKUTANO
PO Box 255
Tel: 2075

LAKE ELMENTEITA
LODGE
PO Box 561 Nakuru
Tel: 2074

Homa Bay
HOMA BAY HOTEL
PO Box 42013
Tel: 229751/223488

Isiolo
LEWA DOWNS
Wildlife Trails
PO Box 42562 Nbi

Kabarnet
KABARNET HOTEL
PO Box 42013
Tel: 22134/22094
Nairobi 227828

SAFARI HOTEL
PO Box 112
Tel: 2378

Kakamega
BENDERA HOTEL
PO Box 423
Sudi Rd
Tel: 20777

GOLF HOTEL
PO Box 118
Tel: 20125/30150
Nbi 330820

Kangundo
KANGUNDO MOTEL
PO Box 1156
Tel: 21433

Kapenguria
BWAKIRE HOTEL
Market St
Tel: 2447

Kapsabet
KAPSABET HOTEL
PO Box 426,
Tel: 2172

KUNJO HOTEL
Market St
Tel: 43001

SPLASH HOTEL
Market St
Tel: 43061

Karatina
BLUE STAR HOTEL
PO Box 175
Tel: 71055

ELEPHANT & CASTLE
PO Box 370
Tel: 29615

KARATINA
TOURIST LODGE
Private Bag
Tel: 71522/71772

NEW KARATINA
LAMU LODGE
PO Box 918
Tel: 2176

Kericho
TEA HOTEL
PO Box 75
Tel: (0328) 30004-5

MID-WEST HOTEL
Tel: 20611-4

Kerugoya
MUNYAKA HOTEL
PO Box 75
Tel: 21067

Kiambu
HOTEL NOVA PARK
Kiambui Rd
Tel: 20162-7

(Karuri)
UTUGI HOTEL
PO Box 50839
Tel: 22061

Kisii
KINANGO HOTEL
PO Box 973
Tel: 21190

KISII HOTEL
PO Box 26
Tel: 30134

RIVERSIDE
TOURIST RESORT
PO Box 2401
Tel: 21646

YORKSTAR HOTEL
PO Box 885
Tel: 21653

Kisumu
EAST VIEW HOTEL
PO Box 857
Omoto Aggar Rd
Tel: 41871

FANANA HOTEL
Tel: 44462/3

FARID HOTEL
Accra St
PO Box 374
Tel: 41591

GET IN HOTEL
PO Box 807
Tel: 42682

HOTEL BEOGRADA
PO Box 920
Tel: 45165

HOTEL CASSANOVA
PO Box 920
Tel: 41743

IMPERIAL HOTEL
PO Box 1866
Tel: 41485/55–57

LAKE VIEW HOTEL
PO Box 1216
Oginga Odinga Rd
Tel: 45055

LERN LERN HOTEL
Angawa Ave
Tel: 22021/40603

NEW KISUMU
PO Box 1690
Tel: 40336-7

NEW VICTORIA
PO Box 276
Tel: 2909/41849

PINE CONE HOTEL
Kisumu/Busia Rd
Tel: 22921

SILICON MOTEL
Kisumu/Nairobi Rd
Tel: 21636

SUNSET HOTEL
PO Box 215
Telex: 31177
Tel: 41100

Kitale
ALAKAPA HOTEL
Kenyatta St
Tel: 20395

BOMEN HOTEL
Church Rd
Tel: 2389/2225

BONGO HOTEL
PO Box 530
Moi Ave
Tel: 20593

KITALE CLUB
PO Box 30
Tel: 20030

HOTEL MAMBOLEO
Moi Ave
Tel: 20172

Kitui
KITUI RIVERSIDE
MOTEL
Kitui/Machakos Rd
Tel: 22006

Lake Baringo
LAKE BARINGO
ISLAND CAMP
PO Box 58581 Nbi
Tel: 216940
Telex: 22066
Fax: 254-2-216796

LAKE BARINGO
CLUB
Block Hotels
PO Box 47557 Nbi
Tel: 335807/830
Telex: 22146
Fax: 254-2-340541

Lake Naivasha
FISHERMAN'S CAMP
Lets's Go Travel
PO Box 60342 Nbi
Tel: 340331/213033

FOUR SEASONS
Sokori Rd
Tel: 20377

KEN-VASH HOTEL
Posta Lane
Tel: 30039

LA BELLE INN
Naivasha
Moi Ave
Tel: 21007

LAITOLIA RANCH
Governors' Camps
PO Box 48217 Nbi
Tel: 331871/2, 331041
Telex: 22678

LAKE NAIVASHA
COUNTRY CLUB
Block Hotels
PO Box 47557 Nbi
Tel: 335807/830
Telex: 22146
Fax: 340541
Tel: 20804/20925/
21004

OTHAYA ANNEX
Kariuki Chotara Rd
Tel: 20770

NAIVASHA
SILVER HOTEL
Kenyatta Ave
PO Box 989
Tel: 20580

UPENDO HOTEL
Kariuki Chotara Rd
Tel: 20258

SAFARILAND
LODGE
PO BOX 72
Tel: 20926

Lake Turkana
ELIYE SPRINGS
LODGE
PO Lodwar
Radiocall Nairobi
Tel: 2064

LAKE TURKANA
FISHING LODGE
PO Box 41078 Nbi
Tel: 226623/808

OASIS LODGE
PO Box 56707 Nbi
Tel: 225255

Lake Victoria
RUSINGA ISLAND
Lonrho Hotels
PO Box 58581 Nbi
Tel: 216940/723776
Telex: 22060

MFANGANO
ISLAND CAMP
Governors' Camps
PO Box 48217 Nbi
Tel: 331871/2, 331041
Telex: 22678

Lodwar
COSMOS SIDE
VIEW HOTEL
PO Box 26
Tel: 21424

NEW LODWAR
LODGE
PO Box 123
Tel: 21223/31

Machakos
FIVE HILLS VIEW
LODGE
Off Machakos Rd
Tel: 20153/30112

T TOT HOTEL
PO Box 841
Tel: 20157

Magadi
MASAI DEN HOTEL
PO Box 72587
Tel: 24198

Makindu
HUNTERS LODGE
PO Box 77
Tel: 221439/220592

Maralal
MARALAL SAFARI
LODGE
PO Box 45155 Nbi
Tel: 211124/334177

Maragoli
AMBWERE
ALLIANCE HOTEL
PO Box 193
Tel: 51475

Maua
MAUA HOTEL
Tel: 21117/42/3

Marmanet
MEDINA HOTEL
Box 1653
Tel: 2

Matuu
MATUU NDALLAS
Ruka/Garissa Rd
Tel: 55425/6

Mazeras
COUNTRY MOTEL
PO Box 81969
Tel: 88

Mbale
MBALE HOTEL
PO Box 193
Tel: 51270

Meru
ELBAJA HOTEL
Kenyatta Highway
Tel: 20427-8

MERU COUNTY
PO Box 1386
Tel: 20427/32

PIG AND WHISTLE
PO Box 1809
Tel: 20433/20574

STANSTED HOTEL
Tom Mboya St
Tel: 20360

THREE STEERS
PO Box 2318
Tel: 20082

TRAVELLERS HOTEL
PO Box 1855
Tel: 30793

Molo
HIGHLANDS
PO Box 142
Tel: 50

HIGHWAY HOTEL
PO Box 168
Tel: 41469

HOTEL EEL
Njoro/Molo Rd
Tel: 31271/31471

Mtito Andei
TSAVO INN
Kilimanjaro Safari
Club
PO Box 30139 Nbi
Tel: 227136/337150

Mweiga
ABERDARE
COUNTRY CLUB
PO Box 449
Nairobi bookings:
Tel: 216940
Fax: 254-2-216796

Nakuru
CRATER VIEW HOTEL
Oginga Odinga Rd
Tel: 41304

LAKE BOGORIA HOTEL
PO Box 542
Tel: 40896/42696

LANET COUNTRY
HOTEL
Tel: 40457

MIDLAND HOTEL
Geoffrey Kamau Way
Tel: 212125/6

NEW HONEY
MOON HOTEL
PO Box 9549
Tel: 44953

PIVOT HOTEL
PO Box 1369
Tel: 40822/42473

SATELITE HOTEL
PO Box 1413
Tel: 210061

SEASONS HOTEL
Government Rd
Tel: 42518

SHIRIKISHO HOTEL
Kenyatta Avenue
Tel: 212345/6

Namanga
NAMANGA RIVER
PO Box 30471 Nbi
336858

Nanyuki
AL-ASWAD HOTEL
PO Box 664
Tel: 30614

EL KARAMA RANCH
AA Travel
PO Box 14982 Nbi
Tel: 742926

JAMBO HOUSE
Tel: 22951

JASKAKI HOTEL
Bazaar St
Tel: 22820

KUNGU MAITU
Laikipia Rd
Tel: 22912

LANDVIEW HOTEL
Willy/Jimmy Rd
Tel: 32545

MOONLIGHT HOTEL
Namanga Rd
Tel: 22503

MOUNT KENYA
SAFARI CLUB
PO Box 35
Tel: 22960/22961
Lonrho Hotels
PO Box 58581 Nbi
Tel: 216940
Fax: (254-2) 216796

OL PEJETA RANCH
Lonrho Hotels
PO Box 58581 Nbi
Tel: 216940
Fax: (254-2) 216796

OL PEJETA LODGE
PO Box 763
Tel: 23414

NANYUKI RIVER
LODGE
Nanyuki/Meru Rd
Tel: 32523

SPORTSMAN'S ARMS
PO Box 3
Tel: 22895

SWEETWATERS
TENTED CAMP
Lonrho Hotels
PO Box 58581 Nbi
Tel: 216940
Fax: (254-2) 216796

Narok
ELEO HOTEL
PO Box 197
Tel: 2362

KANDAS HOTEL
PO Box 119
Tel: 2236

Naro Moru
NARO MORU
RIVER LODGE
Alliance Hotels
PO Box 49839 Nbi
Tel: 337501/227103
Fax: 254-2-219212

Nyahururu
BARON HOTEL
Kenyatta Ave
Tel: 32056

THOMSON'S FALLS
LODGE
PO Box 38
Tel: 22006/32170

Nyeri
BAHATI HOTEL
PO Box 233
Tel: 71491

CENTRAL HOTEL
Kanisa Rd
Tel: 2906

GREENHILLS HOTEL
PO Box 313
Tel: 2017/2687-8

HIGHLANDS HOTEL
PO Box 1264
Mau Summit Rd
Tel: 21036

JOHRENE MOTEL
Commercial St
Tel: 71606

MACHACHARI HOTEL
PO Box 1360
Tel: 4617

MOUNTAIN ROCK
Naromoru Rd
Tel: 62098/9

MOUNTAIN VIEW
PO Box 316
Tel: 4598

OUTSPAN HOTEL
Block Hotels
PO Box 47557 Nbi
Tel: 335807/830
Fax: 254-2-340541

PARESIA HOTEL
Sports Rd
Tel: 2765

SPORTSVIEW HOTEL
Kimathi Way
Tel: 4011

WHITE RHINO
PO Box 30
Tel: 2189/2031

Ol Kalou
BULL HEAD HOTEL
PO Box 122
Munyeki Rd
Tel: 72051

Siaya
VILLA HOTEL
Siaya/Kisumu Rd
Tel: 21200

Soy
SOY COUNTRY CLUB
PO Box 2
Tel: Soy 32037/8

Taveta
CHALLA HOTEL
Taveta Rd
Tel: 2212

Thika
BLUE POSTS HOTEL
PO Box 42
Tel: (0151) 22241

CHANIA TOURIST
LODGE INN
Mugo Kibiru Rd
Tel: 22547

DECEMBER HOTEL
Commercial Rd
Tel: 22140

MARJOE HOTEL
PO Box 856
Tel: 21531

PETROCK PALACE
Tel: 21503

SAGRET HOTEL
Upper Rd
Tel: 21219

WHITELINE HOTEL
PO Box 290
Tel: (0151) 22857

Tigoni
KENTMERE CLUB
PO Box 49666
Tel: 41053/42101

Turbo
SPRING PARK
PO Box 59
Tel: 53016

Voi
SAGALLA VIEW
LODGE
PO Box 123
Kariakoo Area
Tel: 30053

Wajir
MALAB HOTEL
PO Box 323
Tel: 21211

Parks and Reserves

Aberdares
THE ARK
Lonrho Hotels
Norfolk Hotel
PO Box 58581 Nbi
Tel: 216940
Telex: 22066
Fax: 254-2-216796

TREETOPS
Block Hotels
PO Box 47557 Nbi
Tel: 335807/830

Amboseli
AMBOSELI LODGE
KILIMANJARO
SAFARI LODGE &
KIMANA LODGE
Grindlays Building
PO Box 30139 Nbi
Tel: 227136/337150/
338888

AMBOSELI SERENA
Williamson Hse
PO Box 48690 Nbi
Tel: 711077/8,710511
Telex: 22878
Fax: 254-2-718100

KILIMANJARO
BUFFALO LODGE
Aardvark Safaris
PO Box 49718 Nbi
Tel: 331718/334863

OL TUKAI LODGE
Block Hotels
PO Box 47557 Nbi
Tel: 335807/830
Fax: 340541

Buffalo Springs
BUFFALO SPRINGS
TENTED LODGE
African Tours & Hotels
Utalii Hse
PO Box 30471 Nbi
Tel: 336858

Lake Nakuru
LION HILL CAMP
Sarova Hotels
New Stanley Hotel
PO Box 30680 Nbi
Tel: 333233/333249

Maasai Mara
FIG TREE CAMP
PO Box 40693 Nbi
Tel: 221439/220592/

GOVERNORS' CAMP,
LITTLE GOVERNORS,
GOVERNORS'
PRIVATE CAMP

Governors' Camps
International Hse
PO Box 48217 Nbi
Tel: 331871/337344
Telex: 22678
Fax: 726427

KEEKOROK LODGE
Block Hotels
Rehema Hse
PO Box 47557
Tel: 335807/830

KICHWA TEMBO
Conservation
Corporation (EA)
PO Box 74957
Tel: 750298/780
Fax: 254-2-746826

MARA INTREPIDS
Talek Limited
PO Box 14040 Nbi
Tel: 335208/331688

MARA SAFARI CLUB
Lonrho Hotels
PO BOX 58581 Nbi
Tel: 216940/723776

MARA SERENA
PO Box 48690 Nbi
Tel: 711077/8, 710511
Fax: 254-2-718100

MASAI MARA
SOPA LODGE
PO Box 72630 Nbi
Tel: 336088/724
Fax: 223843

MAASAI MARA
RIVER CAMP
PO Box 48019 Nbi
Tel: 331191/29009

SAROVA MARA
Sarova Hotels
PO Box 30680 Nbi
Tel: 333248-51
Fax: (305) 2371-2

SIANA SPRINGS
Conservation
Corporation (EA)
PO Box 74957 Nbi
Tel: 750298/780
Fax: 254-2-746826

Marsabit
MARSABIT LODGE
Msafiri Inns
PO Box 42013 Nbi
Tel: 229751/223488/
330820

Meru National Park
LEOPARD ROCK
SAFARI LODGE
AA Travel
PO Box 14982 Nbi
Tel: 337900

MERU MULIKA
LODGE
PO Box 42013
Nairobi
Tel: 229751/223488

Mount Elgon
MOUNT ELGON
LODGE
PO Box 42013
Nairobi
Tel: 229751/22348

Mount Kenya
MOUNTAIN LODGE
African Tours
& Hotels
PO Box 30471 Nbi
Tel: 336858

Salt Lick
SALT LICK/TAITA
HILLS LODGES
Hilton International
PO Box 30624 Nbi
Tel: 334000

Samburu
LARSENS TENTED
CAMP/SAMBURU
LODGE
Block Hotels
PO Box 47557 Nbi
Tel: 335807/830

SAMBURU SERENA
Serena Lodges
PO Box 48690 Nbi
Tel: 711077-8
Fax: 725184

Shaba
SAROVA SHABA
Sarova Hotels
PO Box 30680 Nbi
Tel: 333233/333249

Tsavo East
ARUBA LODGE
Kenya Wildlife
Services
NAtional Park HQ
Nairobi

CROCODILE
TENTED CAMP
Repotel
Caltex Hse
Koinange St
PO Box 46527 Nbi
Tel: 227828

TSAVO SAFARI
CAMP
Kilimanjaro Safari
Club
PO Box 30139
Nairobi
Tel: 227136/337150
Telex: 22371

VOI SAFARI LODGE
African Tours &
Hotels
PO Box 30471 Nbi
Tel: 336858

Tsavo West
KILAGUNI &
NGULIA SAFARI
LODGES
African Tours
& Hotels
PO Box 30471 Nbi
Tel: 336858

KITANI LODGE &
NGULIA SAFARI
CAMP
Let's Go Travel
Standard St
PO Box 60342 Nbi
Tel: 213033/229540

LAKE JIPE SAFARI
LODGE
PO Box 31092 Nbi
Tel: 218376/334966

Shimba Hills
SHIMBA LODGE
Block Hotels
PO Box 47557 Nbi
Tel: 335807/830

Business Associations

African Business
Consortium
PO Box 40093 Nbi
Tel: 718408/9

Agricultural Society
of Kenya
PO Box 30176 Nbi
Tel: 566655

Architectural
Assoc of Kenya
Professional Centre
Parliament Rd
PO Box 44258 Nbi
Tel: 224806

Assoc of
Accountants
in East Africa
PO Box 20716 Nbi
Tel: 338446

Assoc of Civil
Engineering
Surveyors of Africa
PO Box 40915 Nbi
Tel: 332195

Assoc of Consulting
Engineers of Kenya
PO Box 72643 Nbi
Tel: 222543

Assoc of Professional
Societies in East Africa
PO Box 72643 Nbi
Tel: 212660

Automobile Assoc
of Kenya
Argwings Kodhek Rd
PO Box 40087 Nbi
Tel: 720382/723195

Automobile Assoc
of Kenya
Nkurumah Rd
PO Box 86250 Msa
Tel: 492431

Brewers Assoc
of East Africa
Ronald Ngala St
PO Box 30161 Nbi
Tel: 220962

Commonwealth
Parliamentary Assoc
PO Box 41842 Nbi
Tel: 221291

Cotton and Lint Seed
Marketing Board
Uchumi Hse
PO Box 30477 Nbi
Tel: 331006

East African Tea
Trade Assoc
Nkrumah Ave
PO Box 42281 Nbi
Tel: 337521

Federation of Kenya
Employers
Oginga Odinga Rd
PO Box 1449 Kisumu
Tel: 41504

Federation of Kenya
Employers
Nyerere Ave
PO Box 84115 Msa
Tel: 311112

Federation of Kenya
Employers
Arwings Kodhek Rd
PO Box 48311 Nbi
Tel: 721929/948

Institute of Certified
Public Accountants
Red Cross Building
Paliament Rd
PO Box 59963 Nbi
Tel: 224629

Insurance Assoc of
Eastern Africa
Silopark Hse
Mama Ngina St
PO Box 45338 Nbi
Tel: 220212

Inter-Governmental
Standing Committee
on Shipping
Digo Rd
PO Box 99329 Msa
Tel: 220160

Kenya Assoc of Hotel
Keepers & Caterers
Wabera St
PO Box 46046 Nbi
Tel: 726642/721505

Kenya Assoc
of Manufacturers
Peponi Rd Westlands
PO Box 30225 Nbi
Tel: 746005-7

Kenya Assoc
of Tour Operators
Mama Ngina St
PO Box 48461 Nbi
Tel: 225570/103

Kenya Bankers Assoc
PO Box 73100 Nbi
Tel: 336681/221704

Kenya Clearing,
Forwarding &
Warehousing Assoc
Ambalal Hse
PO Box 87227 Msa
Tel: 311778

Kenya Coffee
Growers Assoc
Haile Selassie Ave
PO Box 72832 Nbi
Tel: 221725

Kenya Farmers Assoc
PO Box 50 Nakuru
Tel: 41800/8

Kenya Film Corporation
Uchumi Hse
PO Box 30674 Nbi
Tel: 226651/331745

Kenya Hospital Assoc
Nairobi Hospital
PO Box 30026 Nbi
Tel: 722160/725237

Kenya Medical Assoc
PO Box 46999
Tel: 716811

Kenya Medical
Research Institute
Mbagathi Rd
PO Box 54840 Nbi
Tel: 722541-3

Kenya National
Chamber of
Commerce &
Industry
Ufanisi Hse
PO Box 47024
Nairobi
Tel: 220866/334413
(Branches in: Busia,
Kisumu, Kakamega,
Mombasa, Kilifi,
Nakuru, Nyahururu,
Thika, Nyeri, and
Murang'a)

Kenya Pilots Assoc
Kimathi St
PO Box 46041 Nbi
Tel: 227055

Sisal Board
Inspectorate
Mozambique Rd
PO Box 81764 Msa
Tel: 224325

Kenya Tea
Development Authy
PO Box 30213 Nbi
Tel: 221441-4

Kenya Tourist
Development
Corporation
PO Box 42013 Nbi
Tel: 229751/223488

Kenya Transport
Assoc
Lunga Lunga Rd
PO Box 78198 Nbi
Tel: 541876

Law Society of Kenya
Parliament Rd
PO Box 72219 Nbi
Tel: 225558

Mombasa & Coast
Tourist Assoc
Tom Mboya St
PO Box 99596 Msa
Tel: 225428/311231

National Nurses
Assoc of Kenya
PO Box 49422 Nbi
Tel: 229083

Clubs

NAIROBI
Aero Club
Wilson Airport
PO Box 40813 Nbi
Tel: 501772

Aga Khan
5th Ave Parklands
PO Box 10843 Nbi
Tel: 742930/749540

Amateur Boxing
Assoc of Kenya
PO Box 47769 Nbi
Tel: 802701/28919

Barclays Sports Club
Thika Rd
PO Box 30120 Nbi
Tel: 802847

Caltex Sports Club
PO Box 49693 Nbi
Tel: 222104

County Sports Club
PO Box 53407 Nbi
Tel: 567120

East Africa
Kennel Club
PO Box 14223 Nbi
Tel: 566067

East Africa Motor
Sports Club
Mombasa Rd Nbi
PO Box 42786
Tel: 822843

Harlequin (Rugby)
Football Club
Ngong Rd
PO Box 42999 Nbi
Tel: 568565

Impala Club
Ngong Rd
PO Box 41516 Nbi
Tel: 565684/560638

Jockey Club
of Kenya
PO Box 40373 Nbi
Tel: 566108/9

Karen Country Club
PO Box 24816 Karen
Tel: 882801/2

Kenya Amateur
Athletic Assoc
Nyayo Stadium
Uhuru Highway
PO Box 46722 Nbi
Tel: 229301/337406

Kenya Football Fdn
Nyayo Stadium
Uhuru Highway
PO Box 40234 Nbi
Tel: 226138

Kenya Golf Union
Muthaiga
PO Box 49609 Nbi
Tel: 763898

Kenya Karate Assoc
PO Box 32184 Nbi
Tel: 553226

Kenya Lawn Tennis
Assoc
Hospital Rd
PO Box 43184 Nbi
Tel: 725084

Kenya Olympic
Assoc
Caltex Hse
Koinange St
PO Box 40872 Nbi
Tel: 331355

Kenya Regiment
Assoc
PO Box 42216 Nbi
Tel: 724135

Kenya Rugby
Football Union
PO Box 48322 Nbi
Tel: 340936

Kenya Taekwondo
Assoc
Koinange St
PO Box 61002 Nbi
Tel: 336389

Muthaiga Country
Club
Muthaiga Rd
PO Box 30181 Nbi
Tel: 767754

Muthaiga Golf Club
Kiambu Rd
Tel: 762414/761262

Nairobi Club
Ngong Rd
PO Box 30171 Nbi
Tel: 725726

Nairobi Gymkhana
Forest Rd
PO Box 40895 Nbi
Tel: 742804/882

Nairobi Sailing &
Sub Aqua Club
PO Box 49973 Nbi
Tel: 501250

Ngara Sports Club
PO Box 42804 Nbi
Tel: 501631

Parklands Sports Club
Ojijo Rd
PO Box 40116 Nbi
Tel: 747991/745164

Premier Club
Forest Rd
PO Box 40143 Nbi
Tel: 763331-2

Public Service Club
Mara Rd
PO Box 41185 Nbi
Tel: 711785

Railway Club
Haile Selassie Ave
PO Box 40476 Nbi
Tel: 729820

Railway Golf Club
Haile Selassie Ave
PO Box 40476 Nbi
Tel: 724084

Rugby Football
Union of East Africa
Ngong Rd
PO Box 45766 Nbi
Tel: 567473

Royal Nairobi
Golf Club
Ngong Rd
PO Box 40221 Nbi
Tel: 725768/724215

Shell & BP
Gigiri Rd
PO Box 41221 Nbi
Tel: 749462

Simba Union Club
Forest Rd
PO Box 40114
Tel: 764069

Sir Ali Muslim Club
Park Rd
PO Box 41284
Tel: 767613

Sir Yusufali
Sports Club
Thika Rd
PO Box 11700
Tel: 860238

Vet/Lab Sports Club
Kabete
PO Box 29105
Tel: 592108

MOMBASA
Aga Khan Club
Aga Khan Rd
PO Box 82289
Tel: 313710/312186

Bahari Club
PO Box 90413
Tel: 471316

Coast Gymkhana
PO Box 84895
Tel: 313343/314895

Coast Province
Sports Council
Mama Ngina Drive
PO Box 82573

Ghaze Social &
Sports Club
Haile Selassie Rd
PO Box 80299
Tel: 21281/749619

Jaffery Sports Club
Nyerere Ave
PO Box 81452
Tel: 313093

Mombasa Club
PO Box 90270
Tel: 312449/316547

Mombasa Sports Club
PO Box 90241
Tel: 224705

Mombasa Golf Club
PO Box 90164
Tel: 313352

Mombasa Deep Sea
Fishing Club
PO Box 84958
Tel: 311532

Mombasa Sea
Angling Club
Ras Liwatoni
PO Box 82345 Msa
Tel: 20823

Mombasa Water
Sports Club
Rassini Rd
PO Box 81315 Msa
Tel: 20008

Mombasa Yacht Club
Liwatoni Rd
PO Box 90391 Msa
Tel: 313350

Nyali Golf &
Country Club
PO Box 95678 Msa
Tel: 471038/471589

United Sports Club
Nyerere Ave
PO Box 81607 Msa
Tel: 313546

UP-COUNTRY
Eldoret Club
PO Box 78
Tel: 31395

Eldoret Sports Club
Tel: 22736

Kericho Club
PO Box 82
Tel: 20860

Kitale Club
PO Box 30
Tel: 20030

Limuru Country Club
PO Box 10
Tel: 40033

Nakuru Golf Club
PO Box 652 Nakuru
Tel: 40803

Nyanza Club
PO Box 29 Kisumu
Tel: (035) 44965-58

Nyeri Club
PO Box 74 Nyeri
Tel: (0171) 2574

Sigona Golf Club
PO Box 10 Kikuyu
Tel: (0154) 32431

Thika Sports Club
PO Box 257 Thika
Tel: (0151) 21101/
31088

Service Clubs

Kiwanis Club
of Olive Branch
PO Box 45259 Nbi
Tel: 333056/332500

Lions International
District 411
PO Box 41981 Nbi
Tel: 554098

Rotary International
District 920
PO Box 41910 Nbi
Tel: 224128

Round Table
PO Box 41504 Nbi
Tel: 336858

United Kenya Club
PO Box 42220 Nbi
Tel: 728346/348

Tour Operators

NAIROBI
Aardvark Safaris
IPS Building
Kimathi St
PO Box 69496
Tel: 331718/334863

Abercrombie & Kent
Mama Ngina St
PO Box 59749
Tel: 226274/228700

Across Africa Safaris
Bruce Hse
Standard St
PO Box 49420
Tel: 332744/7

Action Tours
& Safaris
PO Box 52510
Tel: 243513

Addy Tours
& Safaris
Gilfillan Hse
Kenyatta Ave
Tel: 212984

Adventure Safaris
PO Box 44899
Tel: 228961

African Adventure
Safaris
Ridgeways Rd
PO Box 40414
Tel: 512328

African Alpine
Safaris
PO Box 20224
Tel: 334955

Africa Expeditions
Argwings Kodhek Rd
PO Box 24598
Tel: 561054/457

African Holidays
& Safaris
Uhuru Highway
Tel: 211992

African Quest
Safaris
Kimathi St
Tel: 336735

Africa Safari
Adventures
Koinange St
Tel: 223402

African Tours & Hotels
Utalii Hse
Uhuru Highway
PO Box 30471
Tel: 336858/156

African Travel
& Safaris
Standard St
PO Box 47839
Tel: 338080

African Tropical
Safaris
IPS Bdg
Kimathi St
Tel: 215432

Afrikan Cultural
Safaris
Hilton Hotel Arcade
PO Box 42468
Tel: 335581

Afro Aviation Services
Rahimtulla Trust Bdg
PO Box 49250
Tel: 226944/336136

Ahmedi Expeditions
NCM Hse
Tom Mboya St
PO Box 22129
Tel: 338840

Airland Tours
& Travel
Reinsurance Plaza
PO Box 70509
Tel: 338869

Albatros Travels
& Safaris
Uganda Hse
Kenyatta Ave
Tel: 243387

Alfaraj
Rehema Hse
Standard St
PO Box 44444
Tel: 227989

Alick Roberts Safaris
PO Box 24405
Tel: 891338

Andrew Holberg
Safaris
Ridgeway Rd
PO Box 30328
Tel: 512558/289

Andrew James
PO Box 24874
Tel: 882625

Archer's Tours
Lonrho Hse
Standard St
PO Box 40097
Tel: 331825/223131

Aruba Tours & Safaris
Cameo Bdg
Kenyatta Ave
Tel: 224864

Balloon Safaris
PO Box 43747
Tel: 502850-1

Banko Tours
Latema Rd
PO Box 11536
Tel: 226736

Bateleur Safaris
Hilton Hotel
PO Box 42562
Tel: 227048

Bee Safaris
PO Box 54712
Tel: 570913

Best Camping Tours
Nanak Hse
Kimathi St
PO Box 40223
Tel: 229667/675

Big Five Tours
Kenyatta Ave
PO Box 10367
Tel: 213102/216045

Big Safari Services
Siloma Hse
Koinange St
Tel: 339756

Bike Treks
PO Box 14237
Tel: 581719

Bill Winter Safaris
PO Box 24871
Tel: 882526/146

Blue Bird Tours
Kenyatta Ave
PO Box 42350
Tel: 337337/8

Blue Quail
Corner Hse
Mama Ngina St
Tel: 214799

Bon Voyage
Safaris & Travel
Mercantile Hse
Loita St
Tel: 332298

Bonham Safaris
Nandi Rd
Karen
Tel: 884475/882521

Bookings Ltd
New Stanley Hotel
Standard St
PO Box 56707
Tel: 219178/336570

Bongo Tours
Silopark Hse
PO Box 59487
Tel: 229696

Bruce Travel
Koinange St
PO Box 40809
Tel: 226794

Bruce Safaris
Caxton Hse
Standard St
PO Box 40662
Tel: 223647/339094

Bushbuck
Adventures
Hughes Building
Muindi Mbingu St
PO Box 67449
Tel: 212975/218478

Bunson Travel Svce
Pan Africa Hse
PO Box 45456
Tel: 221992

Camel Trail Safaris
Ngara Rd
Tel: 745896

Carr Hartley Safaris
PO Box 59762 Karen
Tel: 882453

Centrex Tours
Hughes Bdg
Muindi Mbingu St
PO Box 41830
Tel: 332267

Charity Tours & Safaris
Cameo Hse
Kenyatta Ave
Tel: 214901

Cheli & Peacock
PO Box 39806
Tel: 222551

Chinato Tours & Safaris
Mpaka Plaza
Mpaka Rd
Tel: 446704

Come to Africa Safaris
Rehema Hse
Kaunda St
Tel: 213186/213254

Courtes Wide
Tour & Safaris
Uganda Hse
Kenyatta Ave
Tel: 340300

Crombic Tours & Safaris
NHC Hse
Aga Khan Walk
Tel: 245929/241089

Crossway Car Hire
Banda St
PO Box 10228
Tel: 220848/223949

Dallago Tours & Safaris
Mercantile Hse
Koinange St
Tel: 339497/331197

Dalma Tours
Corner Hse
Kimathi St
Tel: 215551/215546

Davanu Tours
Windsor Hse
University Way
Tel: 222002/242403

David Penrose Safaris
Muthangari Rd
Lavington
Tel: 445214

Delamere Camps
Fedha Towers
PO Box 48019
Tel: 335935

Desert Expeditions
PO Box 42628
Tel: 245195

Dik Dik Safaris
Hilton Hotel
PO Box 43004
Tel: 223268

Discover Kenya Safaris
IPS Bdg
Kimathi St
Tel: 213566/227648

Donlen Tours & Safaris
Tom Mboya St
Tel: 225078

Dosojin
Standard Building
Wabera St
PO Box 74612
Tel: 339780/218951

Drumbeat of
Africa Safaris
Diamond Trust Bdg
Ronald Ngala St
Tel: 336013

Duma Tours & Safaris
Songoot Walk
PO Box 48167
Tel: 764518

Dynamic Tours & Safaris
Utali Hse
Uhuru Highway
Tel: 220429

EA Ornithological
Safaris
Fedha Towers
PO Box 48019
Tel: 331684

EA Wildlife Safaris
Fedha Towers
PO Box 43747
Tel: 227217/331228

Ebra Tours & Safaris
Standard Building
PO Box 43457
Tel: 213243

Eclipse Safari Svces
Heron Court Hotel
PO Box 59863
Tel: 720640

Ellerman Lines Safaris
City Hse
Wabera St
Tel: 339158

EMM International
Reinsurance Plaza
PO Box 48017
Tel: 331801/227883

Eric Risley Tours
Langata
PO Box 24751
Tel: 891370

Flamingo Tours
Langata Hse
Wilson Airport
PO Box 44899
Tel: 600900

Format Tours & Travel
Kalyan Hse
Tubman Rd
Tel: 225825

Four by Four Safaris
PO Box 24397
Tel: 564945

Fourwinds Travel
Norwich Union Hse
Mama Ngina St
240275-7

Franz Lang Safaris
PO Box 42026
Tel: 891745/566245

Frontier Safari
PO Box 21090
Tel: 558093

Fun Tours & Safaris
Embassy Hse
Harambee ave
Tel: 214369/214281

Funga Safaris
Caltex Hse
PO Box 41558
Tel: 337751/422

Furaha Travel
Mamujee Building
Tom Mboya St
PO Box 41641
Tel: 333696/340866

Galdesa Safaris
PO Box 38807
Tel: 570587/570055

Gametrackers
Kenya Cinema Plaza
Moi Ave
PO Box 62042
Tel: 335825/212830

Gamewatchers Safaris
Old Mutual Bdg
Kimathi St
Tel: 212957-8

Gateway Travel
Utalii Hse
PO Box 22522
Tel: 223449

General Tours & Safaris
Norwich Union Hse
Kimathi St
PO Box 30585
Tel: 222303/331325

Geosafaris
Karen
Tel: 884258-9

Glen Cottar Safaris
Kaunda St
PO Box 44626
Tel: 330297/221990

Global Tours
Muindi Mbingu St
PO Box 30458
Tel: 333624

Glory Car Hire Tours
Tubman Rd
PO Box 66969
Tel: 225024/224428

HAT
PO Box 55182
Tel: 224079/728002

Haidery Tours Travel
Tom Mboya St
PO Box 45728
Tel: 336201

Highway Tours & Safaris
PO Box 30984
Tel: 545253/558537

Hippo Inns
Tours & Safaris
PO Box 50711
Tel: 218120/246305

Holiday Tours
Panafric Hotel
PO Box 72171
Tel: 720418

Homeland Travel
Utalii Hse
Uhuru Highway
PO Box 57571
Tel: 339151/222125

Inside Africa Safaris
Autorama Corner
Haile Selassie Ave/
Jubilee Insurance Hse
Wabera St
PO Box 59767
Tel: 223304/224081

Intasun Holidays
Kenwood Hse
Kimathi St
PO Box 42977
Tel: 340161/224037

Intercontinental Tours
Texcal Hse
Koinange St
PO Box 49473
Tel: 339518

Intra Safaris
College Hse
University Way
PO Box 50096
Tel: 229961

Ivory Safaris
Esso Plaza
Muthaiga
PO Box 44982
Tel: 760546/760226

Jet Travel
Rehani Hse
Koinange St
PO Box 58805
Tel: 330144/186/7

J H Safaris
University Way
PO Box 42238
Tel: 228168/334112

Jambo Tours Scandinavia
Corner Hse
PO Box 34187
Tel: 336767

Ken Travel
Shretta Hse
Kimathi St
PO Box 30537
Tel: 225130/230708

Kenebco Tours
& Travel
Nanak Hse
Kimathi St
PO Box 20640
Tel: 227203

Kenya Mystery Tours
Phoenix Hse
Standard St
PO Box 30442
Tel: 336876/227101

Kenya Photographic
Safaris
PO Box 25253
Tel: 569870/566223

Kenya Wildlife Trails
Kimathi Hse
Kimathi St
PO Box 44687
Tel: 228960/942

Kenyafonic Touring
Muindi Mbingu St
PO Box 51239
Tel: 332292

Ker & Downey
Enterprise Rd
PO Box 41822
Tel: 556164/556466
Fax: 552378/556183

Kimbla Kenya
Langata
PO Box 40089
Tel: 891592/890047

Kobo Safaris
PO Box 72763
Tel: 446118/562108

Langwenda Safaris
PO Box 56118
Tel: 444494/440878

Leon Travel & Tours
Mbagathi Rd
PO Box 57767
Tel: 711460-2
Fax: 711461

Let's Go Travel
Caxton Hse
Standard St
PO Box 60342
Tel: 340332/213033

Lobelia Tours & Safaris
Mercantile Hse
Koinange St
Tel: 211426

Low Budget Car Hire
Tubman Rd
PO Box 20393
Tel: 229488

Lucky Cabs Safaris
Mamlaka Rd
PO Box 49461
Tel: 728707

Maggie Tours & Safaris
Accra Hse
Tom Mboya St
226463/214712

Malaika Safaris
Kenyatta Avenua
Tel: 332429

Maridadi Safaris
PO Box 46992
Tel: 242678

Mashariki Tour
Mashariki Motor Hse
PO Box 30179
Tel: 558144

Mathews &
Roberts Safaris
PO Box 47448
Tel: 882559

Menno Travel Svce
Gen. Kago St
PO Box 40444
Telex: 22119
Tel: 333051/332439

Micato Safaris
View Park Towers
PO Box 43374
Tel: 220743/246270

Michaelides Safaris
Old Mutual Bdg
Kimathi St
PO Box 48010
Tel: 212861/521042

Mikawa Tours & Safaris
Mama Ngina St
Tel: 333162

Mongoose Tours
Ambassadeur Hotel
PO Box 70192
Tel: 220048/336803

Mountain Rock
Hotel & Tours
Jubilee Insurance Hs
Wabera St
Tel: 210051/242151

Mugumu Safaris
MagadiRd
Langata
Tel: 891356/891490

Nairobi Travel Centre
Fedha Towers
PO Box 41178
Tel: 227939/335327

New Horizon
Travel Agency
Kimathi Hse
PO Box 40193
Tel: 338837/222416

Nile Safaris Aviation
Normandy Court
Tel: 716872

Njambi Tours
Hotel Inter-
Continental
PO Box 30618
Tel: 331762/216805

Orbit Travel
Gilfillan Hse
Kenyatta Ave
PO Box 11038
Tel: 222936/223236

Oryx Tours & Safaris
Woodvale Grve
Westlands
Tel: 746613/747076

Ostrich Holiday
Adventures
Uniafric Hse
Koinanage St
Tel: 242273/77

Pelizzoli Safaris
PO Box 48287
Tel: 891381

Perry Mason Safaris
Jubilee Hse
Kimathi St
PO Box 49655
Tel: 882249

Pollman's Tours
Arrow Hse
Koinange St
PO Box 45895
Tel: 337253/337898

Prestige Safaris
Warren Hse
Loita St
Tel: 227977

Private Safaris
Caxton Hse
Kenyatta Ave
PO Box 45205
Tel: 337104/332153

Reachout Safaris
Koitobos Rd
Langata
Tel: 891457

Reggie Destro Safaris
PO Box18143
Langata
Tel: 891716/890430

Resident's Travel Den
Centro Hse Westlands
PO Box 14960
Tel: 743414/748629

Rhino Safaris
PO Box 40354
Telex: 22081
Tel: 228102/332372

Richard Bonham Safaris
PO Box 24133
Tel: 882521

Robin Hurt Safaris
PO Box 24988
Tel: 882826/088

Rolling Hills
Tours and Travel
Westend Plaza
Chiromo Rd
Westlands
PO Box 53913
Tel: 445911/443364

Safari Camp Services
PO Box 44801
Tel: 228936/330130

Safari Seekers
Jubilee Hse
Kaunda St
PO Box 9165
Tel: 241408-9

Safari Travel Kenya
KCS Hse
Mama Ngina St
PO Box 31120
Tel: 223141/222290

Safaris Unlimited
PO Box 24181
Tel: 891168/890435

Safariworld Kenya
PO Box 56803
Tel: 330506

Samson Tours
& Safaris
Lonrho Hse
Standard St
Tel: 211547

Sapieha Tours
PO Box 48682
Tel: 512283

Sasamoto Tours
& Safaris
Lonrho Hse
Standard St
Tel: 212294/219580

Scenic Safaris
Westminster Hse
PO Box 49188
Tel: 226526/229092/
335122

Senator Travel
Standard St
PO Box 46654
Tel: 222855/224410

Shimba Tourist Service
Langata Rd
PO Box 41942
Tel: 501366/488

Somak Travel
Corner Hse
PO Box 48495
Tel: 332346/220557

Southern Cross
Safaris
Pan Africa Hse
Standard St
PO Box 48363
Tel: 221172/221276

Special Camping
Safaris
Gilfillan Hse
Kenyatta Ave
PO Box 51512
Tel: 338325

Star Travel
& Tours
New Stanley Hotel
Standard St
PO Box 48225
Tel: 226996

Sunny Safaris
Portal Place
Banda St
PO Box 74495
Tel: 211036/339809

Suntrek Tours
Monrovia St
PO Box 48146
Tel: 334965/225679

Thorn Tree Safaris
Jubilee Hse
Mama Ngina St
PO Box 42475
Tel: 225941/213453

Tippett's Safaris
Karen
PO Box 43806
Tel: 882613

Tor Allan Safaris
Langata
PO Box 41959
Tel: 891190

Tour Africa Safaris
Arboretum Rd
PO Box 34187
Tel: 715517-9

Trans-African Guides
Langata
PO Box 49538
Tel: 891172

Transworld Safaris
Corner Hse
PO Box 44690
Tel: 333129

Travel Mart
Nanak Hse
PO Box 46085
Tel: 222508/227637

Travelour
Longonot Place
PO Box 12547
Tel: 222942

Travel Promoters
Sarit Centre
PO Box 39651
Tel: 749473/7

Tropical Ice
Muthaiga
PO Box 57341
Tel: 740826/811

Tropical Land
Tours & Safaris
Westlands Rd
PO Box 14874
Tel: 749259

Tropical Nature
& Cultural Safaris
Jubilee Hse
PO Box 42794
Tel: 225363
Fax: 217029

Ulf Aschan
Wilson Airport
PO Box 44715
Tel: 605508

United Touring Co
Fedha Towers
PO Box 42196
Tel: 331960

Unlimited Travel
New Stanley Hotel
PO Box 30722
Tel: 223752/334664

Universal Safari Tours
Cotts Hse
PO Box 49312
Tel: 221446/339818

Utali Tours & Safaris
University Way
TeL: 333285/212372

Vacational Tours
PO Box 44401
Tel: 220256/229942

Visit Africa
Queensway Hse
Kaunda St
PO Box 59565
Tel: 223257/220838

Waku Waku Safaris
PO Box 58989
Tel: 729116

Wanderlust Safaris
Kenyatta Ave
Tel: 212281/214579

Westminster Safaris
Langata
PO Box 15097
Tel: 891973

Wildlife Safaris
Hilton Hotel
Tel: 333094

Yare Safaris,
Union Towers
Moi Ave,
PO Box 63006
Tel: 214099/213445

Zirkuli Expeditions
Portal Chambers
Banda St
PO Box 34548
Tel: 223949/220848

Zodiac Travel
Hughes Building
PO Box 46851
Tel: 340304

BARINGO
Baringo Bird &
Game Safaris
PO Box 1375 Molo
Tel: Molo 51Y4

KITALE
David Read Safaris
PO Box 183
Kitale

MOMBASA
Archer's Mombasa
Ambalal Hse
PO Box 84618
Tel: 311884

Galu Safaris
Nkurumah Rd
PO Box 99456
Tel: 314174/229520

Highways Tours
Moi Ave
PO BOX 84787
Tel: 228514-5

Ketty Tours Safaris
PO Box 82391
Tel: 312204/315178

Kuldips Touring Co
Mji Mpaya Rd
PO Box 82662
Tel: 228751/223780

Leisure Car Hire
Tours & Safaris
Moi Ave
PO Box 84902
Tel: 313880/314846

Marajani Tours
Moi Ave
PO Box 86103
Tel: 312703/315446

Pollman's Tours
Taveta Rd
PO Box 84198
Tel: 20703/312565-7

Southern Cross
Safaris
PO Box 90653
Tel: 20737/26765

Turkana Safaris
Moi Ave
PO Box 99300
Tel: 21065

NANYUKI
Flame Tree Safaris
PO Box 82
Nanyuki 2053

Olechugu Safaris
Ol Doinyo Farm
PO Box 295
Tel: Timau 24

Car Hire Companies

NAIROBI
Across Africa Safaris
Bruce Hse
Standard St
PO Box 49420
Tel: 332744/223013

Avenue Service Station
Kenyatta Ave
PO Box 14673
Tel: 227849

Alamo
PO Box 60418
Tel: 331648
Fax: 212041

Apollo Tours & Travel
PO Box 42391
Tel: 216969
Fax: 214026

Avis
Union Towers
PO Box 49795
Moi Ave
Tel: 336794/334317
Kenyatta Ave
Tel: 336703/4
Hilton Hotel
Tel: 229576
Jomo Kenyatta Airport
Tel: 822186

Barlany Car Hire
City Hall Way
Tel: 217456

Bentley Car Hire
Mama Ngina St
Tel: 215687

Big Apple Tours
& Car Hire
PO PO Box 44025
Tel: 540630/1299

Bonfree Car Hire
Service
Haile Selassie Ave
Tel: 213470

Borabora Tours
& Travel
Uganda Hse
Tel: 245148

Budget Rent A Car
Vedic Hse
Mama Ngina St
Tel: 334908/213100

Budget
Utalii Hse
PO Box 48555
Tel: 223098/9
Fax: 223074

Car Hire Services
Unga Hse
Muthithi Rd
Tel: 743270/1

Central Rent-A-Car
Fedha Towers
Standard St
PO Box 49439
Tel: 222888/332296

City Shuttle
Prudential Building
Wabera St
Tel: 229224

Concorde Car Hire
Agip Petrol Station
Waiyaki Way
PO Box 25053
Tel: 448953/4/134/5

Coast Car Hire
New Stanley Hotel
PO Box 56707
Tel: 219182/178

Crossways Car Hire
Tours and Travel
Portal Chambers
Banda St
PO Box 10228
Tel: 223949/220848

Empire Car Hire
2nd Parklands Ave
Tel: 751590/5/6

Europcar
Bruce Hse
Standard St
PO Box 49420
Tel: 332744
Jomo Kenyatta Airport
Tel: 335290

Expert Car Hire
& Safaris
PO Box 57066
Rehema Hse
Kaunda St
Tel: 218076/335290

Faceters Agency &
Car Hire
Latema Rd
Tel: 245202/553

Gametrackers
Kenya Cinema Plaza
PO Box 62042
Tel: 338927/212831

Glory Car Hire
Tubman Rd
PO Box 66969
Tel: 225024/224428

Gramons Car Hire
Kencom Hse
Moi Ave
Tel: 215697

Gupta's Car Hire
Moi Ave
PO BOX 83451
Tel: 311182/20728

Habib's Car Hire
Agip Hse
Haile Selassie Ave
PO Box 48095
Tel: 220463/223816

Hertz
Muindi Mbingu St
PO Box 42196
Tel: 331960/331974

Inside Africa Safaris
Haile Selassie Ave
PO Box 59767
Tel: 225884/223304

Intasun Holidays
Kenwood Hse
Kimathi St
PO Box 42977
Tel: 340161/334438

Karibu Car Hire
& Safaris
Rehema Hse
Kaunda St
Tel: 335354/246487

Kesana
Muthaiga centre
Limuru Rd
Tel: 749062/363

Kenya Rent A Car
College Hse
University Way
Tel: 336703/4

Kenya Wildlife Trails
Kimathi Hse
PO Box 44687
Tel: 228960/942

Let's Go Travel
Caxton Hse
Standard St
PO Box 60342
Tel: 340331/213033

Market Car Hire
Koinange St
PO Box 49713
Tel: 225797/335735

Moto Tours
Anniversary Towers
Loita St
Tel: 220690

Mt Kenya Car
Hire Services
PO Box 52231
Tel: 749742/5/9055

Njagi Mugo
Fourway Towers
Muindi Mbingu St
Tel: 227324/215458

Payless Car Hire
Hilton Hotel
Simba St
Tel: 223581
Fax: 223584

Protocol Car Hire
Meru South Hse
Tom Mboya St
Tel: 334476

Rasuls Car Hire
Butere Rd
Tel: 541355/530018

Samken
Vedic Hse
Mama Ngina St
Tel: 334904/545737

Scenic Safaris
Westminster Hse
Kenyatta Ave
PO Box 49188
Tel: 335122

Splinters Tours
& Travel
Arrow Hse
Koinange St
Tel: 217908/230307

Texcal Service Stn
Koinange St
PO Box 49473
Tel: 331327/330787

Westlands Car Hire
PO Box 14655
Tel: 440785/660/007

Vacational Tours
PO Box 44401
Tel: 220256/229942

Wheels Car Hire
PO Box 42821
BP Ngong Rd
Tel: 568113

Wina Car Hire
PO Box 55354
Tel: 241747

Yaya Car Hire
Yaya Centre
Tel: 565651/63
Fax: 565663

MOMBASA
Avis
Moi Ave
PO Box 84868
Tel: 223048/220465
Two Fishes Hotel
(01261) 2101
Moi International
Airport
Tel: 433211
Mombasa Beach Hotel
Tel: 471861

Coast Car Hire
Ambalal Hse
Tel: 311752/311225

Glory Car Hire
Trans Ocean Hse
Chembe Rd
PO Box 85527
Tel: 314284/220265

Herz
Moi Avenue
Tel: 316333/221286
Moi International
Airport
Tel: 434085
Jadini Beach Hotel
Tel: 2149
Safari Beach Hotel
Tel: 2726
Indian Ocean Beach
Club
Tel: 3730
Kaskazi Beach Hotel
Tel: 3171
Diani Beach Office
Tel: 2128
Nyali Beach Hotel
Tel:471827
Whitesands
Tel: 485926
Sun N Sand
Kikambala
Tel: 3 2621

MALINDI
Avis
Sitawi Hse
PO Box 197
Tel: 20513
Lawfords Hotel
Tel: 20440
Watamu Beach Hotel
Watamu 1

Herz
Harambee Ave
Tel: 20040
Turtle Bay Hotel
Watamu
Tel: 3 2003

Kisumu
Azmak Car Hire
Obote Rd
Tel: 44957

Hamara Tours
Esmail Noor Rd
Tel: 23603/4

Kesho Investments
Kenyatta Highway
Hotel Royale Bdg
Tel: 43247

OBS Academy
Bank St
Awori Hse
Tel: 22083

Bus Companies

NAIROBI
Akamba
Lagos Rd
PO Box 40322
Tel: 222027

Coast Bus Services
Accra Rd
PO Box 16030
Tel: 214819

Goldline
PO Box 28016
Tel: 225279/221963

Karim Bus Co
Kirinyaga Rd
PO Box 43802
Tel: 338515

Kenya Bus (Stagecoach)
PO Box 30563
Tel: 764706/764754

Kirima Bus Service
New Pumwani Rd
PO Box 28470
Tel: 229136

MPS (Kenya)
Duruma Rd
PO Box 43940
Tel: 334431

Malindi Bus Services
Duruma Rd
Tel: 229662

Malindi Taxis
Kirinyaga Rd
PO Box 47960
Tel: 224315

Mawingo Bus Services
Landhies/Cross Rd
Tel: 229411

Merali Bus Services
Racecourse Rd
Tel: 224812

Nairobi Bus Union
Lagos Rd
PO Box 10219
Tel: 221642

Rift Valley Peugeot
Latema Rd
PO Box 458817
Tel: 226374

United Peugeot Svce
Duruma Rd
PO Box 43940
Tel: 227739

Shore Line Coach
PO Box 45274
Tel: 557218

MOMBASA
Ambiance Bus Service
Jomo Kenyatta Ave
PO Box 82199
Tel: 494693

Goldline
Mwembe Tayari Rd
PO Box 83542
Tel: 220027/226757

Ivenya Bus Service
Jomo Kenyatta Ave
PO BOX 81664
Tel: 491544

MPS
Haile Selassie Rd
PO Box 83614
Tel: 220368

Malindi Taxis
Jomo Kenyatta Ave
PO Box 83857
Tel: 225441/225411

Mawingo Bus Services
Jomo Kenyatta Ave
Tel: 314318

Nairobi Deluxe
Jomo Kenyatta Ave
PO Box 83857
Tel: 492431

Tawakal
Jomo Kenyatta Ave
PO Box 87630
Tel: 491960

Taxis

NAIROBI
Airporter
Jomo Kenyatta Airport
PO Box 19027
Tel: 822348

Archers Cabs
Koinange St
PO Box 40097
Tel: 220289/221935

Jambo Taxis
PO Box 75057
Jomo Kenyatta Airport
Tel: 822011
University Way
Branch
Tel: 227377

Kenatco Taxis
Uchumi Hse
PO Box 52684
Tel: 221561/338611

Kenya Taxi Cabs Assoc
PO Box 74526
Excelsior Hotel
Branch
Tel: 726047
Koinange St Branch
Tel: 726330
Lilian Towers
Branch
Tel: 332416
Muindi Mbingu St
Branch
Tel: 726048
Utalii St Branch
Tel: 726241

MOMBASA
Archers
PO Box 84618
Tel: 225362

Kenatco Taxis
PO Box 88988
220340/331456

Taxi Service Voda
PO Box 81030
Tel: 223701

Major Hospitals

NAIROBI
Nairobi Hospital
Arwings Kodhek Rd
Tel: 722160-6

Aga Khan Hospital
3rd Parklands Ave
Tel: 742541

Mater Misericordia
South 'B'
Tel: 556666

Gertrude's Garden
Children's Hospital
Muthaiga Rd
Tel: 763474-5

MP Shah Hospital
Parklands Rd
Tel: 742754/742771

MOMBASA
Aga Khan Hospital
Vanga Rd
Tel: 312953

Coast Provincial
General Hospital
Kisauni Rd
Tel: 314201

Katherine Bibby
Hospital
Makadara Rd
Tel: 312190

Lady Grigg
Maternity Hospital
Abdel Nasser Rd
Tel: 314201

Mombasa Hospital
Mama Ngina Dve
Tel: 312191/316552

Banks

African
Development Bank

Algemene Bank

Bank of Baroda

Bank of India

Bank of Tokyo Ltd

Barclays Bank Kenya

Biashara Bank

Central Bank of Kenya

Citibank N.A.

Commercial Bank
of Africa

Co-operative Bank
of Kenya

Delphis Bank

East African
Development Bank

First American
Bank of Kenya

Habib Bank

Habib AG Zurich

Industrial
Development Bank

Kenya Commercial
Bank

Kenya Post Office
Savings Bank

Middle East
Bank Kenya

National Bank
of Kenya

Pan African Bank

Stanbic Bank Kenya

Credit Cards

American Express
Bruce Hse
Standard St
PO Box 40433
Nairobi
334722

Visa/Barclaycard
Barclays Bank
Moi Ave
PO Box 30120
226386

Casinos

NAIROBI
Casino De Paradise
Box 47166
Tel: 802105

Cassanova
Esso Plaza
Muthaiga
Tel: 766191/766054

Four Aces Limited
Waiyaki Way
Tel: 442667/74/91/
4064

Inter-Continental
Hotel Casino
City Hall Way
Tel: 744477

International Casino
Museum Hill
Tel: 742602

Mayfair Casino Club
PO Box 39701
Parklands Road
Tel: 743300
Fax: 746596

Safari Park Hotel
& Casino
PO Box 45038
Thika Road
Tel: 802493/222846
Fax: 802477

MOMBASA
International Casino
Leisure Lodge
Diani Beach

International Casino
Oceanic Hotel
Light House Rd

Nyali Beach
Hotel Casino
Tel: 471733

Night Clubs

NAIROBI
Beat Hse
Kimathi St

Bedouin Complex
Mombasa Rd

Bombax Club
Ngong Rd

Brilliant
Murang'a Rd

Cantina
Langata Rd

Carnivore
Langata Rd

Club Boomerang
Westlands Rd

Club le Chalet
Chiromo Rd

Florida 2000
Moi Ave

Garden Square
City Hall Way

Hollywood
Moktar Daddah St

Hillock
Enterprise Rd

Imani Night Club
Ronald Ngala St

JKA Resort Club
Mombasa Rd

Lost World
Mombasa Rd

New Florida
Koinange St

Zanzibar
Moi Ave

MOMBASA
Bora Bora
Malindi Rd

Bird
Behind PO next
to Bristol Hotel

Banda Disco
(Africana Sea Lodge)
Diani Beach

Breakers
(Bamburi Beach
Hotel) Malindi Rd

Casablanca Day &
Night Club
Moi Ave

Club Jade
(Neptune Beach)
Bamburi

Discongoma
(Diani Reef Hotel)
Diani

Kasbah
Digo Rd

Le Club
(Hotel Inter-
Continental)
Shanzu Beach

Mamba Disco
Mamba Village

New Florida
Mama Ngina Drive

New Star Night Club
Nkurumah Rd

Rainbow
Mnazi Moja Rd

Salambo Club Disco
Moi Ave

Tiffanys
Ambalal Hse

The Pitt
(Robinson Baobab
Hotel)
Diani Beach

NAIVASHA
A to Z Night Club
Kariuki Chotara Rd
Tel: 20055

Cinemas

NAIROBI
ABC
Yatta Rd

Bellevue Drive-In
Mombasa Rd

Cameo
Kenyatta Ave

Casino
Ndumberi Rd

Embassy
Latema Rd

Fox Drive-In
Thika Rd

Kenya
Moi Ave

Nairobi
Uchumi Hse
Aga Khan Walk

Odeon
Latema Rd

Rainbow
Biringo Square

Sun City
2nd Ave, Eastleigh

20th Century
(Duplex)
Mama Ngina St

MOMBASA
Kenya
Nkrumah Rd

Lotus
Makadara Rd

Majestic
Nehru Rd

Moons
Khalifa Rd

Theatres

NAIROBI
Braeburn Theatre
PO Box 45112
Tel: 567901

Kenya National
Theatre
Harry Thuku Rd
PO Box 43031
Tel: 220536

Phoenix Players
Parliament Rd
PO Box 52383
Tel: 225506

MOMBASA
Little Theatre Club
Mnazi Moja Rd
PO Box 81143
Tel: 312101/35497

Art Galleries

Africa Cultural
Gallery
Mama Ngina St
PO Box 10320
Tel: 3334044

African Heritage
Kenyatta Ave
PO Box 17871
Tel: 554378/555501

Gallery Watatu
Standard St
PO Box 41855
Tel: 228737

Handcarvers Gallery
City Hall Way
PO Box 41133
Tel: 228903

Paa Ya Paa Gallery
Ridgeways Rd
PO Box 49646
Tel: 512257

Tazama Art
Rehema Hse
Standard St
PO Box 21130
Tel: 335597

The Art Gallery
Corner Hse
Mama Ngina St
PO Box 48725
Tel: 337159

Wood & Stone Gallery
Bruce Hse
Kaunda St
PO Box 21558
Tel: 222505/225648

Media Directory

Magazines
Autonews
PO Box 30339 Nbi
Tel: 225502

Beyond
PO Box 22027 Nbi
Tel: 338211

Business Contact
PO Box 72732 Nbi
Tel: 221044

Consumers Digest
PO Box 50795 Nbi
Tel: 333322/330557

East African
Computer News
PO Box 67335 Nbi
Tel: 332219

Economic Review
Argwings Kodhek Rd
PO Box 48647 Nbi
Tel: 741503

Executive
PO Box 47186 Nbi
Tel: 555811/557868

Finance
PO Box 44094 Nbi
Tel: 221581/331457

Golf News
PO Box 31283 Nbi
Tel: 339738

Health Digest
PO Box 60481 Nbi
Tel: 226556

Mashambani
PO Box 43350 Nbi
Tel: 338869

Mother & Care
PO Box 57640 Nbi
Tel: 338462

Overdrive
PO Box 78479 Nbi
Tel: 213227

Parents
PO Box 50795 Nbi
Tel: 221431/333222

Personal Secretary
PO Box 56795 Nbi
Tel: 224987

Presence
PO Box 10988 Nbi
Tel: 220196

Step Magazine
PO Box 58070 Nbi
Tel: 802281

Swara
PO Box 20110 Nbi
Tel: 227047/331888

Student's Tribune
PO Box 30344 Nbi
Tel: 334244

The Service Guide
PO Box 12697 Nbi
Tel: 337027

Trade & Industry
PO Box 30339 Nbi
Tel: 225502

Trade Guide
PO Box 61356 Nbi
Tel: 220853

Tradeways
PO Box 70287 Nbi
Tel: 225445

Transport
PO Box 44094 Nbi
Tel: 340482

Weekly Review
PO Box 42271 Nbi
Tel: 227596

Youth
PO Box 45245 Nbi
Tel: 223641

Newspapers
Coastweek
Nkrumah Rd
PO Box 87270 Msa
Tel: 313767/589

Kenya Times
Haile Selassie Ave
PO Box 30958 Nbi
Tel: 224251/340700

Daily Nation
Nation Centre
PO Box 49010 Nbi
Tel: 221222/337710

East African Standard
Kaunda St
PO Box 30080 Nbi
Tel: 540280
Fax: 553939

The People
Waiyaki Way
PO Box 48647 Nbi
Tel: 449269
Fax: 446640

Foreign newspapers
are available the day
after publication.

Radio
Kenya Broadcasting
Corporation
Three services —
English, Kiswahili,
and vernacular.
Hours of transmis-
sion: 0500-2400

Broadcasting Hse
Harry Thuku Rd
PO Box 30456 Nbi
Tel: 334567

Television
Kenya Broadcasting
Corporation
One service. English
and Kiswahili.

Broadcasting Hse
Harry Thuku Rd
PO Box 30456
Nairobi
Tel: 334567

Kenya Television
Network
Hours of
transmission:
1400-2400 then with
Cable News
Network (CNN) to
provide a 24-hour
English language
service.

Kenya Television
Network (KTN)
Nyayo Hse
PO Box 30958
Nairobi
Tel: 339380/227122

KBC Channel 2:
(Multi-Choice
subscription) 24 hrs

Stella Television
24 hrs a day Nairobi
area only

Cultural Centres

NAIROBI
Alliance Francaise
ICEA Building
Kenyatta Ave
Tel: 340054/079

American Cultural Ctre
National Bank Bdg
Harambee Ave
Tel: 337877

Bomas of Kenya
Forest Edge Rd
Tel: 891802

British Council
ICEA Bdg
Kenyatta Ave
Tel: 334855

French Cultural Ctre
Loita St
Tel: 336263

Goethe Institute
German Cultural Ctre
Maendeleo Hse
Tel: 224640

Italian Cultural
Institute
Wabera St
Tel: 220278/340966

Kenya National
Archives
Moi Ave
Tel: 228959/020

Japan Information
Centre
Post Bank Hse
Market Lane
Tel: 331196

Kenya National
Library Service
Ngong Rd
Tel: 227871/229186

McMillan Memorial
Library
Banda St
Tel: 221844

National Museum
of Kenya
Museum Hill Rd
Tel: 742161

Railway Museum
Moi Ave
Tel: 221211

KITALE
Kitale Museum
Tel: 20670/20311

KISUMU
British Council
Oginga Odinga Rd
Tel: 2957

Kisumu Museum
Tel: 40804

LAMU
Lamu Museum
Tel: 3073

MARALAL
Kenyatta Hse
Tel: 2092

MERU
Meru Museum
Tel: 20482

MOMBASA
Alliance Francaise
Freed Building
Moi Ave
Tel: 225048

British Council
Biashara Bank Hse
Nyerere Ave
Tel: 223076

Fort Jesus Museum
Tel: 312839/225934

Kenya National
Library Service
Msarifu Kombo Rd
Tel: 226380

Bibliography

The African Letters (1988), edited by G F V Kleen, published by St Martin's Press, New York.

Africa's Rift Valley (1975), by Colin Willock, published by Time-Life Books, New York.

The Beautiful Birds of Kenya (1985), by John Karmali, published by Westlands Sundries, Nairobi.

The Beautiful People of Kenya (1989), by Mohamed Amin, Duncan Willetts, and Brian Tetley, published by Westlands Sundries, Nairobi.

The Beautiful Plants of Kenya (1986) by John Karmali, published by Westlands Sundries, Nairobi.

The Beauty of Kenya (1984), by Mohamed Amin and Duncan Willetts, published by Westlands Sundries, Nairobi.

The Beauty of the Kenya Coast (1986), by Mohamed Amin and Duncan Willetts, published by Westlands Sundries, Nairobi.

The Book of Kenya (1980), by Gerald Cubitt and Eric Robbins, published by Collins and Harvill Press, London.

Cradle of Mankind (1981), by Mohamed Amin and Brian Tetley, published by Chatto & Windus, London.

Faces of Kenya (1977), by David Keith Jones, published by Hamish Hamilton, London.

Facing Mount Kenya (1965), by Jomo Kenyatta, published by Mercury Books, London.

A Far Off Place (1978), by Laurens Van Der Post, published by Harcourt Brace Jovanovich, Inc., New York.

A Field Guide to the Birds of East Africa (1967), by J G Williams, published by Collins, London.

A Field Guide to the Butterflies of Africa (1969), by J G Williams, published by Collins, London.

A Field Guide to the National Parks of East Africa (1967), by J G Williams, published by Collins, London.

Flame Trees of Thika (1987), by Elspeth Huxley, published by Penguin Books, Inc., New York.

Fodor's Kenya (1987), Random House, New York.

A Guide to Kenya and Northern Tanzania (1971), by David F Horrobin, published by East African Publishing House, Nairobi.

Guide Book to Mount Kenya and Kilimanjaro (1971), by John Mitchell, Mountain Club of Kenya, Nairobi.

Harambee Country (1970), by Kenneth Bolton, published by Geoffrey Bles Ltd, London.

Ivory Crisis (1983), by Mohamed Amin and Ian Parker, Published by Chatto & Windus, London.

Journey through Kenya (1982), by Mohamed Amin, Duncan Willetts, and Brian Tetley, Bodley Head, London.

Journey to the Jade Sea, by John Hillaby, published by Paladin, London.

Kenya (Insider's Guide series) (1989), Hunter Publishing, New York.

Kenya: The Magic Land (1968), by Mohamed Amin, Duncan Willetts, and Brian Tetley, published by Bodley Head, London.

Kenya Travel Guide (1988), (Berlitz Travel Guides series), Macmillan Publishing Co., New York.

Kenya: A Visitor's Guide (1987), by Arnold Curtis, published by Hunter Publishing, Inc., New York.

The Kenya Pioneers (1985), by Errol Trzebinski, published by W. W. Horton & Co., New York.

The Last of the Maasai (1987), by Mohamed Amin, Duncan Willetts, and John Eames, published by Bodley Head, London.

Maasai (1980), by Carol Beckwith and Tepilit Ole Saitoti, published by Elm Tree Books, London.

The Maasai: Herders of East Africa (1964), by Sonia Bleeker, published by Dobson Books, London.

Malindi (1975), by Esmond Bradely Martin, published by East African Literature Bureau, Nairobi.

The Marsh Lions (1982), by Jonathan Scott and Brian Jackman, published by Elm Tree Books, London.

My Pride and Joy (1987), by George Adamson, published by Simon & Schuster Inc., New York.

The Orphans of Tsavo (1966), by Daphne Sheldrick, published by Collins & Harvill Press, London.

Out of Africa (1981), by Isak Dinesen (Karen Blixen), published by Modern Library, New York.

Out in the Midday Sun: My Kenya (1987), by Elspeth Huxley, published by Viking Penguin, New York.

People of Kenya (1967), by Joy Adamson, published by Collins & Harvill Press, London.

Portraits in the Wild: Animal Behaviour in East Africa (1975), by Cynthia Moss, published by Elm Tree Books, London.

Portraits of Africa (1983), by Mohamed Amin and Peter Moll, published by Collins & Harvill Press, London.

Railway Across the Equator (1986), by Mohamed Amin, Duncan Willetts and Alastair Matheson, published by Bodley Head, London.

Rhinos: Endangered Species (1988), by Malcolm Penny, published by Facts On File, New York.

Run Rhino Run (1983), by Esmond and Chryssee Bradley Martin, published by Chatto & Windus, London.

Shepherds of the Desert (1984), by David Keith Jones, published by Elm Tree Books, London.

A Story like the Wind (1978), by Laurens Van Der Post, published by Harcourt Brace Jovanovich, New york.

Treetops Hotel (1969), by Eric Sherbrooke Walker, published by Robert Hale & Co, London.

The Tree where Man was Born (1972), by Peter Matthiessen, published by E. P. Dutton, New York.

An Unfinished Journey (1987), by Shiva Naipul, published by Viking Penguin, New York.

The Tsavo Story (1973), by Daphne Sheldrick, published by Collins & Harvill Press, London.

White Man's Country: Lord Delamere and the Making of Kenya (1935), by Elspeth Huxley, published by MacMillan & Co, London.

White Mischief (1984), by James Fox, published by Random House, New York.

The White Nile (1967), by Alan Moorhead, published by Penguin, London.

Index

(Illustrations are indicated in bold)